MASS MEDIA/
MASS CULTURE

AN INTRODUCTION

McGraw-Hill Series in Mass Communication

Anderson: Communication Research: Issues and Methods
Dominick, Sherman, and Copeland: Broadcasting/Cable and Beyond: An Introduction to Modern Electronic Media
Dominick: The Dynamics of Mass Communication
Dordick: Understanding Modern Telecommunications
Fink: Media Ethics: In the Newsroom and Beyond
Fink: Strategic Newspaper Management
Gamble and Gamble: Introducing Mass Communication
Hickman: Television Directing
Holsinger: Media Law
Richardson: Corporate and Organizational Video
Sherman: Telecommunications Management: The Broadcast and Cable Industries
Walters: Broadcast Writing: Principles and Practice
Whetmore: American Electric
Wilson: Mass Media/Mass Culture: An Introduction
Wurtzel and Acker: Television Production
Yoakam and Cremer: ENG: Television News and the New Technology

MASS MEDIA/ MASS CULTURE

AN INTRODUCTION
Second Edition

77862

STAN LE ROY WILSON
College of the Desert

McGraw-Hill, Inc.
New York St. Louis San Francisco Auckland Bogotá
Caracas Lisbon London Madrid Mexico Milan
Montreal New Delhi Paris San Juan Singapore
Sydney Tokyo Toronto

Mass Media/Mass Culture
An Introduction

Copyright © 1992, 1989 by McGraw-Hill, Inc. All rights reserved. Printed in the United States of America. Except as permitted under the United States Copyright Act of 1976, no part of this publication may be reproduced or distributed in any form or by any means, or stored in a data base or retrieval system, without the prior written permission of the publisher.

2 3 4 5 6 7 8 9 0 HAL HAL 9 0 9 8 7 6 5 4 3 2

ISBN 0-07-070816-9

This book was set in Times Roman by Better Graphics, Inc.
The editors were Hilary Jackson, Carol Einhorn, and Tom Holton;
the designer was Karen K. Quigley;
the production supevisor was Denise L. Puryear.
The photo editor was Elsa Peterson.
Arcata Graphics/Halliday was printer and binder.

Cover Photo Credits
Top L: UPI/Bettmann; Lower L: Copyright © 1991 by The New York Times Company, reproduced with permission; Top R: CBS/Everett Collection; Center R: MGM 1939/Bob Cosenza/Superstock; Lower R: Copyright © 1989 by Random House, Inc.

Library of Congress Cataloging-in-Publication Data

Wilson, Stan Le Roy.
    Mass media/mass culture: an introduction / Stan Le Roy
Wilson.—2nd ed.
        p.   cm.—(McGraw-Hill series in mass communication)
    Includes bibliographical references and index.
    ISBN 0-07-070816-9
    1. Mass media.   2. Communication and culture.   I. Title.
    II. Series.
    P90.W494   1992
    302.23—dc20
                                                    91-16406

ABOUT THE AUTHOR

STAN LE ROY WILSON is professor of mass communication at College of the Desert in Palm Desert, California. He holds a doctorate from the University of Southern California and earned his bachelor's and master's degrees from California State Universities, Fresno and Stanislaus. Prior to his 30-year teaching career at California State universities and community colleges, he worked as a newspaper and radio journalist and as a public relations consultant.

In addition to holding leadership positions in state and national journalism and mass communication organizations, Wilson has had an active political life. He is currently serving his fourth elected four-year term on the Palm Desert City Council and has served three terms as that city's mayor. He also serves on regional governing boards, including the Riverside County Transportation Commission and the South Coast Air Quality Management District, where he is one of 12 directors charged with cleaning up the Los Angeles air basin—the dirtiest in the nation.

CONTENTS

Preface   xiii

PART ONE ▪ CULTURE AND COMMUNICATION

Chapter 1   Culture and Communication: Basic Concepts   3

  Culture   4
    Box 1.1 Pop Culture Becomes Academic   5
  The EPS Cycle   5
  The Communication Process   7
  Information Processing by the Media   16
    Box 1.2 Cartoons against Drugs   17
  Information Processing by the Consumer   19
  Summary   20

Chapter 2   Culture and Mass Communication: How They Interact   25

  The Beginning of Mass Communication   26
  The Protestant Reformation   28
  Development of the Novel   29
  Industrialization   29
  Mass Media in Mass Society   32
  Mass Mediation of Leisure   33
    Box 2.1 The Super Bowl: Exporting Popular Culture   34
  Criticism of Mass Society   36
    Box 2.2 Mass Culture Shapes the Mass Media   38
  Commercialization of Culture   38
    Box 2.3 Selling the Persian Gulf War   40
  Cults in Popular Culture   42
    Box 2.4 The Trekkies "Star Trek" through the Media   44
  Summary   46

Chapter 3   Media Controls: Philosophical   49

  Authoritarian Theory   51
  Libertarian Theory   53
  The Soviet Communist Concept   55
  The Social Responsibility Concept   57
    Box 3.1 The Society of Professional Journalists Code of Ethics   58

The Press in Foreign Lands 60
    Box 3.2 An Independent Communist Party Newspaper? 61
    Box 3.3 Profile: Two Media Moguls 63
Summary 68

Chapter 4 Media Controls: Legal 73
    Government Regulation of Print 74
    Government Regulation of Broadcasting 77
        Box 4.1 FCC's Section 315: Facilities for Candidates
        for Public Office 78
    Court Regulations 81
    Laws against Obscenity 82
    Laws to Protect the Public 84
        Box 4.2 Libel Takes a Variety of Forms 87
        Box 4.3 What Constitutes an Invasion of Privacy? 89
    Summary 90

PART TWO ▪ DEVELOPMENT
OF PRINT MEDIA

Chapter 5 Book Publishing: Past and Present 95
    Origins of Books 98
    Early Books and the Elite 100
    Stages of Book Publishing in the United States 102
        Box 5.1 Horatio Alger, Jr.: Writing Books for Industrial
        Age Youth 106
        Box 5.2 *Barbie: Her Life and Times* by BillyBoy 108
        Box 5.3 Comic Books: International Classics 110
        Box 5.4 The Diary of Anne Frank 114
        Box 5.5 Keep Bookbusters out of Our Libraries 115
        Box 5.6 Working in Book Publishing 117
    Summary 117

Chapter 6 Magazines: The Specialized Medium 121
    History of Magazines 124
        Box 6.1 Magazines Reflect Cultural Changes 129
        Box 6.2 Profile: Henry R. Luce 130
    Decline of General-Interest Magazines 133
    Types of Magazines 135
        Box 6.3 Specialized Magazines 137
        Box 6.4 The Teenzines 139
    Specialization and Popular Culture 140
        Box 6.5 Low Times for *High Times* Magazine 141
    Consumer and Business Trends 142
    Summary 142
        Box 6.6 Working in Magazine Publishing 143

Chapter 7   Newspapers: Past, Present and Problems   147

Early Origins of Newspapers   150
The Colonial American Press (1690–1820s)   151
The Penny-Press Era (1833–1865)   156
    Box 7.1 Night Court—Nineteenth-Century Style   157
The Yellow Journalism Era (1865–1900)   159
    Box 7.2 Women in Journalism   163
The Twentieth Century Press   163
    Box 7.3 Supermarket Journalism: Giving Us What Enquiring
    Minds Want to Know   165
Newspapers as Businesses   168
    Box 7.4 Working in Newspaper Publishing   169
News Wire Services   171
Biases and Other Problems   173
Summary   174

PART THREE ▪ DEVELOPMENT
OF ELECTRONIC MEDIA

Chapter 8   Motion Pictures: Cultural Reflections   181

Early History   184
Movies and the EPS Cycle   187
The Rise of Comedy   187
Sound Joins Motion   189
A Way of Life   191
The Giant Is Crippled   195
Youth, Sex, Violence and Special Effects   198
Current Trends   202
Business Trends   203
    Box 8.1 Working in the Movie Industry   203
Summary   204
    Box 8.2 Is Hollywood Becoming the "Foreign Film Capital"?   205
    Box 8.3 Holdings of Paramount Communications, Inc.   206

Chapter 9   Radio: A Wireless Wonder   211

Harnessing Sound Waves   214
Beginning of Radio as a Mass Medium   216
Development of Radio News   218
Development of Radio Entertainment   221
    Box 9.1 Edward R. Murrow: A Tongue as Descriptive
    as a Paintbrush   222
Radio Loses Its Niche   226
Specialization Gives Radio a New Niche   227
Technology and Specialization   228
    Box 9.2 Working in Radio   230
Summary   231
    Box 9.3 Companion to "Prairie" Lovers Ends His Reign   232

Chapter 10   Television: From Soaps to Satellites   237
How It Began   240
Evolution of Television Entertainment   242
    Box 10.1 Profile: Fred Silverman—TV's Tarnished
    "Golden Boy"   246
    Box 10.2 The Soap Operas of Television   248
Development of Television News   251
    Box 10.3 CNN Leads World News Media into Battle   257
The Cultural Impact of Television   258
    Box 10.4 TV News in the '90s: The Battle for Ratings   259
    Box 10.5 Women in Television   262
Television Specializes   267
Business Trends   269
    Box 10.6 Working in Television   269
Summary   *270*

Chapter 11   Recorded Music: Powerful and Controversial   275
How It All Began   278
Recorded Music Enters the Popular Culture   279
    Box 11.1 The Changing World of the Jukebox   282
Rock Music Changes   283
    Box 11.2 Is Paul Dead? Some in the 1960s Thought So   288
    Box 11.3 "Heavenly Metal Music"   289
Rock Specializes   289
The Music Video Phenomenon (MTV)   291
Controversies Surrounding Rock Music   293
    Box 11.4 Rock against Drugs   296
Other Forms of Recorded Music   297
Business Trends   298
    Box 11.5 Working in the Music Industry   298
Summary   *299*

PART FOUR ■ MEDIA SHAPERS
AND CULTURAL EFFECTS

Chapter 12   Advertising: Selling the Message   303
How Advertising Developed   304
    Box 12.1 Procter & Gamble and Soap Operas   307
Theories on Advertising Effectiveness   307
    Box 12.2 Green Marketing   309
Propaganda Devices   311
Controversies Surrounding Advertising   315
Television Advertising   317
Motivational Research   320
    Box 12.3 VALS Research Leads to New Magazine Genre   324
Summary   *324*
    Box 12.4 Working in Advertising   325

Chapter 13   Public Relations: Creating an Image   331
  What Is Public Relations?   333
  The History of Public Relations   335
  Opportunities and Duties of PR Practitioners   338
    Box 13.1 Working in Public Relations   339
  Examples of Public Relations Activities   339
    Box 13.2 Philip Morris Bill of Rights Promotion
      Sparks Controversy   340
    Box 13.3 Even the Roman Catholic Church Uses PR   341
  Controversies Surrounding PR Practices   343
  Summary   344
    Box 13.4 Declaration of Principles of the Public Relations
      Society of America   345

Chapter 14   The Selling of American Politics   349
  Opinion Leader Theory   350
  The Rise of the Political Consultant   351
    Box 14.1 Profile: Hal Evry, a Political Consultant   352
  The Rise of Political Ads and Media Influence   354
    Box 14.2 Television Political Advertising, Reagan Style   360
  Effective Political Media   361
    Box 14.3 Pretesting Political Campaign Ads   363
  News Coverage of Elections   364
  Summary   367

Chapter 15   Changing Trends in Media Technology   373
  Communication Revolution   374
  Cable Television   375
    Box 15.1 Cable TV Alters Viewing Habits   377
    Box 15.2 "People Meters": High-Tech Media Monitors   378
  Satellite Communication   380
  Computers   382
    Box 15.3 Computers Can Pose Problems   383
  Home Video Equipment   384
  Merging Print and Electronics   387
  Other Technological Advances   389
  Implications for the Future   393
    Box 15.4 Working at Home on the Rise   394
  Summary   394

Chapter 16   Media Ethics and Effects   399
  News-Media Ethics   400
    Box 16.1 Ethics in Journalism: Do You Kill a Story That
      Might Make Someone Kill Himself?   402
    Box 16.2 Sometimes Invasions into Privacy Are
      Just Plain Stupid   407

Media Ethics and Economics 408
Box 16.3 Profile: Peggy Charren 409
Media Ethics and Entertainment 410
Box 16.4 Were There Racial Implications to Press Coverage
in the Stuart Murder? 414
Media Effects 415
Cultural Consequences 420
Summary 422

GLOSSARY 426
INDEX 435

PREFACE

Mass Media/Mass Culture came into being for two primary reasons. First and foremost, I wanted to present the importance and relevance of mass communication to our world, as well as the excitement caused by the technological revolution as our rapidly changing culture makes its way through the information age. I remain convinced that a thematic approach to teaching the introductory material in mass communication is the best approach and, toward that end, I have attempted to show not only how the media affect our popular culture today, but how this interrelationship of media and culture has influenced civilization since the invention of mass communication.

This text was also conceived out of a frustration that most textbooks in this area discuss mass communication and the mass media without relating the importance of the material to students' own lives. This may be fine when students are sufficiently self-motivated to study the subject, as when they have selected the area as their major and future profession. However, *all* students are, and will continue to be, consumers of the mass media and deserve to understand the significance of that role. I have observed a need for students to be made aware of how the media touch and change them and I wrote *Mass Media/Mass Culture* to address that need.

APPROACH OF THE BOOK

In addition to explaining the relationship between mass communication and our popular culture, this book uses another unifying theme to transmit information about how the media have evolved—the media progression concept developed by John Merrill and Ralph Lowenstein. This concept traces how the various mass media move through three stages of evolution—the elitist, popular and specialized stages.

In this book, I also advance the theory that new technologies are outpacing media content and that there is a need for our culture to upgrade its media content to keep pace with new delivery systems.

If at times the tone of this book seems critical, it does not stem from an antimedia bias but rather from an effort to stimulate thinking by presenting the whole media picture—warts and all. The reader can be assured that I am not antimedia. Before becoming a student and teacher of mass communication, I worked as a newspaper and radio journalist and as a public relations practitioner. As the son of a newspaper publisher, I have been associated with mass communication my entire life. I believe, however, that we can get a higher level of performance from the media if we actively scrutinize them.

NEW FEATURES

This edition has been expanded in content in the areas of legal controls on the mass media and media effects. Media controls, both philosophical and legal, are now discussed in the new Chapters 3 and 4. Chapter 16, also new, examines what we must immediately consider after pondering any of the media: media ethics and effects.

Those familiar with the first edition will find a number of new features in this volume. In addition to a complete updating of examples and topical information, I have created the following new elements and learning aids to enhance teaching and learning with *Mass Media/Mass Culture:*

- *Operations Boxes*—Boxed inserts on "Working in . . ." each of the individual media will give students a sense of the steps taken to produce the media product, as well as what a job in each of these industries might entail.
- *Profile Boxes*—A second group of new inserts highlight the lives and careers of those who have influenced the media in important ways. Henry Luce, Fred Silverman, and Peggy Charren are among those profiled.
- *Business Trends*—A section in each individual medium chapter now focuses on the quantitative aspects of the medium: earnings, growth and scope.
- *Thought Questions*—These questions have been added at the end of each chapter to stimulate critical thinking about the concepts covered.
- *Expanded Graphics*—The program of charts and graphs has been expanded to more comprehensively present audience data, media trends and business information.
- *New Design*—Most of the media discussed in this text reach us through visual messages. Accordingly, *Mass Media/Mass Culture* has been redesigned to catch the student's eye and present material in a visually dynamic and pleasing way. Of special note are the two full-color photo essays in the chapters on television (Chapter 10) and Advertising (Chapter 12).

Throughout the text I have used an informal, conversational writing style to insure that the material is accessible to students. Furthermore, I have tried to keep the discussions as brief as possible while covering necessary information: my goal is to enlighten, not to overwhelm.

ORGANIZATION OF THE BOOK

Mass Media/Mass Culture is organized into four sections: "Culture and Communication," "Development of Print Media," "Development of Electronic Media," and "Media Shapers and Cultural Effects."

Chapter 1, *Culture and Communication: Basic Concepts,* defines and explains popular culture, the EPS (media progression) cycle, and the communication process. It includes discussions of such items as agenda setting, gatekeeping and information processing.

Chapter 2, *Culture and Mass Communication: How They Interact,* reviews the impact of mass communication on our culture since the introduction of moveable type by Gutenberg in the fifteenth century. Rapid changes in mass culture since the Industrial Revolution are highlighted, as are modern-day cultural impacts.

Chapter 3, *Media Controls: Philosophical,* describes the four basic theories of media operations in the world today and provides an overview of how the mass media operate in several different countries. It also addresses the impact of Mikhail Gorbachev's *glasnost* and the role new media technologies played in the recent political revolutions in Eastern Europe.

Chapter 4, *Media Controls: Legal,* is a new chapter that addresses media regulations from a variety of sources. Included in the discussion are such issues as government regulations, court regulations, laws of libel and invasion of privacy, and laws providing access to public information such as sunshine laws and the federal Freedom of Information Act.

Chapter 5, *Book Publishing: Past and Present,* begins a chapter-by-chapter media analysis by exploring the development of the most permanent medium, books. It traces this medium from early clay tablets to today's mass market paperbacks and specialized publications, focusing on the impact books have had on Western civilization, as well as on the historical evolution of censorship.

Chapter 6, *Magazines: The Specialized Medium,* examines the evolution of magazine publishing and how magazines have found a niche in our culture by serving highly specialized interests. The rapid expansion of new magazines in the 1980s and the resulting industry economic slump in the early 1990s are also discussed.

Chapter 7, *Newspapers: Past, Present and Problems,* first recounts the historical development of newspapers and then focuses on the tension between the need for newspapers to make money and their constitutional obligation to keep the public informed. It also discusses changing trends in newspapers and examines major news wire services.

Chapter 8, *Motion Pictures: Cultural Reflections,* begins the examination of electronic media by tracing the development of motion pictures from Edison's mechanical kinetoscope to the special effects wizardry of George Lucas and Steven Spielberg. It shows how the movie industry changed the culture, and how the culture changed the industry.

Chapter 9, *Radio: A Wireless Wonder,* describes the three very different roles radio has played in our society: a device for ship-to-shore communication, the primary home news and entertainment medium in the 1930s and 1940s, and a specialized medium of music, news and talk during the television era.

Chapter 10, *Television: From Soaps to Satellites,* explores the evolution and cultural impact of television on American popular culture. In particular, the chapter examines three major concerns about the pervasive medium: the excessive portrayal of violence, television's influence on children, and the rise of televangelism. It also examines the rapid rise of CNN to a position of world-wide dominance as a news medium and its leadership role in covering the Persian Gulf War.

Chapter 11, *Recorded Music: Powerful and Controversial,* concludes the electronic media section with a discussion of the role of popular music and the controversies that have surrounded it since the jazz era of the 1920s. Readers are given a perspective on the current debate over rock and rap lyrics as well as an insight into how culturally powerful popular music has become among young people.

Chapter 12, *Advertising: Selling the Message,* begins a discussion of how others use the mass media to influence the culture. This chapter examines various theories on advertising effectiveness and describes the many propaganda devices used to sell messages. The controversy surrounding subliminal imbedding is examined as well as the use of values and lifestyle (VALS) research to market products.

Chapter 13, *Public Relations: Creating an Image,* explores how public relations has evolved since the nineteenth century. Modern professional PR practices are described and contrasted with early-day press agentry. Focus is placed on recent examples of crisis management PR.

Chapter 14, *The Selling of American Politics,* looks at how the mass media are used to sell candidates and issues in the Amerian political system. The role of political consultants and the use of vote videos, television advertising and direct mail are examined. The chapter also discusses some of the controversies surrounding media news coverage of American politics.

Chapter 15, *Changing Trends in Media Technology,* provides an overview of the rapidly developing technology used in mass communication. It covers cable television, satellite communication, computers, home video equipment, videotext, teletext, fiber optics, digital sound, multichannel multipoint distribution service (MMDS), direct broadcast satellites (DBS), high-definition television (HDTV) and low-power television (LPTV). The chapter concludes with a discussion of home information centers and telecommuting and their implications for the future.

Chapter 16, *Media Ethics and Effects,* discusses ethical issues facing the mass media and the results of research on the effects of mass media on individuals. The chapter concludes with a discussion of cultural consequences and how we, the consumers of the mass media, can influence change in media content.

I hope that old and new users of this book will find this second edition even more academically valuable, exciting and enjoyable to read than the first edition. No textbook can serve as the final word on mass communication as the field is changing daily. Rather, this book is intended as a background for classroom discussions and contemporary reading on current media issues.

RESOURCES FOR INSTRUCTORS

An Instructor's Manual has been prepared to assist instructors in their teaching. It provides sample syllabi and assignments, instructional resources, and suggested audio and video resources for enriching the presentation of material. A computerized test bank is available in IBM, MacIntosh and Apple formats.

ACKNOWLEDGMENTS

In developing this second edition of *Mass Media/Mass Culture,* I have become indebted to many people. My sincere thanks go to the following people who assisted in the preparation of this edition, either as user-contributors or reviewers: Don Alexander, Golden West College; David Clark, Colorado State University; Bob Gassaway, University of New Mexico; Roger Graham, Los Angeles Valley College; Earl Grow, University of Wisconsin at Milwaukee; Dennis Hart, California State University, Northridge; Randall Hines, Texas A & M University; Joli Jenson, University of Texas, Austin; William McKeen, University of Florida; Jerry Medley, Auburn University; Alston Morgan, Oral Roberts University; Robert Ogles, Purdue University; David Rapaport, City College of San Francisco; Marshel Rossow, Mankato State University; James Sayer, Wright State University; Sam Slade, Rose State College; Michael Turney, Northern Kentucky University; Jianglong Wang, Western Washington University; and James R. Wilson, California State University, Fresno.

Credit for any success of this second edition also must go to an outstanding team of professionals at McGraw-Hill. Although there are too many to mention, I'd like to give special thanks to Roth Wilkofsky, who has supported this book since its inception; Hilary Jackson, who assembled and supervised the editing team; Carol Einhorn, who worked closely with me and guided me throughout every stage of development; and Tom Holton, who supervised the editing.

I also wish to thank my wife and family for having the patience to put up with my absences while I worked on this project.

And lastly, special thanks must go to the many students who have given me feedback on the first edition and encouragement and ideas to compile this revised edition. It is for them and those who follow that this book is written.

Stan Le Roy Wilson

MASS MEDIA/
MASS CULTURE

AN INTRODUCTION

CULTURE AND COMMUNICATION

The mass media have tremendous influence on our popular culture, including helping to determine the clothes we wear and the cultural icons we worship.

CULTURE AND COMMUNICATION: BASIC CONCEPTS

Communication is mankind's most important single act. When improperly performed it turns friends into enemies and plunges nations into wars.

—Anonymous

—On July 15, 1985, the lead news story on two of the three major television network newscasts was the announcement that Coca-Cola had decided to go back to its old taste after experimenting with a new one. The rebirth of "classic" Coke was also a major news item in most daily newspapers around the country that day despite the fact that far more important news events had occurred. The main headline of *The Denver Post,* for example, read: "The Real Thing Is Back" in type as large as the name of the newspaper. Below the banner headline was a two-color photograph of a can of Coke.

—On October 18, 1989, a group of aging rock stars—the Rolling Stones— opened a four-day, sold-out concert appearance to crowds in the Los Angeles Coliseum. The performers were in their 40s and 50s.

—On January 31, 1990, 30,000 Russians stood in line for hours at the grand opening of a Moscow McDonald's to get their first taste of an American Big Mac.

—Also in 1990, a list of the 15 top ranked television shows of all time—those with the largest audiences—included eight Super Bowl games.

—Each year millions of Americans tune their TV sets to the "Miss America" contest and other beauty pageants to see who will be crowned for being most beautiful.

What do Coca-Cola, rock concerts, McDonald's, the Super Bowl and beauty pageants have in common? They are all important elements of our popular culture that have been either created or perpetuated by the mass media.

The mass media play an important role in our society. To understand that role better, we need to know a little about how our Western culture developed and how the mass media have helped to change and shape it.

If you are wondering why you should be interested in such things as culture and its relationship to the mass media, stop for a minute and look around you. Did you ever wonder why you comb your hair the way you do, why you wear a certain style of clothing and why you spend your money on the things you do? Most people would answer by saying they do these things because they want to. But the answer goes much deeper than that.

Other questions you might ask yourself are "Why and how did the Super Bowl come to be one of the biggest mass-media events in American society?" and "How and why did rock-'n'-roll become such an important form of music in our culture?" The answers to these questions and many more may be found by studying our American popular culture and its interrelationship with the mass media.

CULTURE

To understand clearly our study of culture and media, it is essential to define precisely what we mean by *culture*. For anthropologists, culture includes every- thing that occurs in a society—all the customs and practices handed down from generation to generation. Culture covers the various forces that contribute to our behavior in society. These contributions usually come from our formal institu- tions, such as churches, the state, and now, the media; mores, or standards of behavior; laws; and conventional practices and customs.

Popular Culture.   *Popular culture* can be defined as the culture of everyone in a society. It can be so pervasive that we seldom notice it. In order for us to notice it, we must step back and consciously observe it. We can do this by really looking around us at the objects in our society and asking ourselves why we idolize the things we do, why we buy the things we do, and why we believe in the things we do (see Box 1.1).

Throughout history, every society has had its own popular culture. Most of

BOX 1.1

▪ POP CULTURE BECOMES ACADEMIC ▪

During the past 20 years, the study of popular culture on college and university campuses has been growing. Such topics as rock-'n'-roll, comic books and detective novels are rigorously examined in many academic settings. Many additional courses examine the relationship of the mass media to popular culture.

It is estimated that more than 2,000 students a year enroll in popular culture classes and at one university—Bowling Green State University in Ohio—students can earn degrees in popular culture. There are even professional organizations, the Popular Culture Association and the American Culture Association, which attract some 3,000 members to annual conventions where such papers as *The Reconciliation of Archie and Meathead, All in the Family's Last Episode,* and *The Tupperware Party and the American Dream* are presented.

In the early years pop culture was looked down upon by many academics who felt that the study of everyday culture was not appropriate in a university setting where students examined Western civilization, philosophy and the sciences. Supporters of the study of popular culture point out that it is part of our history and holds as much relevance as war, slavery and revolutions. They note that by examining the themes and styles of a culture we can better understand the values of the people.

---

today's popular culture is mass-produced and is disseminated in large quantities through the mass media. Popular music, cheap paperback novels, soap operas, videocassette movies and a myriad of advertised products from designer jeans to disposable razors make up our everyday environment. Stephen King novels, Levi's jeans and the golden arches of McDonald's are instantly recognizable symbols in our modern-day pop culture.

Because of the mass mediation of our popular culture, another term, *mass culture,* has developed. This refers to the things in our culture that are mass-produced and/or shared through the mass media. In today's American society, that represents almost everything in our popular culture. It is so difficult to think of anything in our modern popular culture that isn't either mass-produced or promoted in the mass media that the terms mass culture and popular culture have come to be used almost interchangeably.

THE EPS CYCLE

While our mass culture today is a popular one, with distinctions between classes blurry at best, this was not always the case. Throughout this book we will be referring to a media progression cycle called the elitist-popular-specialized (EPS) cycle. This progression cycle concept was developed by mass-communication scholars John Merrill and Ralph Lowenstein, who in 1971 first pointed out that all media develop in three stages.[1]

A mass-communication medium usually starts out in the elite stage. Here the media appeal to, and are consumed by, the affluent leaders in the culture. After a nation breaks through the barriers of poverty and illiteracy, its media enter the popular stage and are enjoyed by the mass culture. Eventually, as the elements of

▪ Popular culture and the mass media play ever-changing roles in our lives. Here a woman shops for a compact disc in what once was called a "record store." Records have been replaced by CDs and tapes.

higher education, affluence, leisure time and population growth coalesce, the mass media begin to enter a third stage of the EPS cycle—specialization. In this stage the media are consumed by highly fragmented segments of the population, each with its own interests and cultural activities.

While media in the United States are entering the age of specialization, in many underdeveloped nations the media are still in the early stages of this cycle. A closer look at these stages can help us see where we've been and where other countries may be headed.

Elitist Stage. Down through the ages, *elite culture* has been the culture of the educated, aristocratic and wealthy. Elite culture is sometimes referred to as *high culture*. Until less than two hundred years ago, there was a distinct separation between high culture and that of the common, peasant class, which was known as *folk culture*. The elite were people whose lives revolved around fine art, literature and classical music. The peasants had their folk culture, which consisted of street carnivals, tavern drinking and singing and the telling of folktales. Although people who participated in the elite culture could also enjoy folk culture, the reverse was not true.

Popular Stage. In the nineteenth century, the distinction between elite and folk culture began to blur following the development of political democracy, public education of the masses and the Industrial Revolution. These forces ushered in the era of popular and mass culture. Although folk culture can be described as a forerunner of popular culture, the term popular culture was not coined until the nineteenth century. Pop culture scholar Ray B. Browne defined *popular culture* as

> *the cultural world around us—our attitudes, habits and actions: how we act and why we act; what we eat, wear; our buildings, roads and means of travel, our entertainment, sports; our politics, religion, medical practices; our beliefs and activities and what shapes and controls them. It is, in other words, to us what water is to fish: it is the world we live in.*[2]

Thus we use the term *popular culture* in this book to describe what surrounds us in our everyday lives. Pop culture is our mainstream culture; it encompasses all the objects, customs, fads and activities we take for granted.*

Specialized Stage.   The United States was the first nation in which all the factors necessary for specialization converged. During the latter half of the twentieth century, there has been a great deal of movement by the American mass media toward specialization. Futurist Alvin Toffler calls this trend the "demassification of the mass media," and he believes it will continue as we complete our move from the industrial age to the information age.[3]

Although magazines are the most specialized of the mass media (see Chapter 6), during the latter part of this century all American mass media have been accelerating toward specialization.

THE COMMUNICATION PROCESS

Before we examine how American mass media have evolved through this EPS cycle, we need to take a look at how the communication process—and mass communication in particular—works.

Communication can be defined simply as *the process by which individuals share information, ideas and attitudes*. A key word in this definition is "share." The word means to give or receive a part of something, or to enjoy or assume something in common. Some people use the term send rather than share when they discuss the communication process. However, "sending" merely implies transmitting a message with little concern for the person receiving the message, while "sharing" implies that the source and the receiver are actively working together for common understanding.

You will also note that we call communication a *process*. This means that communication is ongoing and dynamic. It also means that it encompasses various components that interact with one another, causing specific consequences. For

---

*Even today, however, a few things remain in the elite culture. Going to the movies is considered popular culture, but attending the opera is deemed elite. A Rembrandt painting is part of the elite culture, whereas a poster of Vanna White is a popular culture artifact. Bowling is a leisure activity of the popular culture, while polo is definitely a part of elite culture.

However, the differences between elite and popular culture are subject to change. Golf and tennis were once considered elite sports. Increased mass-media exposure has led to greater availability of public golf courses and tennis courts and has shifted these activities to the popular culture.

example, what information, ideas and attitudes are shared, how much is shared, when is it shared and what tools are used to share it are all variables in the process.

Types of Communication. Various types of communication exist. *Intrapersonal communication* describes a person talking to himself or herself. In *interpersonal communication,* two or three people are talking with one another in close physical proximity. *Group communication* describes a process whereby groups of people communicate with one another in a face-to-face encounter. In *mass communication,* professional communicators use a mass medium to communicate over some distances to large audiences.

There are several basic components in the communication process. While these components can be presented in a variety of diagrams or models, our basic model includes the source, the message, the channel and the receiver (see Figure 1.1).

Source. The source (sometimes called the *sender, communicator* or *encoder*) is the person who shares information, ideas or attitudes with another person. The writer of this textbook is sharing his ideas on the definitions of the term *source* with you. The message is being disseminated to you through the process of mass communication—in this case, book publishing.

In mass communication, the source is usually a professional communicator who shapes the message to be shared. He or she might be a newspaper or television reporter or an entertainer who must gather information or ideas and then share them with the audience.

Message. The *message* is whatever the source attempts to share with someone else. It originates with an idea, which then must be encoded into *symbols* that are used to express that idea.

Symbols are words or objects that the source uses to elicit meaning in the mind of the receiver of the message. Words and pictures are the most common symbols used in communication. Words attempt to describe an object or concept, while pictures actually show a representation of the object or idea. If you were to give some friends directions on how to find your home, you might use words to identify the directions they should follow and the various cross streets that they need to look for. Or, if you preferred, you could draw them a map.

The process of selecting symbols for an idea or object is a very important step in communication because poorly selected symbols will result in a confusing or misunderstood message. Care must be taken to choose symbols that will elicit responses in the mind of the message receiver that are similar to those intended by the source.

In selecting symbols for their messages, communicators must keep in mind that each person has a different frame of reference and that, as a result, certain

Figure 1.1 Communication model

∎ The source of a message in mass communication is a professional communicator. Shown working at her computer terminal is a reporter for the *Knoxville Journal* in Knoxville, Tennessee.

symbols may mean different things to different people. A *frame of reference* (sometimes called *field of experience*) is the set of individual experiences each person possesses; no two people have exactly the same experiences.

Each experience or event in our life leaves some sort of an impression on us, and we use the accumulation of these experiences to give meaning and interpretation to symbols. For example, a person who has been rescued by a police officer will respond differently from a criminal to the message "The police are coming." These different reactions are based on the meanings given to the word *police* that have been developed as a result of the individual's experiences.

Although we primarily use words and pictures to send our messages, we also communicate in other ways. Facial expressions, gestures and body language can effectively send messages. For example, a television newscaster might be reporting on the outcome of a presidential election by stating only the facts about the vote, while his facial expressions and/or tone of voice reveal his biases against the winner.

Channel. The *channel* is the way in which we send our message. In interpersonal communication we use the senses of sight, sound and touch to communicate messages. These are our channels. In mass communication such technological devices as books, newspapers, magazines, movies, radio and television are our communication channels.

Mass communication differs from interpersonal communication in that its messages must be moved over greater distances. This movement is achieved through the use of technological devices. Radio and television messages are transmitted electronically, while newspaper and magazine messages are reproduced on high-speed presses and distributed through the mails or via carriers. Today, however, even some print-media messages are transmitted electronically. Wire services send news via satellite, and *USA Today* transmits the entire contents of the newspaper by satellite to printing plants around the country and to other parts of the world.

Receiver.   The *receiver* (sometimes called the *destination, audience* or *decoder*) in the communication process is the person with whom the message is intended to be shared. Without a receiver, there is no communication. In fact, if any one of the above four communication components is missing, there is no communication. To properly share your message, you also must be sure that the receiver is listening and understanding what it is you have to communicate.

Just because a story is carried in a newspaper or broadcast over radio or television does not mean that everyone has received the message. If some people do not read the story or pay attention to the broadcast, it has not been communicated to them.

The receiver in mass communication is usually a large audience that is often referred to as the *masses*. Because of the audience's size and diversity, mass communication requires careful choice of symbols that will elicit correct interpretations among receivers, who each has a different frame of reference.

Feedback.   If the receiver or audience in the communication process transmits back to the source an observable response to the message, you have an added component called *feedback*. Feedback provides the source with an opportunity to determine if the message was correctly understood and, if it wasn't, with an opportunity to modify it (see Figure 1.2).

Feedback can take many forms. It can consist of words, gestures, facial expressions or any other observable act. A person making a pass at an attractive member of the opposite sex might get a clear message to "get lost" without a word being spoken.

Feedback is absent or at best very much delayed in mass communication. This makes mass communication much more difficult than face-to-face communication. Messages in mass communication must be clearly constructed because there is seldom a chance to restate their meaning. It is true that if a newspaper story is

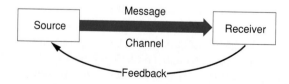

Figure 1.2 Communication process with feedback

erroneously interpreted, people will write letters to the editor, and if a broadcaster's statement is incorrectly perceived, the station may get telephone calls. However, this feedback comes too late to do much good.

Certain additional factors—called communication noise—can complicate the communication process. Three examples of this are channel noise, semantic noise and psychological noise.

Channel Noise.   *Channel noise* refers to external interference in the communication process. The message doesn't make it through as sent. You might be listening to your car radio when, all of a sudden, a large blast of static blocks out the music. This is a case of channel noise in mass communication. Other examples of channel noise might be print that is too small, a voice that is too soft or a picture that is blurred.

Semantic Noise.   What if you heard on the radio that someone had just found a Polyphemus moth or that your mayor was suffering from hyperbilirubinemia? Chances are you would not clearly interpret the messages. This act of communication would be suffering from *semantic noise*.

When semantic noise occurs, the message gets through as sent but you don't understand what it means. Symbols causing semantic noise do not have to be long, technical terms. If a receiver of the message does not have a background in electricity, for example, he or she may find ohm and watt just as confusing as hyperbilirubinemia.

Semantic noise can occur even when we know the other person is familiar with the symbol we have selected. We must remember that words evoke mental pictures in the minds of both the source and the receiver. For example, if a newspaper article mentions that a dog seriously injured a child, the reporter might have had a German shepherd in mind. However, the story can lead to misunderstanding if the receiver of the message, who has been aware of numerous stories describing attacks on humans by pit bull terriers, automatically pictures a pit bull when reading the story. Or perhaps the reader owns a Mexican hairless and pictures her pet when reading the word *dog*. In fact, we have no assurance that certain people will even think of a four-legged animal when the word *dog* is used; perhaps they are accustomed to using the term to describe members of the opposite sex whom they dislike.

Semantic noise can also occur when words take on connotations or emotional meanings that are based on experiences rather than on the word's dictionary meanings. Take the words *socialist, liberal* and *conservative,* for example. These mean different things to different people, based on individual political points of view. A great deal of confusion can thus arise in mass communication if these terms are thrown around too loosely.

The mass media also run into problems with semantic noise when reporters get caught up in the jargon of the beats they are covering. Government and education are two areas in which jargon is used extensively. When a reporter quotes the mayor as saying that the city has a "long-range strategic plan to interface the environmental negative declaration process with the private sector," the reader may decide to turn to the comic pages. Mass communicators must interpret ideas and information and select clearly understood symbols to transmit that information to the masses. In other words, they must constantly guard against semantic noise.

Psychological Noise.   We refer to internal factors that lead to misunderstandings in the communication process as *psychological noise*. People try to protect themselves from information that they might find offensive in three ways: selective exposure, selective perception and selective retention. The concept of psychological noise comes from consistency theory research that found that people usually prefer to seek out information and ideas that are consistent with their beliefs, attitudes and behavior, and tend to avoid information that is inconsistent.

Selective exposure holds that, as a general rule, we expose ourselves to information that reinforces rather than contradicts our beliefs or opinions. For example, Republicans are far more likely than Democrats to watch a Republican candidate on television.

Selective exposure also helps to explain why people with extreme political views have difficulty getting their ideas across to the general public: the audience just "tunes them out."

One of the most colorful episodes in American journalism in the twentieth century—the flourishing of the underground press movement during the 1960s—best demonstrated this phenomenon. Various countercultural groups expressed a frustration that the "Establishment" press was not telling people about their ideas, such as opposition to the war in Vietnam, "blissful" experiences with psychedelic drugs and the joys of sexual freedom. So, in an effort to get their message out to the masses, many of these countercultural movements started up alternative, "underground" newspapers.

After a few years the messages were still not reaching the masses, and the underground press movement started to decline. The reason was selective exposure: the only people reading the newspapers were those who already subscribed to the philosophy of the counterculture.

The second kind of psychological noise is *selective perception:* we tend to see, hear and believe only what we want to see, hear and believe. As the late Canadian philosopher Marshall McLuhan pointed out, "Everyone has his own set of goggles," and we all think that what we see with our set of goggles is what everyone else sees. The Swiss biologist and psychologist Jean Piaget, who has been influential in twentieth-century educational philosophy, called this autistic thinking and defined autism as "thought in which truth is confused with desire."

Many studies have demonstrated selective perception at work. One involved showing people an editorial cartoon from a Northern newspaper ridiculing the Ku Klux Klan; the cartoon was repeatedly interpreted as pro-Klan when shown to Southern Klan sympathizers.

Paul Conrad, the popular and controversial *Los Angeles Times* political cartoonist, deals with this phenomenon all the time. Letters to the editor in response to his June 13, 1985, cartoon on the death of Karen Ann Quinlan—whose parents had much earlier obtained a court order to get her released from a hospital life-support system—included the following two:

KAREN ANN QUINLAN IS FINALLY GRANTED THE RIGHT TO DIE.

■ Selective perception may cause an editorial cartoon, such as this one by Paul Conrad of the *Los Angeles Times,* to produce opposing reactions among readers; people see what they want to see.

Conrad's work of art on the death of Karen Ann Quinlan was so touching it brought tears. He outdid himself this time. I do hope he sent the original to the Quinlan family. It would be a precious gift I'm sure they would treasure.

L.C.M.

Conrad's cartoon with regard to Karen Ann Quinlan was repugnant.

L.W.S.

Another classic example of selective perception appeared in the early 1970s, when television producer Norman Lear first started experimenting with controversial situation comedies (sitcoms). After much effort, he persuaded CBS to air *All in the Family,* which featured Archie Bunker, a classic bigot. Bunker's prejudices were reflected in a number of controversial topics, such as sex, religion and racism, that previously had been considered unsafe topics for discussion on prime-time television. The character of Archie Bunker was designed to satirize American bigotry. But what developed were Archie Bunker fan clubs and Archie Bunker T-shirts proclaiming America's No. 1 television bigot a folk hero. Many people thought what he said was true and thus failed to get the message or see the satire.

In the late 1980s selective perception was evident during the congressional Iran-Contra hearings. When Lt. Col. Oliver North testified before the committee, millions of Americans proclaimed him a national hero and wanted him to run for president—while others were convinced he should be sent to jail for breaking the law and figuratively "shredding" the Constitution.

Selective retention is the third basic psychological defense. It means that we tend to remember those things that reinforce our beliefs better than those that oppose them. For example, try to remember some good things about someone you dislike. Or try to come up with a list of faults for someone you really idolize. Chances are you will remember mostly bad things about your enemies and good things about your idols.

By now you should see that the communication process is more complicated than indicated by the simple definition first offered. Let's consider a more comprehensive definition that attempts to recognize some of the complexities we've covered.

> **COMMUNICATION** *is a process involving the sorting, selecting and sharing of symbols in such a way as to help a receiver elicit from his or her own mind a meaning similar to that contained in the mind of the communicator.*

Mass Communication. We also need to define the more complex process of mass communication. Before we do, however, we will describe one more aspect of mass communication that makes it controversial and important to study if we are to better understand our culture. Previously we noted that mass communication consists of (1) professional communicators shaping and sharing messages, (2) then transmitting them over some distance using technological devices called mass media, (3) to reach large audiences.

These three factors have an effect on the receivers of the message, and this effect should be included in a definition of mass communication. The effect, for example, can be as simple as expanding a person's knowledge about a certain topic by describing an injury someone received in an automobile accident. Or the effect might consist of making people feel good after they watch a movie or television show. However, media effects can also be far more significant, such as changing a person's cultural attitudes and behavior.

This latter, more complex effect causes many people to be disturbed by the mass media and their influences on our culture. Concern about excessive sex and violence in the media and explicit rock-music lyrics has generated a great deal of mass-media criticism in recent years. These issues will be discussed in more depth later in this book.

If we take these factors of mass communication and place them into an operational definition, we might say that:

> **MASS COMMUNICATION** *is a process whereby professional communicators use technological devices to share messages over some distance to influence large audiences.*

Channels of Mass Communication. The technological devices or mass media used to send messages over some distance include books, pamphlets, magazines, newspapers, direct-mail circulars, newsletters, radio, records, audiotapes, television, motion pictures, videotapes and computer networks.

You will note that we have not included telephones, stage plays or rock concerts. One could certainly argue that telephones transmit messages over some distance and that long-running plays or huge rock concerts are seen by large audiences. Then why aren't they considered mass media? Let's examine each of these in relation to our definition of mass communication.

The telephone does use technological devices to transmit messages across some distance, but it does not reach large audiences. Instead, it usually transmits a one-on-one conversation and is an electronic extension of interpersonal communication. Although new technologies such as teleconferencing expand the size of the audience, it is still not sufficient to meet the concept of a *large* mass-media audience.

Although stage plays and rock concerts use some technological devices (lighting and sound systems) to reach large audiences, such shows are limited to a confined area and thus do not transmit those messages over some distance. If these events are broadcast or if audio or videotapes are made, then the broadcast medium or the tapes become the mass medium, not the stage play or concert itself. The Live Aid concert in 1985, for example, made an impact on our popular culture largely because it was shown on network and cable TV.

There is one more thing about the media that we must always keep in mind—the American mass media are businesses and their purpose is to make a profit. If they don't, they go out of business. Collectively, the mass media in the United States are one of the largest industries, with an annual income of more than $125 billion, and they employ more than 1 million people (see Figure 1.3).

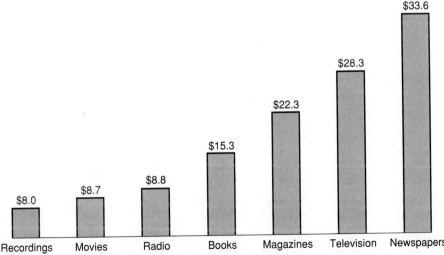

Figure 1.3   1990 annual income of U.S. mass media (in billions of dollars). SOURCE: *U.S Industrial Outlook, 1990* (Washington, D.C.: U.S. Government Printing Office, 1990) and *Media Current Analysis* (Standard and Poor's Industrial Surveys, August 2, 1990).

INFORMATION PROCESSING BY THE MEDIA

The importance of mass communication increases as we develop into adulthood. After early childhood, we learn very little firsthand. Once we learn to talk and then read, we start gathering information from secondhand sources—other people, and eventually, the mass media.

In our early education, television and textbooks become important sources for our secondhand information. Other media, such as newspapers and magazines, join them as we grow older. For example, we might ''know'' that terrorists have taken hostages in the Middle East or that an earthquake has devastated a major city, but we probably didn't experience this information firsthand. We relied on secondhand sources—usually the mass media—to inform us. Because we depend on secondhand sources for information, the mass media play a major role in determining the content of our culture.

Agenda Setting.   A process whereby the mass media determine what we think and worry about is called *agenda setting*. The word agenda means a list, plan, outline or the like of things to be considered. Mass-media agenda-setting theory contends that the mass media, not we, determine what will be news and what won't.

According to researchers Maxwell McCombs and Donald Shaw: ''Here may lie the most important effect of mass communication, its ability to mentally order and organize our world for us. In short, the mass media may not be successful in telling us what to think, but they are stunningly successful in telling us what to think about.''[4]

A newspaper editorial board sets the news agenda during daily meetings.

BOX 1.2

▪ CARTOONS AGAINST DRUGS ▪

Sometimes the media cooperate in a conscious effort to set the agenda for media consumers. Television networks occasionally join together in interrupting their regular programming to broadcast a speech or press conference by the president of the United States. Other times there are simulcast broadcasts of major news events.

In April of 1990 ABC, CBS, NBC and Fox networks joined with cable networks and independent TV stations across the nation to saturate the Saturday morning airwaves with an anti-drug message aimed at children.

At 9:30 A.M. most TV channels carried an animated half-hour show entitled *Cartoon All-Stars to the Rescue.* Organized by the Academy of Television Arts & Sciences and produced under the auspices of Walt Disney Co., the program used such characters as Bugs Bunny, Miss Piggy and the Smurfs to send a strong message to youngsters about the dangers of using illegal drugs.

The story focused on a 9-year-old girl who learns that her 14-year-old brother has broken into her piggy bank to steal money to buy marijuana. The cartoon characters, who come to life from the girl's books and stuffed toys, help her figure out what's going on and eventually persuade the brother to stop using drugs.

The McDonald's Corporation and its Ronald McDonald Children's Charities provided $2 million for the production and a related anti-drug abuse campaign that involved passing out 250 million pamphlets about the program at McDonald's restaurants and distributing tapes to video stores and schools.

The anti-drug effort did not go without criticism, however. Some felt that such an organized effort to send a single message to the nation's youth was setting a dangerous precedent. Others criticized the fact that the program ignored the No. 1 substance abuse problem—alcohol. However, the program's defenders hailed the broadcast as a major step in using the mass media for serious educational purposes.

The professional communicators working for the mass media set the news and information agenda for us. If they determine that something isn't important, it most likely won't be, because it will receive very little, if any, media attention. And, of course, the reverse is true. Often the media give far more extensive coverage to stories than they actually deserve. Sensational murder cases, for example, sometimes get week after week of front-page news coverage, even when very little new information has been uncovered. Such headlines as "No New Clues in Hillside Strangling" are not uncommon.

Most professional communicators, particularly those involved in processing the news, attempt to be objective and fair in their selection of news items. Very few purposely slant the news to fit their own particular biases. Yet there is far more news than space or time available to disseminate it. This means that selections must be made as to what is news on any given day and how much space or time will be devoted to it. Stories of limited interest, such as activities of the local water district, church ladies' aid society or Boy Scout troop, frequently go unreported (see Box 1.2).

Political candidates have a great deal of trouble with media agenda setting at election time. For example, in 1980 President Jimmy Carter felt that there were other important issues in the presidential election besides the American hostages being held in Iran. The media, however, seemed to disagree, and for over a year a count of the number of days Americans had been held hostage and a recap of the hostage story led the evening news each day. The American people were frustrated by the government's inability to free these Americans, and the media would not let them forget the incident. Jimmy Carter lost the election.

In 1984, while President Ronald Reagan was seeking a second term, seven Americans were being held hostage in the Middle East. This time the news media didn't feel the situation was that important, and the plight of the hostages went largely unreported. Ronald Reagan won reelection.

Media treatment of the hostage issue was obviously not the sole reason for Reagan's victories in 1980 and 1984, but the examples do illustrate inconsistencies in media agenda setting. These examples also do not suggest that the news media favored Reagan over Carter. In fact, in October 1986, this "tough-on-Iran" Reagan found his administration in turmoil after the news media revealed that members of his staff had been secretly selling arms to Iran and using the profits to fund rebel forces in Nicaragua. Much to President Reagan's displeasure, the content of the mass media during the summer of 1987 dealt primarily with the congressional hearings on the Iran-Contra scandal. It was their agenda, not his.

It is important to understand, however, that agenda setting can differ greatly from one news medium to another. The content of a suburban weekly newspaper will not be the same as that of a nearby metropolitan daily, for example. The suburban weekly may set as its primary agenda local activities in the community, while the metropolitan daily probably feels obligated to include more coverage of national and international news.

Gatekeeping.   Another way that the media control our access to news, information and entertainment is through *gatekeeping*. This sociological term was coined in 1947 by Kurt Lewin, who used it to describe the fact that news must travel through a series of checkpoints (or gates) before it reaches the public.

In the gatekeeping process, numerous people make decisions as to whether or not we are going to see or hear a story or be exposed to a new musical or entertainment performer or group. A story about the United States shifting its policy toward a Middle Eastern country may or may not reach the American people, depending on the decisions made by the gatekeepers. A group of rock musicians may or may not make it to the top of the charts, depending on decisions by gatekeepers.

Let's take a hypothetical example of the president of the United States changing his policy on a Middle Eastern country. Whether the American people learn about this shift in policy is not necessarily in the hands of the government. Government officials may issue a press release or hold a news conference announcing the change. However, a number of news media personnel must determine that the announcement is important before it becomes news.

Before appearing in a newspaper, the news item must pass to the reporter as a news release or in a news conference. He or she then decides whether the item is important enough to be covered and how much coverage should be given to it. If the reporter decides the item is important, he or she may rewrite the press release or write a story about the press conference or perhaps dictate the item over a telephone to a rewrite person at the newspaper. The rewrite person then functions as the next gate in evaluating the story's importance. Next a copy editor edits the item and judges its importance. The story may also appear before additional

■ Even personnel in this CNN TV control room, who make decisions as a program airs, serve as gatekeepers in the communication process.

gates—the national or international editors and perhaps even the entire editorial board of the newspaper—before a determination is made as to if and where the story will be run in the next edition.

Before this same story appears on television, it must go through a similar set of gates: writers, editors and videotape editors all make judgments as to what portions of the news conference will be aired. (If no videotape footage accompanies the news item, it might be stopped at this gate because television depends on visuals to keep the news interesting.)

Similarly, a rock group that may be the rage at a local college may never "make it" in the entertainment world because gatekeepers feel that they have enough performers with a similar sound. A pilot program for a new television series may never make it on the air because gatekeepers decide that it is not what the public wants. A potential best-selling book may never see print because a gatekeeper makes a decision to reject the manuscript.

INFORMATION PROCESSING BY THE CONSUMER

Although the mass media determine what news and entertainment the public will see and hear, people absorb only a fraction of all the information that they receive. Instead, people process information by condensing it, selecting aspects of interest to them and integrating what they select into their own thinking.

People pay attention to only a small amount of the information available to them. To do otherwise would be to risk *information overload*. Can you imagine reading or remembering everything that has been printed or broadcast during your lifetime? As the years go by, most of us accumulate a substantial backlog of information. This allows us to filter new information into our memories to update and refresh previously developed perceptions and to reject information that we deem unimportant.

Communication researcher Doris Graber found that people "tame the information tide quite well." Her study in Evanston, Illinois, discovered that newspaper readers ignored two out of three stories, read no more than 18 percent of the stories in full and looked at only the first and second paragraph of the rest.[5] (Reading only the beginning of a story is actually an efficient process because it takes advantage of the inverted-pyramid writing style, the most common style of news writing: the most important aspects of the story are summarized in the first paragraph, the next most important information follows and the least important angles appear at the end.)

Graber also found that a similar screening process goes on for television news: of all the stories on a typical half-hour newscast, only one is retained sufficiently to be recalled shortly afterward. Despite this haphazard news-selection process, however, she found that people manage to stay on top of the most important stories.

In addition to ignoring large numbers of stories, people reduce the amount of information they need to store by extracting only the essential points from news stories they do pay attention to.

An example of how this works is the public's understanding of the reasons for the space shuttle *Challenger's* explosion in January 1986. A presidential commission was appointed to determine the cause of the tragedy, and volumes of testimony and study were printed and broadcast during the six months of the investigation. However, most people read, heard and remembered only enough to know that the failure of a booster rocket's O-ring had caused the tragedy.

As a result of her study, Graber concluded:

Average Americans are capable of extracting enough meaningful political information from the flood of news to which they are exposed to perform the moderate number of citizenship functions that American society expects of them. They keep informed to a limited extent about the majority of significant publicized events. They also learn enough about major political candidates to cast a thoughtful vote and make some judgments about post-election performances.[6]

These are the basic definitions and concepts needed to understand your study of popular culture and mass media. In the next chapter we will provide an overview of how popular culture and mass communication have been influencing one another since the fifteenth century.

SUMMARY

Culture is a term that refers to everything that occurs in a society. It represents all of the customs and practices handed down from generation to generation. Popular culture is the culture of everyone in a society. It is so pervasive that we seldom see it. Mass culture is a term often used synonymously with popular culture. It refers to everything in our culture that is either mass produced or disseminated through the mass media.

Most mass media evolve through a progression cycle called the elitist-popular-specialized (EPS) cycle. The media usually start out in the elitist stage, then progress to the popular stage and finally settle into a stage of specialization.

Several basic components are important to the proper functioning of the communication process. These include the source, message, channel and receiver. In addition, communication has such important elements as feedback, symbols, frames of reference and a variety of noises that include channel, semantic and psychological noise.

Mass communication is one of the more complex forms of communication. It is a process whereby professional communicators use technological devices to share messages over some distance to influence large audiences.

The mass media are the channels used in mass communication. In addition to providing information and entertainment, U.S. mass media are in the business of making money, more than $125 billion each year.

Information processing by the media includes agenda setting and gatekeeping. Agenda setting is a process whereby the mass media help us decide what is important and what isn't. People who work for the mass media serve as gatekeepers, determining what news, information and entertainment reach us.

Consumers also exercise information-processing techniques that help them prevent information overload. They very selectively filter information of interest to increase their knowledge about that which they deem important while screening out a great deal of nonessential material.

THOUGHT QUESTIONS

1 Can you make a list of cultural events you have attended that were created or perpetuated by the mass media?

2 Are there any popular cultural items or activities that are neither mass produced nor shared through the mass media?

3 Can you think of instances in your own life where communication has been hindered by psychological noise? Make a list.

4 What are some recent examples where the mass media have set an agenda for what you should think about?

5 After watching a TV newscast, can you make a list of five or more stories that you remember?

NOTES

1. John C. Merrill and Ralph L. Lowenstein, *Media Messages and Men: New Perspectives in Communication* (New York: McKay, 1971), pp. 33–44.

2. Ray B. Browne, "Popular Culture—The World Around Us," in *The Popular Culture Reader*, ed. Jack Nachbar, Deborah Weiser and John L. Wright

(Bowling Green, Ohio: Bowling Green University Press, 1978), p. 12.

3. Alvin Toffler, *The Third Wave* (Des Plaines, Ill.: Bantam Books, 1980), pp. 155–167.

4. Maxwell E. McCombs and Donald L. Shaw, "The Agenda-Setting Function of the Press," in *Enduring Issues in Mass Communication,* ed. Everette E. Dennis, Arnold H. Ismach and Donald M. Gillmore (St. Paul, Minn.: West, 1978), p. 97.

5. Doris A. Graber, *Processing the News* (New York: Longman, 1984), pp. 201–216.

6. Ibid., p. 204.

ADDITIONAL READING

Berlo, David K. *The Process of Communication.* New York: Holt, Rinehart & Winston, 1960.

Browne, Ray B., and Ambrosetti, Ronald J. *Popular Culture and Curricula.* Bowling Green, Ohio: Bowling Green University Popular Press, 1972.

Dance, Frank E. X., and Larson, Carl E. *The Functions of Human Communication: A Theoretical Approach.* New York: Holt, Rinehart & Winston, 1976.

Fisher, B. Aubrey. *Perspectives on Human Communication.* New York: Macmillan, 1978.

Fishwick, Marshall, and Browne, Ray B. *Icons of Popular Culture.* Bowling Green, Ohio: Bowling Green University Popular Press, 1970.

Glessing, Robert J. *The Underground Press in America.* Bloomington: Indiana University Press, 1970.

Hopper, Robert. *Human Message Systems.* New York: Harper & Row, 1976.

Schramm, Wilbur. *Men, Women, Messages and Media.* New York: Harper & Row, 1982.

Bette Midler played a saddened Mother Earth in the twentieth anniversary Earth Day television special produced for ABC by Time Warner.

CULTURE AND MASS COMMUNICATION: HOW THEY INTERACT

*In my opinion,
we are in danger
of developing
a cult of the
Common Man,
which means
a cult of
mediocrity.*
—Herbert
Hoover,
31st U.S.
President

On April 22, 1990, millions of Americans celebrated the 20th anniversary of Earth Day with a wide variety of special environmental festivals and celebrations. That evening on ABC, Bette Midler played an abused Mother Earth attended to by Dr. Doogie Howser in a star-studded two-hour television special.

Dustin Hoffman, one of the stars on the TV special, said, "I think I am every man. This is the 20th anniversary of Earth Day and yet it is the first one I am aware of."

Why was the 20th anniversary of this annual event the first one that most Americans were aware of? Why after 20 years did Earth Day suddenly become an important event in American popular culture? Why, after years of expressing concern over deteriorating environmental conditions, did environmentalists find their cause a pop cultural event? Why, after years of environmental neglect, were the American masses proclaiming that the decade of the '90s would be the environmental decade?

The answer to these questions, in part, is that the American mass media had blessed Earth Day by deciding that it was an important event in 1990. They had not done so in 1989, or any of the previous years since the first Earth Day in 1970.

Hollywood had started to focus on the environment in 1990 by making environmental issues a part of motion picture plots. Books, newspapers, magazines and television were devoting more attention to environmental issues. In addition to news and feature articles, newspapers and magazines were running advertisements by major corporations, long considered polluters by environmentalists, that were promoting the coming Earth Day observance. These corporate ads were saying, "We love the environment too."

By April of 1990, environmental issues had been the focus of prime time television programming on 30 separate occasions. (A group called Environmental Media Association, formed largely by entertainment industry executives, was promoting the inclusion of environmental themes in TV shows.) Earth Day had been the subject of features on ABC's *Good Morning America* and NBC's *Today* show in the week before the event. ABC's Earth Day special was not the only program on the subject, but rather the culmination of a series of environmental specials. Preceding it on April 20th had been a CBS special entitled *Save the Planet* hosted by *Married . . . With Children*'s Katey Sagal and comedian Bobcat Goldthwait. The music video cable network VH-1 broadcast 52 hours of Earth Day programming over that weekend.

The media showcasing of this event is just one example of how mass media agendas influence American popular culture. Recognizing and understanding this pervasive influence is critical to understanding our basic cultural institutions, customs and behavior.

THE BEGINNING OF MASS COMMUNICATION

In Western culture, mass communication began in the fifteenth century when the German printer Johannes Gutenberg (1398–1468) invented the process of movable type. Movable type allowed molds of alphabet characters to be rearranged to form any message desired. After enough copies of a particular page were printed, the letter molds could be reused to form new words and pages.

Prior to that time, most books were handwritten and very time-consuming to produce. Because of this, reading material was scarce and limited to those in the elite culture—the clergy and nobility. Printing from carved wooden blocks was attempted in the fourteenth century, but did not become a popular form of mass communication. Gutenberg's invention increased the number of books and made them available for a new emerging middle class.

Cultural Changes. The development of printing, which led to the spread of literacy to the middle classes, plus the development of trade and commerce caused major cultural changes. The medieval economy, particularly from the eighth to the twelfth centuries, was very regional and agrarian. Except for religious pilgrimages, wars and Crusades, people did not travel, and they produced consumer goods only to meet local needs.

During the Middle Ages, society was highly stratified; people belonged to one of three groups—clergy, nobility and peasants/artisans—and their social rank virtually never changed. Organizations such as guilds and monasteries, though established for different purposes, helped preserve the stratification of social ranks. Moreover, a strict equality was enforced among peers. Guild masters, for example, had to follow closely a set of rules governing their output and their conduct; no master was allowed to produce more work than any other.

Life in medieval society was very stable. People were born into a social class and remained there throughout their life. However, by the fourteenth century, Europeans had started to travel and explore the world beyond them. They began to discover different cultures and different types of consumer goods, and these discoveries led to the development of long-distance trade.

Pictorial Prints. Printing became the first mass-produced and mass-distributed commodity in this new Western culture. And pictorial prints had a special place in the early history of printing: they were the first form of mass-produced images for popular markets. Albrecht Dürer (1471–1528) was one of the most successful Renaissance artists to use the art forms of woodcuts and engravings to mass-produce pictorial prints. These prints became an early form of mass culture that helped foster consumerism in the lower classes of society.[1]

Modern scholars do not consider works of mass-produced graphic art made before the eighteenth century as examples of mass culture; their antiquity and their display in museums give them the status of fine art. But this view reflects a social redefinition that began in the late seventeenth century, when collectors in Holland and France started treating prints as works of art that could be enjoyed, like paintings, both for their esthetic merits and as investments. Before this time, printmaking primarily involved images for a popular audience.[2] (This same phenomenon can be found today as such popular cultural items as old comic books, baseball cards, posters and magazines are collected and exhibited as art. The current value of such items far exceeds their original selling price.)

In addition to books and pictorial prints, maps were also widely published and circulated. They not only facilitated trade and travel, but were used like pictorial prints as decorative wall hangings.

Early Books. Most books published during the first century of printing were reproductions of traditional religious works, such as the Bible, the Book of Hours (which contains the prescribed order of prayers, readings from the Scriptures, etc.) and the like. Although produced with movable type, they were made to look like their handwritten predecessors by using traditional layouts and typefaces designed to resemble handwriting. Woodcut illustrations were used in these books not so much to illustrate a scene but rather to decorate the pages.[3] As the accuracy of illustrations became more important in the latter half of the fifteenth century, woodcuts gave way to metal engravings, which could be reproduced better.[4]

According to the Canadian media theorist Marshall McLuhan, the development of printing had a profound impact on the thinking process in Western culture. In his popular books written in the 1960s—*The Gutenberg Galaxy* and *Understanding Media*—McLuhan contended that print restricted our thinking to linear patterns—one thought follows the next in an orderly fashion. Not until the advent of the electronic media was our culture given alternatives to linear thinking. Electronic media—particularly television—he said, give us an ''all-at-onceness'' that breaks down the logic of linear thought.[5]

THE PROTESTANT REFORMATION

Although printing flourished during the fifteenth century, mass distribution of these first mass-produced products was not yet possible. Then in the sixteenth century, as the Protestant Reformation spread across Europe, rulers began to fear printing because it permitted the wide distribution of pamphlets criticizing political and religious authorities. They attempted to control it by licensing printers and suppressing books. King Henry II of France, for example, vowed to stamp out all heretical books, and both books and printers were put to the torch during the reign.[6]

Mass Movement. The Reformation, led by a German monk, Martin Luther, was the first mass movement made possible by mass communication. Print was used to mobilize people of all social classes. Luther's main argument was that the pope and his agents should no longer be the sole authority for the interpretation of the Bible and that people should read and study the Bible on their own. He translated the Latin Bible into German, and through mass communication it was made available to the people.

Luther and his followers used mass-produced pamphlets to distribute the new religious thoughts to the masses. They communicated with the illiterate through pictorial prints, much like present-day editorial cartoons, which carried propaganda messages against the Catholic Church and the pope.

Despite the efforts to censor these materials by rulers who remained faithful to the Catholic Church, the Reformation spread. In fact, censorship led to the development of international printing. Publishers in one country would print a book censored in another for distribution in the prohibited country. Protestant Geneva, Switzerland, for example, became a center for the publication of the works of French Protestants.

Also developing at this time were agents who worked as book distributors. Printing became firmly entrenched as the first successfully mass-produced and mass-distributed technology. Venice was the center of printing in this early period, and Italy had the most print shops, 50, followed by Germany, with 30.

DEVELOPMENT OF THE NOVEL

After mass communication developed, more and more people learned to read and write, especially among the middle classes. However, in those days, the elite did not think of literacy as being merely the ability to read and write. Only those who could read critically and understand the Greek and Roman classics were considered truly literate.

Chapbooks. The new readers were not interested in the ancient classics, however. In addition to the Bible, they read small, inexpensive books called chapbooks, which contained folk stories and romances. People read chapbooks simply for enjoyment, not to produce erudite literary analysis. Reading was a new way to enjoy the ancient art of storytelling, only now stories were told in printed versions rather than orally.

The Novel. Middle-class readers also provided a market for a new form of book in the eighteenth century—the novel. Writers, no longer reliant on the patronage of the elite and obliged to satisfy their expectations of elevated, stilted language, began to use the everyday language of the masses.

A major characteristic of the novel was its realism. Each new novel was supposed to be different. Novels emphasized individual experience over collective experience. They were concerned with morality and attempted to present moral themes. To make the novels affordable and widely available, many—such as the works of Charles Dickens in the nineteenth century—were published in serial form. (That is, a few chapters would be published each week or month in pamphlet form.) With the evolution of the novel, the language of the written word became descriptive rather than conceptual or abstract.

INDUSTRIALIZATION

Printing technology remained virtually unchanged during the first several centuries of mass communication. Movable type and hand-cranked presses were state-of-the-art until the early nineteenth century, when a steam-powered cylinder press was perfected in England. This new development allowed for the rapid reproduction of printed materials. In 1846 a rotary press was developed that could produce about 20,000 copies of a newspaper per hour.

The rotary press was just one tiny part of the great technological explosion known as the Industrial Revolution. The Industrial Revolution irreversibly changed Western culture and lifestyles. It opened up new jobs in the cities and caused a migration of people from family farms to urban areas. Immigrants and migrants left their traditional popular culture behind and moved into the cities, where their work was regimented, standardized and homogenized.

Artisans and craftsmen were displaced by semiskilled workers who could operate machines. The use of these machines caused society to be restructured into one that focused on mass production and mass consumption. It also brought about the eventual lowering of the workweek from 12-hour days, six days a week, to the current 40-hour (or less) week.

Sociologist Louis Wirth described the new urban culture as one that saw "the weakening of bonds of kinship, and the declining social significance of the family, the disappearance of the neighborhood, and the undermining of the traditional basis of social solidarity."[7] Set adrift from their familiar surroundings and the age-old rhythms of rural life, the new urban working class had new needs—a way to learn about their new environment and ideas for spending their leisure time. These needs helped transform our culture.

The Metropolitan Newspaper.   One of the first things to develop to meet these needs in the new industrial society was the metropolitan newspaper—often called the penny press—which was aimed at common people in the city. The first such paper in the United States was the *New York Sun,* which was established in 1833, shortly after the invention of the steam-driven press.

Although newspapers had existed since the late seventeenth and early eighteenth centuries, they had been read by the educated elite, not the general public. The costs of printing were too high to reach a mass audience, and the content was not everyday news items but rather dated information from abroad and political reports and essays.

Early issues of the *New York Sun* sold for a penny—rather than the usual six cents—and carried stories about ordinary people. Other penny-press newspapers followed, running news items about local events and common people's problems and interests. This new form of journalism helped to reduce anxiety and solitude by revealing to the lonely, displaced city dwellers their common humanity and their mutual pursuit of money as the common denominator of urban life.[8] According to sociologist Michael Schudson, the penny papers "expressed and built the culture of a democratic market society, a culture that had no place for social or intellectual difference."[9]

Entertainment.   Although not directly related to mass communication at that time, two other institutions developed during the latter part of the nineteenth century to meet the needs of the new urban dwellers—the ballpark and vaudeville. Both kinds of entertainment helped to fill the growing amount of leisure time that workers enjoyed. Both later were transformed into mass-mediated activities.

The first professional baseball team, the Cincinnati Red Stockings, was founded in 1869, and soon there were teams in all the major Eastern and Midwestern cities. The *ballpark* brought together crowds of strangers who could experience a sense of community within the big city as they watched a baseball game. Immigrants were able to shake loose their ethnic ties and become absorbed in the new national game, which was becoming representative of the "American spirit." The green fields and fresh air of the ballpark were a welcome change from the sea of bricks, stone and eventually asphalt that dominated the city scene.

Workers could temporarily escape the routine and dullness of their daily lives by vicariously participating in the competition and accomplishment that baseball games symbolized. Baseball reflected the competitiveness of the workplace and

■ The vaudeville team of Drane and Alexander, photographed in 1912.

the capitalist ethic, as players were bought and sold and were regarded as property. The ballpark also provided a means for spectators to release their frustrations against authority figures: the umpire became a symbol of scorn and frequent cries of ''kill the umpire'' were heard, accompanied by tossed debris.

As professional baseball emerged as a popular pastime, it became an increasingly commercial enterprise. Stadiums were built to seat the spectators, and the hawkers of beer, soda, hot dogs, peanuts and Cracker Jack soon appeared. Advertising on signboards, streetcar posters, handbills, balloons and in newspapers helped ''sell'' the ballpark to the public.[10] With the advent of the electronic media in the twentieth century, baseball and other sports would become a form of mass-mediated entertainment.

Vaudeville was the other popular form of entertainment in the nineteenth century. Vaudeville took the traditional forms of popular entertainment or folk art, such as ethnic humor, juggling, dancing and clown acts, and made them part of the new mass culture.

Vaudeville set the mold for entertainment programs on the electronic media that eventually displaced it in the twentieth century. Radio incorporated the style and humor of vaudeville, and television in turn took over the entertainment format of radio when it developed in the late 1940s and 1950s. The quick cuts and action of modern-day television are ultimately based on the conventions of vaudeville entertainment.[11]

In the late nineteenth century the ballpark and vaudeville were followed by the first two mechanized mass communication media—the phonograph and motion pictures. These media and their cultural impact will be discussed in separate chapters.

MASS MEDIA IN MASS SOCIETY

In the nineteenth century the role of mass communication was to supplement face-to-face communication and provide a means of disseminating—and creating—the new mass culture.

Cultural Niches. As new technologies developed in the industrial age, they had to find a way to serve the new society. Among the mass media, for example, the newspaper found its niche by becoming a medium where the common person could learn about what was happening in his or her city.

The *telephone* was invented by a person working on the invention of a hearing aid and at first was considered as a possible device for broadcasting. However, its developers found a better use for it as an electronic extension of interpersonal communication.

Photography was invented in the nineteenth century as a quicker and less expensive alternative to family portraits produced by an artist. It later became an essential part of the way metropolitan newspapers covered events. Today photography is important in many fields of mass communication.

Radio was developed in the early twentieth century for ship-to-shore communication and for military use; messages could now be transmitted without having to string wire between two points. However, radio's more important function was as a mass medium for news and entertainment. For the first time people could hear news as it was happening and listen to a variety of free vaudeville entertainment in their own homes. Radio became a mass medium just before the Great Depression hit in 1929, and free entertainment was one of the few bright spots in the bleak 1930s.

Besides providing free entertainment, radio allowed members of the newly mobile society to take their favorite entertainment with them when they moved from the family farms and small towns to the large cities. Still to be able to hear such familiar voices as Amos 'n' Andy and Jack Benny when they left their homes in Iowa or Oklahoma for the impersonal cities or agricultural lands of California was an enormous comfort to the migrants of this era.

Television was invented as a potential replacement for radio by adding a picture to the sound. When radio programs—comedies, variety shows and soap operas—moved to television, the format of radio changed to specialized music and news. Radio became a different medium, thus finding a new place for itself in mass society. This trend continues as new technologies come on the scene.

MASS MEDIATION OF LEISURE

As leisure became an important ingredient in the new mass culture—both as a means of stimulating consumerism and of providing activities for the increased hours away from the workplace—the mass media started to promote this leisure.

Sports.   The metropolitan press began to cover the ballpark in the latter part of the nineteenth century. First came the sports page, pioneered by Joseph Pulitzer in his *New York World,* followed by the sports section, introduced by his rival, William Randolph Hearst, in the *New York Journal.* Sports magazines also developed during this period.

When radio became a mass communication medium in the 1920s, it soon found that sporting activities in the ballpark were ideal for programming.

As television developed, network executives eventually decided that baseball—the national pastime—was not as "visual" a sport as football, so TV turned professional football into that medium's number one electronic sports entertainment. (It is interesting to note that professional football was the first team sport to call time outs for commercials.)

Prior to this time, professional football had not become a major sport because of the popularity of collegiate football and the long tradition of baseball as America's favorite professional sport. The National Football League (NFL) was barely holding its own, and the American Football League (AFL) was about to disappear when the television networks came to the rescue. If NBC hadn't put down money for the television rights to its games, the AFL would have folded long before it merged with the NFL.

A third professional football league, the United States Football League (USFL), began play in 1983. However, in 1986 the USFL had to suspend operations when it secured only $1 in damages in a lawsuit it had filed against the NFL. The USFL claimed that the NFL had kept the television networks from giving the USFL a broadcasting franchise—and a guaranteed source of income. The need for mass mediation for a professional sport to survive was made brutally clear.

In 1990, the NFL signed a record breaking $3.6 billion four-year contract with five broadcast and cable networks, including Turner Broadcasting System and ESPN. The contract added two more teams to the play-offs and, by the fall of 1992, two more weeks to the professional football season. To help the networks recoup some of their investment, the contract allowed for the addition of five more 30-second commercial spots to each game by 1992. By 1990, time-outs for commercials had extended the average length of a professional football game from 2 hours, 57 minutes in 1978 to 3 hours, 11 minutes. This marriage for profit between television and the ballpark became very lucrative by the 1990s.

One of the biggest popular cultural events in American society today comes, after months of media hype, as the conclusion of the professional football season—the Super Bowl. This media-created and media-promoted event has traditionally been held on the third or fourth Sunday of January. However, the $3.6 billion NFL contract signed in 1990 had a provision to extend the season so that starting in 1993 the Super Bowl could be played in February, which just happens

BOX 2.1

▪ THE SUPER BOWL: EXPORTING POPULAR CULTURE ▪

On January 15, 1967, CBS and NBC gathered in the Los Angeles Coliseum for a television ratings battle and the creation of one of the biggest popular cultural events in American society—the Super Bowl. The playoff featured the NFL's Green Bay Packers and the AFL's Kansas City Chiefs.

CBS won the ratings battle 16–12, but NBC had a large share of the audience, having promoted the event on its highly rated *Today* and *Johnny Carson* shows. CBS's victory was attributed to the fact that it had been broadcasting NFL football since the 1950s and its television signal reached more American households. NBC had been broadcasting AFL football only since 1965.

This arrangement of two networks broadcasting the same football game was unusual. CBS provided pictures for both networks from 11 cameras set up in the stadium. Each network provided its own commentators.

The Super Bowl has come a long way since those early days. It is now one of the highest rated television shows in the United States, with 30-second commercial spots selling for as much as $700,000 by the 1990s. Americans gather in front of their TV sets on Super Bowl Sunday; many hold parties. Some who normally don't watch professional football find themselves cheering for one team or the other. Some retail outlets that once closed only on Christmas Day and Easter are now closing on Super Bowl Sunday as well.

An entire cultural souvenir industry has developed around the Super Bowl, with everything from T-shirts to team photographs available for those lucky enough to actually attend the event. Even the coin that is flipped to determine who will kickoff at the beginning of the game sells for $4,000.

What, really, is the Super Bowl? It is a mass-media created and promoted cultural event. Is it strictly an American phenomenon? In the beginning, but not anymore.

Twenty years after Super Bowl I, Super Bowl XXI was broadcast via satellite to 60 countries around the world. In some countries TV stations competed to obtain the rights to broadcast the event. In Britain, for example, Channel 4 began broadcasting the game at 11 P.M. with Frank Gifford, one of the original CBS commentators on Super Bowl I doing the British commentary. It was estimated that 3.6 million people stayed up to watch the late-night event in the United Kingdom.

Rupert Murdoch's News Corporation broadcast the Super Bowl live in several countries, and his satellite Sky Channel beamed the game into 18 other countries. Super Bowl XXI aired at 10 A.M. Monday in Australia, just prior to the America's Cup sailing competition finals. In Japan, the Tokyo Broadcasting System had 20 sponsors for a delayed broadcast of the game on Monday night. China Central Television, which carried Super Bowl XX the previous year as its first-ever televised football game, taped Super Bowl XXI for airing in May. It had an estimated audience of more than 300 million.

Thus the mass-media created Super Bowl game of today has come to profoundly affect not just the American popular culture but international popular culture as well.

to fall during a television ratings "sweeps" period in which audiences are measured to determine advertising rates (see Box 2.1).

Super Bowl Sunday, like Monday night football, fulfills many of the socialization functions that the early ballpark met. People come together for Super Bowl parties or Monday night football cocktail hours in order to share a common interest. Strangers with nothing else in common can talk about the electronic ballpark festival for days and weeks afterward. Those who attend a football game in person are happy to find the same features of the electronically broadcast

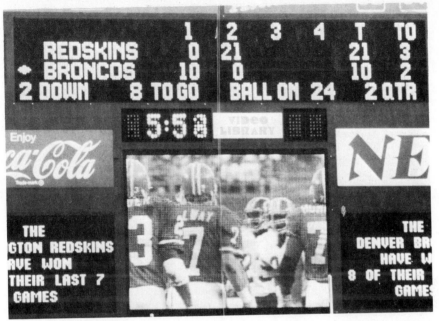

■ Instant replays on large TV screens mounted on scoreboards are now available for fans attending the games.

version available to them—instant replays shown on a large TV screen on top of the scoreboard.

Football, however, is not the only sport that has been changed by television. The World Series is played in freezing October temperatures at night on the East Coast and in late afternoon on the West Coast so that the games will be shown in prime time in other time zones. Professional basketball play-offs now include 16 of the 27 NBA teams and the season stretches into June so TV can have more high-rated games. The National Hockey League has expanded the pauses in play following certain penalties to more than 30 seconds to allow time for a commercial. In preparation for the first U.S. hosted World Cup soccer matches in 1994, the international federation proposed switching from two 45-minute halves to four 25-minute quarters to make the games more appealing to American commercial television.

Sports has proven over the years to be a major money winner for television (see Table 2.1). Unlike sitcoms, which have to be promoted to build an audience, sports is a form of programming that comes with a built-in audience—the fans. During large-audience sports events, the networks can—in addition to making money on commercials—promote their own season's programming.

Consumer Goods. By covering a variety of other leisure-time activities, the mass media influence people to buy things so they can participate too. Recreational vehicles, boats, all-terrain scooters, ski outfits and designer jeans are just some of the consumer goods that have become a part of our popular leisure

TABLE 2.1 TOP RANKED TV SHOWS

Below is a list of the 15 TV shows that have drawn the largest audiences over the years. Note that over half of them are Super Bowl games.

Rank	Program	Date
1.	M*A*S*H Special	2-28-83
2.	Dallas	11-21-80
3.	Roots Part VIII	1-30-77
4.	Super Bowl XVI	1-24-82
5.	Super Bowl XVII	1-30-83
6.	Super Bowl XX	1-26-86
7.	Gone With the Wind—Part 1	11-7-76
8.	Gone With the Wind—Part 2	11-8-76
9.	Super Bowl XII	1-15-78
10.	Super Bowl XIII	1-21-79
11.	Bob Hope Yule Special	1-15-70
12.	Super Bowl XVIII	1-22-84
13.	Super Bowl XIX	1-20-85
14.	Super Bowl XIV	1-20-80
15.	ABC Special—"The Day After"	11-20-83

SOURCE: 1989 Nielsen Media Research.

culture through the mass media's establishment of a need. Advertisements and reflections of active lifestyles on TV and in the movies create these needs.

CRITICISM OF MASS SOCIETY

The new mass culture ushered in by the Industrial Revolution was not accepted without criticism. Intellectuals found the new society debased and felt that it encroached on the elite or high culture. This critique by some European intellectuals, Germans in particular, led in the nineteenth century to the development of Romanticism and the first real study of popular culture. Leaders of the Romantic movement examined the traditional folk culture that was symbolic of the good old days. Such things as folk costumes, customs, foods and history took on a new importance. (Perhaps the most famous and enduring of these efforts was the collection of fairy tales by the Brothers Grimm.)

Other critics of mass culture believed that it had transformed our culture into just another commodity to be bought and sold and that it was intellectually destructive because it provided escapism and created a narcotic function in society. They saw the new mass culture consuming rather than preserving cultural objects that were being mass produced to meet society's entertainment needs. These critics also detested the fact that the mass media conformed to average tastes and did nothing to elevate the cultural level of the masses.

Current Complaints.   This criticism of mass culture still exists today (and in fact seems to be inceasing), with primary focus on the mass media and their influences on society in general. Some intellectuals still believe that television entertainment is "low culture" and is undermining the elite arts. Critics complain that most TV programming is nothing more than a mindless pacifier with no educational or artistic value. Sociologist Dwight MacDonald theorized that a significant part of the population is "chronically confronted with a choice of going to a concert or to the movies, of reading Tolstoy or a detective story, of looking at old masters or at a TV show."[12]

Defenders of high culture express concern that the proliferation of commercialized mass culture is blurring the distinction between elite and mass culture. They point out that this fusion of the two types of culture is not raising the level of mass culture but instead is corrupting high culture. MacDonald says, "There is nothing more vulgar than sophisticated kitsch" (a German term for mass culture).[13]

Critics contend that art in popular or mass culture is predigested so that spectators are spared the effort of understanding genuine art and given a shortcut to appreciating its pleasures. It is much easier to view a Norman Rockwell painting and instantly understand it than it is to quickly comprehend the meaning of an expressionistic Van Gogh.

This democratization of art, critics continue, leads to a homogenization of our culture that is analogous to the homogenization of milk—the globules of cream are evenly distributed throughout the milk, instead of floating separately on top.[14] In other words, the qualities of high and low culture have been blended together, and the demand for the "cream" has all but disappeared.

Another major criticism leveled at the mass media, particularly television, is that both news and entertainment are treated superficially. Critics charge that there seems to be a preoccupation with conflict and celebrity status and the major focus is to entertain rather than inform or educate.

In the 1980s a new criticism of the mass media developed. A group of Americans, led by the Reverend Jerry Falwell and his Liberty Foundation (a new name for his Moral Majority political lobby), began expressing fear that the mass media were corrupting our society sexually and morally. In 1985 a group called Fairness in Media attempted, without success, to take over the CBS network so that it could "take the bias out of its programming." Other groups attempted to get Congress to investigate allegedly obscene lyrics and satanic messages in recorded music, and a mid-1980s government commission on pornography was urging chain stores to stop selling erotica magazines like *Playboy* and *Penthouse*. These attacks continued into the 1990s with efforts by police, with the backing of some courts, to jail sellers and performers of rap musical lyrics that were considered obscene. The target of these arrests were the group 2 Live Crew and performer Luther Campbell.

Criticism of the mass media has grown in recent decades as a result of the rapid expansion of popular music, paperback novels, television soap operas, violence-ridden movie thrillers and videocassettes which are now available at video rental stores, in vending machines and even at some supermarkets. Although the artistic

BOX 2.2

▪ MASS CULTURE SHAPES THE MASS MEDIA ▪

Although the mass media have long been criticized for the way they shape our popular culture, the culture itself plays a role in shaping media content.

An example of this came in the late 1980s when the movie and television industries started reversing their trend of showing promiscuous sex and began returning to the era of old-fashioned romance. This was prompted by the life-and-death AIDS (acquired immune deficiency syndrome) issue, which had become one of the most serious health threats facing the culture in the late 1980s.

Television was one of the first to address the problem in such specials as NBC's *An Early Frost,* about a young man trying to cope with the disease; CBS's *An Enemy Among Us,* about a teenager with AIDS; Showtime's *Brothers,* produced by Gary Nardino and Paramount Productions; and in individual episodes of such programs as *Hill Street Blues, St. Elsewhere,* and *L.A. Law.* By the 1987–88 season, the producers of such shows as *Cagney & Lacey, Cosby, The Golden Girls* and *Cheers* were attempting to address the issue.

The most dramatic change in media sexual attitudes came in daytime soap operas, which had frequently featured regular characters engaging in casual sex. By 1987, casual sex was on the decline, and soap opera themes were returning to old-fashioned romance. NBC's *Days of Our Lives,* one of the pioneers in teenage sexuality, began inserting story lines such as a young boy going to a pharmacy to "get protection," and eventually toned down its use of promiscuity. When Justin Kirakas was first introduced in the show, he had a girl in every port and plenty in his hometown of Salem, Massachusetts. By 1987, Justin was involved in a serious relationship and was not going to touch the woman until after they married. Although casual sex on soap operas hasn't disappeared, it has declined some and efforts are made to suggest that participants are more careful.

The motion-picture industry also felt the need to recognize the AIDS threat. Producers were concerned about showing unsafe sex yet were reluctant to go back to the days of stringent self-censorship. One of the ways they dealt with this issue was to include a box of condoms in the bedroom during love scenes. Among the first to do so were *Dragnet* and *Skin Deep. Masquerade* had to change its title from *Dying for Love* because of the AIDS sensitivity. Other producers required scripts to be altered to take out the unsafe sex scenes. Producer Steve Tisch told a *Los Angeles Times* reporter that his biggest hit, *Risky Business* (1983), "could not and should not be made in 1987."

Even the advertising industry was affected by the AIDS problem. Many media that had shied away from condom ads, such as local TV stations, began carrying sensitive ads promoting condom use for safe sex. However, network television continued to ban such ads.

The media and our culture are closely entwined and what happens to one affects the other.

merits of media-produced culture and its impact on society have been debated for generations, at no time has the criticism been greater than in recent years (see Box 2.2).

COMMERCIALIZATION OF CULTURE

The Industrial Revolution brought into our culture the concept of rapid production and consumption of goods and services. As our mass culture grows and expands and new forms of mass media develop, consumerism grows with it (see Box 2.3).

Individuals in our new mass society are still struggling to regain their identity,

■ Despite the growing criticism of the mass media and charges that media content often causes anti-social behavior, crusaders sometimes use the media to disseminate their own social agendas. Pictured is former First Lady Nancy Reagan appearing with Gary Coleman on the TV sitcom *Diff'rent Strokes* to promote her "Just Say No to Drugs" campaign.

but many of them now seem to believe that the best way to establish that identity is through the purchase of the "right" types of consumer goods. The automobile they drive, the clothes they wear and the type of house they live in tell the world "who they are." The industrial-age American myth holds that the more material goods a person acquires, the better off he or she is. Since having more symbolizes being better, there is never enough, and the society of production and consumption continues to grow.

Product Images.   The meanings symbolized by these material goods are disseminated to the masses through the media. The multibillion-dollar industry of advertising in the United States is not the only way in which consumer goods are "sold." The way products are portrayed on television, in motion pictures, in popular songs, on record-album covers and in special-interest magazines plays a very important role in transmitting meaning and generating desire for products.

The importance of the role the media can play in transmitting product images can best be illustrated by the roller-coaster successes and failures of the hat industry. Hats were an important element in men and women's wearing apparel in

BOX 2.3

▪ SELLING THE PERSIAN GULF WAR ▪

The American consumer culture is quick to find new opportunities to expand and advance our popular culture. By the time the Persian Gulf war broke out in 1991, the American consumer culture was geared up for the event. Months prior to the outbreak, Saddam Hussein had been the target of novelty songs on the radio, bumper stickers and even effigy dolls that were regularly burned in public places. Radio disc jockeys led blood bank drives and yellow ribbon campaigns.

Following the outbreak of the war, a Maryland software firm released "F-15 Eagle," a Gulf-based video war game; fans at a monster truck event cheered while a 12,000-pound modified pickup was driven over a car containing a Saddam Hussein dummy; a New York suburb turned a computer bulletin board into a high-tech war debate; and consumer advocate Chuck Harder's syndicated satellite radio show "For the People" changed its format to accept only callers with messages for the troops in the Middle East (these messages were then rebroadcast by shortwave to the war zone). Holly-

wood film studios quickly prepared and released action films based on the war.

Both hawks and doves began using the likeness of Bart Simpson, without authorization from his creator, on pro- and anti-war T-shirts and buttons. Caught in the middle, Bart's creator, Matt Groening, issued the following statement: "Bart Simpson is against the war—until he's old enough to start one."

Even Super Bowl XXV, which was played a week and a half after the outbreak of the war, capitalized on the conflict. Miniature American flags were sold by vendors to fans at the Tampa, Florida, stadium so they could wave their patriotism in front of TV cameras. The half-time festivities even had sons and daughters of service men and women in the gulf parading and flag-waving in the stadium.

Although this was not the first time the American consumer culture had taken advantage of war to expand sales (it has been evident in every war since the Revolution), our high-tech mass culture was able to speed up the effort to deliver products to the consumer this time around.

the new mass society. Until the 1940s well-dressed gentlemen, for example, always wore a hat when they went outdoors. Then Clark Gable and a few other Hollywood stars appeared outdoors in movies without hats. The bottom dropped out of the hat industry as thousands of men started copying the new hatless style. It took the character of J. R. Ewing in *Dallas* and the one played by John Travolta in the film *Urban Cowboy* to stimulate the desire for 10-gallon hats before the industry bounced back in the late 1970s. (Assisting the hat industry's comeback has been the promotion of caps that advertise popular culture products and brand names.)

An entire profession, called product brokerage, has developed around the need to portray consumer goods favorably in the entertainment business. Product brokers work with the people responsible for acquiring props for movies and TV shows to encourage them to use certain products in their shows. For example, Mercedes-Benz of North America, Inc. will lend its automobiles to film producers free as long as they agree not to let the "bad guys" drive them. The best-known of these brokers is Associated Film Productions (AFP), which represents more than 150 brand names. Examples of product-broker efforts in the past ten years include the placement of Wheaties in *Rocky III*, Pampers in *Three Men and a Baby*, Milk

■ Reese's Pieces helped cement the relationship between these two characters in the film *E.T.* The scene caused sales of this Hershey candy to skyrocket.

Duds in *The Formula,* a Nikon camera in *Hopscotch,* Coca-Cola in *Missing,* Blue Diamond almonds in *Arthur* and a Dynavite exercise machine in *Being There.*[15]

The effectiveness of product portrayal in movies can best be illustrated by the results of the use of Reese's Pieces, the candy used to cement a friendship between the extraterrestrial creature and the young boy, Elliott, in Steven Spielberg's film *E.T.* With promotional help from Hershey, sales of Reese's Pieces jumped 70 percent the month after the film was released, and within two months the candy was being sold at the refreshment counters of 800 theaters that previously had not carried it.[16]

Exporting Commercialized Pop Culture. The commercialization of our popular culture is not limited to the confines of the United States. For many years America has been exporting its popular culture, first as images in motion pictures, magazines, music and television and finally as commercial enterprises.

Coca-Cola and its icon logo and Levi's jeans have long been popular around the world. Even replicas of the ultimate American leisure playground, Disneyland, can now be found in France and Japan.

One noteworthy news story in 1990 was the opening of the first McDonald's restaurant in Moscow. On January 31, 1990, 30,000 Russians stood in line up to an hour and 45 minutes to get their first taste of Big Macs, French fries, and chocolate and strawberry "milk cocktails." Billed as the largest McDonald's restaurant in the world, the Moscow facility seats 700 and has 605 employees. The facility still serves about 5,000 sandwiches an hour and the lunchtime line is 90 minutes and 1,200 people long. Although it was the first one in the Soviet Union, some 19 more have been scheduled to be built in this communist country. (This is a relatively small number compared to the 714 McDonald's restaurants in Japan and 11,300 world-wide. Japan also has 875 Kentucky Fried Chicken outlets.)

■ One of the more successful efforts to export American popular culture has been accomplished by McDonald's, which has over 11,000 outlets to sell "Big Macs" worldwide, including 741 in Japan alone.

CULTS IN POPULAR CULTURE

Many of the mass media we will be studying have already entered the specialization stage of the EPS cycle (see Chapter 1). Our studies will show that this move toward specialization has been assisted by a need that has existed in our mass culture since the early days of the Industrial Revolution—a need for individuals to stand apart from the masses while still having a sense of belonging to something, such as a subcultural group or "cult." Thus, it is important that we understand what a cult is and how it fits within our mass culture.

The words *cult* or *cultists* may evoke the image of religious worshipers with shaved heads and saffron-colored robes passing out literature at airports. Or we may remember the Jonestown suicides by cultist followers of the Reverend Jim Jones or recall some of the TV specials on satanic cult worship.

Cults, however, do not necessarily have to be bizarre or evil. *Webster's Third New International Dictionary* includes among its definitions of cult: "a. great or excessive devotion or dedication to some person, idea or thing . . . such devotion regarded as a literary or intellectual fad or fetish; b. the object of such devotion; c. a body of persons characterized by such devotion." Under such a definition cults can range from skateboard enthusiasts to baseball card collectors.

Many cults are interrelated with the mass media. Some develop as a result of media attention given to a "person, idea or thing" while others are catered to by specialized media publications that help perpetuate the interest in the cult.

Rock Fans.   One category of cults that has developed around the popular music industry focuses on "great or excessive devotion" to rock stars. In the eyes of their followers, they can do no wrong. Long after the Beatles split up and Elvis Presley died, cultlike followers have continued to worship these performers. Elvis Presley, for example, was the subject of a cover photo on the June 1990 issue of *Life* magazine and a series of features on television's *Current Affair* in the fall of 1990, over a decade after his death. With many cultlike followers still worshiping him, he is still able to sell magazines and attract audiences for TV shows.

Movie–TV Buffs.   A large cultlike following developed around the movies *Star Wars, The Empire Strikes Back* and *Return of the Jedi.* Some people say they have seen these movies hundreds of times, and box-office receipts seem to support these claims.

Probably the largest and most interesting television-produced cult has been the "Trekkies," who are devoted followers of the *Star Trek* series (see Box 2.4). The Trekkies have long outlasted the original TV series of the late 1960s. Each year thousands gather at conventions, many of them dressed in Star Trek costumes complete with pointed plastic ears. Exhibitors at these conventions sell a variety of Star Trek memorabilia.

In the 1990s, TV once again helped form a subculture. Soon after the Fox network introduced the cartoon family *The Simpsons* to prime time, young people began wearing Bart Simpson T-shirts with such messages as "Underachiever and Proud of It." Some schools reacted to the new youth subculture by banning the T-shirts.

Gang Members.   Inner-city gangs provide still another subcultural identification for individuals attempting to establish their own identities in a mass society. The glamour of gangs has been perpetuated through the media for years, particularly in motion pictures. In 1990, there were more than 500 gangs with some 80,000 known members in Los Angeles County alone. These gangs usually reflect ethnic and territorial identities. However, rival gangs with similar ethnic origins often find themselves "at war" because of territorial disputes. The two largest gangs in Los Angeles, the Bloods and the Crips, are predominantly African-American and are the most bitter rivals.

Subcult Characteristics.   It is important to examine cults or subcultures to see how they fit into the larger cultural scene and to see how mass media affect them. Many of our subcultures, particularly those involving youth, are music oriented. Subcultures consist of the practices, fashions and styles of subgroups in society. Members of subcultures tend to stigmatize themselves and thus establish roles as social outcasts.

Members of a subculture use signs or badges of identification. Punk rockers, for example, used safety pins, patches, earrings and so forth to set themselves

BOX 2.4

▪ THE TREKKIES "STAR TREK" THROUGH THE MEDIA ▪

Star Trek was a 1960s television series that wouldn't die. Instead it became the catalyst for a complete subculture, called the Trekkies, and became multimedia entertainment.

The science-fiction show had been modeled after a previously popular television genre—the Western. As Robert L. Shayon pointed out in *Saturday Review*, "*Star Trek* is a space version of *Wagon Train*."* The ratings for the series were not very high and it was taken off the air after three seasons. Although its viewers had not been many, they were loyally devoted fans. An effort to cancel the show after its first season produced one of the largest outpourings of protest mail in television's history.

The story of *Star Trek* continues to live, thanks to the high-tech world of multiple mass media. The science-fiction adventures of the spaceship U.S.S. *Enterprise* and its crew are now disseminated in a variety of mass-media forms. Although canceled by the network, *Star Trek* continued on TV in syndicated reruns. The story later spawned books, fotonovels, movies and audio books (see Chapter 5). Simon & Schuster's audio division brought out the audio book *Star Trek IV: The Voyage Home* as the first in a series in the fall of 1987. It was based on Vonda McIntyre's novelization of the 1986 *Star Trek* movie by the same name. Also released at the same time was *Strangers from the Sky* by Margaret W. Bonanno, an audio book based on the latest installment of Pocket Books' *Star Trek* series. Finally in 1987—some 20 years after its first television debut—a new version of *Star Trek*, called *Star Trek: The Next Generation,* was introduced to television audiences.

What makes *Star Trek* so popular? According to Wm. Blake Tyrrell, writing in a 1977 issue of the *Journal of Popular Culture, Star Trek* was a product of the dreams and nightmares of the 1960s. The show blends the imagination of a high-tech world of the twenty-third century with the human needs and emotions of the twentieth century. It gives *Star Trek* fans hope for the future by showing them that good old American values and ingenuity will still be important in the world of tomorrow.

*Robert L. Shayon, "Interplanetary Spock," Saturday Review, *June 17, 1967, p. 46.*

apart from and ridicule mass society. Styles become a signal to the mass culture that the subculture wants to be "different."

Punks gave hidden meanings to style and objects. They used their badges and style to symbolize anarchy, and they wanted people in mass society to dislike them. Their goal was to be in opposition to the usual practices of society.

Thus the style of a subculture has two points: (1) to oppose everyday life and (2) to establish acceptance within the subculture. This need to establish an identity different from the masses through dress existed at the beginning of the Industrial Revolution, when workers in different occupations adopted certain wearing apparel to give them collective identities. Their clothes became their badges of identity and set the "blue-collar" workers apart from the merchants. Among punks, hair color, tattoos and markings on leather jackets all signified something within the subculture and at the same time attempted to provoke disgust from the mass culture. Contrary to popular myth, which portrays subcultures as lawless forms, "the internal structure of any particular subculture is characterized by an extreme orderliness: each part is organically related to other parts and it is through the fit between them that the subcultural member makes sense of the world."[17]

Although punk started in England as an effort by some young people to reject mass society, it wasn't long before the mass media had transmitted their styles and customs throughout the world. People with spiked and dyed hair, tattoos and safety pins in the cheek could soon be seen in such scattered locations as San Francisco, Vienna and Tokyo.

Cultural Industries.   Although subcultures attempt to reject the larger mass culture and establish their own identities, they are an important part of the mass-culture industries. They are promoted and perpetuated by the mass media and mass industry—and not just the music industry, around which many of them develop.

Manufacturers of mass-produced consumer goods soon get on the bandwagon and merchandise the subculture. Even major chain drugstores carried washable colored hair spray for punk rockers. Sales of safety pins, earrings and leather jackets multiplied after the punk movement began. In the United States, the mass media toned down the punk subculture into "new wave" and the subcultural fashions entered the main culture. Women paid several hundred dollars for ripped dresses because they were part of the trendy "new wave" fashion.

Another subculture, the biker subculture, started out as youth-oriented in the 1940s, but today its members are gray-haired and middle-aged men and women. This subculture grew dramatically after the motion picture *The Wild One,* starring Marlon Brando, was released for a youth-oriented audience in the 1950s. The movie, based on a true incident that took place in Hollister, California, depicted a motorcycle gang taking over a town and wreaking havoc. Brando played a tough-talking gang leader who was seen as an anti-Establishment hero. As numerous biker cults developed, it became necessary for them to establish their own subcults within the larger subculture by adopting their own gang names and proudly displaying "their own colors," which give them individual identities.

The Harley-Davidson Motorcycle Company has made millions from this sub-culture. All kinds of paraphernalia have been marketed with the now-famous Harley-Davidson wings on them. Several new products entered the marketplace in the late 1980s, including a wine cooler and a brand of cigarettes catering to the "macho" smoker. The cigarettes were produced by Lorillard, the nation's fourth-largest cigarette maker. The Harley insignia has become an icon as commonly recognized as McDonald's golden arches and the Coca-Cola logo.

Although subculture members try to be different from and antagonistic to the mass culture, they cannot escape from the commercialization of mass society. Each time a new subculture develops, the economy of the main mass culture benefits by providing products for the subculture, and the mass media also are right there to get a piece of the action—either through recorded music or special-interest magazines catering to the new subculture.

Wherever possible, marketing efforts of subcultural products are designed to expand the market into the mass culture as well. The blue jeans of the youth subculture of the 1950s and 1960s, for example, eventually found their way into the mass culture as an acceptable form of dress. The mass culture also attempts to water down the subculture until it becomes acceptable to the masses. For example, the health-food movement was once a fringe subculture but now is big business in the mass culture.

These interrelationships among our mass society, its subcultures and the mass media will be further explored when we examine the various media and how they function later in the book.

SUMMARY

Political democracy, public education and the Industrial Revolution of the nineteenth century ushered in a new mass society that depended on mass production and mass consumption of goods and services. The mass media developed as an integral part of this new mass society and became the disseminators and creators of the new mass culture.

With the new culture came more leisure time; to fill people's leisure hours new cultural industries were developed, which the mass media marketed. Among the first cultural institutions to develop in the new mass society were the metropolitan newspaper, the ballpark and vaudeville. Each helped the new city dwellers to cope with their new lifestyle.

As new technologies developed, they had to find a niche in society. Some of the communication media finding a role in the new mass society were newspapers, telephones, photography, radio and television.

Our new mass culture has been commercialized to the extent that our economy revolves around selling us consumer goods as cultural items. The mass media play an important role in this commercialization of culture and even help to export it.

Even the subcultures in our society that consciously reject mass culture and are antagonistic to it are caught up in the cultural industry. Members of these subcultures buy items that identify their subcultures. These items are produced by the mass society and often become fads in the mainstream culture.

THOUGHT QUESTIONS

1 Can you think of any existing cultures in the world that are similar to the strict stratified system that existed in the Middle Ages prior to Gutenberg's invention? Could this stratification be changed if the mass media in that society became entrenched in the popular culture? What would these changes be like?

2 What role did mass communication play in the development of the industrial society? Are there similar activities at work as our culture moves into the information age?

3 What examples can you list of current efforts to commercialize our leisure culture?

4 What are some of the latest issues being advanced in the ongoing criticism of the mass media?

5 Can you make a list of different subcultures that are prevalent in today's mass culture?

NOTES

1. Chandra Mukerji, *From Graven Images* (New York: Columbia University Press, 1983), p. 38.

2. Ibid.

3. Ibid, p. 53.

4. William Ivins, *Prints and Visual Communication* (Cambridge, Mass.: MIT Press, 1953), pp. 47–49.

5. Marshall McLuhan, *Understanding Media: The Extensions of Man* (New York: Signet Books, 1964), pp. 84–90.

6. Mukerji, p. 45.

7. Louis Wirth, "Urbanism as a Way of Life," *American Journal of Sociology* 44 (July 1938): 21.

8. Gunther Barth, *City People* (Oxford: Oxford University Press, 1980), pp. 58–109.

9. Michael Schudson, *Discovering the News: A Social History of American Newspapers* (New York: Basic Books, 1978), p. 60.

10. Barth, pp. 148–191.

11. Ibid., pp. 192–228.

12. Dwight MacDonald, "A Theory of Mass Culture," in *Mass Media and Mass Man*, ed. Alan Casty (New York: Holt, Rinehart & Winston, 1968), pp. 13–14.

13. Ibid., p. 17.

14. Ibid.

15. Michael Schudson, *Advertising, The Uneasy Persuasion: Its Dubious Impact on American Society* (New York: Basic Books, 1984), p. 102.

16. Joseph Winski, "Hershey Befriends Extra-Terrestrial," *Advertising Age,* July 19, 1982, pp. 1, 66.

17. Dick Hebdige, *Subculture: The Meaning of Style* (London: Methuen, 1979), p. 113.

ADDITIONAL READING

Burke, Peter. *Popular Culture in Early Modern Europe.* New York: Harper & Row, 1978.

Cantor, Norman F., and Werthman, Michael S., eds. *The History of Popular Culture.* New York: Macmillan, 1968.

Geist, Christopher D., ed. *Popular Culture and the Mass Media: A Reader.* Bowling Green, Ohio: Bowling Green University Popular Press, 1977.

Jacobs, Norman, ed. *Culture for the Millions?: Mass Media in Modern Society.* Princeton, N.J.: Van Nostrand, 1959.

McLuhan, Marshall. *The Gutenberg Galaxy: The Making of Typographic Man.* Toronto: University of Toronto Press, 1962.

———. *Culture Is Our Business.* New York: Ballantine, 1970.

Real, Michael R. *Mass-Mediated Culture.* Englewood Cliffs, N.J.: Prentice-Hall, 1977.

Williams, Raymond. *Television: Technology and Cultural Form,* New York: Schocken, 1975.

Media coverage of news events, such as this 1989 demonstration at Tiananmen Square in Beijing, China, differs according to the prevailing political philosophy in a given country.

MEDIA CONTROLS: PHILOSOPHICAL

Congress shall make no law respecting an establishment of religion, or prohibiting the free exercise thereof; or abridging the freedom of speech, or of the press or the right of the people peaceably to assemble, and to petition the Government for a redress of grievances.

—First Amendment, Constitution of the United States

News Item: In the tense early-morning hours of June 4, 1989, thousands of army troops stormed Tiananmen Square in Beijing, China, killing students and other pro-democracy demonstrators. Chinese television showed youthful protesters attacking army trucks, tanks and armored cars, but no pictures of the attacks by the army on the protesters. The only dead and injured shown by the government-owned TV were identified as army personnel. Three days earlier, China had placed restrictions on foreign reporting in Beijing, prohibiting interviews and

■ Chinese students demonstrating for democracy in Tiananmen Square in 1989 were portrayed as the aggressors on Chinese television when troops moved in to squelch the protest. Government-controlled news media present the "official government" position on controversial issues.

banning photography and videotaping in the areas around Tiananmen Square. Despite these restrictions, news and photos of the government's massacre were printed and broadcast outside of China and the free world was outraged.

News Item: The Berlin Wall and the Communist regimes in Eastern Europe both tumbled during 1989, ending four decades of Soviet Communist domination. Political reform swept through East Germany, Hungary, Poland, Czechoslovakia, Bulgaria and Romania. The decade of the '90s saw Western capitalist investments stimulating the Eastern European economies.

News Item: After two Supreme Court decisions ruling that desecration of the American flag was political expression protected by the First Amendment, the U.S. Congress in 1990 narrowly defeated a populist effort to amend the Bill of Rights by placing restrictions on freedom of expression.

News Item: The United States celebrated the 200th anniversary of the Bill of Rights in 1991, the document that granted unprecedented rights to the people of this nation.

What do these news items have to do with our study of mass communication and its relationship to our culture? Each incident relates to a differing or changing philosophy regarding how the mass media should function in a society. In this chapter we will examine four different mass media philosophies and how they operate in selected countries. Hopefully, this discussion of the philosophical limitations on the media will give you a better understanding of how the media function in our society.

Two basic political approaches to the operation of mass communication exist,

■ A demonstrator pounds away at the Berlin Wall as East German border guards look on from above.

and each of these has an offshoot. These four theories—authoritarian, libertarian, Soviet Communist and social responsibility—are characterized by Siebert, Peterson and Schramm in their classic book, *Four Theories of the Press*.[1]

AUTHORITARIAN THEORY

The *authoritarian theory* is the oldest. When mass communication began expanding in the sixteenth century, this theory developed quickly in Europe to protect the autocratic monarchies and the Church from heretical publications.

When the printing press was invented, authoritarian states saw it as an important tool. Many attempts were made to use printing to unify the people. This was done by printing only *wisdom* and *truth*—which, of course, were identified by the heads of the Church and state.

Thus the early press—starting with Gutenberg—published mostly authorized religious materials and—as people became more literate—chapbooks, the forerunner to the romance novel. Only after Martin Luther's challenge to the Catholic Church in 1517 led to the Protestant Reformation did books begin to appear that threatened the authoritarian state or religious order. Attempts were immediately made to censor "heretical" books by burning them and their printers. Less drastic, in order to limit printing to those who would operate for the "good of the state," governments established a system of state licensing for printers.

American Colonies.   England was one of the countries to require the licensing of printers, and this policy, as well as other aspects of the authoritarian theory, was carried over to her American colonies. Although the British Parliament allowed the Licensing Act to expire in 1694, colonial governors retained controls on the press. When John Campbell received permission to establish the first regularly published newspaper in the colonies in 1704, he agreed to permit the authorities to screen all material before it was published.

The official attitude toward printing in the American colonies was best summed up in a 1671 statement attributed to Sir William Berkeley, governor of the Virginia colony: "But, I thank God, we have no free schools nor printing; and I hope we shall not have [them] these hundred years. For learning has brought disobedience and heresy and sects into the world, and printing has divulged them and libels against the government. God keep us from them both."[2]

Authoritarian states that did not have licensing laws attempted to exercise prior censorship by requiring that all printed material be approved by an official government censor before it could be printed and distributed. As the number of presses and the volume of printed materials grew, however, this approach proved too cumbersome.

In the eighteenth century, control by *prior restraint* was largely replaced by the threat of punishment *after* publication. The laws of treason (the act of intending to overthrow the government) and sedition (the act of showing disrespect for the government) were used to prosecute printers of materials that were considered dangerous to the state.

Modern Examples.   Although the authoritarian theory of the press waned in many Western cultures by the second half of the eighteenth century, versions of it are still manifested in authoritarian states today. In 1989, for example, the government of the People's Republic of China, after sending out a horrifically authoritarian message by massacring the Tiananmen Square demonstrators for democracy, clamped down on foreign reporters and directed its own media to show the protesters as the aggressors. The government then started a series of raids, seizing underground presses to ensure that only the official version of the story was spread. In June of 1990, the Chinese government warned foreign journalists to cease "illegal" news after two nights of protests at Beijing University. When foreign correspondents reported on the fact that students were demonstrating on the anniversary of Tiananmen Square, several of the correspondents were beaten, kicked, harassed and forced at gunpoint to leave the campus.

Press controls in South Africa were prevalent during the apartheid struggles of the 1980s. Journalists were prohibited from being "on the scene, or at a place within sight of any unrest, restricted gathering or security action" and were forbidden to report any "subversive" comments criticizing the government. Violators faced jail terms up to ten years and fines up to $10,000 or suspension of publication. Although the strict apartheid news censorship regulations were lifted by the end of the decade, there still remained more than 50 laws in South Africa that curtailed freedom of the press.

In Turkey there are 153 laws and rules governing the press; these laws have been implemented by the Turkish government since 1921. By 1990, it was reported that nearly two dozen Turkish editors and reporters were in jail at any given time for publishing political views unacceptable to the government.

Similar censorship restrictions exist in authoritarian states throughout third world countries.

LIBERTARIAN THEORY

In contrast to the authoritarian view that the media should be controlled so that they do not interfere with the mission of the government, the *libertarian theory* emerged from a premise that the government should exist solely to serve the interests of the individual. It holds that the media should serve the people rather than the government and that the best way to find the truth is to have as many opinions aired as possible. Wilbur Schramm said that the libertarian movement was "foreshadowed in the sixteenth century, envisioned in the seventeenth, fought for in the eighteenth and finally brought into widespread use in the nineteenth."[3]

The Age of Enlightenment, during which the libertarian theory emerged, resulted from a number of developments in Europe during the early modern period (fifteenth to eighteenth centuries). These developments included scientific and geographical discoveries; the rise of trade and consumerism; the rise of the merchant class, which led to the growth of a middle class; the Protestant Reformation, which freed the individual from established church dogmas; and political and social revolutions that challenged the authoritarian concept and championed individual rights and freedoms.

Libertarians.   Many philosophers and writers contributed to the formation of the libertarian concept. Among them were John Milton (1608–1674), John Locke (1632–1704), Isaac Newton (1642–1727), Adam Smith (1723–1790), Benjamin Franklin (1706–1790), Thomas Jefferson (1743–1826), James Madison (1751–1836) and John Stuart Mill (1806–1873). The philosophy behind the libertarian theory of the press is described in the following letter, which Thomas Jefferson wrote to a friend in 1787:

> *I am persuaded that the good sense of the people will always be found to be the best army. They may be led astray for a moment, but will soon correct themselves. The people are the only censors of their governors; and even their errors will tend to keep these to the true principles of their institution. To punish these errors too severely would be to suppress the only safeguard of the public liberty. The way to prevent these irregular interpositions of the people, is to give them full information of their affairs through the public channel of the public [news]papers, and to contrive that those papers should penetrate the whole mass of the people. The basis of our government being the opinion of the people, the very first object should be to keep that right; and were it left to me to decide whether we should have a government without newspapers, or newspapers without a government, I should not hesitate a moment to prefer the latter.*[4]

Jefferson, who also felt strongly about the need for a literate society, qualified his statement favoring a society with free newspapers by saying, "I should mean that every man should receive those papers, and be capable of reading them."

James Madison, another framer of our constitution, expressed his views on the importance of a free press to our country's experiment in democracy as follows:

> *Nothing could be more irrational than to give the people power and to withhold from them information without which power is abused. A people who mean to be their own governors must arm themselves with power which knowledge gives. A popular govern-*

■ Thomas Jefferson felt so strongly that a free press was essential to a democracy that he stated that if he had to select between a government without a free press or a free press without a government, he would prefer the latter.

ment without popular information or means of acquiring it is but a prologue to a farce or a tragedy, or perhaps both.[5]

American Democracy. Because of people like Jefferson, Madison and others, the libertarian theory of the press was an inherent part of the American experiment in democracy. The First Amendment in the Bill of Rights guarantees not only free speech but a free press as well.

Under the libertarian theory, it is the press that keeps the individual informed about the operations of government. It is important to remember that the American experiment in democracy was based on a system of checks and balances. Three separate and independent branches of government were established—the judicial, legislative and executive branches. In addition, the First Amendment provided that the press serve as a "watchdog" of government. This is why the press is often considered a fourth branch—the "fourth estate"—of the governmental power structure. Likewise, with the recent advent of the electronic press, those media have been referred to as the "fifth estate."

In the First Amendment the founders of our country installed a mechanism to protect the public's right to be informed. Thus the American press operates under the libertarian premise that the people's right to know is an essential ingredient of a free society. This right prevails over the right of any government official to silence a critical press. (Limited efforts to restrict this press freedom, such as the Alien and Sedition Acts, will be discussed in Chapters 4 and 7.)

Modern Examples. Examples of the libertarian theory at work appear in American newspapers daily. The seriousness of the savings and loan crisis in the early 1990s—and the burden its bailout would be on the taxpayers—would probably never have become known to the public if government officials had been able to keep it and their deregulation blunders secret. The same can be said for other major scandals in preceding decades—Iran-Contra, Watergate, Vietnam War, etc.

THE SOVIET COMMUNIST CONCEPT

The *Soviet Communist theory,* a modern offshoot of the authoritarian theory, seemed to work well for Communist bloc countries until Mikhail Gorbachev introduced *glasnost* (openness) as part of the restructuring of the Soviet society in the mid-1980s. The theory prior to *glasnost* held that the media should be extensions of the state and should foster unity and social cohesiveness. The Soviets contended that theirs is a "people's press": the Communist party serves the people and the press helps the party carry out that function.

In the Soviet Union, all mass media are owned and operated by the state. The mass communicators needed to be loyal party members so they would know how to interpret all communications correctly, from the party's point of view. Westerners criticized this control of the press, saying that the media cannot serve two masters: the press is either a publicist for the government or a voice of the people.

Thus this state-owned and state-operated press prior to *glasnost* was even more regulated than the authoritarian press. Lenin, the founder of the Soviet state, explained why an unregulated press would be such a threat to Soviet society:

> *Why should freedom of speech and freedom of the press be allowed? Why should a government which is doing what it believes to be right allow itself to be criticized? It would not allow opposition by lethal weapons. Ideas are much more fatal things than guns. Why should any man be allowed to buy a printing press and disseminate pernicious opinion calculated to embarrass the government?*[6]

Although the authoritarian and Soviet Communist theories are similar in their belief that the state must be protected from a free and unregulated press, only the latter system makes use of the media to communicate party and state doctrines to the masses. Governments adhering to the authoritarian theory merely exercise control to ensure that the media do not publish anything that might harm the state. The mass media in an authoritarian system can be private as long as they are subject to licensing, prior censorship, postpublication prosecution, government subsidization or some other form of government control. Thus the Soviet Communist theory results in a *planned system,* whereas the authoritarian theory results in a *controlled system.*

Glasnost and New Technologies. The Soviet Communist theory of the media allows for a closed society where the government controls what people know and think. Gorbachev's *glasnost,* allowing people and the media to express views in opposition to the official position, was diametrically opposed to this closed-society concept. Some say that Gorbachev had no choice but to open up the society because modern mass communication technologies—namely TV, the

■ Satellite dishes such as this one played a major role in bringing Western ideas and information into Eastern bloc countries.

VCR, camcorders, and satellites—were making it impossible to keep people within the society shielded from other viewpoints.

These new electronic technologies are given partial credit for the fall of the Communist regimes in Eastern Europe and with the political unrest in certain Soviet republics. Although television in Eastern Europe was state owned and controlled, videocassette recorders gave people a choice over what they could watch. In 1988, the Soviet newspaper *Izvestia* talked about the "current fashionable passion for videotapes."[7] In Poland the Solidarity movement used VCRs and video documentaries to sustain itself.

Satellite dishes were used behind the Iron Curtain to obtain news and information not provided on the official government television channels. The U.S. Cable News Network (CNN) became one of the most watched channels in Eastern Europe among those with access to satellite dishes. In Poland and Hungary the manufacture and sale of satellite dishes were legal. The effect of this satellite technology was to force the official Polish and Hungarian television stations to become more open or to become irrelevant, and they chose the former.

Adding to the problem was the "spillover" of TV signals across national boundaries. People in East Germany could watch West German television. Hungarians could see Austrian TV, and the liberalized Polish television signals were seen in East Germany, Czechoslovakia and parts of the Soviet Union. In Romania, where dictator Nicolae Ceausescu personally controlled the content of government television, people watched Bulgarian, Soviet and the liberalized Hungarian TV stations.

What Lenin had feared when setting up the Soviet Communist theory of the press came to pass as a result of the emergence of pervasive electronic mass communication technologies.

THE SOCIAL RESPONSIBILITY CONCEPT

As early as the late nineteenth century, critics began to identify flaws in the libertarian theory. The free press was evolving in a manner that fell short of the idealistic libertarian goals.

As the metropolitan press developed, it became large and centralized. More and more media outlets became controlled by fewer and fewer owners, as chain ownership of newspapers grew. The press also became profit-oriented: selling newspapers and advertising space took precedence over the need to keep the public fully and accurately informed.

Major criticism of how the press was functioning in the American society began to be heard and by the twentieth century, the voices for change were loud. The main areas of concern were the following:

1 The press has wielded its enormous power for its own ends. Its owners have propagated their own opinions, especially in matters of politics and economics, at the expense of opposing views.
2 The press has been subservient to big business and at times has let advertisers control editorial policies and content.
3 The press has resisted social change.
4 The press has often paid more attention to the superficial and sensational in its coverage of current happenings, and its entertainment has often been lacking in substance.
5 The press has endangered public morals.
6 The press has invaded the privacy of individuals without just cause.
7 The press is controlled by one socioeconomic class, loosely the "business class," and access to the industry is difficult for the newcomer; therefore, the free and open market of ideas is endangered.[8]

In 1947 an influential report issued by the Commission on Freedom of the Press, chaired by Robert Maynard Hutchins, then chancellor of the University of Chicago, called for a socially responsible press. The report made it clear that freedom and responsibility go hand in hand and that the press should be periodically reminded of its responsibility. Siebert, Peterson and Schramm later expanded on this theory:

Freedom carries concomitant obligations; and the press, which enjoys a privileged position under the Constitution, is obliged to be responsible to society for carrying out certain essential functions of mass communication in contemporary society. To the extent that the press recognizes its responsibilities and makes them the basis of its operational policies, the libertarian system will satisfy the needs of society. To the extent that the press does not assume its responsibilities, some other agency must see that the essential functions of mass communication are carried out.[9]

BOX 3.1

THE SOCIETY OF PROFESSIONAL JOURNALISTS
CODE OF ETHICS

The SOCIETY of Professional Journalists, Sigma Delta Chi, believes the duty of journalists is to serve the truth.

We BELIEVE the agencies of mass communication are carriers of public discussion and information, acting on their Constitutional mandate and freedom to learn and report the facts.

We BELIEVE in public enlightenment as the forerunner of justice, and in our Constitutional role to seek the truth as part of the public's right to know the truth.

We BELIEVE those responsibilities carry obligations that require journalists to perform with intelligence, objectivity, accuracy, and fairness.

To these ends, we declare acceptance of the standards of practice here set forth:

I. RESPONSIBILITY: The public's right to know of events of public importance and interest is the over-riding mission of the mass media. The purpose of distributing news and enlightened opinion is to serve the general welfare. Journalists who use their professional status as representatives of the public for selfish or other unworthy motives violate a high trust.

II. FREEDOM OF THE PRESS: Freedom of the press is to be guarded as an inalienable right of people in a free society. It carries with it the freedom and the responsibility to discuss, question, and challenge actions and utterances of our government and of our public and private institutions. Journalists uphold the right to speak unpopular opinions and the privilege to agree with the majority.

III. ETHICS: Journalists must be free of obligation to any interest other than the public's right to know the truth.

1 Gifts, favors, free travel, special treatment or privileges can compromise the integrity of journalists and their employers. Nothing of value should be accepted.

2 Secondary employment, political involvement, holding public office, and service in community organizations should be avoided if it compromises the integrity of journalists and their employers. Journalists and their employers should conduct their personal lives in a manner that protects them from conflict of interest, real or apparent. Their responsibilities to the public are paramount. That is the nature of their profession.

3 So-called news communications from private sources should not be published or broadcast without substantiation of their claims to news values.

4 Journalists will seek news that serves the public interest, despite the obstacles. They will make constant efforts to assure that the public's business is conducted in public and that public records are open to public inspection.

5 Journalists acknowledge the newsman's ethic of protecting confidential sources of information.

6 Plagiarism is dishonest and unacceptable.

This concept of placing power in the hands of other agencies to ensure that the press acts responsibly has been applied to the broadcast media in the United States to the extent that they are licensed by the government. Although there have been recent efforts to deregulate the broadcast media, the Federal Communications Commission (FCC) has the authority to revoke a broadcaster's license if it is determined that he or she is not serving the public interest. This type of regulation does not apply to the print media in this country, although some other Western democracies do license their journalists. Thus social responsibility for the print media in the United States is voluntary and is adhered to by some print media officials, but not by all.

BOX 3.1 (continued)

IV. ACCURACY AND OBJECTIVITY: Good faith with the public is the foundation of all worthy journalism.

1 Truth is our ultimate goal.
2 Objectivity in reporting the news is another goal that serves as the mark of an experienced professional. It is a standard of performance toward which we strive. We honor those who achieve it.
3 There is no excuse for inaccuracies or lack of thoroughness.
4 Newspaper headlines should be fully warranted by the contents of the articles they accompany. Photographs and telecasts should give an accurate picture of an event and not highlight an incident out of context.
5 Sound practice makes clear distinction between news reports and expressions of opinion. News reports should be free of opinion or bias and represent all sides of an issue.
6 Partisanship in editorial comment that knowingly departs from the truth violates the spirit of American journalism.
7 Journalists recognize their responsibility for offering informed analysis, comment, and editorial opinion on public events and issues. They accept the obligation to present such material by individuals whose competence, experience, and judgment qualify them for it.
8 Special articles or presentations devoted to advocacy or the writer's own conclusions and interpretations should be labeled as such.

V. FAIR PLAY: Journalists at all times will show respect for the dignity, privacy, rights, and well-being of people encountered in the course of gathering and presenting the news.

1 The news media should not communicate unofficial charges affecting reputation or moral character without giving the accused a chance to reply.
2 The news media must guard against invading a person's right to privacy.
3 The media should not pander to morbid curiosity about details of vice and crime.
4 It is the duty of news media to make prompt and complete correction of their errors.
5 Journalists should be accountable to the public for their reports and the public should be encouraged to voice its grievances against the media. Open dialogue with our readers, viewers, and listeners should be fostered.

VI. PLEDGE: Adherence to this code is intended to preserve and strengthen the bond of mutual trust and respect between American journalists and the American people.

The Society shall—by programs of education and other means—encourage individual journalists to adhere to these tenets, and shall encourage journalistic publications and broadcasters to recognize their responsibility to frame codes of ethics in concert with their employees to serve as guidelines in furthering these goals.

(Adopted 1926; revised 1973, 1984, 1987)

Early Proponents.   During the latter part of the nineteenth century, newspaper editors such as Horace Greeley of the New York *Tribune* and Henry J. Raymond of the *New York Times* recognized the need for some form of press responsibility and started to promote social good and community welfare. Then at the turn of the century, Joseph Pulitzer, whose *New York World* had been embroiled in a war of sensationalism with William Randolph Hearst's *New York Journal,* began reflecting on the dangers of circulation at any cost and started speaking out for more press responsibility. He wrote: "Without high ethical ideals a newspaper not only is stripped of its splendid possibilities for public service, but may become a positive danger to the community."[10]

Shortly thereafter, journalism education programs began to be established in colleges and universities. These programs not only offered career training in journalism but also stressed higher ideals and professional standards consistent with the social responsibility concept.

Self-regulation within the industry also reflected the press's acceptance of social responsibility. The American Society of Newspaper Editors adopted its Canons of Journalism in 1923. These guidelines call for the press to serve the public with truthfulness, impartiality, a sense of fair play, decency, respect for individual privacy and concern for the general welfare. Since then other professional journalism associations have stressed ethics and standards as a means of upgrading the profession (see Box 3.1).

Current Efforts.   Today some American media organizations voluntarily adhere to the social responsibility theory; others do not. Those that do, attempt to present all sides of issues and strive to see that minority views and issues, as well as those of the Establishment, are covered. They may even open up editorial comments to dissenting opinions, usually on the "op-ed" (opposite editorial) page.

THE PRESS IN FOREIGN LANDS

In order to understand how these philosophical theories work, it might be well to review briefly the mass media operations in a few other countries. It probably is already clear how the media in authoritarian or Communist states differ from those in the United States, but there are also differences in media operations among Western countries—particularly when it comes to the broadcast media.[11]

Soviet Union.   Since we are already aware of the Soviet Communist theory of the press, let's begin our examination of the press in foreign lands by looking at the media in the Soviet Union.

Tass is the official Soviet news service, which provides the official news to media outlets. It operates similarly to the major wire services in this country (Associated Press [AP] and United Press International [UPI]) except that it is state owned and controlled. *Pravda* (Truth) is the Soviet party newspaper, which serves as the official record of party policies and government actions. It usually carries a front-page photograph glorifying the common person to stress that the party is dedicated to the "good of the common man." In recent years—as a result of severe economic conditions and *glasnost*—even this tried and true Communist party newspaper has started to change (see Box 3.2).

Izvestia is a government-published newspaper that is more popular and less theoretical than *Pravda*. In addition to these national publications, many ministries of government publish their own newspapers, and each of the 15 republics of the Soviet Union has its own regional and local media.

Because the Soviet press until *glasnost* operated under the principles of the Soviet Communist concept, all of the newspapers in the country functioned as interpreters of the "truth" as seen by the Communist party. The press's function

BOX 3.2

■ AN INDEPENDENT COMMUNIST PARTY NEWSPAPER? ■

Glasnost has had a profound impact on all forms of mass media in the Soviet Union. Strict government and Communist party control over the Soviet media has given way to a wide range of independent voices.

In 1990 *Pravda,* the official Communist party newspaper in the Soviet Union, joined the list of media undergoing radical change when it announced that it would begin accepting advertising from foreign firms and would liberalize its ties to the Party Central Committee by publishing the "pluralism of opinion" that existed within the party.

Publication of the newspaper, which had been run by the Central Committee, was turned over to an independent association that not only published this official party newspaper, but produced a television program, an international edition and a string of advertising supplements as well.

In addition to *glasnost,* there were economic reasons for the overhaul of *Pravda.* During the previous two years circulation of the newspaper dropped from 10 million to 7.7 million and it was expected to drop to 3 million by 1991 if improvements weren't made.

Hurting the circulation figures were a number of new publications available to Soviet citizens. These publications ranged from the weekly *Moscow News* and *Tema,* a newspaper that supported gay and lesbian rights, to the business weekly *Commersant* and *Protestant,* a Baptist newspaper.

Although *Pravda's* editor in chief Ivan Frolov began offering full-page ads to U.S. businesses for $50,000 each, there were not many takers. To strengthen the new independent operation, *Pravda* executives began looking abroad for investor capital from media moguls. One of the most prominent being courted by the Soviet Union was publishing tycoon Robert Maxwell.

■ The front page of the Soviet Communist newspaper *Pravda* is being readied for publication. The page features a photograph of ordinary citizens, a common practice of this newspaper.

was to provide proper information for the people. Sometimes national and international news events were not covered in the Soviet press because they were considered not to be in the best interests of the state. However, since *glasnost,* such omissions are less frequent.

In 1986, for example, the Soviet Union initially attempted to keep secret the explosion and fire at the Chernobyl nuclear power plant. However, when high radiation levels were recorded in Scandinavia and other parts of Europe, the Soviet news media were forced to disclose some information. A terse radio broadcast seven days after the disaster released the first information of the event inside the Soviet Union: "There has been an accident at the Chernobyl nuclear power plant in the Ukraine. One of the nuclear reactors has been damaged. Measures for eliminating the consequences of the nuclear accident have been undertaken and victims are being rendered assistance. And now sports." A year later when six Chernobyl plant employees went on trial for causing the nuclear accident, *glasnost* policies allowed coverage of the trial and even permitted foreign journalists to cover some of the court proceedings.

The broadcast media in the Soviet Union are also state owned and operated. They consist of four radio and four television networks. Programming consists of music (more than half of the music broadcast in the country is classical and free from controversial or potentially subversive lyrics), drama and news. In 1990, Gorbachev expanded *glasnost* to radio and television by ordering the immediate diversification of state-run broadcast systems so that all political movements could have access to the airwaves, ending the Communist party's monopoly.

United Kingdom.   Great Britain operates under the libertarian theory but does not have a First Amendment prohibiting government regulation of the media. Its newspapers enjoy one of the world's most successful national markets and are conveniently divided into two categories, the *popular* press and the *quality* press.

The popular press has by far the higher circulation, with two of the most successful publications—the *Sun* and the *Daily Mirror*—each topping 4 million copies per day. These publications are owned by two of the world's most successful media barons—Rupert Murdoch and Robert Maxwell (see Box 3.3). The popular press is tabloid in format (half the size of a regular newspaper) and has content resembling parts of the *National Enquirer* and parts of the *New York Daily News* in this country. The popular tabloids are designed to appeal to those with lower levels of education. The *Sun,* for example, features a "page 3 girl" (a different topless model appearing each day on page 3) and Bingo to entice readers. In 1990, then British Prime Minister Margaret Thatcher ordered the popular press to "clean up their act" or face government controls by a statutory tribunal.

An alternative to the popular press in the United Kingdom is the quality press, which consists of full-size newspapers written in a sophisticated manner for the more discriminating reader. Unlike most newspapers in this country, the British quality press makes no effort to write down to the average reader. Only one quality newspaper, the *Daily Telegraph,* has a circulation of more than a million. All others, including the famed *Times* of London (also owned by Murdoch), have national circulations of a few hundred thousand. Local and regional newspapers are also published in Great Britain, but none is as popular as the national press, which is distributed daily by train and plane to all parts of the United Kingdom.

BOX 3.3

■ PROFILE: TWO MEDIA MOGULS ■

They called one an arrogant Aussie, the other a tough-minded British-Czech. But names didn't stop them. After establishing themselves as media moguls in the United Kingdom, these tycoons have ever since been influencing the direction of mass media development worldwide, and in particular in the United States.

Rupert Murdoch and Robert Maxwell are becoming major players in the arena of U.S. media. Although their backgrounds are different, their global view of the media business is similar.

Murdoch was born in Australia where he inherited a small media company from his father. He built it into a major corporation by starting and acquiring Australian newspapers. He then turned his attention to Great Britain.

Murdoch, who became a U.S. citizen in 1986 in order to purchase a group of Metromedia television stations (U.S. law prohibits foreign ownership of broadcast media), has vast holdings in Australia, Britain, Western Europe and the United States. After the restructuring of Eastern Europe in 1989, he began acquiring newspapers in those countries as well. By 1990, Murdoch's acquisitions had become so numerous that his stockholders became worried about his company's $8.7 billion debt, even though his enterprises individually were worth about $20 billion.

Murdoch's company assets include 20th Century Fox, seven TV stations, more than 100 newspapers, the *Daily Racing Form, TV Guide, Premiere, Seventeen, New York* and HarperCollins Publishers. His newly formed Fox Television network is rapidly expanding, moving from one night of prime-time programming to five nights in 1990. Known for his flair for tabloid newspapers, he has successfully introduced this style of sensationalism into American television and his direction has had a major impact on U.S. network TV.

Maxwell, on the other hand, was born in 1923 as Labji Hoch, the son of a Czechoslovakian farm laborer. After most of his family were killed by the Germans during World War II, Hoch escaped and joined the resistance forces and later became a highly decorated officer in the British Army. He changed his name to Robert Maxwell after the war and built a British printing and communications corporation into an international empire worth billions of dollars.

The London-based Maxwell Communications Corporation owns book publishing firms, newspapers, nearly 400 specialized magazines and cable-TV systems. He is now heavily investing in U.S. media holdings. In 1988 he paid $2.7 billion to acquire Macmillan Inc., a major U.S. book publisher. In 1991 he acquired the New York *Daily News,* which up until the 1980s had been the largest circulating newspaper in the United States. Also in 1991, Maxwell launched a U.S. horse racing newspaper, *Racing Times*, to compete directly with the 96-year-old *Daily Racing Form*, acquired by Murdoch in his 1988 purchase of Triangle Publications. Maxwell was also being courted by Mikhail Gorbachev as a possible investment capitalist to help bail out the failing but prestigious Communist party newspaper, *Pravda.*

In 1989 Murdoch and Maxwell signed a five-year agreement to allow Murdoch's European TV-movie satellite to deliver programming through Maxwell Cable Television, the largest cable-TV system in Britain. The effort was successful in forcing another British satellite cable system to merge with Murdoch's Sky Channel.

The future of worldwide mass communication most likely will continue to be influenced by these two individuals with diverse backgrounds but similar goals. Call them what you like, but watch them carefully.

The broadcasting media in the United Kingdom are also quite different from those in this country. For example, only four television channels are available over the airwaves to viewers in the United Kingdom, all of them closely regulated by the government to protect consumer interests. Two of these channels are operated by the British Broadcasting Corporation (BBC), which was formed in the

1920s when radio was becoming a mass-communication medium. The BBC is financed by government funds and by license fees levied on everyone who owns a television set.

The BBC also operates four radio channels. BBC 1 and BBC 2 carry popular music—one similar to American Top-40 and the other to American album-oriented stations. BBC 3 airs classical music, drama and educational discussion programs. BBC 4 broadcasts news and talk-oriented programs, including popular newsmagazine shows.

BBC television, which started broadcasting in 1936, produces more than 85 percent of its own programming. The remainder includes independently-produced shows and a few American imports, such as *Dallas*. BBC-produced programming is considered to be of high quality and is distributed worldwide, with more than a hundred stations carrying BBC shows.

The BBC was the only broadcasting outlet in Great Britain until 1954, when Parliament, after years of debate, established the Independent Broadcasting Authority (IBA). The IBA oversees the Independent Television (ITV) and Independent Local Radio (ILR) stations throughout the country.

Unlike the BBC stations, these independent radio and television stations carry commercials. However, the IBA regulates their number and types and even the points at which they interrupt the programs. Protection of consumer interests is the regulating criterion for the IBA.

ITV channels are regional in nature, and one is broadcast in each of the 15 regions (two stations broadcast in the London area at different times on the same frequency, for a total of 16 ITV stations). In addition to the two BBC channels and one ITV channel, Britishers receive a fourth channel—also independent and regulated by the IBA—called Channel 4. This channel was authorized by Parliament in 1982 to provide for "minority" programming needs.

In addition to the four channels over the airwaves, the newer technologies of cable and satellite TV were in their infancy in providing expanded programming in the early 1990s. Murdoch was the first to offer satellite TV. His Sky Television began providing four channels—mostly carrying American reruns—to Britishers in 1989. However, his dominance in the field was challenged in 1990 by the launching of British Satellite Broadcasting, a $2.1 billion satellite programming service that offered five national channels. It was anticipated that newly developing cable companies would expand the availability of these satellite channels to those who could not afford satellite dishes.

Japan. There are numerous *shinbun* (the Japanese word for newspapers, taken from the words for *news* and *hear*) in Japan both in the tabloid format for easy reading on trains and subways and in broadsheet format. There are also English-language versions, such as the *Japanese Times,* to accommodate English-speaking people in this international country. Some female nudity in photographs and comic strips can be found in many of the tabloids reflecting a Western European influence (British and German). Although most of the newspapers are local and regional in nature, four of them are considered national in scope and are distributed out of Tokyo by satellite transmission to other population centers.

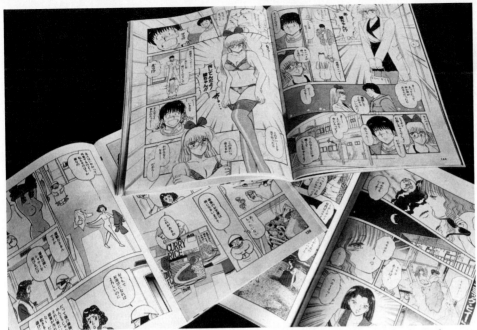

■ This Japanese version of a comic book—called a *manga*—provides adult entertainment for readers, including violence, nudity and sexually violent themes.

One of the most popular forms of reading material in Japan is comic books, called *mangas,* which are usually about one inch thick and contain adult-oriented stories filled with violence, nudity and sexual violence.

Television broadcasting in Japan is an expanded version of the British system with both a national noncommercial system broadcasting over two channels (one is educational) and numerous commercial stations. NHK is the national noncommercial network, with headquarters in Tokyo. The programming is carried throughout Japan. In addition, Japan has five commercial networks, four of them owned by large Japanese newspaper companies. FM radio dominates Japanese radio as it does in the United States. Several of these stations broadcast in English.

The expanding and pervasive influence of electronic mass media, much of it exporting American popular culture, has been influencing and changing the culture of many Japanese young people in recent years. Called *Amekaji* (American casual), this trend is depicted in dress, musical tastes and attitudes about the importance of an education and work ethic. Media contributing to this change are movies, videocassettes, audio tapes and CDs, television and radio. Major FM stations such as FM Yokohama and FM Tokyo regularly play such programs as *Rick Dees Weekly Top-40* and *Pop Town.* Video rock tapes, similar to those seen in this country on MTV, are available in video rental outlets and music stores. Young people of varying ages can be seen on the streets and in the subways with small radios and cassette players pumping out American music through headphones.

Canada.   Turning closer to home, we find Canada's mass media influenced by the cultures of Britain (Canada is a member of the British Commonwealth of Nations) and America (90 percent of the population lives within 100 miles of the U.S. border). Canada's vast size (the third largest country in the world) and small population (26 million) have resulted in the domination of most media by two or three giant companies in each medium. Since approximately one-fourth of the population is French speaking, Canada has developed both French and English systems of mass media.

Most of Canada's major newspapers are controlled by two companies: Southam Communications, Ltd., which owns many papers, including Toronto's influential *Globe* and *Mail;* and Thomson Newspapers, a syndicate founded by Roy Thomson, the owner of the *Times* of London before Rupert Murdoch. There are very few independent newspapers.

Canadian Press (CP), co-owned by over 100 Canadian daily newspapers, is the only Canadian wire service. Most papers supplement it by subscribing to America's AP and UPI, Britain's Reuters or France's AFP.

Books and magazines in Canada consist of a mixture of Canadian-owned and foreign publications. The dominant Canadian book publisher is McClelland and Stewart, although the most successful Canadian publisher internationally is Harlequin Enterprises, leader of the romance-novel market. Subsidiaries of American and British firms play an important part in Canadian book publishing.

Until the late 1960s, both *Time* and *Reader's Digest* marketed a Canadian version in Canada. *Time,* for example, included an 8-10-page section on Canadian news before the section of U.S. news. When the Canadian government passed legislation limiting the deductibility of advertising costs in foreign media (including radio and television), advertising support for the Canadian version of *Time* died. Today, there is an occasional page of Canadian news in the issues of *Time* distributed in that country, but not much more than that.

Filling the void has been *Maclean's,* formerly a Canadian news and opinion monthly along the lines of *Harper's* or *Atlantic.* It is now Canada's weekly newsmagazine and the flagship of the country's dominant magazine publisher, Maclean-Hunter.

Lifestyle publications are as big in Canada as they are in America. In addition to Canadian magazines like *Chatelaine,* the magazine racks are filled with American, British and French publications.

Radio and television in Canada are provided by both national networks and independent stations. The first national networks were the Canadian Broadcasting Corporation (CBC) for English speakers and Radio Canada for French speakers (that name is somewhat confusingly used for both the radio and television networks). These networks are similar to the British BBC in that they are funded by the government. However, unlike the BBC, they do carry commercials. Despite the government funding, these networks are independent of political control. The government does, however, require all radio stations playing popular music to have at least 30 percent Canadian content.

The nation's second TV network, CTV, provides television programming that is a little less "highbrow" than the CBC's. The newest television network, Global, provides programming only to major metropolitan areas. In addition to the networks, there are numerous independent radio and television stations. All stations are regulated by the Canadian Radio-Television Commission (CRTC), a government agency similar to Britain's IBA or America's FCC.

Until recently, Canada's main contribution to the motion-picture industry was to export its most talented citizens—from Mary Pickford to Michael J. Fox—to Hollywood. However, in recent years many Hollywood movie producers have been lured by generous tax breaks to make their pictures on location in Canada. Although the tax breaks have now been scaled back, the practice still continues because of lower production costs in Canada. The most famous Canadian movie production company is the National Film Board, which has been making award-winning documentaries for decades. It is funded by the government.

Mexico.   The mass media in Mexico operate somewhat differently from those of the neighboring United States. The first newspaper in Mexico was started in 1722, 18 years after the first one was established in the British colonies in America. Because the Mexican literacy rate lagged behind that of the United States, the Mexican press lingered longer in the elite culture.

Although Mexican newspapers are privately owned, they do not operate with the same freedom as American newspapers. The Mexican government, for example, owns all of the nation's newsprint. The fact that a newspaper is able to get newsprint suggests that it has the blessing of the government.

One antigovernment newspaper, *Zeta,* which circulates in Baja California, survives only because it prints its copies across the border in nearby San Diego, where newsprint is available. Ominously, in 1988 the co-owner and editor of *Zeta* was murdered on his way to work in Tijuana. He joined more than two dozen Mexican journalists who have been murdered in the past 16 years. Although none of the murders has been solved, the Mexican government in 1989 did accuse a former police chief in the previous administration of masterminding one of the murders.

Broadcasting in Mexico is much like that in Western Europe. Governmental entities regulate broadcasting, which consists of a combination of government owned stations and strictly regulated private stations that must give up to 12.5 percent of their air time to the government.

Third World Nations.   The developing nations in Latin America, Africa, the Middle East and Asia are considered Third World nations. (The First World consists of the so-called Western powers and the Second World the Communist-bloc nations.) In some Third World countries media operations are strikingly different from those in more developed Western nations.

Economic, political and cultural factors strongly influence Third World countries. In the East African nation of Tanzania, for example, the average person's income is the equivalent of $136 a year. The media do not carry any advertising; the reason is not political, as it is in the Soviet Union, but economic—people cannot afford to buy what would be advertised.

In most Third World countries, advertising-supported media are possible only in large urban centers where there are large numbers of middle- and upper-middle-class citizens. Thus, for the most part, the Third World media exist for the elite class.

Many Third World nations operate state owned television stations, which function more to impress neighboring countries than to inform the people (the majority of whom don't own television sets). Yet that doesn't mean that TV doesn't sometimes reach large audiences. In Egypt and Kenya, for example, many people will come together to share a single TV set.

Government-operated radio, on the other hand, is emerging in many Third World countries as the first mass-communication medium to reach the masses because radios are relatively inexpensive and can reach the illiterate. Mass media censorship is prevalent in Third World countries, and in many regions—Africa, for example—this censorship traces its heritage to earlier days of colonialism.

Foreign press domination in Third World countries, particularly from the Communist East and the capitalist West, has caused resentment because much of the news flowing in and out of these emerging nations must come from the Communist-controlled Tass or Western press services such as AP and UPI. This resentment has led in recent years to numerous discussions before the United Nations Educational, Scientific, and Cultural Organization (UNESCO) on how to protect the sovereignty of nations from the flow of international information.

Several UNESCO-sponsored conferences have recommended a "new world information order," which would give each country the right to control who could send information out and what information could come in. A system of licensing all journalists (both foreign and domestic) working within the country would be used to control what news could leave a nation.

The UNESCO recommendations generated a great deal of controversy in the international journalistic community and strong resistance from many Western journalists. The United States cited these recommendations as one of the reasons why it dropped its membership in UNESCO in 1985.

SUMMARY

In this chapter we have examined the philosophical controls that govern mass media operations. These controls stem from four basic theories of how the mass media should operate: authoritarian, libertarian, Soviet Communist and social responsibility.

The authoritarian theory is the oldest and requires that the press be regulated so as not to hinder the state in any way. The libertarian theory offers the opposing viewpoint that the press should function to serve the governed, not the governors.

Each of these theories has an offshoot. The Soviet Communist theory is an extension of the authoritarian theory and makes the press a planned, integral part of the state. Under this theory, the media are state owned and operated for the purpose of advancing the state's ideals and beliefs. Social responsibility is an offshoot of the libertarian theory. After determining that the libertarian theory was not functioning as intended by the founders of our nation, proponents of social responsibility contended that freedom of the press must go hand in hand with responsibility.

The mass media in the Soviet Union, United Kingdom, Japan, Canada, Mexico and the Third World nations differ from those in the United States. The media in each country reflect economic conditions, the political philosophies of the government and the popular culture.

THOUGHT QUESTIONS

1   Can you think of any modern-day examples of authoritarian restrictions on the press?
2   From your knowledge of American current events, can you think of any current examples of the libertarian theory of the press at work?
3   What newspapers in your area practice social responsibility? Can you cite some specific examples to support this conclusion?
4   What additional changes do you foresee in the Soviet Union as a result of *glasnost*? Do you think the Soviet society will allow it to continue? Why?
5   Why do Western journalists and societies oppose the "new world information order"? Do you think this position is justified?

NOTES

1.   Fred S. Siebert, Theodore B. Peterson and Wilbur Schramm, *Four Theories of the Press* (Urbana: University of Illinois Press, 1956), p. 33.

2.   Frank Luther Mott, *American Journalism*, 3rd ed. (New York: Macmillan, 1962), p. 6.

3.   Wilbur Schramm, *Responsibility in Mass Communication* (New York: Harper & Row, 1957), p. 72.

4.   Quoted in Warren K. Agee, Phillip H. Ault and Edwin Emery, *Introduction to Mass Communication*, 6th ed. (New York: Harper & Row, 1979), p. 31.

5.   Quoted in *Speaking of a Free Press* (New York: ANPA Foundation, 1970), p. 15.

6.   Speech in Moscow, 1920. From H. L. Mencken, *A News Dictionary of Quotations on Historical Principles from Ancient and Modern Sources* (New York: Alfred Knopf, 1966), p. 966.

7.   Thomas B. Rosenstiel, "TV, VCRs Fan Fire of Revolution," *Los Angeles Times,* January 18, 1990, Section A, p. 1.

8.   Siebert, Peterson and Schramm, *Four Theories of the Press,* pp. 78–79.

9.   Ibid., p. 74.

10.   Joseph Pulitzer, "The College of Journalism," *North American Review,* 178 (May 1904): 667.

11.   Much of this information was gathered from personal interviews with media personnel in various countries.

ADDITIONAL READING

Cullen, Maurice R., Jr. *Mass Media and the First Amendment*. Dubuque, Iowa: Brown, 1981.

Handlin, Oscar. *The History of the United States*. 2 vols. New York: Holt, Rinehart and Winston, 1968.

Lipscomb, A. A. (ed.). *The Writings of Thomas Jefferson*. Washington: Thomas Jefferson Memorial Association, 1904.

Mill, John Stuart. ''On Liberty [1858],'' in *Great Books of the Western World*. Chicago: Encyclopedia Britannica, 1952.

Schramm, Wilbur. *Mass Media and National Development*. Palo Alto, Calif.: Stanford University Press, 1964.

Carol Burnett, one of a number of entertainers to sue the National Enquirer *for libel, was successful in winning her lawsuit. Laws of libel and invasion of privacy allow individuals to seek monetary compensation for careless or malicious actions by the media.*

MEDIA CONTROLS: LEGAL

Defamation.
*Holding up a
person to
ridicule, scorn or
contempt in a
respectable and
considerable
part of the
community; may
be criminal as
well as civil.
Includes both
libel and slander.*
—Black's Law
Dictionary

Within several weeks of one another, in the fall of 1990, a jury found a Florida record store owner guilty of breaking an obscenity law by selling an audiotape (a form of mass communication); an Oregon jury ordered a Ku Klux Klan leader to pay $10 million in damages to the family of an African student who was killed by skinheads incited by the Klan leader's racist speeches; and a Florida judge was threatening the Cable News Network (CNN) with contempt of court for airing a tape of a telephone conversation that he had previously banned.

If indeed the mass media in the United States are protected by the libertarian theory (see Chapter 3), how could such actions be possible in a country where the First Amendment says that Congress shall make no law abridging the freedom of speech or of the press?

Even though the First Amendment does make regulation of the mass media in the United States different from that in most other countries, the American mass media are regulated by various laws of the land. Although some contend that the First Amendment was meant to be absolute, the courts have disagreed. In 1919, Supreme Court Justice Oliver Wendell Holmes, Jr., said the First Amendment was not absolute and that under certain conditions free speech could be prohibited by Congress. He cited his famous "you can't shout fire in a crowded theater" analogy to support the Court's position that if there were clear and present dangers involved in free speech it could be abridged.

Although the most stringent regulations are imposed by the government on broadcasting media, the print media are subject to some regulation as well, and audio- and videotapes and records are subject to laws governing obscenity.

GOVERNMENT REGULATION OF PRINT

Efforts by the government to restrain the print media from publishing objectionable material have been around almost as long as the First Amendment.

The Alien and Sedition Acts represented the first efforts by the government to impose restrictions on the press in our new republic. After a decade of partisan press attacks on the Federalists who were in power, these laws were passed in 1798—just seven years after the First Amendment became law—to suppress some critics. (At the time, the reason given for passing these laws was to protect the United States in a war against France that was never declared.) Among other things, these acts outlawed false, scandalous and malicious publications against the U.S. government, the president of the United States and Congress. Fifteen people were prosecuted under these laws, some for making offhand, humorous remarks about President John Adams. Anti-Federalist Thomas Jefferson challenged President Adams in his reelection bid in 1800 and his supporters used the Alien and Sedition Acts as a campaign issue. After his victory, Jefferson pardoned everyone convicted under the laws, and the acts were allowed to expire.

The Espionage Act of 1917 and the Sedition Act of 1918 enacted similar First Amendment restrictions in the twentieth century. These laws made it illegal for anyone to openly oppose the nation's involvement in World War I. Some 2,000 people were prosecuted, and major restrictions were placed on ethnic newspapers, particularly German-language papers.

This time, however, the First Amendment restrictions were fought in the federal courts and ultimately in the Supreme Court. (This was not done in 1798, probably because the Supreme Court justices were Federalists and supporters of President John Adams.) The first challenge to these laws was *Schenck v. United States*.[1] In this case a socialist leader, Charles T. Schenck, was prosecuted for circulating antiwar leaflets to army recruits and draftees. Schenck contended that the First Amendment protected his right to express his opinions, but the Supreme

Court ruled otherwise. It was in this case that Justice Holmes used his fire-in-a-crowded-theater analogy.

After the Schenck decision a number of other convictions of socialists were upheld, including the conviction of Eugene V. Debs, who later received nearly a million votes for president of the United States while serving time in prison.

In 1957 the Supreme Court took a significant step toward expanding First Amendment protections in *Yates v. United States* by overturning the convictions of 14 persons who had been charged with pro-communist subversive activities.[2] The Court said that teaching unpopular ideas was protected by the First Amendment.

In 1969, in *Brandenburg v. Ohio*, the Supreme Court ruled that even advocacy of violence was protected by the First Amendment as long as there was no threat of imminent lawless action.[3] This case involved a Ku Klux Klan leader.

In 1971, however, the Executive branch of government challenged the First Amendment in the *Pentagon Papers* case. Several newspapers had begun printing the papers in serial form based on documents compiled by the Rand Corporation,

■ Although the U.S. Supreme Court ruled that the Pentagon Papers could be published, Daniel Ellsberg (above) found himself in legal difficulties for "leaking" the documents to the press. He was tried for stealing the papers from Rand Corporation files. After illegal activities by government officials, including breaking into the office of Ellsberg's psychiatrist, were disclosed during the trial, the judge dismissed the charges, citing government misconduct.

a California-based think tank. The papers were basically a critical history of the Vietnam war. The Nixon administration obtained a prior restraint order, barring the *New York Times, Washington Post* and *Boston Globe* from continuing to print the series until the courts could rule on whether the material would endanger national security.

The case quickly went to the U.S. Supreme Court, which ruled that the government could not prove that anything in the papers would harm the national security. The newspapers won the case and resumed printing the documents. Joining the newspapers was the book publishing industry, which released books carrying the *Pentagon Papers* immediately after the Court's decision. (Although many people supported the right of the media to print these documents, few of them bothered to read the newspaper series or books after the court-authorized publication.)

In 1979, *The Progressive* magazine was restrained by a court from printing an article entitled, "The H-Bomb Secret: How We Got It and Why We Are Telling It," following action filed by the Carter administration. The article, which had been compiled from nonclassified public documents, accurately told readers how to make a hydrogen bomb. Before the case reached the U.S. Supreme Court, an almost identical article appeared in the *Madison Press Connection*. The government eventually dropped its case against *The Progressive,* which then printed the story. A U.S. Supreme Court showdown between the government and the media as to *The Progressive*'s right to publish the article versus the government's right of prior restraint was avoided.

Prior Restraint.   Despite the efforts of the Nixon and Carter administrations, it has long been believed that the intent of the First Amendment was to prevent prior restraint. Prior restraint is the ability of the government to prevent something from being published. This differs from the ability to punish someone afterward. Support for First Amendment protection comes from the belief that the framers of the Bill of Rights intended the First Amendment to provide for a free marketplace of ideas and that no idea should be suppressed.

This belief was affirmed in 1931 by the Supreme Court in the case of *Near v. Minnesota.*[4] The case stemmed from a Minnesota law that allowed courts to declare scandalous newspapers to be public nuisances and order them closed. When a court declared his newspaper—which had been critical of government officials in Minnesota—a public nuisance and ordered it closed, publisher J. M. Near appealed the ruling to the Supreme Court.

The Court declared that the Minnesota action was a form of prior restraint and a violation of the First Amendment. (It did say, however, that Near could be sued for libel if his paper printed untrue defamation.)

In November of 1990, the Supreme Court reversed this precedent by letting stand a federal judge's gag order forbidding CNN from broadcasting tapes of Manuel Noriega's jailhouse telephone conversations. The government had secretly recorded the tapes of the former Panamanian dictator while he was awaiting trial on drug charges. CNN had acquired the tapes and was broadcasting them when the judge implemented the prior restraint order. The Supreme Court ruled 7-2 on its decision, with the dissenters expressing concern that prior restraint should not be allowed. (Later the federal judge lifted the prior restraining order because the damaging tapes had already been aired.)

GOVERNMENT REGULATION OF BROADCASTING

In the 1920s, as the new medium of radio spread across the country, many stations tried to get on the air and jammed each other's frequencies with overlapping signals. At that time there were few regulations of radio broadcasting. Previous legislation had dealt only with ship-to-shore types of radio communication. In fact, the only laws on the books required the Secretary of Commerce to grant radio license requests; he did not have the authority to reject any such requests or to assign power and frequencies for radio operations.

Chaos on the airwaves resulted. Many broadcasters, as well as Secretary of Commerce Herbert Hoover, became concerned. As a result, Hoover held a series of four Radio Conferences during the 1920s to allow all interested parties to discuss the problem and suggest possible solutions. These conferences involved educators, legislators, labor officials, businessmen and religious leaders. Each time, proposals were made and presented to Congress but no action was taken— until President Calvin Coolidge finally urged Congress to deal with the problem.

The Radio Act of 1927 established the Federal Radio Commission, a five-member board that was instructed to establish a system for licensing new radio stations and assigning frequencies and power to stations already established. Congress wanted the FRC to complete the project in one year and then disband; future enforcement of broadcast regulations and further licensing action were reserved for the Secretary of Commerce.

But the FRC was still operating seven years later when President Franklin D. Roosevelt asked Congress to update the act by bringing telephone and telegraph operations under the same communications blanket. The result was the Communications Act of 1934, which in addition to including most of the regulatory legislation of the 1927 act, replaced the "temporary" FRC with a seven-member Federal Communication Commission. The act now covers television as well.

The FCC made it clear from the very beginning that broadcasters would have to operate under the congressional mandate and broadcast in the "public interest, convenience and necessity" if they were to keep their licenses. As did the FRC, the FCC and Congress have acted on the premise that the airwaves belong to the public, not to private broadcasters. The basis for decisions concerning broadcasters is thus how responsibly they serve the public.

When the Commission's right to refuse to renew licenses of stations involved in questionable broadcast practices was first tested, the courts ruled that while the government cannot tell a station in advance not to broadcast something (that would be prior restraint), it can review past performance to determine if a station has been operating in the public interest. If it has not, the government can refuse license renewal.

Although clauses in both the 1927 Radio Act and the 1934 Communications Act stated clearly that "Nothing in this Act shall be understood or construed to give the licensing authority the power of censorship," the U.S. Criminal Code *does*

BOX 4.1

FCC'S SECTION 315: FACILITIES FOR CANDIDATES FOR PUBLIC OFFICE

SEC. 315. (a) If any licensee shall permit any person who is a legally qualified candidate for any public office to use a broadcasting station, he shall afford equal opportunities to all other such candidates for that office in the use of such broadcasting station: *Provided,* That such licensee shall have no power of censorship over the material broadcast under the provision of this section. No obligation is hereby imposed under this subsection upon any licensee to allow the use of its station by any such candidate. Appearance by a legally qualified candidate on any—

1 bona fide newscast,
2 bona fide news interview,
3 bona fide news documentary (if the appearance of the candidate is incidental to the presentation of the subject or subjects covered by the news documentary), or
4 on-the-spot coverage of bona fide news events (including but not limited to political conventions and activities incidental thereto),

shall not be deemed to be use of a broadcasting station within the meaning of this subsection. Nothing in the foregoing sentence shall be construed as relieving broadcasters, in connection with the presentation of newscasts, news interviews, news documentaries, and on-the-spot coverage of news events, from the obligation imposed upon them under this Act to operate in the public interest and to afford reasonable opportunity for the discussion of conflicting views on issues of public importance.

(b) The charges made for the use of any broadcasting station by any person who is a legally qualified candidate for any public office in connection with his campaign for nomination for election, or election, to such office shall not exceed—

1 during the forty-five days preceding the date of a primary or primary runoff election and during the sixty days preceding the date of a general or special election in which such person is a candidate, the lowest unit charge of the station for the same class and amount of time for the same period; and
2 at any other time, the charges made for comparable use of such station by other users thereof.

(c) For purposes of this section—

1 the term "broadcasting station" includes a community antenna television system; and
2 the terms "licensee" and "station licensee" when used with respect to a community antenna television system mean the operator of such system.

(d) The Commission shall prescribe appropriate rules and regulations to carry out the provisions of this section.

SOURCE: The Communications Act of 1934 as amended. Federal Communications Commission, U.S. Government Printing Office, Washington, D.C., 1983, pp. 63–65.

prohibit the broadcasting of anything obscene, indecent or profane. In addition, the FCC established rules regarding fraud and lottery information.

For many years the FCC required broadcasters to air certain types of program content, noting that news, public affairs, educational, informational and agricultural programs were in the public interest.

Congress included Section 315 in both the 1927 and 1934 legislation to protect candidates for political office (see Box 4.1). It requires broadcasters to give bona fide political candidates *equal opportunities* for air time on their stations. This requirement—which does not apply to any print medium—means that a station must grant all candidates for office the same opportunities that other candidates receive on the station's airwaves. This applies not only to free time given to a candidate (in which case all of his or her opponents would receive the same free access on that station) but also to political commercials. If one candidate purchases a certain amount of time for commercials, the station must give all his or her opponents an equal opportunity to purchase advertising in the same time periods at the same cost.

This equal-opportunity section has been modified to exempt certain types of programs, including newscasts and bona fide news interview programs, such as *Meet the Press, Face the Nation* and *Nightline*. Candidate debates were also excluded as long as they were sponsored by an outside agency, such as the League of Women Voters, and were covered by radio and television stations as a news event. This kept control of the debates out of the hands of the candidates and their supporters. However, in 1983, the FCC abolished this sponsorship requirement; broadcasters can now set up and sponsor the debates themselves.

The *fairness doctrine* was another important requirement of the FCC up until its abolition in 1987. Not written into the Communications Act, the doctrine applied to controversial issues and evolved from Commission rulings over the years.

In the early 1940s the FCC decided that it was not in the public interest for radio stations to air editorials. However, the Commission reversed itself in 1949 and encouraged broadcasters to take stands on controversial issues—provided that reasonable time was given to opposing viewpoints. Over the years, this fairness doctrine ruling has required broadcasters to be aware of important community and national issues and to devote broadcasting time to airing all sides of those issues.

The fairness doctrine was applied to advertising content in 1967, when the FCC ruled that because cigarette smoking was a controversial public issue, broadcasters carrying commercials for cigarette companies had to give *free* time to antismoking groups (such as the American Cancer Society and the American Lung Association). This ruling eventually led to congressional legislation banning all cigarette commercials from radio and television as of 1971 (see Chapter 12).

In 1969, in the *Red Lion* decision (named after a five-year-old personal attack case involving the Red Lion Broadcasting Company in Pennsylvania), the U.S. Supreme Court reaffirmed the fairness doctrine by declaring that the rights of the public, not the broadcaster, are paramount. In that decision the Court ruled that Congress and the FCC were not violating the First Amendment when they required broadcasters to devote air time to replies to personal attacks and editorials.

However, a federal court of appeals challenged this decision in the 1980s when it ordered the FCC to reconsider its position on the fairness doctrine—implying that it might not be constitutional. The case resulted from a suit filed by a Syracuse broadcasting company that challenged the FCC's ruling that it had violated the fairness doctrine by not broadcasting anti-nuclear power plant ads after running advertisements in the plant's favor. The broadcaster argued that the rule violated its First Amendment rights.

The FCC did rethink its position and in 1987 abandoned the fairness doctrine, saying that it wished to "extend to the electronic media the same First Amendment guarantees that the print media have enjoyed since our country's inception."[5] Anticipating this ruling from a deregulation-oriented FCC, both houses of

Congress had passed legislation earlier in the year to codify the fairness doctrine. However, President Reagan vetoed the bill, stating that it was "antagonistic to the freedom of expression."[6]

Deregulation of the broadcasting industry has been a goal of some members of Congress since 1978 and was a prime objective of the FCC during the Reagan administration in the 1980s. By the mid-1980s radio had experienced major deregulation. Stations were no longer obligated to devote a certain percentage of their on-air time to news and public affairs programs, to ascertain the needs and interests of their communities through interviews and surveys, or to maintain program logs (although most stations continue to do so for billing purposes). In addition, the requirement that stations could have no more than 18 minutes of commercial time per hour was lifted.

Much of the deregulation activities of the Reagan FCC were aimed at radio; there was more hesitancy toward getting involved with television deregulation. However, by the 1990s the FCC was encouraging the major television networks to work out a compromise settlement with representatives of the motion-picture producers to allow them to again have involvement in the financial benefits of producing and syndicating their own programs—a benefit the FCC had taken away years earlier.

FCC censorship of broadcasting stations is technically prohibited by the broadcasting acts of 1927 and 1934. However, the Supreme Court ruled in 1977 that the Commission does have the right to ban the broadcast of indecent speech during hours when children might be in the audience. The case involved a New York radio station that played a George Carlin comedy recording, *Seven Words You Can Never Say on Television*. Some listeners didn't think they should be said on afternoon radio either.

Although the FCC has adopted a philosophy of deregulation and believes that the marketplace should regulate the airwaves, it is not averse to punishing broadcasters who air objectionable material. In 1989, for example, the FCC levied fines on four radio stations for broadcasting "indecent" material in the daytime, and threatened to fine four others who were sent letters of warning. Most of the fines and charges revolved around explicit language during talk shows and music with explicit lyrics. Shock radio talk-show hosts like Howard Stern, who mixes sexual innuendos and double entendres with news, music, traffic and weather reports, have been targets of the FCC since the mid-1980s.

In 1990, the FCC launched an investigation into the well-known Boston public broadcasting station, WGBH-TV, for showing examples of Robert Mapplethorpe's controversial photography on its 10 P.M. newscast. This same year the FCC reaffirmed its complete ban on what it considers indecent radio and television broadcasts. Although Congress had attempted to implement a 24-hour ban on material that depicted graphic "sexual or excretory activities" or sexual organs, a U.S. appeals court had blocked such a move until evidence could be provided that children under the age of 17 were being exposed to late-night programming. Broadcasters had been pushing for a window of late night hours, and had generally agreed to avoid such material between the hours of 6 A.M. and 10 P.M. In making its decision, the members of the FCC ruled unanimously that new data compiled by the Arbitron rating service indicated that some children listen to the radio and watch TV at all hours of the day and night. Also helping to convince the commissioners were some 90,000 letters from the public favoring a 24-hour ban on indecent material, while less than 5,000 were received in opposition to the proposed ban.

In addition to the FCC, more than 80 government entities have regulations that affect broadcasters—including the Federal Aviation Administration, which regulates the placement of lights on broadcasting towers and antennas so that they can be seen by aviators. A major federal agency involved in broadcasting is the Federal Trade Commission (FTC), which monitors advertising on radio and television as well as in the print media. Of particular concern to the FTC by the mid-1980s was TV advertising directed at children, particularly on Saturday morning shows. The Food and Drug Administration, the U.S. Postal Service and the Alcohol, Tobacco and Firearms Bureau are also involved in regulating and monitoring mass-media advertising.

COURT REGULATIONS

There are a number of legal regulations of the media imposed by the judicial branch of our government. For years the media and the courts have clashed over two sometimes conflicting constitutional provisions—the First Amendment right of a free press and the Sixth Amendment guarantee of a fair trial.

The free press versus fair trial conflict occurs most often when the press attempts to cover sensational or highly publicized trials. In 1954, for example, Dr. Sam Sheppard was tried in Ohio for the murder of his wife. The Cleveland press sensationalized the case and even pronounced Sheppard guilty before the jury did. In 1966 the Supreme Court overturned Sheppard's conviction, citing unfair publicity.

Many judges and attorneys believe that the press's efforts to cover every detail of a case before the trial is concluded prejudices the jury's ability to render an impartial verdict. As a result, many judges have barred the press and the public from pretrial hearings.

In 1986, however, the U.S. Supreme Court overturned a California Supreme Court decision that pretrial hearings could be closed. In the 7–2 decision, the Court found in favor of the *Riverside Press-Enterprise,* ruling that "public access in criminal trials and the selection of jurors is essential to the proper functioning of the criminal justice system. California preliminary hearings are sufficiently like a trial to justify the same conclusion." The Court added, however, that judges may close pretrial proceedings in rare circumstances when there is no other way to protect the defendant's right to a fair trial.[7]

Voluntary press-bar guidelines have been set up in some states in an effort to balance the needs of the press, the bar and the public. To date, 26 states have adopted such guidelines, which, however, have no legal force and are effective only as long as all involved parties act reasonably and responsibly.

Courts can also restrain the press by issuing gag orders, which limit what attorneys and court officials can say to the press and what the press can print or broadcast. Journalists who have violated gag orders, believing that the restrictions infringe on their First Amendment rights and the public's right to know, have been found in contempt of court by judges.

The refusal to disclose sources or turn over personal materials such as notes, tapes, photographs and film has also led courts to jail journalists for contempt of court. Although some states have *shield laws,* which allow journalists to protect the identity of their sources, no such protection exists at the federal level. In a 5–4 decision in 1972, the Supreme Court ruled that journalists have no absolute privilege to protect sources of information if they are subpoenaed to testify in court proceedings.

Other court regulations of press conduct have been relaxed, however, particularly in regard to longstanding rules banning cameras, tape recorders and microphones from the courtroom. By the 1990s these rules had been lifted in more than 40 states.

The rule against cameras was instituted in the 1930s, when loud, popping flash units were used. In 1935 cameras caused a major disturbance at the trial of Bruno Hauptmann (who was accused of kidnapping and murdering the young son of national hero Charles Lindbergh) and many members of the bar felt that they upset courtroom decorum. Two years after Hauptmann was convicted, the American Bar Association called for a complete ban on courtroom photography. In 1952 and 1963 the ban was extended to include radio and television equipment.

Photography and broadcast equipment have since become miniaturized and less conspicuous, and journalists have been fighting to get the ban lifted. As noted above, these efforts have finally achieved results.

Televising trials has also been slowly gaining acceptance. In recent years 39 states have experimented with these televised trials. Opponents say that televising trials turns attorneys and judges into actors and makes a mockery of justice. However, in states where trials have been televised, the conclusion seems to be that the judges and attorneys are more alert and better prepared.

LAWS AGAINST OBSCENITY

Laws against obscenity or pornography have been constantly in conflict with First Amendment rights of free and artistic expression. The 1990 conviction of a Miami, Florida, record store owner for selling a recording of 2 Live Crew's *As Nasty As They Wanna Be,* and congressional efforts to stop funding of artists whose work is considered obscene are two current examples of an age-old problem.

Laws governing obscenity have undergone some clarification during the latter half of the twentieth century. In 1957, in a case against a New York publisher of erotic books, Samuel Roth, the Supreme Court issued a decision that liberalized the definition of obscenity. The court said that the test for obscenity would be "whether to the average person, applying contemporary community standards, the dominant theme of the material taken as a whole appeals to prurient interest."[8] Although Roth went to jail, this decision was the first to liberalize the interpretation of obscenity. (Prior to that time obscenity was defined as anything that had a tendency to deprave or corrupt anyone's mind. Thus if one page of a book contained a statement that could corrupt anyone—a child, for example—the

■ The rap group 2 Live Crew became a well-known musical group when a Florida court ruled that their album *As Nasty As They Wanna Be* was obscene. Sales of the album soared while the courts wrestled with cases against the group and those who sold its music.

book was judged to be obscene.) Then in 1973 the Supreme Court tightened up the standards again, setting these new guidelines for defining obscenity *(Miller v. California):*[9]

- ■ The work taken as a whole must appeal to the prurient interests of the average person applying contemporary community standards.
- ■ The work must depict or describe, in a patently offensive way, sexual conduct specifically defined by the applicable law.
- ■ The work taken as a whole must lack serious literary, scientific, political, or artistic value.

One of the problems resulting from this interpretation was the difficulty of measuring "contemporary community standards" and the inconsistencies that could exist in various regions of the country. What might be judged obscene in one part of the country might not be so judged in another.

In 1987 the Supreme Court *(Pope v. Illinois)* applied the "reasonable person standard" rather than the "contemporary community standard" in judging the third part of the Miller test. In this latest court interpretation of obscenity, the Court said:

Only the first and second prongs of the Miller test—appeal to prurient interest and patent offensiveness—should be decided with reference to "contemporary community standards." The ideas that a work represents need not obtain majority approval to merit protection, and value of that work does not vary from community to community based on the degree of local acceptance it has won. The proper inquiry is not whether an ordinary member of any given community would find serious value in the allegedly obscene material, but whether a reasonable person would find such value in the material as a whole.[10]

Along with the liberalization of the definition of obscenity has been a gradual change in the culture toward acceptance of sexual discussions and representations heretofore considered taboo. Sexually explicit themes in books, magazines, records/tapes and movies have become acceptable to many in the popular culture; nevertheless, others still find them immoral and pornographic. As a result there have been numerous efforts to curb the proliferation of this so-called pornography. In 1967 a presidential commission was set up and funded with $2 million to study the effects of pornography on our culture. The two-year study found no causal relationship between the dissemination of pornography, and crime and other antisocial behavior. Government panels in Great Britain in 1979 and in Canada in 1984 came to similar conclusions.

However, in 1986 an 11-member panel put together by U.S. Attorney General Edwin Meese released very different and controversial findings. The Meese commission, which had spent a year and $500,000 studying pornography, issued a 1,960-page report that said that it had found a causal relationship between exposure to sexually violent books, films and magazines, and aggressive behavior toward women. It called for stringent enforcement of the nation's antismut laws and the extension of those laws into new areas. Soon after, a new harsh anti-obscenity law was passed in North Carolina; supporters of the legislation hoped that it would set a nationwide precedent.

The American Civil Liberties Union and other opponents of censorship in any form immediately criticized the commission's findings. Even two of the commissioners, both women, wrote dissenting opinions claiming that "no self-respecting investigators would accept conclusions based on such a study." However, the report was lauded by religious, conservative and feminist groups that had been complaining about pornography for years.

Opponents claimed that the report was not objective because the commission had been stacked with conservatives who supported the Reagan administration's point of view against pornography. Supporters said that the report was the first step in "defense of decency and the sanctity of the family"*

LAWS TO PROTECT THE PUBLIC

In addition to court-imposed restrictions on the media, there are the laws of *libel* and *invasion of privacy* that give the public legal recourse when harmed by media abuses of power.

---

*Even before the report was issued, lawsuits had been filed alleging that the commission had intimidated major retail chains into removing magazines like *Playboy* and *Penthouse* from their shelves. Letters signed by Alan Sears, executive director of the commission, had been sent to 23 major American companies, advising them that they had been identified in testimony before the commission as being "involved in the sale or distribution of pornography." Several of these companies, including the 7-Eleven chain, subsequently removed "adult"-type magazines from their inventory.

Libel laws are designed to protect people from uncalled-for attacks or careless errors by members of the press. Libel is the defamation of a person's character through the print or broadcast media. *Defamation* is any communication that exposes people to hatred, ridicule or contempt; lowers their esteem in the community; causes them to be shunned; or injures their careers.

The media have three major defenses against libel suits:

1   *Truth* is an absolute defense against libel. If it can be proven that a report is true, the plantiff has no case. For many years the burden of proof rested with the media. However, in 1986 in the case of *Philadelphia Newspapers v. Hepps,* the Supreme Court ruled that the person suing the media must prove that the statements are false.[11]

2   *Privileged statements*, those made at legislative, judicial and other official public proceedings, are immune to libel suits. For example, if a witness makes a false (or libelous) statement at a trial, the news media can report it as long as the judge doesn't order it stricken from the record. If the witness were to make the same statement in the courthouse hallway, to print it would be libelous and a suit could be filed.

3   *Fair comment and criticism* is the defense that holds that it is permissible to publish critical comments as long as they consist of opinion, rather than fact, about issues of public interest. This defense protects writers of editorials and critics of plays, books, movies, records, sporting events and so on, as long as they are expressing opinions about the public performances of the people involved, rather than their private lives. This defense was significantly weakened in 1990 when the U.S. Supreme Court ruled that a writer or speaker may be sued for statements that expressed "opinion." The ruling resulted from the writing of a sports columnist who had claimed that a Cleveland, Ohio, wrestling coach had "lied" his way out of a suspension.

Another defense against libel suits involving public officials is the absence of malice. A landmark Supreme Court decision in 1964 *(New York Times v. Sullivan)* ruled that a public official must prove malice before he can win a libel suit.[12] Others need only to prove carelessness. This landmark decision gave the press much greater latitude to criticize public officials than private citizens.

Some libel cases involving public persons have attempted to collect judgment for special considerations. In a 1988 case, *Falwell v. Hustler,* the Reverend Jerry Falwell, founder of the conservative Moral Majority organization, sued *Hustler* magazine for publishing a satirical pseudo-advertisement that implied that the minister had had his first sexual experience with his mother in an outhouse.[13] A jury which couldn't find in favor of libel because malice couldn't be proved—the ad was clearly labeled as satire—awarded Falwell $200,000 for emotional stress. The Supreme Court overturned the verdict, citing the need for the media to have freedom to make satirical comments about public officials even though they might be stressful. It noted that political cartoons were a longstanding American tradition.

Any person who believes he or she has been libeled by the mass media may bring a civil suit against those responsible and seek payment for damages. Since actual damages are hard to prove in a libel suit, the plaintiff can seek punitive

■ Often targets of libel suits, the *National Enquirer* and the *Star* thrive on running sensational stories about celebrities.

damages, whose purpose is to punish the libeler. Some punitive damages have run into millions of dollars, especially in cases where actual malice has been proved.

Carol Burnett's suit against the *National Enquirer* initially won a $1.6 million judgment in a California court, but the damages were lowered to $750,000 by an appeals court. The *Enquirer* had run a story that Burnett was seen drunk and disorderly in a Washington, D.C., restaurant. Burnett, who had been active in an antidrug campaign, filed a suit charging that the story injured her reputation and was untrue.

Another large judgment levied by a jury in a libel case occurred in 1986 when singer Wayne Newton won a $19.3 million libel suit against NBC, after charging that the television network had seriously injured his reputation when it wrongly broadcast that he had Mafia connections. The judgment was reduced by a judge to $5.3 million and was finally overturned by a federal appeals court in 1990 when it ruled that NBC had not been deliberately false or reckless. Although NBC finally won the case, it spent millions of dollars over a 10-year period on legal fees.

Other cases where the mass media ended up spending large sums of money before winning libel suits include *Time*'s defense against Israeli defense minister Ariel Sharon and CBS's battle with retired U.S. General William Westmoreland.

Although Sharon was able to prove that *Time* had indeed printed false and defamatory information about him, he was unable to collect from the magazine because he couldn't prove malice (Sharon was a public person). Still, Sharon considered the fact that he had cleared his name a victory in itself.

BOX 4.2

▪ LIBEL TAKES A VARIETY OF FORMS ▪

Libel results from a variety of printed and broadcast information, not just news stories.

For example, a jury recently found *Soldier of Fortune* magazine liable for $9.4 million for publishing a classified advertisement that led to a contract killing. The case began when the son and mother of a slain Texas woman sued the publication because the woman's husband had hired the killer through a classified ad in the magazine. The ad read: "Ex-marine. '67–'69 Nam vet. Ex-DI, weapons specialist—jungle warfare. Pilot. ME. High-risk assignments. U.S. or overseas."

Lawyers for the publication unsuccessfully argued that the publication should not be found liable for the slaying because the magazine's executives had no way of knowing the ad was for an illegal activity. The jury disagreed.

In another case, a Chicago newspaper was sued for libel for running a map attempting to show the location of a house of prostitution. The newspaper contended that these illegal bordellos existed in the city and that the Chicago police were not doing anything about them. The only problem with the map was that the "X" locating the brothel was placed on the house next-door, and its owners sued for defamation.

A professional wrestler, in another Chicago case, sued a newspaper for running his photograph next to one of a gorilla. A sports editor had noted a similarity in features in the two photos and had run them side by side with a humorous caption suggesting that there was something to the theory of evolution.

Westmoreland, who claimed that CBS had inaccurately portrayed him in a 1982 documentary as having tried to deceive his superiors about the size of the enemy forces in Vietnam, withdrew his suit before the trial was concluded. His charges that CBS had deliberately attempted to discredit him by biased editing and interviewing went unanswered but the network's legal defense fund was significantly reduced.

In 1990, the two largest libel verdicts in the history of the American news media were handed down. In *Sprague v. Walter,* a Pennsylvania jury awarded $34 million in damages—including $31.5 million in punitive damages—against the *Philadelphia Inquirer* for a 1973 story that questioned the handling of a homicide case by a local prosecutor. In *Srivastava v. Harte-Hanks Communications, Inc.* a Texas jury awarded $29 million—including $17.5 million in punitive damages—as a result of a series of news broadcasts examining the activities of a local heart surgeon.[14] These decisions are being appealed.

Many other libel suits occur from carelessness in what *Editor and Publisher* magazine calls "nickel and dime" stories. These are small stories where reporters mix up the names and identify an innocent person as the accused or leave out the "not" in a not guilty story. These stories are also actionable (see Box 4.2).

Large awards of punitive damages in libel cases have had a chilling effect on the mass media and some claim that these awards, which seem to be getting larger each year, are responsible for weakening freedom of the press by discouraging investigative reporting and aggressive journalism.

Invasion of privacy suits offer another form of legal recourse against the media.

■ Former first lady Jacqueline Onassis (Mrs. John F. Kennedy) has been hounded by photographers who have often invaded her privacy to get pictures.

Citizens can recover damages from the media for any of the following reasons: (1) intrusion into a person's physical solitude; (2) public disclosure of embarrassing private facts; (3) placing the person before the public in a false light; and (4) commercial exploitation of a person's name or likeness.

Intrusion into a person's physical solitude involves trespassing on private property to interview or photograph a person. In one case, *Galella v. Onassis,* a celebrity photographer (Ron Galella) was ordered to stay 24 feet away from the wife (Jacqueline Onassis) and children of the late President John F. Kennedy even when they were in public places.

Public disclosure of embarrassing private facts deals with information that is considered so intimate that it should remain private. Revealing that a person has had a sex-change operation, and exposing the criminal record of a rehabilitated ex-convict have been found to be invasions of privacy.

Placing a person before the public in a false light deals with instances where the media incorrectly place a person in a position or social status that embarrasses him or her. One such case involved a photograph of an office worker sitting on a park bench during a lunch break. The photo had been used to illustrate a story on the homeless and implied that he was one of them.

Commercial exploitation of a person's name or likeness without permission involves using the pictures or names of famous people and others to advertise or

BOX 4.3

■ WHAT CONSTITUTES AN INVASION OF PRIVACY? ■

Media lawyers have been pulling their hair out over what constitutes an invasion of privacy and what doesn't. Where does a reporter's right to legitimately cover a news story stop and a person's right to privacy begin?

Should journalists be allowed to go onto private property to cover a story of a drug bust or some other crime, or is this an intrusion into the criminal's privacy?

If a person—famous or not so famous—dies of AIDS, is it okay to print the cause of death, or does that constitute the disclosure of embarrassing private facts?

Did the disclosure by the *Miami Herald* that Donna Rice had spent the weekend with presidential candidate Gary Hart place her before the public in a false light? When are such things legitimate news and when do they invade a person's privacy?

The Supreme Court has intervened in privacy cases in only a few instances. In one such case, *Cox Broadcasting v. Cohn,* the court ruled that the media cannot be held liable under privacy law for the accurate publication of information legally obtained from public records. The case stemmed from the publication of the name of a rape-murder victim in Georgia where the law prohibits the publication of the names of rape victims. Reporters for an Atlanta television station had broadcast the name of the victim after obtaining it from a police report.

promote commercial ventures. Photographs and names can be used in news stories without permission, but not in ads or commercial endeavors (see Box 4.3).

Although invasion of privacy laws are designed to protect people from general nuisances and intrusions into their privacy, recent court actions have blurred the line between invasion of privacy and legitimate news coverage. In 1989 the *Los Angeles Times* settled an invasion of privacy case out of court for an undisclosed amount following a charge by a San Diego woman that she became a "walking target" after the *Times* named her as a witness in a murder case. The plaintiff had discovered the raped and murdered body of her roommate while the intruder was still in the apartment. California's 4th District Court of Appeals ruled that a jury should decide whether publication of the woman's real name was newsworthy and necessary to the story.

The two basic defenses for the mass media in an invasion of privacy case are newsworthiness (or public interest) and consent. Any legitimate news story should qualify in the newsworthy category (although the *Los Angeles Times* case places a shadow of doubt over this defense). Consent, however, usually takes proof of a contractual agreement, such as a signed model release (a standard form permitting one's likeness to be published).

Truth is not always a defense for the media in invasion of privacy cases, even though it is in libel suits. Newsworthiness, on the other hand, is not necessarily a libel defense. Something that is perfectly nonlibelous may be an invasion of privacy, and vice versa.

As you can see from this discussion of legal controls on the media in the United States, the strict interpretation of the libertarian theory is somewhat tempered by our laws and regulations. However, the net effect of this seems to be the creation of a climate in which the media can operate with more social responsibility.

Access to Information.   In addition to laws that protect the public from the press, there are laws that protect the public's right to know by giving the media and citizens in general access to public information.

The most important public access law on the national level is the Freedom of Information Act (FOI) passed by Congress in 1966. This law requires agencies of the federal government to declassify and divulge certain information that is no longer considered sensitive or harmful to the national security. Although there are several categories of information that are not affected by this legislation, the FOI has enabled the press and public to obtain significant data that has shed light on important government activities. The federal government also has a "Sunshine Act" that allows about 50 federal agencies to be open to the public.

In addition to these federal laws, numerous states have sunshine laws giving the public and the press access to government agencies and requiring open meetings of governmental bodies. Many states also have public records acts that make public documents available to the press and public.

SUMMARY

Legal controls are levied on the media through a variety of government and judicial statutes. Despite First Amendment protections, laws have been passed that restrict First Amendment provisions of free speech and press. The first such laws were the Alien and Sedition Acts of 1798. Similar laws during World War I were challenged, but they were upheld by the Supreme Court.

Efforts to exercise prior restraint have been made in recent times, despite a Supreme Court ruling that such actions violate First Amendment provisions.

Since the 1920s, the federal government has had laws that restrict the operations of the broadcast media. Although originally established to protect broadcasting stations from overlapping each other's frequencies, these laws have been extended to content as well.

The courts also have legal restrictions on mass-media operations. These laws range from prohibitions on cameras and microphones in courtrooms to gag orders on the press.

Laws against obscenity restrict content of the mass media. Although many feel such laws violate the First Amendment protections of free expression, prosecutions continue in the 1990s.

The people also have legal recourse—through civil suits for libel and invasion of privacy—against injuries inflicted by the media.

The rights of the public to be well informed in a democracy are protected by a variety of state and federal laws giving the press and public access to government information and meetings.

THOUGHT QUESTIONS

1 Why did the Supreme Court uphold convictions of socialists who distributed antiwar leaflets during World War I?

2 Do you support the FCC's position on a complete ban of broadcasting indecent material? If so, how should "indecent" be defined and by whom? If you do not support the ban, how would you protect children from hearing such material?

3 Should records, tapes, books, magazines, videos and movies be censored if they are considered pornographic by community standards? Why or why not?

4 Why should "truth" be a defense in libel cases but not in invasion of privacy cases? Do you think this inconsistency hinders freedom of the press?

5 How can we ensure that monetary judgments in libel and invasion of privacy cases do not inhibit freedom of the press?

NOTES

1. *Schenck v. United States*, 249 U.S. 47 (1919).

2. *Yates v. United States*, 354 U.S. 298 (1957).

3. *Brandenburg v. Ohio*, 395 U.S. 444 (1969).

4. *Near v. Minnesota*, 283 U.S. 697 (1931).

5. Raymond L. Fischer, "The FCC and the Fairness Doctrine," *USA Today*, magazine, May 1988, p. 42.

6. Ibid.

7. *Press-Enterprise v. Superior Court of California for Riverside County* (1986).

8. *Roth v. United States*, 354 U.S. 476 (1957).

9. Quoted in *Publishers Weekly*, May 22, 1987, p. 20.

10. Ibid.

11. *Philadelphia Newspapers v. Hepps*, 105 S.Ct. 1558 (1986).

12. *New York Times v. Sullivan*, 376 U.S. 254 (1964).

13. *Falwell v. Hustler*, 485 U.S. 46 (1988).

14. Lee Levine and David L. Perry, "No Way to Celebrate the Bill of Rights," *Columbia Journalism Review*, July/August 1990, pp. 38–39.

ADDITIONAL READING

Ashley, Paul P. *Say It Safely: Legal Limits in Publishing, Radio, and Television*, 5th ed. Seattle: University of Washington Press, 1976.

Ashmore, Harry S. *Fear in the Air: Broadcasting and the First Amendment: The Anatomy of a Constitutional Crisis.* New York: Norton, 1973.

Carter, Barton, Franklin, Marc, and Wright, Jay. *The First Amendment and the Fourth Estate.* Mineola, N.Y.: Foundation Press, 1988.

Gillmor, Donald, and Barron, Jerome. *Mass Communication Law*. St. Paul, Minn.: West Publishing Co., 1984.

Holsinger, Ralph. *Media Law*. New York: Random House, 1987.

Middleton, Kent, and Chamberlin, Bill. *The Law of Public Communication*. New York: Longman, 1988.

Nelson, Harold, and Teeter, Dwight. *Law of Mass Communication*. Mineola, N.Y.: The Foundation Press, 1989.

Rowan, Ford. *Broadcast Fairness: Doctrine, Practice, Prospects*. New York: Longman, 1984.

DEVELOPMENT OF PRINT MEDIA

Books are not only the oldest form of mass communication, but one of the most controversial as well. Here author Kitty Kelley is shown with her latest controversial unauthorized biography.

BOOK PUBLISHING: PAST AND PRESENT

A book is the only place in which you can examine a fragile thought without breaking it, or explore an explosive idea without fear it will go off in your face. . . . It is one of the few havens remaining where a man's mind can get both provocation and privacy.

—Edward P. Morgan

Surgeon General's Warning: Writing and publishing novels can be injurious to your health.

Such warnings have not yet appeared on jacket covers of novels, but to Salman Rushdie, author of *The Satanic Verses,* it might seem like a good idea.

In 1989 Rushdie went into hiding where he remained in the 1990s after Iran's Ayatollah Khomeini issued the following statement: ''I inform the proud Muslim people of the world that the author of *The Satanic Verses,* a book which is against Islam, the prophet and the Koran, and all those involved in its publication who were aware of its content, are hereby sentenced to death.''

THE CULTURAL HISTORY OF BOOKS

ELITIST	POPULAR	SPECIALIZED		
■			c. 2500 B.C.	Sumerian clay tablets.
■			c. 600 B.C.	Papyrus scrolls used in Egypt.
■			540 B.C.	First public library founded in Athens.
■			1st century A.D.	Books regarded as household treasures by the elite.
■			5th century	Great Library of Alexandria, Egypt, destroyed.
■			5th–10th centuries	Books preserved in monasteries.
■			9th century	Chinese invent printing.
■			13th century	Rise of European universities.
■			1456	Gutenberg Bible printed from movable type.
■	■		16th century	Books become the first mass-produced and mass-distributed commodity.
■	■		16th century	Books help spread the ideas of the Protestant Reformation; authorities invoke censorship to control printers.
■	■		1640	*Bay Psalm Book* published at Harvard College.
	■		18th–19th centuries	Industrial Revolution.
	■		19th century	Rise of American novelists and publishing houses.

The Iranians put up a $5.2 million reward for the person who carried out the death sentence if the person were Iranian, $2 million if he or she were not. A year later, following the death of Khomeini, his successor, Ayatollah Ali Khamenei, reaffirmed the death sentence.

Although the non-Islamic world was shocked by this latest attempt at book censorship, it certainly wasn't the first time that books had been controversial. This oldest form of mass communication has a history of generating extreme reactions to its contents, such as the torching of printers by King Henry II (see Chapter 2).

Despite the controversy and occasional hazards, book publishing is still a very successful and profitable enterprise. More than 20,000 firms, employing some 74,000 people, were in the U.S. book publishing business in the early 1990s. Most of these firms were small publishing houses, with only 2,264 firms releasing four or more book titles a year. According to the U.S. Industrial Outlook, the book

THE CULTURAL HISTORY OF BOOKS

Elitist	Popular	Specialized	Year	Event
	■		1852	*Uncle Tom's Cabin* is published; sells 7 million copies, helps spark Civil War (1861–65).
	■		1867	Horatio Alger, Jr., publishes his first "rags-to-riches" story, *Ragged Dick.*
	■		1873	Anthony Comstock founds the New York Society for the Suppression of Vice.
	■		1920s	Novelists used publicity from having their books "banned in Boston" to promote sales elsewhere.
		■	1945	Books begin serving a variety of specialized interests as post–World War II years change American culture.
		■	1957	Supreme Court begins to liberalize its interpretation of obscenity in *Roth v. United States.*
		■	1960s	Wide range of books published, reflecting new subcultures and protest movements.
		■	1973	Supreme Court adopts stricter "contemporary community standards" test to define obscenity *(Miller v. California).*
	■		1980s	Book publishers begin marketing audio books.
	■		1990s	Consolidation of large publishing firms continues.
	■		1990s	Censorship of books continues.

publishing industry was publishing over 60,000 titles a year by the beginning of the 1990s.

Gross revenue from U.S. book sales was estimated to be $15.3 billion in 1990 and was expected to grow to $17.9 billion by 1994. Textbooks represent the largest category in book publishing, with 31 percent of the sales. The recent growth in elementary and secondary school textbooks (called el-hi textbooks) was caused by growing enrollments from the children of baby boomers. An influx of college reentry students over the age of 25 helped stimulate the sales of college textbooks during the decade of the 1980s. Trade book sales were in second place at 21 percent, followed by technical, scientific and professional books at 18 percent of the market share (see Figure 5.1).

There are five major distribution channels for books: retail outlets such as book stores, department stores, drug and proprietary stores, gas stations, train and bus depots, airports and convenience stores, which account for approximately 36

■ Textbooks, used in nearly every classroom in America, generate the highest income of any U.S. book publishing category.

percent of total sales; book clubs and mail order, 20 percent of sales; college bookstores, 18 percent; primary and secondary schools, 16 percent; and libraries and other institutions, 10 percent. Although books are one of the few mass media that do not rely on advertising to produce revenue, the book publishing industry does use advertising—and talk shows—to stimulate sales.

Books play an important role in preserving the ideas, thoughts and histories of civilizations. Since these records are handed down from generation to generation and are collected in libraries—a practice that has been going on for thousands of years—books have become the most permanent of all the mass media. For example, to learn about the Persian Wars of 500 years B.C., one need only to read *The History of the Persian Wars* by Herodotus, who lived at that time. To learn about early Greek literature and the Homeric age, which fell between the thirteenth and ninth centuries B.C., one can turn to Homer's *Iliad* and *Odyssey*, written around the eighth or ninth centuries B.C.

ORIGINS OF BOOKS

In order to understand how books influence our culture today, it is necessary to review how this mass-communication medium developed and how it has been influencing and changing cultures for centuries.

Early Forms. We can trace book publishing back to Sumerian clay tablets, which were used 4,500 years ago to record various items of religious, legal and

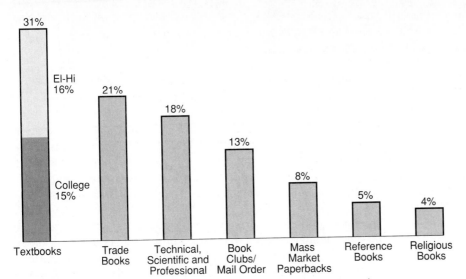

Figure 5.1 Percentage breakdown of U.S. book sales by categories.
SOURCE: *U.S. Industrial Outlook, 1990* (Washington, D.C.: U.S. Government Printing Office, 1990).

medical interest, as well as narrative tales. These are the oldest written documents known to mankind.

Next came papyrus scrolls, which were used throughout ancient Egypt, Greece and Rome. These large rolls of papyrus were attached to two rods that permitted the book to be held and rolled from either end. Although the lengths of the manuscripts varied, some rolls contained entire books. Archeologists have unearthed ancient handwritten scrolls in Egyptian, Greek, Latin, Arabic, Hebrew and Syrian. In addition to religious writings, these scrolls contained the philosophies, history, oratory, drama, poetry and anthologies of such ancient writers as Eustathius, Plato, Aristotle, Demosthenes, Homer, Sophocles, Euripides, Archilochus and Ascepiades.

Public Libraries.   The first public library was established in Athens in 540 B.C. Later, around 300 B.C., Ptolemy I founded the Great Library in Alexandria, Egypt. The library became the intellectual center of the Hellenistic Empire, and the most famous scholars, scientists, poets, philosophers and artists of the day gathered there to study and work.

At its peak, the library contained between half a million and a million hand-copied papyrus volumes—almost all of Western civilization's recorded knowledge. Transcribers were often sent there to copy manuscripts for other libraries. This great repository of learning was burned and ravaged by Romans, civil war and even the Christian emperor Theodosius I; by A.D. 400 the world's greatest intellectual treasury up to that time had been lost forever.

The selling and collecting of papyrus scrolls in ancient Rome reached its peak around the time of Christ, with some households reportedly having libraries containing thousands of volumes. As the Roman Empire began its decline and libraries were ravaged and burned during barbarian invasions, books found sanctuary in Christian monasteries, especially in Ireland.[1]

Middle Ages. Although relatively little is known about the development and use of books during the Middle Ages (A.D. fifth through fourteenth centuries), there were some improvements in how knowledge was recorded. For example, in the fifth century the Saxons began using books made of animal skins; these more resembled paged books as we know them today. About this same time the Romans were replacing the awkward scroll with the codex, which was a stack of folded leaves that was bound along one side and protected by wooden covers. The more durable animal parchment was replacing papyrus as the medium on which books were written.

Also at about the same time, the Chinese were perfecting and using paper made from tree bark, old rags, hemp waste and fishnets. The art of making paper slowly spread through Europe around the twelfth century, although paper wasn't produced in England until the late fifteenth century or on the American continent until the late seventeenth century. The Chinese were also the first to develop printing, sometime during the ninth century. The oldest existing printed book is *The Diamond Sutra*, printed in China in A.D. 868 from carved wood blocks and containing Buddhist wisdom.

However, printing did not spread from China to the Western world. Bookmaking and manuscript copying by cloistered clergy in monasteries remained a handcrafted process in Europe through the Middle Ages. Thus most of the medieval codex production consisted of sacred works such as Bible texts and interpretations, liturgical manuscripts and the works of those philosophers and classical authors whose thoughts were believed to contribute to Christian principles.

The Renaissance. Six centuries after the Chinese began to print books, printing technology was introduced into the Western culture. Credit for bringing mass communication to the Western World belongs to the German inventor Johannes Gutenberg, who used movable type and a converted wine press to publish a 42-line-per-page Bible in 1456. This large-sized Bible, in Latin, was a replica of existing hand copied manuscripts. Gutenberg's Bible was a work of great precision and beauty, and the reproduction of 200 identical copies was astonishing in a world that was used to handwritten books.

Although Gutenberg died a pauper shortly after his press was confiscated to pay his debts, by the end of the fifteenth century this new craft was established in every major capital in Europe. The first printer in England was William Caxton, who published his first book in 1476.

EARLY BOOKS AND THE ELITE

From the days of clay tablets to well beyond the invention of mass communication, books were limited to the elite. Thousands of years passed before the medium began to enter the popular culture.

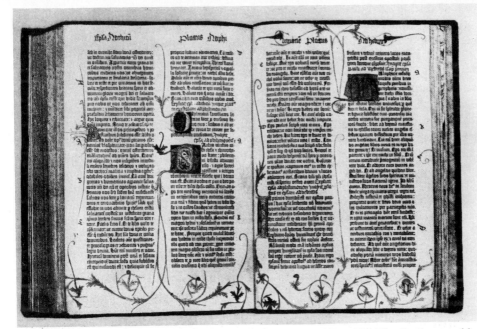

■ Two hundred copies of the Gutenberg Bible were printed in 1456. The book resembled the handwritten Bibles that preceded it.

Even after Gutenberg's new technology spread throughout Western Europe, books remained in the elite phase of the elite-popular-specialized (EPS) cycle (see Chapter 1). Illiteracy among the poor was the main cause. Books were read primarily by the clergy, educators, scientists, professionals and members of the aristocracy.

However, the Renaissance also saw a great expansion of trade and commerce and the creation of a new middle class. These prosperous merchants and bankers had a practical interest in secular learning and proved a ready market for books. Thus the first mass-communication medium began at last to reach beyond a tiny elite to mainstream society.

The Reformation.   By the time of the Protestant Reformation, in the sixteenth century, printing was able to reach the developing middle class. In the 1520s, for example, Martin Luther became the first person to use this new mass-communication technology for propaganda purposes. He wrote a series of pamphlets in German attacking the doctrines of the Roman Catholic Church. Luther's revolt caused the printing of books in Germany to rise from 150 in 1518 to 990 in 1524. Four-fifths of these books favored the Reformation. Soon his works were being printed in other languages and were spreading throughout Western Europe. As one historian has written, "Printing was the Reformation; Gutenberg made Luther possible."[2]

Part of Luther's new religious doctrine was the idea that the people—not the Catholic Church—should be the interpreters of the Bible. To facilitate this premise, he translated both the Old and New Testaments of the Latin Bible into conversational German. During his lifetime, 100,000 copies of the New Testament were printed, and it became and has remained the best-selling book in Germany.[3]

Censorship.   The practice of censorship developed at the time of the Protestant Reformation. It did not take long for those in authority—kings and popes—to realize that Gutenberg's new technology, which allowed ideas to be mass produced and distributed, posed a threat to those in power. As previously noted, King Henry II in Catholic France made it a practice to burn books and printers who attempted to distribute Protestant thought. In England, King Henry VIII established a list of prohibited books and by 1529 had developed a system of licensing printers. Even Martin Luther advocated the censorship of books written by Huldreich Zwingli and John Calvin—Protestants with views different from his own. This era of religious censorship and suppression lasted over a hundred years, and many people were executed for expressing their beliefs. The voice of religious and political dissent was never completely stilled, however, as printers could always find a haven somewhere to publish "heretical" writings.

STAGES OF BOOK PUBLISHING IN THE UNITED STATES

England's policy of strict censorship of the press and the licensing of printers was transported to the new English colonies in America in the seventeenth century. Although this helped curtail the early development and spread of books in the colonies, book publishing did eventually grow and flourish. To better understand the development of book publishing in America, we will examine this industry as it evolved through each stage of the EPS cycle.

The Elitist Stage.   Printing remained in the elite culture in the American colonies from the seventeenth to the nineteenth century. The conditions necessary for books to enter the popular culture (see Chapter 1) were slow to develop. Most colonists had few luxuries. Like all frontiersmen, they worked hard and had very little leisure time for the cultivation of aesthetic and intellectual values. With the exception of the elite and clergy, most colonists could not read or write.

Religion, which played a major role in the expansion of book publishing in sixteenth-century Europe, was also instrumental in getting this industry started in the colonies. Many settlers belonged to strict religious sects, such as the Puritans who settled in the Massachusetts Bay colony. The Puritans were responsible for establishing the first printing press in North America in 1638 at Harvard College near Boston; two years later it published the first book in the Thirteen Colonies, the *Whole Booke of Psalmes,* better known as the *Bay Psalm Book.* Harvard controlled this press until 1662, when the Massachusetts legislature took it over. The early Harvard press was used to produce religious books, pamphlets and sermons, as well as some government and educational materials.

One of the first successful secular contributors to the development of book publishing in the American colonies was Benjamin Franklin. He began publishing one of America's most famous early books, *Poor Richard's Almanack,* in 1733. It became successful—selling about 10,000 copies a year—by giving people something besides the Bible to read in the home. The almanac contained a wide variety of useful and entertaining information, including poetry, short stories, mean temperatures in various parts of the country, lists of public officials and public affairs articles. In 1744 Franklin published the first novel in America, *Pamela,* by English novelist Samuel Richardson. Franklin was also the first person to establish a subscription library in the colonies.

Publishing developed slowly in the North American colonies. However, a number of important pamphlets produced by political dissenters around the time of the American Revolution stimulated an interest in reading. In 1774 three separate publications challenged the right of England's Parliament to govern the colonies: James Wilson's *Considerations on the Nature and Extent of the Legislative Authority of the British Parliament,* Thomas Jefferson's *A Summary View of the Rights of British America* and John Adams's *Novanglus Papers.* In 1776 Englishman Thomas Paine, who had come to the colonies two years earlier, published *Common Sense.* In 47 pages it spelled out the meaning of the American revolutionary movement and made it clear that the Americans were not quibbling over the details of taxation but were standing up for their liberties as a nation. The pamphlet sold 120,000 copies in three months, a tremendous number when one considers that the colonial population at the time was only about 400,000.[4]

Following the Revolutionary War, book publishing centers were established in New York, Boston and Philadelphia, and the new industry began to expand. According to historian Oscar Handlin, "the exciting current events of the Revolution fortified the desire for printed matter. Americans wished to learn what was going on in every part of the continent, and they were anxious to follow the political arguments provoked by the debate over their rights. The result was a steady rise in the volume of publications."[5]

A number of American novelists soon began publishing. Although some were writing in a style similar to that of their European counterparts, others were developing a uniquely American style of writing. Examples include Hugh Henry Brackenridge's *Modern Chivalry* (1792), a satire on the first few years of the politics of the new nation; Charles Brockden Brown's *Wieland* (1798), a romantic tragedy in a genre of horror and remorse that Edgar Allan Poe would later cultivate; and Washington Irving's *A History of New York, by Diedrich Knickerbocker* (1809), a humorous parody of an earlier work about New York City. Noah Webster helped establish an American language by publishing a national dictionary.

The Popular Stage. As the new nation struggled with its destiny as a republic dedicated to the common wealth of all its people, its economy and culture began changing. The nation underwent an expansion to the West. To accommodate this vast new country a transportation system of canals and eventually steam-engined railroads developed. The new methods of transportation furthered economic, political and social unity by bringing the vast regions of the nation closer together. This growth stimulated trade and commerce, and the nation's cities grew.

Conditions in Europe—landlords were ousting tenants from their land to put larger acreages together for more profitable farming and famine was sweeping across Ireland and Germany in the 1840s—caused hundreds of thousands of people to immigrate to the United States annually. This large unskilled labor pool stimulated the growth of industries, and by the mid-nineteenth century the agrarian American culture was being transformed into an industrial society as the Industrial Revolution swept the land.

The Industrial Revolution also brought new technology to printing. Cylinder and rotary presses and Ottmar Mergenthaler's Linotype machine greatly sped up book production. Large numbers of trees were also available, making wood-pulp paper abundant.

At the same time the concept of compulsory public education was taking hold; only an educated citizenry, it was argued, could uphold and protect the new democracy from the threat of tyrannies. By the 1840s universal public education had been established in most Northern cities, and a large literate population began to emerge. By the 1850s all states had accepted the principle of tax-supported elementary schools. (In the South, however, blacks were barred from this education.) By 1861 the United States had the highest literacy rate in the world: 94 percent of the population in the North and 83 percent of the whites in the South (58 percent of the total population). Industrialization and universal public education together created the conditions that moved book publishing from the elite into the popular culture.

Books by American writers like Ralph Waldo Emerson, James Fenimore Cooper, Henry David Thoreau, Catherine Sedgwick, Lydia Sigourney and Edgar Allan Poe were finding their way into the popular culture. In addition, many Americans enjoyed the works of popular British authors such as Charles Dickens and William Wordsworth. By 1855, U.S. book sales far exceeded sales figures in England.

Recognizing the immense market for books, an entrepreneur named Erastus Beadle decided to mass produce a line of inexpensive books that appealed to common interests. He and his brother Irwin published huge printings of paperback books that followed a set formula of praising the spirit of individuality and the virtue of common people. A typical title was *Malaeska: Indian Wife of the White Hunter*, by Mrs. Ann S. Stephens. He sold these books—called Beadle's Dime Novels—for ten cents each and began advertising them as "Dollar Books for a Dime!" Between 1860 and 1865 he sold over 4 million copies.

During this period a number of other individuals established major publishing houses, many of which are still prominent today. Among these entrepreneurs were the brothers James and John Harper, John Wiley, George Palmer Putnam, Dan Appleton, Charles Scribner, E. P. Dutton, Henry Oscar Houghton and George Harrison Mifflin (Houghton Mifflin) and Charles Little and James Brown (Little, Brown).

These publishing houses opened up opportunities for a newly developed crop of American authors to publish their works, and many outstanding literary works resulted. Nathaniel Hawthorne's *The Scarlet Letter* (1850) is said to be one of the greatest books ever written in the Western hemisphere. Herman Melville's *Moby-Dick* (1851) is still considered one of the finest novels in American literature. Harriet Beecher Stowe's *Uncle Tom's Cabin* (1852), which helped forge antislavery thinking before the Civil War, established the American novel as a powerful

■ Harriet Beecher Stowe helped forge antislavery thinking prior to the Civil War. Her book *Uncle Tom's Cabin* sold 7 million copies and influenced such leaders as Abraham Lincoln, who later as president abolished slavery in the United States.

literary and social force. The story of a literate, kindly slave known as Uncle Tom, who was abused and finally killed by the evil Simon Legree, was published first in serial form in a magazine and later as a two-volume novel. Although banned from sale in the South, the book was an early success, selling about 1,000 copies a week; a total of 7 million copies were eventually sold. *Uncle Tom's Cabin* had a profound influence on public opinion and evoked sympathetic responses from various national leaders, including the future president of the United States, Abraham Lincoln.

By the end of the nineteenth century a number of writers had large followings and fan clubs similar to those that idolize today's rock stars. They included Mark Twain, who wrote about growing up on the Mississippi with Tom Sawyer and Huckleberry Finn, and the English poets Robert Browning and Rudyard Kipling.

However, the most commercially successful author in this period was Horatio Alger, who wrote more than 120 books about growing up in the new industrial society. His books, which offered hope for the young in the new mass culture, were all rags-to-riches tales of the American dream—a pious, intelligent young boy makes his way to the top by hard work and virtue. The theme of upward mobility seemed to strike a responsive chord in the hearts of many (see Box 5.1).

This era also saw the development of a free public library system, which made books available to all segments of the public regardless of whether they could afford to purchase them. This library system helped to establish the concept of egalitarianism in the American culture.

As industrialization spread and the number of immigrants in the United States increased (there were 4 million foreign born in 1860 but 9 million by 1890), worker exploitation through poor working conditions and low wages became common. To expose these conditions, a new kind of book emerged in the popular culture. Novels like Upton Sinclair's *The Jungle* (1906), which described intolerable working and sanitation conditions in Chicago's meat-packing plants, helped raise the public's social consciousness during this era. This and other books like it were

BOX 5.1

HORATIO ALGER, JR.: WRITING BOOKS ▪ ▪ FOR INDUSTRIAL AGE YOUTH

Often a series of books can play an important role in shaping American popular culture and they can even help to promote American mythology.

One such series was written by Horatio Alger, Jr., during the late nineteenth century. He wrote over 120 novels—all rags-to-riches stories for boys. His books were melodramatic accounts of the trials and tribulations of young, energetic, hard-working young boys who developed into "honorable, manly characters." The books carried such titles as *Ragged Dick, Only an Irish Boy, The Cash Boy, Making His Way, Strong and Steady, Try and Trust, Bound to Rise, Tony the Tramp, Joe's Luck, Julius the Street Boy* and *Facing the World*.

In *Facing the World* young Harry Vane, a poor orphan boy, goes to live with a mean, stingy guardian after his father dies. He encounters numerous hardships and obstacles but manages to save lives, survive shipwrecks, emerge as a hero and live happily ever after.

These books played a role in giving young people growing up in impoverished conditions during the emerging Industrial Revolution a sense of hope and a desire to climb out of poverty and into a life of success and happiness. This helped promote the American myth that success is within reach of all hard-working citizens.

Publishers promoted these books by pointing out that "their high moral character, clean, manly tone and the wholesome lessons they teach without being *goody-goody*, make Alger Books as acceptable to the parents as to the boys."*

* *Quoted from inside cover of* Facing the World *(New York: New York Book Company, 1909).*

instrumental in changing public attitudes about the benefit and dangers of unfettered free enterprise. Eventually laws were passed to protect consumers and employees, such as statutes that required federal inspection of food products and child-labor laws, which prevented the exploitation of children in sweatshops.

Meanwhile, as book publishing became firmly entrenched in the popular culture, major efforts were still being made to censor books. One of the first such efforts in the new nation came in 1821 when the book *Fanny Hill,* published before the Revolution by the famed printer Isaiah Thomas, was found to be obscene at a trial in Massachusetts.

A major push came in 1873 when Anthony Comstock, a New York City dry-goods store employee, founded the nonprofit New York Society for the Suppression of Vice. Its stated purpose was to "clean the filth out of the wickedest city in the world." Comstock devoted 40 years to this effort and was successful in getting federal legislation passed that made it illegal to send anything obscene through the mail. One result was that providing information about contraception was illegal in many states for almost a hundred years (until a Supreme Court decision in 1965).

According to historian Paul Boyer, the vice-society movement grew "in response to the deep-seated fears about the drift of urban life in post-Civil War years." As Boyer notes, the migration of Americans away from the familiar sources of guidance and support—family, church and close-knit communities— and into the metropolitan areas made people like Comstock feel there was a need to protect the nation's young from the "filth" that could be found in popular literature.[6]

Efforts at censorship continued well into the twentieth century. It took court action before certain books, like Erskine Caldwell's *God's Little Acre* and James Joyce's *Ulysses,* could be sold in the United States. (Both books were attacked by censors because they contained sexually explicit language.)

One of the most famous censoring efforts of this century was conducted in Boston. This community, which still had strong religious influences, established a book-censoring commission; books found objectionable by the commission were "banned in Boston." Some of the writers whose works were banned were John Dos Passos, Theodore Dreiser, Ernest Hemingway, Sinclair Lewis, Upton Sinclair and H. G. Wells. Boston's strict censorship codes did not reflect national attitudes toward literature and conflicted with many people's desire for a wide range of reading material. As a result, the city's efforts seemed to do more to stimulate sales in other parts of the country than to suppress books in Boston. As Upton Sinclair once said, "We authors are using America as our sales territory and Boston as our advertising department."

Whatever impact censorship had on sales, there is no doubt that publishing houses flourished in the first half of the century, as reading became one of the most popular leisure activities in both the elite and popular cultures. An example can be found in the success story of Bennett Cerf and Donald S. Klopfer. In 1925 Cerf—a book salesman for Boni & Liveright—persuaded his wealthy friend Klopfer to invest $100,000 to purchase the Modern Library, Boni & Liveright's classical-book division. Two years later the partners formed an additional company so that they could print books other than classical reprints, "sort of at random," Cerf later noted. To suit their aim, they called this new publishing operation Random House. In 1966, they sold Random House to RCA for $40 million (RCA later sold Random House to Samuel I. Newhouse, Jr.). The value of book-publishing firms has continued to climb. In 1987, media baron Rupert Murdoch paid $300 million for Harper & Row.

The Specialized Stage.   The period from 1945 to the present has seen a dramatic shift in the book-publishing industry, as the business responded to new and changing audiences. For example, after World War II ended, many military personnel enrolled in college under the GI Bill, which paid veterans' educational expenses. As a result, the textbook business boomed, and it wasn't long before textbook publishing led the list in revenue generators for the book-publishing industry (a position it still retains).

In addition, people began to take up or renew other interests, such as their family and children, suburban living, and leisure activities like hunting, fishing, bowling, tennis, golf and spectator sports. The book-publishing industry responded by bringing out more nonfiction "lifestyle" titles each year, rather than relying so heavily on a few blockbuster popular novels. Child care manuals, books on how to landscape the backyard or fix up the house and tell-all biographies became hot sellers in the marketplace. With these expansions, book publishing began to enter the third stage of the EPS cycle—the age of specialization. (See Box 5.2 for perhaps the ultimate specialized book.) The ratio of literary works— fiction, biography, poetry and drama—to nonliterary works, such as textbooks,

BOX 5.2

▪ *BARBIE: HER LIFE AND TIMES* BY BILLYBOY ▪

Books have been reflecting our culture for thousands of years. These reflections can take many forms. Even a twentieth-century popular-culture icon—the Barbie doll—has been chroniclized for future civilizations in a book called *Barbie: Her Life and Times.* Written by the French jewelry designer BillyBoy, the book includes over 300 full-color photos of the doll, taken from BillyBoy's collection of over 11,000 Barbie dolls.

This study of the Barbie doll does more than reflect BillyBoy's affection for it, however. It also provides an insight into changing American attitudes toward the role of women in our culture by charting the evolution of the Barbie doll from its early days as a petticoated prom queen to a doctor, astronaut and fitness-conscious business-woman in the 1980s.

Sociologists study the role children's toys play in changing sexist stereotypes; perhaps BillyBoy's book on Barbie will provide them with new insights.

Courtesy of Crown Publishers, Inc., New York, 1987

professional books, reference books, cookbooks and "self-help" and "do-it-yourself" guides, shifted dramatically. By the 1970s new *non*literary works outnumbered new literary works by more than two to one.[7]

How-to books represent one of the most successful categories of specialized book publishing. As people became absorbed with "who they were" and "self," the publishing industry started catering to their interests. Popular topics included such things as how to pan for gold, fix up your home, straighten out your psyche, exercise your body and lose weight through the "perfect" diet plan. Many of these how-to-books feed on the American myth that everyone in this country can succeed if he or she is determined and has the "inside scoop" on how to do it. Book titles in this genre in the 1990s ranged from *The Secret Language of Success: Using Body Language to Get What You Want* to *Woodworking with Your Kids.*

As the book-publishing industry adapted to providing reading material for special interests, the promotion of these books helped expand the special-interest area into larger segments of the culture. Specialized books on diets and exercise, for example, helped form a new cultural belief that "being thin" meant being healthy and "everybody should lose weight." It is interesting to note that with this new cultural attitude came an increase in cases of anorexia being reported in the late twentieth century.

Instant books, another extremely successful form of specialization, put book publishing in competition with news-oriented mass media by providing immediate, detailed coverage of news events. The instant book is a paperback about a current topic that is published immediately after the event. When a special review board appointed by the president—known as the Tower Commission—released its report on the Reagan administration's involvement in the Iran-Contra scandal in 1987, paperback books containing the complete report were available for sale 47 hours and 29 minutes later. Copies were rushed to bookstores across the country and large chain bookstores like B. Dalton were selling out as quickly as they were getting them in. When newspaper heiress Patty Hearst was kidnapped in 1974, several paperbacks about the kidnapping were on sale shortly thereafter. It was reported at the time that FBI investigators were buying the books in search of leads in the case. When rock idol John Lennon was murdered outside his New York apartment in 1980, instant books about his life and its tragic end were on the market within days. Most other types of books take at least nine months to manufacture.

Nonfiction novels also compete with the news media by presenting more detailed interpretation of news events than the news itself. Some of the pioneering examples of this approach are Truman Capote's *In Cold Blood,* a nonfiction novel based on the true story of two murderers who killed a Midwestern farm family, and investigative works like Bob Woodward and Carl Bernstein's *All the President's Men* and David A. Yallop's *In God's Name: An Investigation into the Murder of Pope John Paul I.* (The Woodward-Bernstein book details how the two Washington Post reporters uncovered the Watergate scandal; Yallop's book alleges that the death of Pope John Paul I was not due to natural causes, as reported).

Personalized books have become possible as a result of new computer technology. These publications, composed and printed entirely by computer, are designed primarily for children. The computer stores a complete text of the book, with a few key items left blank. To purchase such a book, a person gives the publisher the name, address and other personal data about the child who will be given the book. This information is fed into the computer and out comes a book (obviously not a great literary work, but rather something simple or mundane) that incorporates the specified data in the story. Thus the recipient of the book becomes the hero of the story.

Fotonovels are part printed text, part picture book and part comic book. They usually develop as spinoffs of a popular movie or television program. *Star Trek* became one of the first successful topics for a fotonovel in this country. The books were a hit with the "Trekkies" (see Chapter 2). Although fotonovels have been popular in South America and Europe for more than 40 years, they are relatively new in the United States and seem to reflect the fact that specialized interests in our multimedia world tend to overlap from one medium to another.

BOX 5.3

▪ COMIC BOOKS: INTERNATIONAL CLASSICS ▪

The comic book is a relatively new American publishing genre that has become an international phenomenon. These books became popular in the late 1930s with the introduction of *Detective Comics* and *Action Comics*, publications that featured original stories rather than comic strip reprints.

Soon youngsters in the American popular culture were reading about the fantastic achievements of such superheros as *Superman* and *Batman and Robin*. Following these flying crime fighters onto the comicbook pages were animal characters developed by *Terrytoons Comics* and Walt Disney's *Comics and Stories*. In 1939 60 different series of comic books were being published. This figure grew to 650 by 1954 (the year a strict self-censorship code was enforced), and included such comic characters as Airboy, Captain America, Captain Marvel, The Phantom, Dick Tracy, Popeye, Flash Gordon, Donald Duck, Mickey Mouse and Tarzan. There was even a series of classical literature tales told in the comicbook format, such as Huckleberry Finn, Robin Hood, Ivanhoe and King Arthur and the Knights of the Roundtable.

The development of the American comic book was influenced by other twentieth-century mass media, particularly motion pictures, radio and eventually television. The Western genre of the motion picture became a popular subject for comic books. Even singing cowboy radio and movie stars like Gene Autry and Roy Rogers became comic book characters, as did fictitious action/adventure characters like *The Lone Ranger, The Shadow, Sergeant Preston of the Yukon* and *The Green Hornet.* In the 1950s, following television's entry into the popular culture, some comic books began featuring TV action/adventure themes such as *Have Gun Will Travel, Gunsmoke, Lawman* and *77 Sunset Strip.*

Although created in the United States, the modern comic book never really gained respectability here as an art or literary form. It was perceived as children's entertainment and as such became a target for concerned parents and others who feared that the comic book would corrupt the youth. Strong objections developed over the use of themes of sex and violence in comic books. The Comics Magazine Association of America (CMAA) attempted to establish a code of ethics in the 1940s.

The government got into the act when the Kefauver Crime Committee began holding hearings on the effect of comics on children. A stringent code of conduct was enforced by the CMAA in 1954, and approved comics began carrying a seal indicating that they contained only wholesome material. In 1955 the State of New York passed a law making it illegal to sell obscene, objectionable comics to minors or to carry such words as *crime, sex, horror* or *terror* in the title of any comic book. Other states followed with similar legislation. The number of comic books in this country declined significantly after that. It wasn't long before those who had been concerned about sex and violence in comic books shifted their efforts toward the newer medium of television.

In Europe, Japan, Central and South America, on the other hand, people of all ages read comic books. Some of the American superheros, such as Superman, became popular speaking in foreign tongues. The American genre of the Western be-

Graphic novels are a spinoff of the comic books that have been gaining popularity since the 1980s. This book form consists of an original self-contained story told in the comic-book format. By the 1990s, graphic-novel titles ranged from the *Thief of Baghdad,* selling for $12.95, to *The Legend of Kamui,* priced at $16.95. There were also official movie adaptations in comic-book format that included *Arachnophobia, Who Framed Roger Rabbit* and *Teenage Mutant Ninja Turtles.* Even Fox's TV series *Married . . . With Children* was depicted in the graphic-novel format. This genre of books is designed to appeal to visually-oriented

BOX 5.3 Cont.

came very popular abroad. Other comic characters were developed that were unique to the foreign cultures. In France and Japan, for example, comic books represent a very large publishing market. In Japan in the late 1980s, 20 percent of all publications sold were comic books, called *mangas*. This translated into approximately 70 million copies a month. The themes or plots of these comic books range as widely as American popular novels and are mostly aimed at adults. Sex, violence and even nudity is not uncommon in many of these foreign comic books.

There is new hope for the comic-book genre in the United States, however. Numerous book publishers are bringing back a version of the American comic book with a new name and a new target audience—adults. These new comics are called graphic novels. Each graphic novel contains a complete story—like any other novel—and the quality of writing is very high. The graphics are also more spectacular than the old comic books and the production quality is far superior to ordinary paperbacks.

individuals who do not read much. Publishers are hopeful that the graphic novel will introduce these individuals to reading and that the experience will lead them to try other types of books (see Box 5.3).

Novelization is a book genre that developed in recent years from the book industry's symbiotic relationship with motion pictures. Books and motion pictures have been linked together since the early days of film. Many books have been made into movies through the years, and the ability to sell the movie rights to a best-seller means a great deal to publishers and authors. Recently a reverse trend, called novelization, has occurred, whereby book publishers print novels based on successful movies. In 1990, after the movie *Dick Tracy* did well at the box office, paperback Dick Tracy novels flooded the bookstores.

Mass-market paperback books, often sexy romance, western or mystery novels, also account for large revenues in book publishing. These high-volume books often have press runs that exceed a million copies. These paperbacks, which once sold for around 75 cents, now bring $4.95 to $12.95 a copy and prove that despite the variety of other media for recreation and escape the novel still appeals to the masses.

Audio books are a new publishing industry genre that by the mid-1980s had become very lucrative. As more and more people found themselves on freeways fighting the traffic to and from work, the concept of listening to books on audio cassette tapes became popular. By the 1990s, some businesses in Southern California were establishing audio book libraries for their employees as an incentive to rideshare. In 1991, Carol Publishing expanded this category by starting to publish audio books on compact disks.

Censorship

Efforts at censorship not only continued but increased during the period of specialization. In the late 1940s and 1950s the book-publishing industry was attacked for printing materials that critics believed to be pro-Communist or anti-American. Alleged obscenity also remained a popular target for censors. For example, in 1950 the Chicago Police Bureau of Censorship banned a novel called *A Diary of Love* which had been written by Maude Hutchins, the estranged wife of the president of the University of Chicago.

The attacks on books increased during the 1980s. From 1980 to 1984 censorship complaints brought to the attention of the American Library Association increased from 300 to almost 1,000 cases a year. According to Judith Krug, director of the American Library Association's Office of Intellectual Freedom, the number of annual complaints took another jump above the 1,000 level in 1989.[8] Efforts were being made to censor a variety of books for various reasons. Topics popular for attack included sex, race, politics, religion and drugs. Some of the more popular works that have been targeted because they contain references to one or more of these tabooed topics include *The Adventures of Huckleberry Finn, 1984, Slaughterhouse Five, Go Ask Alice, The Diary of Anne Frank, Of Mice and Men, To Kill a Mockingbird* and *The Catcher in the Rye* (see Box 5.4).

In a Northern California lumber community, there was even an effort in 1989 to ban Dr. Seuss's *Lorax* because it told a story about a fuzzy little creature losing its home in the forest because the greedy "Once-lers" cut down all the trees.

In 1990, a California school board found itself facing a recall election when it refused to remove a set of state-approved schoolbooks from its classrooms. Parents claimed the new readers, called *Impressions,* carried satanic, immoral and violent messages and were unfit for children. After setting up a study committee, the Yucaipa School Board decided to continue to use the readers but agreed to set up special classes—using the traditional "Dick and Jane" readers—for children

■ Cries for censorship of printed material comes from a wide variety of people, as this antipornography rally in New York City demonstrates.

whose parents found *Impressions* unacceptable. School officials and the study group found that the new readers stimulated an interest in reading among the youngsters who used them and that more books were checked out of the library by these students than by those who used the traditional readers. The compromise wasn't good enough for the angry parents who began circulating the recall petitions.

A 1990 study of 421 California school districts by a California State University, Fullerton, professor disclosed that 150 of the districts had been challenged by parents and organizations unhappy with the content of school materials during a two-year period. Of those challenges, 13 percent of the time the objectionable materials were removed. About half of the 300 reported challenges were based on religious grounds, including depictions of Satan or witchcraft in such classics as *Macbeth* and *Snow White*.

In 1987 a federal judge in Alabama upheld a fundamentalist Christian group's effort to ban 44 state-approved textbooks that allegedly contained "secular humanism," a philosophy that the judge equated with religion. He ruled that secular humanism was a form of religion because it places man, not God, at the center of existence and advocates situational ethics and morals instead of absolute religious values. The banned books covered such fields as home economics, history and social studies. This decision was later overturned by a federal appeals court.

Although book banning is usually a tactic of conservative movements and tends to be criticized by liberals, there are no clear-cut political categories when it

BOX 5.4

▪ THE DIARY OF ANNE FRANK ▪

On July 6, 1944, four months before Anne Frank was arrested and sent to a German concentration camp where she died, she wrote in her now-famous diary the following thoughts about her first and only boyfriend, Peter van Daan:

Poor boy, he's never known what it feels like to make other people happy, and I can't teach him that either. He has no religion, scoffs at Jesus Christ, and swears using the name of God; although I'm not orthodox either, it hurts me every time I see how deserted, how scornful and how poor he really is.

People who have a religion should be glad, for not everyone has the gift of believing in heavenly things. You don't necessarily even have to be afraid of punishment after death; purgatory, hell and heaven are things that a lot of people can't accept, but still a religion, it doesn't matter

which, keeps a person on the right path. It isn't the fear of God but the upholding of one's honour and conscience.*

Do you think this statement is blasphemous and unworthy of the eyes of teenagers with religious backgrounds? In 1986, because of this passage, a group of parents in Greenville, Tennessee, went to court to prevent the local schools from making their children read the book. A judge ruled in their favor.

The book provides an earnest and humane statement about the value of religion from a young girl who died because of a doctrine of supremacy that had no room for religious freedom. Yet it ended up on a list of books some people felt should be banned in the United States—200 years after the country was founded on a premise of religious freedom.

* The Diary of Anne Frank *(London: Pan Books, 1954) p. 212.*

comes to reacting emotionally to the contents of books. Twain's *Huckleberry Finn,* which describes the evils of racism in the nineteenth century, has been branded as racist by many who find the use of the word *nigger* offensive. Other books have been condemned by feminist groups who claim that pornography degrades women. A 1991 novel, *American Psycho,* was the subject of a boycott against the publishers by the National Organization of Women (NOW) because of its "violent and women hating" content. The novel, by Bret Easton Ellis, deals with a yuppie serial murderer who sexually mutilates women. On the more conservative side of the political spectrum, the Reverend Jerry Falwell was condemning the censorship of conservative books in the 1980s (see Box 5.5).

According to historian John Tebbel, this "virtual epidemic of censorship" that has been sweeping the country in recent years is the result of a combination of cultural factors: (1) a militant advocacy of fundamentalist values by nearly 70 million evangelicals organized by radio and television evangelists; (2) a large number of traditionalists who found themselves unable to accept a changed world and longed for what they considered the peaceful days of repression and rigid traditional morals and manners; and (3) the Supreme Court's decision to leave the definition of obscenity to local community standards.[9] Others say that this trend is a reflection of cultural paranoia, and they cite Supreme Court Justice Potter Stewart's comment that "censorship reflects a society's lack of confidence in itself."

BOX 5.5

▪ KEEP BOOKBUSTERS OUT OF OUR LIBRARIES ▪

The following is an editorial that appeared in the July 12, 1985, issue of USA Today.

If you're spooked by a story or a thought or a word, who're you going to call? Bookbusters!

In the past several years, attempts to get books pulled from library shelves have tripled, the American Library Association reported this week.

This year, the ALA expects to hear about 1,000 efforts to remove books from classrooms or libraries. Volumes that have come under fire recently include literary classics, like *Adventures of Huckleberry Finn* and *1984*.

Some communities have a review process that gives a book a chance to stay on the shelves once it has been challenged. Others simply yank the book.

In Racine, Wis., it was *Slaughterhouse Five*—Kurt Vonnegut's novel of the fire-bombing of Dresden. In Rankin County, Miss., it was *Go Ask Alice*, which describes a teenager's death from drug abuse. In Anniston, Ala., it was—yes—Doris Day's autobiography.

In New Jersey, Arizona, and many other states, the banned books were the novels of Judy Blume, who writes about the growing pains of adolescents.

Conservatives complain they are the victims of censorship, too. For example, Jerry Falwell says libraries tend to exclude books that have conservative or fundamentalist Christian points of view.

Lately, books thought to be racist have been targets. In Waukegan, Ill., an alderman tried to rid classrooms of *Uncle Tom's Cabin* and *Huckleberry Finn*—he didn't like the way they portrayed blacks. In Fairfax, Va., a teacher succeeded in getting Huck Finn temporarily banned from—ironically enough—Mark Twain Intermediate School.

The educator published his own version that substituted "slave" or "black man" for the word "nigger." Never mind that part of the book's purpose was to underscore the evils of the racism of that day. It's all been smoothed over now.

In the 19th century, it was bad grammar and blasphemy that helped get books banned. Today, it is racism, ageism, and sexism. Books are targeted because they promote creationism, or because they don't promote creationism.

The Bookbusters must think that words will hurt us. And not just words, but—eeeeek!—ideas.

Of course, ideas need a context. A kid who knows nothing of the racism that thrived when *Huckleberry Finn* was written won't understand the author was attacking racism.

Parents who object to depiction of premarital sex or drug abuse in novels intended for teens should use the opportunity to explain their family's values to their children.

But censorship is dangerous. There's no limit to beefs about books. If Mark Twain and Doris Day offend, why stop there? There's always the Constitution: Censorship is a hallmark of totalitarian regimes everywhere.

When the world has been made safe from ideas, the Bookbusters will have won. The library shelves will be empty—and ignorance will have triumphed.

Another way the courts have been used in the latter part of the twentieth century as a tool of censorship is through the threat or institution of libel suits. One reason for this trend may be the fact that there are more attorneys per capita in the United States than in any other major civilized nation in the world. Although libel laws were designed to protect the innocent from defamation by the mass media and were clearly not intended as a form of censorship, some people have used the threat of a suit to pressure publishers into removing material from books before they go to press.

Book publishers started taking this new threat very seriously in 1979, when Doubleday and its author Gwen Davis Mitchell lost a $75,000 judgment to a California psychologist. (He argued that although his name wasn't used in the novel *Touching,* one of the fictitious characters who used nude therapy had been modeled after him.) Since then, many book publishers have involved lawyers in the review and editing of manuscripts. As a result, much of the content of these books has been altered.

Some of the books that were threatened with libel suits before publication were *Two of a Kind: The Hillside Stranglers* and biographies of John F. Kennedy, Ernest Hemingway, Frank Sinatra, Errol Flynn, Katherine Graham and Claus von Bülow. According to Rodney Smolla, author of *Suing the Press,* more and more books are being censored because of the threat of a libel suit.

In the 1980s, even the government was using the courts to censor the contents of books. A 1980 U.S. Supreme Court decision upheld an injunction against Frank Snepp, a former CIA officer, that required him for the rest of his life to get the CIA's approval before speaking or writing on CIA activities. The case resulted from a book written by Snepp that was critical of the way the CIA had treated Vietnamese intelligence aides, including leaving their names behind in files when the United States withdrew from Vietnam. Before writing the book he attempted to get the CIA to investigate the incident. When they refused, he wrote *Decent Interval,* describing what happened. The CIA charged that he had violated a secrecy agreement by publishing the material; the Supreme Court agreed and ordered him to turn over his profits from the book—some $180,000—to the government. In 1986 CIA director William J. Casey warned two journalists who were working on books about his agency that they would be violating the law if their books included any secret "communications intelligence."

If we use history as a basis for predicting the future, it is safe to assume that there will always be attempts to impose censorship as long as book publishing and other forms of mass communication play a major role in disseminating information and ideas in our culture.

Current Business Trends

As a major industry in the United States, book publishing has not been immune to the takeover fever that swept American business in the 1980s. Many privately owned publishing houses—as well as medium and large-sized companies—have been taken over by large conglomerates. Just before the first edition of this textbook was to be released by Random House in 1989, the college and school textbook division of Random House was acquired by McGraw-Hill Publishing Co. Soon after, McGraw-Hill merged its school textbook division with Macmillan and together they purchased the Merrill Publishing Co. to make the new Macmillan/McGraw-Hill the nation's largest el-hi publisher.

Some worry that this consolidation trend will eventually limit the number and variety of books available, as profit-minded executives are less willing to take chances when deciding which books to publish. Just as troubling to many people in the industry is the fact that many of the buyers have been foreign companies stimulated by the currency advantage. Doubleday, Dell and Henry Holt were sold

BOX 5.6

▪ WORKING IN BOOK PUBLISHING ▪

A lot happens between the time a writer signs a contract to publish a book and the moment a finished product reaches a bookstore. The process can take 18 months or longer and involve many people. Although the process varies depending on the publishing house and the size of the publishing firm, the following steps usually occur.

First an *author* must contact an acquisitions editor. He or she usually has an outline or overview of the book and some sample chapters. Sometimes an *agent* does the contacting and negotiates a contract.

The *acquisitions editor*'s job is to look for potential authors and to work out contract agreements. Contracts usually call for an advance and a percentage of the book's sales to be paid to the author. The acquisitions editor also manages one or more "lists" of books in a particular discipline or area, overseeing projects and making sure that books are emerging as planned.

A *development editor* sometimes works with the author during the development of the manuscript. In the case of textbooks, the development editor sets up and handles the task of getting multiple reviews from teachers who are potential users of the book and uses that information to help shape the finished product. A development editor may also edit and help to rewrite the manuscript and guides the selection and creation of artwork for the book.

The *production editor* manages the book during the various stages of production, which include copyediting, design, typesetting, proofreading and printing. Usually the book is typeset and printed by outside firms.

The *marketing department* is responsible for advertising the book and getting reviews for promotional purposes. Marketing activities include writing advertising, catalog and back-cover promotion copy; developing thematic promotion campaigns for books; and getting the author booked for lectures or guest appearances on television and radio talk shows.

The fulfillment department is responsible for getting the book to bookstores and making sure that additional copies are printed when supplies run low. In the case of textbooks, there is a staff of *sales representatives* responsible for visiting schools or college instructors and telling them about the book.

---

to West German publishers; New American Library, E.P. Dutton, South-Western, Gale Research and Grove Press were acquired by British companies; and both Harper & Row and William Collins & Son are owned by Australian-born Rupert Murdoch. Following the merger of Time Inc. with Warner Communication in 1989, the new Time Warner, Inc. sold its Scott Foresman publishing company to Murdoch's Harper & Row for $455 million.

In 1988, British-conglomerate Pearson bid $283 million to buy Addison-Wesley. It publishes the educational textbook line of Addison-Wesley-Longman, which has worldwide sales of about $440 million. This, along with British-owned Macmillan's entry into the textbook field as the largest el-hi publishing company with annual sales in excess of $550 million raises new concerns about foreign control of American educational materials.

As long as the dollar remains weak abroad and the book publishing industry continues to be lucrative, the forecast for the 1990s seems to be more of the same.

SUMMARY

Books are the most permanent form of mass communication because they are durable, designed to be passed from person to person and are housed in libraries.

Civilizations have been recording permanent messages in portable form since the Sumerians used clay tablets 4,500 years ago. Other ancient forms of books included papyrus scrolls and the codex; these were the predecessors to the handwritten book on paper made from wood pulp.

In the mid-fifteenth century Johannes Gutenberg's invention of movable type turned the ancient art of bookmaking into a mass-communication medium. Soon after the invention of mass communication, those in authority saw the medium as a threat to their rule and took steps to regulate it. Despite these efforts at censorship, books became an important part of the Protestant Reformation in the sixteenth century.

In the United States, book publishing has gone through three stages of development—the elitist, popular and specialized stages. Specialized books outsell novels by two to one, and book publishing is a major cultural industry.

Throughout the history of book publishing, censorship and book banning have remained an integral part of society. In recent years many people have used the courts in an effort to censor books.

Book publishing is a major industry in the United States, generating more than $15 billion in sales annually. In the 1980s many smaller firms were taken over by huge conglomerates, and some of the major American publishers were sold to foreign companies.

THOUGHT QUESTIONS

1 What cultural factors made Western civilization ready for the mass production of books in the fifteenth century?

2 What kind of a picture will today's mass market paperbacks leave for future anthropologists who might use them to study our civilizations thousands of years from now?

3 Why did it take longer for comic books or graphic novels to reach the adult population in the United States than in other countries?

4 Should books be censored to protect classes of people and society in general from abuses and potential harm? If yes, how should this be done and if no, how can we protect our culture from such abuses?

5 What are some of the potential dangers ahead if the trend of conglomerate takeovers of the book publishing industry continues, particularly takeovers of U.S. companies by foreign interests?

NOTES

1. Edward Edwards, *Libraries and Founders of Libraries: From Ancient Times to the Beginning of the Nineteenth Century* (Amsterdam: Gerard Th. Van Heusden, 1968; originally published 1865), p. 25.

2. Will Durant, *The Reformation: A History of European Civilization from Wyclif to Calvin: 1300–1564* (New York: Simon & Schuster, 1957), p. 368.

3. Ibid., p. 369.

4. Oscar Handlin, *The History of the United States,* vol. 1 (New York: Holt, Rinehart & Winston, 1967), p. 234.

5. Ibid., p. 258.

6. Paul S. Boyer, *Purity in Print: The Vice Society Movement and Book Censorship in America* (New York: Scribner's, 1968).

7. Curtis G. Benjamin, "Book Publishing's Hidden Bonanza," in *Readings in Mass Communication: Concepts and Issues in the Mass Media,* ed. Michael C. Emery and Ted C. Smythe (Dubuque, Iowa: Brown, 1972), p. 182.

8. Alan Parachini and Dennis McDougal, "Censorship: A Decade of Tighter Controls of the Arts," *Los Angeles Times,* December 25, 1989, p. F-1.

9. John Tebbel, *Between Covers: The Rise and Transformation of Book Publishing in America* (New York: Oxford University Press, 1987), p. 460.

ADDITIONAL READING

Cerf, Bennett. *At Random: The Reminiscences of Bennett Cerf.* New York: Random House, 1977.

Compaine, Benjamin M. *The Book Industry in Transition.* White Plains, N.Y.: Knowledge Industry Publications, 1978.

Dessauer, John P. *Book Publishing: What It Is, What It Does,* 2nd ed. New York: Bowker, 1981.

Exman, Eugene, *The House of Harper.* New York: Harper & Row, 1967.

Handlin, Oscar. *The History of the United States,* 2 vols. New York: Holt, Rinehart & Winston, 1968.

Lehmann-Haupt, Hellmut. *The Book in America: A History of the Making and Selling of Books in the United States.* New York: Bowker, 1951.

Madison, Charles A. *Book Publishing in American Culture.* New York: McGraw-Hill, 1966.

Merryweather, F. Somner. *Bibliomania in the Middle Ages.* London: Woodstock Press, 1933.

Reitberger, Reinhold, and Fuchs, Wolfgang. *Comics: Anatomy of a Mass Medium.* London: Studio Vista, 1972.

Smolla, Rodney A. *Suing the Press.* New York: Oxford University Press, 1986.

Stern, Madeleine B. *Publishing for Mass Entertainment in Nineteenth Century America.* Boston: G. K. Hall, 1980.

Tebbel, John. *A History of Book Publishing in the United States,* 4 vols. New York: Bowker, 1972, 1975, 1978 and 1981.

Wroth, Lawrence C. *A History of the Printed Book.* New York: Limited Editions Club, 1938.

Magazines are the most specialized of the mass media. Browsing through the wide range of selections at a magazine stand provides a good overview of our ever-changing popular culture.

MAGAZINES: THE SPECIALIZED MEDIUM

Of all the literary scenes
Saddest this sight to me:
The graves of little magazines
Who died to make verse free.
—Keith Preston,
The Liberators

The 1990s started out as a bust for the magazine industry. Tobacco and automotive advertising dollars were off sharply and other ad categories were weak. Adding to the problem was the fact that there were many more magazines competing for the advertising revenue.

The sales slump could have been predicted by examining the record-breaking trend that the industry had set during the 1980s. More than 2,500 new magazines were started during the 1980s, including such flashy upstarts as *Vanity Fair, Spy, Elle, Spin, Wigwag, New York Woman, L.A. Style, Child, Sassy, European*

THE CULTURAL HISTORY OF MAGAZINES

ELITIST	POPULAR	SPECIALIZED		
▨			1704–14	First English-language magazines—*Review, Tatler, and Spectator*—published in London.
▨			1741	First two American magazines published within days of each other.
▨		▨	1743	*Christian History* founded, America's first unit-specialization magazine.
▨			1821	*Saturday Evening Post* founded.
▨			1830	*Godey's Lady's Book* becomes first women's magazine.
	▨		1865–1900	First magazine boom, following the end of the Civil War.
	▨		1893	McClure and Munsey reduce prices of their magazines to make them truly affordable; *Saturday Evening Post* follows.
	▨		1890s–1900s	Magazine muckrakers expose political corruption and unsafe working conditions.
	▨		1920	Magazine advertising tops $129 million annually.
	▨		1922	*Reader's Digest* is founded to serve the busy culture of the Roaring '20s.
	▨		1923	Henry Luce starts *Time*, America's first newsmagazine.
	▨		1936	Luce starts *Life* to fill the visual void created by radio.
	▨		1947	*Reader's Digest*, with more than 9 million subscribers, becomes largest-selling publication in U.S.

Travel & Life, Fame, Egg, Details, Victoria, Premiere, Smart, Condé Nast Traveler, Manhattan Inc., 7 Days, Model and *Taxi*. In 1989 alone, 584 new magazines were launched.

In 1990, *Manhattan Inc.* was sold to Capital Cities/ABC to be merged with their ailing *M* magazine; *7 Days, Taxi* and *Model* had folded. Even some veteran publications that predated the boom decade, like *Psychology Today*, suspended publication in 1990.

Advertising revenue declines were hurting many long-time favorites as well. Murdoch's News Corporation's *TV Guide* ad revenue declined 12 percent, Time Warner's *People* revenue was down 10.1 percent, *Time*, 8.2 percent, *Newsweek*, 12.2 percent, *Woman's Day*, 18.1 percent, and *Family Circle*, 18.3 percent.

THE CULTURAL HISTORY OF MAGAZINES

ELITIST	POPULAR	SPECIALIZED		
	■		1948	*TV Guide* begins in New York City; later expands nationally.
	■		1950s	General-interest magazines begin to decline in circulation as specialized publications develop.
	■		1952	*Mad* is founded; pokes fun at consumer culture.
	■		1953	Hugh Hefner's *Playboy* gives popular culture a sex life.
	■		1960s	Specialized publications take over circulation lead from general-interest magazines.
	■		1972	*Life* ceases publication.
	■		1972	*Ms.* becomes first magazine with a feminist viewpoint.
	■		1974	Time Inc. introduces *People* magazine as a smaller version of old movie fan magazines.
	■		1978	*Life* resumes publication as a monthly.
		■	1980s	More than 12,000 specialized magazines are available; new ones start daily. Computer, family and lifestyle magazines are the latest to find a niche in the specialized culture.
		■	1980s	The decade of major magazine expansion with more than 2,500 new magazines founded during this period.
		■	1990s	This decade began with an advertising revenue slump caused by many new publications competing for the same dollars and by a decline of tobacco and automobile ads.

Experts in the field predicted that the industry was merely going through a readjustment period after the boom decade and that the industry would emerge from the slump into a period of prosperity by 1993. Such readjustments with successful years following had been common for the magazine industry since it first entered the popular culture in the nineteenth century. Magazines are the most specialized of all the mass media, with new publications emerging each year to reflect our ever-changing popular culture and its subcultural needs.

Although it took thousands of years for books to move from the elitist stage to the popular stage and a hundred more years before they reached the specialized stage, magazines evolved much more rapidly. In fact, magazines have been specializing in one way or another since they began in the eighteenth century.

■ Magazines appeal to a wide range of interests, as these examples suggest.

According to mass media scholars John Merrill and Ralph Lowenstein, all magazines have either *unit* specialization or *internal* specialization.[1] Unit specialization occurs in magazines that target audiences with special interests: *Hot Rod Magazine, Surfer* and *Personal Computing,* for example. Most magazines produced in the United States today fall into this category. Internal-specialization magazines are general-interest publications that appeal to a larger audience and offer a wider variety of articles. The readers then select the articles that are of interest to them. Although many of these magazines have gone out of business during the past 30 years, some are still very successful—consider *Reader's Digest.*

HISTORY OF MAGAZINES

British Publications.   The first English-language magazines were started in London in the early eighteenth century. The first such publication, the *Review,* was actually a cross between a newspaper and a magazine. It was published by Daniel Defoe (the author of *Robinson Crusoe)* in 1704. In 1709 Richard Steele began publishing the *Tatler.* He was soon joined by Joseph Addison, and together they published both the *Tatler* and its short-lived successor, the *Spectator.* In 1731 the first British publication to carry the word magazine in its title began: Edward Cave's *Gentlemen's Magazine.* Cave later hired the famed man of letters Dr. Samuel Johnson as one of his writers. Johnson started his own magazine, the

■ In 1741, Benjamin Franklin lost by three days his race to become the first American magazine publisher to fellow Philadelphia printer Andrew Bradford. Yet Franklin's publication, *General Magazine and Historical Chronicle,* outlasted Bradford's efforts by three issues.

Rambler, in 1750. These magazines sought an audience among the elite—both men and women—by providing witty and stimulating reading in periodical form.

Early American Efforts.   In 1741 two prominent printers in Philadelphia—Andrew Bradford and Benjamin Franklin—vied to publish the first magazine in the American colonies. Bradford was the victor, publishing his *American Magazine, or a Monthly View of the Political State of the British Colonies* three days before Franklin's *General Magazine, and Historical Chronicle, for All the British Plantations in America.* Franklin was more successful, however, as his magazine lasted for six issues compared to Bradford's three. The content of these American magazines consisted mostly of material reprinted from British magazines; only about 10 percent of the material in the six issues of the *General Magazine* was original.[2]

These early American magazines were designed for the elite, the relatively few literate members of society. Thus they carried essays and articles on religion, philosophy, natural science, political affairs and literature.

In 1743 a publication that might be described as the first specialized magazine in America was printed. It was *The Christian History,* a religious magazine. Due to the low literacy rate in the eighteenth century and the slowness of the mails, the development of magazines during this period was less than spectacular. Indeed, prior to the nineteenth century, no American magazine lasted for more than 14 months.

Successful Expansion. By the 1820s, however, American magazine publishing began to develop into a lucrative and long-lasting enterprise. One of the more famous magazines of this era was the *Saturday Evening Post,* which was founded in 1821. It lasted as a weekly publication until 1969. In 1825 there were fewer than 100 magazines in the United States. Twenty-five years later, there were 600.

This tremendous growth in magazine publishing resulted from advances in printing technology (steam power and cylinder and rotary presses), the eventual development of a literate society as a result of compulsory education, and major reform movements that generated topics for printed discussion. In 1820, for example, the first abolitionist magazine, *The Genius of Universal Emancipation,* was published in Ohio. As slavery became hotly debated and as the nation moved toward the Civil War, magazines played an important role in informing and influencing the people. As mentioned in Chapter 5, Harriet Beecher Stowe's *Uncle Tom's Cabin* first appeared as a series of magazine articles before it was published in book form.

Nevertheless, before the Civil War, magazine readership was still drawn primarily from the elite. The *Saturday Evening Post* and other successful publications founded in this period—the *North American Review* (1815), *Harper's* (1850), and *Atlantic Monthly* (1857)—carried mostly short stories, novels, poems, scholarly essays and political and social commentaries.

Expansion into Popular Culture. By the end of the Civil War (1865), compulsory education had helped give the United States the highest literacy level in the world and the railroads had provided a means of transporting people and goods (including publications) across the continent. American magazines could now start to enter the popular culture. Numerous publications featuring both unit and internal specialization appeared. Two of the most popular genres of unit specialization were farming and women's magazines. Some of the more popular publications of the late nineteenth century were *Ladies' Home Journal, McCall's* and *Woman's Home Companion.* (*Godey's Lady's Book,* the forerunner of these specialized women's publications, was first published in 1830.)

The 1880s and 1890s saw the debut of a number of mass-circulation, general-interest magazines featuring fiction and nonfiction articles. The most important were *Collier's, Cosmopolitan* and *McClure's. McClure's,* founded by the newspaper magnate Samuel S. McClure, was the first inexpensive mass-circulation magazine, selling for 15 cents a copy. This prompted Frank Munsey to cut the price of his *Munsey's Magazine* to 10 cents. Soon the *Saturday Evening Post* was selling for a nickel. Now that they were very affordable, magazines became entrenched in the popular culture. The variety of their articles enabled these magazines to appeal to a wide range of Americans. Farmers in the Midwest could enjoy certain stories in *Saturday Evening Post,* for example, while other articles appealed to merchants and bankers in New York. The magazine industry thrived. In 1865 there were about 700 magazines, by 1900 more than 5,000.

The Muckrakers. The millions of Europeans who immigrated to the United States during the latter part of the nineteenth century provided a large labor force for the new industrial economy. Many workers were forced to live in deplorable slums and work long hours in sweatshops for abysmally low wages. Reformers turned to such magazines as *The Nation* and *Harper's Weekly* for support in their efforts to improve living and working conditions. In the 1890s, the Populist movement attacked the great disparity between rich and poor and accused industrial capitalists of a greedy disregard for the common welfare. The medium for their crusading articles was magazines.

By the beginning of the twentieth century, this new form of journalism, called *muckraking,* had become an important part of magazine content. Muckraking journalists sought out and exposed corruption and scandal. President Theodore Roosevelt coined the term *muckraker* to express his dislike for this negative form of journalism. For him, these journalists were like the "Man with the Muckrake" in *Pilgrim's Progress,* who would not look up from the filth on the floor even when he was offered a glittering crown. But the muckrakers themselves considered the term a compliment to their crusading efforts.

Although *Harper's Weekly* had exposed political corruption in New York as early as the 1870s and the nineteenth-century magazine *The Arena* had attacked slums, sweatshops and prostitution, it was not until the turn of the century that campaigns against corruption became commonplace in such mass-circulation magazines as *McClure's, Everybody's* and *Collier's.* Soon both general-interest and opinion magazines were carrying muckraking articles exposing deplorable living conditions, corrupt business practices, exploitation of workers and political corruption.

Among the more prominent muckrakers were Lincoln Steffens, Ida Tarbell, Ray Stannard Baker, David Graham Phillips and Upton Sinclair. Steffens tackled the slums in his widely praised "Shame of the Cities" series; Tarbell exposed the

▪ Ida Tarbell was one of the courageous muckrakers at the turn of the century who challenged large corporate giants during the Industrial Revolution. Her article *History of the Standard Oil Company* exposed corrupt business practices of the company's founder, John D. Rockefeller.

corrupt business practices of John D. Rockefeller in the "History of the Standard Oil Company"; Baker wrote a series on the problems of corrupt labor unions entitled "The Right to Work"; Phillips attacked politicians who favored special interest groups in "Treason in the Senate"; and Sinclair wrote about worker exploitation and unsanitary conditions in Chicago's meat-packing houses in "The Condemned Meat Industry."

Muckrakers created popular sentiment for reform legislation, most notably the Pure Food and Drug Act and the Meat Inspection Act, both sponsored by President Theodore Roosevelt.

World War I.   As World War I approached, muckraking journalism declined—attention was increasingly focused on the war in Europe. Magazines played a role in eventually getting the United States involved in the war. The British conducted an overt campaign to get pro-Allies propaganda before the American people, some of which made its way into American magazines. Numerous stories (many of them false) about German atrocities in Belgium circulated throughout the United States. Even President Woodrow Wilson was influenced by the British magazines that he regularly read.[3]

Postwar Trends.   Although Wilson overcame considerable domestic opposition to secure the entry of the United States into World War I in 1917, he was unsuccessful in persuading the nation to guarantee the peace. The U.S. Senate refused to ratify the treaty that would have made the United States a member of the new League of Nations. Many Americans believed that peace and economic prosperity could best be achieved by isolating our nation from alliances and commitments with other countries. This isolationist attitude grew after the war. As the country turned inward, it began to focus on the cultural changes that were occurring in the 1920s. They included changes in the family structure, women's suffrage, prohibition, growth of urban life, a rising crime rate and more permissive moral attitudes—which many people blamed on the invention of the automobile (which allowed young people to court one another away from the home), jazz music and dance halls.

As the culture changed, so did magazine content (see Box 6.1). A variety of new magazines emerged. For example, as our popular culture became fast-paced with prohibition, popular music and fast living during "The Roaring '20s," the stage was set for a magazine that would save the reader time by condensing its articles. In 1922 *Reader's Digest* was founded by DeWitt and Lila Wallace; their idea was to take the best articles from other publications and reprint them in a condensed form, and their magazine became the largest-selling one in the nation.

Because the United States did not have a strong system of nationally circulating newspapers, as in England, magazines filled the void. The first "newsmagazine," a term coined by its founders Henry R. Luce and Britton Hadden, was introduced in 1923 as *Time. Newsweek* followed in 1933 and in 1948 *U.S. News & World Report* entered the field.

As the trend toward urbanization continued, metropolitan magazines, featuring articles about lifestyles in our large urban centers, became popular. The first and most successful was the *New Yorker,* introduced in 1925.

BOX 6.1

▪ MAGAZINES REFLECT CULTURAL CHANGES ▪

American popular culture changed dramatically during the first part of the twentieth century. As the culture changed, so did the content of the nation's magazines. One of the best ways to study the changing popular culture is to look at magazines over a period of time. Each new trend, fad, hobby or subculture is reflected in our magazines. These changes are seen in general-interest as well as special-interest publications.

One of the first studies of our changing culture as seen through the pages of magazines was published in *Radio Research* (edited by Paul F. Lazarsfeld) in 1942–43. In this study, Leo Lowenthal compared the biographical articles in *Collier's* and the *Saturday Evening Post* for 1901 and 1940–41; he found that in the 40-year interval the proportion of articles about business and professional men and political leaders had declined, while those about entertainers had gone up 50 percent.

The study showed how our culture had changed from the days of the Industrial Revolution—when men of production played a paramount role in society—to a new age preoccupied with leisure pursuits and the popular, rather than the elite, arts. It confirmed too that our popular culture had moved from an interest in elite or high culture to mass-cultural interests: in 1901 the entertainers featured were mostly serious artists, such as opera singers, sculptors or pianists, while the 1941 entertainers were all movie stars or baseball players.*

Probably more so than any other mass medium, magazines serve as a barometer for measuring our changing American culture.

* Alan Casty, Mass Media and Mass Man *(New York: Holt, Rinehart & Winston, 1968), p. 20.*

Life.   Henry Luce had another idea for making magazine history in 1936, when he brought out a large-size pictorial weekly called *Life* (see Box 6.2). By this time radio had become an important mass-communication medium and was taking listeners to the scenes of important news events. (It also competed with magazines for consumers' leisure time.) *Life* was able to fill the visual void radio created by providing pictures of major news events each week.

Life was an almost instant success and soon was found in most households. Its excellent photojournalism is still admired today. Teams of *Life* photographers were sent out on news and feature stories, and only the very best of the photos were used.

Although *Life* became a very popular magazine, its development was not without controversy. A 1938 photo essay on the birth of a baby shocked many people, and the magazine was banned in 33 cities—to cite just one instance in which the content was too graphic or controversial for the conservative elements in the popular culture.

A year after *Life* began publishing, Gardner Cowles introduced *Look* magazine as an imitator. It too became a popular general-interest magazine. In 1945, *Ebony* was founded as another version of *Life,* this time aimed at a burgeoning black audience.

TV Guide.   When television started entering the popular culture in 1948, *TV Guide* was established as a magazine catering to New York television-set owners. Sold soon after to Walter Annenberg's Triangle Publications, it became the national television guide, offering local area listings. In 1974 it replaced *Reader's*

BOX 6.2

▪ PROFILE: HENRY R. LUCE ▪

Henry Robinson Luce was born April 3, 1898, in Tengchow, China, to American Presbyterian missionaries. His Christian upbringing in the Chinese culture would years later play an important role in shaping American foreign policy.

At the age of 14, Luce left China to attend preparatory school in the United States. He later attended Yale University. At 25—in 1923—Luce and a former Yale classmate, Britton Hadden, founded *Time* magazine, the first weekly news magazine in the United States. A millionaire by the time he was 30, Luce founded *Fortune* magazine in 1930 (following the death of Hadden) and *Life* in 1936. Time Inc. (now Time Warner) publications also include *Sports Illustrated, Money, People Weekly* and *Entertainment Weekly.*

As publisher of a major magazine empire, Luce became one of America's most influential citizens in the twentieth century. With his help, Luce's second wife, Clare Boothe Luce, became a U.S. congresswoman and later U.S. ambassador to Italy under the Eisenhower presidency. News articles in *Time* were often biased toward Luce's political causes and leanings. On occasion, *Time* "Man of the Year" selections were made to advance a Luce political cause.

Luce was an avowed anticommunist who detested the "godless" Russians and strongly supported China's General Chiang Kai-shek's efforts to fight Mao Tse-tung's communist government. To assist Chiang Kai-shek's efforts to increase U.S. aid and support for his cause, *Time* featured him on its cover seven times. When President Lyndon Johnson supported Luce's desire to fight communist aggression in Vietnam by committing troops to the cause, *Time* named him "Man of the Year."

In a 1962 interview when Luce was asked about the allegations that his magazine was biased, he responded: "I am a Protestant and a free enterpriser, which means I am biased in favor of God, Eisenhower and the stockholders of Time Inc. and if anyone who objects doesn't know this by now, why the hell are they still spending 35 cents for the magazine?"*

* *Quoted in* The Reader's Digest Dictionary of Quotations *(New York: Funk and Wagnalls, 1968), p. 125.*

Digest as the largest-selling magazine in the country, and today its weekly circulation figures exceed 16 million. These two publications have been competing for first place ever since, with both publications topping 18 million circulation at one time or another. In 1988 media baron Rupert Murdoch paid $3 billion for Triangle Publications, publishers of *TV Guide, Seventeen* and *Racing Forum.* In recent years, *Modern Maturity,* a free publication for members of the American Association of Retired Persons, has jumped ahead of both *TV Guide* and *Reader's Digest* in annual circulation figures (see Tables 6.1 and 6.2).

TABLE 6.1 THE 30 TOP U.S. MAGAZINES IN CIRCULATION

Modern Maturity, *which is sent to every member of the American Association of Retired Persons, is the nation's leader in magazine circulation. The publication serves one of the largest and most politically powerful subcultural groups in our society and is mailed free to association members. In second place is* Reader's Digest, *which has long been this country's most successful internal-specialization publication followed closely by* TV Guide, *a successful unit-specialization magazine. The rest of the top 30 is dominated by women's interest, travel, news, health, lifestyle, sports, science and erotica publications. (One publication,* Philip Morris *magazine, which technically ranks fourth with 12 million circulation, is not listed because it has no paid circulation. It is mailed free to cigarette smokers as an advertising periodical.)*

Magazine	Circulation (millions)
Modern Maturity (Amer. Assn. of Retired Persons)*	20.3
Reader's Digest	16.4
TV Guide (News America Publications)	16.3
National Geographic	10.8
Better Homes and Gardens (Meredith)	8.0
Family Circle	5.2
McCall's	5.1
Good Housekeeping (Hearst)	5.1
Ladies' Home Journal (Meredith)	5.1
Woman's Day (Diamandis)	4.4
Time (Time Warner Inc.)	4.3
Redbook (Hearst)	3.9
Sports Illustrated (Time Warner Inc.)	3.7
Playboy	3.6
People Weekly (Time Warner Inc.)	3.3
Newsweek (Washington Post)	3.2
Prevention (Rodale)	3.1
Cosmopolitan (Hearst)	2.8
Smithsonian	2.3
U.S. News and World Report	2.3
Glamour (Condé Nast)	2.3
Southern Living	2.3
Penthouse	2.0
Field and Stream (Times-Mirror)	2.0
Popular Science	1.8
Motorland	1.8
Money (Time Warner Inc.)	1.8
Country Living (Hearst)	1.8
Seventeen (News America Publications)	1.7
Life (Time Warner Inc.)	1.7

SOURCE: *Gale Directory of Publications and Broadcasting Media*, vols. 1–3 (Detroit: Gale Research, 1990).
*The corporate owner is included only when it differs from the name of the magazine.

TABLE 6.2 THE 30 TOP U.S. MAGAZINES IN GROSS REVENUE

Circulation is not the only way to list America's leading magazines. For comparison purposes, the following lists the 30 top magazines according to their 1989 gross revenue.

Magazine	Total Revenue	Ad Revenue	Circulation Revenue
TV Guide	$928.3	323.0	605.3
Time	636.5	373.4	263.1
People	605.6	326.2	279.4
Sports Illustrated	565.9	336.7	229.2
Reader's Digest	419.2	113.6	305.6
Newsweek	397.8	255.9	141.9
Parade	314.5	314.5	n/a
Business Week	298.7	260.6	38.1
Better Homes & Gardens	275.7	152.4	123.3
Family Circle	249.3	152.2	97.1
Good Housekeeping	245.2	148.0	97.2
U.S. News & World Report	244.8	152.9	91.9
National Geographic	226.1	33.2	192.9
Woman's Day	212.8	135.6	77.2
Ladies' Home Journal	207.2	104.7	102.5
Cosmopolitan	204.3	125.7	78.6
Fortune	202.8	168.7	34.1
Forbes	195.4	157.7	37.7
PC Magazine	182.8	147.3	35.5
McCall's	167.8	74.8	93.0
Money	143.2	79.7	63.5
Glamour	141.9	88.8	53.1
Vogue	140.8	101.1	39.7
Redbook	130.6	75.0	55.6
New York Times Magazine	126.8	126.8	n/a
Cable Guide	123.1	33.8	89.3
Penthouse	118.3	25.1	93.2
Life	117.1	56.8	60.3
Southern Living	113.7	61.2	52.5
Rolling Stone	113.0	71.1	41.9

*In millions of dollars.
SOURCE: *Advertising Age,* June 18, 1990, pp. 5–6.

Mad. As the American popular culture became ever more obsessed with technology and conspicuous consumption, it was not surprising that a magazine developed to criticize these trends. In 1952 William Gaines established *Mad,* a satirical humor magazine that used a sophisticated comic book format. Much of *Mad*'s success seems to come from its ability to poke fun at the materialistic and commercialized American culture and mass media's role in it. *Mad*'s willingness to satirize the very commercial products that other magazines rely on for advertising revenue endears it to many Americans. Until 1990, when *Ms.* magazine stopped running advertisements, *Mad* held the distinction of being the only major magazine to survive without accepting paid advertisements.

▪ *Life* magazine provided Americans with a weekly pictorial report on world news for 36 years. This spectacular photo of a dam at Fort Peck, Montana, on the cover of the first issue was taken by the famous *Life* photographer Margaret Bourke White.

Playboy.   A year after *Mad* began publishing, *Playboy* appeared on the scene. It has since been credited by some and criticized by others for launching the sexual revolution in America. The first issue in 1953 was put together on a card table in the kitchen of the founder, Hugh Hefner, a former *Esquire* magazine employee.

Hefner enlisted the assistance of a freelance artist on the promise of some stock in his new company, and the first issue of *Playboy* was polished and released featuring a nude centerfold of movie actress Marilyn Monroe. By 1954 *Playboy* was selling more than 100,000 copies a month, and this figure climbed to nearly 800,000 two years later. It now sells 3.7 million copies a month, down from its best years, when it sold more than 7 million.

Intent on building a sophisticated image for his nudie magazine, Hefner also ran articles by well-known and respected writers. At first he refused to accept advertising, but later he carefully added this form of revenue by accepting only "quality-image" advertising; he rejected more than 80 percent of the ads submitted for publication. His plan paid off, as in a few short years his magazine became accepted by many in the popular culture. John Brady, former editor of *Writer's Digest,* said that Hefner "gave popular culture a sex life."[4]

DECLINE OF GENERAL-INTEREST MAGAZINES

As many new special-interest magazines were launched in the 1950s, it soon became apparent that general-interest magazines were in trouble. In 1956 *Collier's* was the first modern mass-circulation general-interest magazine to go bankrupt and cease publication.

Demographic and Regional Breakouts.   By 1967, *Look* turned to alternative ways to survive. It began publishing *demographic breakout* editions, which allowed advertisers to pay less by placing their ads in editions of the magazine that went only to certain demographic categories. An advertiser could run an ad, for example, in a portion of the copies printed, such as those going to people with incomes above $24,000. Despite these efforts, *Look* went out of business in 1971.

Many surviving general-interest magazines and the successful national news-magazines sell ads on a *demographic* or *regional breakout* basis. Regional break-outs allow advertisers to purchase ads in the copies circulated in particular geographic regions.

Death of *Life*.   The biggest shock for the millions of people who depended on general-interest magazines came in 1972, when *Life* announced that its December issue would be its last. Although American popular culture had changed greatly in the 36 years since *Life* was born, the magazine had reared a generation of Americans—and life without *Life* seemed too much for many of them to take.

A number of factors contributed to the demise of these general-interest maga-zines. One was higher production costs and postal rates. Another was the com-petition for leisure time posed by the new medium of television. Television filled the same visual void for pictures of news events that *Life* did. It provided both pictures and sound—and did it daily. Another factor in the demise of many general-interest magazines was the fact that many readers were turning to more specialized magazines.

Specialization.   Since advertising revenue is the "life's blood" of the magazine industry, the nail in the coffin for many general-interest magazines came when advertisers realized that they could better target the specialized audiences they were seeking by using specialized publications. With the increase in numbers and variety of special-interest magazines available, many advertisers no longer wanted to pay the higher cost of reaching the general-interest masses. The homogeneous interests of specialized magazine readers were superior to regional and demographic breakouts.

Despite *Life*'s demise, 1972 was not all gloom for the magazine business. This was the year that a new special-interest magazine, *Ms.*, was founded. Devoted to women's rights and the feminist movement, it found a niche in American popular culture by recognizing that women should be something more than sex objects and housewives. The magazine was an overnight success.

In 1974 Time Inc. launched *People* magazine, a smaller, livelier version of the old movie fan magazine. (Movie magazines had been popular during the heyday of the movies in the 1930s and '40s, but their readership had declined after the motion-picture industry was forced to move into the era of specialization in the 1950s.) Some felt that *People* was an attempt to satisfy some of the diehard former *Life* readers with a more focused publication that was less expensive to produce. It has become successful, with 85 percent of its sales coming from newsstands, particularly in supermarkets.

Life's Rebirth.   Despite these new magazines, many who had grown up with *Life* still missed it. In response, Time Inc. began issuing a number of special editions of *Life*. Their success prompted Time to reintroduce the magazine as a monthly in 1978. The new *Life* still features quality photojournalism but does not have the weekly "news" orientation it once had.

High Risk.   In 1983 Time Inc. created yet another new magazine, this time with disastrous results. As cable television spread across the nation, Time Inc. decided to try to reach this affluent and growing market by publishing a cable TV program guide. In April it produced the first issue of *TV-Cable Week,* spending $100 million to move into the specialized market dominated by *TV Guide.* The goal was to supply cable TV subscribers with better information than was available from Annenberg's publication.

   TV Guide, however, did not stand still, and it easily fought off the competition by simply adding cable programs to its listings. In September 1983, after five months, Time Inc. published its last issue of *TV-Cable Week.* A staff of 250 was laid off, and losses totaled $50 million. (Time Inc.'s [now Time Warner] latest entry into the magazine field came in February of 1990 when it introduced *Entertainment Weekly.*)

   Many other new magazines have had experiences like that of *TV-Cable Week.* The costs of establishing and sustaining a new publication are great and many magazines go under before they can establish themselves in the market place.

TYPES OF MAGAZINES

According to the 1990 *Gale Directory of Publications and Broadcast Media,* there were 12,205 magazines being published in the United States by the beginning of the decade of the '90s. This figure had increased from 6,950 in 1950. Of these 12,000-plus publications, only about 800 were general-interest magazines; the rest were devoted to special interests.

   U.S. Industrial Outlook, 1990 breaks magazines down into three broad categories: consumer magazines, business publications and farm magazines (see Figure 6.1.). However, within these categories are numerous subcategories reflecting a

Figure 6.1   Percentage breakdown of U.S. magazines by categories.
SOURCE: *U.S. Industrial Outlook, 1990* (Washington, D.C.: U.S. Government Printing Office, 1990).

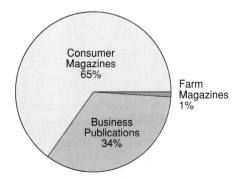

high level of specialization. Most of the new publications launched during the 1980s, for example, fit into the following narrowly focused special-interest categories: health & fitness, sports, travel/leisure, lifestyles, ethnic, regional, business, age-specific women's and men's magazines and special-interest regional publications such as *Pacific Diver, Southern Bride* and *California Basketball*. Among the new business publications, subject areas included medicine, technology, business management, computers and computer software. We now turn to some of the narrow special-interest categories for magazines.

Family Magazines.   One of the newest categories of magazines to become popular in the late 1980s was the family magazine. These publications reflected a revived interest in the family by a segment of the population that had previously been regarded as interested in self only—the Yuppie generation. New magazines in this category include *Parenting, Fathers, Child, Children* and *Grandparents*.

Computer Magazines.   Another successful new magazine category in the 1980s was computer magazines. As more and more people used computers at home and at work, they created a market for publications like *Byte, PC World, MacWorld, PC Magazine* and *Publish* (see Box 6.3).

Erotica Magazines.   Erotica or sex magazines began reflecting more permissive attitudes toward sex and nudity in the 1950s. Always controversial, this category came under renewed criticism in the 1986 report by the Meese Commission on Pornography (see Chapter 4). At the request of the Commission's executive director, some companies, including 7-Eleven, removed these publications from their shelves. However, the report did not put an end to the popularity of these publications. Of the 584 new magazines started in 1989, 72 were sex magazines. Publications in this category include *Playboy, Penthouse, Playgirl, Hustler, Oui* and *Screw*.

Sports Magazines.   A genre that caters exclusively to our culture's interest in leisure activities is the sports magazine. These publications range from the specialized general-interest magazines like *Sports Illustrated* and *Sport,* to more specialized publications covering just one sport—such as *Runner's World, Boating, Backpacker, Flying* and *Skiing*. Sports magazines, like erotica magazines, once seemed to be intended for men only. However, women now make up a large segment of the audience for general sports magazines, and some sports magazines are designed just for women.

Men's Magazines.   Although men are the prime audience for most erotica and sports magazines, there are many other men's magazines, especially ones that focus on adventure and fashion. *Field & Stream, Guns & Ammo, Esquire, GQ, Men, Men's Life, Details, M. Inc., FYI* and *Assets* are just a few publications in this field.

BOX 6.3

▪ SPECIALIZED MAGAZINES ▪

In 1981, an investor approached David Bunnell with the idea of starting a magazine about computers. Bunnell jumped at the chance, and he put together the first issue of *PC Magazine* in his home. This was not Bunnell's first experience in the computer field, however. In 1974 he stumbled onto a job writing instruction manuals for a small electronics firm in New Mexico. In 1975 the firm brought out the first personal computer—the MITS Altair.

In 1982, after Ziff Davis Publishing purchased a majority interest in *PC Magazine,* Bunnell and 48 of his 52 staff members started a competing publication, *PC World.* The 324-page publication made history as the fattest first issue ever published. By 1986 the 38-year-old Bunnell, serving as editor-in-chief of *PC World* and *MacWorld,* was making over $1.6 million a year.

Bunnell is one of a number of people who became successful during the 1980s by publishing specialized magazines. Other new publications that found success in the 1980s were family-oriented magazines, which were popular with the Yuppie generation in the late 1980s, and health and sports magazines, which reflected growing interests in health-oriented leisure activities. In 1986, for example, 33 new sports magazines began publishing in the United States. Six of them were wrestling magazines, including one called *Beauties of Wrestling* about female grapplers.

One of the best ways for a person to stay abreast of the changing popular culture in the twentieth century is to browse in the magazine directory of publications.

Women's Interest. As discussed earlier, women's magazines have been popular since the nineteenth century and today include some of the highest circulating magazines in the country, with at least a dozen of them selling between 1 million and 8 million each month. With more than 50 titles devoted to women's interests, there are actually subcategories within this one: women's general interest, health and fitness, parenting, style and fashion and women's career magazines to name a few.

Among some of the more popular women's publications are *Harper's Bazaar, Bridal Guide, Bride, Cosmopolitan, Family Circle, Good Housekeeping, Ms., Woman's Day, Woman's World, Complete Woman, Better Homes and Gardens, Mirabella, Modern Bride, Lear's, McCall's, Redbook, Self, Shape, Elle, Glamour, Fashion Guide, Vogue, W., Savvy, Working Mother* and *Working Woman.*

Youth Magazines. Magazines for young people—ranging from *Boy's Life* to *Seventeen*—have been around for a long time. As American youngsters mature earlier, their magazines have been tackling more adult topics. One such magazine, *Penny Power,* is designed to make young people consumer activists. In 1988 an Australian publishing firm began challenging *Seventeen* in the U.S. market by bringing out a sexier publication for teenage girls. Called *Sassy,* the magazine's first issue included articles on "How to Flirt" and "Losing Your Virginity." By the end of its second year, it had toned down its emphasis on sexuality and had gained a circulation of over 500,000, impressive but nowhere near *Seventeen*'s 1.8 million. An important subcategory of youth magazines is the wide range of rock-'n'-roll fan magazines commonly referred to as *teenzines* (see Box 6.4).

▪ A teenage girl reads a copy of *Seventeen*. In 1988 an Australian
publishing firm challenged *Seventeen*'s domination of the market
niche with a racier teenage publication called *Sassy*.

Ethnic Magazines.   Virtually all ethnic minorities have found magazines to be an
effective way to communicate with one another. Some of the more successful
ethnic publications are *Ebony, Jet, Black World, Tan, Essence and Identity.* In
recent years there has been a growing number of Asian magazines in the American
culture.

Subcultural Magazines.   Other subcultures, from motorcycle gangs to marijuana
smokers, have magazines specializing in their interests. Such publications include
Easyrider for bikers, *Advocate* for gay-rights supporters and *High Times* for
marijuana smokers (see Box 6.5).
   Other magazine categories include newsmagazines, opinion, intellectual, quality, humor, city, regional, travel/leisure, hobbies, religions, romance, cars,
gourmet foods, environmental, health and fitness and lifestyles. During the magazine boom years of the 1980s, a publication for the affluent was launched with the
appropriate title: *Millionaire.* Among the many environmental magazines to come
along to join the original "mother" of them all, *Mother Jones,* was a publication
launched in 1989 called *Garbage.*

Video Magazines.   The information age of the 1990s saw magazines take on a
new technological twist—video magazines for the VCR. Like print magazines,

BOX 6.4

▪ THE TEENZINES ▪

One of the most popular categories of youth-oriented magazines is the *teenzines*. These magazines play an important role in shaping and reflecting the popular culture of teenagers. Most teenzines are fan magazines for 11- to 13-year-old girls. They are offshoots of such traditional movie magazines as *Photoplay* and *Motion Picture* that focus primarily on rock stars rather than movie stars. Teenzines got their start in the 1950s, when popular music and the motion-picture industry first started targeting young people as a potential audience.

The early teen fan magazines had a preachy, parental tone that attempted to set and preserve moral standards. The popularity of these magazines grew in the 1960s, as Beatlemania and Monkeemania caused monthly circulation figures to skyrocket. Since then, rock music has dominated the content of the magazines. As a result, the magazines have reflected the changing attitudes in popular music and given their young readers what they want: the inside scoop on the public and private lives of their rock stars. Today these magazines feature intimate interviews with sexy superstars such as Billy Idol and Prince and discuss rock stars' attitudes on romance, drugs and sex.

Although the content of the female-oriented teenzines is more worldly than it was in earlier days, these publications still attempt to avoid four-letter words and lewd poses. Their goal is to feature "wholesome" pinup shots of rock stars that girls can post on their bedroom walls and school lockers.

Some of the more popular teenzines are *Tiger Beat, Teen Beat, Bop, Topless Hunks* and *16*, all for girls. Male-oriented teenage fan magazines include *Circus, Hit Parade, Metal* and *Creem*. These publications have macho overtones and are not immune to four-letter words or photos that border on lewdness.

The teenzines, like all magazines, must reflect the desires of their audience if they are to remain successful. In so doing, they reflect the popular culture that influences teens today, even to the exasperation of adults. As one teenzine editor noted in an interview with a *Los Angeles Times* reporter, "It's not our role to play the part of parents. Kids are picking up the magazines to get away from that. To read about these people [rock stars]—it's sort of rebellious."

---

video magazines are published on a regular basis. *Persona* launched a show-business oriented magazine featuring interviews and features to be sold at supermarket check-out stands and other retail outlets for a cost of $4.95, not much more than the cost of a blank cassette. Ads for the new magazine point out that the cassette can be reused for other recording purposes after the magazine has been viewed. Like the print version, video magazines include advertising—about 20 minutes worth in the two-hour program.

Additional Periodicals.   In addition to the 12,000 publications that are widely available, there are thousands of periodicals with limited circulation. The *Standard Periodical Directory* lists over 62,000 journals and magazines in this category, including academic publications, alumni magazines, trade journals, monthly reports from professional associations, industry magazines, free-circulation magazines (like those produced by airlines) and business publications.

■ John H. Johnson founded *Ebony* in 1945 to give African-Americans a picture magazine that reflected their culture. He is the most successful African-American publisher in the United States.

SPECIALIZATION AND POPULAR CULTURE

Many people have tried to explain the trend away from general-interest publications to highly specialized periodicals. The trend was slow at first, starting in 1945 at the end of World War II, and has rapidly accelerated in recent years.

In 1973 sociologist Richard Maisel suggested that the United States had moved from an industrial society to a postindustrial society, which is characterized by increased specialization and the growth of service industries. In such a society, he says, the populace tends to fragment into segments with various interests and concerns.[5]

Jean-Louis Servan-Schreiber, a Frenchman, made the same point in his book *The Power to Inform:* "Americans today find that, as a result of an era of progress from which their country benefited before any of the other industrialized nations, their immense, reputedly homogeneous society of 200 million individuals is fragmenting."[6] In other words, the human resistance to the mass culture that developed during the Industrial Revolution has finally caused that culture to fragment into subcultures with individualistic interests.

Meeting Consumer Needs. This fragmentation has caused magazines to specialize. From their beginnings in the eighteenth century, magazines have had to give readers what they wanted in order to survive. As Americans had more money to spend and more leisure time to spend it in, people developed special interests to consume their time and money. Coupled with this has been the desire of individuals to find their own identities in our mass culture.

The need to break away from the mass identity created by the Industrial Revolution and find individuality through cults and other subcultural forms (see

BOX 6.5

■ LOW TIMES FOR *HIGH TIMES* MAGAZINE ■

The federal government's "War on Drugs" has created problems for one subcultural specialization magazine. *High Times,* which caters to those interested in marijuana cultivation and smoking, has been left with few advertisers to support its business endeavor.

As part of its efforts to curtail the use of illegal drugs, the government has targeted merchants who sell drug paraphernalia—such as "roach clips" and water pipes—and that decision has spelled trouble for *High Times,* the publication that has provided advertising opportunities for merchants of such products.

The advertisers, fearing government reprisals, have shied away from this publication in recent years, leaving the magazine without its main source of revenue.

Chapter 2) has created an interesting paradox. It seems that in addition to our desire to be valued as individualists, we also need to "belong" to some identifiable group—smaller, of course, than the masses as a whole. Thus we seem to be seeking a compromise in the American popular culture between being faceless entities in mass society and individuals who belong to something. As one mass-media scholar puts it:

> We are young, middle-aged, or old. Many of us find an attachment to a racial or ethnic minority more important than a status as an American. We are Easterners or Southerners or Westerners or Texans or Californians—and proud of it. We are environmentalists, runners, women's liberationists, part of the counter culture, Jesus freaks, skiers, sports car enthusiasts, concerned parents, swinging singles; we collect stamps and coins and beer cans and model trains and antique cars and nostalgia items; we ski, surf, hike, climb mountains, scuba dive, sail, camp, fish, hunt, bowl, golf, ice skate, and swim.[7]

All consumer industries have tried to cater to at least some of these widely varying interests. Our mass media—particularly the magazines—have simply done so more visibly.

One policy of the Hearst Corporation, one of the more successful publishing firms, helped it move quickly into the age of specialization: "Find out what your readers want and give it to them."[8] By 1955 Hearst was already publishing mostly special-interest magazines, including *Motor, Motor Boating, American Druggist, Harper's Bazaar, House Beautiful, Town and Country, Good Housekeeping, Sports Afield* and *Cosmopolitan.* And when *Cosmopolitan,* for example, started to show signs of decline, the old, rather conservative format was abandoned and a new format developed to appeal to a sophisticated, sexually liberated woman. Its circulation climbed as a result.

Advertising's Role.   A magazine's success depends on its ability to attract advertising, and advertisers want magazines that can deliver readers. But not all readers are equally valuable to advertisers. As reader interests began to fragment, advertisers found that they could reach their target audience more effectively and at a lower cost by advertising in special-interest publications with smaller circulations. Magazine advertisers have changed their focus from a "shotgun blast" at the masses to a rifle shot at particular groups. From the first, the success or failure of any magazine has depended on its ability to predict reader interests and meet those interests with appropriate reading material. Specialization has made it easier to do so.

CONSUMER AND BUSINESS TRENDS

Despite the slump that the magazine industry experienced in the early 1990s, the twentieth century as a whole has seen a remarkable expansion of this mass communication business. The estimated revenue for magazines in 1990 was a record-breaking total of $22.2 billion with advertising receipts accounting for 55 percent and circulation revenue 45 percent. Of the total amount of money spent on advertising in the United States, 7.6 percent of it is spent on magazines.

As in the book publishing industry, consolidation and conglomerate takeovers were the name of the game for the magazine industry during the 1980s and this is expected to continue through the 1990s. According to the 1990 edition of *U.S. Industrial Outlook,* the Time-Warner merger in 1989 "added momentum to what is becoming a world-wide media consolidation trend."[9] Increased foreign ownership is anticipated, with major publishing firms throughout the world forming partnerships to ease entry into less familiar markets. The U.S. is seen as an attractive magazine market for foreign firms because of its currency advantage, access to capital and opportunities for media growth.

Along with mergers and conglomerate takeovers has come controversy. Shortly after the merger of Time Inc. and Warner Communications, Time Publications ran a 32-page advertising insert commemorating the 50th birthday of Warner Brothers' Bugs Bunny. The insert reached some 80 million people by appearing in *Time, Life, People, Fortune* and *Entertainment Weekly.* Some media critics said "it was a prime example of intra-company back-scratching that is 'anti-competitive' and smacks of 'self-dealing' by the giant media concern."[10] When Murdoch purchased *TV Guide* in 1988, critics complained that it would give unfair advantage to his efforts to develop the Fox television network. Although coverage of the Fox network by *TV Guide* has not been blatant, it has been apparent.

The magazine industry will face new challenges in the 1990s as well. Demographic changes from the aging baby boomers will require more focus on the home, parenting, schooling, financial management and careers. The industry has already begun focusing on these demographic changes and will surely give increased attention to them in this decade.

SUMMARY

Since their beginning in the eighteenth century, magazines have provided a wide variety of material for their readers. All magazines, by their very nature, spe-

BOX 6.6

▪ WORKING IN MAGAZINE PUBLISHING ▪

There are usually six divisions in the business operation of a magazine: administration, editorial, advertising sales, circulation sales, production and distribution.

The *administration* department handles the business operation of the company. Duties range from paying the bills and keeping the books to insuring that overhead expenses do not exceed the company's income. Cost of this area of the operation is about 10 percent of the total overhead.

The *editorial* department is in charge of gathering stories and photographs, editing the copy and designing the pages. The size of this department will vary greatly depending on the type of publication. A news magazine, for example, might have many reporters and photographers. Other magazines might have a very small editorial department because they rely on freelance writers and photographers to contribute materials. About 10 percent of the overhead goes to paying editorial costs.

The *advertising sales* department is responsible for keeping the magazine profitable. Without advertising revenue, most magazines would go out of business. The cost of advertising in a publication depends on the circulation. Magazines usually spend about 10 percent of their overhead on this department.

The *circulation sales* department has the responsibility of getting readers for the publication. The more circulation, the more advertisers will want to support a publication. There are two modes of circulation sales: single-copy sales on newsstands and mail delivery copies to subscribers. Because of the large number of magazines available, getting the publication on newsstands is not easy. Obtaining mail subscribers involves numerous promotional activities including media and direct-mail advertising. About 30 percent of the publication's overhead is spent on this activity.

Production of the magazine is the most expensive part of the process and usually runs about 32 percent of the entire cost of operation. Some magazines have their own typesetting and printing plants, while most rely on outside firms.

The *distribution* department of the magazine handles the transportation of the publication to numerous newsstands and to mailing houses for distribution to subscribers. Speed is an essential ingredient in handling the distribution of publications. Despite the importance of this activity, only about 8 percent of the overhead goes toward distribution.

---

cialize in some way. They either have unit specialization or internal specialization.

Magazines did not really begin to flourish until the 1820s, when new technologies, coupled with a new literate society brought on by compulsory education, paved the way for their expansion. By the end of the nineteenth century, magazines had entered the popular culture with general-interest, special-interest and low-cost publications.

The beginning of the twentieth century was the heyday of muckraking articles in magazines, but by 1917 the public's attention had shifted to concern about World War I in Europe. In the 1920s a new variety of magazines developed to meet the needs of the new, fast-paced American culture. After World War II, general-interest magazines started to decline, and the age of specialization was firmly established.

Magazines can be classified in a variety of ways, but what is abundantly clear is that there seems to be a magazine for just about every interest and taste in both our popular and elite cultures.

Individuals in our culture have gone from faceless cogs of a mass society to members of one sort or another in a variety of interest groups. Magazines, which must deliver readers to their advertisers, have changed to cater to these various special interests and as a result have become the first mass medium to effectively reflect these changes.

THOUGHT QUESTIONS

1 What cultural factors contributed to the movement of magazines into the popular stage of the EPS cycle?

2 Why did magazines move so solidly into the stage of specialization?

3 Select a popular magazine that has been around for a long time and spend some time examining early copies on microfilm in your college library. What does such an examination tell you about changes in our culture?

4 Go to a major bookstore or newsstand that carries a wide variety of magazines. What does your examination of the types of magazines available tell you about our society's subcultural interests? How many different subcultures can you identify from these publications?

5 What changes do you anticipate for the magazine industry based on your knowledge that the 1980s saw a major expansion of publications, which in turn caused a decline in advertising revenue for many publications in the 1990s?

NOTES

1. John C. Merrill and Ralph L. Lowenstein, *Media, Message and Men: New Perspectives in Communication,* 2nd ed. (New York: Longman, 1979), p. 39.

2. Frank Luther Mott, *History of American Magazines 1741–1850* (New York: Macmillan, 1930), p. 232.

3. Oscar Handlin, *The History of the United States,* vol. 2 (New York: Holt, Rinehart & Winston, 1968), p. 322.

4. John Brady, "The Nude Journalism," in Edward Jay Whetmore, *Mediamerica: Form, Content and Consequences of Mass Communica-* *tion,* 3rd ed. (Belmont, Calif.: Wadsworth, 1985), p. 76.

5. Richard Maisel, "The Decline of Mass Media," *Public Opinion Quarterly* (Summer 1973), p. 161.

6. Jean-Louis Servan-Schreiber, *The Power to Inform* (New York: McGraw-Hill, 1974).

7. Don R. Pember, *Mass Media in America,* 4th ed. (Chicago: Science Research Associates, 1983), p. 89.

8. John Tebbel, *The American Magazine: A Compact History* (New York: Hawthorn, 1969), p. 211.

9. *U.S. Industrial Outlook, 1990* (Washington, D.C.: U.S. Government Printing Office, 1990), p. 48-6.

10. Paul Farhi, "Time Warner Inc.'s 32-page Ad Insert Bugs a Media Critic," *Los Angeles Times,* May 5, 1990, p. D-2.

ADDITIONAL READING

Anderson, Elliott, and Kinzie, Mary. *The Little Magazine in America: A Modern History.* Yonkers, N.Y.: Pushcart Press, 1978.

Ford, James L. *Magazines for the Millions.* Carbondale, Ill.: Southern Illinois University Press, 1970.

Mogel, Leonard. *The Magazine: Everything You Need to Know to Make it in the Magazine Business.* Englewood Cliffs, N.J.: Prentice-Hall, 1979.

Mott, Frank Luther. *History of American Magazines 1850–1905,* 3 vols. Cambridge, Mass.: Harvard University Press, 1938–1957.

Peterson, Theodore. *Magazines in the Twentieth Century.* Urbana: University of Illinois Press, 1964.

Riley, Sam G. *Magazines of the American South.* Westport, Conn.: Greenwood Press, 1986.

Taft, William H. *American Magazines for the 1980s.* New York: Hastings House, 1982.

Although not as fast as the newer electronic media, newspapers are the print media's fastest form of mass communication. When presses, like the one shown here, begin to roll, they set in motion a sophisticated distribution system that provides our culture with its first rough draft of history.

NEWSPAPERS: PAST, PRESENT AND PROBLEMS

It is well to remember that freedom through the press is the thing that comes first. Most of us probably feel we couldn't be free without newspapers, and that is the real reason we want the newspapers to be free.

—Edward R. Murrow

In 1990, Frank Deford, a former *Sports Illustrated* writer and NBC commentator, and Mexican media tycoon Emilio Azarraga Milmo launched a $100 million gamble to bring to the United States a national "sports-only" newspaper, the *National.*

The 32- to 48-page daily used color, quality writing and numerous box scores to bring to avid sports fans the latest information about their favorite teams and athletes. Initially, the paper targeted New York City, Chicago and Los Angeles for its distribution but planned to expand to all regions of the nation during its five-

CULTURAL HISTORY
OF NEWSPAPERS

ELITIST	POPULAR	SPECIALIZED		
			1st century	Romans post news sheets in town squares.
			16th century	Italians sell printed news sheets for a coin called a *gazetta*.
			17th century	Corantos (newspaper forerunners) begin in Germany.
			1665	*Oxford Gazette* founded, first English-language newspaper.
			1690	First newspaper published in 13 colonies, *Publick Occurrences;* lasts one issue.
			1704	*Boston News-Letter* becomes first regularly published American newspaper.
			1735	John Peter Zenger tried in New York for libeling the governor.
			1765–83	American newspapers promote revolution.
			1791	Bill of Rights ratified: press is given protection from government censorship by First Amendment.
			1798	Alien and Sedition Acts passed, leading to prosecution of newspaper editors for criticizing government.
		▓	1827	*Freedom's Journal* founded, first African-American newspaper in the United States.
	▓		1833	*New York Sun* founded, first penny press.
	▓		1841	Horace Greeley begins *New York Tribune;* introduces the editorial page and attacks slavery.
	▓		1848	Associated Press (AP) founded, first news wire service.

year start-up period. Those plans, however, were dashed after 17 months when low circulation caused the paper to cease publication in June of 1991.

The *National* had joined *USA Today* and the *Wall Street Journal* as a national newspaper designed to use telecommunication technology to compete in the television era. Much of the start-up strategy was based on a more successful effort in 1982 when Al Neuharth, then chairman and chief executive officer of Gannett Co. Inc., the largest newspaper chain, launched *USA Today* as the newspaper industry's answer to television. Filled with short "TV style" news stories, many features and ample color and graphics, the newspaper was distributed to Gannett-owned printing plants around the country by satellite.

CULTURAL HISTORY OF NEWSPAPERS

ELITIST	POPULAR	SPECIALIZED		
			1883	Joseph Pulitzer begins publishing *New York World.*
			1895	William Randolph Hearst buys *New York Journal;* circulation war with Pulitzer is branded "yellow journalism."
			1896	Adolph Ochs buys *New York Times* and ushers in objective journalism.
			1907	United Press (UP) becomes second news wire service.
			1909	Hearst starts third news wire service, International News Service (INS).
			1920s	Tabloids begin reflecting Roaring '20s lifestyles.
			1923	Society of Newspaper Editors adopts Canons of Journalism, stressing social responsibility.
			1958	United Press and International News Service merge to become United Press International (UPI).
			1965–70	Underground newspapers reflect new American subcultural lifestyles.
			1972	Two *Washington Post* reporters expose the Watergate scandal that eventually leads to President Nixon's resignation.
			1982	*USA Today* founded as a national daily, using satellite technology and innovative color graphics.
			1985	Desktop publishing, using computers, makes possible inexpensive publication of specialized newspapers.
			1990	The *National* (sports daily) is launched as a specialized national newspaper.

Soon after *USA Today* was launched, other newspapers were utilizing computerized color graphics and condensing much of their news into brief summaries to allow more space for human interest articles. The look and content of newspapers, which had remained relatively unchanged during the past century, was undergoing a transformation in an effort to adapt to TV-influenced popular culture.

This was not the first time the new medium of television had had an impact on newspapers, however. TV's more immediate coverage of news events brought an end to the use of sensationalism to sell newspapers. Home delivery subscriptions replaced street hawkers screaming out lurid headlines.

■ *USA Today* was launched in 1982 using satellite technology, specially decorated newsstands, and an innovative design featuring short stories, color and graphics to compete with television as an attractive and concise news medium.

Since their nineteenth-century introduction into the popular culture, newspapers have been the recorders of the first rough draft of history. Newspapers quickly chronicle and disseminate to the masses the daily actions within any given culture. Although newspapers are not as quick to disseminate information as the newer electronic mass media, they are the fastest of the print media.

EARLY ORIGINS OF NEWSPAPERS

Early attempts to disseminate printed information to the public can be traced back some two thousand years to the official news sheets, called *acta diurna* (daily acts), posted by the Roman government in public places. However, it wasn't until the mid-sixteenth century that efforts to sell printed news began. Leaders in Venice made news regularly available to the public on printed sheets that sold for a coin called a gazetta. Later many newspapers would adopt the name *Gazette* for their publications.

Corantos. Another forerunner of today's newspaper began appearing in Germany around 1609 and in London in 1621. Called corantos, they consisted of printed single sheets containing current news that was published at regular and frequent intervals—often once or twice a week.[1] Amsterdam, where corantos were published in Dutch, German, French and English, became the first major newspaper center.

First English Papers.   In 1665 the first real English-language newspaper—the *Oxford Gazette*—started publishing twice weekly under the authority of the English Crown. Later renamed the *London Gazette,* it continued publishing into the twentieth century.

The first daily newspaper in English was the *Daily Courant,* which began publication in London on March 11, 1702. This high-quality, highly literate paper was aimed at the educated elite. Like newspapers of today, it relied on advertising for its revenue.

Like all other publications, these early English newspapers were subject to censorship by the Crown, although censorship was rarely enforced after the late seventeenth century. In the American colonies, however, colonial governors continued to censor newspapers well into the eighteenth century.

THE COLONIAL AMERICAN PRESS (1690–1820s)

The Cradle of American Journalism.   Credit for the first effort to found a newspaper in the American colonies belongs to Benjamin Harris, a former London publisher. He brought out the first edition of *Publick Occurrences Both Foreign and Domestick* in Boston on September 25, 1690. Harris had fled to the colonies after being arrested in England for printing seditious material against the Crown.

The first issue of *Publick Occurrences* apparently didn't please those in authority any better than his previous efforts in England. Among other things, the paper carried unfavorable comments about some Indians who were allies of the English and about the French king, who, it was alleged, had seduced his daughter-in-law. The newspaper's first issue was therefore its last. The governor of Massachusetts Bay colony banned Harris's paper on the grounds that it had been published without authority and contained material disapproved by the government.

In putting Harris out of business, the authorities reaffirmed their right to *prior* censorship: publishers had to first secure permission from the government before publishing anything. A firmly established authoritarian principle dictated that the press be controlled to protect the interests of the Crown, and in the colonies the governors represented the Crown.

It was not until April 1704 that the *Boston News-Letter* became the first newspaper to be published regularly in the colonies. Its publisher was the postmaster of Boston, John Campbell, and under its nameplate were the words "published by authority."

The post-office connection was important for several reasons. First, the postmaster was the governor's appointee and in effect was "approved" by him. Second, the post office was an effective place for gathering news because people assembled there to read aloud to each other letters from England.

Because most colonists were English, it was not surprising that the *Boston News-Letter* was similar in appearance and content to the *London Gazette.* Two-thirds of the *News-Letter* consisted of news taken from London journals. Thus most stories concerned English politics and European wars. The rest of the space was filled with very brief articles about ship arrivals, sermons, deaths, political appointments, court actions, the weather and the activities of Indians and pirates.

■ This copy of the first and only issue of *Publick Occurrences Both Foreign and Domestick* was the first newspaper published in the British-controlled American colonies.

When Campbell retired from his job as postmaster in 1718, his successor, William Brooker, seemed to consider newspaper publishing a part of the job. But when Campbell refused to relinquish the *News-Letter,* Brooker started a second paper, the *Boston Gazette,* in 1719. Unlike Campbell, when Brooker lost his job as postmaster a year later, he turned the paper over to his successor. Five postmasters, including Brooker, served as publisher of the *Gazette.*

The Spread of Newspapers. Philadelphia's first newspaper, *The American Weekly Mercury,* was founded by the William Bradford family in 1719. Although it too was an authorized publication, Bradford's son Tom, the publisher, soon got into trouble for writing that he hoped the General Assembly "will find some effectual remedy to revive the dying credit of the Province and restore to us our former happy circumstances."[2] Tom went to jail for the statement; he was later released and was allowed to continue publishing the paper until his death in 1742.

In 1721 James Franklin, the older half-brother of Benjamin Franklin, started the *New England Courant* in Boston. Unlike the two older Boston papers, the *Courant* was not "published by authority" and had no connection with the post office.

The *Courant* did not resemble the *London Gazette,* as its predecessors had, but modeled itself after English literary essay papers such as the *Spectator* and *Guardian.* Its content was thus more entertaining than informative. The *Courant* ran humorous literary essays, most of them satirically critical of the Puritans and the colonial government. Eventually James Franklin was thrown in jail for a month and forbidden to publish the *Courant* or any paper "of like nature."

Franklin circumvented that government order by naming his brother, Benjamin, an apprentice in his print shop, publisher.

Ben Franklin, who had perfected his writing style by reading and rewriting Joseph Addison's essays in the *Spectator,* which his brother kept in the print shop, started contributing satirical essays to the *Courant.* Appearing under the pseudonym of Silence Dogood, the articles soon became a popular feature.

In 1723 Benjamin Franklin left his apprenticeship to strike out on his own. He moved to Philadelphia, where he worked for Tom Bradford for several years. Then, in 1729 he bought an interest in an unsuccessful newspaper, *The Universal Instructor in all Arts and Sciences and the Pennsylvania Gazette.* He shortened the name to the *Pennsylvania Gazette* and turned it into a highly regarded newspaper—thus launching a successful publishing career that was to include a chain of newspapers as well as *Poor Richard's Almanack* and his *General Magazine.*

New York became the third colony with a newspaper when William Bradford started the *New York Gazette* in 1725. Bradford had left Philadelphia to become the official printer for the New York colony. Although not a postmaster, he benefited from the status of being an agent of the government.

Struggle Against Authority. In 1733 a young German immigrant by the name of John Peter Zenger began publishing the *New York Weekly Journal.* Zenger had the backing of a number of anti-Establishment merchants who disliked the colonial governor, William Cosby. Zenger printed one attack after another on the governor and his council until he was arrested for seditious libel. During the nine months he was held in jail awaiting trial, Zenger continued to edit his newspaper, which was printed and distributed by his wife and friends.

The trial began ominously, as Zenger's two attorneys were disbarred for attempting to get the judge to disqualify himself (on the grounds that he had been appointed by Governor Cosby). Zenger's supporters then hired Andrew Hamilton, a Philadelphia attorney, to represent him. At that time truth was not a defense in a libel suit (it is today), and the jury needed only to decide whether or not Zenger had printed the papers in question. The judge would decide if the material was criminally libelous.

During the trial in 1735, Hamilton argued for truth as a defense of libel. He challenged the jury to ignore the technicalities of the law and recognize the greater issues at stake: "The question before the court . . . is not the cause of the poor printer. . . . No! It may in its consequences affect every freeman . . . on the main[land] of America. It is the best cause; it is the cause of Liberty . . . the liberty both of exposing and opposing arbitrary power . . . by speaking and writing Truth."[3]

The jury responded to Hamilton's oratory, ignored the letter of the law and returned a verdict of not guilty. Although the Zenger decision set no legal precedent, it sent a clear signal that the people were no longer compliant toward government suppression of the press. The press was beginning to play an important role in shaping cultural attitudes in the colonies.

Following the Zenger case, other newspapers started up in the colonies. By 1765 all but two—Delaware and New Jersey—had newspapers. There were four papers in Boston, three each in New York and Philadelphia, and two each in Connecticut, Rhode Island and North and South Carolina. The other four colonies had one paper each, published weekly at the seat of government.

With the exception of Benjamin Harris, John Campbell and the various postmasters who published the *Boston Gazette,* most newspaper editors and publishers in colonial days were printers by trade. Besides publishing a newspaper, these printers usually had a job-printing business and also printed books and pamphlets. Sometimes the printer-publisher was the postmaster, a magistrate and in many cases, the official printer for the colony. Frequently they ran bookstores where they sold their own publications as well as books from London—and occasionally general merchandise. Ben Franklin, for example, advertised coffee, soap, wines, patent medicines, eyeglasses, Rhode Island cheese and lottery tickets for sale along with his books and stationery.[4]

The Press and the Revolution.   Slowly the colonial culture, with its strong loyalty to England, was changing. This loyalty was severely strained in 1765, when the British Parliament passed the Stamp Act imposing a tax on all legal documents, official papers, books and newspapers. To ensure that the tax was collected, all printing had to be done on taxed paper. This law was followed by the Townshend Acts, which placed taxes on tea, wine, oil, glass, lead and paint.

Hostility toward this "taxation without representation" was building in the colonies, and colonial printer-publishers started speaking out boldly against second-class colonial citizenship. Soon many newspapers were at the center of the controversy. Samuel Adams's *Boston Gazette* and Isaiah Thomas's *Massachusetts Spy* were leaders in the patriotic movement that was sweeping the colonies. A number of those prominent in the American Revolution were writers for the colonial press: John Adams, John Dickinson, Benjamin Franklin, Thomas Jefferson, Richard Henry Lee and Thomas Paine.

When the Revolution broke out in 1775, the press attempted to cover the war. However, there were no effective ways of gathering the news, and papers often had to rely on hearsay and secondhand reports from the battlefield. Facts were not always a major element in some of the war reports, as the partisan press helped to sustain the spirit of the American people. Typical was the May 3, 1775, *Massachusetts Spy* report on the first battle of the war:

> *Americans! forever bear in mind the BATTLE OF LEXINGTON!—where British troops, unmolested and unprovoked, wantonly and in a most inhuman manner, fired upon and killed a number of our countrymen, then robbed, ransacked, and burnt their houses! Not could the tears of defenseless women, some of them were in the pains of childbirth, the cries of the helpless babes, not the prayers of old age confined to beds of sickness, appease their thirst for blood!—or divert them from their design of MURDER AND ROBBERY!*

The Press in the New Republic.   Neither the Articles of Confederation of 1781 nor the Constitution drawn up in 1787 included protection for the press. Nevertheless, the practice of prior censorship had died with the end of British rule, and newspapers participated vigorously in public debate. In particular, the New York newspapers played an important role in securing the ratification of the Constitution by publishing the *Federalist Papers,* a series of essays in defense of the new document. Finally, in 1791 the First Amendment, the constitutional foundation for freedom of the press in the United States, was ratified.

In the early days of the new republic, the press played a major role in American politics. The new nation split into two parties—the Federalists, led by Alexander Hamilton, and the Republicans, or anti-Federalists, led by Thomas Jefferson. Newspapers became partisan, lining up with one party or the other. Some even became party organs, directly subsidized by the party. The development of a highly partisan press has caused some historians to see the 1790s as the beginning of the "dark ages" of American journalism.

Pro-Federalist papers included John Fenno's *Gazette of the United States,* William Coleman's *New York Evening Post,* Noah Webster's *American Minerva* and William Cobbett's *Porcupine's Gazette.* Pro-Republican newspapers included Philip Freneau's *National Gazette,* Samuel Harrison Smith's *National Intelligencer* and Benjamin Franklin Bache's *Aurora* (Bache was a grandson of Ben Franklin).

The content of these postrevolution newspapers was not all political, however. The American culture still placed a great deal of importance on foreign news, particularly from England. Even though the new nation had won its independence through a bloody war, the culture was still dependent on the "mother country" for many things, including cultural leadership, the models for newspapers and magazines and news about English customs and thought.

However, the partisan postrevolutionary press differed in many ways from the tame colonial newspapers with their noncontroversial accounts of foreign and domestic news. Now the papers were run by strong-minded editors, who routinely expressed their political convictions and attacked those who held opposing points of view.

Alien and Sedition Acts. In 1798—just seven years after the First Amendment gave the press explicit constitutional protection from government interference—the Federalist-controlled Congress passed the Alien and Sedition Acts. The Sedition Act placed serious restrictions on a person's right to criticize the government, the president or any members of his cabinet. Some Republican newspaper editors, at least one Republican congressman and other critics of the government were tried under the new law. Those convicted were fined and sent to jail. Citizens became so angry at this government high-handedness that they voted Federalist President John Adams out of office in 1800 and elected Thomas Jefferson, who had campaigned against the acts. Jefferson pardoned those who had been imprisoned under the acts, and all fines were repaid with interest. The laws expired with the end of the Federalist reign.

Early Nineteenth Century. The dark ages of American journalism continued into the nineteenth century, as Thomas Jefferson, a long-time defender of a free press in a democratic society, suffered outrageous personal attacks from Federalist newspapers. Even President James Madison, the "Father of the Constitution" and the author of the First Amendment, was harshly criticized by certain elements of the press when he succeeded Jefferson to the presidency.

In the meantime, a new kind of paper, the mercantile newspaper, had emerged in the new nation. The *Courier,* the *Enquirer* and the *Journal of Commerce* carried business news, shipping information and advertisements. In the early nineteenth century the mercantile press and the political press began to merge, forming the prototype of today's American newspaper.

As the American experiment in democracy unfolded in the years after independence, the press played an important role in shaping and reflecting political culture and values. Political leaders and thinkers differed on how the new democracy should function, and their lively war of ideas was amplified and disseminated through the mass medium of newspapers.

It is important to note, however, that in this period newspaper readers consisted primarily of a rather select, educated elite of politically aware citizens and merchants. Newspapers did not reach out to the general public until 1833.

THE PENNY-PRESS ERA (1833–1865)

By the 1830s New York had emerged as the metropolitan center of America's emerging industrial culture. Its population quadrupled to over 800,000 people between 1830 and 1860, as immigrants from Europe and migrants from rural New England arrived daily.

Popular Culture Newspapers.   On September 3, 1833, Benjamin Day, a printer, launched a daily newspaper called the *New York Sun*. This paper represented a major departure from previous newspapers in terms of its content, cost and target audience. Instead of aiming the paper at the elite, who could afford to pay the customary six cents per copy, Day priced his paper at one cent, within reach of the new urban masses—the industrial-age immigrants and migrants.

Day hired newsboys to sell the four-page newspaper on the streets. He borrowed this "London plan" of circulation from English newspapers. To capture the interest of the newly arrived city dwellers, Day concentrated on stories of crime, violence, murder, fires, trials, executions and other sensational topics. Another popular feature in the *Sun* was a humorous column that summarized the daily police-court activities in New York (see Box 7.1). Day's approach proved successful, and by the end of his first year the *Sun* had a circulation of 10,000.

With such a large audience, the *Sun* was very attractive to advertisers, and increasing advertising revenues meant new independence for the newspaper. Up to now, most papers had either served the business interests (the mercantile press) or been tied to political parties, which restricted editorial freedom. But with advertisers footing the bills instead, Day could take the editorial stands he believed in.

There were 11 competing newspapers in New York when Day started the *Sun*. After five years, the *Sun*'s circulation was over 30,000—more than the combined circulation of all the other papers. Day had successfully launched the metropolitan newspaper as a mass medium of popular culture.

BOX 7.1

▪ NIGHT COURT—NINETEENTH-CENTURY STYLE ▪

One of the most popular items in the New York Sun *was George W. Wisner's report of the police-court news. The following example of his work appeared in the July 4, 1834, edition.*

Margaret Thomas was drunk in the street—said she never would get drunk again "upon her honor." Committed, "upon honor."

William Luvoy got drunk because yesterday was so devilish warm. Drank 9 glasses of brandy and water and said he would be cursed if he wouldn't drink 9 more as quick as he could raise the money to buy it with. He would like to know what right the magistrate had to interfere with his private affairs. Fined $1—forgot his pocketbooks, and was sent over to bridewell.

Bridget McMunn got drunk and threw a pitcher at Mr. Ellis, of 53 Ludlow st. Bridget said she was the mother of 3 orphans—God bless their dear souls—and if she went to prison they would choke to death for the want of something to eat. Committed.

Catharine McBride was brought in for stealing a frock. Catharine said she had just served out 6 months on Blackwell's Island, and she wouldn't be sent back again for the best glass of punch that ever was made. Her husband, when she last left the penitentiary, took her to a boarding house in Essex st., but the rascal got mad at her, pulled her hair, pinched her arm, and kicked her out of bed. She was determined not to bear such treatment as this,

and so got drunk and stole the frock out of pure spite. Committed.

Bill Doty got drunk because he had the horrors so bad he couldn't keep sober. Committed.

Patrick Ludwick was sent up by his wife, who testified that she had supported him for several years in idleness and drunkenness. Abandoning all hopes of a reformation in her husband, she bought him a suit of clothes a fortnight since and told him to go about his business, for she would not live with him any longer. Last night he came home in state of intoxication, broke into his wife's bedroom, pulled her out of bed, pulled her hair, and stamped on her. She called a watchman and sent him up. Pat exerted all his powers of eloquence in endeavoring to excite his wife's sympathy, but to no purpose. As every sensible woman ought to do who is cursed with a drunken husband, she refused to have anything to do with him hereafter—and he was sent to the penitentiary.

Dennis Hart was fighting in the street. Committed.

John Movich, of 220 Mott St., got drunk and disturbed his neighbors. Committed.

Others soon copied Day's innovations. In 1835 James Gordon Bennett founded the *New York Herald,* which refined and expanded the popular content of the penny press. He designed his paper to "cover the city" by sending reporters to Wall Street, churches, social events and the courts.

Bennett's newspaper took a middle-of-the-road approach. Although it too featured crime news as an essential ingredient, it was more serious and responsible than the *Sun.* Just as important, it was more lively and entertaining than the mercantile, or Wall Street, papers, which quickly struck back. In an effort to discourage sophisticated New Yorkers from reading the *Herald,* the Wall Street press implied that Bennett's newspaper was "not suitable for ladies and gentlemen."[5] This was the first major struggle between the elite and popular press in the United States.

Many other penny-press newspapers followed Day's and Bennett's lead. One of the more significant was Horace Greeley's *New York Tribune,* which was

■ Benjamin Day introduced news carriers to the streets of New York to sell his successful *Sun,* the newspaper that launched the penny press and made newspapers available to the masses.

founded in 1841. Greeley—whose exhortation "Go West Young Man, Go West" is legendary—hired others to handle the business side of the newspaper and concentrated his efforts on editorial work. He introduced the idea of separating news and opinion and developed the editorial page as we know it today. Greeley became one of the most influential editorial writers in the nineteenth century. He even ran unsuccessfully for president of the United States in 1872 on the Republican ticket.

Ten years after Greeley established the *Tribune,* Henry J. Raymond founded the *New York Times.* Modeling his newspaper after the *Times* of London, Raymond concentrated on news interpretation and background reporting and developed a strong editorial policy. He personally accompanied presidential candidates so he could write campaign stories firsthand. He also hired European correspondents to cover foreign stories exclusively for the *Times.*

New Technology. The Industrial Revolution had a major impact on printing technology, which had been virtually unchanged since the mid-fifteenth century. Newspapers began using the new rotary and cylinder presses, first driven by steam and later by electricity. It was now possible to print nearly 100,000 copies of a 12-page newspaper in an hour—a far cry from the early days of hand-fed presses.

The Associated Press. Soon after Samuel F. B. Morse invented the telegraph in 1844—the first glimmer of the electronic age—American newspapers started to take advantage of this new technology. By 1848 six New York newspapers had joined together to use the telegraph to pool their news-gathering resources. This first wire service was called the Associated Press of New York, later simply the Associated Press.

The debut of electronic technology affected the content of newspapers, just as television would in the second half of the twentieth century. Because telegraph lines were sometimes cut and news transmissions were often interrupted for military use during the Civil War, journalists started to put a complete summary of the story in the first paragraph. All of the traditional elements—who, what, when, where, why and how—were crowded into the lead paragraph so that the important information could be received before the transmission was interrupted. This style of newswriting, called the *inverted pyramid,* is still used in a modified version today. Use of the telegraph also led to the demise of editorial comment in news stories. Because editorial opinions varied from newspaper to newspaper, a reporter writing for a number of newspapers could not come up with a slant that would fit them all. It was better to stick to the facts and let the individual newspapers editorialize as they wished.

Newspaper Syndicates.   The first independent newspaper syndicate was founded in 1865 to supply feature materials to rural newspapers. Then, in 1884, Samuel S. McClure (who later published *McClure's Magazine*) established the first large-scale newspaper syndicate to furnish nonnews features and entertainment material to participating newspapers. McClure concentrated on women's features and the serialization of popular novels. Today's syndicated materials include comic strips, editorial cartoons, columnists, humor material and crossword puzzles.

THE YELLOW JOURNALISM ERA (1865–1900)

Between 1865 and 1900 the United States was transformed into a major industrial state. According to Agee, Ault and Emery,

> *Industrialization, mechanization and urbanization brought extensive social, cultural and political changes: the rise of the city, improved transportation and communication, educational advances, political unrest and the rise of an extensive labor movement. The mass media could not fail to go through great changes along with the society they served.*[6]

The 35-year period between the end of the Civil War and the turn of the century is known as the ''yellow journalism'' era to some and the period of ''new journalism'' to others. It was a time when the metropolitan press took on a flamboyance characteristic of the new industrial age. Newspapers became a major force in disseminating the new mass culture.

During this period the population of the country doubled, the national wealth quadrupled and manufacturing output increased sevenfold. The United States was completing its transformation from an agrarian culture to an industrial society. One-third of the population was urban, and by 1900, 62 percent of the labor force was engaged in nonagricultural work.

As the nation changed, so did its newspapers. Urban workers looked to the press for crusading reporting on corruption and editorial support for laws to ban the worst abuses in mines and factories. Among the many crusading journalists who led the effort to provide newspapers for the new mass audience, three stand out. Of these, two fought head-to-head in New York in one of the century's fiercest circulation battles: Joseph Pulitzer, later named by his colleagues as the leading American editor of this period, and William Randolph Hearst. The third was Edward W. Scripps.

Joseph Pulitzer.   The new nation of immigrants was ready for one of its own to take a leading role in American journalism. Born in Hungary in 1847, Joseph Pulitzer came to the United States at the age of 17 to fight in the Civil War.

After his discharge in 1865, Pulitzer moved to St. Louis, where he studied law and worked as a newspaper reporter for a German-language newspaper. In 1878 he bought the *St. Louis Post-Dispatch* and soon turned it into the city's leading newspaper. In 1883 he left the *Post-Dispatch* in the hands of an editor to move to New York. There he bought the run-down *World,* with similar results. Within four years the *World* was New York's leading newspaper, with a record-breaking circulation of 250,000.

Although Pulitzer was not above using entertainment and sensationalism to capture readers' attention, he did not neglect the basic purpose of a newspaper. He believed in accuracy, an aggressive and crusading editorial policy and good news judgment. One of his famous commands to his staff was "Accuracy! Accuracy!! Accuracy!!!" Another was: "Terseness! Intelligent, not stupid, condensation." Still another showed his concern for the lighter side of the news: he reminded reporters to look for both the significant news and the "original, distinctive, dramatic, romantic, thrilling, unique, curious, quaint, humorous, odd, apt to be talked about" news.[7]

Pulitzer was constantly crusading for just causes. He was particularly concerned about the plight of his fellow immigrants, who were the victims of discrimination, poverty, ignorance and crowded slum conditions. Pulitzer believed that his paper should

> . . . *always fight for progress and reform, never tolerate injustice or corruption, always fight demagogues of all parties, always oppose privileged classes and public plunderers, never lack sympathy with the poor, always remain devoted to the public welfare, never to be satisfied with merely printing news, always be drastically independent, never be afraid to attack wrong, whether by predatory plutocracy or predatory poverty.*[8]

Despite his high ideals, Pulitzer allowed himself to be pulled into one of American journalism's most degrading circulation wars. His opponent was William Randolph Hearst, who had become a successful publisher by using some of Pulitzer's techniques of entertainment and sensationalism.

William Randolph Hearst.   In marked contrast to Pulitzer, William Randolph Hearst was born into a wealthy San Francisco family. As part of his privileged upbringing, Hearst was sent to Harvard for an education. While there he served as

■ Despite his involvement in the sensational circulation war with William Randolph Hearst during the Yellow Journalism era, Joseph Pulitzer (pictured) is considered to be the best American newspaper editor of his time.

business manager of Harvard's *Lampoon* and became familiar with Pulitzer's style of journalism by working briefly for Pulitzer's *World*. About this time Hearst's father, George, purchased the *San Francisco Examiner* to use to manipulate the California legislature into appointing him to the U.S. Senate. (U.S. senators were appointed by state legislators until the adoption of the Seventeenth Amendment in 1913.)

When Hearst returned to San Francisco in 1887 he persuaded his father (now a senator) to turn the *Examiner* over to him rather than sell it. Then, employing some of the techniques he had learned from Pulitzer's *World,* he turned the *Examiner* into a mass-circulation newspaper that found a niche in San Francisco's popular culture.

Hearst, like Pulitzer, attempted to protect the public from abuses by the rich and powerful and from political corruption. He even crusaded against his father's friend Senator Leland Stanford, the millionaire owner of the Southern Pacific Railroad. Hearst opposed Stanford's efforts to get government subsidies for the railroads and made that crusade a major topic of his paper. He also fought corruption in San Francisco politics.

In 1895 Hearst, seeking new worlds to conquer, moved to New York. There he bought the *New York Journal* to compete head-to-head with Pulitzer's *World,* which at the time had the largest circulation of any paper in the country. Although Hearst had Pulitzer's crusading zeal and his flair for sensationalism, he did not share his rival's concern for accuracy and fairness. As one book has pointed out,

"Hearst did not blink at coloring, stealing, or even faking the news; he did not hesitate to appeal to jingoism and a variety of other cheap emotions; and the tone of discourse in his papers often fell to mere abuse."[9]

In the circulation war, which reached a peak in 1898, both publishers resorted to journalistic excesses, including bold, misleading headlines, intensive coverage of crime, sex and violence, sensationalistic photojournalism and bizarre promotional stunts. Hearst was even accused of provoking the Spanish-American War through his sensational coverage of Spain's activities in Cuba.

Eventually people started calling these tactics "yellow journalism." The term came from "The Yellow Kid" comic strip, which was drawn for the *World* by Richard Outcault, one of the most popular comic-strip cartoonists of the time. (Pulitzer had introduced color comic strips to American newspapers in 1894.)

The strip featured a bald, toothless, grinning boy dressed in a yellow sacklike garment. Because of the strip's popularity, Hearst offered Outcault a tremendous salary to quit the *World* and draw for the *Journal,* an offer he couldn't refuse. But Pulitzer, claiming he had sole rights to the comic strip, simply hired another cartoonist to draw it. For a while New York had two "Yellow Kids."

Although the two newspapers together sometimes sold more than a million copies a day during the circulation war, Pulitzer eventually lost his appetite for the competition and withdrew from the contest, leaving the field of yellow journalism to Hearst and a few of his imitators.

Hearst went on to build a major publishing empire consisting of a chain of newspapers throughout the country, four feature syndicates (which merged in 1931 to form the King Feature Syndicate), a wire service (International News Service, which he founded in 1909 when his papers were denied membership in the Associated Press) and numerous magazines, including *Cosmopolitan, Good Housekeeping,* and *Harper's Bazaar.*

One of Hearst's more significant contributions to the field of journalism was the introduction of women reporters into the newsrooms, mostly human-interest feature writers who became known as "sob sisters" (see Box 7.2). He also hired promotion managers to increase readership and led the way in proving the importance of strong circulation departments.

Edward Wyllis Scripps.   The third crusader during this flamboyant period of American journalism was Edward Wyllis Scripps (1854–1926). Scripps concentrated his efforts in the nation's smaller cities, building a chain of newspapers with headquarters at the *Cleveland Press* in Ohio.

Like Pulitzer and Hearst, Scripps used his papers to champion the people's rights, but he never stooped to sensationalistic abuses. Scripps's goal was to improve the position of the new industrialized masses through better education, labor-union organization, collective bargaining and a reasonable redistribution of wealth. In this way, he reasoned, the ideal of a peaceful and productive society could be realized.

Scripps started many newspapers by sending an editor and business manager into a community with $25,000 and instructions to establish a newspaper. If they succeeded, they received 49 percent of the stock; if they ran out of money, they were replaced. If the paper did not show a profit within 10 years, it was shut

BOX 7.2

▪ WOMEN IN JOURNALISM ▪

The term *sob sister* was coined around the turn of the century to describe the women who wrote sentimental human-interest stories for William Randolph Hearst's newspapers. Although the hiring of women by Hearst helped to open up the field of journalism to women, it was by no means a first for women in the field.

Ann Smith Franklin, widow of Benjamin Franklin's older brother, is considered to be one of the first female journalists. She took over her husband's printing business after his death in 1735. About this same time the wife of John Peter Zenger was helping her husband publish the *New York Weekly Journal* while he was in prison awaiting trial on a charge of libeling the governor. The first female printer, however, was Dinah Nuthead, who took over her husband's printing business after he died in 1695.

Today there are many women in the editorial offices of American newspapers. However, not too many women hold top editorial positions. According to a 1986 survey by the American Society of Newspaper Editors, 12.4 percent of the country's senior newspaper editors were women, though only a fraction of them were top newsroom executives. In fact, by 1988 only seven women held the top editorial position in newspapers with circulations over 100,000. They were Katharine Fanning, *Christian Science Monitor;* Barbara Henry, *Rochester* [N.Y.] *Democrat & Chronicle;* Sandra Mims Rowe, *Virginian-Pilot/Ledger-Star* (Norfolk, Va.); Janet Chusmir, *Miami Herald;* Beverly Kees, *Fresno Bee;* Deborah Howell, *St. Paul Pioneer Press Dispatch;* and Jane Amsterdam, *New York Post.*

In addition to these top editors, several other women have had distinguished careers as publishers after inheriting newspapers from their husbands. They include Katharine Graham, chairman of the Washington Post Co. and Helen K. Copley, chairman of the San Diego–based Copley Newspaper chain.

down. In addition to his chain of 30 newspapers, Scripps also founded the Newspaper Enterprise Association (NEA) syndicate in 1902 and the United Press wire service in 1907.

THE TWENTIETH-CENTURY PRESS

By the late 1890s many readers were looking for something better than what Hearst, Pulitzer and others like them had to offer, and yellow journalism began to wane.

Objectivity. What was lacking in New York and many other cities was a newspaper that was objective in its coverage of the news. Seeing an opportunity to improve the state of journalism in New York, Adolph Ochs purchased the near-bankrupt *New York Times* in 1896 and set out to make it the ''newspaper of record.'' He introduced the slogan that still appears on the paper's front page today: ''All the news that's fit to print.''

Ochs guided the *Times* for 40 years and turned it into a paper that was respected worldwide for its comprehensive, accurate and balanced news coverage. As Ochs hoped, the *Times* has become the newspaper of record, and today it can be found indexed in most scholarly libraries. The standards set by the *New York Times* became respected by readers and journalists alike and soon other papers followed its lead.

Social Responsibility.   The second trend at work at the beginning of the twentieth century was an emphasis on the *social responsibility* of newspapers and journalists (see Chapter 3). Schools and departments of journalism were established in colleges and universities, and attempts were made to teach high standards. The Graduate School of Journalism, established at Columbia University in 1912 by a legacy from Joseph Pulitzer, took the lead in this field. (The school still administers the most prestigious awards in newspaper journalism, the Pulitzer Prizes.) Various professional newspaper organizations drew up codes of ethics during this period.

Many observers of the American press were convinced that the libertarian theory of the press, which forbade government interference with the press, would not work if the mass media were not socially responsible. Some of the major newspapers in the country accepted this view and tried to make their publications more socially responsive by striving for fairness in news coverage and downplaying sensationalism.

Jazz Journalism.   Although newspaper content was more responsible and objective during this period, sensationalism was not dead. Hearst publications continued to use bold headlines, sensationalized photography and stunts to sell papers. Indeed, there was another wave of sensationalism during the "Roaring '20s." This was called jazz journalism, and it reflected the Jazz Age of the time.

Helping to usher in this period of jazz journalism was Joseph Medill Patterson, copublisher of the *Chicago Tribune*. Patterson introduced a tabloid newspaper (half the size of a regular newspaper and similar in size to today's *National Enquirer*) to New York City.

Patterson's *New York Illustrated Daily News* featured large photographs (sometimes one covered the entire front page), crime, violence, and sex stories and sensational headlines to sell papers at newsstands. There was still a huge market for this type of journalism, and the New York *Daily News* ("Illustrated" was later dropped) soon became the nation's largest-selling daily newspaper, with a circulation that exceeded 2 million copies for many years. It finally surrendered first place in 1980 to the *Wall Street Journal*.

Soon Hearst and others started bringing out tabloid newspapers in New York City too. It is interesting to note that the largest-selling *weekly* newspaper in the United States is also a sensational tabloid—the *National Enquirer,* which sells nearly 5 million copies per week (see Box 7.3).

The Electronic Press.   The most significant change in the way people got the news was the introduction of electronic journalism—first radio and then television news. (These are discussed at length in Chapters 9 and 10.) In the following discussion, we use the term *press* to include both print and electronic news gathering.

Interpretative Reporting.   Although *interpretative reporting* was first introduced in the 1930s, there has been a marked increase in this type of reporting during the past decade or so. These articles, often labeled "news analysis," appear alongside straight news stories and try to explain the implications and possible conse-

BOX 7.3

SUPERMARKET JOURNALISM: GIVING US WHAT ENQUIRING MINDS WANT TO KNOW

Not all successful newspapers are delivered to the home or sold on newsstands. Some are strategically marketed at supermarket checkout counters. Here grocery shoppers are enticed with sensational headlines and teasers for unbelievable stories that supposedly will be found on the inside pages.

The leader of these supermarket journals also happens to be the largest-circulating newspaper in the United States—the *National Enquirer*. The *Enquirer's* success can be traced back to 1952, when Generoso (Gene) Pope purchased the *New York Enquirer*. He immediately began filling the newspaper with stories about sex and violence (topics that the *Enquirer* now downplays). In the 1960s Pope expanded it into a national publication and began selling it in supermarkets. He toned down the sex and violence to appeal to a broader audience and began focusing on stories about celebrity gossip, government waste, haunted houses, ghosts, psychic predictions, honest people who find and return money, life-threatening accidents, successful people who never went to college, heroic activities, fat people who learned how to lose weight, ideas on saving money and medical advice. In short, Pope had learned how to market our popular cultural interests through news columns.

Through the years the *National Enquirer* has become one of the most successful and controversial newspapers in American society. It has been sued by numerous celebrities and has reached out-of-court settlements with many of them. Lawsuits against the *Enquirer* have been filed by Carol Burnett, Johnny Carson, Frank Sinatra, Tom Selleck, Richard Pryor and Shirley Jones, to name a few. Despite large settlements to the plaintiffs, the *National Enquirer's* flamboyant style does not change.

In 1987 the *Enquirer* angered many by publishing a front-page photo of former Democratic presidential frontrunner Gary Hart with actress Donna Rice sitting in his lap. The headline read: "GARY HART ASKED ME TO MARRY HIM." Other newspapers, magazines and television networks had carried the Donna Rice–Gary Hart story in previous weeks, but none of the stories came near the revelations of the *Enquirer.* The *Enquirer* had reportedly paid $25,000 for the photograph, and the cover helped the publication climb above the 5 million circulation mark that week.

When Marine Lt. Col. Oliver North became a folk hero during his 1987 testimony before a congressional committee investigating the Iran-Contra scandal, the *Enquirer* began featuring him on its cover. Months after his testimony the *Enquirer* was still catering to his popularity by running cover photos proposing him as a candidate for president.

The *National Enquirer* does not represent anything new in American journalism, however. What it does represent is a continuation of the style of journalism that has been in existence here since newspapers first began catering to the popular culture in the early nineteenth century. The publications of Benjamin Day and James Gordon Bennett in the early days of the penny press, William Randolph Hearst and Joseph Pulitzer in the yellow journalism period, and the tabloids of New York in the jazz journalism age of the 1920s were not too much different in content from the *National Enquirer*. And they too were popular with the masses. This style of journalism is also the most popular form of journalism in the United Kingdom.

National Enquirer reporters are among the highest paid in the nation, and the paper covers major news events with teams of journalists and photographers, as *Life* magazine did in its heyday. The *Enquirer* often rushes journalists to the scene of news events to sign up eyewitnesses to "exclusive stories." While the popular entertainer Liberace was dying of AIDS in 1987, for example, eight *National Enquirer* reporters and photographers camped outside his Palm Springs home attempting to arrange exclusive stories.

Although highly criticized for its approach and style, the *National Enquirer* seems to be giving many people what they want—sensational stories concerning events that "enquiring minds want to know."

quences of certain events. They have become an important part of modern journalism.

For example, after George Bush and Michael Dukakis had sewed up the nominations of their parties for president in May 1988, the *New York Times* carried an article on its front page about possible running mates. Written by the *Times*'s leading political reporter, R. W. Apple, Jr., the article explained how the process of picking vice presidential nominees had worked in the past and speculated on who might be the best choices this time.

Investigative Reporting.　*Investigative reporting* has a longer history; it dates back to the turn of the century, when muckraking reporters began exposing the corruption and abuses of the new industrial society (see Chapter 6).

Classic examples of investigative reporting are Seymour Hersh's revelations about the My Lai massacre during the Vietnam war and Bob Woodward and Carl Bernstein's uncovering of the Watergate scandal in 1972–74.

In 1969 Hersh discovered that American soldiers had killed over 300 Vietnamese civilians at the village of My Lai the previous year. His reports led to congressional hearings and the indictment of military personnel involved in the episode. The incident shattered the myth that American soldiers were always the good guys who protected the innocent in times of war.

The Watergate story started with a police report about a burglary at the Democratic National Headquarters in a Washington, D.C. office and apartment complex called Watergate. Woodward and Bernstein, investigative reporters for the *Washington Post,* tried to find out what was behind the break-in. With the help of an anonymous source within the government, called "Deep Throat," they began discovering a series of illegal activities that they traced to the White House. When President Richard Nixon himself was implicated in a cover-up, he resigned from office. This event shook the foundation of our American culture because it ran counter to the myth that we could trust our presidents to respect the laws of the land.

In both of these investigative news events, many Americans blamed the press for revealing the information. Nevertheless, in a free society the role of the press is to keep the people informed and reflect all of the culture, including its unpleasant secrets.

Advocacy, Subjective or New Journalism.　Not all journalists subscribe to the standard of strict objectivity. In the 1960s some reporters began to practice what they called *advocacy journalism, subjective journalism* or even *new journalism.* Believing that they should report the truth "as they see it," these reporters became personally and emotionally involved in the events they covered. This type of reporting has not been welcomed by the Establishment press, but it has found a home in certain specialized publications. One of the more successful subjective journalists is Hunter S. Thompson, who wrote "Fear and Loathing: On the Campaign Trail 1972" for the magazine *Rolling Stone.*

Although new journalism has had many meanings over the years, today the term refers to a twentieth-century writing style that applies literary techniques to journalism. The result is a semiobjective, journalistic view of reality written from

■ Frederick Douglass, an ex-slave and abolitionist, published the most important pre–Civil War newspaper in the United States to feature African-American views. His weekly *North Star* contributed to anti-slavery sentiment, which, in turn, led to the Civil War.

a subjective, first-person viewpoint. Some writers who have used this style are Tom Wolfe, Jimmy Breslin, Truman Capote, Norman Mailer and Gay Talese.

Limited Specialization.   As our popular culture continues to fragment, American journalism is changing only slowly. Although newspapers do specialize in the sense that they serve a specific community or region, they generally attempt to appeal to almost everyone in that area. Thus they trail the other media in moving into the final stage of the EPS cycle.

However, there are some newspapers that do cater to specialized audiences, particularly ethnic groups. The first African-American newspaper, *Freedom's Journal,* was founded in 1827 by John B. Russwurm and the Reverend Samuel Cornish. The most important African-American pre–Civil War newspaper was Frederick Douglass's weekly, *North Star.* By the mid-1970s there were more than 325 African-American newspapers in the United States, with a total circulation of more than 7 million. Most African-American papers represent the middle of the road African-American Establishment position. However, two—*Muhammad Speaks* and *Black Panther*—took a more militant position. Other ethnic newspapers in this country include the more than 50 Hispanic newspapers started since 1960 and the foreign-language newspapers originally founded to serve the wave of European immigrants at the turn of the century. Despite the number of minority publications, figures released in 1988 by the American Newspaper Publishers Association indicated that only about 7 percent of American newsroom employees are minorities.

Another type of newspaper specialization flourished in the 1960s to serve the alienated youth and political radicals of the period. Many people wanted an alternative source of news and information, and the *underground press* was born. Although thousands of underground newspapers were established, few were successful. Some of the better-known ones included the *Village Voice* and the *East Village Other* in New York, the *Los Angeles Free Press*, Chicago's *Seed*, Boston's *Avatar* and *Phoenix*, the *Berkeley Barb* and San Francisco's *Rolling Stone*. This latter publication is now an Establishment rock music magazine.

NEWSPAPERS AS BUSINESSES

Although newspapers perform a crucial public service by keeping our society informed, we cannot forget that newspapers—like all mass media—are businesses that have to make a profit. If they don't, they die. Newspapers, in fact, generate the largest revenue of all mass media: $42.5 million each year.[10]

The price of a newspaper does not begin to pay for the cost of producing it; the major source of newspaper revenue, 79 percent, is advertising. Of that figure, 51 percent is earned from retail advertising, 38 percent from classified and 11 percent from national ads. The more circulation a newspaper has, the more it can charge for its advertising. Fatter newspapers do not necessarily have more news. They do, however, carry more advertising and are usually more financially successful.

Decline of Competition.   The competitive nature of newspapers as businesses is causing changes in American newspaper publishing—some of them less desirable than others. For example, when Americans started moving out of the cities to the suburbia in the mid-twentieth century, the number of newspapers serving many metropolitan areas started a steady decline. Cities that once boasted many newspapers now had only one. Lack of competition within a city is always a cause for concern, since it can result in complacency and newspapers' shirking their responsibility to keep their community well-informed.

In 1989, the Los Angeles *Herald Examiner* ended 118 years of service to the community by closing. Its major competitor, the *Los Angeles Times* editorialized that its competitor would not be easily replaced and that its absence "will place an even greater responsibility on the *Times* to be fair, accurate and complete in its reporting and to be attentive to the views and concerns of all segments of this increasingly diverse community."[11]

In the beginning of the 1990s, newspapers were suffering from very slow growth. Daily and Sunday circulations were stagnant. Only weekly circulations were rising. Some large national and metropolitan newspapers, such as the *Wall Street Journal, Chicago Sun-Times* and *Los Angeles Times,* were reporting decreases in circulation.

Due to increased competition from television in recent years, some evening newspapers have been changing to morning publications, which tend to have higher circulations. However, there are still more evening newspapers than morning: 1,150 evening, 525 morning (see Figure 7.1).

Although daily newspaper circulations are larger, weekly newspapers far outnumber dailies: 7,606 weekly, 1,675 daily (see Figure 7.2).

BOX 7.4

▪ WORKING IN NEWSPAPER PUBLISHING ▪

There are two separate and distinct operations in the average American newspaper: editorial and business. Although all American mass media are in the business of making a profit, most responsible newspapers attempt to keep these two parts of their operation as separate as possible so that business decisions don't influence editorial content.

The *editorial* department is in charge of gathering and writing the news and feature stories, editing the copy, designing the pages, gathering, selecting and processing photographs and writing editorials. These activities are usually divided into two divisions: *reporting,* which involves gathering news and feature stories and photographs and *desk work,* which is the processing of this information. Those who work in the first category are usually reporters and photographers, while the latter category consists of men and women called editors. All of these functions are overseen by either a main editor (sometimes called editor in chief) or the publisher.

The business side of a newspaper's operation consists of the advertising department, circulation department, production department and business department.

The *advertising* department is responsible for bringing in advertising revenue to keep the newspaper profitable. Advertising rates depend on the size of circulation.

The *circulation* department is responsible for obtaining subscribers and distributing the newspaper in a timely manner. Activities in this department include promotion activities to obtain additional readers and the daily or weekly process of getting the newspapers from the pressroom to the newsstands and homes of subscribers. This usually involves a large staff of truck drivers and motor route carriers.

The *production* department handles the typesetting, page makeup, printing and insertion of advertising supplements into the publication.

The *business* department handles all of the accounting, billing and clerical operations of the newspaper.

Each of these departments has a manager in charge of its operations who usually reports directly to a business manager or to the publisher.

Figure 7.1 Comparison of morning and evening newspapers by number and circulation.
SOURCE: *U.S. Industrial Outlook, 1990* (Washington, D.C.: U.S. Government Printing Office, 1990).

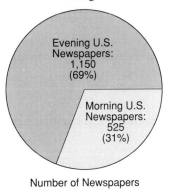
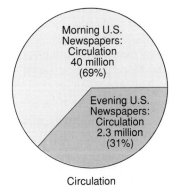

Number of Newspapers   Circulation

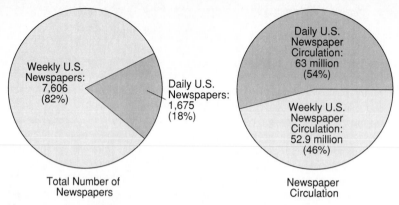

Figure 7.2 Comparison of number of newspapers by type and circulation.

SOURCE: *U.S. Industrial Outlook, 1990* (Washington D.C.: U.S. Government Printing Office, 1990).

Soft News.   Another way newspapers have responded to the challenge of television is to expand the amount of space devoted to *soft* news, or *fluff journalism*. Designed to entertain the readers, it includes such varied material as background stories that accompany news events, features on health and fitness, money management and diet, as well as comics, crossword puzzles and columns, from Erma Bombeck to Dear Abby. Soft news is constrasted with *hard* news—straight factual reports on current events.

Chain Ownership.   Like the other print media, newspaper ownership is being increasingly monopolized by a few media conglomerates, called *chains*. The four largest newspaper chains in the United States are Gannett, Knight-Ridder, Newhouse and Times-Mirror. By the early 1990s, there were 143 companies that owned two or more newspapers and these chains controlled 76 percent of the daily newspapers and 83 percent of the daily circulation.

The advantage of chain ownership is that a chain's local newspapers enjoy strong financial backing. The disadvantage is that, as control of the nation's newspapers fall into fewer and fewer hands, local community interests may be subordinated to corporate interests. Where newspapers once acted as the voice of their communities, they now often serve as the mouthpiece of the corporation that owns them. Some chains have been known to require that their corporate philosophy be reflected on news and editorial pages.

And who controls the chain? Although most chains are media companies, there is nothing to stop a large oil company, for example, from buying newspapers. If this were to happen, would the newspapers remain impartial in reporting news about the oil business?

Some people worry that foreign investors may buy up American newspapers. What is there to prevent political leaders of a wealthy country with a controlled press from buying a major interest in Gannett, for example? Would these newspapers—many of them the only paper in their community—be unbiased in their coverage of the controlling country? This concern became a reality in the summer of 1986, when a Mexican newspaper magnate with reported close ties to the Mexican government purchased America's second-largest news service, United Press International.

Libel Suits.   Meanwhile, the recent rash of libel suits has already had a chilling effect on many newspapers. Since juries have awarded huge damages in a few well-publicized cases, some newspapers have cut back on their investigative reporting to minimize their risk of being sued.[12] This trend could have serious implications for a democracy based on the premise that only an informed citizenry can determine its political destiny.

But the bottom line cannot become the only consideration in deciding what to publish. After all, as Tom Goldstein reminds us in his book *The News at Any Cost,* the press is not merely a business; newspapers were given constitutional protection "because the founding fathers felt a vigorous and independent press was essential to let people know what government was doing."[13] This conflict in roles will be discussed further in Chapter 16.

Future Challenges.   The newspaper industry is facing many changes in the '90s. Experts predict that to survive, newspapers will have to more fully enter the specialization stage of the EPS cycle. Forcing this specialization are major demographic changes in our culture: larger ethnic populations, a shift of the baby boomers into middle age, changing roles of women in the culture, increased time pressures on readers and increasing elderly populations.

Newspapers are also facing greater competition for advertising revenue from direct mail, telemarketing and home shopping TV channels. Metropolitan newspapers are finding increased competition for readers coming from suburban daily and weekly newspapers and city magazines.

Environmental concerns will also play a role in future newspaper changes. By 1990, more than a dozen states had proposed laws that would require newspapers to use recycled newsprint. Other environmental regulations controlling air pollution emissions from inks, solvents and other newspaper products were passed. These tighter environmental regulations are expected to force the industry into new, less polluting technologies, such as flexographic printing, a process that uses water-based paint and eliminates the need for traditionally toxic ink and air-polluting cleaning solvents.

NEWS WIRE SERVICES

The American press's coverage of our popular culture has been greatly assisted since the nineteenth century by press wire services. Wire services were established as news-gathering and disseminating services for newspapers after the invention of the telegraph in the 1840s. Today wire services work for radio and television as well.

■ News wire services send photographs as well as stories to members and subscribers. Shown here is an Associated Press laserphoto distribution center set up at the Democratic National Convention.

American Wire Services.   As mentioned earlier, the first wire service was the Associated Press, which was established in New York in 1848. AP, which remains the largest American wire service, has always been a nonprofit organization; newspapers that use and pay for the service "belong" to the Associated Press. Thus members share as well as receive news stories.

United Press International, the second major American wire service, was founded as United Press by E. W. Scripps in 1907. It operates like other businesses, with users subscribing to its service. Thus AP has members, while UPI has clients or customers.

The third wire service to be formed in the United States was International News Service, which William Randolph Hearst established in 1909. In 1958 United Press merged with International News Service to become United Press International.

Foreign Wire Services.   AP and UPI are not only the two major news services in the United States; they are dominant worldwide services as well. However, three others are equally influential in global news coverage: Agence France-Presse (AFP), headquartered in Paris; Reuters, in London; and the Telegrafnoie Agentsvo Sovetskovo Soyuza (Tass), in Moscow.

AFP, which was organized in 1945 at the end of World War II, has 100 foreign bureaus. Like AP, it is a nonprofit service. Reuters was founded in the 1850s and has more than a thousand correspondents in 180 countries, including a half-dozen bureaus in the United States. In recent years its revenues have come to exceed AP's, thanks mostly to the addition of financial news and information-retrieval services.

Tass, like all Soviet news media, is the official voice of the Soviet Union. Its foreign correspondents in more than a hundred countries gather and report local and international news in accordance with official Soviet policy.

Although UPI was established as a profit-making wire service, it has been losing money since 1963. In 1982 it was sold by its co-owners, the E. W. Scripps Company and the Hearst Corporation, to the Media News Corporation. But the new owners were not able to turn the service around either, and in the summer of 1986, they sold UPI to Mexican newspaper magnate Mario Vazquez Rana, who owned Mexico's largest chain of newspapers. This alarmed American journalists, who were concerned about Vazquez Rana's ties to the Mexican government.

Foreign ownership of such an essential news source was unprecedented. At the time of the sale, UPI's subscribers included about 850 American newspapers and some 3,300 radio and television stations. In addition, it was a major news source for numerous Third World nations, many in Latin America.

UPI's ownership was returned to American control in 1989 when it was sold to Infotechnology, Inc. Its financial woes continued, however, and by late 1990 Infotechnology forced its employees to take a 35 percent pay cut to avoid bankruptcy. During the past 30 years, UPI had reported annual profits only twice. Unlike the nonprofit AP, the heavily subsidized Reuters and government owned news wire services, a profit-oriented company such as UPI has a tough time competing.

BIASES AND OTHER PROBLEMS

There are five basic functions of the American press (both print and electronic): (1) to inform, (2) to entertain, (3) to influence through editorials, (4) to present advertisements and (5) to transmit the culture. Most of the criticism of the press focuses on how it carries out the first of these—to inform. Reader, listener or viewer biases account for much of this criticism.

Blaming the Messenger.   For one thing, it is simply human nature to blame the messenger for bad tidings. (In an ancient Greek play by Sophocles, for example, a king beheads a messenger who has brought him some bad news.)

For example, when there were riots on American streets and university campuses in the 1960s, many people blamed the press for causing the disturbances. They claimed that by publicizing riots in one place, the media were giving others the idea to riot elsewhere. Similarly, during the unraveling of the Watergate scandal in 1972–1974, many people criticized the press for "harping on Watergate" because they didn't want to hear about crimes being committed by the highest government officials. More recently, the press's coverage of terrorist activities has been criticized for encouraging more terrorist attacks. After particularly intense criticism of its coverage of the TWA hijacking in 1985, ABC television announced that it would no longer publicize the demands of terrorists.

This is one reason the press ranks near the top of most lists of the nation's most controversial institutions. Researchers have found that criticism of the press rises in direct proportion to the amount of unpleasant news being reported.

Watchdog Function.   Of course, under the libertarian theory, it is an essential function of the American press to serve as a watchdog of government. Keeping the citizenry informed about its government necessarily puts the press and government in an adversarial relationship, at least some of the time. When the press reports on activities that do not reflect favorably on the government and its leaders, it often receives a great deal of criticism from the government.

Bad News Only Myth.   Many people also suffer from a misconception that the press prints "only bad news because that's what sells newspapers." In fact, newspapers carry both good and bad news, but readers often ignore the good. Stories about the Boy Scouts, PTA and church socials tend to interest only Boy Scouts, PTA members and people who attend church socials.

There is some disagreement on just what constitutes bad news. Although an obituary should be considered bad news, just ask your newspaper editor what happens if he or she leaves one out of the paper. Editors are bombarded with angry telephone calls from family and friends. And for that matter, a story about a blizzard might be bad news for residents of a community but great news for people elsewhere planning a ski trip.

Myth of Media Truth.   Another problem the media have is the popular misconception that if something appears in print or is heard over the airwaves, it has to be true. How many times have you heard someone attempt to win an argument by saying "I saw it in the newspaper" or "I saw it on television"? So when the media do make mistakes—as they inevitably will—people are bitterly critical.

Biases.   Finally, many people blame the press for being biased. Certainly everyone has his or her own biases, and newspeople are no exception. Good journalists do try to keep their biases out of their stories and present all sides of the story fairly, objectively and accurately. However, most readers and viewers forget that they too have biases. And often when they read or hear a story that is trying to present several sides, they react negatively to those parts that conflict with their own biases.

More specific complaints about television news will be discussed later in Chapter 10.

SUMMARY

The history of American newspapers has paralleled the history of our culture. As our society has changed, so have its newspapers.

Early colonial newspapers were designed for the elite—those who were interested in political and business information. With the advent of new technology, compulsory education and the major cultural changes brought on by industrialization and urbanization, newspapers moved into the popular culture with the advent of the penny press.

The significant changes in our society as the United States was transformed into a truly industrial nation between the end of the Civil War and the turn of the century brought about many changes in American journalism, including the era of sensationalism, or yellow journalism.

Twentieth-century newspapers, for the most part, have attempted to blend objectivity and social responsibility. This era also has seen the development of electronic news media, interpretative reporting, investigative reporting, advocacy journalism, ''new journalism'' and specialized newspapers.

Despite the role news media play in our democratic society, it must be kept in mind that they are businesses and that business decisions play an important role in their operation.

Unlike other mass media, most newspapers have resisted the trend toward specialization (other than local or regional specialization). However, there are some specialized newspapers, mostly religious and ethnic publications.

Wire services play an important role in gathering news and information for the mass media. The two largest American wire services are the Associated Press and United Press International. The other dominant worldwide news sources are AFP, Reuters and Tass, headquartered in Paris, London and Moscow, respectively.

Individual biases and other problems play a role in making mass communication a complex activity. Although the various functions of the media—to inform, entertain, influence, advertise and transmit culture—are criticized, the most severely criticized is the function to inform. Reasons for this are that people (1) tend to blame the messenger for unpleasant information, (2) fail to understand the *watchdog* function of the media, (3) believe the myth that the mass media dwell only on bad news and (4) bring their own biases into the information-sharing process.

THOUGHT QUESTIONS

1   In your opinion, why did the *National* sports daily fail? Does its demise signal difficulties for newspapers to enter the stage of specialization?

2   What other factors—besides government restrictions—do you think were responsible for it taking so long to establish newspapers in the American colonies?

3   How did each of the four eras of American newspaper journalism differ from each other?

4   The underground press era of the 1960s failed as a serious movement to take newspapers into the stage of specialization. Do you think we will see another such movement soon? If so, what will be the social forces stimulating the movement?

5   If you were a newspaper publisher in a local community, what types of stories and issues would you cover to make the publication appeal to young people?

NOTES

1. Peter Burke, *Popular Culture in Early Modern Europe* (New York: Harper Torchbooks, 1978), p. 264.

2. George Henry Payne, *History of Journalism in the United States* (Westport, Conn.: Greenwood Press, 1970), p. 40.

3. Quoted in Warren K. Agee, Phillip H. Ault and Edwin Emery, *Introduction to Mass Communications,* 9th ed. (New York: Harper & Row, 1988), p. 67.

4. Frank Luther Mott, *American Journalism: A History 1690–1960,* 3rd ed. (New York: Macmillan, 1962), p. 49.

5. Michael Schudson, *Discovering the News: A Social History of American Newspapers* (New York: Basic Books, 1978), pp. 50–56.

6. Agee, Ault and Emery, p. 83.

7. Ibid., p. 85.

8. Quoted in Edwin Emery, *The Press and America: An Interpretive History of the Mass Media,* 3rd ed. (Englewood Cliffs, N.J.: Prentice Hall, 1972), p. 311.

9. W. Phillips Davison, James Boylan and Frederick T. C. Yu, *Mass Media: Systems and Effects* (New York: Praeger, 1976), p. 15.

10. *U.S. Industrial Outlook, 1990* (Washington, D.C.: U.S. Government Printing Office, 1990), p. 48–3.

11. "End of Herald Examiner," *Los Angeles Times,* Nov. 2, 1989, p. B–4.

12. Michael Massing, "The Libel Chill: How Cold Is It Out There?" *Columbia Journalism Review* (May–June 1985), pp. 31–43.

13. Tom Goldstein, *The News at Any Cost: How Journalists Compromise Their Ethics to Shape the News* (New York: Simon & Schuster, 1985), p. 83.

ADDITIONAL READING

Boyd-Barrett, Oliver. *The International News Agencies.* Beverly Hills, Calif.: Sage, 1980.

Carlson, Oliver. *The Man Who Made News: James Gordon Bennett.* New York: Duell, Sloan & Pearce, 1942.

Chancellor, John, and Mears, Walter R. *The News Business.* New York: Harper & Row, 1983.

Glessing, Robert. *The Underground Press in America.* Bloomington: Indiana University Press, 1970.

Janowitz, Morris. *The Community Press in an Urban Setting.* New York: Free Press, 1967.

Liebling, A. J. *The Press.* New York: Pantheon, 1981.

Manoff, Robert, and Schudson, Michael, eds. *Reading the News: A Pantheon Guide to Popular Culture.* New York: Pantheon, 1986.

Mott, Frank Luther. *The News in America.* Cambridge, Mass.: Harvard University Press, 1952.

Peck, Abe. *Uncovering the Sixties: The Life and Times of the Underground Press*. New York: Pantheon, 1985.

Pickett, Calder M. *Voices of the Past*. Columbus, Ohio: Grid, 1977.

Rivers, William L. *News in Print*. New York: Harper & Row, 1984.

Sim, John Cameron. *The Grass Roots Press: America's Community Newspapers*. Ames: Iowa State University Press, 1969.

Swanberg, W. A. *Citizen Hearst*. New York: Scribner's, 1961.

———. *Pulitzer*. New York: Scribner's, 1967.

Van Deusen, Glyndon G. *Horace Greeley: Nineteenth Century Crusader*. Philadelphia: University of Pennsylvania Press, 1953.

Wolseley, Ronald E. *The Black Press, U.S.A.* Ames: Iowa State University Press, 1971.

DEVELOPMENT OF ELECTRONIC MEDIA

PART THREE

Geena Davis and Susan Sarandon sparked controversy in their starring roles in **Thelma & Louise** *after the movie was released in 1991. While some critics claimed the file was antifeminist, others felt it was filled with "male bashing" feminism. Most of the negative discussion seemed to come from male reviewers. Regardless of the wide-ranging interpretations, the movie generated a great deal of media attention and met with box-office success.*

MOTION PICTURES: CULTURAL REFLECTIONS

*People tell me
that the movies
should be more
like real life. I
disagree. It is
real life that
should be more
like the movies.*
—Walter
Winchell

"Why fix it if it isn't broken?" That was the reaction of Motion Picture Association of America's president Jack Valenti when in the summer of 1990 he found himself confronted with controversy over his motion picture rating system.

Valenti—who launched the rating system in 1968 to shift the burden of censorship from the industry to the audience—was under pressure to come up with a new rating for adult-oriented films that carried the skull-and-crossbones "X."

Valenti, however, changed his tune in September of 1990 when the MPAA voted to change the X designation to NC-17, meaning no one under 17 admitted.

CULTURAL HISTORY OF MOTION PICTURES

ELITIST	POPULAR	SPECIALIZED		
▓			1888	First motion-picture camera developed in Thomas A. Edison's laboratory.
	▓		1895	Lumière brothers start projecting motion pictures in a Paris café.
	▓		1896	Films shown in vaudeville theaters.
	▓		1903	Edwin S. Porter's *Great Train Robbery,* first American film to tell a complete story.
	▓		1905–10	Era of the nickelodeon, movie theaters that charged a nickel for admission.
	▓		1912	Mack Sennett begins Keystone Company, which specialized in slapstick comedy.
	▓		1915	D. W. Griffith releases *Birth of a Nation,* first full-length film to have an impact on the culture.
	▓		1917	Charlie Chaplin becomes first entertainer to earn $1 million a year.
	▓		1923	Lee De Forest begins experimenting with sound motion pictures.
	▓		1927	*The Jazz Singer* ushers in talking motion-picture era.
	▓		1930	Motion-picture industry tightens its code of standards to avoid censorship.
	▓		1930s–40s	Golden Age of movies; movies provide an escape from Depression and war.
	▓		1939	*Gone With the Wind* breaks box-office records.
	▓		1941	Orson Welles's *Citizen Kane* is released; voted greatest classic of all times in 1987.

The problem developed when the hard-core pornographic film industry adopted the X rating to symbolize its adult-only contents. Most theater chains refused to book X-rated films and many newspapers would not run advertisements for films that carried the rating.

The legitimate film industry found itself cutting out violent and explicitly sexual scenes to avoid the "kiss of death" that an X rating would bring. When serious filmmakers failed to cut deep enough, they found themselves facing the economic ruin that an X rating could bring.

What brought the issue to a head in 1990 was the awarding of X ratings to four films, which although not hard-core pornography, contained adult-intended

CULTURAL HISTORY OF MOTION PICTURES

	ELITIST	POPULAR	SPECIALIZED		
		■		1941–45	Hollywood promotes patriotism during World War II with propaganda films and rousing war movies.
		■		1946	Hollywood's biggest box-office year—$1.7 billion gross income, 87 million Americans attending movies each week.
		■		1947	Red Scare leads to congressional investigation of Hollywood.
		■		1948	Supreme Court requires movie studios to sell their theaters.
		■		1948	Motion-picture audiences decline after television's breakthrough year.
			■	1950s	Hollywood experiments with 3-D, Cinerama, CinemaScope and movies for youth subculture.
			■	1960s	Movie industry abandons self-censorship and adopts a movie-rating system.
			■	1960s	Youth, sex and violence help sell movies to new audiences.
			■	1970s	Disaster films become popular with movie audiences.
			■	1977	George Lucas's *Star Wars* is released; its computerized special effects give movies a new image and excitement.
			■	1980s	Video movies expand industry revenues; multiplexes replace large-screen theaters.
			■	1990	*Dick Tracy* becomes a box-office hit, another in a string of comic strip movies.
			■	1990	Movies featuring Julia Roberts (*Pretty Woman*) grossed $278 million, making her the all-time box-office movie star.

themes and scenes. The films were Peter Greenaway's *The Cook, The Thief, His Wife & Her Lover,* John McKnaughton's *Henry: Portrait of a Serial Killer,* Pedro Almodovar's *Tie Me Up, Tie Me Down,* and Zalman King's *Wild Orchid.*

Earlier in the history of the MPAA rating system, several X-rated films were box office successes—*Midnight Cowboy, Last Tango in Paris* and *Clockwork Orange.* However, by the 1990s, the rating had become associated with hard-core pornography.

This was the second time in the 22-year history of the rating system that controversy forced a change in the rating designations. In 1984 there was a storm of protests over the PG-rated *Indiana Jones and the Temple of Doom* because of a

■ When explicit but not pornographic movies like *The Cook, The Thief, His Wife & Her Lover* received X ratings in 1990, the push began to find a new category for serious movies with adult content. The result was NC-17.

scene where a beating heart was ripped out of the chest of a man. The MPAA responded to the controversy by adding a PG-13 category designating that children under 13 should not be allowed to see the film.

The controversy over the rating system is just one of many in the history of motion pictures. The profound role that this medium has played in our culture has made its content the subject of much discussion and concern. This industrial-age mass communication medium was the first to move almost immediately into the popular stage of the EPS cycle. Starting out as a mechanical medium and later becoming electronically operated, motion pictures also became one of the first electronic media to be forced by changing media technologies into the stage of specialization.

EARLY HISTORY

In the late nineteenth century, as city dwellers were experiencing more leisure time, they began looking for new pastimes beyond reading, the ballpark and vaudeville (see Chapter 2). This was the industrial age, and mechanical inventions of all kinds were dramatically changing the American way of life. It was only natural that some inventors turned their attention to developing mechanical devices for leisure use.

Edison.   The leading American inventor of leisure technology was Thomas A. Edison, probably best known for inventing the light bulb. But he was also responsible for devising the phonograph in the 1870s, and by the late 1880s he was trying to come up with something similar for the eye. The concept behind motion pictures, however, actually dates back to the second century A.D., when the Greek astronomer Ptolemy discovered that the human eye retains an image on the retina for a moment after the image disappears. This is called persistence of vision. Over the years many people theorized that a series of still pictures of similar yet slightly different images could give the illusion of movement if flashed before the eye quickly, because persistence of vision would fill in the gaps. Experimentation with this theory took place in Edison's laboratory until his assistant, William Kennedy Dickson, constructed the first crude motion-picture camera.

The first commercial use of motion pictures was a kinetoscope—a four-foot-tall box that one person at a time could peer into to see a series of still photos "move" across a light source. Edison unveiled the kinetoscope to the world in 1894, and the "peep show" became a popular attraction in penny arcades. One of the first films made by the Edison Co. for the arcades was a 30-second strip called *Anabelle*. Sex and violence soon became the predominant theme for these arcade films.

Projection.   In 1895 two brothers in France, Auguste and Louis Lumière, perfected Edison's invention by developing a projection device. They produced films and began showing them for an admission price in the basement of a Paris café. The motion-picture industry was born.

In the United States the novelty of Edison's kinetoscope soon began to wear off. In the meantime, two inventors of a movie-projection system known as the vitascope, Thomas Armat and Francis Jenkins, joined forces with Edison, and in April 1896 motion pictures began showing in vaudeville houses, supplementing the live entertainment.

Vaudeville theaters remained the primary showplace for motion pictures until about 1905, when nickelodeons took over. These were motion-picture parlors where admission cost a nickel. The average length of a motion picture was about 12½ minutes, and most programs featured two to three films. By 1909 there were nearly ten thousand nickelodeons in the United States.

Early Classics.   Another major innovator was the Frenchman Georges Méliès, who began producing films in 1896 and soon became an international distributor. He introduced the concept of special effects. Méliès's most famous film, *A Trip to the Moon* (1902), showed a group of scientists and chorus girls launching a rocket to the moon. The rocket hit the "eye" of the man in the moon, and space travelers encountered moon men. The special effects in the film, although not up to today's standards, were fascinating for the time and included the earth rising on the moon's horizon and moon people disappearing in smoke.

But the father of the story film was not Méliès but the American film producer Edwin S. Porter, an Edison Company camera man. In his most famous film, *The*

Great Train Robbery (1903), he developed new editing techniques to piece together different scenes to create a story line. The film—filled with gunfights, chases and action as a band of desperadoes hold up a westbound train—was only 12 minutes long, but it set standards for drama and excitement that would become basic to American films for years to come. Incidentally, it also introduced the enduring Western theme into American filmmaking. The significance of *The Great Train Robbery* has been summed up this way:

> For years The Great Train Robbery *was the nickelodeon's most widely exhibited picture and it is said to have insured the permanence of the movies. It became the bible for all film makers until Griffith's films further developed Porter's editing principle. The efforts of all movie makers to imitate its form and content stimulated the industry as nothing— not even Méliès' films—had ever done before.*[1]

The next milestone in the development of American motion pictures was *Birth of a Nation,* directed by D. W. Griffith and released in 1915. Originally titled *The Clansmen, Birth of a Nation* was a masterpiece that lasted more than three hours. Although all early films were silent, Griffith's film was accompanied by a complete musical score to be performed by a symphony orchestra. The movie impressed the nation and led President Woodrow Wilson to say it was "like writing history with lightning."[2]

Griffith began his career in motion pictures in 1907 as an actor for the Mutoscope and Biograph Company in New York. Because his acting skills were limited, he became a director a year later. He was the first to use close-ups and a variety of camera angles to add emotional impact to his films. Through new editing techniques he showed how emotion and tension could be generated by the length of the scene, with shorter scenes creating greater excitement. An innovator who defied the conventions of moviemaking, Griffith insisted on hiring established stage actors and holding rehearsals. He was also among the first to shoot on location—at San Gabriel Mission outside Los Angeles in 1910.

Birth of a Nation, filmed in Los Angeles, used all of Griffith's innovations in shooting, lighting and editing to capture the emotion of the Civil War. It was the first motion picture to attempt to portray a part of U.S. history in dramatic terms, covering the period from pre–Civil War days through Reconstruction. Griffith, the son of a Confederate officer, had a flawed, sentimental attachment to the old South. His sympathetic portrayal of the Ku Klux Klan and stereotyping of African-Americans offended many. The National Association for the Advancement of Colored People, the president of Harvard University and liberal politicians all damned the work for its bigoted portrayal of African-Americans. Despite this, the movie was a box-office success, and it clearly demonstrated what a dramatic impact this new art form could have on popular culture. As a result of its showing in major cities there were race riots and a rebirth of the Ku Klux Klan in the South.

Griffith was stung by the uproar created by his film. He decided to invest some $2 million of the profits from the film to create a new movie, *Intolerance,* which preached against the evils of bigotry. He reportedly chose the name because he felt that *he* had been a victim of intolerance. Despite high production costs and lavish sets, the film was a box-office flop.

MOVIES AND THE EPS CYCLE

Unlike the print media, motion pictures did not spend a long period in the elite culture before moving into the popular stage of the EPS cycles (see Chapter 1). In fact, there are more culturally elite films today than there were in the early days of motion pictures. A more realistic description of the media progression cycle for motion pictures would be: P-E-P-S cycle.

Both social and economic factors explain why this new medium moved immediately into the popular culture. Silent movies appeared at a time when American cities sheltered large numbers of foreign workers. Even though many of these immigrants spoke no English, they could still enjoy the drama and comedy of silent films: pantomime is a universal language.

In addition to meeting a social need, movies were relatively inexpensive. The first movie houses—the nickelodeons—were inexpensive storefront theaters. Their five-cent admission made the movies affordable for immigrants and others in the popular culture. In fact, their admission price and melodramatic, slapstick acting actually discouraged the elite from attending. It wasn't until after the peak of the nickelodeons in 1909 that efforts were made to attract the elite to the motion picture studios. By the 1920s large palace-like movie theaters were being built. They were modeled after the opera houses and concert halls of the nineteenth century. Between 1920 and 1930, 250 of these magnificent theaters were built. Admission to these theaters usually cost 65 cents (35 cents before 6 P.M.) and the elite started attending films often for the theater experience rather than for the movies being shown.

THE RISE OF COMEDY

In the early days of the motion pictures, comedy came to play a special role in the socialization of immigrants and other workers who were often the victims of exploitation. It had a special appeal for this new work force of the industrial society because it gave them an opportunity to laugh at the disappointments, frustrations and confrontations of daily living.

Sennett.   One of the first to make a major contribution to motion-picture comedy was Mack Sennett. Sennett, who worked for Griffith in his early days in the film industry, was the son of Irish immigrants. In 1912 he struck out on his own, founding the Keystone Film Company. Sennett fascinated his audiences by showing them the new twentieth-century America. Typical scenes were of automobiles beginning to replace the horse and buggy, dusty roads, policemen in slapstick chase scenes, men with large moustaches and women wearing full-length dresses and huge hats. Sennett's comedy effectively brought to the screen the visual and

■ Jackie Coogan, shown here with Charlie Chaplin in *The Kid* (1921), launched his acting career as a child star with this performance and began a trend for child stars to follow. This classic comedy evoked tears and laughter to entertain movie audiences.

physical elements of burlesque, and his Keystone Kops became a Hollywood trademark.

Chaplin. An English stage comedian, Charlie Chaplin came to this country in 1913 to tour vaudeville stages with a music-hall act. Although leery of the new medium of film, he was enticed to start working for Sennett at Keystone for an attractive salary of $150 a week. One year later he signed a contract with the Essanay Company of Chicago for $1,250 a week, plus a $10,000 bonus for signing and a guarantee of $75,000 for 1915 (a huge amount of money in those days). The contract allowed him to act, direct and produce his comedies. By 1917 Chaplin was making more than $1 million a year, a figure that was almost incomprehensible at a time when many people earned less than a thousand dollars a year and new automobiles sold for several hundred dollars.

In 1915 Chaplin produced *The Tramp,* in which he played a vagabond in baggy pants who comes to the rescue of a pretty girl. The tramp and his girl were the heroes of many of the Chaplin movies that followed. While giving people an opportunity to laugh at the plight of the downtrodden in society, Chaplin also used comedy to make social commentary on good and evil in our society. Only relatively few had prospered from the years of unfettered industrial expansion, while a vast and growing army of workers struggled to cope with low salaries and harsh working conditions. Chaplin's films depicted the dark and often cruel distances between the haves and have-nots.

Chaplin became the first twentieth-century superstar. Millions of fans rushed to novelty shops to purchase mechanical dolls and plaster Tramp statuettes in his image, much as later generations have bought Mouseketeer, Beatle, *Star Wars* and Teenage Mutant Ninja Turtle paraphernalia.[3]

Laurel and Hardy. Other popular comedy stars in the silent-film era were Stan Laurel and Oliver Hardy, who, in the Sennett and Chaplin style, portrayed the downtrodden against the world. Although they started out separately, they got together in 1926 and remained a popular movie comedy team well into the sound era. Indeed, of all the comedians from the silent-film era, they were the most successful in making the switch to sound motion pictures.

Keaton and Lloyd. Although not a team, two other master comedians of the silent era were Buster Keaton and Harold Lloyd. Keaton came close to rivaling Chaplin in his ability to provide funny and serious insights into human relationships and to dramatize the conflict between individuals and the immense industrial society that surrounded them. Like Chaplin, Lloyd was small in physical stature, which was a disadvantage as the characters he portrayed struggled against various misfortunes in a hostile world.

SOUND JOINS MOTION

The genres of comedy and drama helped the American film industry flourish. The American film industry moved permanently to Hollywood, California, where good weather and wide open spaces allowed for year-round outdoor moviemaking. Since World War I inhibited European filmmakers from developing this new industry, American moviemakers took the lead. By the early 1920s, Hollywood was producing three-quarters of the world's films.

By 1925, 46 million Americans were attending movies weekly. The American film industry had become big business. Movies made in Hollywood set standards of excellence throughout the world. This was the decade that sound was synchronized with film and a new medium emerged.

Early Efforts. For 30 years inventors had attempted to connect sound to motion pictures. Dickson, Edison's assistant, claimed to have produced a rough synchronization of word and picture as early as 1889. Others experimented with synchronizing recording discs with motion pictures in France between 1896 and 1900. However, live sound was preferred during the nickelodeon days in the United States. Pianos, organs or trios of musicians provided musical accompaniment to many films. Actors sometimes recited the lines behind the screen. Sometimes narrators explained or commented on the scenes in the movies. (Oliver Hardy's first job in cinema, incidentally, was singing in a quartet behind the screen at an Atlanta nickelodeon.)

Serious problems continued to exist with efforts to put sound and motion together. Separate disc machines, such as the Vitaphone, could easily get out of sync with the film. After World War I, three German inventors discovered a way of putting sound directly on film using light beams. In the United States, Dr. Lee De Forest developed a similar sound-on-film process. De Forest, whom many consider to be the father of American radio (see Chapter 9), started demonstrating sound motion pictures in 1923.

The Jazz Singer. However, it wasn't until audiences heard Al Jolson sing "Mammy" on screen in *The Jazz Singer* (1927) that people realized that sound motion pictures were really possible. Produced by Warner Brothers, a small movie company, the film was an instant success and changed the movie business forever.

In 1930 the trade paper *Variety* summed up the impact of sound this way: ". . . it didn't do any more to the industry than turn it upside down, shake the entire bag of tricks from its pocket and advance Warner Brothers from last place to first in the league."

The public's rapid acceptance of sound initially caught the film industry off guard, but soon all the studios were scrambling to produce "talkies." By 1930 the silent-film era was history, and so was its universal language of pantomime. Also at an end were the careers of actors and actresses with unsuitable voices or accents.

During this period some studios also experimented with Technicolor sequences in a few of their movies, though complete Technicolor films did not become common until the mid-1930s.

Cultural Changes. The 1920s were a period of immense technological and social change in American culture. The automobile, radio, advertising and the motion picture combined to change American lifestyles and help usher in an age of "New Morality." Many films glamorized the fast and loose life of the Roaring '20s. They showed men and women dancing, smoking and drinking in public, activities previously considered unacceptable, particularly for women. The movies helped break down these taboos and changed cultural attitudes. Today critics note that since the 1920s there has been an increase in the number of cases of lung cancer and alcoholism among women.

A number of scandals in Hollywood during the 1920s led some to refer to the movie capital as a "twentieth century Babylon."[4] A director named William Desmond Taylor was murdered; actor Wallace Reid, on the screen a symbol of virtuous young American manhood, died of a narcotics overdose; and comedian Fatty Arbuckle was charged with manslaughter in the death of a girl at a party in his hotel suite.

Self-Censorship. In this era of Prohibition, when many people felt that government should police public morals, it was not surprising that many cried out for some form of government censorship of the motion-picture industry. To forestall such an effort, the industry established its own organization to draw up a code of ethics. The Motion Picture Producers and Distributors of America (MPPDA) was founded in 1922. Its first president was Will H. Hays, who was a former postmaster general, the chairman of the Republican National Committee and an elder in the Presbyterian church. His credentials gave the office the political and moral stature needed to avert government censorship.

The MPPDA established a list of forbidden subjects that corresponded to the most frequent targets of critics. In 1927 this list was adopted as the Code of the Motion Picture Industry. Criticism continued, however, primarily from the Catholic Church. In 1930 the MPPDA, now commonly called the "Hays Office," tightened the code to spell out more clearly what could not be shown in motion pictures. Depiction of immoral behavior and nudity was still permissible, so long as it was made clear that such behavior was wrong and that those who indulged in it were punished. According to film historian Arthur Knight, "The studios could present six reels of ticket-selling sinfulness if, in the seventh reel, all the sinners came to a bad end."[5]

The fast and "loose" life portrayed in movies eventually led to the Catholic Church's formation of a Legion of Decency, which advocated boycotts of motion pictures that the Church felt were indecent.[6] Protestant and Jewish groups backed the Legion's efforts, and Hollywood felt the impact of the boycotts on a national scale.

The Hays Office responded to this pressure in 1934 by issuing a stringent set of rules, the "Code to Govern the Making of Motion and Talking Pictures," to be enforced by a new Production Code Administration (PCA). Movies released without PCA approval were fined $25,000. These self-imposed guidelines prohibited profanity, replaced skimpy-dress scenes with full clothing and restricted bedroom scenes to married men and women only (and even they had to be shown in separate beds). Not only were such words as *God, hell* and *sex* banned, but so were everyday slang terms like *guts, nuts* and *louse*. The Hays Office even got involved in timing the length of screen kisses. The movies became so pure during this period that there was a major national furor in 1939 when Clark Gable used the word *damn* in his now-immortal line, "Frankly, my dear, I don't give a damn," at the end of *Gone With the Wind*.

A WAY OF LIFE

In the 1930s and 1940s, moviegoing was not merely a form of entertainment but a way of life. People no longer went to see a particular picture, they "went to the movies" much as many people today sit down for an evening of watching TV.

Big Studios and Stars. To serve the rapidly growing audience, large motion-picture studios developed. MGM, Paramount, Warner Brothers, 20th Century-Fox and RKO all put actors and actresses under contract and made them into "movie stars." Some of the all-time greats were Mary Pickford, Douglas Fairbanks, W. C. Fields, the Marx Brothers, Gary Cooper, Jimmy Stewart, Clark Gable, Clara Bow, Jean Harlow, Spencer Tracy, Katharine Hepburn, John Wayne, James Cagney, Fred Astaire, Ginger Rogers, Humphrey Bogart, Rita Hayworth, Joan Crawford, Edward G. Robinson and Judy Garland.

Studios started mass-producing motion pictures. Since each major studio owned its own chain of theaters across the country, it had to produce one feature

■ Vivien Leigh (pictured with leading man Clark Gable) won the Academy Award for best actress in David O. Selznick's *Gone With the Wind*. This blockbuster movie broke box-office records in 1939 and won the Academy Award for best picture.

film and one "grade B" movie (an inexpensive film for second billing) for each of the 52 weeks in a year. Cartoons and newsreels were also needed to round out the evening's entertainment.

Great Depression.   Offering a complete evening of entertainment for the price of one show became very important during the Great Depression of the 1930s. Although there was a decline in attendance in 1934, more than 60 percent of the American public found a way to afford to go to the movies during the Depression. The lavish spectaculars of this period helped people forget the dreary reality of daily living and escape into a make-believe world created by Hollywood.

Trends and Celebrities.   Even in these lean years, movies played their role in keeping our consumer culture alive. For example, one of the top box-office stars of the decade was a curly-haired little girl named Shirley Temple. The star of 21 relentlessly upbeat films, she spurred the sale of Shirley Temple dolls, books and clothing.

What the stars did influenced everything in our popular culture from what people wore to how they did their hair. Peroxide hair-rinse sales skyrocketed in the 1930s, thanks to Jean Harlow, Carole Lombard and Mae West and movies like *Platinum Blonde* (1931). In 1934 Clark Gable nearly destroyed the undershirt industry when he took off his shirt and exposed a bare chest in *It Happened One Night*. Soon men all over the nation were following suit and abandoning their longstanding habit of wearing undershirts.

Motion-picture stars, beginning with Charlie Chaplin, became the first "celebrities" of our popular culture. Celebrities have replaced political and military heros as the objects of public adulation. Although heroes do things, celebrities tend to be passive objects, whose popularity is created and maintained by the media. According to sociologist Daniel Boorstin, a celebrity is "a person who is well known for his well-knownness."[7]

Film Genres.   In addition to the traditional film genres—like the Western, which began with *The Great Train Robbery*—a variety of new ones developed during the 1930s. One of the most popular was the gangster movie, which depicted the typical criminal activity of the Prohibition era (1920–1933). Since many normally law-abiding citizens violated the law and continued to drink, a large underground developed to supply their need. Gangsters got involved in the manufacture, distribution and sale of alcohol.

This world was graphically recreated in such films as *Little Caesar* (1930), *The Public Enemy* (1931) *City Streets* (1931) and *Scarface* (1932), which was based on the exploits of Chicago gangster Al Capone. These were followed by tough-talking cop movies and prison films. Although most of these movies depicted the gangster in an unfavorable light, some glamorized his get-rich-quick image.

One of the problems with the Western and gangster film genres was the fact that as Hollywood exported its films, they created a distorted view of American culture. For example, until very recently many foreigners believed that the United States was a land where gangsters ruled the cities and cowboys and Indians fought on the prairies. (These stereotypes have now been replaced by perceptions of wealth and ruthlessness, following the export of such TV shows as *Dallas* and *Dynasty*.)

Following the election of Franklin D. Roosevelt to the presidency in 1932 and the repeal of Prohibition the following year, the mood of the country seemed to be improving. This upswing was reflected in a series of musical extravaganzas that were produced in Hollywood as alternatives to the gangster films. Three Busby Berkeley musicals, for example, were 1933 box-office successes: *42nd Street*, *Gold Diggers of 1933* and *Footlight Parade*. These surrealistically choreographed fantasies allowed the audience to become absorbed in the singing, dancing and comedy depictions of backstage show-business life.

Also popular during this period were a variety of comedies ranging from the slapstick of the Marx Brothers in *Duck Soup* (1933); to more sophisticated, fast-paced romantic comedies such as *It Happened One Night* (1934), starring Clark Gable and Claudette Colbert; *Twentieth Century* (1934), starring John Barrymore and Carole Lombard; and *Bringing Up Baby* (1938), with Katharine Hepburn and Cary Grant. *It Happened One Night*, about a journalist in professional and amorous pursuit of a runaway heiress, established the romantic comedy as a popular genre for the rest of the 1930s.

■ Orson Welles portrayed a newspaper tycoon from the yellow journalism era in *Citizen Kane* (1941). The tycoon's idiosyncrasies resembled those of William Randolph Hearst, and Hearst threatened to sue the producers. Welles introduced many new sound and camera techniques to the film industry, and by 1987 *Citizen Kane* was voted by movie critics as the best motion picture of all time.

Hollywood also developed the film series, featuring continuing episodes much like modern television. These included the Andy Hardy pictures, Charlie Chan films, Flash Gordon, Henry Aldrich, the Thin Man and *Young Doctor Kildare*.

The fantasies depicted in the films of this period gave Americans hope and a way to cope with the harsh realities of the Depression. Many films had strong moral themes and showed that decent, honest people could overcome obstacles. The films all had a warm, happy ending. One of the best at turning out these films was Frank Capra, who directed *It Happened One Night* (1934), *Mr. Deeds Goes to Town* (1936), *You Can't Take It With You* (1938) and *Mr. Smith Goes to Washington* (1939). One of his all-time classics, *It's a Wonderful Life* (1946) starring Jimmy Stewart, is still shown on television each year during the Christmas season. Its heart-warming message is that everyone's life has value because of the other lives it touches.

When the United States entered World War II in December 1941, Hollywood was there to rouse patriotic enthusiasm. Numerous propaganda films were produced during the war, while entertainment movies showed the Americans triumphing over their Japanese and Nazi enemies. Such movies as *30 Seconds over Tokyo* helped reassure Americans that they were winning the war and that the cultural myth of an indestructible American spirit was a reality.

Although Hollywood mass-produced many motion pictures during the Depression and war years, it managed to turn out a number of classics. Among the all-time greats were *Gone With the Wind,* which broke box-office records in 1939, and Orson Welles's *Citizen Kane* (1941), which did not do well at the box office at first but was later—in 1987—voted the best film of all time.

THE GIANT IS CRIPPLED

In 1946 the motion-picture business was on top of the world, with 87 million Americans going to the movies each week (about half as many go every *month* now). The industry was putting out between five and six hundred movies a year. This was the industry's peak box-office year; the American film business grossed $1.7 billion domestically. However, during the next two years, 1947 and 1948, three events rocked the industry and toppled it from its peak of success.

Red Scare. In 1947 a subcommittee of the House Committee on Un-American Activities (HUAC) alleged that members of the Communist party had infiltrated the movie industry and were using films to disseminate Communist propaganda.

After World War II ended in 1945, a Cold War broke out between the United States and the Soviet Union. As Americans saw country after country in Eastern Europe being occupied by the Soviet army, rumors ran rampant that the Soviet Union was attempting to take over our country as well, with the help of American Communists. The government responded by conducting congressional investigations to see whether national security had been breached, and the motion-picture industry became one of the targets for their inquiries.

The HUAC hearings, which began on October 20, 1947, led to the fining and imprisonment of 10 Hollywood writers who refused to answer the committee's questions about their alleged Communist party affiliation. The writers—who came to be known as the "Hollywood 10"—were also blacklisted by motion-picture executives, who feared that if they took no action the government, supported by public opinion, would take control and censor their industry. The blacklisting, which spread far beyond the original Hollywood 10, lasted for more than a decade. Many blacklisted entertainers and writers went without work for a dozen or more years.

The Hearst newspapers gave the hearings major coverage and called for restrictive laws: "The need is for FEDERAL CENSORSHIP OF THE MOTION PICTURES. The Constitution PERMITS it. The law SANCTIONS it. The safety and welfare of America DEMAND it."[8] Many Americans supported this point of view.

In fact, many Hollywood studios were more than willing to accommodate the new public mood. In the late 1940s the industry turned out such anti-Communist movies as *I Was a Communist for the FBI, I Led Three Lives, I Married a Communist* and *The Red Menace,* films which only helped to fuel the anti-Communist terror that gripped the nation.

A few films, however, subtly criticized the witchhunting of this period. The most successful was *High Noon* (1952), a Western that offered an allegory on McCarthyism.[9] The film, starring Gary Cooper, told the story of a courageous marshal who when facing the threat of attack from four gunmen found his friends and fellow town folks turning their back on him. Like many people during the witchhunting days, "they didn't want to place their own lives at risk by getting involved." Another, to be produced long after that period, was Woody Allen's *The Front* (1976), which told the story of Hollywood writers who had to get their work accepted under another name because they had been blacklisted.

■ Humphrey Bogart and Lauren Bacall (right) were among many Hollywood stars who appeared before the House Committee on Un-American Activities (HUAC) during its investigation of alleged Communist infiltration of the motion-picture industry.

Antitrust.   The next setback for the motion-picture industry came in 1948, when the U.S. Supreme Court ruled that the major studios were operating an illegal monopoly on the production, distribution and exhibition of films (*U.S.* v. *Paramount Pictures, Inc., et al.*). At this time, for example, Paramount owned 1,239 theaters, 20th Century-Fox 517, and Warner Brothers 507. The five major studios owned 77 percent of the first-run movie houses in the 25 largest American metropolitan areas.

The Supreme Court decision forced the major studios to sell all their theaters. Warner Brothers sold its Stanley Warner Theaters, MGM got rid of its Loews Theaters, RKO divested itself of RKO Theaters, 20th Century-Fox sold its National Theaters and Paramount Pictures severed its connection with Paramount Theaters. No longer did the studios have guaranteed outlets for their movies; from now on they would have to compete in the marketplace to get theaters to show their films. This opened up movie production to many independent film producers and reduced the dominance of the large studios.

Television.   But the greatest blow of all was yet to come. In 1948 two major radio networks began the process of transforming television from a rich man's toy to a new mass medium for the popular culture. At first major studio executives ignored TV and told themselves that it was a passing fad. After all, they thought, no tiny television screen could compete with the larger-than-life "silver screens" in motion-picture theaters. But they were quickly proved wrong, as more and more people chose the convenience of staying home to watch the free entertainment. One factor encouraging home viewing was a shift in demographics. After the war many Americans started moving from the cities to the suburbs, and most movie theaters were concentrated in the big urban centers.

Television also hurt movie viewing indirectly by creating new interests in the popular culture. Telecasts of team sports like baseball and football stimulated an interest in professional and collegiate sporting events. And TV programs featuring such previously elite individualistic sports as golf, tennis and skiing helped create an interest in these activities. Soon many more people were spending some of their leisure time enjoying these sports.

Fight for Survival. Movie attendance continued to decline in the 1950s. Weaker studios, such as Republic, Allied Artists and Monogram, soon collapsed. Others followed. While the number of television sets in homes was increasing 400 percent between 1948 and 1960, weekly theater attendance declined 50 percent. The demand for the second features eventually vanished altogether.

The motion-picture industry fought back by introducing a variety of technical gimmicks to attract audiences. For example, studios began experimenting with three-dimensional (3-D) films (which required special glasses, given to people at the theater, to view them). In 1952 alone Hollywood released such 3-D movies as *Bwana Devil, House of Wax, Creature from the Black Lagoon, The French Line, Kiss Me Kate* and *Murders in the Rue Morgue*. Audiences left their TV sets to experience the visual illusion of knives, arrows, avalanches and chemicals being hurled at them, but they quickly tired of the novelty. The industry even experimented with ''smell-o-vision,'' where smells were piped into theaters. But movie audiences continued to dwindle.

Finally, the industry introduced Cinerama, a process of using three projectors and three screens to wrap around the audience. Whereas 3-D had attempted to bring the picture into the audience, Cinerama put the audience into the picture. Cinerama previously had been used for special-effect travelogues but not by Hollywood to tell a story. An MGM film editor, Harold Kress, disputed the claim of Cinerama executives that this special-effects flim could not be edited. After he proved that a powerful story could be told in this new film technology, Hollywood talent banded together and produced the first Cinerama story—*How the West Was Won*—as a benefit for a Santa Monica, California, hospital. Many major Hollywood stars appeared *gratis* in the film. It was a box office success in an era of low movie-theater attendance—and it won Kress his first Academy Award for film editing.

A second Cinerama production—*Brothers Grimm*—lost money, and Hollywood soon abandoned the new technology. Cinerama required larger screens as well as extra theater personnel to operate the three projectors and sophisticated sound equipment that gave the film its unique qualities. It was just too expensive to be practical.

The third gimmick the industry tried was CinemaScope. It too used a larger screen, but it was more successful than the other two techniques because it required no special glasses and only one projection system. The first CinemaScope film was *The Robe* (1953), a Biblical epic starring Richard Burton. It was followed by other large-scale, expensive films, such as *The Ten Commandments* (1956) and *Ben Hur* (1959). Some CinemaScope features were successful; others were not.

■ Three-dimensional (3-D) films, which required special glasses to view them, were introduced in the 1950s in an attempt to bring movie audiences lost to television back to the theaters.

The film industry's struggle to regain its audiences from television was also partially responsible for the almost total conversion to color motion pictures in the 1950s. Although a few successful color films had been produced in the 1930s, including *Gone With the Wind* and *The Wizard of Oz* in 1939, color shooting was slow and expensive. Black-and-white films thus remained the rule rather than the exception until the more competitive years of the 1950s.

Despite all of these efforts to attract back its mass audiences, the motion-picture industry was finding that the popular cultural interests had changed and that the new medium of television was more than a gimmick—it had become a new way of life. By the mid-1950s the film industry decided to end its boycott and permit old films to be shown on television. Some companies even rented out their movie studios for TV productions.

YOUTH, SEX, VIOLENCE AND SPECIAL EFFECTS

The motion-picture industry now realized that, in order to survive as a mass-communication medium in the age of television, it had to move from the popular stage of the EPS cycle to specialization. This change in focus began in the mid-

■ Youth films found a niche in the American culture and propelled such stars as James Dean (shown here in a scene from *Rebel Without a Cause*) to folk-hero status.

1950s, when the industry discovered that, though many adults were staying home to watch television, there was a potential audience among young people, who wanted to get out of the house and socialize.

Youth.   Social-commentary films about young people, such as *Blackboard Jungle* (1955) and *Rebel Without a Cause* (1955), appealed to the young and made box-office idols out of young actors. For example, James Dean, an unknown actor from a small town in Indiana, became a teenage idol overnight after appearing in *Rebel Without a Cause*. Although he starred in only three hit movies before his death in a traffic accident in 1955, Dean remains a legend today. His memory has been kept alive in our popular culture in a number of ways: television stations have continued to show his movies, video stores feature his films and poster companies still sell blow-ups of publicity stills from his movies.

The youth-oriented movies of the 1950s catered to a new American subculture—the youth subculture. These films portrayed the restlessness and rebellion of young people in a sympathetic way that they could easily relate to. Also developing at this time was a youth-oriented form of popular music—rock-'n'-roll (see Chapter 11). In fact, the theme song for *Blackboard Jungle* was the first rock-'n'-roll hit of the 1950s, *Rock Around the Clock*.

The 1950s were also the years for such low-budget films as *I Was a Teenage Werewolf, I Was a Teenage Frankenstein, Joy Ride* and *Riot in Juvenile Prison*. Then as now, horror and violence were popular genres in the youth subculture. Braving a horror movie became a rite of passage for young men, while their dates screamed in terror. (Surveys show that among dating couples the male usually chooses the movie; among older married moviegoers, the choice generally falls to the wife.)

A string of beach movies followed, featuring teenagers enjoying life at the beach, with all of its sun, bikinis, surfing, volleyball and romance. These films reflected the party flavor of the new youth subculture and featured similar plots with such titles as *Beach Blanket Bingo* and *How to Stuff a Wild Bikini*. Movies featuring the new rock-'n'-roll stars of the period, like Elvis Presley and the Beatles, were also box-office successes of the 1960s.

By the latter part of the 1960s, the influence of the youth "counterculture" began to be felt. Some films were now featuring antiheroes—social misfits, deviates or outlaws who usually lost out in the end, but for whom the audience felt sympathy. The youth subculture had become anti-Establishment, opposing the war in Vietnam and defying the laws against drugs. Thus when other lawbreakers, like the notorious bank-robbing team of *Bonnie and Clyde* (1967), were portrayed as heroes, the film was a hit with youths. Other films that glorified lawlessness were *The Dirty Dozen* (1967), *Cool Hand Luke* (1967), *Easy Rider* (1969) and *Butch Cassidy and the Sundance Kid* (1969). More sophisticated anti-Establishment films that satirized the "hypocrisy" of middle-class values included *The Graduate* (1967), *Bob and Carol and Ted and Alice* (1969) and *Goodbye, Columbus* (1969).

Sex. A major departure for the film industry in the 1960s was the explicit presentation of sexual themes, reflecting the new sexual permissiveness of the time. Since sexual themes were not allowed on television at the time, movie producers saw a golden opportunity. As the sexual genre developed during this period of specialization, a more explicit variety with actual nudity became commonplace as an effective tool to pull people away from their relatively sexless TV sets.

The sexual themes of such films as *Barbarella*, *Midnight Cowboy* and *Carnal Knowledge* helped lure people to the box office. Three hard-core pornography films also became popular during this period: *Deep Throat*, *Behind the Green Door* and *The Devil in Miss Jones*.

Obviously, the industry could only make such films by completely ignoring the standards of the Production Code Administration. By the late 1960s the motion-picture industry officially abandoned the former self-censorship by devising a rating system that placed the burden of censorship on the moviegoer. The ratings ranged from "G," which designated wholesome movies for the entire family, to "X" (now NC-17), which prohibited anyone under 18 from attending and warned that anything might be found in the movie, from brutal violence to hard-core pornography. Although profanity and explicit sexual themes and scenes were originally restricted to R- and X-rated movies, they now can be found in today's PG (parental-guidance recommended) films.

At first, most movies received a rating of either G or M (later changed to PG), with 25 percent of the films rated G and 43 percent M or PG. However, within a decade the movie industry found that moviegoers preferred more violent and sexually explicit films. By 1979 movies rated PG had content similar to that of the early-day R-rated movies. The R category grew from 25 percent in 1969 to 45 percent in 1979; the G category fell from 25 to 6 percent.

Disasters and Violence. When television began toning down its depiction of violence in the 1970s to comply with consumer group complaints, the motion-picture industry turned to disaster films and explicit violence as film genres. Disaster films became the big box-office draws of the 1970s. These films were filled with suspense as passengers scrambled for their lives in a sinking luxury ship (*The Poseidon Adventure*), summer vacationers were gobbled up by a giant shark (*Jaws*), Los Angeles was shaken by destruction (*Earthquake*) and a giant skyscraper was consumed by flames (*The Towering Inferno*).

As people became accustomed to disasters, the films got more violent in an effort to keep the audience interested. Some of the more popular superviolent films were *The Wild Bunch* and *Dirty Harry*, a movie starring Clint Eastwood as a tough San Francisco cop who doesn't let the law get in his way of capturing, torturing and eventually killing a rooftop sniper. Although these films depicted people being gunned down in cold blood, it was still the ''bad guys'' who lost out in the end. However, as the 1970s drew to a close, many innocent people were being axed and mutilated in films such as *Halloween*, the *Texas Chain Saw Massacre* and *Friday the 13th*. All of these films had sequels.

Of course not everyone wanted to spend Saturday nights watching people being hacked to pieces. Some viewers, especially women, wanted good, clean, wholesome family-type entertainment, and movies were also made for this segment of the market. Some of the more successful included the musical about the life of the legendary singing Von Trapp family of Austria, *The Sound of Music* (1965), *Oliver!* (1968) and a long string of Walt Disney movies.

Special Effects. As space-age technology and space exploration became part of our culture, the movies began to use this technology and depict these themes. With the help of such directors as Steven Spielberg and George Lucas, films started featuring amazing computer-generated special effects. These special effects created graphic depictions of everything from interplanetary war to extraterrestrial beings. The first to dazzle audiences was Lucas's *Star Wars* (1977), which broke box-office records. It was followed by *Close Encounters of the Third Kind*, *The Empire Strikes Back*, *Return of the Jedi*, *Poltergeist*, *Raiders of the Lost Ark*, *E.T.*, *Poltergeist II*, *Aliens*, *Indiana Jones and the Temple of Doom* and *The Fly*.

Films of the '80s. The 1980s saw a continuation of the specialized productions that had helped the industry rebound from the decline of the 1940s. Among the better and more successful releases of the decade were *Raging Bull* (1980); *E.T.* (1982); *The Purple Rose of Cairo, Prizzi's Honor, Out of Africa* and *Brazil* (1985); *The Fly* and *Blue Velvet* (1986); *The Last Emperor* (1987); *Wings of Desire* (1988); and *Batman* (1989).

Comics. The summer blockbuster of 1990 was *Dick Tracy*, a movie adaptation of the famous Chester Gould comic-strip character of the same name. Starring Warren Beatty as the famous detective and Madonna as the sexually provocative ''Breathless Mahoney,'' the movie followed a trend established the previous year by *Batman*, another comic-strip-inspired movie. These comic films used media hype and the sales of cultural artifacts to generate instant box office success. Earlier comic strip successes on the magic screen had been several sequences of *Superman*.

TABLE 8.1 TOP-GROSSING FILMS (1985–1990)

Year	Film	Distributor	Gross*
1990	*Ghost*	Paramount	$206.1
1989	*Batman*	Warner Bros.	$251.2
1988	*Rain Man*	MGM/UA	$171.2
1987	*Three Men and a Baby*	Buena Vista	$167.8
1986	*Top Gun*	Paramount	$176.8
1985	*Back to the Future*	Universal	$200.1

*In millions of dollars
SOURCES: Exhibitors Relations Co., Entertainment Data Inc., and *Los Angeles Times*

What made *Dick Tracy* stand out was the fact that it was released by Walt Disney—long known for its family-oriented films—and was the first Disney film to feature contents loaded with double entendres and sexually provocative costumes and scenes featuring America's sex symbol, Madonna.

Prior to the release of *Dick Tracy,* Disney had protected its name by releasing only the tamest of family-oriented films. Other films were released under the name of its companion division, Touchstone. Even *Who Framed Roger Rabbit* was considered too racy for the Disney name and became a Touchstone production.

CURRENT TRENDS

Today movies deal with every social and antisocial theme; graphic scenes of violence, bondage and explicit sex are not uncommon. As a result, the motion-picture industry still finds itself under attack from a variety of groups, ranging from concerned parents and religious leaders to women's rights activists. All are calling for some form of censorship.

Censorship. Parent and religious groups are concerned that the movies' depiction of brutal violence, permissive sex, alcohol and drug abuse, reckless driving and wanton destruction of property encourages such behavior among young people. Women's groups believe that movies that show women in stereotyped roles, portray them as sex objects and show explicit scenes of bondage and violence are hurting women's movement toward equality and are contributing to an increase in violence against women.

The central issue in this ongoing controversy is whether motion pictures shape our popular culture or merely reflect it. The groups that advocate censoring motion-picture content believe that the "silver screen" is a powerful force in our culture that sets trends and lifestyles; directors and producers maintain that they merely reflect the lifestyles and interests that exist in our society and are giving people the type of entertainment they want.

BOX 8.1

▪ WORKING IN THE MOVIE INDUSTRY ▪

The production of motion pictures today differs greatly from the "golden age" when large studios did everything. Current practices are usually separated into four operations: (1) moviemaking or production, (2) investors, (3) distributors and (4) exhibitors.

Production is a highly collaborative process involving many different people. Major players in the production can include an executive producer, producer, writer, director, composer, editor, director of photography and the actors and actresses. These people are supported by a crew of hundreds of other workers, usually unionized, who handle specific details ranging from building the sets to applying make-up to catering meals on location.

Investors are the venture capitalists who put up the money to fund the production. There is high risk in investing in movies as many of them become box-office flops. However, when a picture is successful, these venture capitalists stand to make a good return on their investments.

Distributors are responsible for making prints of the film and getting them delivered on time. The method of producing multiple prints and distributing these prints to each theater dates back to the early days of the industry. It is envisioned that in the not-so-distant future satellite technology will be used to modernize this process (see Chapter 15).

Exhibitors are the theater owners who make showing of the movies possible. One of the biggest competitors for these exhibitors today is video-rental outlets. The theaters have changed greatly during the past century from nickelodeons to grand theatrical palaces to the current multi-screen operations featuring 10 to 12 film showings at a time. Some predict that there may be a return to the large movie palaces when large-screen high-definition television arrives (see Chapter 15), in order to provide an experience competitive with the home VCR. In addition to making their money on admission tickets, these exhibitors make about 10–20 percent of their income from the refreshment counters.

BUSINESS TRENDS

Ever since the motion-picture industry got over its initial shock from television and began taking advantage of new market opportunities developed by this in-home visual medium, profits and business opportunities have improved.

Estimated revenue for 1990 was $8.7 billion. Box-office receipts accounted for $4.8 billion; $2.5 billion came from foreign exports (U.S. films are distributed in more than 100 countries); and $1.4 billion came from domestic rentals, which included satellite, cable and videocassette rentals (see Figure 8.1). This final category is expected to expand as the Direct Broadcast Satellite industry develops (see Chapter 15). However, piracy in foreign countries—the unauthorized recording of videocassettes—is estimated to be costing the movie industry $1.2 billion a year.

By the 1990s there were more than 23,000 theater screens in the United States and an annual attendance of nearly 1.1 billion. The average cost of ticket prices across the country was $4.11.

Video Movies.   Although the industry was cranking out more than 500 films a year by 1990, eight out of ten did not recover their investment in box-office

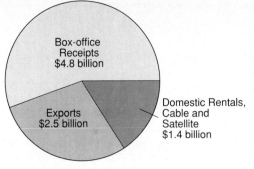

Figure 8.1 Percentage breakdown of U.S. motion-picture industry revenues in 1990, by categories. SOURCE: *U.S. Industrial Outlook, 1990* (Washington, D.C.: U.S. Government Printing Office, 1990).

receipts. However, the advent of video rental businesses gave all films—including the less successful ones—another opportunity to generate revenue.

The introduction of home video equipment in the late 1970s created a profitable market for the movie industry. Movies found a whole new audience as many people who had not been to a theater in years began watching films on video-cassettes.

As videocassette recorders (VCRs) and video-rental businesses spread throughout the country in the 1980s, Hollywood began recording old films onto videotape. New movies are also released after their run at the box office for a considerable amount of extra income. Although motion picture producers receive a percentage of the box-office receipts from theaters, they receive no such share from video rentals. However, the many rental outlets are a prime market for videocassette sales. When Steven Spielberg's *The Color Purple* was released on videocassette, for example, it had already made nearly $100 million at the box office. It sold more than 275,000 videocassettes at $89 each to video-rental outlets, providing an additional $25 million in income.

Conglomerates.   Like the print media, the motion-picture industry is not immune to conglomerate takeovers (see Box 8.2). Recent takeover and merger activity includes: Matsushita's $6.1 billion purchase of MCA; Sony's $3.4 billion purchase of Columbia; Pathé's acquisition of MGM/UA; and Time Inc.'s merger with Warner Communications, owner of Warner Bros. Paramount, which until 1989 had been a subsidiary of Gulf and Western, became Paramount Communications Inc., with extensive holdings in the entertainment and publishing fields (see Box 8.3).

SUMMARY

The motion-picture industry has had a major impact on our popular culture, and our popular culture has in turn affected the industry, as new media, cultural attitudes and changing lifestyles have forced it to change.

Soon after the invention of the motion-picture camera in Thomas Edison's laboratory, film found its way to mass audiences. It was first used as a moving

BOX 8.2

▪ IS HOLLYWOOD BECOMING THE "FOREIGN FILM CAPITAL"? ▪

Ownership of Hollywood's movie studios in recent years has been shifting to foreign control. Japanese-, Italian- and Australian-based organizations have been paying large amounts for some of the major U.S. motion-picture companies.

In late 1990, Matsushita, the Japanese manufacturer of video and audio equipment, paid $6.1 billion for Universal Pictures and its parent company MCA Entertainment. Matsushita produces electronic equipment under the names of Panasonic, Quasar and Technics. Earlier this year, MGM/UA had been acquired by Italian financier Giancarlo Parretti. In 1989, Japan's Sony paid $3.4 billion for Columbia Pictures and in 1985 Rupert Murdoch's Australian based News Corp. purchased 20th Century-Fox.

These recent acquisitions left only three major Hollywood motion-picture studios under American ownership: Disney, Paramount and Warner Brothers.

The foreign interest in American moviemaking was prompted by the global success of the American entertainment industry. Each year $300 billion is spent worldwide on movie tickets, compact discs, videotapes and other American entertainment products. One-fourth of these sales are overseas. In Europe, American films account for half of the box-office receipts; in Japan in 1989–90 some $32 million was spent for tickets to see *Indiana Jones and the Last Crusade,* while other American films account for most of the rest of the movie showings in that country.

And there is an added benefit for Matsushita and Sony: the acquisition of American entertainment companies provides them with the ability to own a large supply of the software (movies, records and films) that can be played on the machines they manufacture.

peep show in penny arcades, then in vaudeville shows, nickelodeons and eventually in large palace-like theaters.

Films such as Edwin Porter's *The Great Train Robbery* and D. W. Griffith's *Birth of a Nation* proved that the motion picture could be a powerful storytelling medium. Film moved quickly into the popular culture because it was invented at a time when immigrants in our industrialized urban society needed an entertainment medium with no language barrier. The international language of the silent film's pantomime and comedy provided that medium. Soon the likes of Mack Sennett, Charlie Chaplin, Stan Laurel, Oliver Hardy, Buster Keaton and Harold Lloyd were silently communicating to the masses.

Although experimental sound pictures were made in the early days of the industry, it wasn't until Warner Brothers brought out *The Jazz Singer* in 1927, with Al Jolson singing on screen, that the full potential of "talking" pictures was realized. The success of the early "talkies" changed the industry and helped make Warner Brothers into a major studio.

In the 1930s and 1940s going to the movies became a way of life in the United States. The major movie studios turned out hundreds of films a year and created movie stars who became as familiar to American audiences as members of their own families. These films also provided an effective escape from reality during a time of depression and war.

In 1947 and 1948 three events rocked the industry and toppled it from its peak of economic success. First came the congressional hearings into alleged Communist infiltration of the motion-picture industry. The second was a Supreme Court

BOX 8.3

▪ HOLDINGS OF PARAMOUNT COMMUNICATIONS INC. ▪

When the U.S. Supreme Court ruled in 1948 that major motion-picture studios were violating antitrust laws by owning theaters as well as studios, they were apparently operating in a different world from the conglomerate era of the 1990s. Today owners of motion-picture studios have a wide variety of holdings, as the following partial listing for Paramount Communications Inc. suggests:

Entertainment

Paramount Pictures	Madison Square Garden Center	Miss Universe Pageants
Paramount Television	Madison Square Garden Network	Cinamerica Theaters
Paramount Home Video	MSG Television Productions	United International Pictures
Wilshire Court Productions	New York Knicks	Cinema International Corporation
USA Network	New York Rangers	United Cinemas International

Publishing & Other

Simon & Schuster	Allyn & Bacon	Modern Curriculum Press
Prentice Hall	Appleton & Lange	Macdonald Children's Books
Summit Books	Globe Book Company	Arco
Pocket Books	Coronet/MTI Film & Video	Betty Crocker
Poseidon Press	Brady Computer Books	Harvester/Wheatsheaf

ruling that forced major studios to sell their theaters. The final blow was the entrance of television into our popular culture.

The motion-picture business changed from a big-studio-dominated industry that owned most of the stars and the distribution outlets to one of independent producers and theaters. The industry experimented with a variety of films and technology—such as three-dimensional pictures and large screens—but it could not win back its mass audience.

Soon Hollywood discovered that films aimed at specialized audiences helped revive low box-office receipts. Finding popularity at the box office were films aimed at youth and films that contained sex, violence and special effects.

Today the motion-picture industry is thriving. Its acceptance of the new video technology has provided it with a significant additional source of revenue.

THOUGHT QUESTIONS

1 What social factors contributed to the rapid movement of motion pictures into the popular culture?

2   What similarities are there between comedy of the silent film era and today's humor? Are these similarities driven by cultural needs?

3   Why are topics like sex and violence popular in motion pictures? Is this a case of Hollywood giving us what we want or us liking what we're given?

4   If you were a motion-picture producer, what changes would you make to create box-office hits during the 1990s?

5   Do you think new technology, which will allow homes to have television sets as large as living-room walls with the clarity of motion-picture screens, will create a decline in motion-picture theater audiences? Why or why not?

NOTES

1.   Lewis Jacobs, *The Emergence of Film Art,* 2nd ed. (New York: Norton, 1979), p. 27.

2.   Gerald Mast, *A Short History of the Movies,* 4th ed. (New York: Macmillan, 1986), p. 63.

3.   Ibid., p. 93.

4.   David Robinson, *The History of World Cinema* (New York: Stein and Day, 1973), p. 104.

5.   Arthur Knight, *The Liveliest Art: A Panoramic History of the Movies* (New York: New American Library, 1957), pp. 112–113.

6.   Robinson, p. 190.

7.   Pamela S. Ecker, "My Affair With Farrah," in Jack Nachbar, Deborah Weiser and John Wright, eds., *The Popular Culture Reader* (Bowling Green, Ohio: Bowling Green University Popular Press, 1978), pp. 211–212.

8.   Walter Goodman, *The Committee: The Extraordinary Career of the House Committee on Un-American Activities* (New York: Farrar, Straus & Giroux, 1964), p. 218.

9.   Robinson, p. 253.

ADDITIONAL READING

Boorstin, Daniel J. *The Image: A Guide to Pseudo-Events in America.* New York: Harper & Row, 1964.

Bordwell, David, and Thompson, Kristin. *Film Art: An Introduction,* 3rd ed. New York: McGraw-Hill, 1990.

Charters, Werrett Wallace. *Motion Pictures and Youth.* New York: Arno Press & The New York Times, 1970.

Ellis, Jack C. *A History of Film.* Englewood Cliffs, N.J.: Prentice-Hall, 1979.

Fulton, Albert R. *Motion Pictures: The Development of an Art from Silent Films to the Age of Television.* Norman, Okla.: University of Oklahoma Press, 1960.

Griffith, Richard, and Mayer, Arthur. *The*

Movies, rev. ed. New York: Simon & Schuster, 1970.

Higman, Charles. *Hollywood at Sunset.* New York: Saturday Review Press, 1972.

Jacobs, Lewis. *The Rise of the American Film: A Critical History.* New York: Harcourt, Brace, 1939.

Kauffman, Stanley. *A World on Film.* New York: Harper & Row, 1966.

Lee, David, and Berkowitz, Stan. *The Movie Business.* New York: Vantage, 1981.

Schickel, Richard. *Movies: The History of an Art.* New York: Simon & Schuster, 1963.

The gift of gab of the live disc jockey, like New York's Jay Thomas, remains popular with radio audiences.

RADIO:
A WIRELESS WONDER

*Radio was really
do it yourself
television.
Instead of a big
ugly glass picture
tube, you saw
the performers in
your own mind.
You were not
restricted by the
boundaries of a
21-inch tube, but
instead painted
your own big as
life version of
each moment
with that loving
creative brush we
call imagination.*
            —Jack Benny

At 1:30 A.M. each weekday, Bob Edwards climbs out of bed in his Arlington, Virginia, home and prepares for his trip to the office in downtown Washington, D.C.

Arriving at work between 2:30 and 3 A.M., Edwards begins putting together his two-hour morning news program. At 6 A.M. he goes on the air with what is considered to be one of the best radio news broadcasts in the nation—National Public Radio's (NPR) *Morning Edition.*

ELITIST	**POPULAR**	**SPECIALIZED**		

CULTURAL HISTORY OF RADIO

			1888	Heinrich Hertz transmits wireless sound waves.
			1901	Guglielmo Marconi sends wireless sound across the Atlantic.
			1906	Lee De Forest adds grid to vacuum tube, making voice transmission possible.
			1917	U.S. enters World War I; U.S. Navy takes over broadcasting from American Marconi Co.
			1919	Radio Corporation of America (RCA) founded; Frank Conrad transmits music over the airwaves in Pittsburgh.
			1920	KDKA (Pittsburgh) goes on the air for Westinghouse—first fully licensed station with continuous broadcasting.
			1922	WEAF (New York) begins commercial broadcasting.
			1926	AT&T gives up effort to build a radio network; NBC (an RCA subsidiary) starts two networks.
			1927	UIB/Columbia network begins (later becomes CBS).
			1927	Federal Radio Act sets up commission to regulate the airwaves.
			1928	*Sam and Henry* (later *Amos 'n' Andy*) becomes popular network sitcom.
			1930s	Radio soap operas offer escape from the Depression.
			1933–45	President Franklin Roosevelt uses radio for fireside chats with the nation.

Edwards's soothing voice and friendly interviewing style have made him a favorite with *Morning Edition* fans across the nation. His weekly interview with sportscaster Red Barber, long retired in Florida, has become a regular feature each Friday. Unlike most radio newscasts, music is interspersed throughout the program to create the appropriate mood and signal changes in subjects.

Morning Edition, along with its afternoon counterpart *All Things Considered,* is carried by public broadcasting stations throughout the nation. It first went on the air in November of 1979 with Edwards, who was the cohost on *All Things Considered,* filling in for 30 days while his bosses at NPR found a permanent

CULTURAL HISTORY OF RADIO

ELITIST	POPULAR	SPECIALIZED		
	▓		1934	Federal Communication Commission (FCC) established.
	▓		1934	Mutual Broadcasting System goes on the air as fourth radio network.
	▓		1938	Orson Welles's *War of the Worlds* panics nation.
	▓		1939	First FM radio station goes on the air in New Jersey.
	▓		1940–45	Edward R. Murrow broadcasts vivid descriptions of the war in Europe on CBS for American audiences.
	▓		1943	Federal government forces NBC to sell one of its two networks; it eventually becomes ABC.
	▓		1948	Network radio revenues reach a peak.
		▓	1950s	Radio loses its programs and stars to television.
		▓	1950s	Radio begins to specialize with individual musical formats and disc jockeys; promotes rock-'n'-roll.
		▓	1959	Payola scandal rocks radio industry.
		▓	1970s	Country-and-western music and all-talk shows grow in popularity on radio.
		▓	1981	FCC begins deregulating radio.
		▓	1980s	AM radio adds stereo broadcasting to fight growing popularity of FM stations.
		▓	1990s	AM stereo begins to catch on after U.S. auto makers place stereo receivers in new cars.

anchor. The new audience for the show liked Edwards and he became fond of the challenge the new program provided. He even found himself adjusting to the early-to-bed, early-to-rise routine. As a result, his 30-day stint became a permanent assignment.

Although public (noncommercial) radio has a strong, loyal following, the audience accounts for only a small percentage of total radio listeners. Since its beginning as a mass-communication medium in the 1920s, radio has achieved most of its success as a commercial enterprise. As the first electronic medium to enter the homes of the masses, radio played an important role in changing our popular

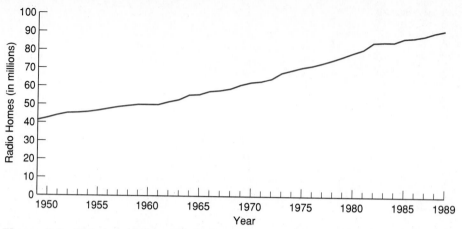

Figure 9.1 U.S. households with radios. SOURCE: *The Broadcasting Yearbook 1990* (Washington, D.C.: Broadcasting Publications, Inc., 1990).

culture by transforming our living rooms into entertainment centers featuring the live sounds of vaudeville, theaters and ballrooms. Many families stopped reading and conversing in the evenings and began listening to the radio together.

Today there is more than one radio for every person in the United States: 91.1 million homes have radios (see Figure 9.1) and 95 percent of all automobiles in this country are equipped with them. Radio has a larger audience than television does for a sizable part of the day, usually around the "drive times" of 6 to 10 A.M. and 3 to 7 P.M. According to statistics compiled by the Radio Advertising Bureau, on average high school and college students spend more hours a day listening to radio than they do watching television.

HARNESSING SOUND WAVES

The invention of radio was the culmination of 70 years of technological advances in communicating messages.

The need for instant communication first arose in the 1830s, as the great era of railroad building got under way. The efficiency and safety of the railroads required a system that could send messages to distant stations faster than the trains traveled. Experimentation soon began on harnessing sound waves to meet this need.

The Telegraph.   In 1844 a portrait painter and experimental photographer named Samuel F. B. Morse invented a system of sending sound waves over long-distance telegraph wires. To demonstrate his discovery, he strung 40 miles of telegraph lines between Washington, D.C., and Baltimore, Maryland, and transmitted the now-famous message: "What hath God wrought?"

Soon telegraph lines were crisscrossing the country; by 1861 a transcontinental line was in place. This electronic communication system was adequate for the railroads' needs, but it was unsuitable for public use, since the telegraph messages were limited to coded signals of dots and dashes, the well-known Morse code.

The Telephone.   Many scientists went to work to find a way to send the human voice over telegraph lines. Although some claim that an Italian-American inventor named Antonio Meucci first laid out the plans for a voice transmitter and converter, credit for developing a workable system in 1876 goes to Alexander Graham Bell. His telephone consisted of a microphone, which converted sound into electrical energy, and a receiver, which changed it back into sound.

Three years earlier, the Scottish physicist James Clerk Maxwell predicted that someday it would be possible to generate electronic signals that could be sent through space at the speed of light without the use of wires. The German physicist Heinrich Hertz proved Maxwell's theory correct in 1888, when he sent a wireless signal from one point to another in his laboratory. (The unit of frequency called *hertz* is named in his honor.)

Development of the Wireless.   A wealthy young Italian, Guglielmo Marconi, experimented with Hertz's theories in Bologna, Italy, where he successfully sent signals across the hillside near his family home. Unable to interest the Italian government in his invention, Marconi and his mother traveled to England, where his mother's family had important social contacts. There he demonstrated his invention and obtained support from the British Post Office Department. Marconi received his first patent on radiotelegraphy equipment in England in 1896, when he was 22 years old. The following year he formed the British Marconi Company, which continued to experiment with radio signal transmission over greater distances.

Marconi made history in 1901 when he set up a radio receiver in Newfoundland and picked up three dots (the Morse code for the letter S) that had been sent across the Atlantic by a colleague in England. He then developed a number of companies that expanded the ability of Morse code communication to mobile points. Radio thus found its first niche in the culture transmitting messages ship-to-ship and ship-to-shore.

Meanwhile, scientists were still struggling to find a way to send voices through the air. They were looking for a wireless telephone. The essential step came in 1906, when an American, Dr. Lee De Forest, perfected the vacuum tube by inventing a grid that became an amplifier when inserted into the tube. This improved vacuum tube, called an Audion, enabled radio receivers to pick up voice and music sounds. The vacuum tube remained a fundamental component of radio receivers until the transistor was invented in 1947. Although De Forest is generally given credit for being the "father of radio," his patent rights to the Audion were disputed by J. Ambrose Fleming, who had patented a vacuum tube called the Fleming valve in 1904; De Forest's invention had been an improvement on Fleming's vacuum tube rather than a completely new invention.

On Christmas Eve 1906, University of Pittsburgh professor Reginald A. Fessenden, working with General Electric engineers, used wireless technology to broadcast music to ships at sea. Although a new era of wireless transmission had

■ Guglielmo Marconi, a key figure in the development of wireless technology.

arrived, few people at the time had any idea that they were experimenting with a
mass-communication technology that would transform the culture.

BEGINNING OF RADIO AS A MASS MEDIUM

One person who did foresee radio's future as a mass-communication medium—
and who later became a force in making it so—first learned of radio's potential at
the age of 21, while working as a wireless operator for the American Marconi
Company on April 14, 1912. Through the static on his radio receiver came a series
of dots and dashes that told that the *Titanic* had hit an iceberg in the North
Atlantic and was sinking fast.

The young radio operator was David Sarnoff. The *Titanic*, which was considered unsinkable, had been on its maiden voyage from Europe to the United States
and was carrying many socially prominent passengers. The news of the tragedy
spread fast, and soon many amateur radio operators were trying to make contact
with the sinking ship. President Taft ordered all of the stations shut down except
one—David Sarnoff's.

Sarnoff received and transmitted messages about the disaster and fed the
information, including reports about survivors, to the waiting nation. Although he
gained fame during the event, Sarnoff later went to work for the Radio Corporation of America (RCA) and earned his place in radio history as the head of its
subsidiary the National Broadcasting Company (NBC).

Voice transmission continued in the experimental stages for a number of years. In 1916 De Forest sent out an experimental transmission of the Wilson-Hughes presidential election returns, which is now considered to be the first radio news broadcast.

That same year, David Sarnoff sent the following message to his boss at the American Marconi Company:

I have in mind a plan of development that would make radio a "household utility" in the same sense as the piano or phonograph. The idea is to bring music into the house by wireless. . . . The receiver can be designed in the form of a simple "Radio Music Box" . . . supplied with amplifying tubes and a loud speaking telephone, all of which can be neatly mounted in one box. . . . Aside from the profit derived from this proposition, the possibilities for advertising for the company are tremendous for its name would ultimately be brought into the household, and wireless would receive national and universal attention.[1]

Like most memos, this "Music Box Memo" was largely ignored. However, in 1919 a Westinghouse engineer, Dr. Frank Conrad, started broadcasting music at an experimental station in Pittsburgh. A department store started running newspaper ads suggesting that people could hear "Dr. Conrad's magical music" come out of thin air by purchasing a crystal set (a small tubeless radio receiver that used a crystal detector) at their store.

Also in 1919 General Electric purchased the equipment and patents held by the American Marconi Company and joined forces with Westinghouse, American Telephone & Telegraph (AT&T), Western Electric Company and United Fruit Company to pool electronic patents and form RCA. Each company owned a percentage of RCA and Sarnoff became RCA's general manager in 1921. The decision to form an American radio distribution firm was prompted by the nation's involvement in World War I in 1917–18 and the realization that Marconi, the major company in the field of radio at that time, was foreign-owned. During the war, the U.S. navy took over all U.S. commercial and amateur wireless stations, dismantling some and operating others as part of its own facilities. (Marconi, incidentally, served in both the Italian army and navy during the war.)

The rapid sale of crystal sets to hear Dr. Conrad's music proved that Sarnoff had made a good suggestion in his 1916 music box memo. The next year, on November 2, 1920, Westinghouse went on the air in Pittsburgh with station KDKA, the first fully licensed commercial broadcasting station to have continuous programming. Its opening broadcast featured returns from the Harding-Cox presidential election, along with a request for people to write the station if they heard the broadcast.

Early Commercial Broadcasting.　The success of Westinghouse's KDKA led the other electrical companies to open their own stations. RCA went on the air with WDY in New York City, AT&T began WEAF in New York City and General Electric started WGY in Schenectady, N.Y. Westinghouse later added stations in Massachusetts, New Jersey and Illinois. The motivation for these electrical companies to start commercial radio stations was financial. While the sale of radio transmitters and receivers for ship-to-shore broadcasting was limited, by expanding radio to the masses, the entire population became a potential market.

WEAF went on the air in 1922 as a toll station; that is, it sold air time to advertisers. The print media resented the competition and criticized the idea of radio advertising, calling it offensive. Even broadcasters disagreed as to whether commercials belonged on radio.

The Beginning of the Networks. As more and more stations were founded around the country, AT&T started linking them together in 1923 using its telephone lines. This "chain broadcasting," which allowed stations to share programming, was the forerunner to network broadcasting.

In 1926 AT&T bailed out of the broadcast distribution business and began leasing its wires to RCA's subsidiary NBC. This launched the era of network broadcasting, with NBC establishing and operating two radio networks—NBC Red and NBC Blue. The company operated both networks until the Federal Communications Commission intervened and forced the sale of the Blue network in 1943. The Blue network thus became the American Broadcasting Company (ABC).

In 1927 another broadcasting system was organized by the United Independent Broadcasters (a group of rival stations not affiliated with NBC), with the help of the Columbia Phonograph Record Company. First called UIB/Columbia, it was renamed the Columbia Broadcasting System (CBS) after it was reorganized and purchased in 1928 by a 27-year-old cigar-company heir named William S. Paley. Paley, who still chaired the board of CBS in the 1980s, had been impressed with the success of radio advertisements in boosting the sales of his family's cigars.

A fourth radio network, the Mutual Broadcasting System, was started in 1934 by four non-network-affiliated stations. By 1935 Mutual had 60 affiliates. It was the only major network to remain exclusively in radio after the other three expanded into television.

The Need for Government Regulations. By the latter part of the 1920s, the expanding radio industry found itself in need of stricter regulations to allocate radio frequencies and keep stations from jamming each other's signals. It turned to the federal government for help and the Radio Act of 1927 was passed, which set up the Federal Radio Commission (FRC). Soon the number of radio stations in the country was reduced to avoid interference in reception. The FRC was expanded and renamed the Federal Communications Commission (FCC) by the Communication Act of 1934.

DEVELOPMENT OF RADIO NEWS

Although KDKA's debut broadcast was a report on election returns, early radio newscasts were limited. For the most part, announcers simply read headlines from the local newspaper—with an advertising tag line that if listeners wanted the complete details, they should buy a copy of the paper. Some newspapers actually started radio stations to advertise themselves.

Early radio news was also unscheduled. Not until the 1930s were regularly scheduled newscasts offered—usually only one or two in the morning, one at midday and a couple in the evening.

Newspaper Opposition.   Network radio grew rapidly after 1927, and by 1930 radio had become firmly entrenched in the popular culture. The new medium's popularity, coupled with the decline in newspaper advertising revenue following the Great Depression in 1929, alarmed many newspaper publishers.

Not only was the advertising revenue of radio increasing while that of newspapers was declining, but this new mass medium was becoming a credible news source as well. For the first time in history, listeners could hear news events as they were happening without being on the scene. To many, this was far superior to reading about the event the next day. When the stock market crashed in October 1929, people became even more interested in "instant" news.

After radio broadcast both the Democratic and Republican conventions coast to coast in 1932 and the Associated Press provided radio with election returns for instant airing, the newspapers had had enough. The American Newspaper Publishers Association issued an ultimatum to the press associations: stop providing news to radio. Most AP members voted to comply with this request in 1933, and all three press associations stopped selling news to radio stations. Forced to gather news on its own, radio was soon giving newspapers more competition than they had bargained for.

CBS took the lead in creating a first-rate news-gathering service. Under the direction of former newspaperman Paul White, CBS opened bureaus in major U.S. cities and in London. A string of news commentators such as H. V. Kaltenborn, Boake Carter, Lowell Thomas, Edwin C. Hill and Gabriel Heatter became household voices.

Within several years after the wire-service ban, United Press and International News Service were selling news to radio again. UP even set up a service specifically for radio broadcasting. AP resumed its news feed to radio in 1940, and it too developed a special radio news service.

Radio Meets Cultural Needs.   President Franklin D. Roosevelt assisted radio in becoming a major information source. After his election in 1932, Roosevelt started using the new medium to communicate directly with the people through broadcasts that he called fireside chats. Many Americans were in states of panic over their financial troubles. Their only hope, they believed, was the leadership of the new president. For the first time in history, average people had the opportunity to listen directly to the reassuring voice of their president. (In the 1980s, a new president, Ronald Reagan, used radio to talk directly to the people. His weekly Saturday broadcasts often included the first formal announcement of major policy decisions.)

Reports about the activities of a madman in Germany—Adolf Hitler—were also causing concern among Americans. Radio kept a concerned nation informed about Hitler's activities, as network radio newscasters took the ears of the American people to the scenes of the action.

■ Franklin D. Roosevelt was the first U.S. president to use radio to communicate regularly with the public. His "fireside chats" reassured anxious Americans during the Depression.

Radio and World War II. In 1937 CBS sent a then-unknown Edward R. Murrow to Europe as its director of educational broadcasting. He and an assistant, newspaperman William L. Shirer, soon found themselves covering history in the making. On March 12, 1938, as Hitler sent his troops into Austria, Murrow described the scene live from Vienna, while Shirer reported on reactions from London and other CBS reporters gave their impressions from Berlin, Paris and Rome. This was radio's first multiple pickup news broadcast; it demonstrated the scope and diversity of radio as a news medium and left no doubt about its importance in the American popular culture.

In 1940 Americans vicariously lived through the bombings of London, as Murrow broadcast eyewitness accounts of the air raids in his famous *This Is London* series. Murrow could describe any event in such a way that listeners could picture it in their minds (see Box 9.1). Americans could almost feel the impact of the war on Europe through Murrow's reports.

Radio's coverage of the war in Europe set the stage for the fateful Sunday on December 7, 1941, when radio bulletins announced to the nation that Japanese planes had bombed the American fleet in Pearl Harbor. The next day a record-sized audience listened to President Roosevelt deliver his war message to Congress. As FDR declared that December 7 was a "date which will live in infamy," he inspired a spirit of patriotism and dedication that has never been equalled in American history.

Throughout World War II radio reporters kept the people at home informed about the war with firsthand broadcasts from the battle scenes in the Pacific and Europe. For the first time, Americans experienced a war being fought on distant soil almost as it was happening. There was, however, a great deal of censorship of news from the front, self-imposed as well as governmental, and the horrors of war were downplayed.

DEVELOPMENT OF RADIO ENTERTAINMENT

Radio's impact on American culture was not limited to its "ear-witness" news coverage. It also became a powerful entertainment medium.

Shortly after radio entered the popular culture, the nation experienced the most serious economic depression in its history. Many wealthy families lost their fortunes in the stock market crash, large numbers of poor and middle-class families lost their sources of income as their breadwinners were laid off, and many people lost their life savings as banks collapsed across the country.

Radio had come along at just the right time. It provided free entertainment in the comforts of the home. Families that could no longer afford to go out for entertainment gathered together in their living rooms to escape reality by laughing, fantasizing and dreaming of happier times.

Electronic Vaudeville.   Radio had become a first-class entertainment medium after the networks were established in 1927. Variety shows, dramatic productions and comedy series soon dominated the airwaves. Most comedy programs consisted of a series of jokes, gags and short skits that were a form of burlesque comedy borrowed from vaudeville. Many vaudeville stars found jobs in this new entertainment medium, and eventually radio, coupled with motion pictures, led to the death of vaudeville.

Situation Comedy.   After a few years, radio comedy shows had evolved into a new form of comedy—situation comedy (sitcom). Early radio sitcoms were originally 15 minutes long and ran five nights a week. Episodes were in serial form, with the average plot or story line lasting for most of the week. This format was later changed to the 30-minute, once-a-week, self-contained situation comedy, as we now have on television.

The first successful situation comedy, which started in the 15-minute format and then converted to 30 minutes, debuted in 1928 as *Sam and Henry;* it later changed its name to *The Amos 'n' Andy Show*. It soon became the nation's most popular radio program—so popular, in fact, that movie theaters stopped their shows and turned on the radio when it was "Amos 'n' Andy time."

The stars of this series, Freeman Gosden and Charles Correll (both white men), played four to five characters each, all African-American men (it was common for one radio actor or actress to play more than one part on the same show). Although not as racist as D. W. Griffith's *Birth of a Nation,* the show did perpetuate the negative stereotypes of African-Americans that were common at the time.

BOX 9.1

EDWARD R. MURROW: A TONGUE AS DESCRIPTIVE AS A PAINTBRUSH

Edward R. Murrow worked for the CBS network from 1935 to 1961, when he resigned to become director of the United States Information Agency. His ability to calmly describe news events on radio in a manner that left no confusion in the minds of the audience helped bring the realities and the horrors of World War II home to Americans. The following is an excerpt of Murrow's April 15, 1945, broadcast describing what he found when he visited the German concentration camp Buchenwald.

Permit me to tell you what you would have seen, and heard, had you been with me on Thursday. It will not be pleasant listening. If you are at lunch, or if you have no appetite to hear what Germans have done, now is a good time to switch off the radio, for I propose to tell you of Buchenwald. It is on a small hill about four miles outside Weimar, and it was one of the largest concentration camps in Germany, and it was built to last. As we approached it, we saw about a hundred men in civilian clothes with rifles advancing in open order across fields. There were a few shots; we stopped to inquire. We were told that some of the prisoners had a couple of SS men cornered in there. We drove on, reached the main gate. The prisoners crowded up behind the wire. We entered.

And now, let me tell this in the first person, for I was the least important person there, as you shall hear. There surged around me an evil-smelling horde. Men and boys reached out to touch me; they were in rags and remnants of uniform. Death had already marked many of them, but they were smiling with their eyes. I looked out over that mass of men to the green fields beyond where well-fed Germans were ploughing.

A German, Fritz Kersheimer, came up and said, "May I show you round the camp? I've been here ten years." An Englishman stood to attention, say-

Other popular situation comedy shows were Fred Allen and his *Allen's Alley,* which featured conversations between Allen and a cross-section of ethnic Americans, and *The Jack Benny Show,* which focused on Benny being a very stingy man. A number of other shows featured husband-and-wife teams where one spouse would handle the straight lines and the other would provide the comedy by being a dimwit. Popular among these shows were the *Burns and Allen Show* and *Fibber McGee and Molly.*

Many of these early radio entertainers had started their show-business careers in vaudeville. Edgar Bergen and his wooden dummy Charlie McCarthy, Eddie Cantor, Don Ameche, Nelson Eddy, Bing Crosby and Bob Hope were just a few of the entertainers who became well known as members of the family. Fictional heroes such as the Lone Ranger, the Green Hornet and the Shadow added suspense to the lives of millions. Good radio drama, which required the audience to use its powers of imagination to visualize what was happening, was provided by such weekly shows as *Lux Radio Theater* and the *Mercury Theater on the Air.*

The Soap Opera. Radio introduced another entertainment genre that is still with us today—the soap opera. Radio soap operas (named after the early sponsors of

BOX 9.1 cont.

ing, "May I introduce myself, delighted to see you, and can you tell me when some of our blokes will be along?" I told him soon and asked to see one of the barracks. It happened to be occupied by Czechoslovakians. When I entered, men crowded around, tried to lift me to their shoulders. They were too weak. Many of them could not get out of bed. I was told that this building had once stabled eighty horses. There were twelve hundred men in it, five to a bunk. The stink was beyond all description.

When I reached the center of the barracks, a man came up and said, "You remember me. I'm Peter Zenkl, one-time mayor of Prague." I remembered him, but did not recognize him. He asked about Benes and Jan Masaryk. I asked how many men had died in that building during the last month. They called the doctor; we inspected his records. There were only names in the little black book, nothing more—nothing of who these men were, what they had done, or hoped. Behind the names of those who had died there was a cross. I counted them. They totaled 242. Two hundred and forty-two out of twelve hundred in one month.

As I walked down to the end of the barracks,

there was applause from the men too weak to get out of bed. It sounded like the hand clapping of babies; they were so weak. The doctor's name was Paul Heller. He had been there since 1938.

As we walked out into the courtyard, a man fell dead. Two others—they must have been over sixty—were crawling toward the latrine. I saw it but will not describe it.

In another part of the camp they showed me the children, hundreds of them. Some were only six. One rolled up his sleeve, showed me his number. It was tattooed on his arm. D-6030, it was. The others showed me their numbers; they will carry them till they die.

An elderly man standing beside me said, "The children, enemies of the state." I could see their ribs through their thin shirts. The old man said, "I am Professor Charles Richer of the Sorbonne." The children clung to my hands and stared. We crossed to the courtyard. Men kept coming up to speak to me and to touch me, professors from Poland, doctors from Vienna, men from all Europe. Men from the countries that made America.

Source: From Edward R. Murrow, In Search of Light: The Broadcasts of Edward R. Murrow, 1938–1961 *(New York: Knopf, 1967), pp. 91–92. Copyright © 1967 by the Estate of Edward R. Murrow. Reprinted by permission of Alfred A. Knopf, Inc.*

the shows, which were mostly soap companies) were similar to the daytime soaps on television today—with a couple of exceptions. First, radio soaps were only 15 minutes long and their characters had "romances" (such as *The Romance of Helen Trent*) rather than affairs. Today's TV soap opera characters also tend to be younger and sexier than their radio counterparts.

Early radio soap operas, particularly during the Depression, provided listeners with an escape from their troubles; they were often comforted to find that the radio characters had worse problems than their own. Up to 80 soap operas a day were broadcast during radio's golden years (1930s–40s). Although many made the transition to television, only one—*The Guiding Light*—was still on the air in the 1990s. Television, of course, has introduced new, faster-paced soap operas tailored for prime-time, such as *Dallas, Dynasty, Knots Landing* and *Falcon Crest*.*

* Prime time is 8-11 P.M. on both coasts, 7-10 P.M. in the midwest and mountain states.

▪ Charles Correll and Freeman Gosden played Amos and Andy on radio for decades. They were able to play multiple characters, all with African-American dialects, and the show became one of the most popular in America. When television entered the popular culture, Correll and Gosden had to find African-American actors and actresses to play the parts they had created in order for the show to make a successful transition to the new entertainment medium. It was later taken off the air for being racially stereotyped.

▪ Vaudeville comics Gracie Allen and George Burns were among many husband-and-wife comedy teams to be successful on radio.

A Mobile and Credible Medium.   Radio has always been a mobile form of entertainment. The Great Depression forced many Americans to leave their homes in search of jobs, but their favorite programs were always waiting for them when they reached their destinations. And now that the transistor has made radios portable by eliminating the need for bulky vacuum tubes, people can take radios with them anywhere. Sony "Walkmans," headsets and other portable radios can be seen today as constant companions for sunbathers, joggers, bicyclists and other people on the go.

Radio's credibility as a news medium also affected the culture. As radio news bureaus developed in the 1930s, regular programs were frequently interrupted for special news bulletins. An ear-witness account in 1937 of the fiery crash of the German dirigible *Hindenberg,* which killed 36 people in New Jersey, helped establish radio's credibility. As more and more people came to depend on radio to take their ears to the scenes of major news events, the stage was set for one of the most famous hoaxes ever played on the American public.

On the eve of Halloween in 1938, a 23-year-old radio producer and actor, Orson Welles, broadcast his rendition of H. G. Wells's novel *War of the Worlds* on the *Mercury Theater of the Air.*

All week the cast had been struggling to adapt the story to radio and was finding it difficult to make the drama believable. So Welles decided to present the story as an interruption of a regular music broadcast, with news reporters breathlessly cutting in to describe the landing of creatures from Mars.

▪ On Halloween eve in 1938, 23-year-old Orson Welles drove the nation to panic with his radio adaptation of H. G. Wells's *War of the Worlds,* which was about Martians landing on the planet earth.

Although the broadcast included four announcements that the attack was just a dramatization, many people were listening to the Edgar Bergen and Charlie McCarthy show on another network when *War of the Worlds* started. During the first commercial on the McCarthy program, many people turned the dial to see what else was on. They tuned in to an announcer describing a strange creature climbing out of a vessel in Grovers Mill, New Jersey. Then they heard the announcer being annihilated by the creature's ray gun. National panic set in, as people telephoned friends and relatives to warn them of the impending disaster.

By the end of the hour-long broadcast, people had attempted suicide, jammed long-distance telephone lines and caused national pandemonium. Military personnel were called back to their bases. In Concrete, Washington, a power failure during the broadcast caused a traffic jam, as most of the town's residents fled to their automobiles to escape the invading Martians.

To understand how so many people could be fooled by a radio drama, one must remember that times were tense. The nation was in its eighth year of economic depression, Hitler had taken over Czechoslovakia and world war was imminent. And radio was a new and believable news medium. Psychologists and sociologists spent years afterward studying Welles's national panic. In the meantime, the FCC quickly stepped in and banned fictional news bulletins from the airwaves.

RADIO LOSES ITS NICHE

Radio prospered during World War II and the years right after the war, but soon the cloud of television began to cast its shadow over the medium.

The radio networks were turning their attention to TV, and numerous station owners were applying for TV licenses. Many people saw television as an improvement on radio, since it provided pictures as well as sound.

The CBS Raid. Television's breakthrough year was 1948, when radio network advertising revenue reached an all-time high of $210 million. This was also the year that CBS made its famous raid on NBC radio personalities, signing such stars as Jack Benny, Amos 'n' Andy, Burns and Allen, Edgar Bergen and Bing Crosby to CBS television contracts.

According to broadcast historian Erik Barnouw, CBS's coup was made possible by the American income-tax laws. CBS convinced these radio stars that they would reduce their taxes by ''selling'' their shows to CBS, since money from the sales would be taxed at the lower capital gains rate. CBS succeeded in buying all of NBC's highly rated Sunday night entertainers and gained control of important talent for the new television age.[2]

NBC's Recovery Efforts. NBC responded by signing for its TV network the popular vaudeville and nightclub comedian Milton Berle. To ensure that he wouldn't be stolen away, they offered him a 33-year contract. It seemed like a wise investment as Berle became ''Mr. Television'' and gave NBC several years of high ratings. He used many of his vaudeville and burlesque routines on television, such as dressing in outlandish costumes (many times in drag or in gorilla suits), and he featured lots of slapstick. However, TV shows proved not to have the staying power of their radio predecessors. After eight years people began to tire of Berle, ratings declined and the show was taken off the air. Milton Berle was forced to retire—on full salary for another 25 years.

SPECIALIZATION GIVES RADIO A NEW NICHE

As the networks focused their attention on television, there was a steady decline in radio ratings and earnings. However, radio did not die, as some had predicted. Television had stolen radio's programming format and left it with a choice— change or die. It chose the former. After a period of transition it found its new niche in the specialization stage of the EPS cycle.

Music and News.   Gradually radio eliminated its programming of ballroom music, quiz shows, soap operas, sitcoms, dramas and action/adventure shows and replaced them with a basic format of music and news. Network affiliate stations, which had formerly all sounded alike, now took on their own identities. One station in an area might play Top 40 music, while others would feature rhythm-and-blues, country-and-western, jazz or classical music. Born with this new era of radio was the disc jockey—an announcer who developed a following for his or her on-the-air personality and choices of music.

The development of the disc jockey era was not without controversy, however. In 1959 the radio industry was rocked by the "payola scandal." A number of disc jockeys, including Alan Freed, the man who coined the term *rock-'n'-roll,* were charged with taking money and gifts from the recording industry to plug certain records. Many disc jockeys lost their jobs, and stations now hired program directors to select the music that would be played on the air. Radio-station employees must still sign a form acknowledging awareness of the FCC payola rules and promising to report to management any record company gift worth more than $25.

The new era of specialization of radio and its popular music formats coincided with the development of rock-'n'-roll as the most successful form of popular music. Ever since the 1950s, the success of radio and that of popular recordings have been dependent on one another.

All-News and All-Talk.   Not all radio stations feature music, however. All-news stations broadcast a complete news show every 20 minutes or so—20 minutes is the average driving time for an all-news listener.

All-talk shows feature a host with guests and/or telephone call-ins. Topics for the call-in shows range from personal and sexual problems to politics; popular hosts include Chuck Harder and his *For the People* show, sex therapist Dr. Ruth Westheimer and political journalist Larry King. The call-in format has become very popular in our culture, as it gives listeners a chance to get advice for personal problems or to "sound off" about current issues.

■ Dr. Ruth Westheimer became a well-known sex therapist by voicing her views on talk radio.

Sports.   Radio still plays a major role in broadcasting sports events, despite television's inroads in this field. Credit for this must be given to radio's mobility. Radio can be taken to work, on picnics and so forth. Some people even take their radios to the sporting event, to give themselves an opportunity to "hear" as well as "see" the activities. In addition, the advent of pay-TV and cable sports networks with exclusive contracts has limited many people's access to televised sporting events.

Programming Potpourri.   According to the 1990 *Gale Directory of Publications and Broadcasting Media,* radio stations are now categorized under no less than 25 programming formats (see Table 9.1). The advantages of this new formula radio are many. Not only do radio stations now focus on specialized listening needs, but they can deliver well-defined audiences to advertisers.

Recently TV has mounted a new challenge to radio, as TV itself enters the specialization stage. Cable channels such as MTV and VH-1 are competing with contemporary hit radio stations by showing music videos, while other channels have begun to feature talk shows and radio personalities such as Dr. Ruth.

TECHNOLOGY AND SPECIALIZATION

A number of technological improvements have also helped radio to find its new niche in our popular culture.

TABLE 9.1 RADIO STATION FORMATS   **229**

9 ■
RADIO: A
WIRELESS
WONDER

Adult Contemporary
Agricultural
Album-Oriented Rock
Alternative/New Wave/Progressive
Big Band/Nostalgia
Blue Grass
Classic Rock
Classical
Contemporary Country
Contemporary Hit Radio (CHR)
Country
Easy Listening
Electric/Full Service
Ethnic
Jazz
Light Soft Rock
Middle-of-the-Road (MOR)
News
Oldies
Public/Educational
Religious
Sports
Talk
Top 40
Urban Contemporary

SOURCE: *Gale Directory of Publications and Broadcasting Media,* vol. 3 (Detroit: Gale Research, 1990).

FM Radio.   Radio reception quality was enhanced by the development of FM (frequency modulation) broadcasting. FM operates on a higher frequency and sends its signals in a straight line. Thus it avoids the atmospheric distortion that is common in AM (amplitude modulation) broadcasting, which bounces its signals off the ionosphere. FM has less static and higher quality and was the first to broadcast in stereo.

Although FM was introduced before World War II, it did not become a successful alternative to AM broadcasting at first. However, in the 1960s the FCC made several decisions that assisted the development of FM radio. One was a freeze on the allocation of new AM licenses, leaving FM as the only avenue for new radio stations. The second was an FCC ruling that allowed FM to broadcast in stereo. The third was the 1967 "nonduplication rule," which required AM–FM combination stations to limit the duplication of their programming on both frequencies. (This regulation was abandoned in the mid-1980s.) In 1945 only 50 FM stations were on the air. In 1960 there were 688. By 1990 there were more than 5,600 FM stations reaching 95 percent of American households.[3] In the 1980s some AM stations began fighting back against the growing popularity of FM radio by broadcasting in stereo. This effort was aided in the 1990s when automobile manufacturers started placing AM stereo radios in cars.

The future of radio continues to look bright. By 1990 there were 10,650 radio stations operating in the United States: 4,972 AMs, 4,258 commercial FMs and

BOX 9.2

▪ WORKING IN RADIO ▪

Experience is important when it comes to getting a job in radio. Most people start at small stations and work their way up the ladder. Getting that first job at a small station often requires working for very low wages. However, this is necessary because larger stations won't hire a person without experience.

Departments within a radio station depend on the size of the station. Usually, there are six divisions that offer employment. These include management, programming, sales, news, traffic and engineering.

The *management* of a radio station is essential to ensure that profits are made, departments operate efficiently and bills, paperwork, personnel and payroll are handled. Depending on the size of the station, there is a general manager and perhaps a station manager. These positions can be combined at smaller stations. The general manager is in charge of the overall operation of the company. The station manager handles the day-to-day operations.

The *programming department* consists of the program director, who is responsible for the station's on-the-air content, the announcers and the disc jockeys. The content of the station depends on the format that management has selected. It might be a specialized type of music or all-talk or news. Some stations today rely on satellite-fed programming that is made available through syndicated services. Others use computerized equipment to cut down on the need for music selection and announcers.

The *sales department* is responsible for generating the revenue to keep the station on the air and

make a profit. This department has a sales manager and a sales force that usually works on a commission, selling air time to clients who wish to advertise. Each station has a rate card that gives the costs for commercials. The rate card is usually dependent on the station's share of the audience in the market—the bigger the audience at given times, the higher the station can charge for commercials.

The *news department* is composed of a news director, on-the-air newscasters, reporters and writers. Some stations have large news staffs that gather news from the community, while others rely on announcers to "rip and read" stories from the wire services. All-news operations have much larger staffs than music-oriented stations.

The *traffic department* is in charge of the daily program log that shows when programs and commercials are aired. Today this log is usually computerized. The log is the official blueprint for all on-the-air talent to follow and becomes the permanent record of the station for billing purposes.

The *engineering department* is responsible for keeping the station on the air and for maintaining the equipment. The chief engineer is trained in electronics and must not only keep the station's transmitter and other equipment in good repair but must be up-to-date on new equipment and technologies to keep the station "state-of-the-art." In large stations, the engineering department is responsible for operating the turntables and mixing boards. At smaller stations this is handled by the disc jockeys and announcers.

1,420 noncommercial FMs.[4] The commercial stations were generating an $8.8 billion in advertising revenue.[5]

Public Radio.   Another avenue for specialization—primarily for elite rather than mass cultural tastes—is provided by noncommercial educational radio stations. Many of these stations are owned and supported by educational institutions, others by private foundations.

There are two networks that serve these noncommercial stations—National

Public Radio (NPR) and American Public Radio (APR). NPR, founded in 1970, receives its funding through the Corporation for Public Broadcasting (CPB), which was established by the Public Broadcasting Act of 1967. The sources of CPB's funding are the federal government, private donations and station membership fees.

NPR provides about 50 hours of programming each week for some 300 affiliates. Its two in-depth news programs—*Morning Edition* and *All Things Considered*—are highly regarded. Another popular show produced by NPR is *Car Talk* featuring Tom and Ray Magliozzi. In 1979 NPR became the first radio network to use satellites to transmit its programming.

Unlike NPR, APR does not produce programs, but instead distributes programming produced by its member stations. It uses some of NPR's satellite distribution facilities to accomplish this. For many years, APR distributed the popular *Prairie Home Companion* starring Garrison Keillor. The weekly show, with its fictitious little Minnesota town called "Lake Wobegon," went off the air in 1987 after Keillor decided to retire and devote more time to writing. However, by popular demand, APR has been featuring *Prairie Home Companion* in rebroadcasts and in an annual live broadcast, which Keillor produces, on the anniversary of the last regular *Prairie Home Companion*. The program still remains a favorite with its cultlike following (see Box 9.3).

SUMMARY

Although radio is a twentieth-century mass-communication medium, its beginnings date to the nineteenth century, when scientists were attempting to discover ways to convert sound waves into electrical energy. Samuel Morse's invention of the telegraph, Alexander Graham Bell's discovery of the telephone, Guglielmo Marconi's wireless telegraphy and Lee De Forest's amplifier vacuum tube all contributed to the development of radio.

Radio became a mass-communication medium in the 1920s, when stations started broadcasting music and news bulletins. Companies such as Westinghouse, General Electric, RCA and AT&T played major roles in converting radio from a maritime communication system to a mass medium. They did so to sell more radio receivers.

The development of the networks in the late 1920s launched radio into its golden age as a news and entertainment medium. American lifestyles were drastically changed as people were able to hear major news events live from the scene and enjoy the very finest entertainment free in their homes.

During the Great Depression, many people escaped their troubles by listening to radio. They were also able to take their entertainment with them when they migrated to find new jobs in distant places.

After television adopted radio's programming in the 1950s, radio entered the specialized stage. Stations learned to cater to distinct segments of the listening audience and adopted music and news as the basis of their programming. The

BOX 9.3

■ COMPANION TO "PRAIRIE" LOVERS ENDS HIS REIGN ■

The following article was written for the Los Angeles Times *by staff writer Dennis McDougal, who covered the last broadcast of Garrison Keillor's* A Prairie Home Companion.

ST. PAUL, Minn.—Garrison Keillor shut down Ralph's Pretty Good Grocery, Bertha's Kitty Boutique and the Chatterbox Cafe with style and grace Saturday, declining to accept "cheap bronze plaques" commemorating his 13-year run as host of radio's *A Prairie Home Companion* and returning to the stage for no fewer than a half-dozen encores following his final public appearance.

Outside the World Theatre where the gangly, iguana-eyed radio personality has performed for nearly a decade, the mayor of St. Paul, George Latimer, released 10,000 yellow, orange and blue balloons and a local theater troupe serenaded Keillor. A crowd of 500 strong women, good-looking men and above-average children jockeyed for a glimpse of their departing hero while a brass band played.

It was wholesome Americana: a scene straight out of *The Music Man, Our Town* . . . or *Blue Velvet.*

The 44-year-old storyteller—hailed as the new Mark Twain—told a sold-out audience several times during the 2½-hour show that he would miss them more than they would miss him. He packs for Denmark next week, where he claims he will resume his life as a shy, retiring writer of fiction.

With his backup orchestra and the show's soloists playing a spate of melancholy melodies ranging from *Remember Me* to *Till We Meet Again,* his farewell radio program very nearly crossed over the line from the climax of a broadcast phenomenon to a sentimental sob fest.

Handkerchiefs and Kleenex came out all over the tiny World Theatre when Keillor sang farewell to Lake Wobegon in his low flannel voice:

"I looked back and shed a tear, to see it in my rear-view mirror, I said I'd just be gone a couple of weeks, and now it's been 30 years," he sang.

Lake Wobegon, "The little town that time forgot," sprang from Keillor's own tragic-comic memories of his Midwestern fundamentalist upbringing just 50 miles north of St. Paul in suburban Anoka County.

But that all changed after his national radio audience grew in recent years to more than 3.5 million listeners. After more than a million sales of his novel, *Lake Wobegon Days,* in 1985, Keillor and his sad little Minnesota town became more American than Mayberry, Muncie or apple pie.

The Disney Channel has been televising the show since March, and fan mail protesting the demise of *A Prairie Home Companion* has poured in by the bag load at Minnesota Public Radio, the show's producer. Director Sydney Pollack bought the film rights to the novel and explored upper Minnesota with Keillor some months ago in search of the non-existent town and its archetypal residents for the purposes of making a movie.

In the most recent tour books, even the American Automobile Club has felt compelled to print a descriptive paragraph, warning summer travelers not to go searching for Lake Wobegon because it exists "only on a popular Saturday night radio program."

But true Keillor fans are undaunted by such

development of FM radio also enhanced the medium. There are two national public radio networks that service noncommercial education stations. They are National Public Radio and American Public Radio.

Radio continues to have a strong impact on our culture, with nearly everyone owning radios and young people spending more time with radio than with any other mass medium.

BOX 9.3 cont.

facts. What they are after, says Van Nuys resident Don Browne who personally paid more than $1,000 for tickets, air fare and hotel charges to see the last show, is Truth with a nostalgic capital *T*.

"I first heard the show in June of 1980 and I immediately went to the library looking for Lake Wobegon," said the UCLA research scientist. "They can say it doesn't exist, but there's a lot of it right here (in St. Paul). Everything's a lot simpler, a lot more honest. You try to cash a check in Westwood, they ask you for three pieces of ID and a blood sample. But it's not like that here at all."

In Lake Wobegon, Bob's Bank operates out of a green mobile home on Main Street, "where your money is safe and the door is always open," according to a "commercial" that aired from time to time on *A Prairie Home Companion*.

Every check issued by the bank carried both Bob's picture and the inscription: "Cash this. They're friends of mine," according to Keillor's vision.

Garrison's friends flocked in from all over the United States this last show: Philadelphia; Shreveport, La,; Honolulu; Los Angeles . . . In fact, there were very few from St. Paul or Minneapolis in the audience. When he asked for a hand from his fellow Minnesotans in the audience, the applause was scattered.

Carroll and Joyce Lehman drove all the way from Keene, N.H., to see the last of Keillor and counted themselves lucky to get $100 tickets. What more wholesome way could they spend their 22nd wedding anniversary.

"It was wonderful! It was just wonderful!" Joyce squealed.

"She grew up in Iowa and she says that Garrison knows just how it was," Carroll Lehman said of his effervescing mate.

Keillor spun his final weekly report of the news from Lake Wobegon by freezing Mayor Clint Bunsen, Pastor Ingqvist, a half-dozen Norwegian bachelor farmers and all the rest of his Minnesota characters in the timeless fantasy of a quirky wholesome town that disappeared amid freeways and fast-food franchises long before Keillor decided to abandon his show and go to Denmark.

In his finest storytelling hush, Keillor told his audience that the last day he spent in his imaginary hometown was Wednesday, June 10, 1987.

It was raining, ending a long spring drought. A great long rain, he called it.

Everyone crowded into the Chatterbox Cafe because it was that kind of a day—a cream of mushroom soup and toasted cheese sandwich kind of a day in Lake Wobegon. With Keillor's voice growing quieter and more confidential with each sentence, he described in loving detail how the rain turned into a surrealistic mist as his characters faded from view.

"And here it is. This mist. You could get to anywhere you wanted to get in it," he told his rapt and weepy audience. The talk in the cafe had turned to the planting of the last sweet corn, now that the drought was done. The great, long rain would mean that the crop would not fail, the river would rise and it would be possible to sail on down the river and see at last what was around the bend.

Outside the World Theatre on Saturday it was a hot, muggy June afternoon. Inside it was cold and misty and the 925 people who watched the last show shared a final grilled cheese sandwich with Keillor before he said goodby.

"That's where I leave them," he said. "If you see them, give them my best and tell them I think of them. That's the news from Lake Wobegon."

THOUGHT QUESTIONS

1 What cultural factors were at work to create the need for the development of wireless communication?

2 What social and economic forces contributed to the conversion of radio into a mass-communication medium?

3 Why did so many Americans believe the *War of the Worlds* broadcast was true? Could something similar happen today? Why or why not?

4 What other mass media helped radio move smoothly into the stage of specialization? Be able to identify and explain the role of three other media.

5 Why have the number of AM and FM radio stations and the number of radios in our culture grown during the era of television?

NOTES

1. Quoted in Archer Gleason, *History of Radio to 1926* (New York: American Historical Society, 1938), p. 85.

2. Erik Barnouw, *The Golden Web: A History of Broadcasting in the United States* (New York: Oxford University Press, 1968), p. 245.

3. *The Broadcasting Yearbook 1990* (Washington, D.C.: Broadcasting Publications, Inc., 1990), p. A-3.

4. Ibid.

5. *Media Current Analysis* (Standard & Poor's Industrial Surveys, August 2, 1990).

ADDITIONAL READING

Aitken, H. G. *Syntony and Spark—The Origins of Radio.* New York: Wiley, 1976.

Allen, Robert C. *Speaking of Soap Operas.* Chapel Hill: University of North Carolina Press, 1985.

Baker, W. J. *A History of the Marconi Company.* New York: St. Martin's, 1971.

Barnouw, Erik. *A Tower of Babel.* New York: Oxford University Press, 1966.
————. *The Image Empire.* New York: Oxford University Press, 1970.

Brooks, John. *Telephone: The First Hundred Years.* New York: Harper & Row, 1976.

Campbell, Robert. *The Golden Years of Broadcasting: A Celebration of the First 50 Years of Radio and Television on NBC.* New York: Scribner's, 1976.

Davis, Stephen. *The Law of Radio.* New York: McGraw-Hill, 1927.

Dunning, John. *Tune in Yesterday: The Ultimate Encyclopedia of Old-Time Radio, 1925-1976.* Englewood Cliffs, N.J.: Prentice-Hall, 1976.

Fang, Irving E. *Those Radio Commentators!* Ames: Iowa State University Press, 1977.

Friendly, Fred. *Due to Circumstances Beyond Our Control.* New York: Random House, 1978.

Head, Sydney W. *Broadcasting in America: A Survey of Television and Radio,* 3rd ed. Boston: Houghton Mifflin, 1976.

Hettinger, Herman S. *A Decade of Radio Advertising.* Chicago: University of Chicago Press, 1933.

Post, Steve. *Playing in the FM Band.* New York: Viking, 1974.

Sarnoff, David. *Looking Ahead: The Papers of David Sarnoff.* New York: McGraw-Hill, 1968.

Schubert, Paul. *The Electric Word: The Rise of Radio.* New York: Macmillan, 1928.

Settel, Irving. *A Pictorial History of Radio,* 2nd ed. New York: Grosset & Dunlap, 1967.

Sterling, Christopher H., and Kittross, John M. *Stay Tuned: A Concise History of American Broadcasting.* Belmont, Calif.: Wadsworth, 1978.

Instant television news coverage of the Persian Gulf war in 1991 added a new dimension to war reporting and catapulted Cable News Network (CNN) to a leadership position as a global news source. CNN news reports by Peter Arnett, who remained in the enemy capital of Baghdad throughout the war, sparked complaints by some who felt he was being used by Saddam Hussein to give an anti-American view of the results of allied bombings.

Peter Arnett
Baghdad, Iraq

CNN
LIVE

TELEVISION AND PEOPLE OF COLOR

People of color have been portrayed in a variety of ways on American television screens over the years. The first sitcom to feature African-Americans was *Amos 'n' Andy.* Although it had long been a favorite on radio, it was taken off the air after several successful seasons on television because it was felt that it negatively stereotyped black people. On radio the parts of Amos and Andy were played by two white men. An all-black cast had to be assembled when the show made its transition to television. *(Everett Collection)*

(Left) *Julia,* which starred Diahann Carroll as an African-American nurse, began featuring blacks in professional roles in the 1960s. It was one of the first shows to feature people of color in roles that were not demeaning. *(Photofest)*

(Right) *All in the Family,* starring Carroll O'Connor as the classic bigot Archie Bunker, dealt with racial prejudice as one of its themes. The show portrayed Lionel Jefferson, Bunker's next door neighbor, as a likable young black man who forced Bunker to deal with his prejudices. Later the Jefferson family got a show of their own. *(Henry Gris/FPG International)*

(Top, facing page) *Diff'rent Strokes* was another sitcom that dealt with the issue of blacks and whites living together. In this show Todd Bridges and Gary Coleman played African-American brothers who were adopted into an upper-class white family. *(NBC/Globe Photos)*

(Center) Oprah Winfrey broke the all-white talk show host barrier in the 1980s by becoming the host of her own popular daytime show. Another popular daytime talk show, hosted by a Hispanic, featured Geraldo Rivera. (Globe Photos)

(Bottom) Arsenio Hall began challenging the popular late night talk show king Johnny Carson in the late 1980s. His style of comedy drew a large audience. Here he is shown being interviewed by Connie Chung during a CBS television special in 1990. (Everett Collection)

(Top) Rap star Will Smith got a TV sitcom of his own in the fall of 1990 in *Fresh Prince of Bel Air.* The plot revolved around Smith, who leaves his ghetto home to live with his upper-class aunt, uncle and cousins in their Bel Air mansion and takes his cool rap culture with him. The sitcom not only featured Smith performing rap songs but also had a rap musical beat in the background. *(NBC/Globe Photos)*

(Bottom) *In Living Color* was one of a long list of offbeat shows developed in the 1990s for Rupert Murdoch's Fox network. The show featured an almost all African-American cast (with two token whites) and used ethnic humor to create spoofs on racism and other cultural biases. *(Everett Collection)*

TELEVISION: FROM SOAPS TO SATELLITES

Children will watch anything, and when a broadcaster uses crime and violence and other shoddy devices to monopolize a child's attention it's worse than taking candy from a baby. It is taking precious time from the process of growing up.

—Newton Minow, former chairman, Federal Communications Commission

"This is home, not a restaurant," Peg Bundy replies to her husband Al's request for dinner. "I know. If it was a restaurant, we'd have a clean bathroom," Al retorts.

After four decades of sweet, wholesome families depicted on the television screen, the Fox network's *Married . . . With Children*, featuring the Bundy family, was in sharp contrast to the stereotype that TV had created for the "typical" nuclear family. It was one of several nontraditional family sitcoms that climbed into the top of the ratings during the early years of the 1990s.

CULTURAL HISTORY OF TELEVISION

ELITIST	POPULAR	SPECIALIZED		
▓			1923	Vladimir Zworykin, working for Westinghouse, develops a television camera tube.
▓			1927	Philo Farnsworth applies for electronic television patents.
▓			1936	Great Britain is the first country to begin regular television broadcasting.
▓			1939	Large numbers of Americans see television for the first time at New York's World's Fair.
▓			1941	FCC authorizes commercial television broadcasting in the United States.
▓			1946	Color television demonstrated by CBS and NBC.
▓	▓		1948	Television's breakthrough year; CBS and NBC begin offering regular news and entertainment on TV.
	▓		1951	Microwave provides coast-to-coast television broadcasts.
	▓		1952	Edward R. Murrow changes radio's popular *Hear It Now* to *See It Now.*
	▓		1952	FCC lifts the freeze on new stations that it had imposed in 1948.
	▓		1954	Army-McCarthy hearings are televised; Murrow risks career to challenge McCarthy on *See it Now.*
	▓		1956	*Playhouse 90* brings high-quality live drama to television.
	▓		1956	Television begins extensive coverage of presidential elections.
	▓		1959	Westerns dominate TV entertainment.

A second Fox show that skyrocketed to the top of the ratings was an animated, bickering family known as *The Simpsons*. Homer Simpson's son, Bart—a brat spouting such phrases as "don't have a cow, man"—soon became a folk hero stimulating sales in the consumer culture with products ranging from T-shirts and dolls to posters.

Over on ABC in 1990 *Roseanne* was displacing the last of the real nuclear families—*The Cosby Show*—as the number-one-rated show in prime time. Episodes of *Roseanne* would find this working mother of the Conner family wishing she could trade her husband and nagging kids for a dishwasher. Soon Fox, which was boldly attempting to become the fourth major network, was pitting *The*

CULTURAL HISTORY OF TELEVISION

ELITIST	POPULAR	SPECIALIZED		
	▓		1963	Television's coverage of Kennedy assassination demonstrates its power to unite nation in one emotion.
	▓		1967	Congress establishes Corporation for Public Broadcasting to fund educational and cultural programs.
	▓		1968	Riots outside Democratic convention televised; TV blamed for nation's unrest.
	▓		1969	World watches man's landing on the moon live on television.
	▓		1971	*All in the Family* brings Archie Bunker and controversial issues to TV comedy.
	▓		1973–74	Watergate hearings and impeachment proceedings televised; Nixon resigns.
	▓		1977	*Roots* becomes most popular mini-series; this program format becomes an effective way to increase ratings.
	▓		1978	*Dallas* revives popularity of evening soap operas.
		▓	1980s	Cable television and VCRs change American viewing habits; network popularity begins to decline.
		▓	1982	Home Shopping Network debuts—advertising becomes programming.
		▓	1987	Iran-Contra hearings televised; Oliver North becomes a folk hero.
		▓	1988	ABC preempts two weeks of prime-time programming to televise the Calgary Winter Olympics.
		▓	1990s	Fox network programming forces Big 3 to adopt tabloid-TV style to compete.

Simpsons up against NBC's longstanding ratings success, *The Cosby Show,* at the 8 P.M. Thursday time slot.

Third-place CBS launched a nontraditional family sitcom, *Uncle Buck,* as part of its efforts to boost ratings in the fall of 1990. A spinoff of the 1989 movie of the same name, the show featured an uncle who was somewhat of a slob, strapped with taking care of his brother's children—two smart-aleck girls and a boy.

The longstanding TV tradition of depicting the father as a pillar of wisdom, the mother as guardian of the home and the kids as sweet but mischievous, has been changed by shows which present the father as a slob or oaf, the mother as a sarcastic incompetent and the kids as disrespectful brats. And the audience,

■ Bart Simpson became a folk hero for his offbeat antics on Fox Network's popular adult cartoon show *The Simpsons*. His character fed the consumer culture with products ranging from T-shirts to posters.

according to the ratings, loves it. Some psychologists attribute the popularity of the antifamily shows to the fact that the audience can breathe a sigh of relief, knowing that their own families are all right by comparison.

Whatever the reason for the popularity of this new trend of family shows, it demonstrates that the American TV industry is constantly searching for and finding new ways to add to its commercial success. Television started out in the 1940s as a novelty—radio with pictures—and by the 1960s it had become this nation's most important entertainment medium. It also has become a powerful and controversial influence on our popular culture, one that not only holds up a mirror to society but also magnifies the forces of change within that society. Some have credited TV with raising the educational level of our young, while others blame it for destroying family life and individuality. Whether its impact has been positive or negative or both, there is no denying that television has transformed our culture and become a major American leisure pastime.

HOW IT BEGAN

Early Experimentation.   The story of electronic television begins in 1923, when Vladimir Zworykin, a Russian immigrant working for Westinghouse Corporation, developed the iconoscope, which was the first practical electronic tube for a television camera. Zworykin later developed the kinescope, or picture tube.

In 1927 Philo Farnsworth applied for a patent on an electronic television system, and by 1928 General Electric was experimenting with telecasting. NBC followed with experimental telecasting in 1930, and by 1939 its station in New York was offering regularly scheduled programs. In Great Britain the BBC began regular television broadcasting in 1936. However, it wasn't until the 1939 New York World's Fair that a large number of Americans saw television demonstrated for the first time.

Early TV Stations.   The FCC authorized commercial television broadcasting in 1941. However, the nation's entry into World War II in December of that year put TV's development on hold, since all electronic research and development was diverted to the war effort. However, six stations remained on the air during the war: two in New York City and one each in Schenectady, N.Y., Philadelphia, Chicago and San Francisco.

Early Programming.   Before 1948 only a small elite of Americans could afford this expensive novelty. In 1946 there were approximately 7,000 television sets in American households. Programming was limited, but it included sporting events, such as football, baseball, tennis, boxing, wrestling and hockey; news; studio productions of plays; dance recitals; musical shows; and old movies.

In the fall of 1947 TV began to generate interest in the popular culture. An estimated 3.5 million people watched the World Series on television that year, most of them in neighborhood taverns. Now they wanted TV sets in their own homes.

Breakthrough Year.   Television's breakthrough year was 1948, the year the CBS and NBC radio networks turned their attention toward it. Since television was offering radio programming with the added novelty of pictures, interest in network radio began declining and so did radio network advertising revenues. In this year CBS made its famous raid of NBC's radio stars, signing them for the new CBS television network; Milton Berle went on television for NBC, becoming "Mr. Television"; and New York newspaperman Ed Sullivan began his long-running variety show, *Toast of the Town,* on CBS.

In the fall of 1948 the FCC, recognizing that this new medium was going to grow rapidly, placed a freeze on TV-station authorizations, restricting the number to 124 (although only 108 stations actually got on the air). During the freeze, which lasted until 1952, the FCC developed a comprehensive plan to allocate television frequencies to all parts of the United States. The plan authorized 2,000 channels in 1,300 communities. The FCC also worked on a proposal to standardize color television systems and allocate educational television frequencies.

Despite the freeze, television expanded as a mass medium in 1948 to 1952. A microwave relay system was developed that allowed for the first coast-to-coast network broadcasts in 1951. The number of TV sets in American homes rose from 172,000 to 17 million during this period.

Lifting the Freeze.   After the freeze was lifted, television expanded even more rapidly. NBC and CBS were far along in their efforts to shift their interests from radio to television. A third network—DuMont—was struggling to compete. ABC merged with Paramount Theaters and followed the other three networks into television. Mutual remained a radio-only network. DuMont was unable to compete with the three former radio networks and went out of business in 1955. However, DuMont earned its place in television history by producing *The Honeymooners,* with Jackie Gleason, and using kinescopes to preserve early television on motion-picture film. Thirty-some years later, Americans were enjoying *The Honeymooners* in syndicated reruns.

EVOLUTION OF TELEVISION ENTERTAINMENT

TV entertainment started out as nothing more than a novelty. The shows consisted of pointing a camera at some action and letting it be transmitted. The early programs included variety shows, puppet-comedy shows, stand-up comedians, domestic comedies and game shows. Many of these latter programs were carbon copies of radio shows, but with pictures. People watching early television were dazzled to be able to see action and watch their longtime radio stars present familiar sitcoms in their living rooms.

Early Entertainers.   Some of the leading entertainers during the beginning years of television were Milton Berle, Ed Sullivan, the puppets Cecil the Seasick Sea Serpent and Howdy Doody, Sid Caesar, Imogene Coca, Lucille Ball, Art Carney, Jackie Gleason, Art Linkletter, Arthur Godfrey, Jack Benny, Amos 'n' Andy, ventriloquist Edgar Bergen and his dummy Charlie McCarthy, Bing Crosby, Red Skelton and the witty comedy team of George Burns and Gracie Allen.

Most of these entertainers had started their careers in vaudeville and made the transition to radio. Now they were transmitting re-creations of the early days of vaudeville into the living rooms of the United States. The content of popular cultural entertainment had not changed much since the nineteenth century. Only the delivery system had changed.

Live Drama.   Some of the best dramas ever shown on television were the plays broadcast live from New York studios in the 1950s. The major Hollywood studios, fearing competition from the new medium, refused to allow their facilities to be used to produce television programs. Two of the best-known live dramas of this "golden age" of television were Rod Serling's *Requiem for a Heavyweight* and *Days of Wine and Roses* starring Cliff Robertson and Piper Laurie. These high-quality dramas focused on character development and analysis, rather than on car chases and elaborate scenery.

Quiz Show Scandal.   Quiz shows, which had been popular on radio, offered greater rewards when transferred to television. Radio's *$64 Question* became TV's *$64,000 Question,* for example. The popularity of these shows grew as people could vicariously share in the delight of winning big money by knowing the right answers to questions.

In 1959 television was rocked by its first major scandal when it was revealed that certain quiz-show contestants had been given the questions prior to the programs. This was done to ensure that the most popular contestants would win and return the next week. Until this time, TV programs had been produced by advertising agencies and the shows' sponsors. As a result of the scandal, the FCC required quiz shows to issue disclosures whenever assistance was given to contes-

■ James Arness played Marshall Matt Dillon on television's *Gunsmoke*. This TV version of the popular radio Western had to make adjustments when it made the shift to television. Portly actor William Conrad (*Jake and the Fatman*) had been Matt Dillon on radio.

tants and the networks were forced to take over production of the programs to ensure compliance with ethical standards.

The Westerns.   By the late 1950s TV entertainment had moved from live quiz and variety shows, domestic comedies and drama to prerecorded dramatic series. The first genre to develop was the Western, which had long been popular in movies and on radio. Such shows as *Gunsmoke* and *Have Gun, Will Travel,* which had been popular on radio, *Wyatt Earp, Colt 45, The Rifleman* and *The Virginian* occupied the TV screen during prime time. By 1959 there were 30 Westerns on prime time each week.

Also in 1959 *Bonanza* began airing on NBC at 7:30 on Saturday evenings to sell color television sets for its parent company, RCA. It was the only color show on TV, and its time slot was important because department stores were open at that time and color sets could be demonstrated by showing *Bonanza*.

Bonanza transmitted the American myth that the rugged rural life of the "good old days" was a glamorous and comfortable time. The program revolved around three grown sons, at least two of them in their 30s, still at home and subject to the authority of their father. Some sociologists felt that the show appealed to people who missed the parental authority and support they had given up to leave home and marry.[1] Whatever the reason, *Bonanza* was one of the most popular shows on the air for 15 years.

Urban Westerns.   Other genres that became popular during this period were doctor, police, detective and courtroom shows, in which—as in the Westerns— good always prevailed over evil. These adventure stories were sometimes referred to as "urban Westerns" because the moral themes were the same as in the Westerns; only the location and time period were changed. Some of the urban Westerns were *Dragnet, Highway Patrol, Racket Squad, The Lineup, Perry Mason* and *The Defenders.* A few years later came *The Man from U.N.C.L.E.* and *Mission Impossible,* series dealing with international intrigue and spy chasing, as the "good guys" pursued the forces of evil around the world.

Variety Shows.   Variety shows, hosted by such performers as Carol Burnett, Bob Hope and Sonny and Cher, provided cheerful escape during the 1960s. However, by the late 1960s one variety show—*The Smothers Brothers*—was introducing realism and social commentary into evening entertainment. In keeping with the cultural unrest and growing displeasure with the Vietnam war that was sweeping the country, the show ridiculed the war and other social ills and soon was canceled by CBS in a dispute over censorship. Audiences, the network executives felt, did not want controversy and realism mixed with their entertainment.

Another variety show that debuted in 1968, *Rowan and Martin's Laugh-In,* became popular with younger audiences by dealing with sexual and political themes, topics that reflected the new openness that had swept the nation during the 1960s. Its hosts, Dan Rowan and Dick Martin, were able to touch on these topics without irritating network executives the way the Smothers Brothers did. This type of programming survived in the 1990s on such shows as *Saturday Night Live* and *Late Night with David Letterman.* In the meantime, the more traditional variety shows had all but disappeared by the mid-1970s, except for an occasional special.

Sitcoms.   From the beginning the most popular of all the TV entertainment genres has been the situation comedy. Other forms of television entertainment— such as the Western and variety shows—have come and gone, but the sitcoms have endured.

In an effort to appeal to middle-class America, early TV continued to produce the family sitcoms that had been popular on radio. The settings were always the same—a happy, white, middle-class home with humorous but bland family problems to cope with and solve by the end of each 30-minute show. *Father Knows Best, Make Room for Daddy, Leave It to Beaver, I Love Lucy, The Adventures of Ozzie and Harriet* and *My Three Sons* were a few of the more popular shows in this category. There were also sitcoms like *Bewitched, I Dream of Jeannie* and *The Munsters,* which featured supernatural characters trying to act like ordinary middle-class folks.

As the American culture passed through the troubled 1960s and entered the 1970s, TV sitcoms reflected changing cultural attitudes. One of the most innovative departures was *All in the Family,* a new kind of sitcom produced by Norman Lear, which debuted on January 12, 1971. For the first time, a TV sitcom was dealing with—and joking about—the culture's social issues: sex, politics and racial prejudice, issues that theretofore had been taboo on television. The show starred Carroll O'Connor as Archie Bunker, who was characterized as a classic bigot. Archie unexpectedly became a folk hero in American popular culture. Many people apparently did not recognize the satire in the program and felt Archie's bigotry reflected their own latent or not-so-latent feelings.

The show was so successful that it generated a number of spinoffs. Archie's wife, Edith, had a cousin named Maude, who eventually got a show of her own, as did Maude's maid, Florida, and the Bunker's black next-door neighbors, the Jeffersons. *All in the Family* and its spinoffs opened up the sitcom format to allow for biting social commentary in a humorous framework.

The Mini-series.   In the mid-1970s the networks tried to break down traditional viewing habits by introducing a new format, the mini-series. The idea was to get people hooked on the series in the first episode—usually broadcast on Sunday night—so they would tune in again the next several evenings. Mini-series have proven very popular and they are often scheduled during "sweep periods," when TV stations are monitored to determine audience sizes. (Sweeps are usually conducted three times a year—November, February and May—and are used to set advertising rates. High ratings means higher ad rates for the local stations and networks.)

The mini-series concept actually came from public broadcasting, which began showing BBC-produced serials such as *The Forsyte Saga* in 1969 and *Upstairs Downstairs.* In 1975 CBS attempted to emulate PBS's successful *Upstairs Downstairs* with a short-lived American version called *Beacon Hill.* This led ABC to introduce a 12-hour version of Irwin Shaw's novel *Rich Man, Poor Man* in 1976.

The following season ABC introduced *Roots,* a mini-series based on Alex Haley's book of the same name, which kept millions of viewers glued to the TV set for eight nights. The series, which traced Haley's ancestors from Africa through American slavery and into the twentieth century, set ratings records and helped keep Haley's book at the top of the best-seller lists for months (see Box 10.1). Part of the popularity of *Roots* was its powerful portrayal of one of the darker aspects of American history.

TV Sports.   Sports, which have played an important role in providing leisure enjoyment for the masses since the nineteenth century, have become an important part of television programming. The popularity of electronically mediated athletics grew rapidly after the development in the 1960s of such new technology as instant-replay television recorders. Television permanently took over as the "electronic ballpark" (see Chapter 2).

Last-place network ABC led the way with its innovative *Wide World of Sports,* which cut between live, taped and filmed sports events, some of which had taken

BOX 10.1

■ PROFILE: FRED SILVERMAN—TV'S TARNISHED "GOLDEN BOY" ■

Credit for breaking television ratings records with the successful mini-series *Roots* goes to television's "Golden Boy" Fred Silverman, whose influence on all three major networks has been unparalleled.

Silverman became the chief of programming for CBS in 1970. He was instrumental in leading the network through some major programming overhauls that gave it a wider audience range and made it number one in the ratings. Some of his daring accomplishments included putting the controversial sitcom *All in the Family* on the air in 1971.

Last-place network ABC was so impressed with Silverman's accomplishments that it lured him away in 1975 with a higher salary and the title of vice president in charge of programming. Under Silverman's leadership, ABC quickly moved to first place in the ratings, thanks in part to the popularity of *Roots.* The successful mini-series broke audience viewing habits by getting viewers hooked on the series during the first episode and keeping them tuned to ABC each succeeding night while the network promoted its own line of regular prime-time programming during commercial breaks.

Silverman's successes at ABC enticed the now-last-place NBC to offer him the presidency of the network in 1978. Although his duties were broader—head of the entire network—NBC's intentions were clear. It wanted Silverman to lead the network into the number-one ratings spot. Things were different this time around, however. Silverman found himself competing with some very effective programming strategies that he had left behind at both CBS and ABC. After three years of unsuccessful efforts to boost NBC's ratings, in 1981 the network fired Silverman. Several years later under his successor, Grant Tinker, and with the help of some programs that Silverman had been instrumental in developing while president, like *Hill Street Blues,* NBC did take over the number-one spot in network ratings.

What is he doing today? Silverman is working as an independent producer of TV programs. After several failures with *Thicke of the Night* and *We Got It Made,* he was producing such successful shows as *Jake and the Fatman, Heat of the Night* and *Matlock.* His talent was still contributing to the television industry, but the pressures to produce or else had been significantly reduced.

---

place days before in various places around the world. In 1970 ABC paid $9 million for the rights to *Monday Night Football*. Eventually ABC found itself number one in the ratings thanks to its expanded sports coverage and a new lineup of popular sitcoms like *Happy Days* and *Three's Company*.

Daytime TV.   Despite the fact that prime-time television has the largest audience and highest advertising rates, over the years daytime TV has been the biggest moneymaker. Soap operas and game shows have always been extremely popular and are much cheaper to produce, even though the game shows give away money and prizes. As we have seen, soap operas have been an important part of the American culture since the early days of radio. Today they appeal to a wide range of viewers, from homemakers to business executives (see Box 10.2).

In the 1980s, as our culture became more tolerant of open media discussions of such controversial topics as AIDS, child molestation, gay rights, spouse abuse, alcoholism and drug abuse, the popularity of daytime talk shows increased. Following the success of Phil Donahue, others like Oprah Winfrey and Geraldo Rivera were using this format to launch talk shows of their own.

Prime-time Soaps.   In 1964, ABC premiered the first prime-time soap opera, *Peyton Place,* based loosely on a steamy best-seller by Grace Metalious. Shown two or three nights a week, it launched the careers of Mia Farrow and Ryan O'Neal and demonstrated yet again the durability and versatility of the genre. Other networks were slow to follow ABC's lead, but in 1978, CBS launched *Dallas* as a weekly serial. During the 1980s it and its imitators, *Dynasty, Knots Landing* and *Falcon Crest,* topped the evening ratings by bringing the continuing stories and daytime troubles of TV families to nighttime viewers.

These shows appeal to the average person's interest in the rich and elite, and all seem to revolve around one central theme—that rich families are plagued with turmoil and strife and the American cultural myth that money can't always buy happiness is true. It doesn't matter if your name is Ewing (on *Dallas* and *Knots Landing*), Tyler (on *All My Children*), Quartermaine (on *General Hospital*), Abbott or Chancellor (on *The Young and the Restless*)—if you've got money, you've got troubles. It is worth noting that *Dallas* and *Dynasty* became the most popular American TV shows in Canada, Australia, Chile and many western European countries during the 1980s.

Hybrid TV.   As our culture evolves so do the entertainment genres on television. In the 1980s a new TV format developed that was a combination of a number of others. It borrowed the ongoing story line from the soap operas; character development of early-day TV dramas; action/adventure from the Western, police and lawyer shows; comedy from sitcoms and fast-paced action from vaudeville and TV variety shows. The genre was pioneered by Steven Bochco in 1981 with *Hill Street Blues.* Other shows, like *St. Elsewhere, Miami Vice, L.A. Law, The Wonder Years,* and *thirtysomething,* were soon utilizing these same techniques as the trend continued its popularity throughout the 1980s. Bochco's *Miami Vice* became known as an MTV cop show because of the rock music background.

In 1990, Bochco added a new dimension to MTV cop shows when he launched *Cop Rock.* Unlike *Miami Vice,* where rock music was in the background, *Cop Rock* was a musical that featured cops who actually sang and danced. The departure from regular action/adventure proved to be too radical and the series was canceled in December.

Probably the most hybrid of all TV shows was *Twin Peaks,* a droll, mildly melodramatic soap opera, introduced by ABC during the spring of 1990. The show mixed horror and humor in a witty, avant-garde fashion and soon found itself with a cultlike following. Despite this following it remained low in ratings.

Docudramas.   Another invention of the 1980s was the docudrama, which portrays a real-life situation in fictional form. While the shows take liberties with the facts to heighten the dramatic effect, the impression left in the viewer's mind is that the televised version is the way it actually happened. Although docudramas bring historical topics into the popular culture through the medium of entertainment, they cause some concern because they often blend truth with fiction.

In the summer of 1986, for example, NBC produced a docudrama about the people behind the planning and building of the Statue of Liberty in 1887. The show, called *Liberty,* ran the following disclaimer: "This story is based on actual

BOX 10.2

▪ THE SOAP OPERAS OF TELEVISION ▪
James R. Wilson

One of my students recently told me that she never schedules any of her classes between 2 and 3 P.M. because she's been hooked on *General Hospital,* a daily television soap opera, ever since she came to this country several years ago.

And she's not alone. It has been estimated that some 35 million people watch at least one soap opera every day, and 56 percent of *all* college students watch at least one per week. Is it any wonder that students gather in front of college union TV sets each day to argue over whether to watch the latest activities of Erica, Jill, Rachel or Gina?

The TV soaps have become extremely popular with college students, but others have also "come out of the closet" and admitted that they watch soaps, including business executives who now join their workers in the employee lounge during the lunch hour to watch the daytime shows. But most important, these programs remain quite popular with the homemakers of the United States—just as their radio counterparts were from the 1930s through the 1950s. During the depression years the radio soaps provided a form of escape for listeners—they had found a way to listen to stories of people who were having tougher times than they were.

Several radio soaps made the switch to television in the early days, but only one of those transplants remains on the air today: *The Guiding Light.*

The original TV soaps followed the same basic format as their radio predecessors, including the daily length of 15 minutes per show. The first half-hour soap, *As the World Turns,* made its debut in 1956. One year later, *The Edge of Night*—another 30-minute soap—debuted, and TV soap operas were changed forever as sponsors and producers found that it was a lot cheaper to put together one 30-minute program than to hire actors, writers and technical crews for two 15-minute programs.

In 1975, expansion hit the soap operas again as NBC's *Another World* went to 60 minutes daily. In 1979 it expanded to 90 minutes per day. However, this format was unsuccessful because it took so many story lines and characters to fill the time that viewers were becoming confused. *Another World* returned to its 60-minute format in 1980.

Several other soaps expanded to an hour in the 1970s, with two of them making a stop along the way. In 1976 ABC converted two of its half-hour soaps—*General Hospital* and *One Life to Live*—to 45-minute shows running back to back. Two years later they both expanded to their present one-hour format.

It was also in the 1970s that a new soap opera was introduced in an attempt to lure younger viewers with story lines involving younger people: *The Young and the Restless.*

As the 1990s began, the three major television events. However, some of the characters and incidents portrayed and the names used herein are fictitious." The producers never specified what was real and what wasn't, and viewers were left with a confusing view of a historical event.

Another example occurred in 1989. Former president Richard Nixon fought unsuccessfully to stop the production of a three-hour docudrama on the Watergate scandal that led to his resignation in 1974. Based on the Woodward and Bernstein book *The Final Days,* the ABC production, according to Nixon's lawyers, was filled with inaccuracies and was an invasion of privacy.

But a docudrama can strive for accuracy and still be entertaining. The 1988 ABC mini-series *Baby M* carefully followed the sequence of events and court records of a famous surrogate motherhood case. Winning high ratings, this docudrama brought a complex social issue into focus for the masses.

BOX 10.2 Cont.

networks were running more than 10 hours of soap operas per day and one of them, NBC, was bringing back a soap from the 1960s—one that was scheduled in the later afternoon hours because of its popularity with high school students—*Dark Shadows* (complete with vampires). However, the plan was to make it a prime-time soap.

Soap operas, begun as a radio escape in the depression years of the 1930s, survived wars and radicalism by stressing love, romance and the importance of the family unit. They not only became the most popular form of daytime programming, but they have expanded into prime time as well—from *Peyton Place,* two and three times a week in the 1960s, to *Knots Landing* and *Dallas* in the 1980s and '90s.

In addition, their popularity has been overflowing into other media. There are now magazines specifically for the soap fans, and many newspapers across the country run weekly columns designed to keep readers up-to-date on the daily activities of their favorite soap characters. To top it off, a series of books has been published that deal with the original story lines of some of the more popular shows for fans who weren't born when their favorite shows went on the air. Now those younger members of that audience of 35-million avid soap opera viewers can see how their favorite soaps began.

And the way things are going, the soaps may never end.

■ A. Martinez (Cruz) and Marcy Walker (Eden) on *Santa Barbara*.

Wilson is a professor of telecommunications at California State University, Fresno.

As Americans became more concerned about social issues during the 1980s, some made-for-TV movies began providing information on such topics as alcoholism, AIDS, incest, child kidnapping and spousal abuse.

These educationally oriented movies were very helpful in disseminating important social information in the context of leisure entertainment.

Tabloid TV. By 1988 a TV version of the titillating sensationalism of tabloid newspapers had emerged as a new genre of television programming.

Leading the way was Rupert Murdoch, the king of tabloid newspapers in Australia, Britain and the United States. Murdoch's Fox Broadcasting Company was using sex, murder and mayhem in its attempt to establish a fourth TV network made up of independent stations.

■ Critics and viewers alike began speculating on "who killed Laura Palmer?" when the melodramatic soap opera *Twin Peaks* made its debut on prime-time television in 1990. The show soon developed a cultlike following.

Fox introduced a news magazine show, *A Current Affair,* which featured bloody murder scenes, titillating sex crimes and gore. Another popular Fox show, *America's Most Wanted,* gained invaluable publicity when a number of suspects wanted for crimes (which are reenacted on the show) were apprehended as a result of the weekly broadcasts.

Fox was not the only one getting into the tabloid TV business. The networks were keen to add real-life crime shows to their line-ups, since they are so cheap and easy to produce. NBC began broadcasting *Unsolved Mysteries* as a weekly series and added *Hard Copy* to its nightly line-up, while ABC aired a special by Geraldo Rivera, *Murder: Lives from Death Row,* which included actual film footage of the murder of a convenience store customer as well as interviews with several convicted murderers talking about their crimes. (The most celebrated of these was Charles Manson.)

On the *Morton Downey Jr. Show,* the controversial talk-show host had a guest reenact the strangling of a woman in New York's Central Park by her boyfriend who claimed that he had accidentally killed her during "rough sex."

Still another questionable form of entertainment was aired by ABC during the tabloid TV era—a show featuring America's funniest (or unfunniest) home videos. Spawned by the camcorder, the show invited people to send in their funniest home videos. The 30-minute program then featured what were considered the best of the week's entries. It soon became obvious that people were staging the videos and that many of the scenes could be dangerous—particularly for children or animals—if replicated. Ironically, these seemed to be the themes that were successful in getting on the air and winning the cash prizes. After several months, ABC had to ask the producers of the show to issue warnings when soliciting videos that viewers should not tape anything that could be harmful to the persons or animals involved.

DEVELOPMENT OF TELEVISION NEWS

Networks began experimenting with news at locally owned stations as early as January 1940, when NBC began airing radio newscaster Lowell Thomas on its New York TV station. CBS's first television news broadcasts began in the spring of 1941. Since early television was unable to broadcast film of news events, newscasters simply read the news aloud to the audience. When President Roosevelt delivered his war message to Congress in December of 1941, for example, CBS's New York station put an American flag in front of the camera and turned on an off-camera fan to make it wave while the station carried the president's voice.

Although World War II produced a number of top-notch radio journalists—such as Edward R. Murrow, William L. Shirer, Eric Sevareid, Walter Cronkite, Charles Collingwood and Howard K. Smith—none of them wanted anything to do with television news after the war because they believed that radio was the more serious medium.

CBS and NBC took the first major steps in network television journalism when they broadcast the Democratic and Republican national conventions in 1948. CBS selected Douglas Edwards as its convention broadcaster; NBC named John Cameron Swayze. Their convention coverage launched both men to television stardom. Edwards soon after went on the air with a nightly 15-minute news show called *The CBS TV News.* Six months later NBC put Swayze on a 15-minute nightly newscast sponsored by Camel cigarettes and called *The Camel News Caravan.* NBC led in the ratings until 1955. In 1956, NBC replaced Swayze with co-anchors Chet Huntley and David Brinkley. In 1960 this news team was able to overtake Edwards in the ratings. Walter Cronkite replaced Edwards at CBS in 1962. A year later the networks doubled the length of the evening news to 30 minutes. It took Cronkite until 1967 before his ratings surpassed those of Huntley and Brinkley. He continued to dominate the ratings until his retirement in 1981.

ABC did not launch a news show until the 1950s, when it put radio actor John Charles Daly on the air as its newscaster. ABC news did not become a ratings contender until the late 1970s when Roone Arledge, the producer of ABC's *Wide World of Sports,* was appointed head of the news division. With the help of newsmen like Frank Reynolds, Peter Jennings and Ted Koppel, Arledge was able to make ABC news popular.

Technical Limitations.   Early-day television news could not begin to compare with radio news. Radio could go to the scene of events and broadcast live. TV news required motion-picture cameras, and the film had to be processed after it was shot. Some early network newscasts relied on motion-picture newsreel photographers to provide footage, but often this material was not available until

■ RCA Chairman David Sarnoff holds a magnetic tape used to record television pictures in both color and black and white. This breakthrough in electronic photography was first demonstrated at RCA laboratories in Princeton, N.J., in 1953. It paved the way for a new era in television news and entertainment.

several days after the event. In the meantime, the networks often used still photos, which the newscasters held up in front of them. However, by the 1960s portable cameras and videotape recorders had made television a much more credible news medium because viewers saw pictures of the news events on the day they occurred. Eventually TV provided more people with their news than newspapers and radio combined.

Communist Scare. TV news was not confined to the evening news summaries. In the early 1950s, well-known CBS radio newsman Edward R. Murrow made the switch from radio to television by converting his popular radio show *Hear It Now* to a weekly TV program, *See It Now*. He set a standard for television journalism that has guided the industry ever since. He also was one of the first to show that television could be a powerful force in the culture by tackling some controversial topics, including U.S. Senator Joseph McCarthy.

House and Senate committees that investigated the alleged infiltration of Communists into the movie industry (see Chapter 8) also scrutinized television. Their search was greatly aided in June 1950 by the publication of *Red Channels,* which listed the names of 151 radio- and television-industry personnel who were accused of being either sympathetic to or associated with the communist movement. Many people on the list found themselves suddenly out of work and their careers destroyed as a fearful industry took the easy way out to avoid controversy. Some of the better-known names cited were actors Orson Welles, Howard Duff and Edward G. Robinson; musicians Leonard Bernstein, Burl Ives and Lena Horne; and radio-television newsmen William L. Shirer and Howard K. Smith. Smith was listed because a communist newspaper had praised his reporting of a particular news event.[2]

■ Senator Joseph McCarthy (left) and Attorney Roy Cohn are shown during the televised Army-McCarthy hearings in 1954. Some 20 million Americans were able to see the ruthless tactics of the junior senator in his fight against Communism, and this exposure led to the eventual decline of "McCarthyism."

Despite the fear that gripped the broadcasting industry, Murrow challenged Senator McCarthy and his scare tactics openly on *See It Now*. On March 9, 1954, Murrow told the nation that the senator was giving "comfort to our enemies" by violating the civil rights of the people he had accused; although McCarthy had not created the atmosphere of fear, he had "certainly exploited it." This broadcast was the third-lowest-rated *See It Now* program of the 1953–54 season, but it had an impact in starting to turn public opinion against the senator. Ironically, McCarthy's response, which was aired on *See It Now* in April, was the program's highest-rated show.[3]

Shortly afterward, McCarthy found himself in a controversy with the army. He was accused of abusing a general during an investigative hearing into the promotion of an army dentist whom McCarthy called a "Fifth Amendment Communist." A Senate investigative committee looked into the charges against McCarthy and the 36-day hearing was televised to 20 million Americans. Now the American people could see McCarthy's ruthless and arbitrary tactics firsthand. The senator's popularity began to decline and McCarthyism and the climate of fear subsided. TV had demonstrated that it could be a powerful social force.

Kennedy Assassination. The most profound demonstration of the power of television in bringing news to our popular culture came in November 1963, when President John F. Kennedy was assassinated in Dallas. The three networks provided continuous 24-hour-a-day coverage from Friday through Monday, canceling all commercials at significant cost.

TV cameras at the Dallas jail also captured live the murder of Lee Harvey Oswald, Kennedy's suspected killer, as he was about to be transferred from the Dallas jail to another location.

For four days Americans sat in front of their TV sets watching reruns of both assassinations, historical film of the Kennedy presidency and the emotional burial of the president in Arlington National Cemetery. Television's ability to unite the entire nation in one common emotion demonstrated without doubt just how socially powerful this new mass-communication medium had become.

Vietnam War. As the nation's involvement in the Vietnam war escalated during the 1960s, television was there to bring the war into America's living rooms every night. For the first time in history, Americans could watch ordinary people being killed on foreign battlefields. People could no longer ignore the unpleasantness of war, and soon our involvement in Vietnam began to be questioned. Many blamed television news for turning the Vietnam war into an unpopular one.

The Debate over TV's Newsmaking Role. Television news is profoundly different from newspaper journalism. As TV newsman John Chancellor put it, readers of the print media can be their own editors, selecting what they want to read. With television, people have only two choices—leave the TV on or turn it off—and most people choose to leave their sets on.

Eventually some critics started wondering whether television wasn't shaping the news rather than merely reporting it. In the summer of 1968—after the assassinations of Martin Luther King, Jr., and Senator Robert F. Kennedy, widespread riots in urban ghettos and a battle between Chicago police and antiwar demonstrators outside the Democratic national convention—many Americans became convinced that TV news was the cause of the nation's troubles.

The newly elected Republican vice-president Spiro Agnew articulated this concern in 1969:

> The members of Congress or the Senate who follow their principles and philosophy quietly in a spirit of compromise are unknown to many Americans—while the loudest and most extreme dissenters on every issue are known to every man in the street.
>
> How many marches and demonstrations would we have if the marchers did not know that the ever-faithful TV cameras would be there to record their antics for the next TV show? . . . By way of conclusion, let me say that every elected leader in the United States depends on these men in the media. Whether what I have said tonight will be heard and seen at all by the nation is not my decision; it's not your decision; it's their decision.4

TV Covers the Space Race. Television demonstrated what it could do best in July 1969, when it took the world live to the scene of *Apollo XI*'s landing on the moon. Hundreds of millions of people saw the first human steps on the moon. The American dream of space conquest had been achieved and television brought the event into the world's homes—live.

TV's coverage of the space program again impacted the popular culture in January 1986 when the space shuttle *Challenger,* carrying the first teacher into space, exploded on live TV seconds after liftoff. The nation was plunged into mourning. Many people interviewed at the time indicated that they had not felt such an emotional loss since the assassination of President Kennedy 23 years earlier.

Watergate.   Although the Watergate scandal was first exposed by newspaper reporters (see Chapter 7), TV played a crucial role in bringing the story to the masses. Millions of Americans were glued to their television sets as Congress conducted investigative hearings in 1973–74. As a parade of top Nixon administration officials revealed the web of lies, burglaries, money laundering and obstruction of justice committed on the president's behalf, a growing sentiment for impeachment developed. On August 8, 1974, these same Americans saw their president go on television to announce his resignation.

Iran-Contra Hearings.   Some 33 years after TV news demonstrated its influence on the culture by televising the Army-McCarthy hearings, it again set the national news agenda by broadcasting live congressional hearings into the Reagan administration's sale of arms to Iran and the diversion of profits to the Contra "freedom fighters" in Nicaragua.

Whereas TV had earlier transformed Senator McCarthy from a hero to a villain, during the televised Iran-Contra hearings Lt. Col. Oliver North, who had been fired by President Reagan for his illegal activities in the Iran-Contra scandal, was transformed into a folk hero with a cultlike following. Wearing his Marine Corps uniform decorated with ribbons, North—who had been one of President Reagan's National Security advisers—convinced many Americans that he was a young, patriotric officer who was "just following orders from his superiors." North had previously been cast by the press as a villain, or at best a scapegoat. Within days the American consumer culture was selling "Ollie North for President" bumper stickers and T-shirts.

News vs. Entertainment.   Over the past four decades, television news has been constantly evolving. Improvements in equipment enabled the first changes to occur. These were followed by changes in style, prompted by the desire for TV news to be "entertaining" in order to attract large audiences and generate higher commercial fees.

Local television news has adopted the "eyewitness" news and "friendly newscaster" approaches. Jokes and friendly chitchat between stories have become standard, and human interest stories and feature reports (movie reviews, sports) take up more and more air time.

Some newscasters are selected for their appearances and personalities rather than their news judgment, and weathermen and women are often used to provide comic relief or sex appeal. (This problem was highlighted in the movie *Broadcast News.*) These popular local news "talents" draw large salaries as long as they keep the ratings up. Research on why people watched one newscast instead of another has found that most people prefer programs where the newscasters joke with one another.

A short-lived experiment to enhance the entertainment value of television news was started in 1988 by the Gannett newspaper chain, publishers of *USA Today*. They launched *USA Today: The Television Show,* provided it with four anchors and a fast-paced format, and borrowed sophisticated graphics and an occasional in-depth "cover story" from their national newspaper. The $40 million experiment failed and the show was canceled in 1990.

TV News Sexism. Women, more than men, were finding that an attractive appearance was essential for employment as a television anchorperson. In 1983 a jury awarded Christine Craft, a former Kansas City TV anchor, $500,000 in damages in a sex-discrimination suit. She had been fired from KMBC-TV because a consulting firm had found that she was "too old, too unattractive, and not deferential enough to men." Although a United States District judge threw out the verdict, a new jury awarded her $325,000 in a retrial in 1984. But that award was also overturned, and the Supreme Court refused to hear her final appeal.

The search for the perfect anchor continues, however. One Los Angeles television station faced with declining ratings used galvanic skin response (GSR) tests on randomly selected viewers to measure the perceived attractiveness of various anchors and, in this way, determine whom to keep and whom to fire.

TV News Dominance. Today more Americans claim they get their news from television than from any other source. Since TV cannot begin to provide the variety of stories or the in-depth coverage that newspapers do, this has serious implications for a democracy that needs a well-informed citizenry to function properly.

Although network TV news seems more serious and sophisticated, it too is dependent on ratings and its share of the audience. Often those ratings are dependent on the local news because in most cities, local news immediately precedes network news, and most viewers will watch their favorite local news show and stay tuned to whichever network news follows. The second and third reason people watch one network news show over another, according to William Wheatley, executive producer of *NBC Nightly News,* are the popularity of the anchor and the content.[5]

By the 1990s, the networks had developed the technique of sending their nightly news anchors around the world to the scenes of major news events in an effort to boost ratings. When the Berlin Wall began to fall in 1989, NBC's Tom Brokaw was there to report on it. When U.S. forces were sent to Saudi Arabia in 1990 in preparation for war against Iraq, CBS's Dan Rather and ABC's Ted Koppel went to the Iraqi capital of Baghdad to broadcast live, while NBC sent Brokaw and its morning *Today* show host Bryant Gumbel to Saudi Arabia. Several weeks later, Rather was to win the "battle of the anchors" by becoming the first to televise an interview with Iraqi leader Saddam Hussein.

CNN Debuts. Cable TV tycoon Ted Turner began giving the big-three network news operations a run for their money in the 1980s with the introduction of two 24-hour-a-day satellite/cable news channels—Cable News Network (CNN) and

BOX 10.3

▪ CNN LEADS WORLD NEWS MEDIA INTO BATTLE ▪

When war between the United States and its allies and Iraq's Saddam Hussein broke out in January 1991, the eyes and ears of the world turned to Ted Turner's ten-year-old cable news network—CNN.

Months of sophisticated planning, lobbying efforts to gain special permission from Iraqi officials to broadcast the war, satellite transmitters and a highly reliable two-way overseas telephone connection allowed the world to hear CNN newsmen Bernard Shaw, John Holliman and Peter Arnett describe U.S. bombing raids live from their hotel room in Baghdad, Iraq. Complete with drum rolls and dramatic graphics, the all-news network was able to give television viewers live drama from the scene of an actual war.

Independent TV stations in the U.S. began carrying the CNN programming and even CBS, ABC and NBC were quoting CNN reports on the war. Newspapers and news magazines ran stories hailing CNN as the new number-one network in the ratings. Cable companies were bombarded with requests for subscriptions from people who wanted to watch CNN in their homes.

Advertisers, who had been paying $3,800 for 30-second commercials on CNN prior to the war, saw the cost of these spots skyrocket to $138,000 per 30-second commercial as the network justified the increases with millions of new viewers.

Although the Vietnam war had been the first war to be fought in American living rooms, the coverage of those battles were taped replays aired some 24 hours later. The Persian Gulf war became the first to be seen live in American homes. As the U.S. prepared for a ground war to follow its air offensive, CNN requested permission to set up satellites in the Kuwaiti desert to broadcast the battles. The Pentagon turned down the request, fearful that people back home might be able to see loved ones killed in action as it actually happened and before official notification from the government.

Unfortunately, much of the war coverage was repetitive and not much more than speculation from numerous journalists on hand to report the war. After the initial excitement waned, viewers began to realize that with over a million troops on both sides assembled for the war in the Middle East, the only ones shown and appearing to be in danger were the journalists donning gas masks and scrambling for bomb shelters. Reporters were becoming the celebrities in this war.

Soon the media were focusing on themselves. The strengths and weaknesses of the war coverage became topics on network news shows and PBS. Even CNN went on the air a week and a half after the war broke out with a special program called *The Press at War*.

Headline News. For the first time, the American people were able to watch worldwide TV news whenever they wanted to, rather than when the networks told them they could watch it. This type of independence from the network news "clock" found a niche among many people who were ready to break away from old habits and try something new.

Adding to the network woes was the fact that Turner aggressively built a worldwide news operation that gained respect abroad as well as at home. During the uprisings in Eastern Europe and in Tiananmen Square during 1989, people worldwide were using satellite dishes to learn the latest from the news-gathering forces of CNN. When the U.S. invaded Panama in December of 1989, the Soviet foreign minister didn't call the U.S. Embassy to protest but instead called the Moscow bureau of CNN to announce he wanted to go on camera with a statement condemning the invasion (see Box 10.3).

Local vs. Network News. Recent studies have shown that most people identify with their local news more than with network news. A 1986 NBC survey found that when viewers were asked which they would watch—network or local news if they could watch only one—the margin in favor of local news was 52 percent to 45 percent.

New technology was partially responsible for the increase in popularity of local news by the 1990s. Networks had dominated TV news from 1948 until the mid-1980s because their larger and more global news-gathering forces were able to deliver the major worldwide and national news stories of the day. However, the new satellite technology of the 1980s made these stories available to stations in advance of the network newscast. Stations were able to purchase satellite news from a variety of sources, including CNN, CONUS Communication (a consortium of stations with specially equipped trucks housing satellite dishes that can send and receive television signals) and Group W's NEWS FEED network. In 1990 NBC began offering its 209 affiliated stations a 24-hour satellite news service to use on their local news shows. By 1990, the ratings of local newscasts had become so important that stations were relying on a variety of gimmicks to attract viewers (see Box 10.4).

THE CULTURAL IMPACT OF TELEVISION

Television's impact on our society has been profound. It has changed the life-styles of most Americans and become a major influence in our culture. Unlike printing, which took hundreds of years to influence the culture, TV's impact was almost instantaneous.

During television's breakthrough year there were fewer than 20 television stations on the air. This figure grew to 1,440 by the beginning of the 1990s.[6]

The number of television sets in homes also grew rapidly. From 172,000 sets in 1948, the sale of TV sets increased at a rate of a quarter million per month for the next two years. The sales figures climbed to 5 million sets per year during the 1950s and today exceeds 22 million. By 1962, more than 90 percent of all households had at least one television set and 13 percent had more than one set (see Figure 10.1). By the late 1980s there were 125 million television sets in homes, representing nearly 98 percent of American households (a greater percentage than had indoor toilets).[7]

A.C. Nielsen Co. reports that most American families today own a minimum of two television sets (1.83 is the national average) and most of these sets (87.3 million) are color. These sets are located in vital living areas, such as the living room, family room, bedroom and kitchen. Because they own multiple sets, many families no longer watch television together and parents often do not know what their children are viewing.[8]

Nielsen also reports that the average television usage in U.S. households exceeds seven hours a day, which translates to more than 2,500 hours per year—the most time-consuming activity besides sleeping.[9]

Socialization Effects.　TV's dominance as a household activity often reduces the level of communication among family members and, as a result, much of the culture being disseminated to youngsters today comes from the tube rather than

BOX 10.4

■ TV NEWS IN THE '90s: THE BATTLE FOR RATINGS ■
Dennis Hart

Local television news finds itself in what some observers call a "fight for survival" in the 1990s. Viewers now have many more channels to choose from, and that means diminished ratings for virtually all stations that, just a few years ago, had only a few competitors to worry about.

"I would say in most of the major markets, it's [the competition] as tough as it can be and still remain nonviolent," says Harry Fuller, news director at KPIX-TV in San Francisco.

"The fight for ratings points in a major city like New York or Los Angeles or San Francisco is really critical. A rating point can mean as much as a million dollars a year, either made or lost."

The ratings pressure is most severe during the "sweeps" months of February, May and November, when Nielsen and Arbitron measure the audience for all of the nation's TV stations. Those are the times when broadcast journalism occasionally sinks to levels that dismay some critics.

For example, during one recent May sweeps, a New York station produced a news series called *Sex Tapes,* a three-part look at pornographic videos featuring darkly lit shots of nude bodies. A panel of experts that included Dr. Joyce Brothers debated whether such tapes are valuable as an aphrodisiac.

During that same month in Los Angeles, a station broadcast a multi-part series called *The Search for Sleaze.* A reporter examined night life in the city and exposed viewers to female mud wrestling, gyrating dancers and X-rated cakes. Before the series started, the station bought an advertisement in the *Los Angeles Times,* promising "10 gorgeous girls!" and "9 gorgeous costumes!" and urging viewers to "watch what happens!!"

At the same time, a San Francisco station aired a multi-part series exploring sexual behavior in the Bay Area. The station bought newspaper advertisements with the headline, "If You're Not Having Sex Tonight, Find Out Who Is." At least one paper, the *San Francisco Chronicle,* refused to run that headline, toning it down to "Sex, Truths & Videotape." But the copy underneath remained the same, saying the series would look at people's views on such things as romance, extramarital sex, sexual satisfaction and what the station called the "Big O" (orgasm).

Another common practice in local TV news is spinning off a story from the network program that precedes a late-night newscast. The idea is to interview the star of the network program, promote that interview during prime-time teases and then induce the audience to stay up for the station's newscast.

In San Francisco, the NBC affiliate successfully spun off interviews with the stars of the series, *LA Law,* for two consecutive sweeps months. The interviews provided little new information about the stars, but much of the program's audience stayed through the station's newscast to watch them.

One of the newest tactics to keep the audience awake for late-night local newscasts is being used on the West Coast. Several Pacific Time Zone stations tape the East-Coast feed of their networks' 10 P.M. entertainment shows off a satellite at 7 P.M. The stations then edit out credits, promos or even part of the program, which results in an earlier "off time" for the network show and allows the stations to begin their newscasts earlier than their competitors.

The theory is that most viewers now have remote controls and "flip around" for programming at 11 P.M. Those viewers will, so the theory goes, stay with the newscast that is first on the air.

One station in San Francisco had remarkable success using this tactic. During one sweeps month, the station edited its network's 10 P.M. program every night to get its local newscast on the air significantly earlier than the competition's.

Despite the network's small audience lead-in to that local newscast, the station consistently won the 11 P.M. time period. Station staffers believe the newscast's "early start" was the primary reason.

What about future strategies for maintaining a television news audience? KPIX's Harry Fuller has one answer: "I think what you'll see is a dramatic reaching around for anything that works."

Hart, formerly executive news producer at KPIX-TV in San Francisco, is an assistant professor of journalism at California State University, Northridge.

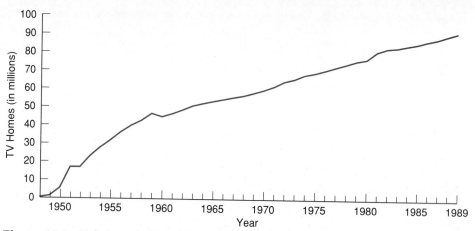

Figure 10.1 U.S. households with television sets. SOURCE: *The Broadcasting Yearbook 1990* (Washington, D.C.: Broadcasting Publications, Inc., 1990).

the family. Television usage in homes with children is the highest and it is believed that the average child has watched more than 18,000 hours of TV by the time he or she reaches the age of 15. This compares with 11,000 hours of schooling and 3,000 hours of church attendance. Television has become the most powerful tool for socialization that civilization has ever devised.

What has made television's significance even more profound is the fact that it took very little time for it to become pervasive in the culture. Unlike many media, TV spent relatively little time in the elite culture. The rich and middle classes were not the only ones to rush to purchase television sets. Many lower-class households went into debt to own this luxury item. However, to most Americans, television was not a luxury but rather a psychological necessity; it provided comfort to a lonely mass culture whose members sought both entertainment and solitude in their homes. Sociologists have been puzzled as to how something previously nonexistent could become a psychological necessity the moment it arrived in the popular culture. The answer seems to be that television found a niche by bringing the world to individuals isolated from the dominant culture. However, by bringing the world into the home, TV replaced many cherished activities—such as after-dinner conversations among family members and parents reading bedtime stories to children—with TV sitcoms, variety shows and action/adventures.

Reflecting Cultural Changes. Television programming has played an important role in reflecting for the masses the cultural changes that have been occurring in American society. When the civil rights movement calling for equality for Americans gained momentum in the 1960s, TV started reflecting these changes. Women and African-Americans began to be portrayed in other than stereotyped roles for the first time. Sitcoms like *That Girl,* starring Marlo Thomas—who portrayed a young woman making it on her own in the world—and *Julia,* featuring Diahann Carroll as an African-American nurse and mother, became popular. Prior to that, singer Nat "King" Cole had been the only African-American to host a network variety show (in the 1950s) and Bill Cosby had been the only one to have a costarring role in a weekly drama series, *I Spy*, in the 1960s. (By the 1990s Cosby was still going strong on television and starred in one of the top-rated shows—a sitcom that promoted the nuclear family much like the white versions had done in the 1950s.)

These trends were significant in that they demonstrated that TV was culturally responsive. Besides merely reflecting these cultural changes, television helped transmit them to the masses and by doing so accelerated their acceptance into the mainstream popular culture.

The action/adventure genre also began reflecting these changing times. Women began playing previously male-only roles of cops, detectives and lawyers. Shows such as *Police Woman, Charlie's Angels, Cagney & Lacey, Moonlighting* and *L.A. Law* all showed women in professional rather than subservient roles. However, early versions, like *Charlie's Angels,* were highly criticized for making the female stars more sexy than professional (see Box 10.5).

Resistance to TV's Cultural Takeover.   Despite television's rapid takeover in the American popular culture, it did meet some resistance. In the early years, many academics and urban intellectuals resisted TV and viewed it as a "low cultural form" unworthy of serious attention from the "refined and thinking" members of our society.

At first it was a status symbol among the "cultured" *not* to own a television set because the new medium appealed to low cultural interests aimed at delivering the largest audiences. But quality live-drama productions of the 1950s—such as *Playhouse 90*—and important news presentations such as the Army-McCarthy hearings made it difficult for intellectuals to resist this new mass medium. It wasn't long before people in intellectual circles could be heard saying rather sheepishly that "We own one, but we never turn it on."

In 1964—only 16 years after television first started to make inroads into the popular culture—a survey of the 1939 graduating class of Harvard University revealed that 92.5 percent owned at least one TV set and that 13 percent had three or more sets in their home. By the 1960s television had become nearly everyone's mass medium.

Despite this universal acceptance, criticism of television continued, with critics regularly expressing alarm that TV content was aimed at the masses and had little if any educational value. Many were calling television an "electronic mind pacifier" that had a narcotic effect on our culture. This was the theme of Paddy Chayefsky's movie *Network* in the mid-1970s. (Ironically, the movie ended up being a movie of the week on network television.) When one of the film's characters, Howard Beale—a TV newsman suffering a nervous breakdown—preached the following lines on his "news-entertainment hour," many TV network executives cringed:

> *Television is not the truth. . . . We lie like hell. . . . We deal in illusions, man. None of it is true. But you people sit there day after day, night after night. . . .We're all you know. You're beginning to believe the illusions we're spinning here. You're beginning to think that the tube is reality and that your own lives are like the tube, you eat like the*

BOX 10.5

■ WOMEN IN TELEVISION ■

Despite more than 20 years of feminism, a 1990 study issued by two women's organizations showed that the television industry has been slow to respond.

Most of the women shown on prime-time television entertainment shows are under 40, white and work as clerks, homemakers or helpmates to male lead characters.

Producers, directors and writers of TV shows remain far below the work force average. At ABC only 8 percent of the producers of programs examined for the study were women, compared to 16 percent at NBC, 20 percent at CBS and 26 percent at Fox.

Women writers did a little better—but not much. At ABC and NBC 22 percent of the writers at each network were women, compared to 29 percent at CBS and 33 percent at Fox.

The study's findings were based on examinations of 80 prime-time network entertainment shows aired during a two-month period in the spring of 1990. Information was gathered on the gender, age, race, occupation, marital and socioeconomic status of recurring characters.

The study found that with exceptions such as NBC's *L.A. Law* and ABC's *China Beach,* the women in dramatic series were not strong characters. CBS's *Murder, She Wrote* was the only dramatic series with a female lead.

The most common female job portrayed during the study was clerical with 14 percent of the women characters working as secretaries, receptionists and clerks. Another 14 percent were employed in other service jobs such as waitresses and bank tellers and 11 percent were full-time homemakers. Only 5 percent were shown as entrepreneurs.

Despite the fact that television is a leader in portraying cultural changes, the industry seems slow in reflecting equal opportunities for women in our changing culture.

Sources: National Commission on Working Women and Women in Film.

tube, you raise your children like the tube. This is mass madness, you maniacs. In God's name, you people are the real thing: we're the illusions.[10]

Even in the 1990s, after an entire generation has grown up with the pacifying effects of television and the medium is firmly entrenched in the culture, critics are still making satirical social commentary about its shortcomings. Picking up on the theme that TV was turning people into mental vegetables was a California group that called themselves the Couch Potatoes. Their goal was to bring to the attention of the masses their belief that television is a passive, antiintellectual medium. When asked by a reporter to comment on a two-way cable TV system that allowed viewers to participate in quiz shows and electronic polling by talking back to their TV sets, a Couch Potato spokesperson said, "Why watch TV if you have to think and respond? As far as I'm concerned, the main point of watching TV is that it lets you avoid having to do that. To put it another way, if you're going to have to respond to your TV, you might as well go out and cultivate friendships or read a book or something."[11]

The cultural impact of TV during that last half of the twentieth century has generated a great deal of discussion and concern in several specific areas: the effects of violence on TV, television's influence on children and the use of the medium to "sell" religion to the masses.

Television and Violence.   The question of violence on TV has been around nearly as long as the medium itself. Many critics claim that TV violence increases violence in our society (see discussion of research on this topic in Chapter 16).

The *information-imitation theory* contends that TV violence plays a prominent role in causing bizarre and violent behavior in society. This theory holds that some people (usually mentally unbalanced individuals) observe information and activities in the media and then proceed to imitate what they saw. Several specific cases illustrating this theory have received a great deal of discussion and have fueled the arguments for eliminating violence on TV.

Fuzz, which first appeared as a book written by Evan Hunter under the pseudonym Ed McBain, was made into a movie starring Burt Reynolds and Raquel Welch. No public outcry developed over the book or the movie. However, when the movie was shown on television, it generated a great deal of concern. Some groups attempted to prevent the movie from being shown by a major network. They objected to a scene in the film in which a group of juvenile delinquents poured gasoline over a skid row vagrant and set him on fire.

The night after the movie was shown on national television, a woman—who had run out of gas in Boston and was carrying a can of fuel back to her car from a corner service station—was accosted by a gang of juveniles. The gasoline was poured over her and she was set on fire. Several nights later, a tramp sleeping along railroad tracks in Florida was doused with gasoline by a gang of youths and set on fire.

When the motion picture *Deer Hunter,* which featured numerous scenes of people playing "Russian roulette," was shown on TV, more than 20 suicides of people playing the deadly game were reported.

Following an NBC-TV network showing of the movie *Born Innocent,* which contained a prison scene in which a female inmate, played by Linda Blair, was raped with a broomstick, a San Francisco girl was raped with a Coke bottle by several other girls who said they had gotten the idea while watching the TV movie. The victim's mother sued NBC and the local TV station, but the court ruled that television could not be held responsible for how some people reacted to scenes in an entertainment program.

Several years later Ronnie Zamora, a Florida teenager, was on trial for murder. His defense attorney, Ellis Rubin, claimed that the youngster was driven to commit the act by watching so much violence on television. The courts found Zamora—not the TV industry—guilty of the murder.

A number of researchers have linked aggressive behavior and television viewing. In a 1982 study the National Institute of Mental Health concluded that "the scientific support for the causal relationship [between violence on TV and aggressive behavior] derives from the convergence of findings from many studies, the great majority of which demonstrate a positive relationship between televised violence and later aggressive behavior."[12]

Over the years television has responded to these concerns by reducing the level of violence. The violent Westerns of the 1950s and 1960s have vanished. Detective shows such as *Starsky and Hutch* were taken off the air for being too violent. They were replaced, however, by action/adventure shows, such as *The A-Team,* that used "make-believe" violence. Some psychiatrists and psychologists charged that shows such as *The A-Team* created a false view of violence by showing the use of automatic rifles, hand grenades and other weapons without ever injuring or killing anyone.

Saturday morning cartoon shows continue to be one of the main targets for antiviolence advocates. A report by the National Coalition on Television Violence reported that by the mid-1980s, there was a "deluge of high-action, violent cartoon shows" aimed at children. Dr. Thomas Radecki, head of the coalition and a psychiatrist, said, "We can only pump so much violence into our people before we explode."[13]

Television and Children.   Parents and other groups are not concerned only with TV violence aimed at children. They are also bothered by some nonviolent content. Research by the National Council on Alcoholism, for example, found that before a child reaches the age of 18, he or she will watch someone drink alcohol on television an average of 100,000 times. George Gerbner, dean of the Annenberg School of Communications at the University of Pennsylvania, points out that having a drink is an effective dramatic device for TV programming.

Another concern regarding TV's influence on children developed in the 1980s when commercial enterprises began exploiting children by reaching into actual program content to sell their products. This new concern developed after the FCC began deregulating the television industry in the 1980s. This hands-off policy toward TV encouraged toy makers to begin producing their own programs, a practice that had been abandoned after the quiz-show scandal of 1959. Such toy manufacturers as Hasbro, Bradley, Mattel, Coleco, Kenner, Tomy, Tonka, Selchow & Righter and even CBS Toys joined forces with animation houses to produce children's shows that featured planned and existing toys. These product-oriented entertainment shows were in reality 30-minute commercials.

Early program-length commercials featured such lovable dolls as Strawberry Shortcakes and the Smurfs, but by 1985 they included such aggression-oriented products as He-Man and the Masters of the Universe, G.I. Joe: A Real American Hero, Transformers, She-Ra: Princess of Power, M.A.S.K. (Medical Armored Strike Command), Thunder Cats, Voltron and Rambo.

Children, who at early ages have difficulty distinguishing between commercials and programs, now found that there was no difference. Efforts by Peggy Charren, founder and president of Action for Children's Television (ACT), to get the FCC to enforce its own regulations, which require sponsors to be identified, fell on deaf ears (see Chapter 16). The FCC philosophy of the 1980s was that the marketplace, not government regulations, should determine what was in the public interest. In any case, by the end of the 1987–88 season, ratings for the animated superhero shows began to decline, as children tuned in to new live action game shows, like cable network Nickelodeon's *Double Dare* and Lorimar's *Fun House,* or watched their own videocassettes.

Concerns about children's TV programming did not start with the product-oriented children's shows, however. They are as old as the medium itself. Early concerns centered around physiological effects (will staring at a picture tube ruin a child's eyesight?) as well as on emotional or psychological effects. Numerous studies have been conducted over the years to examine TV's effects on children. Early research by the National Television and Radio Center in the late 1950s and early 1960s concluded: "For some children, under some conditions, some television is harmful. For other children, under the same conditions, it may be beneficial. For most children, under most conditions, most television is probably neither harmful nor particularly beneficial."[14]

Most research seems to indicate that children do learn behavior and that television does play a role in teaching that behavior. In her book *Mind and Media,* Patricia Greenfield says that children often take well-known TV characters as examples to be imitated. She points out that the day after "Fonzie" took out a library card on *Happy Days,* there was a fivefold increase in the number of children applying for library cards in the United States. She contends that TV can be a very positive force in the lives of children if it is used constructively and if parents actively see to it that their children interact with the programs' content through discussions and parental explanations.[15]

Such parental involvement is not always possible, however. Recent changes in our culture regarding the traditional nuclear family are creating new problems. The traditional family where the father works and the mother stays home has been replaced with situations where either both parents are working or the household consists of a single parent raising the children. Both of these conditions have created a new kind of child in the United States—the "latchkey kid." Millions of American children today go home from school to fend for themselves.

Many observers of this new trend contend that today's American child no longer obtains his or her cultural values from the traditional family structure, but instead gets them from the mass media. And some critics say that what they are getting is a popular culture filled with sex and violence.

However, some research studies have shown that TV has a positive impact on children's learning. These studies have found that vocabulary levels and general cultural awareness of youngsters starting school seem to be much higher than those of television-deprived children of the same age. Some TV programs for children, such as *Sesame Street* and *The Electric Company* (both on PBS), are designed to teach youthful viewers.

Another concern over the impact of television on children came from the explosion of the space shuttle *Challenger*. Millions of children were watching the shuttle's takeoff in their classrooms because it was carrying the first teacher, Christa McAuliffe, into outer space. McAuliffe was to have given some lessons to the nation's school children from space. Concern was expressed that the explosion may have inflicted some long-lasting psychological damage on many of the young viewers.

Follow-up observations, however, have so far shown that some forgot about the incident within days, while others still remember it. Children with stable home lives and family relationships were less likely to remember the incident than single-parent children, who related to it as a case of other children losing parents.

Child psychiatrist Robert Coles says that what children do with television depends on the nature of their own lives. He points out that if a child has an unstable family life, he or she may be more vulnerable to the emotional and moral power of TV, while a child with a stable home life will not "likely be sucked into the moral wasteland that one finds while watching certain programs." What matters, he says, "is not only the quality of television programming for our young people (or for us, their parents) but the quality of American family life."[16]

Television and Religion.   In the late 1980s controversy erupted over another kind of programming—religious broadcasting. Fundamentalist Protestant revivalism has been part of American culture since the religious movement known as the Great Awakening swept the 13 colonies in the 1730s and '40s. Preaching to mass rallies in the open air (and later in tents), ministers from Jonathan Edwards to Billy Graham urged listeners to repent and start a new life.

In the 1950s, as tent revival audiences started to dwindle due to the competition from television, evangelists like Oral Roberts started taking their messages to the home via the TV set. *Televangelism* was born. Television stations began selling air time to evangelical preachers and, since the 1970s, the electronic church has been a successful part of TV programming.

As the cost of air time climbed and the new technology of cable became available, religious broadcasters started turning their attention to this new delivery system. The Christian Broadcasting Network (CBN) built up a cable network that supplemented its own three TV stations. TBN (Trinity Broadcasting Network) and PTL (Praise the Lord or People That Love) followed with their own religious cable networks. Of course, it still costs money to produce telecasts, so pitches for donations are a regular feature of many of these networks' shows.

According to a 1984 survey by the University of Pennsylvania's Annenberg School of Communications—done for the National Council of Churches and the National Religious Broadcasters—an estimated 13.3 million people watched at least 15 minutes of religious programming a week. Most of these viewers were female and nonwhite and were less well educated, older and poorer than the average American. However, they tended to respond to the various calls for contributions to keep the ministries on the air. The Annenberg study found that many viewers contributed regularly to three or more programs.

A 1985 Nielsen survey found an even larger audience for religious programs: 61 million people, representing more than 40 percent of the nation's households, watched one or more of the top-10 syndicated religious broadcasts during the February sweeps period. The most popular program was Pat Robertson's *700 Club,* with 28.7 million viewers. The electronic church has become a multibillion-dollar-a-year enterprise and a significant part of TV programming in our popular culture.

However, in 1987 ratings and revenue dropped after an electronic "holy war" broke out. Popular TV evangelists Jim and Tammy Faye Bakker were forced to turn over their lucrative ministry—The PTL Club—to the Reverend Jerry Falwell, head of the Liberty Foundation. Bakker stepped down from his electronic pulpit after admitting that he had had an affair with Jessica Hahn, a church secretary. Not long afterward, popular televangelist Jimmy Swaggart, who had been instrumental in exposing the affair of his rival Jim Bakker, was himself defrocked after admitting to encounters with a prostitute.

By 1990, Bakker was serving a 45-year prison sentence for embezzling $3.7 million from his followers; his wife, Tammy Faye, was working as an evangelist in a converted warehouse near Disney World, and Swaggart was back on the air with a teleministry that was drawing over 1 million viewers a week.

Although the scandals triggered a decline in the millions of dollars raised each week by television preachers, they did not spell the end of televangelism. By 1990, one TV ministry, Paul F. Crouch's Trinity Broadcasting Network, was the largest single owner of television stations in the United States and it used satellite technology to broadcast around the world. The ministry owned 14 full-powered commercial UHF stations, three full-powered educational noncommercial outlets and 125 low-powered TV stations (see Chapter 15). Its annual revenue in viewer pledges exceeded $40 million.

TELEVISION SPECIALIZES

Television, like many other mass media, has entered the stage of specialization. A variety of specialized programming is now available to meet particular interests.

Public Broadcasting. A noncommercial form of broadcasting, servicing primarily the elite or high culture, is provided through the joint efforts of the Corporation for Public Broadcasting and the Public Broadcasting Service (PBS). Efforts to provide noncommercial educational television (ETV) began in the 1950s. These activities were not too successful, but they did lead to the passage of the Public Broadcasting Act of 1967, which provided for the first interconnected network of ETV stations and federal financial assistance.

PBS programming ranges from in-depth news and Wall Street analysis to opera, classical music and sophisticated British Broadcasting Corporation (BBC) drama and comedy productions. Among the BBC shows are a number of successful serials such as *Civilisation, Masterpiece Theater, Upstairs Downstairs* and *Yes, Minister.* PBS also broadcasts programs developed by the Children's Television Workshop (CTW), such as *Sesame Street* and *The Electric Company.*

PBS programming is carried on noncommercial television stations and is usually transmitted by satellite. The biggest source of revenue for public broadcasting is corporate sponsorship; the second largest source is local station membership dues, auctions and other fund-raisers; and the rest is made up by revenues from federal funding through the Corporation for Public Broadcasting and other federal agencies, such as the National Endowment for the Arts.

Despite some excellent programming, PBS does not reach a mass audience. In every major market where noncommercial broadcasting is available, its audience totals less than 5 percent. However, in 1990—following a successful series on the Civil War—PBS Executive Vice President for Programming and Production, Jennifer Lawson, launched an aggressive promotional campaign to make PBS as much a household product as NBC, ABC and CBS.

Cable and Satellite Television. Although cable television began in the 1940s as a way to relay television signals to remote areas and thus boost the sales of television sets, it wasn't until the 1970s that it shifted its focus to providing specialized programming. The change in emphasis came after Home Box Office leased a satellite transponder and began providing pay-TV services to cable companies. Through the use of these communication satellites, cable companies can now pick up and redistribute a wide range of programming.

By the 1990s, despite the fact that there were more TV households in the United States, the big-three networks found themselves with a much smaller share of the television audience, falling from a household penetration of more than 90 percent to 61 percent.[17] Although most of this was caused by cable programming, the Fox network—which also relies on cable to make many of its weaker-signal UHF affiliate stations accessible—also played a role.

According to A.C. Nielsen, 50.9 million or nearly 56 percent of the nation's 92.1 million television households had cable television by 1990[18] and there were over 9,000 cable systems in operation.[19] In addition to cable and over-the-air transmission, several million homes were taking their television signals directly from satellites via a reception dish, bypassing local stations and advertisers. With the advent of these new methods of TV reception has come an expansion of the number of channels available, with some cable- and satellite-fed homes receiving over 100 channels.

People with cable or satellite reception can now view channels that feature nothing but sports, religion, sitcoms, rock music, country-and-western music, movies, children's shows, soft-core adult shows, news, live congressional sessions and so forth. Many of these programs can be tuned in any time of the day or night.

For example, cable network ESPN provides sports programming 24 hours a day. In 1987 it broke the networks' monopoly on the electronic ballpark by successfully bidding for the rights to Sunday night NFL football games.

Teleshopping. In the mid-1980s *teleshopping* developed as another method of selling consumer goods in the American culture. Unlike regular broadcast commercials that attempt to create an interest in a product or company, teleshopping is designed to stimulate instant sales. Products are shown on the screen with a discount price and viewers are urged to call in their charge-card numbers immediately before the limited number of products are sold. These programs—many of them broadcasting 24 hours a day—sell everything from cubic zirconia diamonds to fur coats and computers. Some viewers admit to watching these marketing channels more than 12 hours a day. All a viewer needs is a TV set, telephone and credit card to make numerous purchases. It was estimated that in 1987 sales figures from these shows exceeded $2 billion. Although teleshopping first began with Home Shopping Network in 1982, by the late 1980s there were over a dozen such operations.

Even major retailers like Sears have discovered teleshopping. Sears, a catalog sales giant for over 100 years, recognized that television's electronic catalog business, which catered to impulse buying, was superior to print catalogs. So Sears began marketing its merchandise on the QVC home shopping network.

By 1988 the popularity of home shopping channels had leveled off and stock market prices for these networks were declining. Although sales were still going strong into the 1990s, some companies, like J.C. Penney, Sears and IBM, were looking to new technology—such as interactive cable systems—to add a new

BOX 10.6

▪ WORKING IN TELEVISION ▪

Most entry-level jobs in television are with local TV stations. These stations usually have seven departments in which a person might find employment: sales, programming, production, engineering, traffic, promotion and administration.

The *sales department* sells the commercials that bring revenue to the station. These commercials are divided into national and local ads. National ads are usually placed by advertising agencies while local ads require direct contact with the local businesses. Sales people often work on a commission basis.

The *programming department* selects and schedules the programs that will be shown. These programs are usually divided into two categories: news and entertainment. There are three types of TV stations and each has different responsibilities for the programming department. Independent stations must buy and program all of the shows that are aired. O & O stations are those that are owned and operated by the networks. These stations air the network programming available to them. Affiliates are independently owned stations that carry network programming. They may also carry their own programs and purchase syndicated programs from other sources. Generally, affiliates carry a limited number of locally produced shows (usually news programs) and rely most heavily on the networks.

The *production department* creates the locally produced programs and all of the local commercials. It usually has entry-level job opportunities ranging from cue card holders and camera operators to master controllers who insert commercials into programs.

The *engineering department* is responsible for seeing to it that all broadcast operations are working. These include the transmitter, antennas, cameras and other production and broadcasting equipment.

The *traffic department* is in charge of monitoring the production schedule to make sure that all advertising sold is aired at the required time. In addition to making sure that the ads are aired, this department is in charge of the billing operation.

The *promotion department* is in charge of publicizing the station and the programs that it carries. Such activities might include on-the-air promos of upcoming shows and advertising on local radio, newspapers and billboards. It also handles special promotional activities such as giveaways and contests.

The *administration department* handles the business operations of the station and is usually headed by the station manager. Activities range from clerical operations, payroll and personnel, to major management decisions.

dimension to teleshopping. Such systems would allow buyers to immediately purchase a televised product by pushing a button on a hand-held TV selector.

TV started out as a mass medium to provide entertaining programming that would deliver large audiences to advertisers. Today, in the stage of specialization, advertising has become some of the programming.

BUSINESS TRENDS

Although the television industry suffered an economic decline during the recession at the beginning of this decade, the fact remains that this industry is the second largest of all the mass media. Advertising revenue for television is second only to newspapers (which also suffered during the recession) and amounts to more than $28 billion a year.

Although the major networks have seen a decline in audiences, which translate into advertising revenue, there has been tremendous growth during the past decade in cable programming as TV moves from the popular to the specialized stage of the EPS cycle.

Television has been very successful in expanding the American consumer culture, which has been prevalent since the Industrial Revolution, into the mass culture by providing new outlets for selling American products. Television delivers audiences to advertisers. The larger an audience watching a show, the more stations and networks can charge for commercials on that show. The average 30-second prime-time network television announcement costs $100,000 (spots on a top-rated series costs $200,000; low-rated programs average about $80,000 per spot). An estimated 120 million people watched the 1991 Super Bowl XXV telecast, for example, and because of this the network was able to sell 30-second spots on that show for $800,000 apiece.[20]

SUMMARY

Originally just a novelty, television has become the most important entertainment medium in American culture. Although TV was invented in the 1920s, it didn't enter the popular culture until 1948, following a short period serving the elite culture. By the 1960s it was playing a major role in reflecting and shaping the culture.

Television borrowed most of its programming genres from radio. Its early days of programming also featured visual comedy, especially slapstick comedians reflecting the earlier era of vaudeville, such as Milton Berle; variety shows, such as Ed Sullivan's *Toast of the Town;* and shows starring puppets like Cecil the Seasick Sea Serpent and Howdy Doody. One of the finest forms of TV entertainment in the 1950s was live drama, which presented character studies rather than action/adventure. Quiz shows and prerecorded action/adventure shows followed these early TV programs.

Television entertainment has changed during the past 40 years to reflect the ever-changing culture. Sitcoms, talk shows and made-for-TV movies are now dealing with controversial and socially relevant topics. One of the latest trends has been the change in image from the "nuclear family" to nontraditional family sitcoms.

Television news was primitive in the development days, but it soon became a powerful force. Eventually it dominated the news scene, with more people reporting that they got their news from TV than from any other source. In the 1960s, when assassinations and riots received major coverage, people started blaming TV for shaping the news.

Local television news began changing in the 1970s to become more entertaining for the masses. Feature stories and humor were added to the evening newscast, and newscasters began to be hired for their looks and personalities rather than their news judgment. Networks, which have been a major source of news and information since the early days of television, found that new technologies, such as satellites, were making local news shows more competitive by the 1990s.

Television's impact on our culture has been staggering. Ninety-eight percent of American homes have at least one TV set. TV has become one of the most powerful socializing agents in our culture. Children spend more hours watching TV than they spend in school. The average American home has the TV set on more than seven hours a day.

Despite the widespread acceptance of television into our culture, it remains a controversial enterprise. Violence on TV has been a concern since the beginning, with many people citing the information-imitation theory to support their argument.

Another concern about television's effect on children developed more recently: in the 1980s toy manufacturers started producing product-oriented cartoons for children. By the mid-1980s these 30-minute commercials dominated children's television.

Television's impact on the learning environment of children has been a concern since the early 1950s. Research has shown that TV does influence children but that the degree of that influence seems to depend on the level of involvement of the parents and the quality of the child's home life. Given the changes in the nuclear family and the growing number of "latchkey kids," there is new concern about TV's influence.

Also drawing attention in the 1980s as a concern over television programming were the scandal-ridden "electronic churches." Following publicity about scandals that some televangelists became involved in, some felt that all televangelists were going too far to get money and support from TV viewers.

By the 1980s television had entered the specialization stage of the EPS cycle. Public broadcasting was providing noncommercial programming for the high or elite culture, while cable and satellite channels offered a large variety of specialized programs to meet particular interests. And perhaps inevitably, television, which had from the beginning been a vehicle to deliver large audiences to advertisers, now offered teleshopping channels that ran nothing but ads 24 hours a day.

Business trends in television have built this relatively new mass communication medium into the second largest generator of advertising revenue with more than $28 billion spent each year on commercials.

THOUGHT QUESTIONS

1 Why do you think television became such a pervasive mass-communication medium in our culture? Why did it catch on in the popular culture so rapidly?

2 What types of entertainment genres do you think will develop during the '90s? What will be the differences from and similarities to genres of past decades?

3 Does television news shape as well as reflect our popular culture? If yes, what are some current examples of this happening? If no, give some examples to refute this argument.

4 Why has televangelism been so successful in viewers and revenue? What are some of the implications of this trend for traditional religious institutions?

5 Will television become any more specialized during the 1990s? What types of programming do you see developing to continue this trend?

NOTES

1. James H. Myers and William H. Reynolds, *Consumer Behavior and Marketing Management* (Boston: Houghton Mifflin, 1967), p. 239.

2. Counterattack, *Red Channels: The Report of Communists in Radio and Television* (New York: Counterattack, 1950), pp. 1–100.

3. James R. Wilson, "Murrow Versus McCarthy: A Historical Study of Two 1954 *See It Now* Telecasts and Their Impact on the Two Participants, Edward R. Murrow and Joseph R. McCarthy," Master's thesis, California State University, Fresno, 1976, p. 53.

4. Quoted in George McKenna, *Media Voices: Debating Critical Issues in Mass Media* (Guilford, Conn.: Dushkin, 1982), pp. 67–74.

5. David Shaw, "Future of Network News: Is the Signal Weakening?" *Los Angeles Times,* December 29, 1986, p. 17.

6. *The Broadcasting Yearbook 1990* (Washington, D.C.: Broadcasting Publications, Inc., 1990), p. A-3.

7. John Brooks, "The Sudden Assault," in *The History of Popular Culture,* Norman F. Cantor and Michael S. Werthman, ed. (New York: Macmillan, 1968), p. 714.

8. *International Television Almanac,* 35th ed. (New York: Quigley Publishing, 1990), p. 26-A.

9. Ibid.

10. *Network,* dir. Paddy Chayefsky, MGM, 1976.

11. B. A. Krier, "Practitioners of the Art of Zen TV Watching," *Los Angeles Times,* June 6, 1982, pp. 1, 14.

12. *Television and Behavior: Ten Years of Scientific Progress and Implications for the Eighties,* vol. 1 (Rockville, Md.: U.S. Department of Health and Human Services, 1982), pp. 89–90.

13. "Why Children's TV Turns Off So Many Parents," *U.S. News & World Report,* February 18, 1985, p. 65.

14. Wilbur Schramm, Jack Lyle and Edwin Parker, *Television in the Lives of Our Children* (Palo Alto, Calif.: Stanford University Press, 1961), p. 13.

15. Patricia Marks Greenfield, *Mind and Media: The Effects of Television, Video Games and Computers* (Cambridge, Mass.: Harvard University Press, 1984), pp. 25–70.

16. Robert Coles, "What Makes Some Kids More Vulnerable to the Worst of TV?" *TV Guide,* June 21–27, 1986, p. 7.

17. *International Television Almanac,* 1990, p. 23 A.

18. *The Broadcasting Yearbook 1990,* pp. A-6, G-16.

19. *International Television Almanac,* 1990, p. 28 A.

20. Rock Du Brow, "Big Figures but Ratings Down for Super Bowl," *Los Angeles Times,* January 29, 1991, p. F-1.

ADDITIONAL READING

Barnouw, Erik. *Tube of Plenty: The Development of American Television.* New York: Oxford University Press, 1975.

Bower, Robert T. *Television and the Public.* New York: Holt, Rinehart & Winston, 1973.

Cantor, Muriel, and Pingree, Suzanne. *The Soap Opera.* Beverly Hills, Ca.: Sage Publications, 1983.

Cross, Donna Woolfolk. *Media-Speak: How Television Makes Up Your Mind.* New York: Mentor, 1983.

Edmondson, Madeleine, and Rounds, David. *From Mary Noble to Mary Hartman: The Complete Soap Opera Book.* New York: Stein and Day, 1976.

Epstein, Edward J. *The News from Nowhere.* New York: Random House, 1973.

Greenfield, Jeff. *Television: The First Fifty Years.* New York: Crescent, 1977.

Gitlin, Todd. *Inside Prime Time.* New York: Pantheon, 1985.

————. *Watching Television: A Pantheon Guide to Popular Culture.* New York: Pantheon, 1986.

Himmelstein, Hal. *Television Myth and the American Mind.* New York: Praeger, 1984.

Horsfield, Peter G. *Religious Television: The American Experience.* New York: Longman, 1984.

Johnson, Nicholas. *How to Talk Back to Your Television Set.* Boston: Little, Brown, 1970.

Kaminsky, Stuart M., with Mahan, Jeffrey H. *American Television Genres.* Chicago: Nelson-Hall, 1985.

Leonard, Bill. *In the Storm of the Eye: A Lifetime at CBS.* New York: Putnam, 1987.

Liebert, Robert M. *The Early Window: The Effects of Television on Children and Youth,* 2nd ed. New York: Pergamon, 1982.

Marc, David. *Demographic Vistas: Television in American Culture.* Philadelphia: University of Pennsylvania Press, 1984.

McCabe, Peter. *Bad News at Black Rock: The Sell-Out of CBS News.* New York: Arbor House, 1987.

McNeil, Alex. *Total Television: A Comprehensive Guide to Programming from 1948 to the Present,* 2nd ed. New York: Penguin, 1984.

Newcomb, Horace. *TV: The Most Popular Art.* Garden City, N.Y.: Anchor Books, 1974.

Powers, Ron. *The Newscasters.* New York: St. Martin's, 1978.

Vaughn, Robert. *Only Victims: A Study of Show Business Blacklisting.* New York: Putnam, 1972.

Westin, Av. *Newswatch: How Television Gathers and Delivers the News.* New York: Simon & Schuster, 1982.

Williams, Raymond. *Television: Technology and Cultural Form.* New York: Schocken, 1974.

Woolery, George. *Children's Television: The First Thirty-five Years, 1946–1981.* Metuchen, N.J.: Scarecrow Press, 1985.

Protests against rock music, like this one on Capitol Hill, have resulted in congressional hearings on whether rock lyrics corrupt young people.

RECORDED MUSIC: POWERFUL AND CONTROVERSIAL

11

I make a living doing things most people get arrested for.
—Ozzy Osbourne

"I'm not guilty and I'm not going to pay the fine," Florida record store owner Charles Freeman angrily exclaimed after a judge fined him $1,000 for selling obscene music.

Freeman had been convicted by a jury for selling a copy of 2 Live Crew's rap album *As Nasty as They Wanna Be*, which had earlier been declared obscene by a Florida court.

During the first part of the 1990s, the recording industry found itself under assault from parents, religious groups, legislators, the courts and police. Since the

CULTURAL HISTORY OF RECORDED MUSIC

ELITIST	POPULAR	SPECIALIZED		
■			1877	Thomas A. Edison invents the "talking machine."
■			1902	Enrico Caruso begins recording opera.
■			1905	Columbia introduces two-sided discs.
	■		1920s	African-American music helps recording industry expand its sales.
	■		1920s	Jazz music evokes charges that music is corrupting young people.
	■		1920s	Covering (white musicians playing African-American music) leads to development of "White Swing."
	■		1925	Electric phonographs replace hand-cranked machines.
	■		1927	Jukebox becomes popular.
	■		1930s	Recording industry declines due to Great Depression and radio's free music.
	■		1930s	Big Band era keeps recording industry alive.
	■		1940s	Frank Sinatra gains fame appealing to a youthful bobbysoxer audience.
		■	1950s	Specialization of radio introduces African-American rhythm and blues to white audiences.
		■	1954	Sam Phillips of Sun Records discovers Elvis Presley, who becomes the king of rock-'n'-roll.
		■	1955	The motion-picture industry, reaching out for a youth audience, uses Bill Haley and the Comets' "Rock Around the Clock" as the theme song for *Blackboard Jungle*.

1980s, parents and religious leaders had been expressing fear that rock music lyrics—particularly those found in heavy metal and rap music—were corrupting the young. Legislators got into the act in numerous states by introducing laws that required warning labels on music. Courts in Florida and Texas began heating up the controversy in the 1990s by finding the music of certain rap groups obscene. Police followed by arresting such groups as 2 Live Crew, Too Much Joy and Kid 'N Play for performing "obscene" music.

Popular music, however, has always been controversial. Despite this fact, the recording industry has grown to be one of the most powerful and influential mass communication media in the American popular culture. Contrary to what critics may contend, not all of music's influence is negative. In the 1980s, for example,

<table>
<tr><th>ELITIST</th><th>POPULAR</th><th>SPECIALIZED</th><th colspan="2"># CULTURAL HISTORY
OF RECORDED MUSIC</th></tr>
</table>

CULTURAL HISTORY OF RECORDED MUSIC

ELITIST	POPULAR	SPECIALIZED		
		▓	1955–63	Rock-'n'-roll becomes firmly entrenched in new youth subculture.
		▓	1960s	Led by the Beatles and the "British invasion," rock music begins carrying less innocent messages that reflect changing American subcultures.
		▓	1970	The Beatles disband.
	▓	▓	1970s	Disco palaces invade American culture.
		▓	1976	Punk rock emerges in Britain.
		▓	1981	Warner-Amex introduces MTV cable channel; popularizes music videos.
		▓	1985	We Are the World and Live Aid concerts raise millions for starving in Africa.
		▓	1985	U.S. Senate committee holds hearings on rock-music lyrics; suggests a rating system to warn listeners of explicit lyrics.
		▓	1986	Michael Jackson pays a reported $40–50 million for the rights to the Beatles' music.
		▓	1990	Jury finds Florida music store owner guilty of obscenity for selling rap music.
		▓	1990	Court finds Judas Priest innocent of causing the deaths of two Nevada suicide victims by placing subliminal messages in their music.
		▓	1990s	State legislatures continue efforts to regulate recorded music by requiring ratings and lyrics on jacket covers.

rock music groups joined together to benefit a variety of worthy causes from hunger in Ethiopia, to the plight of farmers in America. These events included a 16-hour Live Aid concert in Philadelphia and London, which was televised worldwide via 16 communication satellites to more than a billion people in 169 countries, and an annual Farm Aid concert featuring Willie Nelson and a host of country and rock-'n'-roll stars.

Is rock music obscene and corruptive? Or is it rejuvenating, bonding and healing? These contrasting opinions have generated much debate in our culture in recent years. However, one thing seems certain: the global influence of music has gotten the attention of the masses and the industry has grown to be a lucrative media business.

HOW IT ALL BEGAN

The influence and significance of music in our culture has long been recognized. More than two thousand years ago, Plato called for strict censorship of popular music in *The Republic,* a book about his concept of an ideal society. He feared that citizens might be tempted and corrupted by "weak and voluptuous" music and led to indulge in demoralizing emotions. Over the centuries many philosophers and scientists have expressed this fear of music's power to corrupt. However, it wasn't until the nineteenth century that music began to be mass-communicated and the criticism began to grow in intensity. This criticism of popular music seems to have hit full stride in the 1990s.

Sheet Music.   The pervasiveness of recorded music in today's American popular culture sometimes lets us forget that recordings weren't the first form in which music was mass-communicated in our society. In the nineteenth century music was transmitted in print; sheet music was printed and distributed, first in the elite culture and then, in the late nineteenth and early twentieth centuries, in the popular culture. A variety of popular folk songs were widely distributed and people used the sheet music to play pianos or other instruments at family sing-alongs or social gatherings.

The Talking Machine.   Although sheet music was popular, it did not have the cultural impact of recorded music. Thus, when Thomas A. Edison first heard his own words "Mary had a little lamb" repeated back to him from his talking machine in 1877, the stage was set for the development of a powerful mass-communication medium. Edison recognized the potential for his invention and by the following year had formed the Edison Speaking Phonograph Company.

Edison's early *phonograph* used a tin-foil cylinder to record and play back the sound. Two technicians working for Alexander Graham Bell improved on Edison's invention by developing the *graphophone,* which used a wax cylinder instead of tin foil for longer wear and better sound. The new talking machines were first played publicly for vaudeville audiences; later they were leased to saloons, where people could "hear them talk" for a nickel.

The American Graphophone Company and the Columbia Phonograph Company began leasing the talking machines to record dictation in offices during this period. Columbia did well because it had the Washington, D.C., franchise to lease the machines to government offices. The former company failed, and Columbia obtained its patent rights and became known as Columbia-Graphophone.

The next improvement on the early talking machines was the *gramophone.* It changed the way the stylus recorded sound and used a disc instead of a cylinder. The inventor of the gramophone, a German immigrant named Emile Berliner, joined forces with a New Jersey machinist, Eldridge Johnson, to found the Victor Talking Machine Company. They were the first to market the gramophones for use in the home.

The world-famous opera star Enrico Caruso gave people something worthwhile to listen to on their gramophones when he began making records in 1902. Other opera stars followed suit, and the recording industry was on its way. Columbia

■ Thomas Edison, with his newly invented "talking machine."

introduced the two-sided disc in 1905. However, the new talking-machine industry was very much a communication medium for the elite, as only wealthier homes could afford a gramophone and records, which cost 65 cents apiece in a day when $5 a week was a good salary.

RECORDED MUSIC ENTERS THE POPULAR CULTURE

American culture has two distinct forms of folk music, both rooted in American subcultures—African-American music and hillbilly music, now better known as country-and-western. African-American music was the first to be transmitted throughout the popular culture through sheet and recorded music. Hillbilly music remained primarily in the Southern region of its origin until the second half of the twentieth century.

African-American Music. Early African-American music—spirituals, gospel and blues—reflected the poverty and oppression of slaves in the South. The only thing the slaves were able to bring with them to this country was their culture, and that culture was expressed through their music.

African-American music became popular in the nineteenth century after the Civil War as musicians of color were hired to play in saloons and brothels along the Mississippi River. A popular form known as ragtime made the transition from these establishments to the popular culture in the late nineteenth century through the distribution of sheet music.

As ragtime's popularity waned in the early twentieth century, a new form of African-American music known as Dixieland jazz took its place. The 1920s were known as the Roaring '20s or the Jazz Age. This was a decade when prohibition was in effect and illegal drinking was promoted in speakeasies, which played music and allowed people to enjoy themselves by dancing the Charleston.

Until 1925 most phonographs were mechanical and hand-cranked. In that year the industry started selling electric phonographs, and the recording industry moved rapidly from the elite culture into the popular. In 1927 987,000 phonographs were sold, along with 104 million records.

As jazz entered the popular culture, it provoked a great deal of criticism— similar to what we hear today about popular music—that it was destroying the morals of the youth. The themes of popular music in the 1920s were very similar to the ones in today's recorded music.

As early as the 1920s, blues songs on such labels as Okeh and Bluebird carried a variety of sexually suggestive titles. The music, which reflected the emotions and struggles of the poorer segments of the African-American community, often referred to the earthy conditions of everyday life and occasionally included four-letter words. The music was criticized by blacks as well as whites, as the following passage from an African-American leader indicates: "To respectable, middle class, churchgoing Negroes, blues is often considered evil music; the devil's music that beguiles the listener and leads him to damnation."[1]

Such charges against recorded music were prevalent during the Jazz Age. The culture was changing during this period as new music, new dances, new styles of dress, the entrance of the automobile into the popular culture and new moral codes began altering people's behavior. Women began smoking and drinking and listening to jazz in speakeasies. They wore short "flapper" dresses and did the Charleston and other "shimmy dances." Men and women were displaying a new carefree attitude in a culture that had previously been guided by Victorian morality. Even Cole Porter wrote a song about "getting a kick from cocaine" during this period, while Billie Holiday sang about "Love for Sale."

Leaders of such groups as the National Education Association, the Federation of Women's Clubs and various religious organizations took up the anti-jazz cry. The following article in William Randolph Hearst's New York *American* reflected a common view:

Jazz Ruining Girls, Declares Reformer

Chicago, Jan. 21—Moral disaster is coming to hundreds of American girls through the pathological, nerve irritating, sex-exciting music of jazz orchestras, according to the Illinois Vigilance Association.

In Chicago alone the association's representatives have traced the fall of 1,000 girls in the last two years to jazz music.

Girls in small towns, as well as the big cities, in poor homes and rich homes, are victims of the weird, insidious, neurotic music that accompanies modern dancing.

The degrading music is common not only to disorderly places, but often to high-school affairs, to expensive hotels and so-called society circles, declares Rev. Richard Yarrow, superintendent of the Vigilance Association.

The report says that the vigilance society has no desire to abolish dancing, but seeks to awaken the public conscience to the present danger and future consequences of jazz music.[2]

Despite this and similar criticism, the popularity of jazz continued to grow.

Covering. Attempts by the recording industry to sell blues and jazz to the popular culture ran into some difficulties, however. In particular, many whites were reluctant to buy records by African-American artists. To overcome this, the process of covering was developed: white artists were hired to record black music.

White Swing.   Benny Goodman, for example, rode to fame playing the music of African-American songwriter Fletcher Henderson. From blues and jazz came white swing. Swing was a milder, watered-down version of African-American music that did not reflect the raw emotions of the black experience. Swing became a popular style of music that mainstream tastes could accept.

Jukeboxes and Sales.   The recording industry grew and flourished during the last half of the 1920s. The jukebox became popular in 1927 and added another market for the sales of records as well as being a new promotional device for home sales of records (see Box 11.1).

In the 1930s, however, the industry nearly collapsed because the Great Depression seriously curtailed people's ability to spend money on leisure pursuits and because radio was now offering music free. The end of prohibition in 1933 helped record sales, though, by bringing back taverns, which all had jukeboxes playing the latest records.

Radio and Sales.   Radio networks also began to see a future in the recording industry, and in 1938 CBS purchased the Columbia Phonograph Company and started promoting its recording stars on network radio. People were encouraged to go out and buy their records.

In the late 1930s a young singer by the name of Francis Albert Sinatra was discovered. Backed by the popular Harry James and Tommy Dorsey bands, he became the idol of many young "bobbysoxers" throughout the country. Teenage girls would scream and faint when they saw him in concert or heard his voice on records or radio. Many other popular vocalists, some like Peggy Lee who were from the big band era of the 1930s, became successful as recording artists during the 1940s and early 1950s. Among them were Frankie Laine, Vaughn Monroe, Mel Torme, Perry Como, Vic Damone, Dinah Shore and Doris Day.

During this period radio was forced to find a new niche as a specialized medium because of the entrance of television into the popular culture. As a result, numerous radio stations began to feature specialized types of music.

Rhythm-and-Blues.   One of the more popular sounds among young people was coming from the African-American rhythm-and-blues stations that were broadcasting in metropolitan areas. It started to dawn on recording-industry executives that if they could find white performers to sing rhythm-and-blues, they might capitalize on the expanding audience of young people for this new sound.

In 1951 Cleveland disc jockey Alan Freed, who later coined the term rock-'n'-roll, started playing rhythm-and-blues records for a white radio audience.

Rock-'n'-Roll.   Sam Phillips, a Memphis, Tennessee, record promoter—who formed Sun Records in the early 1950s—combed the South for a white country singer who could handle the beat of rhythm-and-blues. "What I need," he said unabashedly, "is a white boy who can sing colored."[3]

BOX 11.1

▪ THE CHANGING WORLD OF THE JUKEBOX ▪

Although electrically driven coin-operated record machines didn't emerge in the popular culture until 1927, the concept for the jukebox dates back to 1889. On November 23 of that year Louis Glass added a coin slot to an Edison recording machine and installed it in a San Francisco saloon. For a penny, patrons could listen to John Philip Sousa's Marine Band.

In 1906 The Gabel Automatic Entertainer provided a mechanical record changer for a coin-operated music box. But it wasn't until the Roaring '20s, when prohibition sparked the speakeasy and jukeboxes became a source of cheap music, that electrical jukeboxes became an integral part of our popular culture. The records in those days were heavy discs (about 10 inches in diameter) that spun at 78 revolutions per minute. Just as popular music has changed over the years, so has the jukebox. In the 1940s when much smaller and lighter phonograph records, known as 45s (because they spun at 45 revolutions per minute), replaced 78s in the singles market, jukeboxes had to be redesigned.

Then in the 1980s, the jukebox industry found itself facing another crisis. The 45s were being phased out of the music industry, and by 1986 they accounted for only 5 percent of the records and tapes made.

In 1987 the old 45-playing jukeboxes were replaced with new machines that played compact discs. The king of the jukebox industry, Seeburg, was the first to develop a CD jukebox that would play 3 songs for $1 or 18 songs for $5. Not only did the new jukeboxes have better sound quality—thanks to the CDs—they contained more selections—700 to 1,000, compared to around 200 in the old 45 jukeboxes.

Other music dispensers developed in the 1980s included jukeboxes with large 25-inch color screens that played laser video discs. Produced by Laser Video Music and Rowe International, these music videos cost 50 cents a selection—10 times the amount of the original jukebox.

In 1954 he found country-and-western singer Elvis Presley and turned him into the "king" of rock-'n'-roll. By 1956 Presley had five songs at the top of the charts. After a hitch in the army he became a motion-picture star as well. Although his recording career faded in the 1970s he was a living legend for many years until his death in 1977.

Rock-'n'-roll was a new form of American music that evolved from a blend of rhythm-and-blues and country-and-western. The motion-picture industry, which was attempting to recover from the television-caused box-office slump by focusing on the youth audience, helped promote rock-'n'-roll in some of its movies. For example, Bill Haley and his Comets' rock-'n'-roll song "Rock Around the Clock" was the theme for *Blackboard Jungle,* a film about juvenile delinquency in the schools. The song became one of the best-selling records of 1955. Television featured rock-'n'-roll shows too, most notably Dick Clark's *American Bandstand,* which played the latest songs each day. The program showed rock stars lip-syncing their hits and teenagers dancing to the music.

The American youth of the 1950s were forming their own subculture with its own fads, clothing styles and music. The early period of rock-'n'-roll—from 1955 to 1963—was an innocent era when a number of teenagers became overnight rock-'n'-roll stars. Recording stars such as Ricky Nelson, Frankie Avalon, Fabian, Paul Anka, Bobby Darin and Bobby Rydell became teen idols. They sang largely about teenage romances. Also popular were female singers and groups such as Lesley Gore, the Shangri-Las, the Ronettes, the Marvelettes and the Crystals.

Not all rock-'n'-roll stars were white, however. As the beat of rock-'n'-roll swept through the youth culture, the music industry began featuring African-American artists to keep up with the demand for this new sound. Indeed, rock-'n'-roll was instrumental in breaking down the color barrier in music once and for all. The young were less prejudiced than their parents and enjoyed the music without caring about its ethnic origins. Many African-American entertainers became popular with white as well as black audiences. Among them were Chuck Berry, Fats Domino, Little Richard, Chubby Checkers, Bo Diddley, the Platters, the Shirelles and the Coasters.

The merging of country-and-western music with rhythm-and-blues also helped move country music into our mainstream popular culture. Many of the early rock-'n'-roll singers were former country stars, and this trend of crossing over from country to popular music helped spark country music's acceptance in the popular culture. The 1970s saw the emergence of such popular country-and-western crossover artists as Kenny Rogers, Dolly Parton, Johnny Cash and Willie Nelson.

ROCK MUSIC CHANGES

Rock-'n'-roll was fun, innocent music for the young, a new genre that adults did not accept. Parents complained that the new music sounded awful and described it as a clattering of pots and pans. To keep it out of earshot, they sent their children to their rooms to listen to it. This helped set the stage for what was termed the generation gap between parents and adolescents in the late 1960s.

Cultural Changes.   Following the assassination of President Kennedy in 1963, rock-'n'-roll music became more sophisticated, and its lyrics reflected the troubled and changing times. The counterculture, with its "flower children," "hippies" and psychedelic drug users, had arrived. The slogan of the day was "Make Love, Not War," as the counterculture preached free sex and opposition to U.S. involvement in the Vietnam war. This agenda was expressed in the rock music of the mid- and late 1960s. Songs like the Rolling Stones' "I Can't Get No Satisfaction" and Bob Dylan's "Blowin' in the Wind," "A Hard Rain's Gonna Fall" and "Talkin' World War III Blues" presented ideas and viewpoints far removed from those of mainstream middle-class America.

Many parents were shocked to find that their children were developing values different from their own. They started to blame the schools for teaching such things to their children, unaware that much of the education was going on at home—through the music they had banished to their children's rooms.

The Beatles.   One of the most popular recording groups of all times was the Beatles, an English quartet that had a profound impact on American popular culture and middle-class culture worldwide during the 1960s. Although the group

■ The Beatles, who had been fans of Elvis Presley, brought their own version of rock-'n'-roll to America in 1964, thus launching the "British invasion" of rock music. Here they are shown performing on the Ed Sullivan television show, which introduced them to the American popular culture.

disbanded in 1970, their cultural influence was so strong that their popularity continues in the 1990s.

The Beatles, from Liverpool, England, consisted of John Lennon, Paul Mc-Cartney, George Harrison and Ringo Starr. In 1964 they led the "British invasion" of rock stars who became household names in the American popular culture. These British performers had grown up with America's Elvis Presley and had popularized American rock-'n'-roll for British youth. Then, in 1964, the Beatles brought their British version of American rock-'n'-roll home to the United States, thus launching an invasion of British performers. The Beatles and other British groups also triggered a youth fashion revolution in the United States, which consisted of long hair and "Beatle" boots for boys and miniskirts and straight long hair for girls.

The Beatles' early hits were simple and innocent songs such as "I Want to Hold Your Hand" and "She Loves You." Their music changed with the times, however, and began to rely on advanced recording techniques. In 1967 the Beatles released *Sgt. Pepper's Lonely Hearts Club Band*. The album took more than 400 hours to record and was highly sophisticated with many hidden messages and meanings in the lyrics, sound track and album cover. Some claimed four-letter words and other messages were imbedded at a level where they could only be heard by the subconscious mind.

One song in particular—"Lucy in the Sky with Diamonds"—was believed by some observers to be about the use of LSD. They pointed out that the key words in the title start with the letters of this hallucinogenic drug and that the lyrics describe a psychedelic acid trip with such phrases as "tangerine trees and mar-malade skies." The Beatles, of course, denied any connection. *Sgt. Pepper* was so successful that 20 years later, in 1987, it was voted by rock critics around the world as the greatest rock album of all time[4] (see Table 11.1).

Some people also zeroed in on the Beatles' top-selling single "Hey Jude" (1968), and said that it too was about the use of drugs. The word *her* was said to refer to heroin in such lyrics as "let her into your heart" and "the minute you let her under your skin then you begin to make it better." However, Beatles business associate and biographer Peter Brown says that Paul McCartney wrote the song to ease the pain of John Lennon's young son, Julian, during his father's divorce from his mother, Cynthia, and new involvement with Yoko Ono.[5]

Brown does confirm that the group was one of many who did get heavily involved in drugs. Although the Beatles had been taking amphetamines to help them through concerts since their early days of performing in Hamburg, West Germany, it was not until their first American tour in 1964 that they were turned on to marijuana. According to Brown, "On August 28 a small but auspicious event occurred at the Delmonico Hotel in New York that would grow to affect the consciousness of the world: Bob Dylan turned the Beatles on to marijuana for the first time in their lives."[6] Brown also confirms the Beatles' experimentation with LSD and admits that John Lennon became dependent on heroin.[7]

The change in the Beatles and their music was what kept them so popular. They led the British invasion with a new sound that the youth of America seemed to be waiting for, as Beatlemania swept over the United States in 1964. In April of 1964 the top five singles in this country were all recordings by the Beatles. Other British groups—Herman's Hermits, the Dave Clark Five and Peter and Gordon—had top-10 hits that year, but only the Beatles became a cultural legend because they were willing to change as rock music "grew up" in the troubled decade of the 1960s (see Box 11.2).

Even though the Beatles broke up in 1970, their impact on our popular culture remains profound. Paul, George and Ringo are still performing. When John Lennon was murdered outside his New York apartment in December 1980, the event became one of the biggest news stories of the year. Hundreds of radio and TV stations throughout the United States honored his wife Yoko Ono's request for 10 minutes of silence. Magazines and newspapers ran extensive stories on the shooting and ordinary people's reaction to his death. In 1986 singer Michael Jackson paid between $40 and $50 million to purchase the rights to almost all of the songs written by the Beatles. And in the 1990s many radio stations were still regularly playing the Beatles' music.

Second Wave of the British Invasion.   The second wave of the British invasion brought the Rolling Stones, a group that sang about alienation and social discontent. Reflecting the hostility of the times, the Stones challenged the Beatles as the most popular group in the United States. However, feminist groups greatly criticized the Stones for the hostility toward women evident in such songs as "Under My Thumb," about a girl who does just as she is told, and "Time Is on My Side," about a dependent woman who keeps running back to her man. In the 1970s feminists protested a billboard advertisement for the Rolling Stones' album

TABLE 11.1 THE TOP 100 ROCK-'N'-ROLL ALBUMS OF ALL TIME
(ACCORDING TO ROCK CRITICS AROUND THE WORLD)

1. *Sgt. Pepper's Lonely Hearts Club Band,* the Beatles
2. *Born to Run,* Bruce Springsteen
3. *Blonde on Blonde,* Bob Dylan
4. *What's Going On,* Marvin Gaye
5. *Born in the U.S.A.,* Bruce Springsteen
6. *The Sun Collection,* Elvis Presley
7. *The Velvet Underground and Nico,* the Velvet Underground and Nico
8. *Pet Sounds,* the Beach Boys
9. *Astral Weeks,* Van Morrison
10. *The Beatles (The White Album),* the Beatles
11. *Exile on Main Street,* the Rolling Stones
12. *Let it Bleed,* the Rolling Stones
13. *Abbey Road,* the Beatles
14. *Songs in the Key of Life,* Stevie Wonder
15. *Dark Side of the Moon,* Pink Floyd
16. *Live at the Apollo, Vol. I,* James Brown
17. *Revolver,* the Beatles
18. *Highway 61 Revisited,* Bob Dylan
19. *Never Mind the Bollocks Here's the Sex Pistols,* Sex Pistols
20. *Who's Next,* the Who
21. *Rubber Soul,* the Beatles
22. *Otis Blue,* Otis Redding
23. *Thriller,* Michael Jackson
24. *The Band,* the Band
25. *Blood on the Tracks,* Bob Dylan
26. *Rumours,* Fleetwood Mac
27. *Avalon,* Roxy Music
28. *My Aim Is True,* Elvis Costello
29. *With the Beatles,* the Beatles
30. *Tapestry,* Carole King
31. *The Clash,* the Clash
32. *Bringing It All Back Home,* Bob Dylan
33. *Beggars Banquet,* the Rolling Stones
34. *Forever Changes,* Love
35. *I Want to See the Bright Lights Tonight,* Richard and Linda Thompson
36. *Live!,* Bob Marley and the Wailers
37. *Court and Spark,* Joni Mitchell
38. *Innervisions,* Stevie Wonder
39. *Get Happy!!,* Elvis Costello
40. *London Calling,* the Clash
41. *Entertainment,* Gang of Four
42. *Bridge Over Troubled Water,* Simon and Garfunkel
43. *Squeezing Out Sparks,* Graham Parker and the Rumour
44. *Grievous Angel,* Gram Parsons
45. *Synchronicity,* the Police
46. *Kate and Anna McGarrigle,* Kate and Anna McGarrigle
47. *The Unforgettable Fire,* U2
48. *Hotel California,* the Eagles
49. *Starsailor,* Tim Buckley
50. *Electric Ladyland,* the Jimi Hendrix Experience

TABLE 11.1 (continued)

287

11 ∎
RECORDED MUSIC:
POWERFUL AND
CONTROVERSIAL

51. *Private Dancer*, Tina Turner
52. *Moondance*, Van Morrison
53. *It's Too Late to Stop Now*, Van Morrison
54. *Green River*, Creedence Clearwater Revival
55. *The Stranger*, Billy Joel
56. *Building the Perfect Beast*, Don Henley
57. *Paris 1919*, John Cale
58. *Hunky Dory*, David Bowie
59. *Darkness on the Edge of Town*, Bruce Springsteen
60. *This Year's Model*, Elvis Costello
61. *For Your Pleasure*, Roxy Music
62. *The Pretenders*, the Pretenders
63. *Dreamer*, Bobbie Bland
64. *Music from Big Pink*, the Band
65. *Here's Little Richard*, Little Richard
66. *Who Sell Out*, the Who
67. *Blue*, Joni Mitchell
68. *Aftermath*, the Rolling Stones
69. *Can't Slow Down*, Lionel Ritchie
70. *Stand!*, Sly and the Family Stone
71. *Beatles for Sale*, the Beatles
72. *Young Americans*, David Bowie
* *Sports*, Huey Lewis and the News
74. *Talking Book*, Stevie Wonder
75. *King Creole*, Elvis Presley
* *The Notorious Byrd Brothers*, The Byrds
* *Stranded*, Roxy Music
78. *The 'Chirping' Crickets*, the Crickets
* *John Wesley Harding*, Bob Dylan
* *Radio City*, Big Star
81. *Trout Mask Replica*, Captain Beefheart and his Magic Band
* *The Velvet Underground*, the Velvet Underground
* *Off the Wall*, Michael Jackson
* *Let's Get It On*, Marvin Gaye
85. *Imagine*, John Lennon
86. *Amazing Grace*, Aretha Franklin
87. *Horses*, Patti Smith
* *Making Movies*, Dire Straits
* *Swordfishtrombones*, Tom Waits
90. *Purple Rain*, Prince and the Revolution
* *The Rise and Fall of Ziggy Stardust and the Spiders from Mars*, David Bowie
92. *L.A. Woman*, the Doors
* *Layla*, Derek and the Dominos
94. *A Christmas Gift for You*, Phil Spector and Artists
95. *Going to a Go-Go*, the Miracles
* *The Last Waltz*, the Band
97. *Are You Experienced*, the Jimi Hendrix Experience
* *Pearl*, Janis Joplin
* *Sweet Dreams*, Eurythmics
100. *Transformer*, Lou Reed

---

*Indicates a tie.
SOURCE: Reprinted by permission from Paul Gambaccini, *The Top 100 Rock 'n' Roll Albums of All Time* (London: Harmony Books, 1987).

BOX 11.2

▪ IS PAUL DEAD? SOME IN THE 1960s THOUGHT SO ▪

In 1969 a rumor started that one of the Beatles, Paul McCartney, had been decapitated in an automobile accident and replaced by a look-alike named William Campbell. The rumor swept through the American popular culture and the world.

Fans started finding clues that Paul was dead subliminally embedded in the Beatles' music and on their album covers. If one listened carefully to the end of "Strawberry Fields Forever" (1967), one was supposed to hear John muttering "I buried Paul." Other clues were found by spinning the Beatles, *The White Album* (1968) backward. In the tune "Revolution 9," the phrase "number nine, number nine" sounded like "turn me on dead man, turn me on dead man" when played counterclockwise. By listening carefully to the gibberish sandwiched between "I'm So Tired" and "Blackbird" on that album, clue seekers could find the message "Paul is dead man, miss him, miss him."

The cover of *Abbey Road* (1969) offered additional clues. The Beatles were pictured leaving a cemetery with John Lennon dressed in white, Ringo Starr dressed as an undertaker and George Har-rison dressed as a gravedigger. McCartney was the only one out of step with the others. He was bare-foot, as British corpses are often buried, and had a cigarette in his right hand, supposedly confirming that this was an impostor for the left-handed Paul. The license plate on a Volkswagen parked on the street was "28 IF," which, clue seekers noted, would have been McCartney's age had he lived.

All the Beatles denied not only the rumor but the existence of the "clues." Nevertheless the rumor developed into a genuine folk tale created and spread by the mass media. Sociologist Barbara Suczek claims it was a twentieth-century version of the ancient Greek myth in which a beautiful youth dies and is resurrected as a god.

By the 1970s, the entire episode was a joke, and even John Lennon referred to it in the lyrics of one of his songs. The "Paul Is Dead" hoax significantly increased the sale of the Beatles' albums, and it proved that all kinds of messages could be cleverly transmitted in the sound tracks and album covers of popular music.

Black and Blue. It showed a woman beaten and tied up with a caption reading "I'm black and blue from the Rolling Stones, and I love it."

However, the Rolling Stones have endured this criticism and have continued to perform through three decades. Now in their 40s and 50s, this group (called the "geezers" by *Time* magazine) has outlasted, outperformed and outsold all other rock stars of the '60s generation. According to the Recording Industry Association of America, the Stones have been awarded five gold singles (representing sales of 1 million copies each) and 28 gold albums (500,000 copies each). In addition they have had two albums go multi-platinum: *Tattoo You*, with 3 million copies sold, and *Some Girls*, with 4 million.

Other Favorites.   Another popular kind of music in the 1960s was the Motown sound, danceable African-American soul music that originated in Detroit. This music featured the sounds of Diana Ross and the Supremes, the Temptations and Stevie Wonder. By the early 1970s these groups were singing socially conscious songs like "Love Child" and "Ball of Confusion."

Other groups that were reflecting the new age of social protest and the drug culture during this period were the Doors and Jefferson Airplane. In a quieter, more subtle way, Simon and Garfunkel were also singing about social protest and bitterness.

BOX 11.3

■ "HEAVENLY METAL MUSIC" ■

While some have been working toward banning heavy-metal music claiming that much of its lyrics promote Satanism, the heavenly metal band Stryper has been fighting the devil's music on the top-40 charts.

Stryper found success blending born-again Christian lyrics with a heavy-metal sound and seemed to have made it in the music world when their first video, from their album *Calling on You*, debuted on MTV in the late 1980s.

Their 1986 album *To Hell with the Devil* found mainstream acceptance among hard-rock fans and gave defenders of heavy metal support for their argument that it's the sound—not the lyrics—that turns on audiences.

The Christian rock band consists of lead singer Michael Sweet, guitarist Oz Fox, drummer Robert Sweet (brother of Michael) and bassist Tim Gaines.

Stryper is just one of a number of rock bands that have taken up the Christian theme in their lyrics in an attempt to combat what many fundamentalist Christian ministers called the "moral corruption" of heavy-metal music.

ROCK SPECIALIZES

From its beginnings in the 1950s, rock music has learned to specialize. Over the years a variety of rock forms—such as pop rock, hard rock, acid rock, punk rock, bubblegum rock, glitter rock, reggae, new wave, heavy metal and even Christian rock—has evolved (see Box 11.3).

Disco. In the 1970s, as the Vietnam war came to an end and people began to tire of protest music, they began searching for a new sound. The discotheque—a cabaret where patrons could dance to popular music—began to grow in popularity. Disco music, like rock, had its roots in the beat of rhythm-and-blues. It created a new cultural industry of disco palaces, like the celebrity haven Studio 54 in New York. Disco music brought a new group of stars, from soloists like Donna Summer to groups like the Village People, which consisted of six men dressed as a cowboy, a construction worker, an Indian, a policeman, a biker and a soldier. One of the hottest disco groups, thanks to the inclusion of their songs in the movie *Saturday Night Fever* (1977), was the Bee Gees.

In the late 1970s, the record industry went into a financial slump similar to the one it had experienced in the 1930s. Part of the problem was an increase in record prices due to the rise in petroleum prices (the vinyl used in records is a petroleum by-product). But some people, like record producer Richard Perry, blamed disco for the decline in record sales: "Everybody spent their money dancing at discos, not on albums. Disco also was limited to . . . 128 beats per minute, which gave it pulse but no solid melody. All disco began to sound alike. It became totally uninspiring to dance to. It got people out of the habit of buying records. It really hurt the whole music industry."[8]

Punk Rock.   Also contributing to the decline of record sales was the recording industry itself, which tried to limit the expenses of promotion by restricting the number of new rock groups allowed to record during the 1970s. (This was a classic form of gatekeeping discussed in Chapter 1.) Rock-'n'-roll had evolved from a youth subcultural movement of the 1950s to become an Establishment medium that was still providing groups from the 1960s, such as the Rolling Stones, Diana Ross and the Who. Establishment control of the recording industry led in 1976 to the *punk rock* rebellion in England. A new youth subculture, known as punks, began developing a new anti-Establishment music. Some of the first punk-rock bands, such as the Sex Pistols and the Clash, denounced the Establishment's control of mass culture and spoke out against our consumer society. The punk movement spread throughout the world, but it did not become the rage in the United States as it was in Britain. Eventually it was watered down and became popular as new-wave music. Punk and new wave both had an impact on American fashion. While some people bought fashionable new-wave clothing promoted by the Establishment consumer culture, others spiked and colored their hair green or purple or attached safety pins to their faces to imitate the British punk look.

New Wave.   Disco's popularity had declined by the 1980s as punk and new-wave music emerged. Among the new groups rising to popularity were the B-52s, Devo, Blondie, Elvis Costello, the Cars, the Motels, the Talking Heads, the Police, Duran Duran and Boy George and the Culture Club. The new music plus the development of music videos and the debut of MTV in 1981 helped restore the financial health of the recording industry.

From Bruce to Madonna.   By the mid-1980s recording artists like Bruce Springsteen, U2, Michael Jackson, Prince and Madonna were leading popularity charts and selling out concerts within hours after tickets went on sale. They also were contributing to the consumer culture by selling concert trinkets that ranged from "Madonna" jewelry to T-shirts. Madonna, who had become a movie star in *Desperately Seeking Susan* (1984) to assist her climb to rock stardom, was featured on the cover of three national magazines in 1985, *Time, Playboy* and *Penthouse.* She was still attracting attention in the 1990s with media coverage of her controversial video "Justify My Love," which was banned by MTV for being too sexually explicit.

Second-Generation Rockers.   Now that an entire generation has grown up with rock-'n'-roll, the generation gap seems to have disappeared and the music has "aged." Half of the number-one singles on the *Billboard* charts in 1986 were by

■ Madonna uses sex and shock to sell her musical talents. Her hot and steamy video "Justify My Love" was banned by MTV in 1991. The ban surprised everyone, including Madonna, because the all-music network was not known for avoiding videos with sexual themes and innuendos.

artists over 35; four singers were over 40. Young and old are now listening to rock-'n'-roll—the younger ones listening to Janet Jackson, George Michael, the New Kids on the Block and U2 while the older ones are still enjoying the music of the Rolling Stones.

THE MUSIC VIDEO PHENOMENON (MTV)

In 1981 Warner-Amex created an album-oriented rock cable television channel that featured videos supplied by record companies. It targets 12- to 23-year-olds and became television's only 24-hour-a-day rock-music station. It has had a phenomenal impact on the American popular culture. By the mid-1980s surveys showed that virtually every new band was making at least one music video and that 70 percent of rock enthusiasts indicated that MTV was important in determining which records they would buy. Eventually music videos became another consumer product in music stores.

Music Video Expansion. In 1982 another cable network, USA, started broadcasting Night Flite, a program devoted to MTV-type videos. Soon HBO and Showtime were playing videos for youngsters to fill the time between movies. Atlanta superstation WTBS developed a music video show called *Night Tracks*, NBC developed *Friday Night Videos* and even ABC and CBS were airing at least an hour of music videos each week by the mid-1980s. In the meantime, a second

■ Although the performers and their audiences have aged, the Rolling Stones (shown above in the 1960s and today) continue to draw large audiences for their concerts and recordings.

24-hour music video channel, VH-1, debuted on cable, featuring soft rock and aimed at an older audience. Country-and-western fans can enjoy video music on cable's The Nashville Network.

Impact on Education.   Some educators have complained that students are spending too much time watching MTV and not enough on homework. Although many teenagers had been studying with rock music in the background since the 1950s, videos required visual as well as audio attention.

Other educators recognized the significance of MTV and began studying it. For example, California State University at Los Angeles offered a course called Music Video 454. Students studied the contents of music video, listened to guest speakers from the video industry and visited sets where some of the videos were produced.

Impact on Other Media.   The influence of music videos has not been limited to the recording industry. Rock videos' pace, style and sound have influenced such television shows as *Miami Vice* and such motion pictures as *Top Gun* and *True*

Stories. (Miami Vice star Don Johnson and Bruce Willis, who played David Addison on *Moonlighting,* became rock recording stars as well as TV stars.) When David Byrne of the Talking Heads starred in the rock video–influenced film *True Stories,* it landed him on the cover of *Time* in 1986 as "rock's renaissance man." In 1987 Michael J. Fox shed his kid-next-door image to play a long-haired, earring-wearing rocker in *Light of Day.* Rock videos of sound tracks from these movies were often used on MTV to plug the films.

Decline in Ratings.   MTV's ratings, however, peaked in 1984 with a high of 1.2 percent of the potential audience. Although the ratings seem to have leveled off at 0.6 percent, the cable channel still delivers a large number of 12- to 23-year-olds to advertisers.

In the 1950s, 1960s and 1970s youngsters grew up listening to the sounds and messages of rock music. Today they are experiencing visual as well as audio creations of the rock music world.

CONTROVERSIES SURROUNDING ROCK MUSIC

Criticism and controversy have surrounded recorded music ever since its entrance into the popular culture. The major focus of criticism has been the music's lyrics.

Editorial Statements.   We usually think of newspapers as the medium in which editorials are most effectively used. However, in reality, the most effective editorial statements are carried in recorded music because the messages are combined with music's ability to interact with our emotions.

Each record or tape contains an editorial statement. It might be an innocent expression of the joys of love or a socially powerful statement about the need to feed starving people. Instrumental music contains melodies or beats that stir up some type of emotion, whether it be sadness, joy, relaxation or an impulse to dance. Whatever type of music it is, it is directing some form of persuasion toward the listener.

Subliminal Messages?   A great deal of criticism has been leveled against the recording industry for releasing music with hidden messages designed to appeal to the subconscious, rather than the conscious, mind. Two types of hidden messages have been singled out in particular: subliminal imbeds and backmasking.

Retail stores have used *subliminal imbeds* for some time. Many department stores and supermarkets now play music that includes a voice, just below the level where it can be consciously heard, that continuously repeats messages such as "You are an honest person; you will not steal." Studies indicate that shoplifting has been reduced significantly when this music is played. People can now buy subliminal tapes that claim to program their minds with various messages that will help them lose weight, stop smoking, think positively and so on.

Many rock music critics charge that subliminal messages are also found in popular music—and often the messages imbedded are quite different from the lyrics.

Backmasking, sometimes called backward masking, is even more controversial. People debate not only whether it can affect the listener, but whether it exists at all.

Religious leaders have played records backward for congressional leaders to point out what they say are satanic messages. For example, in Led Zeppelin's all-time favorite, "Stairway to Heaven," phrases that sound very much like "I live with Satan" and "Here's to my sweet Satan" can be heard when the recording is played backward.

In 1990, the British rock group Judas Priest spent nearly a month in court defending against charges that a subliminally imbedded phrase "Do it" and a variety of backmasking suggestions promoting self-destruction in their 1988 album *Stained Class* had caused two Nevada youths to commit suicide. Although the judge ruled that these messages were contained in the album, he said the plaintiffs failed to prove that Judas Priest and CBS Records had intentionally planted them.

Rap and Heavy-Metal Lyrics.   Today the criticism of popular music is focused on lyrics. In recent years some rock artists have gone to extremes in explicit language and antisocial sentiments. Topics discussed in song lyrics include suicide, incest, homosexuality, bisexuality, illegal drug use, murder of family members and explicit sex and bondage. By most cultural standards, these lyrics are raunchy and vulgar.

Prince has sung about sexual activities that would make almost anyone blush, Luther Campbell and 2 Live Crew rap about ghetto sexual activity that rivals animals in heat, and Ozzy Osbourne has boasted that he has made a living doing things most people get arrested for. (Osbourne also was continually finding himself sued by parents of teenaged suicide victims who claimed their children had been listening to Osbourne's "Suicide Solution" at the time of their death. Although a California judge threw out the first such suit in 1986, similar charges brought Osbourne back into a Georgia court, facing wrongful death charges in two suicide cases in 1990.)

The biggest controversy surrounding popular music at the beginning of this decade centered around rap lyrics. When courts in Florida and Texas ruled in 1990 that 2 Live Crew's album *As Nasty as They Wanna Be* was obscene and could not be sold or performed in those states, many in the music industry were outraged. The outrage turned to shock in the fall of 1990 when an African-American music-store owner was found guilty of selling obscenity by an all-white jury in Florida. He appealed the case.

Other rap groups, such as N.W.A. (Niggers with attitude) and Public Enemy, have been criticized for their antisocial and sometimes explicit lyrics. The African-American community is divided on the issue. Some feel that certain rap groups reflect negatively on their race, while others feel that these groups are being singled out because they are African-American. Advocates of the latter point of view point to groups such as Guns 'N' Roses as examples of white groups that have gotten away with obnoxious and obscene lyrics.

Heavy-metal groups continue with their own controversies, mainly that they are singing about satanic worship, and their music is blamed for the increase in

■ Ozzy Osbourne, who boasts that he makes a living doing things most people would get arrested for, has had to defend himself in court against outraged parents who blame his song "Suicide Solution" for the deaths of their teenage children.

satanic cults in a number of communities. Critics have linked bizarre killings, such as those committed by the Night Stalker in California, as well as sexual abuse of preschool children, to heavy-metal music. Such linkage is not new, however. The Manson family killings in Los Angeles during the late 1960s had been linked to the Beatles' popular hit "Helter Skelter" because the killers had scribbled the phrase in blood on the walls at the murder scenes. Songs about marijuana and cocaine have also been prevalent in the 1980s and 1990s—themes that have been around since the Roaring '20s.

Rating Systems.   One of the most powerful of the lobbying groups was the Parents' Music Resource Center (PMRC), a Washington, D.C., based organization formed by Tipper Gore, wife of Senator Albert Gore of Tennessee, and Susan Baker, wife of Secretary of State James Baker. They began pressuring the recording industry to voluntarily label all explicit records so that parents would know what the music contained. They called for either a rating system similar to that used by the motion-picture industry or the printing of lyrics on album covers. They were instrumental in getting a U.S. Senate subcommittee to hold a hearing on the issue in 1985. Opponents of the PMRC proposal argued that the job of censoring children's listening habits belonged in the home, not with government.

Although no federal laws were passed requiring the labeling, by 1990 more than 25 states had introduced legislation to either require labeling and/or printed lyrics or bans on selling and displaying "obscene" music, and the industry was making efforts to voluntarily comply with the request.

BOX 11.4

▪ ROCK AGAINST DRUGS ▪

While the Parents' Music Resource Center was calling for voluntary warning labels on rock music and First Lady Nancy Reagan was telling young people to "Just Say No" to drugs—both with limited results—rock musicians were doing their own thing to help young people grapple with the temptations of drug and alcohol abuse.

A series of television commercials aired in the late 1980s—many on MTV—featured rock musicians speaking out against drugs. The project, called Rock Against Drugs (RAD), used a refreshing and effective approach to get the antidrug messages before teenagers. Instead of talking down to the teenage audience and attempting to scare them, the RAD commercials attempted to get the message across without betraying the rebellion and energy of rock-'n'-roll.

Steve Jones—whose colleague, Sid Vicious of the Sex Pistols, died of a heroin overdose—was pictured looking up from his motorcycle snarling "Drugs suck." Vince Neil of Motley Crüe was quoted as saying "I still party with the best of them but now I do it clean."

Although it's impossible to measure the effectiveness of these commercials, letters from fans seemed to indicate some success. One high-school student wrote MTV to say that the commercial by Bon Jovi encouraged him to stop taking drugs. "Those guys were the only people I would listen to," he wrote. "They changed my life around," another fan wrote to rocker Ronnie Dio. "Teachers can preach for hours about how bad drugs are and I still went out and got high. But man, once I heard you say how stupid drugs are, I never touched them again!"*

In addition to the antidrug commercials, the rock industry was combating substance abuse in the lyrics of many of its songs. Bob Seger's "American Storm," Huey Lewis's "I Want a New Drug" and Glen Frey's "Smuggler's Blues" all carried antidrug messages. While PMRC and religious groups were condemning KISS for singing satanic messages, one of the group's constant messages for more than 10 years was not to use drugs.

The irony of the decade of the 1980s was that while people were banding together in fear of the evils of rock music, this powerful mass-communication medium was successfully combating one of society's most serious problems—drug abuse.

* *Danny Goldberg, "To Reach Teens: Rock Stars Speak Against Drugs,"* Los Angeles Times, *June 14, 1987, Opinion section, p. 3.*

The Beat, Not the Lyrics.   Despite the controversy over explicit lyrics, research in the mid-1980s showed that lyrics about sex, drugs, violence and satanism had little impact on the vast majority of teenagers. In fact, some rock musicians were using their medium and popularity to combat these social ills (see Box 11.4).

At California State University in Fullerton, Lorraine Prinsky, a sociology professor, and Jill Rosenbaum, a criminal justice professor, wanted to know what teenagers thought about rock lyrics. They used a 40-page questionnaire to get teens to describe their favorite songs. They found that only about 7 percent of the teenagers perceived that the 662 songs listed were about sex, violence, drugs or satanism. The study concluded that specific lyrics seem to be of little consequence to most teens, who are far more interested in the beat or overall sound of a recording.

If the musical themes of the 1990s are not really much different from those of the 1920s, why is such a fuss being made? One answer is that the language used in the 1990s is no longer cute or suggestive; it is often completely explicit. Another is that the age of the audience for recordings has changed. In the 1920s the people who listened to recorded music were mostly in their 20s or, at the very youngest, in their late teens. In the 1990s the audience consists of many impressionable pre-teenagers who worship recording stars like Luther Campbell, Prince and Madonna with cultlike devotion. In addition, radio, television and home audio and video recordings have made popular music a far more pervasive element in our mass-mediated popular culture than it was in the 1920s.

OTHER FORMS OF RECORDED MUSIC

Although rock-'n-'roll remains, in its various specialized forms, the undisputed champion of popular music, two other genres of recorded music deserve mention. They are country-and-western and classical.

Country-and-Western.   Although Southern folk music has been featured on rec-ords and some radio stations for decades, not until recently has country-and-western music climbed to the top of the popular music charts. For example, in 1973 there were about 700 country-music radio stations in the United States; by the 1980s there were almost 1,600.

Hollywood has assisted country-and-western music's move into mainstream America with such movies as *Coal Miner's Daughter* (1980) and *Sweet Dreams* (1985), about the lives of country singers Loretta Lynn and Patsy Cline, respec-tively. In the late 1970s *Urban Cowboy* with John Travolta popularized country-and-western bars and music.

Country-and-western music has been called many things over the years, includ-ing hillbilly music (it originated in the mountains of the South), cowboy music and Okie music (it was brought west by migrants, called Okies, who left the dust-bowl regions around Oklahoma during the Great Depression). In reality, it might best be called white soul music; country songs are about the simpler things in life and about the struggles of rural and small-town working people.

Like rock-'n'-roll, country-and-western has changed over the years. Some of it has adopted the beat of rock—country rock—and the industry is using more sophisticated recording techniques. Efforts to take the "twang" out of country-and-western music also have contributed to its increase in popularity. Today more songs are recorded in the home of country music—Nashville, Tennessee—than in any other American city.

Classical Music.   Although classical music was the first successful form of re-corded music, with opera stars like Enrico Caruso making records, it has re-mained primarily in the elite culture. Classical record sales remain steady, but modest. Commercial classical music radio stations have actually declined over the years, from 50 in 1965 to only 25 today. Most fans turn to noncommercial radio and television stations for classical music and other forms of "high cultural" programming.

BOX 11.5

▪ WORKING IN THE MUSIC INDUSTRY ▪

Popular music is a multibillion-dollar-a-year business that has skyrocketed many to stardom and has kept other talented performers out of the limelight.

How does a musical group make it in the recording industry? The best way is to be discovered by an A & R person—artist-and-repertoire representative. These are the people who discover talent, sign it to the record label they work for, budget the album and then do whatever is necessary to facilitate its production (including finding songs and producers as well as massaging the performers' egos). When the record is pressed, the A & R reps become in-house cheerleaders, pushing the company to mount a campaign to win radio station airplay.

There are fewer than 100 A & R jobs in American record companies. Many such positions are filled by former musicians, record company employees or radio and entertainment managers.

Some A & R reps double as producers, recording the acts they sign and earning royalties on each album, tape or compact disc. A & R rep salaries usually start around $50,000 and go much higher. These reps have liberal expense accounts. Record companies that hire reps look for people with musical expertise and a knowledge of what is current.

What do A & R reps look for when they are seeking new talent? According to John Milward, writing for the *Philadelphia Enquirer,* A & R execs offer the following advice to undiscovered musicians:

- Don't go broke making a slick demo—they're used to hearing things in the raw.
- Don't include more than three or four songs, and make sure the first is a killer.
- Develop as much of a buzz about your live shows as possible, and expand beyond your hometown.
- Don't quit your day job.*

* *John Milward, "Giving Their All for the Record,"* Philadelphia Enquirer, *January 10, 1988.*

However, some classical artists, such as opera star Luciano Pavarotti, have gained popular attention due to the mass media informing the popular culture of "high cultural" participants and activities. The lines separating the elite from the popular cultures are not as clearly defined as they once were.

BUSINESS TRENDS

Despite the controversies threatening to squelch the success of the recording industry, it has emerged as a multibillion dollar per year enterprise. In 1990 the industry made more than $8 billion in revenue from the sale of 976.5 million units of recorded music. This figure had increased from $4.7 billion in 1987.

The most popular form of recordings in the 1990's has been the cassette, although compact discs are growing in popularity. In 1988, for the first time, CDs surpassed the sales of long playing albums. By the 1990s, it was difficult to find LPs in record stores. CDs and cassettes had taken over and made LPs and 45 RPM single records a thing of the past.

The recording business is dependent on young people for its sales, with buyers under the age of 30 accounting for 66 percent of all recordings purchased.

According to the U.S. Industrial Outlet 1990, revenue for the recording industry was expected to grow by 8 percent a year through 1994 (see Box 11.5).

SUMMARY

Recorded music is one of the most influential forms of mass communication among young people and it is one of the most controversial. The industry has also been known to join together in efforts to raise money for worthy causes.

The ability to produce recorded music dates to the invention of the phonograph by Thomas A. Edison in 1877. By the beginning of the twentieth century, opera stars were recording records for home sale in the elite culture.

In the 1920s the recording industry brought African-American music, such as blues and jazz, into the popular culture. However, the color barrier in our society at the time created the need for white performers to "cover" such music. The color barrier was not eliminated until the recording industry targeted the youth of America as its major market in the 1950s.

The expansion of the youth market led to the development of rock-'n'-roll and contributed to the emergence of the generation gap of the 1960s. Parents refused to listen to the new music, while their children grew up with it. As the editorial statements in this new music changed to reflect the changing culture during the 1960s, only the youth were listening. While these young people were listening to the new rock-'n'-roll, the British invasion, featuring the Beatles and Rolling Stones, was taking place. A new youth subculture developed.

Rock was also instrumental in helping the recording industry move into the specialization stage of media development. A wide variety of forms and style of rock music has evolved through the years.

Recorded music is both powerful and controversial. Each CD or tape produced contains an editorial statement that has the ability to persuade. Some of the editorial messages are simple, while others are complex and profound.

Many groups have criticized the lyrics of popular music, and the reported use of subliminal messages and backmasking has generated a great deal of controversy. Eliciting the most furor are heavy-metal and rap lyrics.

Despite the controversies, the recording industry is a rapidly growing commerical enterprise with sales figures exceeding $8 billion in 1990 and projections of an 8 percent annual growth rate through 1994.

Although rock-'n'-roll in its various forms remains the favorite popular music in the American culture, country-and-western and classical music also play an important role in keeping the recording industry healthy.

THOUGHT QUESTIONS

1 Do you think musical lyrics that discuss deviant behavior cause listeners to experiment with such behavior?

2 Are rappers getting a "bum rap" when it comes to court and police efforts to censor them? Do white groups experience similar censorship efforts?

3 Why was such a big deal made of the Beatles' "Paul is dead" controversy? Who do you think was behind the rumor and for what reason?

4 What influence on the youth culture has MTV had? Do you think MTV will continue to be popular among young people? Why or why not?

5   If you were appointed the "Music Czar of America," what would you do to eliminate the controversy surrounding popular rock music?

NOTES

1. Paul Oliver, *The Blues Tradition* (New York: Oak Publications, 1970), p. 23.

2. *New York American,* January 22, 1922.

3. Quoted in Edward Jay Whetmore, *Mediamerica: Form, Content, and Consequences of Mass Communication,* 3rd ed. (Belmont, Calif.: Wadsworth, 1985), p. 129.

4. Paul Gambaccini, *The Top 100 Rock 'n' Roll Albums of All Time* (London: Harmony Books, 1987).

5. Peter Brown and Steven Gaines, *The Love You Make: An Insider's Story of the Beatles* (New York: McGraw-Hill, 1983), pp. 301–303.

6. Ibid., p. 155.

7. Ibid., pp. 250–251, 416.

8. Quoted in Don R. Pember, *Mass Media in America,* 4th ed. (Chicago: Science Research Associates, 1983), p. 162.

ADDITIONAL READING

Adorno, Theodor W. *Introduction to the Sociology of Music.* New York: Continuum, 1976.

Belz, Carl. *The Story of Rock,* 2nd ed. New York: Oxford University Press, 1972.

Chapple, S., and Garofalo, R. *Rock 'n' Roll Is Here to Pay.* Chicago: Nelson-Hall, 1977.

Drake-Chenault Enterprises Inc. *History of Rock and Roll.* Canoga Park, Calif.: Drake-Chenault, 1978.

Eberly, Philip K. *Music in the Air: America's Changing Tastes in Popular Music.* New York: Hastings House, 1982.

Frith, Simon. *Sound Effects: Youth, Leisure, and the Politics of Rock 'n' Roll.* New York: Pantheon, 1982.

Gelatt, Roland. *The Fabulous Phonograph: 1877–1977,* 3rd ed. New York: Macmillan, 1977.

Palmer, T. *All You Need Is Love: The Story of Popular Music.* New York: Viking, 1976.

Passman, Arnold. *The Deejays.* New York: Macmillan, 1971.

Pichaske, David. *A Generation in Motion: Popular Music and Culture of the Sixties.* New York: Schirmer Books, 1979.

Read, Oliver, and Welsh, Walter. *From Tin Foil to Stereo: Evolution of the Phonograph,* 2nd ed. Indianapolis, Ind.: Sams, 1976.

ADVERTISING...

ISN'T IT NICE TO LIVE IN A TIME WHEN WOMEN
AREN'T BEING PUSHED AROUND SO MUCH ANYMORE?

Women have spent the last ten centuries conforming to their lingerie. Fortunately, lingerie has finally gotten around to conforming to women.

M A I D E N F O R M

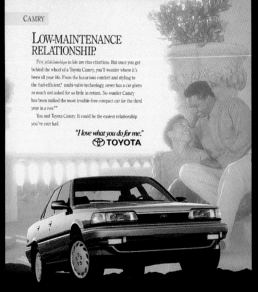

CAMRY

LOW-MAINTENANCE RELATIONSHIP

Few relationships in life are thus effortless. But once you get behind the wheel of a Toyota Camry, you'll wonder where it's been all your life. From the luxurious comfort and styling to the fuel-efficient,* multi-valve technology, never has a car given so much and asked for so little in return. No wonder Camry has been ranked the most trouble-free compact car for the third year in a row.**

You and Toyota Camry. It could be the easiest relationship you've ever had.

"I love what you do for me."

🚗 **TOYOTA**

(Previous page) One can often see a reflection of cultural trends, fashions and social changes in American advertising. The women's equality movement, for example, was first reflected in advertising. In this ad for ASICS GELS running shoes, this confidence in women's equality is used to sell shoes. *(Courtesy ASICS Tiger Corporation)*

(Top) Even advertisements for Maidenform undergarments now play off the "freedom for women" theme to sell products. *(© 1991 Maidenform, Inc.)*

(Bottom) A trend in American advertising that developed in the 1980s was the use of ethnically diverse models. Instead of limiting models to blond blue-eyed Caucasians, ads started featuring African-Americans, Asians and Hispanics as well. Here Toyota uses African-American models to sell their Camry. *(Courtesy Toyota)*

(Top) One of the first advertisers to capitalize on the "rainbow look" was the Italian knitwear maker Benetton. They developed a worldwide ad campaign known as the "United Colors of Benetton" that featured ethnically diverse models. Shown here is one of the most popular ads to feature this "United Colors" theme. (Courtesy Benetton Services Corporation; photographer Oliviero Toscani)

(Bottom) Topical social issues are often featured in advertisements. Here Dakin plays off the increasing concern over violence-oriented toys to help sell their stuffed animals. (© Dakin Inc., 1991)

Is it any wonder the prisons are full?

In the mid 1950's, researchers at the University of Pennsylvania began conducting what has become a landmark study.

Its purpose: to determine the effect violent toys have on our children.

What they found was rather disturbing. The researchers stated that violent toys cause children to become more violent. That they actually may, in fact, teach children to become violent.

At Dakin, we've always tried to produce toys that teach children some other things.

Toys that, rather than teach a child how to maim, would teach a child how to love.

That, rather than teach a child how to hurt, would teach a child how to care for something.

Toys that, rather than being designed to be played with in only

one way, would challenge the child's imagination to use them in a variety of ways. From playing house. To playing veterinarian. To playing Mr. Big Shot Hollywood movie director.

Naturally, researchers and child psychologists have had something to say about toys like the Dakin stuffed animal you see on the left: That they can play a very important role in helping children develop into secure, well-adjusted individuals.

You see, as parents ourselves, we at Dakin don't design toys solely on the basis of whether or not they'll make money.

We design them on the basis of whether we'd want our children playing with them.

Gifts you can feel good about.

DAKIN

© 1990 DAKIN, Inc. Available at fine gift and toy shops everywhere.

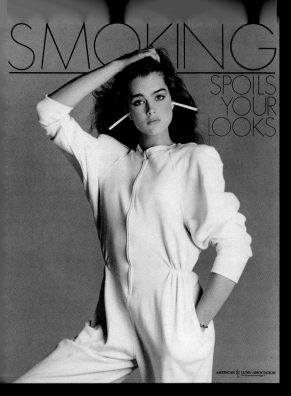

SMOKING SPOILS YOUR LOOKS.

AMERICAN LUNG ASSOCIATION

SISLEY

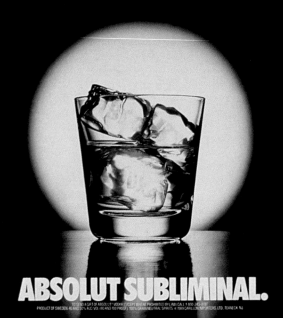

ABSOLUT SUBLIMINAL.

(Top left) Health organizations, such as the American Lung Association, use advertising to promote social attitudes and behavioral changes. It is just one of a number of health organizations that have been campaigning against smoking in recent years. *(Courtesy American Lung Association)*

(Top right) As sexuality became more visible in our society, sexually suggestive images began appearing in ads for a wide variety of products, including Sisley's Cachoeira sportswear. *(Courtesy Sisley, Benetton Services Corporation)*

(Bottom) After years of claiming that subliminal ads existed only in the imagination of a few critics, some advertisers began capitalizing on this publicity by calling attention to intentionally placed imbeds. Here Absolut vodka makes an overt subliminal appeal. *(Courtesy*

MEDIA SHAPERS AND CULTURAL EFFECTS

PART FOUR

If you want power, control and excitement, then you need to buy a Pontiac Bonneville SSE. Or at least that is what the designer of this ad wants you to believe. Advertising sells us images, and often it is the image, rather than the product, that we are purchasing.

Promote Yourself
To A Position Of
Power And Control.

Bonneville SSE.

A quick check inside Bonneville® SSE will reveal that its individual front seats are endowed with 12 power adjustments, and French seams bordering their carefully shaped bolsters.

A technique once reserved for purely handcrafted automobiles, French seams provide a more tailored, pleasing appearance to the Bonneville's sumptuous interior.

Such painstaking craftsmanship won't add to the power of its 3.8L "3800" V6, with sequential port fuel injection (SFI), the precision of its power rack-and-pinion steering, or the confidence of its anti-lock braking system. But it does show Pontiac's commitment to quality, performance and excitement goes right down to the seams.

Which can put you in a very comfortable position for years to come.

PONTIAC. *We Build Excitement.*

Call Toll-Free 1-800-762-4900 For More Product Information.

EPA Est. MPG	
19 City	28 Hwy.

ADVERTISING: SELLING THE MESSAGE

*You can tell
the ideals of a
nation by its
advertisements.*
—Norman
Douglas,
South Wind

It was an automobile ad, but you wouldn't have known it by looking at it. When the new Japanese luxury car—Infiniti—was introduced to the American market in 1989 the print and television ads did not show the curious public the new automobile. Instead they showed landscapes and serene pictures of nature. Although Infiniti dealers weren't too happy with the ad campaign, its purpose was to create an image—the image of what it felt like to drive the ultimate in quality automobiles.

Images play an important role in helping the advertising industry sell the American popular culture both here and abroad. These images are used to create a desire for the products sold. The images used to sell us things reflect sexuality, beauty, youth, fashion, happiness, serenity, success, status and luxury. When Calvin Klein or Guess, for example, advertises blue jeans, each is selling us sex appeal, not jeans. Polo sells us fashion status and Miller beer offers us macho good times.

The average American adult is exposed to approximately 500 advertisements each day and the estimated expenditure on advertising in the United States in 1991 was more than $128 billion. Although these costs are passed on to consumers, advertising can ultimately be economical by delivering more customers to manufacturers, thus making possible mass production, mass consumption and lower prices. Color television sets, for example, cost $800 to $1,000 when they first went on the market in the late 1950s, but thanks to mass production and consumption, some sets now sell for less than $200.

Advertising is an important element of our culture because it reflects and attempts to change our lifestyles. New cultural trends and fashions are first transmitted to the mass culture through advertisements.

It is estimated that, by the time a person raised in the United States reaches the age of 21, he or she has been exposed to 1 million to 2 million advertisements.[1] The cumulative effect of this lifelong exposure plays a significant role in shaping our behavior, social beliefs and values. It influences our choice to wear Reebok running shoes, brush our teeth with Crest and feed our cats Fancy Feast.

Advertising also plays an important role in shaping the kind of mass media we have in the country. Advertisers pay the mass media to disseminate their messages and, without advertising, our newspapers, magazines and radio and television programming would be far different. We would not have the number or variety of media and programming, and the cost to the consumer would be much higher.

HOW ADVERTISING DEVELOPED

Mass advertising as we know it today began in the nineteenth century and developed with industrialization and mass production. It became the vehicle to sell mass consumption in our new consumer-oriented society.

Early Advertising.   The concept of advertising dates to early civilization. In 3000 B.C. Babylonian merchants hired barkers to hawk their wares to prospective customers, and placed signs over their doorways to indicate what they sold. This practice continued in ancient Greece and Rome: advertisements were found on walls in the streets of the excavated Roman city of Pompeii. The use of handbills, posters and newspaper advertisements emerged after Gutenberg developed movable type in the fifteenth century.

When Benjamin Franklin established the *Philadelphia Gazette* in 1729, it soon became a favorite medium for advertisers. When the weekly *Pennsylvania Packet* and *General Advertiser* became a daily in 1784, it featured an entire front page of

■ Early advertisements were posted on walls and other public places.

advertisements for such things as dry goods, food, wine and tobacco products. When the United States began developing into an industrial nation in the nineteenth century and American newspapers and magazines began entering the popular culture, advertising in print media expanded.

First Ad Agency.   Credit for organizing the first advertising agency goes to Volney Palmer, who in 1841 started an agency in Philadelphia. On his heels in this new business was another pioneer, John Hooper. These men perceived a need for someone to help publishers sell space to advertisers. (This new industry developed just four years after William Procter and James Gamble joined forces to make soap and candles. Their company—Procter & Gamble—is today one of the biggest advertisers in the world.) Since they represented publishers rather than advertisers, these early agencies worked quite differently than agencies do today. By the 1870s, however, N. W. Ayer—the nation's oldest ad agency—began representing advertisers, helping them get the best results for their advertising dollars. This is the way all agencies operate today (see Table 12.1).

Expanding advertising from newspapers to magazines was the brainchild of a young ad man named J. Walter Thompson, who at the turn of the century saw the potential of literary magazines for advertising. He put together the so-called "List of Thirty," important women's and general-interest magazines that would be the best vehicles for advertisers. The list included *Harper's, Ladies' Home Journal* and *Cosmopolitan.*[2]

Government Regulations.   A lot of early advertising was deceptive and exaggerated. This was the era of patent medicines that claimed to cure everything from cancer to baldness. These heavily advertised products sold to millions, but cured

TABLE 12.1 TOP 20 ADVERTISING AGENCIES BY 1989 WORLDWIDE REVENUE

Rank	Agency	Location	Gross Revenue*
1	Dentsu	Tokyo	$1,316.4
2	Saatchi & Saatchi	New York	890.0
3	Young & Rubicam	New York	865.4
4	Backer Spielvogel Bates	New York	759.8
5	McCann-Erickson	New York	715.5
6	Oglivy & Mather	New York	699.7
7	BBDD Worldwide	New York	656.6
8	J. Walter Thompson	New York	626.4
9	Lintas: Worldwide	New York	593.3
10	Hakuhodo	Tokyo	585.5
11	DDB Needham	New York	552.9
12	Foote, Cone & Belding	Chicago	510.9
13	Grey Advertising	New York	498.9
14	Leo Burnett Co.	Chicago	483.8
15	D'Arcy Masius Benton & Bowles	New York	471.5
16	EWDB Worldwide	Paris	381.0
17	Publicis-FCB Comm.	Paris	358.8
18	N W Ayer	New York	210.5
19	Bozell	New York	190.7
20	RSCG	Paris	175.3

*In millions of dollars
SOURCE: *Advertising Age,* December 24, 1990, p. 16

very few. Some of the potions gave relief because their high alcohol content deadened pain; some even contained pain-relieving cocaine and morphine. In 1906 Congress passed the Pure Food and Drug Act to control such advertising, and the Federal Trade Commission (FTC) was formed in 1913 to regulate untruthful claims in advertising. Some states adopted "truth-in-advertising" laws and advertising organizations drew up codes of behavior. Today a number of federal agencies enforce truth in advertising, including the FTC, the Federal Communications Commission (FCC), the Food and Drug Administration (FDA) and the U.S. Postal Service.

Electronic Advertising.   Although radio first began to function as a mass-communication medium in 1920, it was not until 1922 that station WEAF in New York began selling air time to advertisers—$100 for 10 minutes. When network broadcasting entered the picture in 1926–27 with the formation of NBC and CBS, the new medium's potential to carry advertisements was fully realized. Ad agencies began producing programs for advertisers. The ad business had become show business. A New York ad agency, Blackett-Sample-Hummert, developed a new type of daytime drama for Procter & Gamble's soap products. The daily serial became known as the soap opera (see Box 12.1).

Although the first commercial on television was aired by the J. Walter Thompson agency in 1930, it wasn't until 1948 that TV's potential as an advertising medium was realized. Many early programs carried the advertiser's name, such as Milton Berle's popular *Texaco Star Theater* and the *Camel News Car-*

▪ PROCTER & GAMBLE AND SOAP OPERAS ▪

Even in the 1990s, Procter & Gamble found soap operas an important part of the company business. In addition to advertising heavily on daytime soap operas, the company owned the rights to such TV soaps as *As the World Turns, The Guiding Light, Another World, Search for Tomorrow* and *Edge of Night.*

When Eastern Europe opened up to Western influence in the 1990s, Procter & Gamble attempted to market its daytime soaps in some of these countries. However, one of the first efforts—to introduce daytime soap operas to Czechoslovakian television audiences—was rebuffed by the head of the Czechoslovak State Television's programming section responsible for foreign acquisitions. His response was that Procter & Gamble's programming offer was "garbage with which we don't want to mess up our TV screens."*

Although some Americans might agree with the Czechoslovakian analysis of this form of American popular culture, the fact remains that American soap operas have been extremely popular since the early days of broadcasting and have sold many products for Procter & Gamble.

Quoted in "Czechs Scrub Soaps," by Milan Ruzicka, Advertising Age, December 17, 1990, p. 8.

avan. And soon television became the preferred advertising medium to reach the masses in the United States.

In the 1980s, with the development of cable and satellite TV, a new form of electronic advertising developed—direct-response home shopping services. These cable networks (HSN, CVN, etc.) sell discounted goods directly to consumers, who telephone in their orders to banks of operators. Instead of purchasing air time from cable operators, home shopping networks pay cable operators a percentage of the profits from sales generated.

THEORIES ON ADVERTISING EFFECTIVENESS

Despite the dominant role that advertising plays in American society, people disagree as to whether advertising is as effective as it is thought to be. There seems to be universal agreement that certain types of price advertising (such as supermarket ads in the local newspaper) are effective in generating sales. However, when it comes to national advertising of consumer product images (most ads we see on television and in magazines), the agreement stops.

Minimal Effects Theory. While some believe that advertising makes our mass production-consumption culture possible, others contend that advertising has almost no effect on consumer buying habits.

The effectiveness of television advertising, in particular, has come under close scrutiny in recent years. Advertising researchers have found that while people may have a television on in their homes much of the time, they pay far less attention to it than previously believed. A study conducted by Gerard Tellis, a University of Iowa professor, found that an examination of products purchased by a study group of 250 people showed very little correlation with the advertisements they saw on television. A greater correlation was found between lower prices and the availability of coupons.[3]

Earlier research by sociologist Michael Schudson led him to the conclusion that, contrary to the common belief that advertising brings an increase in sales, the opposite is true: an increase in sales leads to increases in advertising.[4] This theory was supported by a study conducted by Richard Schmalensee, who found that there was a closer correlation between consumption in a given quarter and advertising in the next quarter than between consumption in the given quarter and advertising in the previous quarter.[5]

Schudson cited numerous examples to support his contention that advertising doesn't automatically increase sales. He noted that heavy advertising by the Ford Motor Company to promote the Edsel resulted in failure. The Edsel appeared on the market in 1957 as the most heavily promoted consumer product in history. The company expected to sell 200,000 cars its first year, but when it took the product off the market two years later, only 109,000 had been sold. The car was ugly, and no amount of advertising was going to get people to buy it. Conversely, he noted that the Hershey Foods Corporation has been a chocolate industry leader since the turn of the century, even though it didn't start advertising until 1970. Schudson also noted that the two largest selling products in the American popular culture—marijuana and cocaine—are never advertised.[6]

Stephen Fox, in his comprehensive history of American advertising, *The Mirror Makers,* supports the idea that, despite increased advertising expenditures, the industry's influence has declined during the twentieth century.

From its peak as an independent force in American life in the 1920s, advertising has been caught in a tightening vise between two contrary forces. Regulation by the government and (finally) by the industry itself has gradually limited Madison Avenue's freedom to lie. When restricted, more or less, to the truth, advertising lost some of its most powerful, frightening devices. Yet even as advertising grew less deceptive, the public grew ever more sophisticated and skeptical.[7]

Cutting Edge Theory. Advertising's role in influencing our attitudes, lifestyles and culture is beyond dispute. The advertising industry is often on the cutting edge of new cultural developments and trends in our society.

For example, when cigarette smoking by women started to become fashionable and suggestive of naughtiness during the Jazz Age of the 1920s, the advertising industry was there to reflect the new trend. One of the first smoking ads directed toward women was for Chesterfield cigarettes in 1926. It showed a romantic couple at night, with the man smoking and the woman sitting next to him. The caption read "Blow Some My Way." When the women's liberation movement first got rolling, ads began to depict women in previously stereotypically "male" roles. Often these women were smoking a "women's cigarette," such as Virginia Slims. When jogging, aerobic exercises and tennis became popular recreations in the 1980s, a glance at magazines showed much money being spent on advertisements for fashionable clothing for these activities.

Another trend in advertising that began in the late 1980s was the use of ethnically diverse models. Instead of exclusively featuring blond Caucasian male and female models, as had been the case for decades, a variety of ads began appearing in magazines, newspapers and on television that featured African-

▪ GREEN MARKETING ▪

On January 29, 1991, the advertising trade publication *Advertising Age* hosted the first of what was planned to become an annual event—a "Green Marketing Summit."

Leaders from the media and advertising communities, corporate America, governmental agencies and the environmental movement gathered to share insights on how they could work together to market environmentally sensitive products.

The 1990s had clearly become the environmental decade and American businesses were facing pressures to become more environmentally sensitive with their products. This was a new challenge for the advertising industry that marketed American consumer goods.

The goal of the summit, according to *Advertising Age,* was to turn confrontation into cooperation and come up with strategies that would help the environment without harming business. The Green Marketing Summit agenda included panel discussions on such topics as "What Is Green?," "What Is a Green Product?," "Who Is the Green Consumer?," "Gallery of Green Advertising" and "How We Green Ourselves."

The green marketing movement was designed to use consumers' environmental concerns to help sell products. It began expanding rapidly in the 1990s. By 1991 such major companies as McDonald's, Procter & Gamble, Lever Brothers, Kraft General Foods, Fuji Photo Film Co., H. J. Heinz Co., Coca-Cola Co. and Pepsi-Cola Co. were all promoting their new-found environmental sensitivity. McDonald's phased out the use of polystyrene foam packaging, Procter & Gamble and Lever Brothers were using recycled resin and polyethylene packaging, Kraft began using recyclable trays in its microwave products, Fuji replaced plastic film containers with recyclable paper containers, Heinz began using recyclable plastic ketchup bottles, and Coca-Cola and Pepsi-Cola both began selling their beverages in recycled plastic bottles.

Advertisements and packages all promoted the products as environmentally friendly, showing once again that the providers of our consumer culture were on the cutting edge in giving us what we wanted.

Americans, Asians and Hispanics. One of the first advertisers to embrace the rainbow look was the Italian knitwear maker Benetton which launched its "United Colors of Benetton" ad campaign featuring youth of diverse nationalities standing arm in arm. The advertising industry was again on the cutting edge reflecting our ethnically diverse culture.

Although some critics blame advertising for creating new cultural trends in order to sell more goods and services, others argue that the message industry merely reflects cultural changes (see Box 12.2).

A-T-R Model. Getting a person to buy a product involves far more than simply running an ad in a newspaper or a commercial on television. To best describe the complexities of advertising, we will use the A-T-R model, which shows that there are three main stages in the selling process: awareness, trial and reinforcement.

Awareness is the easiest step. Through repetition and other advertising techniques, consumers can be made aware that a product exists. Usually the bigger the advertising campaign, the more awareness is generated.

Trial, the second step, is much more difficult to induce. Merely advertising a product is not necessarily going to make someone try it. As a result, many companies use other techniques to get people to try the product, including sending free samples through the mail or giving them out in stores, giving away discount coupons and offering price reductions.

Reinforcement is the necessary third step to get users to buy the product again. Studies have shown that after people try a new brand, they usually go back to their regular brand unless they are constantly reminded about the new brand by effective advertising. Of course, the new brand must be comparable in quality to the old brand. If the product does not please the customer, he or she will probably never purchase it again.

Thus, according to the A-T-R theory, increasing the advertising budget after a product is established will not necessarily increase *new* sales. However, cutting the budget will likely reduce repeat sales because some reinforcement will be lost (see Table 12.2).

Consumers' Information Environment. Advertising is not the only factor in our decision to make a purchase. As Schudson points out, the normal adult consumer brings a lifetime of informational resources to any new advertisement. These

TABLE 12.2 TOP 25 LEADING NATIONAL ADVERTISERS BY 1989 SPENDING

Rank	Advertiser	Total U.S. Spending*
1	Philip Morris Co.	$2,072.0
2	Procter & Gamble Co.	1,779.3
3	Sears, Roebuck & Co.	1,432.1
4	General Motors Corp.	1,363.8
5	Grand Metropolitan	823.3
6	PepsiCo.	786.1
7	McDonald's Corp.	664.4
8	Eastman Kodak Co.	718.8
9	RJR Nabisco	703.5
10	Kellogg Co.	611.6
11	Nestle SA	608.4
12	Unilever NV	604.1
13	Ford Motor Co.	602.1
14	Anheuser-Busch Co.	591.5
15	Warner-Lambert Co.	585.9
16	AT&T Co.	567.7
17	Time Warner	567.5
18	K-Mart Corp.	561.4
19	Chrysler Corp.	532.5
20	Johnson & Johnson	487.1
21	General Mills	471.0
22	American Home Products	456.1
23	Bristol-Myers Squibb Co.	451.6
24	Ralston Purina Co.	429.5
25	Toyota Motor Corp.	417.6

*In millions of dollars
SOURCE: *Advertising Age,* December 24, 1990, p. 18

resources, which he calls the consumer's *informational environment,* include the following:

1 The consumer's own information from personal experience with the product or related products.
2 Word-of-mouth information about the product or related products from family, friends or acquaintances.
3 Information in the media about the product or related products that is not paid advertising. Some of this information will be planted by the public relations efforts of commercial companies and some of it will be independently generated by government reports, consumer groups, journalists and other noncommercial agencies.
4 Information available through formal channels of consumer education, especially the school system, credit institutions and other agencies.
5 Advertisements for rival products and also advertisements for unrelated products, the "clutter" of advertising in general.
6 Skepticism about the credibility of the medium in which the ad is placed.
7 Skepticism about the credibility of advertising in general.
8 Information from nonadvertising channels of marketing.
9 Price. This is a special case, and an especially important one, of a nonadvertising channel of marketing.[8]

Selective Perception. Another factor in determining an advertisement's effectiveness is *selective perception* (see Chapter 1). Advertisers may bombard consumers with television and magazine advertising, sales-promotion discounts and premiums, point-of-purchase displays and other promotional devices, only to find little change in sales figures. Follow-up research will often show that the promotional activities never got through the consumers' *perceptual filters.*[9] In other words, if the public is convinced that the product is worthless, no amount of advertising will change that perception.

Thus it is important to remember that, even though a great deal of money is spent on advertising, the success or failure of these ads to persuade us to buy things is far more complex than one might believe.

PROPAGANDA DEVICES

Although the industry might frown on a discussion of propaganda techniques in a chapter on advertising, there is an important relationship between the two. Webster's dictionary defines *propaganda* as "a systematic effort to promote a particular cause or point of view."

Thus, by definition, propaganda is not evil or deceptive. However, over the years, ever since the British used propaganda to solicit U.S. support for the allies' war effort against Germany in World War I, the word has taken on undesirable connotations. But even though the goals of propaganda may not be evil, some of the techniques used are questionable because they appeal primarily to our emotions rather than to our intellect.

Propaganda was probably used most destructively in the 1930s, when Adolf Hitler used it to take control of Germany and neighboring lands. One of Hitler's first acts when he came to power was to name Dr. Joseph Goebbels minister of propaganda. Goebbels immediately took over the German mass media and turned them into propaganda outlets that endorsed Hitler and his reign of terror.

While Hitler waged his propaganda campaign, the rest of the world sat back and watched. Yet years earlier, in 1925, Hitler had spelled out the importance of propaganda and how he planned to use it in his book *Mein Kampf,* which he wrote in prison.

> *The great masses' receptive ability is only very limited, their understanding is small, but their forgetfulness is great. As a consequence of these facts, all effective propaganda has to limit itself only to a very few points and to use them like slogans until even the very last man is able to imagine what is intended by such a word. As soon as one sacrifices this basic principle and tries to become versatile, the effect will fritter away, as the masses are neither able to digest the material offered nor to retain it. Thus the result is weakened and finally eliminated.* [10]

If this philosophy sounds as though it is alive and well in American advertising today, it is because propaganda techniques are still very much in use. But fortunately the American advertising industry is only trying to sell you consumer goods and political candidates, not the bigotry and totalitarianism of Adolf Hitler.

Propaganda is a daily feature of our popular culture. It is a prime ingredient in political rhetoric and is used extensively in advertising campaigns. For these reasons, it is important for all of us to be familiar with the basic propaganda devices so that we can detect them, ward off their emotional appeal and analyze the messages intellectually. The following are some of the more common forms of propaganda devices used today.

Slogans. The slogan is equally effective in advertising and political campaigns. In the latter, it usually takes the form of a chant that can unite large crowds into one common emotion. Examples of political slogans are ''Four More Years'' used at political conventions; ''On strike, shut it down'' used by labor and student strikers; ''Hey, hey, LBJ, how many babies did you kill today?'' used by protesters during the Vietnam War; and ''America, love it or leave it,'' a common bumper sticker during the 1960s. In consumer advertising the list is endless— ''Come to Marlboro Country,'' ''You've come a long way baby,'' ''Coke Is It,'' ''Join the Pepsi Generation,'' ''The Uncola,'' ''I Tecate my body,'' ''Light my Lucky'' and on and on.

Name Calling. The device of name calling is constantly used in political and ideological battles as well as in commerical advertising campaigns. It tries to make us form a judgment without examining the evidence on which it should be based. Propagandists appeal to our instincts of hate and fear. They do this by giving ''bad names'' to those individuals, groups, nations, races or consumer products that they would like us to condemn or reject. Such names as communist, capitalist, imperialist, pervert, egghead and so on are just a few that have been used to discredit the opposition.

Not all name calling is so blatant or direct, however. Often it can work by inference or association. Presidential candidate Al Smith once used indirect name calling against President Franklin D. Roosevelt by stating "There can be only one capital, Washington or Moscow." He was indirectly calling the incumbent president a communist.

Most name calling in advertising uses this indirect approach: "Our painkiller doesn't give you an upset stomach"—implying, of course, that the competition does. Some advertisers actually name a competing brand and charge it with being inferior.

Glittering Generalities.   Glittering generalities are broad, accepted ideals and virtuous words that are used to sell a point of view. Like name calling, glittering generalities urge us to accept and approve something without examination. Such expressions as "The American way," "It's in the public interest" and "Taste America's favorite bran flake cereal" are examples. Words like "America," "truth," "freedom," "honor," "liberty," "justice," "loyalty," "progress," "democracy" and "America's favorite" are all common glittering generalities.

Transfer.   Some advertisements use symbols of authority, prestige and respect that arouse emotions to sell a cause, candidate or consumer product through the process of subconscious transfer or association. Typical examples are a political candidate photographed next to the American flag ("She's a good American") and cigarette smokers relaxing by a peaceful lake ("Enjoy the natural taste of this brand of cigarette and you too will feel healthy and calm"). Many ads for automobiles feature a sexually attractive person in the passenger seat or at the wheel. The point, of course, is to transfer the sexuality of the person to the brand of vehicle. Designer jeans ads are also effective in transferring sexuality to their product.

Testimonial.   An endorsement of a political candidate by celebrities or other well-respected individuals is called a testimonial. When a movie star endorses a particular savings and loan institution, for example, thousands of people may invest there solely on the rationale that, if it is good enough for their idol, it's good enough for them. How many sports fans have selected a certain brand of shaving cream or deodorant because their favorite professional athlete has endorsed it?

Plain Folks.   The plain folks device creates the impression that the advertisers or political candidates are just ordinary folks like you and me. In every presidential election, you will see candidates visiting coal mines and factories wearing hard hats. They don't go down into the coal mines, so obviously they don't wear the hard hats for protection. Instead the hats are used to give the impression that they are just ordinary folks like the rest of the workers. Have you ever wondered why laundry detergent ads show "ordinary housewives" rather than attractive models promoting the product?

Card Stacking.   Card stacking is the technique by which facts, illustrations and statements are carefully selected to make the maximum impact and sometimes

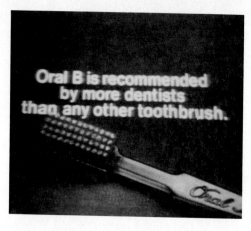

■ Card stacking is a popular propaganda device that leaves out details of why a statement is true.

give misleading impressions. The cliché that "statistics don't lie, but you can lie with statistics" applies to this technique. A politician may tell his constituents that he votes only for bills that help his district, while neglecting to mention that when special-interest groups have opposed such a bill, he has ducked the issue by not showing up for the vote.

An advertisement claiming that "Four out of five dentists surveyed recommend Chewy chewing gum" will certainly be true, but it could be omitting to say that only five dentists were contacted and that four of them were paid to give an anonymous endorsement.

Bandwagon. The bandwagon device is based on the idea that "if everybody else is doing it, so should you." Jump on the bandwagon, follow the crowd and don't throw your vote away by voting for a loser are clichés associated with this device. The psychology behind this technique makes political polling important at election time. The fact that each candidate needs to project the image that he or she is a winner often leads to some conflicting polling results. (Pollsters can skew their results by carefully selecting their samples or by using loaded wording in their questions.) Advertisements telling you to join the Pepsi Generation or to have a good time with the crowd when it's "Miller time" are examples of this type of appeal.

Sex Appeal. We don't ordinarily think of sex as a propaganda device, but it sells products in many ways. In recent years emotional appeals based on sex have been used more and more in product advertising. How about the after-shave-lotion ad that features a sexy female voice saying "Wear English Leather or wear nothing at all"? Or the billboard for Canadian Black Velvet whisky that showed a sexy blonde in a black velvet dress with the words "Feel the Velvet Canadian." And don't forget the Calvin Klein ads that feature partially clad men and women. Sex appeal is used to stimulate emotions and sell consumer products to both sexes.

Music. The last device in our list—music—is also seldom thought of as a propaganda device, yet it is one of the most effective devices in radio and television commercials. Music is an excellent tool for creating specific moods, and it can be used effectively for product identification. Often people will think of a certain product when they hear a tune that has been associated with the product in ads. In politics, music is used to stir the crowds, and the president of the United States uses it effectively to generate a mood of respect when he makes a grand entrance to the strains of "Hail to the Chief."

CONTROVERSIES SURROUNDING ADVERTISING

By its very nature, advertising is controversial. In the early twentieth century people clamored for the regulation of advertising, believing that much of it was exaggerated and untruthful.

As we have seen, government regulations have succeeded in eliminating outright falsehoods from advertising, but many people are still critical. According to Agee, Ault and Emery, most criticism of advertising centers on the following complaints:

1 Advertising persuades us to buy goods and services we cannot afford.
2 Advertising appeals primarily to our emotions, rather than to our intellect.
3 Advertising is biased.
4 Advertising involves conflicting competitive claims.
5 Advertising is unduly repetitious.
6 Much advertising is vulgar, obtrusive, irritating.[11]

The advertising industry has answers for most of these charges. It points out that such criticism merely indicates that advertisers are using natural selling techniques to make customers aware of their products. After all, aren't the above comments true of most types of selling? It is also important to keep in mind that advertising plays a very important role in informing the masses about the many goods and services available.

Subliminal Advertising.   However, since the 1950s some criticism has been far more severe. One of the first critics to lash out was Vance Packard, who pointed out in *The Hidden Persuaders* that advertisers were using motivational research and other techniques to sell consumer goods.[12] Packard charged that advertisers were using "depth manipulation," which causes us to do things that are irrational and illogical. Often, he said, ads were filled with messages that were trying to invade the privacy of our minds through hidden subliminal imbeds.

In 1957 a researcher named James Vicary inserted one-frame Coca-Cola and popcorn ads among the 26 frames that are projected on a movie screen every second. Just as the frames around each still photo cannot be perceived by the eye, the advertisements went unnoticed. However, Vicary claimed that people's subconscious minds perceived the ads: his research found that Coca-Cola sales increased 18 percent and popcorn sales 57.8 percent after the subliminally imbedded films were shown.[13]

When Vicary was asked to replicate his study under controlled conditions, the new test produced no increase in the sales of either Coke or popcorn.[14] But even though Vicary's claim was invalidated, it had long been known that subliminal stimuli could produce certain behavioral effects under laboratory conditions.[15] What was not known was whether consumers could be motivated to purchase a product by subliminal advertising. In the 1970s Wilson Bryan Key, a mass-communication researcher from Canada, took up Packard's and Vicary's charges. Key advanced the theory that advertisers were using sexually explicit hidden messages, called subliminal imbeds, to sell products. According to Key the messages, primarily in magazine ads, were designed to appeal to our subconscious instincts about sex, death and fear.

By the early 1980s Key had written three popular books on the subject: *Subliminal Seduction, Media Sexploitation* and *Clam Plate Orgy.* Key claimed to see such hidden details as castrated penises in Parkay Margarine ads, death masks and skulls in the ice cubes in liquor ads and the word *cancer* in cigarette ads.

Although he couldn't explain how these imbeds worked, Key was convinced that they triggered a subconscious emotional response, ensuring that people would remember the ad and the brand when it came time to buy the product. He has not, however, been able to prove that the ads actually sell more than other ads.

The advertising industry at first ignored Key's charges, claiming that he was nothing more than a "dirty old man" who could see perverted symbols in cloud formations. Some in the industry claimed that the images he saw were mere accidents and were not intended to have any conscious or subconscious effect on consumers.

Finally, in 1984, articles in the industry's trade paper, *Advertising Age,* urged the industry to challenge the lack of evidence for Key's assertions and prove him wrong once and for all. In one article, *Ad Age* reporter Jack Haberstroth published the results of his own survey of 100 randomly selected advertising art directors: of 47 usable responses, only two indicated that they had ever deliberately imbedded a subliminal message.

By 1989 several big advertisers were running parody ads on the subliminal controversy. Schweppes inserted a 90-second commercial spoofing subliminal ads prior to the beginning of the home video of the movie "A Fish Called Wanda." The commercial featured a man expressing concern about subliminal ads while the word *Schweppes* flashed constantly on the screen. In 1990, the House of Seagram introduced a print ad campaign featuring a "hidden pleasure"—a woman swimming in a glass of Seagram's Extra Dry Gin. The image of the barely perceptible woman was enhanced by an arrow pointing to her. The headline on the ad read: "Have you found the hidden pleasure in refreshing Seagram's Gin?"

Nevertheless, some support for Key's contentions has come from other researchers. Warren Breed of the Institute for Scientific Analysis in Berkeley calls imbeds UPOs, or "unidentified printed objects." A study by Breed and James R. DeFoe found hidden images in 45.5 percent of all of the alcoholic-beverage advertisements they examined, a percentage much higher than in ads for other products.[16]

Such discoveries led the Federal Bureau of Alcohol, Tobacco and Firearms to propose rules in 1980 to outlaw subliminal advertising in liquor ads. Although the proposed regulations were distributed for comment and hearings were held, the regulations were never adopted. The executive vice-president of the American Association of Advertising Agencies argued at the hearings that you cannot forbid the use of something that doesn't exist.

During the summer of 1990, Pepsi-Cola was criticized by some consumers who claimed that the word *sex* seemed to be subtly printed on the exterior of a newly released Pepsi "Cool Can." A Pepsi spokesman said that it was merely an "odd coincidence" and that the design was selected only because consumers preferred it over hundreds of other designs.

The jury is still out on whether there is something to the subliminal imbedding theory. Whatever the outcome, more research needs to be done to determine whether or not the imbeds actually help sell consumer goods.

TELEVISION ADVERTISING

The advent of television dramatically changed American advertising. Today the annual expenditure on TV advertising exceeds $28 billion. These ads are creatively produced and are instrumental in changing American attitudes and lifestyles as well as in selling products.

What television ads don't do, according to some consumer organizations, is give the viewer much information. Commericals are a slick attempt to get viewers to "feel good" about the product through effective emotional appeals, mostly directed at sexual instincts.

High Cost. Often more money is spent to produce a 30-second commercial than to make the hour-long program in which it is inserted. And the cost of buying TV time is equally high. In 1986 the top-rated television program, NBC's *The Cosby Show,* began charging $400,000 for each 30-second commercial. That was the highest amount ever paid for a commercial in a regular TV series. Only the Super Bowl, which was getting $700,000 for a 30-second spot in 1990, has been able to charge a higher fee.

15-Second Spots. In 1986 all three television networks started running 15-second ads, which allowed them to reduce the cost per ad, double the number of ads run and not reduce revenue. The 15-second advertisements posed a new creative challenge to the industry—packaging a powerful message in half the time and still selling the product to the consumer.

TV Ad Techniques. Many television advertisements have a tripartite structure: the problem, the advice and the resolution. All three messages must be delivered in 15, 30 or 60 seconds. Let's take a mouthwash commercial as an example. First you establish the problem—someone has bad breath. Then you suggest that the person try the advertised mouthwash. This is followed by the person being chased by attractive members of the opposite sex, an obvious resolution of the problem. Quick as a flash the person has gone from disaster to success.

In addition to delivering a message quickly, TV advertising uses imaginative techniques to make the advertised products attractive. For example, food stylists are hired to make advertised food look appealing. According to TV food stylist Lloyd Davis, Elmer's Glue is added to milk in television ads to make it look white and delightful, roasted chickens are spray-painted to look deliciously golden brown and Ivory Soap is added to give coffee a fresh-brewed appearance.[17]

Criticism of TV Ads.   Because of its impact on our culture, television advertising has become the focus of considerable criticism in recent years. Probably the longest ongoing controversy concerns advertising directed toward children.

Children's advertising on television is a $200-million-a-year enterprise. According to research findings, the average child sees 20,000 television ads a year—about three hours of commercials a week.

According to psychologist Patricia Greenfield, young children equate all of television except cartoons with reality. Youngsters under the age of seven usually cannot distinguish between a commercial and the program, and they learn a great deal from commercials.[18]

Groups such as Action for Children's Television (ACT) have been campaigning to get regulatory agencies to limit commercials aimed at children. A request for an FCC ban on children's advertising was denied. Opponents of such a ban pointed out that it would have meant the end of commercial television programming for children.

For years, concern has been expressed over the number of ads for sugar-coated breakfast cereals and unrealistic toys. The most recent concern (discussed in Chapter 10) centers around the fact that toy manufacturers are now producing programming for children that stars their products.

Parents have also complained about TV ads that entice children to call 900-prefix telephone numbers to hear such messages as "Santa's Christmas stories." Unlike the toll-free 1-800 numbers, 900 telephone prefixes incur charges. Some parents have been shocked to find hundreds of dollars in 900 charges on their monthly bills. By the mid-1980s revenue from 900 calls placed by children was reported to be in the hundreds of millions of dollars. (In 1987 the California Public Utilities Commission ordered telephone companies to allow customers to block their access to telephone numbers with a 900 prefix. Other states soon followed suit.)

Beer and wine commercials have been the subject of controversy in recent years. Groups such as the National Institute on Alcohol Abuse and Alcoholism (NIAAA), Mothers Against Drunk Drivers, (MADD) and Students Against Drunk Drivers (SADD) have pressured Congress to ban beer and wine advertising on television, claiming that it contributes to alcoholism and drunk-driving-related deaths.

The beer, wine and broadcast industries argue that there is no causal relationship between alcohol problems and the commercials. Industry officials say that their ads do not cause people to drink more or entice nondrinkers to drink; they are aimed only at increasing a brand's share of the existing market. Opponents of liquor advertising are skeptical however; they contend that the ads do attempt to attract new drinkers, particularly young people, with their themes of good times, adventure and sex.[19]

It should be pointed out that for years the National Association of Broadcasting has enforced restrictions on liquor advertising. First, no hard liquor can be advertised on radio or television. Second, broadcasters are prohibited from showing anyone drinking beer or wine in a commercial—glasses can be hoisted, but there is never any sipping. (It is all right, however, to show characters in regular programs drinking like fish.) Third, currently active sports figures are not allowed to appear in beer or wine commercials. This is why all of the Miller Lite commercials featured former athletes. In 1990, Coors and other alcoholic beverage companies even started running "safe drinking" and "designated driver" messages in their television commercials. Despite these restrictions and activities, commercials—rather than the program content—continue to be the center of controversy surrounding the issue of booze and the media.

Cigarette advertising on television and radio was caught in a similar controversy in the 1960s. The first result of this debate was a requirement that broadcast stations running cigarette advertising had to air counter ads telling of the harmful effects of smoking. These ads began appearing in 1968, and cigarette smoking started to decline. An alarmed tobacco industry then accepted a total ban on cigarette advertising in the electronic media in 1971. When the advertising stopped, so did most of the counter ads, and soon the sales of cigarettes (which could still be advertised in the print media) began to climb.

If the case of cigarette advertising can be used as a guide, banning beer and wine commercials will not help solve this nation's alcohol problem—but increasing the frequency of counter ads might help.

Infomercials   Another controversy surrounding the advertising business deals with a relatively new technique for selling called "infomercials." These are 30-minute television commercials that resemble news broadcasts but which in reality are promotional vehicles for such items as money-making ideas, kitchenware products, cosmetics and weight-loss programs.

In 1990, after thousands of complaints about the claims made in infomercials, Congress held hearings on the industry. Representatives of the industry met with the congressional leaders and agreed to form a trade association to police their new industry.

Zipping and Zapping.   Another headache for television advertisers is new technology that permits viewers to eliminate commercials entirely: the *double Zs*. First of all, viewers can now sit in their easy chairs and change channels during commercials by remote control; this is called zipping in the industry. Second, the VCR (videocassette recorder) allows people to *zap* commercials out of recorded programs by fast-forwarding right through them.

The threats of zipping and zapping can be credited with continual improvements in the quality of TV commercials. The industry must make television ads extremely entertaining and compelling if they are to compete for viewers against the temptations of zipping and zapping. This, unfortunately, largely precludes providing any product information in commercials.

MOTIVATIONAL RESEARCH

Psychological Advertising. From its inception in the nineteenth century, the advertising industry has relied on creative endeavors to sell goods and services. However, by the mid-twentieth century creativity was no longer enough. What was needed were more sophisticated techniques that would persuade people to buy more, so that the wheels of our mass-production, mass-consumption economy would keep turning. To develop these techniques, the ad industry turned to consumer research, which could provide insights into the personalities and subconscious desires of the consuming public.

According to Vance Packard, who began writing about this research with alarm in the 1950s, the advertising industry started tailoring its ads to meet the needs of the id. (In Freudian psychology, the id is that part of our mind that generates our most basic animal urges and impulses.)[20]

Motivational research, or MR, was the name given to this new area of consumer analysis. Millions of dollars were targeted for MR, and social scientists soon found an industry ready and willing to fund this type of psychological exploration.

MR looked for the hidden "whys" of consumer behavior. It replaced the older statistical research approaches by borrowing from the disciplines of psychology and psychoanalysis. Instead of treating consumers as rational beings who knew what they wanted and why they wanted it, MR examined the subconscious, nonrational levels of motivation and suggested where and how ads should be aimed. The researchers used in-depth interviews, Rorschach (inkblot) tests, stress tests that measured eye-blinking frequencies in stores via hidden cameras, lie detectors, word-association tests and group interviews to compile their data.[21]

One of the leaders in this research was Dr. Ernest Dichter, head of the Institute for Motivational Research. By probing the subconscious, Dichter was able to discover unsuspected areas of tension and guilt that were important to sales psychology. He learned why certain ads had failed in the past and suggested ways to put together advertising campaigns to take advantage of these formerly unknown areas.

Sex sells was an idea that had been around a long time. However, it wasn't until MR came along that it was discovered just how subtle and complex sexual fantasies are in influencing consumer buying patterns. One study found that men were lured into automobile dealerships by ads and window displays of convertibles because they associated convertibles with youth and adventure and they were symbolic of a mistress. However, men usually ended up buying a sedan; it symbolized the girl they would marry because she would make a good wife and mother. What the industry needed in the 1950s was a new car that had the attractions of both a mistress and a wife. Dichter's organization took credit for suggesting the solution—the hardtop convertible.[22]

Another sexually related discovery was made when an ad agency ordered an in-depth study to find out why a campaign for the Cigar Institute of America had failed. The ads had shown a smiling woman offering cigars to a group of men. The study revealved that subconsciously men smoke cigars because they know the smell is offensive to women. Thus the smiling woman enticing them to smoke a cigar turned them off.

Conflicts between MR and creativity developed over this new orientation in developing advertising campaigns. Copywriters and art directors regarded advertising as an art, or at least a craft, and resented the new emphasis on psychological research. As Les Pearl of Batten, Barton, Durstine & Osborn put it, "Merchandising men and research men are statistic-ing the creative man to death."[23]

Since earlier consumer research had dealt only with demographics (statistical information on ages, marital status, income, educational levels, etc.) a new name was coined for motivation-oriented research: *psychographics*.

VALS Research.   In the 1960s MR and Freudian psychoanalytical theories were challenged by a revival of creative, non-research-oriented ads. However, psychographic research continued. The Stanford Research Institute (now known as SRI International) began working on psychographic research in the 1950s, concentrating on VALS (values and lifestyles). SRI issued its first report on the interrelationship of social values and consumer buying habits in 1960. The report, called *Consumer Values and Demands,* suggested that a neglected area of market research involved how people's values influence their spending patterns. This

■ This ad combines opera and a Rolex watch to sell to a specialized audience in the elite culture. VALS research helps to identify the audience and the appropriate sales approach.

Rolex accompanies Te Kanawa.

Kiri Te Kanawa's voice has been called perfect by Sir Colin Davis of Covent Garden. She is so highly esteemed by the Metropolitan Opera that they chose her to star in the coveted new production of Strauss's *Arabella.*

In nineteen eighty-two, her rare talent was recognized when Queen Elizabeth II named her Dame Commander

of the British Empire.

Te Kanawa has won renown in film, recordings and television. She has gained international acclaim in recitals and orchestral concerts. Accomplishments foreseen from an early age for this storied New Zealand prodigy.

But for all her achievements, she remains a delightfully down-to-earth diva. As

energetic on a golf course as on a stage. As enthusiastic a wife and mother as a performer.

One of opera's most revered sopranos, Te Kanawa is accompanied by her equally celebrated Rolex. A duet well-matched for both commanding presence and consistently brilliant performance. **ROLEX**

Lady Datejust, Oyster Perpetual Chronometer in 18kt gold; bezel and dial set with diamonds.

report, which was ahead of its time, had very little immediate influence on advertising research at the time.

One of the early pioneers of this research was Arnold Mitchell, a marketing analyst at SRI. Mitchell and his colleagues continued their "values-oriented" research through the 1960s and into the 1970s to determine how the children of the turbulent 1960s would affect the marketplace. What would happen when a generation that seemed to have rejected capitalism came of age? Business needed a marketing strategy to reach these people, and the SRI studies helped advertisers to determine the needs of the "baby boomers."[24]

One of the findings of this research was an observation that by 1985 some of these consumers were blending the liberal values of the 1960s with more traditional values. This trend—called neotraditionalism—found consumers buying sports utility vehicles such as the Jeep Cherokee and Isuzu Trooper and using them like the station wagons their parents owned.

This quest to learn what motivates consumer buying habits has seen a growing number of companies turning to psychographic research. Users of VALS data range from Christian church groups to Citibank. The growing use of this data coincides with the movement of the mass media into the specialization stage of the EPS cycle. Targeting professional women with children or suburban teenagers requires more detailed information than demographics and that detail is provided by the psychological profiles found in VALS data.

Carnation Co., for example, used lifestyle data to develop its Contadina line of fresh pasta. The product is targeted at two-income couples who like freshly prepared foods that do not take long to cook.

Eight Lifestyles.   SRI has developed and refined several versions of its VALS profile of typical American consumers. An outdated VALS matrix consisting of nine lifestyles developed in the late 1970s was replaced with a refined version called VALS 2 by 1990. This latest matrix groups consumers into eight categories: actualizers, achievers, believers, makers, fulfilleds, experiencers, strivers and strugglers (see Table 12.3).

The Mission of VALS.   In 1978 the VALS project became a separate program at SRI, with a staff of four and 37 clients. By 1984 it had developed into a $2 million operation with 151 clients and a staff of 19.

The VALS program has become more than a market-research project. Its developers see it as a social agent for changing American culture. At its headquarters in Menlo Park, California, the following credo hangs on the wall of each staff member's office:

> *The mission of the VALS program is to exert a positive and creative force in the evolution of the American culture. VALS aims to do this by acquiring, disseminating, and applying insights into how values can aid institutions and individuals to operate in a more humane, productive and ethical way. Specifically, VALS intends:*
>
> ■ *To become a significant part of American business thinking.*
> ■ *To enhance public awareness of the role of values in social change.*
> ■ *To contribute to SRI research, remain financially healthy and operate for the enjoyments and personal growth of the staff.[25]*

TABLE 12.3 VALS 2 SYSTEM CATEGORIES   **323**

ACTUALIZERS
Value personal growth
Varied leisure activities
Well informed; concerned with social issues
Wide intellectual interests
Highly social
Politically active

ACHIEVERS
Have formal social relations
Lives center on career and family
Avoid excess changes or stimulation
May emphasize work at expense of recreation
Politically conservative

BELIEVERS
Enjoy settled, comfortable, predictable existence
Socialize within family and established groups
Respect rules and trust authority figures
Reasonably well informed
Politically conservative

MAKERS
Prefer "hands on" activities
Enjoy outdoors
Spend leisure with family and close friends
Avoid joining organizations, except unions
Distrust politicians, foreigners and big business

FULFILLEDS
Leisure centers on home
Moderately active in community and politics
Value education and travel
Health conscious
Politically moderate and tolerant

EXPERIENCERS
Like exercise, socializing, sports and outdoors
Like the new, offbeat and risky
Concerned about image
Unconforming, but admire wealth, power and fame
Politically apathetic

STRIVERS
Easily bored
Narrow interests
Somewhat isolated
Look to peer group for motivation and approval
Unconcerned about health or nutrition
Politically apathetic

STRUGGLERS
Prime concerns are safety and security
Limited interests and activities
Burdened with health problems
Rely on organized religion
Conservative and traditional

SOURCE: SRI International.

BOX 12.3

▪ VALS RESEARCH LEADS TO NEW MAGAZINE GENRE ▪

In 1987 newsstands across the United States started squeezing in a new type of specialized magazine. This magazine genre was reflecting a new interest among the baby boomers, often referred to as the "Yuppie" generation. In a surprise to some observers who had been watching the "Me Generation" Yuppies for a long time, the Yuppies were now focusing on—of all things—the family.

Publications like *Parenting, Father, Child, Children* and *Grandparents* were finding an audience among Yuppies in the late twentieth century. The trend was based on solid market research and was attracting publishing biggies like Time Inc., which had pumped $5 million into *Parenting,* a San Francisco–based publication.

Values and Lifestyles research had shown that members of the Yuppie generation were finally having children and were now focusing their attention on their families. Advertisers, who closely followed VALS research, were readily available to purchase space in these new magazines. *Parenting,* at $5,400 for a full-page ad, sold 200 more ad pages than it had projected during its first 10 issues. *Child,* with full-page ads costing $7,000, also attracted major advertisers, among them Procter & Gamble, Ford, Eastman-Kodak, Saks Fifth Avenue and Sears.

This was just one way that VALS research was paying off for advertisers and media entrepreneurs during the late 1980s.

VALS Users. At first VALS research was treated rather secretively; only lately has it been fashionable to discuss it. Many ad agencies now boast about their "psychographic capabilities." The mass media now uses VALS to sell advertising space. *Reader's Digest* has used VALS data to persuade reluctant advertisers that its readers were the right type of people to be targeted for the advertisers' products. The *National Geographic* has run a full-page ad in the *New York Times* telling how it uses VALS to help advertisers. The ad was headlined "THE NATIONAL PSYCHOGRAPHIC."

Since 1982 Simmons Market Research Bureau and Mediamark Research Inc. have been polling about 20,000 people annually for VALS data.

Advertisers can use VALS data to determine which media to use to reach specific market segments. Product developers can use the data to project trends and future consumer needs. Many of the new products scheduled for release into the marketplace in the mid-1990s were placed into development years ago on the basis of trends projected by VALS research. (For an example of how publishers have used VALS, see Box 12.3.)

The advertising of consumer goods has become a sophisticated, well-researched industry. The marketing community probably knows at least as much about our American popular culture and its future trends as most sociologists, psychologists and futurists. Whether we like it or not, the advertising industry may know more about us and why we do things than we do ourselves.

SUMMARY

Advertising is a message industry that plays a major role in shaping the content and operation of the mass media. Although advertising has existed since ancient

BOX 12.4

▪ WORKING IN ADVERTISING ▪

There are numerous job opportunities in the field of advertising. They include working for the mass media, working for major companies that advertise and working in a variety of departments in advertising agencies. Women play a major role in advertising, filling about 50 percent of the available jobs.

There are about 6,000 advertising agencies in the United States although only about 500 of them are considered large (with revenues in excess of $1 million). Most agencies usually have five major departments: market research, creative, account management, media selection and administration.

Market research gathers information on the product, who will buy it and where to promote it. Depending on the size of the agency, this activity can be accomplished in-house or can be contracted with market research companies.

The *creative* department writes the copy, develops the graphics and often produces the commercials or print ads.

Account management is in charge of working with the client to ensure that the ad campaign reflects the client's desires. The person in charge of an account is usually called an *account executive*.

Media selection is the department in charge of picking the right mass media for the client. Media selections range from radio, TV, newspapers and magazines to billboards and direct mail.

The *administration* handles the day-to-day business activities. These include billing clients and paying the bills.

In addition to these departments, some agencies offer public relations services for clients who do not have their own PR departments.

times, mass advertising as we know it today began growing up with the mass media in the late nineteenth century.

Advertising plays an important role in our popular culture because it shapes and reflects our lifestyles. It is one step ahead of other elements in our culture and is usually the first to reflect social trends. The average adult is exposed to approximately 500 advertisements each day, and more than $128 billion is spent on advertising in the United States each year.

The first ad agency was established in 1841; since then advertising has developed into an important yet controversial message business. Some of the debate deals with whether or not advertising is an effective tool for selling consumer goods. Some contend that advertising does not change consumer buying habits and others say that its effectiveness cannot be measured because too many other consumer information variables are involved. Some research has suggested that advertisers use sales records as indicators of whether or not to increase advertising. If sales go up, so does the amount spent on advertising.

The use of propaganda devices in advertising appeals to our emotions rather than to our intellect and is prevalent in American culture. Propaganda devices from slogans to sex appeal are used constantly.

Other advertising controversies include the charge that hidden messages are often subliminally imbedded in advertisements to appeal to our subconscious mind. Hidden appeals to the basic instincts of sex, death and fear are said to be used to sell products. Researchers have found that more of these hidden images can be found in liquor ads than in any other type of product advertising, but evidence that proves whether or not these imbeds have any effect on our buying habits is lacking.

As American industrial society grew in the mid-twentieth century, the production of consumer goods reached a level that required new sophisticated techniques to help mass-distribute the mass-produced goods. In the 1950s the advertising industry turned to motivational research to help stimulate sales.

An outgrowth of motivational research was the study of lifestyles and how they affect consumer buying patterns. Although it began in the 1950s, lifestyle research has been undergoing continual research and development. Today the Values and Lifestyles (VALS) system consists of eight consumer categories: actualizers, fulfilleds, achievers, experiencers, believers, strivers, makers and strugglers.

The VALS studies have led to a wealth of data that are now used on a regular basis to target the appropriate audience for a product; determine what media will best reach the target group; explain why the people in the target audience buy what they do; and help the ad agency develop an effective campaign to sell the product. VALS research is also used to help businesses determine what types of products are going to be marketable in the future.

THOUGHT QUESTIONS

1 What cultural factors were responsible for the development of the advertising industry as we know it today? Reflect on the nineteenth-century factors, the mid-twentieth-century needs, and current forces shaping the advertising industry.
2 Can you make a list of all the factors that contributed to a decision that you recently made regarding a major purchase?
3 Do you think advertising is effective? List some examples where it did or didn't play a major role in selling a product.
4 Reflecting on the 10 categories of propaganda devices discussed in the text, can you make a current list of examples for each category being used in advertising today?
5 Do you think the use of motivational research by the advertising industry is ethical? Why or why not?

NOTES

1. Harold Berkman and Christopher Gilson, *Advertising: Concepts and Strategies*, 2nd ed. (New York: Random House, 1987), p. 4.

2. Ibid., p. 34.

3. William F. Allman, "Science 1, Advertisers 0," *U.S. News & World Report*, May 1, 1989, pp. 60–61.

4. Michael Schudson, *Advertising, The Uneasy Persuasion: Its Dubious Impact on American Society* (New York: Basic Books, 1984), pp. 18–19.

5. Richard Schmalensee, *The Economics of Advertising* (Amsterdam: North Holland, 1972), p. 43.

6. Schudson, p. 33.

7. Stephen Fox, *The Mirror Makers: A History of American Advertising and Its Creators* (New York: Morrow, 1984), p. 328.

8. Schudson, pp. 90–91.

9. James H. Meyers and William H. Reynolds, *Consumer Behavior and Marketing Management* (Boston: Houghton Mifflin, 1967), p. 138.

10. Adolf Hitler, *Mein Kampf* [English language edition] (New York: Reynal & Hitchcock, 1939), p. 234.

11. Warren K. Agee, Phillip H. Ault and Edwin Emery, *Introduction to Mass Communications*, 9th ed. (New York: Harper & Row, 1988), pp. 360–361.

12. Vance O. Packard, *The Hidden Persuaders* (New York: Pocket Books, 1957).

13. Walter Weir, "Another Look at Subliminal 'Facts,'" *Advertising Age,* October 19, 1984, p. 46.

14. Ibid.

15. R. S. Lazarus and R. A. McCleary, "Automatic Discrimination Without Awareness: A Study of Subception," *Psychological Review* 58 (1951): 113–122.

16. Warren Breed and James R. DeFoe, "Themes in Magazine Alcohol Advertisements: A Critique," *Journal of Drug Issues* (Fall 1979): 46.

17. *30-Second Seduction,* a *Consumer Reports* special on television advertising, HBO Home Video, 1985.

18. Patricia Marks Greenfield, *Mind and Media: The Effects of Television, Video Games and Computers* (Cambridge, Mass.: Harvard University Press, 1984), pp. 51–53.

19. Michael Jacobson, Robert Atkins and George Hacker, *The Booze Merchants: The Inebriating of America* (Washington, D.C.: Center for Science in the Public Interest, 1983), pp. 44–82, 103–130.

20. Vance Packard, "The Ad and the Id," in *Mass Media and the Popular Arts,* ed. Fredric Rissover and David C. Birch (New York: McGraw-Hill, 1971), p. 9.

21. Ibid., p. 10.

22. Fox, p. 183.

23. Quoted in Fox, p. 182.

24. James Atlas, "Beyond Demographics: How Madison Avenue Knows Who You Are and What You Want," *The Atlantic,* October 1984, p. 51.

25. Arnold Mitchell, *The Nine American Lifestyles* (New York: Macmillan, 1983), pp. 3–37.

ADDITIONAL READING

Engel, Jack. *Advertising: The Process and Practice.* New York: McGraw-Hill, 1980.

Foote, N. N. *Consumer Behavior: Household Decision-Making,* vol. 4. New York: New York University Press, 1961.

Key, Wilson Bryan. *Subliminal Seduction.* New York: Signet, 1974.

————. *Media Sexploitation*. New York: New American Library, 1976.

————. *Clam Plate Orgy*. New York: New American Library, 1980.

Myers, James H., and Reynolds, William H. *Consumer Behavior and Marketing Management*. Boston: Houghton Mifflin, 1967.

Riesman, David. *The Lonely Crowd: A Study of Changing American Character*. New Haven, Conn.: Yale University Press, 1950.

Johnson & Johnson implemented effective crisis management when cyanide-tainted Tylenol capsules were discovered on store shelves.

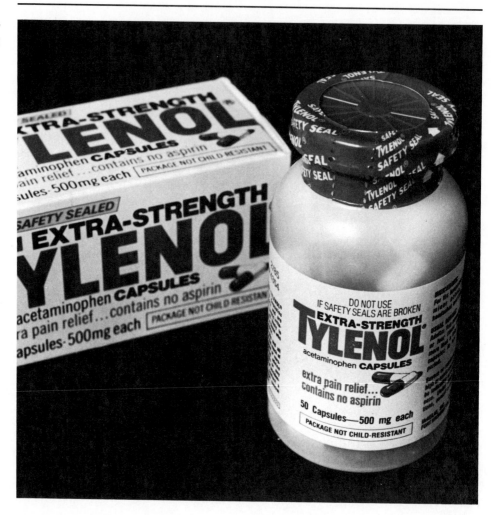

PUBLIC RELATIONS: CREATING AN IMAGE

It is no use putting whipped cream on the manure pile because the sun comes out in the morning and you have the same old manure pile.

—L. L. L. Golden, public relations consultant

Up until 1990 ordering a Perrier was a fashionable thing to do. But within weeks after it was reported in the news media that this chic French bottled mineral water had been contaminated with traces of benzene, Perrier became a forgotten product.

In 1989, when the oil tanker *Exxon Valdez* was grounded in Alaska, spilling nearly 11 million gallons of oil in Prince William Sound, the public turned on this large oil firm, boycotting its gasoline and conjuring up images of a major polluter whenever the name Exxon was encountered.

AN OPEN LETTER TO THE PUBLIC

On March 24, in the early morning hours, a disastrous accident happened in the waters of Prince William Sound, Alaska. By now you all know that our tanker, the Exxon Valdez, hit a submerged reef and lost 240,000 barrels of oil into the waters of the Sound.

We believe that Exxon has moved swiftly and competently to minimize the effect this oil will have on the environment, fish and other wildlife. Further, I hope that you know we have already committed several hundred people to work on the cleanup. We also will meet our obligations to all those who have suffered damage from the spill.

Finally, and most importantly, I want to tell you how sorry I am that this accident took place. We at Exxon are especially sympathetic to the residents of Valdez and the people of the State of Alaska. We cannot, of course, undo what has been done. But I can assure you that since March 24, the accident has been receiving our full attention and will continue to do so.

L. G. Rawl
Chairman

■ Crisis management efforts like this one came too late to head off a major public relations problem for Exxon after the *Exxon Valdez* dumped 11 million gallons of oil into Prince William Sound.

These things should not have happened to these successful companies and illustrate what can occur when a firm poorly handles an important public relations activity known as "crisis management."

Source Perrier bungled its crisis management challenge by first trying to ignore the benzene contamination and then by trying to minimize its extent. The public lost confidence in the company and its product. Exxon at first shrugged off responsibility for the oil spill and was slow to begin cleanup operations. As one public relations practitioner put it: "Exxon should have had the president of the company on the shore cleaning the rocks within 24 hours."

Examples of good crisis management, on the other hand, can be found in the way Bristol-Myers and Johnson & Johnson handled the crises of cyanide-tainted capsules of Extra-Strength Execedrin and Tylenol. Instead of trying to hush up this bad news when the poisoned capsules were discovered, the companies immediately removed the products from the store shelves and publicized both these efforts and their apparent concern for the safety of consumers.

Crisis management is an important function in corporate public relations as our society becomes more complex and news and information is more rapidly and

333

13 ■
PUBLIC
RELATIONS:
CREATING AN
IMAGE

thoroughly circulated. Public relations (PR), like advertising, is a message business that in recent years has become highly sophisticated and respected. However, it is still surrounded by some of the controversies that have plagued it from its early days. Most of the controversy comes from the fact that a greal deal of confusion still exists with regard to exactly what public relations is.

WHAT IS PUBLIC RELATIONS?

The *Random House College Dictionary* defines public relations rather simply: "1. the efforts of a corporation to promote good will between itself and the public. 2. the methods used to promote such good will." In the *Public Relations Handbook* (1971), Philip Lesly expanded on this definition by noting that PR enables institutions and people to learn what others think of them, determine what they must do to earn the good will of others, devise ways to win that good will and carry on programs designed to secure good will.[1]

Throughout the 1970s, confusion existed as to what PR was all about. In 1975 the Foundation for Public Relations Research and Education commissioned a panel of 65 public relations leaders to study 472 different definitions and come up with one single statement that reflected the profession. The outcome was the following 88-word sentence:

> *Public relations is a distinctive management function which helps establish and maintain mutual lines of communications, understanding, acceptance, and cooperation between an organization and its publics; involves the management of problems or issues; helps management to keep informed on and responsive to public opinion; defines and emphasizes the responsibility of management to serve the public interest; helps management keep abreast of and effectively utilize change, serving as an early warning system to help anticipate trends; and uses research and sound and ethical communication techniques as its principal tools.[2]*

In 1978 another attempt was made at defining PR: "Public relations practice is the art and social science of analyzing trends, predicting their consequences, counseling organization leaders, and implementing planned programs of action which will serve both the organization's and the public's interest."[3]

In 1980 a task force chartered by the Public Relations Society of America came up with these two definitions:

1 Public relations helps an organization and its publics adapt mutually to each other.
2 Public relations is an organization's efforts to win the cooperation of groups of people.[4]

What the many attempts to define public relations seem to indicate is that it is a complex field with a variety of functions and activities. What is central in all the definitions is that PR is an organized effort to handle relationships with the public.

Some people confuse PR and advertising. Advertising involves the paid use of time and space in the mass media, usually to sell goods and services. Public relations, on the other hand, often uses free space and time in the media to sell corporate images, individuals and good will. These two practices sometimes overlap when paid advertising is used to sell a corporate image or create good will, and, in fact, advertising often becomes an important part of the PR practitioners' total campaign. Thus, the confusion over these two fields is understandable.

Unfortunately, public relations still means different things to different people. Some who call themselves public relations practitioners are engaged in only a narrow aspect of the field. In its broadest sense, PR includes such activities as policy making, press agentry, spin doctoring, promotion, public affairs, publicity and, as previously noted, paid advertisement. All of these activities play a major role in shaping the content of the mass media and disseminating cultural information throughout our society. To distinguish among these activities, let's look at each separately.

Policy Making. A PR practitioner is a liaison between an institution and the public. He or she is responsible for setting a public relations policy to represent the corporation or agency to the public and for conducting research to provide adequate feedback from the public to the institution. Usually a PR practitioner works closely with top-level management and is instrumental in influencing management's policy changes. The PR person can be described as a strategist who plans and executes large-scale public relations efforts.

Press Agentry. Public relations had its origins in press agentry, and today some people still think the terms are synonymous. Press agentry consists of planning and staging events that will attract favorable attention to an institution, person, idea or product and placing positive news items in the media about the client. Although early press agents sometimes used fraud and deception to achieve their goals, today's practitioners are more honest and professional.

Spin Doctoring. Related to press agentry is an activity that has become rather prevalent in recent years. It is known as spin doctoring. The term *spin doctoring* does not apply to disc jockeys or people in the medical field. It is a relatively new term used to describe people who are able to place a favorable "spin" on media coverage for companies or political causes.

Promotion. Promotional activities go beyond getting publicity and involve generating support or endorsements for a client. Clients range from churches and charities to political candidates and causes and a variety of social concerns, such as the "Save the Whales" and "Right to Life" movements. Promotional activities often involve fund-raising campaigns.

Public Affairs. The term *public affairs* is misleading because some corporations and government agencies use it to describe their entire PR effort. (Many institutions are now calling their directors of public relations "directors of public affairs," for example.) However, properly speaking, the term refers to a narrower

335

13 ∎
PUBLIC
RELATIONS:
CREATING AN
IMAGE

public relations activity: direct institutional involvement with community and government relations.

Publicity.   Publicity involves placing news and information in the mass media. People who work in this field are skilled in writing publicity in a news format; in government agencies they often carry the title of public information officer. Good public information officers need to have some of the skills and training of professional PR practitioners to handle the occasions when the mass media are seeking unfavorable news and information.

Advertising.   Occasionally PR practitioners need to use paid advertising. For example, they may decide to mount an ad campaign to clarify a client's institutional policy or correct an unfavorable image, or to provide assistance with a promotional or press agentry campaign. Public relations personnel who do not have experience in advertising usually call in a professional for assistance. However, many PR agencies today have expanded their operations to include advertising as well.

THE HISTORY OF PUBLIC RELATIONS

Although public relations has been with us in some form through the ages, modern PR traces its roots to early attempts at press agentry in the 1830s, when the metropolitan penny press developed. It was common practice for early press agents to invent stories to promote their clients in these newspapers.

Early Press Agentry.   One of the early users of press agentry was P. T. Barnum, who successfully promoted the midget Tom Thumb and Jenny Lind, a singer known as the ''Swedish Nightingale''; they became popular sideshow attractions for Barnum's circus. He coined the often-quoted phrase ''There's a sucker born every minute.''

However, public relations as we now know it developed to help big businesses combat the negative image they had acquired during the Industrial Revolution. By the late nineteenth century it was becoming apparent that many of these industries needed to create a favorable image to offset the public's growing distrust. This need became even more obvious when muckrakers, such as Lincoln Steffens and Upton Sinclair, painted grim pictures of big-business practices around the turn of the century. Stories of huge profits and employee exploitation became common.

Corporate PR.   Simple press agentry wasn't enough to overcome suspicions about big business. In fact, the lies and distortions association with press agentry at the time were the last thing companies needed.

One of the first to try to change this negative corporate image was journalist Ivy Ledbetter Lee, considered by many to be the first real PR practitioner. Lee started as a political publicist in 1904, but soon he was working for industrial giants. He began distributing press releases explaining business's side of labor

■ P. T. Barnum used press agentry to promote the midget Tom Thumb, shown here with Barnum.

disputes; he told city editors at the local newspapers that he was a "press agent who dealt in the truth."

Government PR.   Government became involved in public relations when the United States entered World War I in 1917. President Woodrow Wilson established the Creel Committee, headed by newspaperman George Creel, to promote the sale of Liberty Bonds to finance the war, to censor news about the war and to convince the American people of the necessity of the nation's participation in the war.

A member of the committee, Edward L. Bernays, emerged as a leader in the development of the PR profession after the war. In 1921 he set up his own firm, becoming the first person to call himself a public relations counsel. Two years later he wrote the first book on the subject, *Crystallizing Public Opinion*.[5] He also taught the first course in public relations, at New York University. Bernays eventually earned the title of "father of modern public relations." As his reputation in PR grew, he found himself rejecting an offer by Adolf Hitler to help propagate Nazism.

The U.S. government again turned to public relations for help when it became involved in World War II in 1941. It established the Office of War Information (OWI), headed by radio commentator Elmer Davis. After the war ended, the OWI became the U.S. Information Agency.

The Great Depression.   The PR industry's road to success as a respected profession was not without setbacks. When the Great Depression hit in 1929, the public

337

13 ■
PUBLIC
RELATIONS:
CREATING AN
IMAGE

■ The U.S. government uses public relations to create support for its efforts during wartime. Here is a World War II poster promoting more production on the home front to aid the war effort against Germany.

was quick to blame big business for the nation's financial woes. A real need existed for corporate public relations people to respond to the critics. However, because businesses were suffering financial hardships and PR was a relatively new field, funds to support institutional public relations were among the first to be cut—at a time when such services were sorely needed.

Post–World War II.   After the Great Depression and World War II, however, public relations prospered. Industry and government both began to recognize the need to present their activities favorably to the public.

By the mid-1980s the Department of Labor was reporting that 143,000 people were engaged in PR activities in the United States. In addition to several hundred public relations firms, every sizable organization, whether public or private, had one or more employees working in the field.

Today's public relations professional requires a broad range of skills, including listening, counseling, planning and communicating. Public relations counselors Carl Byoir & Associates describe their business this way:

Analysis—*of policies and objectives of client . . . of relationships with various publics, including employees, customers, dealers, shareholders, the financial community, government and the press. Continuing research keeps the analysis of these relationships up-to-date.*

Planning and programming—*of specific undertakings and projects in which public relations techniques can be employed to help attain the objectives through effective communication between the client and its publics.*

Implementation—of the programs and projects by maximum and effective use of all avenues of communication, internal and external, to create understanding and stimulate action.[6]

OPPORTUNITIES AND DUTIES OF PR PRACTITIONERS

The field of public relations is fast growing. According to the U.S. Department of Labor, public relations jobs during the 1990s will increase faster than the average for all occupations. This is because major companies have realized how important their image is in selling their products. Employment opportunities are numerous, with some 1,600 PR agencies; corporations employing thousands of PR practitioners, many of them at the top of the management level; and most government and educational institutions having public relations offices (see Box 13.1).

Diverse Responsibilities.   Since the field is so broad, it might be helpful to describe what public relations practitioners actually do. Frank Wylie, a public relations practitioner and an educator, points out that there are major differences between the job duties of an entry-level PR employee and an experienced executive. He says that the average entry-level employees spend 50 percent of their time on techniques, 5 percent on judgment and 45 percent on "running like hell." The experienced executives, on the other hand, spend 10 percent on techniques, 40 percent on administration and 50 percent on analysis and judgment.[7]

Herb Schmertz, vice-president of public affairs for Mobil Oil until his retirement in 1988, described his wide-ranging duties this way:

> *Sometimes I describe myself as a lobbyist who tries to raise certain issues and arguments before the public, the government and the press. But I am also a publisher—of books, pamphlets, reports, and issue-oriented advertisements. In addition, I am a patron of the arts and culture. I am also a corporate spokesman who explains and defends Mobil's point of view. From time to time, I am an advocate who confronts individuals and institutions whose positions are, in our view, wrong or misinformed. And I am a media critic who refuses to allow inaccurate or damaging stories to go unanswered.*
>
> *In addition to all of this, I am responsible for administering a large department and a hefty budget. As a member of Mobil's board of directors, I participate in corporate investment decisions and other policy issues. When evening rolls around, I often represent the corporation at an art or cultural event, or at a political dinner, or as a guest on a TV interview show.*[8]

Campaign Development.   Public relations practitioners use a systematic approach to developing their campaigns. One such approach, developed by Bernays, is called "the engineering of consent" and consists of the following eight steps:

1 Define goals or objectives.
2 Research publics to find whether goals are realistic and attainable, and how.
3 Modify goals if research finds them unrealistic.

BOX 13.1

▪ WORKING IN PUBLIC RELATIONS ▪

There are numerous opportunities for people to work in the field of public relations. Entry-level jobs can be found working for charitable organizations, hospitals, government agencies, colleges and universities, chambers of commerce, trade organizations, entertainment groups, sports organizations and small business firms. In addition, there is employment with large corporations and public relations agencies.

The largest number of job opportunities exists with large corporations, which often have hundreds of people working in various public relations activities. Approximately 85 percent of the 1,500 largest corporations in America have public rela-

tions departments. In addition, about a third of these corporations retain external public relations agencies. These firms can range in size from a one-person operation to 2,000 or more employees. They usually charge clients on a fee-plus-expenses basis.

PR practitioners are usually college graduates trained in the profession. Formal education is offered at more than 160 colleges and universities in the United States, usually in schools and departments of journalism and mass communication. About 12 percent of the graduates of these schools and departments enter the field of public relations.

4 Determine strategy to reach goals.
5 Plan actions, themes and appeals to publics.
6 Plan organization to meet goals.
7 Time and plan tactics to meet goals.
8 Set up budget.[9]

As you can see, PR practitioners are skilled professionals who do much more than issue press releases and plant publicity in the media. They are planners who set goals, research needs, establish systematic campaigns and select and work with the media.

EXAMPLES OF PUBLIC RELATIONS ACTIVITIES

Three major types of PR activity dominate the field: behavior modification, combined marketing and PR efforts and issues and crisis management.

Behavior Modification. Much of the current behavior-modification PR efforts result from an increase in social awareness and concerns. Such campaigns as the need to fasten seat belts, hire the handicapped, say no to drugs and not drink while driving receive much PR attention.

Major milk companies and supermarket chains contribute to creating public awareness of missing children by printing pictures of some of these children on milk cartons and shopping bags. Even alcoholic beverage companies have joined the "don't drink and drive" campaign by promoting responsible drinking in their advertisements. One purpose of these PR efforts is to foster the companies' reputations as concerned institutions (see Box 13.2).

BOX 13.2

PHILIP MORRIS BILL OF RIGHTS PROMOTION SPARKS CONTROVERSY

In conjunction with the 200th anniversary of the Bill of Rights in 1991, the tobacco giant Philip Morris launched a $30 million campaign to promote its corporate image and send a message to the nation on the importance of individual freedoms protected by this national document.

In the campaign, advertisements were run in major newspapers across the country featuring such prominent national leaders as Benjamin L. Hooks, executive director of the National Association for the Advancement of Colored People; Rev. Theodore M. Hesburgh, president emeritus of the University of Notre Dame; Judith Jamison, artistic director of the Alvin Ailey American Dance Theater; actor Charleton Heston; New York City Ballet dancer Valentina Kozlova; and Vietnam prisoner of war Everett Alvarez, Jr. The individuals were all quoted discussing the importance of the Bill of Rights to their individual freedoms. In addition to the ads, Philip Morris gave away copies of the Bill of Rights to anyone who dialed a toll-free number.

However, this particular public relations effort drew criticism in some circles. Antismoking advocates resented the fact that a tobacco company was identifying itself with such a symbol of freedom as the Bill of Rights. Some suggested that the hidden agenda in the PR campaign was the fact that cigarette smokers had lost many of their rights to smoke in public places and the company was trying to win support for smokers' rights.

Philip Morris and the participants in the ads all denied the charges. They asserted that they and Philip Morris were merely interested in affirming the importance of the Bill of Rights.

Combined Marketing and PR Efforts. The growth of the combined efforts of marketing and PR also reflects changing cultural attitudes and practices. These activities attempt to expand the marketing efforts of certain institutions, such as museums, churches and hospitals, which until recently saw no need to market themselves (see Box 13.3).

Museum promotions of traveling exhibits like the Armand Hammer collection of paintings are an example of this successful blend of marketing and PR. Other recent notable examples were the promotion of the 1984 Summer Olympics in Los Angeles, which was privately funded and turned a profit for an activity that had previously been publicly financed, and the refurbishing and celebration of the centennial of the Statue of Liberty in 1986.

Issues and Crises Management. Issues management attempts to identify and correctly interpret problems before they become a crisis; crisis management attempts to react to crises, such as disasters, in as favorable a climate as possible.

In the 1980s some corporations' issues management began taking on a new and controversial tone. Some firms abandoned their longtime practice of handling the mass media with kid gloves and spoke out forcefully when they felt they had been treated unfairly by the press.

One of the first companies to take this posture was Mobil Oil, which started running full-page ads presenting its position on controversial issues. Companies that have followed Mobil's lead include Chevron, Dow Chemical and W. R. Grace.

BOX 13.3

▪ EVEN THE ROMAN CATHOLIC CHURCH USES PR ▪

Public relations is for everyone. Once thought of as the tool for large corporate America, public relations is now regarded as an essential element in our popular culture. So it shouldn't have come as a surprise in 1990 when the Roman Catholic Church awarded a $1 million a year contract for one to five years to one of America's largest public relations firms.

But it wasn't good will with the congregation or a recruiting drive for new converts that the church was interested in. It hired the PR firm of Hill & Knowlton to launch an antiabortion campaign.

However, the PR firm got more than it bargained for when it took on the assignment. About a third of its staff signed a letter protesting its decision to promote antiabortion for the nation's Roman Catholic bishops. Other employees complained individually and one person resigned. In addition, the company lost several accounts over the issue.

The irony of the controversy was the fact that Hill & Knowlton, which had established itself as a leader in helping companies avoid such turmoil, was now in need of some good PR for itself.

Leading Mobil's fight against the media was Herb Schmertz, then its vice-president of public affairs. He challenged biased reporting in major newspapers and the television networks. Although the networks refused to run Mobil's countermedia advertisements, some did appear on independent TV stations and a few network affiliates. Most of the Mobil messages have appeared in newspapers and magazines.

Mobil's counterattacks did not make the company very popular with the media, but Schmertz feels that the ads have made the networks more cautious about airing poorly researched news specials about the oil industry in general and Mobil in particular. On the other hand, Schmertz has cited examples of news reporters going out of their way to "get even" with Mobil.[10] In 1984, after continued run-ins with reporters and editors at the *Wall Street Journal,* Mobil severed all relations with that newspaper. Mobil indicated that it would grant no more interviews, send no more press releases or run advertisements in the *Wall Street Journal.*[11]

Many PR executives, including some in the oil industry, have criticized Mobil's combative approach to issues management. However, two communication researchers studied the new approach and concluded that the news media lost credibility when they attacked firms that responded to the criticism.[12]

Another example of issues management occurred in 1988 after Suzuki, makers of the popular four-wheel drive Samurai, found itself reacting to charges from *Consumer Reports* magazine that the vehicle was unsafe and tipped over frequently. The magazine said Suzuki should recall all 150,000 vehicles on the road and refund the purchase price.

The company first charged that the magazine's claims were "unfounded," "defamatory" and politically motivated. It threatened a libel suit against the publication.

To bypass the possibility of having the wrong "spin" placed on their claims by a few reporters at a press conference, Suzuki's PR practitioners used the new satellite technology to broadcast their rebuttal to reporters around the country.

■ Ivy Ledbetter Lee is considered to be the first real public relations practioner to effectively handle crisis management. He created a positive corporate response to a train crash involving the Pennsylvania Railroad in 1906.

They next saturated television with $1.5 million worth of advertising, much of it shown on network and local newscasts.

The first success in crisis-management public relations is attributed to Ivy Ledbetter Lee, who represented the Pennsylvania Railroad in the early twentieth century. When one of the railroad's trains derailed in 1906, killing and injuring several people, Lee resisted company efforts to hush up the accident (a typical approach to crises at the time). Instead he provided the media with full and accurate accounts of the accident and even ran special trains, at company expense, to take journalists to the scene. He also persuaded the company to conduct a systemwide survey of railroad beds to avoid future derailments and announced that the company would provide financial aid to the families of the killed or injured. As a result, the Pennsylvania Railroad and the railroad industry received their first favorable press coverage in years.[13]

Johnson & Johnson began its first round of crisis-management PR in 1981, after seven people in the Chicago area died from taking cyanide-tainted Tylenol capsules. The company immediately took all Tylenol capsules off the market and reissued the product in tamper-resistant containers, spending millions of dollars. Many believed that negative publicity about the Tylenol-related deaths would spell the end of the popular pain reliever, but it rapidly recovered its number-one position in market sales. In March 1983 the Public Relations Society of America's Honor and Awards Committee presented its Silver Anvil Award to Johnson & Johnson and its PR firm, Burson-Marsteller, for their handling of the crisis.

Johnson & Johnson's success was due in part to a company philosophy of social responsibility. Lawrence G. Foster, vice-president of public relations for Johnson & Johnson at the time, described the company's approach: "During the crisis phases of the Tylenol tragedy, virtually every public relations decision was based on sound, socially responsible business principles, which is when public relations is most effective."[14]

Johnson & Johnson used the same management style and philosophy in 1986, when the tamper-resistant containers proved fallible and another woman died from a cyanide Tylenol capsule. This time the company permanently ceased manufacturing all capsule medication.

343

13 ▪
PUBLIC
RELATIONS:
CREATING AN
IMAGE

CONTROVERSIES SURROUNDING PR PRACTICES

The fact that PR practitioners are involved in creating positive images for their clients often causes public concern and criticism. PR efforts determine much of the content of our mass media, and news consumers seldom know the difference between a story written by a news reporter and a public relations news release. When they find out that what they believed to be an unbiased account by a reporter is actually a press release, they become angry.

Wall Street Journal **Study.**   A study of a typical issue of the *Wall Street Journal* found that 53 news stories were based on PR releases and, of these, 32 were reprinted almost verbatim or in paraphrase. Curiously, 20 of these 53 stories— including some taken nearly verbatim from a press release—were identified as having been written by a *Journal* staffer.[15]

These findings are reflective of media content throughout the country. There would be no problem with the fact that PR practitioners generate a large amount of media content if the sources of that content were identified. People could then evaluate the information on the basis of its source, rather than blindly accepting it as unbiased "news."

Positive Aspects of PR News.   Public relations practitioners argue that they are actually helping the free flow of information in our society. Our nation has grown very large since its founding more than two hundred years ago. For the concept of a democracy dependent on a well-informed citizenry to work today, journalists must have help in gathering news and information. Public relations assists in this process.

Modern PR may also be an important ingredient in our culture because it provides a broader and sometimes more accurate flow of information. According to Herb Schmertz, most news reporters—particularly television reporters—don't understand business. As a result, they often distort business stories to the detriment of corporations. The job of corporate public relations departments, according to Schmertz, is to reflect accurately for the public the truth about business activities.[16]

"Flacks."   Despite the media's dependence on public relations for content and the fact that many PR practitioners have been trained as journalists, a rather cool and distant relationship often exists between journalists working for the media and public relations personnel. Since the early days of press agentry, journalists have called PR people *flacks*. A 1969 edition of the Associated Press Managing Editors (APME) *Guidelines* had the following to say about flacks:

> *A flack is a person who makes all or part of his income by obtaining space in newspapers without cost to himself or his clients. Usually a professional. The term also includes those persons who seek free space for causes which they deem beneficial to the country, to the nation, or to God. Mostly amateurs. Of the two categories, the pros are easier to handle. They are known formally as public relations men. . . . A flack is a flack. His job is to say kind things about his client. He will not lie very often, but much of the time he tells less than the whole story. You do not owe the PR man anything. The owner of the newspaper, not the flack, pays your salary. Your immediate job is to serve the reader, not the man who would raid your columns.*[17]

Lingering Negative Image.   Criticism and distrust of public relations linger on, years after the profession has "grown up." This is one of the reasons that some large companies have changed the name of their public relations departments to public affairs or communications. Changing the name, however, doesn't necessarily change the image, which, by and large, is caused not by the true PR practitioners but rather by some not-so-professional individuals who call themselves public relations people.

One of the reasons that PR retains a poor image is the lingering practice by some companies to attempt to deceive the news media. According to Robert L. Dilenschneider, president of Hill & Knowlton, the largest public relations firm in the United States, too many businesses have damaged their credibility by lying to the media. "If you look at American business over the past 25 years, there's been a lot of deception," he said. "But there's no substitute for telling the truth, no matter how tough that might be."[18]

More constructively, many strides have been made to improve the industry's image. The most effective efforts have been made by the Public Relations Society of America (PRSA), which has adopted a stringent code of ethics and mandatory accreditation procedures for all members (see Box 13.4). There are more than 14,000 members—a figure that represents less than 10 percent of all the people who claim to be working in public relations. Ironically, although the primary function of the public relations industry is the creation of positive public images, it has failed to create good will for itself.

SUMMARY

Public relations, like advertising, is a message business designed to promote and maintain good will for clients. PR is dependent on the mass media to promote this good will, and the media are dependent on PR practitioners for much of their content.

Public relations now involves a variety of activities, including policy making, legitimate press agentry, spin doctoring, promotion, working with government agencies (public affairs), publicity campaigns and paid advertising.

The need for PR developed in the late nineteenth century, when big business found that they had a very poor public image. Early public relations practitioners,

BOX 13.4

DECLARATION OF PRINCIPLES OF
■ THE PUBLIC RELATIONS SOCIETY OF AMERICA ■

This declaration serves as a preamble to the Public Relations Society of America's Code of Professional Standards for the Practice of Public Relations.

Members of the Public Relations Society of America base their professional principles on the fundamental value and dignity of the individual, holding that the free exercise of human rights, especially freedom of speech, freedom of assembly and freedom of the press, is essential to the practice of public relations.

In serving the interests of clients and employers, we dedicate ourselves to the goals of better communication, understanding and cooperation among the diverse individuals, groups and institutions of society.

We pledge:

To conduct ourselves professionally, with truth, accuracy, fairness and responsibility to the public;

To improve our individual competence and advance the knowledge and proficiency of the profession through continuing research and education;

And to adhere to the articles of the Code of Professional Standards for the Practice of Public Relations as adopted by the governing Assembly of the Society.

such as Ivy Ledbetter Lee and Edward L. Bernays, helped elevate PR from an activity of merely getting publicity for a client to one that involved a systematic effort to represent the client favorably to the public and research public perceptions adequately.

The federal government got into the public relations business in World War I when it appointed the Creel Committee to present the U.S. war effort to the public in a favorable light.

During the Great Depression of the 1930s businesses curtailed their PR efforts at a time when they needed them most. The U.S. government again cranked up public relations efforts during World War II by creating the Office of War Information. This agency survives today as the U.S. Information Agency.

Today public relations is recognized as an important activity in our society. More than 140,000 people work in this field, and there are several hundred PR firms. In addition, almost all major companies and government agencies have PR personnel on their payroll.

Although most people don't readily recognize public relations activities as such, their impact on our culture is evident. Many of today's PR efforts are directed toward creating behavior modification, assisting in marketing activities and facilitating issues and crisis management.

The mass media rely on public relations practitioners for information to keep the society informed. The public is also served by PR practitioners who accurately interpret the activities of their corporate or government clients.

Although public relations is a respectable profession today, with its own code of ethics, many people who call themselves PR practitioners still do not adhere to the principles of the profession and often use the same dubious tactics as early press agents.

THOUGHT QUESTIONS

1 How would you have handled the Perrier crisis-management challenge?
2 If you were the chief executive officer of a major chemical company criticized for making toxic substances, how would you combat the negative image?
3 What are some examples of behavior modification PR currently being used in the media today?
4 Do you think the Herb Schmertz approach of attacking negative press works? How would you handle such a situation?
5 Do you think the Public Relations Society of America should seek legislation requiring all PR practitioners to be licensed?

NOTES

1. Philip Lesly, ed., *Public Relations Handbook* (Englewood Cliffs, N.J.: Prentice-Hall, 1971), p. xi.

2. Rex F. Harlow, "Building a Public Relations Definition," *Public Relations Review* 2, no. 4 (Winter 1976): 36.

3. First World Assembly of Public Relations Associations, Mexico City, Mexico, 1978.

4. Philip Lesly, "Report and Recommendation: Task Force on Stature and Role of Public Relations," *Public Relations Journal* (March 1981): 30.

5. Edward L. Bernays, *Public Relations* (Norman: University of Oklahoma Press, 1952), p. 84.

6. Quoted in Don R. Pember, *Mass Media in America,* 4th ed. (Chicago: Science Research Associates, 1983), p. 292.

7. Frank Wylie, "The New Professionals," speech to the First National Student Conference, Public Relations Student Society of America, Dayton, Ohio, October 24, 1976 (published by Chrysler Corporation), p. 5.

8. Herb Schmertz with William Novak, *Good-bye to the Low Profile: The Art of Creative Confrontation* (Boston: Little, Brown, 1986), pp. 16–17.

9. Edward L. Bernays, "The Engineering of Consent," *Industry* 43 (December 1978): 12–13, 36.

10. Schmertz, pp. 66–73.

11. Ibid.

12. David E. Clavier and Frank B. Kalupa, "Corporate Rebuttals to 'Trial by Television,'" *Public Relations Review* 9 (Spring 1983): 24–36.

13. Irwin Ross, *The Image Merchants* (Garden City, N.Y.: Doubleday, 1959), p. 31.

14. Lawrence G. Foster, "The Role of Public Relations in the Tylenol Crisis," *Public Relations Journal* (March 1983): 13.

347

13 ■
PUBLIC
RELATIONS:
CREATING AN
IMAGE

15. "It's in the Journal. But This is Reporting?" *Columbia Journalism Review* (March/April 1980): 34–36.

16. Schmertz, pp. 82–83.

17. *APME Guidelines* (New York: Associated Press Managing Editors Association, 1969), p. 42.

18. Quoted from an address at a Public Relations Society of America convention, June 25, 1990, Palm Desert, California.

ADDITIONAL READING

Canfield, Bernard R., and Moore, H. Frazier. *Public Relations: Principles, Cases, and Problems,* 9th ed. Homewood, Ill.: Irwin, 1985.

Center, Allen H., with Walsh, Frank. *Public Relations Practices: Managerial Case Studies,* 3rd ed. Englewood Cliffs, N.J.: Prentice-Hall, 1985.

Creel, George. *How We Advertised America: The First Telling of the Amazing Story of the Committee on Public Information That Carried the Gospel of Americanism to Every Corner of the Globe.* New York: Harper & Row, 1920.

Cutlip, Scott M., and Center, Allen H. *Effective Public Relations,* 6th ed. Englewood Cliffs, N.J.: Prentice-Hall, 1985.

Henry, Kenneth. *Defenders and Shapers of the Corporate Image.* New Haven, Conn.: College and University Press, 1972.

Larson, Keith A. *Public Relations: The Edward L. Bernayses and the American Scene: A Bibliography.* Westwood, Mass.: F. W. Faxon, 1978.

Public Relations Society of America. Careers in Public Relations. New York: PRSA, 1983.

Simon, Raymond. *Public Relations: Concepts and Practices,* 3rd ed. New York: Macmillan, 1984.

Sperber, Nathaniel, and Lerbinger, Otto. *Manager's Public Relations Handbook.* Reading, Mass.: Addison-Wesley, 1982.

During the Persian Gulf war in 1991, public relations was a key factor in selling our country's involvement in the war to the masses. Here a provocative poster helps sell patriotism.

THE SELLING OF
AMERICAN POLITICS

*Politics is the
gentle art of
getting votes
from the poor
and campaign
funds from the
rich, by
promising to
protect each
from the other.*
—Oscar
Ameringer, labor
organizer and
editor

After 40 years of television image-making and negative advertising, candidates for the 1992 presidential election faced a new challenge—newspapers began to pay less attention to what they said in their speeches and instead were focusing on the candidates' glitzy TV ads.

Ever since television became a powerful force in the popular culture in the 1950s, newspapers had ignored how political candidates were using that medium to sell themselves to the public. Instead, this print medium had continued business as usual; focusing on what candidates said in speeches and what the polls were saying about who was winning and losing.

However, in 1990, newspapers began analyzing the claims in political TV ads and reporting the lies, inaccuracies and distortions that they found. These regular examinations of TV ads soon became known as "truth boxes." Although 1990 was not a presidential election year, it gave the media a chance to focus on gubernatorial races. Truth boxes began during the 1990 primary election in California in the *Los Angeles Times* and were in use in Florida, Texas and California by the time of the campaigns for the general elections in November of 1990.

The public response to these analyses, coupled with the professional satisfaction that newspapers were at last giving the public a dimension of political coverage long ignored, set the stage for this process to become an important part of newspaper coverage of the 1992 presidential election.

The American experiment in democracy is dependent on a well-informed and participating citizenry, thus our survey of the functions of the mass media would not be complete without an examination of how the media treat political campaigns.

OPINION LEADER THEORY

The impact of the mass media on American presidential politics first became a concern to media researchers and political observers in the 1930s. They began to wonder if the new medium of radio, combined with the system of newspapers that was strongly entrenched in American popular culture, might influence voter behavior more powerfully than the traditional political parties.

Lazarsfeld Study. In 1940 a group of researchers headed by Paul Lazarsfeld decided to find out just how much influence the mass media exerted during presidential elections. They examined the media's role in the election between Democratic President Franklin Delano Roosevelt and Republican challenger Wendell Willkie. To gather their data, an extensive study was set up in Erie County, Ohio.[1]

The study's surprising results indicated that neither radio nor print had as much influence on voters as had been suspected. The researchers found that most of the people studied relied more on other people for the information they used to make their voting decisions.

Lazarsfeld then began to study the individuals who were relied on for information, calling them *opinion leaders*. He found that opinion leaders could be just about anyone, from a homemaker next door to a coworker on the assembly line. However, further analysis revealed that these opinion leaders were better informed than the average person and that, in general, they tended to read more newspapers and magazines and listen to more radio news and commentary.

As a result of his findings, Lazarsfeld developed the *two-step flow theory* of communication. This theory advanced the concept that (1) the mass media influence certain individuals and (2) these individuals personally influence others.[2]

Subsequent studies of the 1952 and 1956 presidential elections by Campbell, Converge, Miller and Stokes substantiated Lazarsfeld's findings.[3]

Changing Trends.　However, research in the 1970s and 1980s seemed to indicate that a number of factors were causing the mass media's indirect or secondary role in determining election outcomes to change. Prevalent among these factors were the advent of the political consultant and the prominent role television had come to play in the American culture.

Political scientist Robert Agranoff described the changing political scene as follows:

> *The candidate organization, the news event, the computer-generated letter, and most importantly the electronic media are the prevalent means of getting messages across in the modern campaign. The rise of the candidate volunteer and the electronic media has enabled the candidate to bypass the party and appeal directly to electors.[4]*

THE RISE OF THE POLITICAL CONSULTANT

The decline in the role of party bosses in helping candidates get elected created a need for someone to take their place. According to Sidney Blumenthal, "Political consultants are the new power within the American political system. The consultants have supplanted the old party bosses as the link to the voters."[5]

Early Pioneers.　The pioneers in the political consulting business were a husband and wife team in California, Clem Whitaker and Leona Baxter, who founded a public relations firm in 1934. They were instrumental in getting numerous Republicans elected to office until their retirement in 1958. Other successful consultants include Joe Napolitan, Stu Spencer, Bill Roberts, Sandy Weiner, Gerald Rafshoon, Bob Squier, Dick Woodward, Jack McDowell, Roger Ailes and Hal Evry (see Box 14.1).

Political consultants are professionals with advertising and public relations skills. They also make extensive use of opinion polling in shaping campaigns.

Opinion Polling.　Opinion polling can help win elections by finding out what issues are important to voters and what the majority's sentiments are. Candidates can then take a stand on the "right" side of the issues, telling voters what they want to hear. The extensive use of polling to shape campaign rhetoric has come under a great deal of criticism. Before his own campaign for the Senate, Democrat Paul Simon said, "The me-too illness is now compounded by the dramatic rise in public opinion polling and the spectacle of public officials following the implications of the polls, regardless of national need."[6]

In the 1980s President Ronald Reagan hired a firm called Decision/Making/Information to carry out the most extensive (and expensive) poll taking on a continual basis ever conducted for a president. The information from the polls became an important part of White House strategy and sometimes influenced the president's policy decisions.[7]

BOX 14.1

▪ PROFILE: HAL EVRY, A POLITICAL CONSULTANT ▪

In a June 3, 1966, feature article in *Life* magazine, political consultant Hal Evry was quoted as saying he could "elect you to office if you had $60,000, an IQ of at least 120, and could keep your mouth shut." The IQ, Evry noted, was not necessary for being an elected official but was a requirement for having enough sense to understand why it was important to do as he said and not talk to the press or public during the campaign. (Today, he points out that the cost of getting elected is ten times that amount.)

Evry is one of the more colorful and controversial veteran political consultants in America. He started his political consulting business in Los Angeles in 1955 and has been involved in over 500 political campaigns in the United States, Canada and Japan. He boasts a success rate of over 90 percent. He has managed gubernatorial races for George Wallace in Alabama, William Scranton and Raymond Shafer in Pennsylvania, David Hall in Oklahoma and Winthrop Rockefeller in Arkansas, as well as many senatorial and congressional races and one presidential primary.

The winning formula for election campaigns, according to Evry, consists of "identifying the publics (voters), polling them to learn their opinions, and then communicating with them in such a manner as to win their support" (telling them what they want to hear).

Evry's controversial and unorthodox theories include a strong belief that candidates should not give political speeches. He feels they are a waste of time (usually only people who support a candidate or have already made up their minds on how to vote go to hear politicians speak). Not only that, but the candidate might say something that will offend some of the voters. His advice to candidates is to leave town and let him (Evry) create an image and sell it. (Evry once got a millionaire who wanted to be elected mayor of a California city to vacation in Bermuda during the campaign. When he returned he was the mayor-elect, having won 20 of 21 precincts.)

Many critics of Evry's slick political campaigns claim that keeping the candidates away from the public and press degrades the American political system because the whole idea is for the electorate to be well-informed about the candidates' positions on the issues.

Evry is quick to debate this argument by contending that unqualified candidates are elected all the time under the old system and that his method may be bringing in a new caliber of candidate who would not have bothered to run before. He points out that traditional politics attracts only the noisy, boisterous types who love to "press the flesh" and talk at the top of their lungs. Under Evry's system the refined, introverted type can make it into public office, he says.

Evry also believes very strongly in what he calls his golden rule—"He who has the gold, rules." The more money a candidate spends, the more likely he or she is to win, Evry says. He believes that a person has to be rich to run for political office and tells people planning to run on a limited budget to give their money to the Cancer Society where it might do some good. As he points out, "Money does not necessarily guarantee success in a campaign (if an opponent is equally well financed he may run a better campaign). But, while money is no guarantee of success—the lack of money is a guarantee of losing."

Although Evry's attitude toward the American political process seems cynical, he does have some suggestions—equally controversial—for improving the system. He believes that the United States should have standards for political office seekers and qualifications for voters. He argues that we would not let an unqualified person perform brain surgery on us, yet we let anyone run for political office, where they help run the country and influence world affairs. As for voter qualifications, he points out that when the American experiment in democracy was established, the vote in most states was given only to land owners. "Now," he says, "the vote of any vagrant on the street carries as much weight as the richest man in America."

Sources: Personal interviews with Hal Evry; David Chagall, The New King Makers *(New York: Harcourt Brace Jovanovich, 1981); and Hal Evry,* The Selling of a Candidate: The Winning Formula *(Los Angeles: Western Opinion Research Center, 1977).*

■ On the campaign trail, media events are often contrived photo opportunities to create a favorable image for the candidate. Here George Bush is pictured showing his affection for ethnically diverse children.

Creating Images.   Political consultants are skillful image makers. Their standard operating procedure is to find out what the voters want and then package the candidate to meet those desires. Journalism educators Shaw and McCombs describe this process as follows:

> *The ability of television, newspapers, magazines, movies, radio and a whole host of new communications technologies to mold the public mind and significantly influence the flow of history is a widely ascribed power. In the political arena, candidates spend substantial sums for the services of image-makers—a new kind of mass communication artist and technocrat who presumably works magic on the voter via the mass media.*[8]

Selling Images.   The techniques used to sell political candidates have been changing over the years. Instead of debating issues or defending party goals, candidates are now more likely to be packaged and sold to the American public in almost the same way as laundry detergent. As reporter Joe McGinniss put it in 1968, "Style becomes substance. The medium is the massage and the masseur gets the votes."[9]

But there was more to selling candidates than media advertising. The mass media, which had long set their own news and information agendas (see the discussion of agenda setting in Chapter 1), were now facing competition from the political consultants in the agenda-setting process.

Political consultants often stage *news ploys* (called media events) to get free publicity for their candidates. The news media—fearful they might be scooped

■ Photo opportunities can occasionally backfire as this classic shot of 1988 Democratic presidential candidate Michael Dukakis shows. His posed photo in military gear in a U.S. tank was designed to show him as a strong military supporter. The image conveyed to the masses, however, was one of a foolish-looking misfit.

by the competition if they refuse to cover these contrived events—dutifully co-operate.

Some successful media events staged by political consultants include a U.S. senatorial candidate in scuba-diving gear swimming to the scene of an oil slick caused by offshore drilling, a California candidate for state treasurer attempting to throw a silver dollar across the Sacramento River on George Washington's birthday and another U.S. senator kicking off his campaign by running in a marathon. All of these events received extraordinary media coverage—far beyond their news value.

THE RISE OF POLITICAL ADS AND MEDIA INFLUENCE

The role the mass media play in the political system in the United States has been steadily growing during the twentieth century. Also increasing through the century has been the effective and controversial use of political advertising in the media. Debate over such advertising first emerged in 1916, when both the Republican and Democratic parties hired ad agencies to place advertisements during the presidential election. This activity led Congress in 1917 to consider for the first time regulations on political advertising.[10]

Harding and Coolidge.   From then on, advertising and PR people have played important and varied roles in American politics. In the 1920s these roles ranged from paying $20,000 to keep Warren G. Harding's mistress silent during the 1920 campaign to coining the slogan "Keep Cool with Coolidge" to help elect Calvin Coolidge president in 1924.

Roosevelt-Willkie.   In 1940 so many high-powered advertising men were supporting Wendell Willkie's campaign against President Franklin D. Roosevelt that the fact became a campaign issue. Columnist Dorothy Thompson stated on CBS radio, "These are the boys who have perfected the technique of selling the American people anything on the shelves." She said that she was supporting Roosevelt because "I am at long last fed up with the glib copywriters who think you can slug this nation into an election."[11]

Eisenhower-Stevenson.   Although the Republican and Democratic national conventions were first televised in 1948, it wasn't until 1952 that the new medium was used for advertising during a presidential campaign. General Dwight D. Eisenhower was the first president to use spot TV commercials. In one day, under the supervision of ad man Rosser Reeves, he recorded 40 20-second spots, which were broadcast during the last weeks of the campaign. This led George Ball, a staff member of Democratic challenger Adlai Stevenson, to say: "They have invented a new kind of campaign—conceived not by men who want us to face the crucial issues of this crucial day, but by the high powered hucksters of Madison Avenue."[12]

When Stevenson accepted his party's nomination to challenge Eisenhower again in 1956, he said his opponents would use "shows, slogans and the art of advertising" to get votes, and that "The idea that you can merchandise candidates for high office like breakfast cereal—that you can gather votes like box tops—is, I think, the ultimate indignity to the democratic process."[13] Despite Stevenson's remarks, the convention where he was appearing and the platform on which he was standing had been orchestrated and redesigned by an ad agency hired by his party. Advertising agencies were now firmly entrenched in American presidential politics.

Kennedy-Nixon.   Television was not everyone's medium, however. Some people did not come across well on the TV screen. One of the first politicians to learn this the hard way was Vice-President Richard M. Nixon, the Republican nominee for the presidency in 1960. Nixon agreed to appear in a series of televised debates with his Democratic challenger, the junior senator from Massachusetts, John F. Kennedy.

The relatively unknown Kennedy came across as youthful, witty, intelligent and appealing. Nixon's TV image was less attractive. Kennedy ended up winning the election by a very narrow margin, and many political observers credited the TV debates for his victory. (It is interesting to note that many people who listened to the debates on radio thought that Nixon had won.)

Kennedy also used television effectively while in office. According to McGinniss, the American people forgave John Kennedy for many mistakes, including a

■ John F. Kennedy's ability to project a better visual image during his televised debates with Richard Nixon in 1960 was critical to his narrow victory. Those who watched the debates on television declared Kennedy the winner. Those who heard the debates on radio thought Nixon had won.

botched-up invasion of Cuba, a perilous confrontation with the Soviet Union over missiles in Cuba and a dangerous bluff in foreign policy in Berlin. McGinniss said: "We forgave, followed, and accepted because we liked the way he looked. And he had a pretty wife. Camelot was fun, even for the peasants, as long as it was televised to their huts."[14]

Johnson-Goldwater. Probably the most controversial political advertisement of all times was aired in 1964 by the Doyle Dane Bernbach advertising agency on behalf of President Lyndon B. Johnson (Johnson had assumed the presidency in November 1963 following the assassination of President Kennedy). Known as the "Daisy" commercial, it showed a three-year-old girl plucking the petals of a daisy while miscounting. The soundtrack then shifted to a Voice of Doom, which completed a countdown from 10 and detonated a nuclear explosion. The commercial suggested that Johnson's Republican challenger Barry Goldwater, with his hawkish stand on national defense, would lead the country to nuclear annihilation.

Although Johnson was able to use television advertising effectively to win his own term as president, he soon found that the new medium was not his "cup of tea." Although he had been a very successful politician in Congress, his TV image was stiff and stilted and lacked the charm that Americans had come to expect from their president during the Kennedy years. In 1968 Johnson, whose image and popularity had reached rock bottom due to his escalation of the war in Vietnam, went on television one more time to announce to the nation that he would not seek reelection.

Nixon-Humphrey. In this same year Richard Nixon made another try at the presidency. This time he hired experts to create a warm, friendly and appealing

TV image. A series of commercials showed the "new Nixon" talking with people of all ages and backgrounds. Perhaps not due solely to the new image, Nixon won the presidency in the contest against Johnson's vice-president, Hubert Humphrey.

Raymond K. Price, a former editorial writer for the *New York Herald Tribune* who became a prominent speech writer in Nixon's campaign, was one of the first to suggest that the campaign "attack *personal factors* rather than *historical factors* that were the basis of the low opinion so many people had of Richard Nixon."[15] Feeling there was a problem between the voter and Nixon's image, Price suggested that a new image be created and that the campaign focus on getting a positive response to that image. He said:

> *The response is to the image, not to the man. . . . It's not what's there that counts, it's what's projected—and carrying it one step further, it's not what he projects but rather what the voter receives. It's not the man we have to change, but rather the received impression. And this impression often depends more on the medium and its use than it does on the candidate himself.[16]*

Much of what we know about how Nixon's advisers used television to create a "new Nixon" comes from Joe McGinniss's book *The Selling of the President, 1968*. A newspaper reporter, McGinniss worked on Nixon's advertising and media staff for several months without being detected. The book made it clear that TV images rather than issues had become the new game in American politics.

Nixon-McGovern. Nixon used television effectively again in 1972 to win a landslide victory over Democratic challenger George McGovern. However, when TV began broadcasting the congressional hearings into the Watergate affair in 1973, Nixon's television image began to worsen. Within a year, the man who had won reelection by a landslide was forced to resign from office. Television had made the illegal activities of his administration known to the masses and impeachment was imminent.

Carter-Ford. Gerald R. Ford, who became president following Nixon's resignation, had a difficult time with his television image. Ford's rise to the presidency was the result of a series of unparalleled events. He was a congressman from Michigan when Vice-President Spiro Agnew was forced to resign during a bribery scandal. Nixon appointed Ford vice-president, not expecting that he himself would soon be forced to resign and surrender the presidency to a nonelected vice-president.

At first Ford was treated kindly by the media. Many reporters felt he was a "nice guy" who had become a victim of circumstances. However, when Ford issued a pardon for former President Nixon, the press was outraged. It began scrutinizing his administration and television cameras were there to catch every action. Soon the cameras observed him tumble down the ramp of *Air Force One* in Salzburg, Austria, on his way to a meeting with the Egyptian president, Anwar Sadat. On other occasions he was photographed stumbling, bumping his head and falling while skiing. As the media continued to focus on Ford's apparent lack of coordination, a public image was created of Ford as a stumbler and bumbler.

In 1976 a peanut farmer from Plains, Georgia, challenged Ford for the presidency. James Earl Carter, who wanted people to call him "Jimmy," was a political unknown on the national level, although he had once been governor of Georgia. With the assistance of political consultant Gerald Rafshoon, Carter capitalized on his "plain folks" image (see Chapter 12) and used television and other media to establish a national identity and win the presidency. TV made Carter's face and voice familiar to millions of voters who had never heard of him, and it established his image as a man of the people, a born-again Christian "who had come to rescue them from the Washington devils."[17]

At first Carter was able to use the media to enhance his image as president. Network news people considered the Carter White House more clever in handling TV than earlier administrations. CBS correspondent Bob Schieffer said, "They know when it's to their advantage to be helpful to us. Like the joint swearing in of an antiwar guy [Sam Brown, director of ACTION] and a disabled Vietnam veteran [Max Cleland, head of the Veterans Administration]. You know you're being had, but you do it exactly the way they want it done because they're right, it's good television."[18]

Reagan-Carter.   Television also played a part in Jimmy Carter's downfall. A series of events led to the decline of Carter's public approval ratings from a high of 70 percent to 28 percent in 1979. Among them were scandals involving some of his staff members, the energy crisis, record levels of inflation, his well-publicized and televised flamboyant beer-drinking brother Billy, and finally, on November 4 of that year, the seizure of the American Embassy in Teheran by Iranian students, who captured 63 Americans and held 50 of them hostage for 442 days. As the Americans' captivity continued throughout 1980—an election year—the television networks led each evening's newscast with a count of the number of days Americans had been held (see discussion of agenda setting in Chapter 1).

Jimmy Carter's presidency had faced hard times in a troubled and complex world. His challenger, former California governor Ronald Reagan—who had earlier earned his living performing before movie and TV cameras—developed a television image of a leader who would bring back the glories of the past. According to American mythology, the "good old days" were a time when simple answers solved complex problems and there was no doubt about America's righteousness and superiority. His campaign slogan was "Let's Make America Great Again."

Thanks to his training, Reagan was able to project a relaxed, folksy image as an ordinary man—no politician—during his television debates with Jimmy Carter. Even though Carter was better prepared, Reagan won by appearing to be a calm, confident elder statesman. His now-famous "there you go again" phrase projected an image of a wise and benevolent parent putting down an immature offspring.

After Reagan defeated Jimmy Carter, both Carter and his press secretary, Jody Powell, wrote about what they considered media abuses of power. In his memoirs *The Other Side of the Story,* Powell attacked the country's TV networks and major newspapers. In the *New York Times Book Review,* journalist Lester Bernstein responded:

The fact is that Jimmy Carter as a national figure was almost invented by the media. He owed more to the engines of publicity for his emergence from obscurity to a Presidential nomination than any politician since Wendell Willkie in 1940. If Mr. Powell takes that as a norm, small wonder that he has felt shortchanged ever since.[19]

After his election, Reagan continued to use television effectively. A master at reading scripts, Reagan used Teleprompters to deliver his speeches. He even took his Teleprompter with him to Germany when he was scheduled to deliver a major televised address. His televised State of the Union addresses before Congress (and the ever-faithful Teleprompters) amazed many Americans who thought he was speaking to them without notes. He also used radio to deliver regular Saturday talks with the nation, much as Franklin Delano Roosevelt had done 50 years earlier.

However, despite his mastery of TV, Reagan experienced the same problems with the press that other presidents had faced. The press began zeroing in on erroneous statements he made during news conferences, and there were numerous leaks to the media from within his administration. He soon limited the number of news conferences to a level far below that of his predecessors and attempted to punish anyone in his administration who leaked information. (Other presidents, like Johnson and Nixon, also attempted to stop leaks and punish offenders.) Those news conferences he did hold were scheduled during television's prime time so that his remarks would be carried live and could not be edited by the networks.

The Reagan administration began to stage news events and set up barriers for press access to news it didn't want covered. When the United States invaded the Caribbean island of Grenada in 1983, the news media were not told about it until after the event. Because of Reagan's popularity, the media found little support from the public for their protests over the obvious censorship of the invasion.

Reagan-Mondale.   When Reagan ran for reelection in 1984, he took full advantage of the media to project his "presidential image" (see Box 14.2). Steven R. Weisman, chief White House correspondent for the *New York Times,* summed up Reagan's use of the media during this election:

[I]t is increasingly evident that something extraordinary has happened to the relationship between President Reagan and the press. What is now clear is that Mr. Reagan has ignored some of the unstated ground rules under which reporters have traditionally covered the Presidency. As a consequence, he has dramatically altered the kind of information the public receives about him and his administration.

. . . He and his aides have . . . achieved a new level of control over the mechanics of modern communication—the staging of news events for maximum press coverage, the timing of announcements to hit the largest television audiences. Moreover, the President has displayed his news media artistry at a time when television has become the dominant means by which the public gets its news. From the beginning of his Presidency, Mr. Reagan and his aides have understood and exploited what they acknowledge to be the built-in tendency of television to emphasize appearances and impressions more than information.

BOX 14.2

TELEVISION POLITICAL ADVERTISING, REAGAN STYLE

In 1984, after two incumbents seeking a second term had been voted out of office (Gerald Ford in 1976 and Jimmy Carter in 1980), incumbent president Ronald Reagan won reelection by a landslide. He carried every state except his challenger's home state of Minnesota and the District of Columbia.

Assisting Reagan was a cleverly developed advertising campaign that created an image of success, patriotism and a regal presidency. The image was the work of a team of successful Madison Avenue ad executives called the Tuesday Team, Inc. Although these advertising superstars had limited political experience, they had been successful in developing singing feline lyrics for Meow Mix and bandwagon-inducing commercials for Pepsi-Cola. This was considered an asset rather than liability by the Reagan people, who wanted commercials different from the typical ones that attacked the opponent and defended the incumbent's record.

Masterminding the campaign were White House aides Michael Deaver, a former PR account executive who had been assisting Reagan with his image since his campaign for governor of California in 1966, and James Baker, Reagan's chief of staff. They decided to stress broad themes rather than specific issues in order to play up a feeling of patriotism and prosperity. What they didn't want was to spend time defending Reagan's policies from attacks by challenger Walter Mondale.

The Tuesday Team used 16mm film (rather than inferior videotape), lush music, elaborate lighting and the latest in dubbing and editing techniques to create polished television ads. The country was flooded with TV images of President Reagan looking presidential. There were scenes of him in the White House rose garden, picnicking with an Alabama family, talking to assembly-line workers in Michigan and putting on a Smokey the Bear hat in Kentucky—to show his concern for the environment. Some of the ads featured staged campaign rallies with bands playing and clean-cut-looking kids and ordinary folks waving American flags in support of the president. The slogan and voiceover on the commercials said "President Reagan—Leadership That's Working."

In addition, Reagan's political campaign appearances were staged to recreate the images in the ads. People were given flags to wave and "appropriate"-looking people were moved to the front of the crowd. This was done to ensure that the ads would look like actual news events rather than harsh commercial interruptions of the evening's TV entertainment. The ads were designed to blur the line between political commercials and the 6 o'clock news.

Some 40 variations of the ads were developed and aired on network television, at a cost of $25 million. While Reagan's ads were helping build his landslide, Mondale's television campaign was using 20 different commercials featuring the typical "attacking candidate." Mondale's $20 million expenditure for the commercials translated into relatively few votes.

Mondale was well aware of the role television played in his defeat. In a postelection news conference he said: "Modern politics requires television. I think you know I've never really warmed up to television, and in fairness to television, it's never really warmed up to me."

Central to the President's overall strategy has been his unusual ability to deal with television and print reporters on his own terms—to decide when, where and how he will engage them. In short, the art of controlled access.[20]

The Reagan presidency ran into more difficulty during its second term, when the press disclosed that the administration had been selling arms to Iran and diverting the profits to rebel forces in Nicaragua. After Congress held televised hearings into the activities, a national poll showed that most people didn't believe Reagan when he said he didn't know about the diversion.

Despite this trouble, two phrases came to characterize the Reagan presidency. Friends as well as critics agreed that he was the *Great Communicator*—probably the best one ever to hold the office. Critics also called him the *Teflon President,* because—despite the various troubles in his administration—no blame ever seemed to stick to him.

Bush-Dukakis.   The 1988 presidential campaign between Vice-President George Bush and Massachusetts Governor Michael Dukakis was labeled one of the dirtiest in modern times. It also was a classic example of how political consultants could use the media to completely change the public's perception of a candidate and create a new positive image in less than three months.

When Dukakis was nominated in July as the Democratic party's standard bearer, he led in the polls. Vice-President Bush, who had spent eight years in the shadow of the popular Republican president, Ronald Reagan, had been perceived by many voters as a "wimp" while Dukakis, a new face on the national political scene, was regarded as a reformer who would bring new life to national politics.

Thanks to a cleverly staged showdown with CBS anchorman Dan Rather and numerous TV ads that showed Bush as a tough anticrime candidate, the Republican candidate was able to reverse the polls and win the election. Helping him in his efforts were an effective technique to paint the challenger Dukakis as a "liberal" and capitalizing on the "L" word during the campaign; wrapping himself in the American flag and as a protector of the Pledge of Allegiance while insinuating that his challenger was against the pledge; and a series of "Willie Horton" ads. Horton was an African-American rapist and murderer who was sentenced to life in prison without parole in Massachusetts in 1974. He participated in a weekend furlough program and raped a white woman. Although the furlough program was established by Dukakis's Republican predecessor, blame for the furloughs and Horton's evil deed were placed on the liberal Dukakis. (Many felt the Willie Horton ads exploited racial prejudice.)

Following the 1988 campaign, many called for political campaign reforms. Some suggested that candidates be required to focus on a different issue each week and that television be required to make air time available for the debate of these weekly issues. What did emerge, however, was the efforts by the print media to analyze more critically the content of television political advertising.

EFFECTIVE POLITICAL MEDIA

Although television has emerged as one of the most powerful political tools in election campaigns, it has been by no means the only one. By the 1990s, three forms of media were being used effectively by political consultants—vote videos, direct mail and TV ads. All three of these approaches are extremely expensive and have driven the cost of political campaigns sky high. In fact, this escalation of campaign costs has led to numerous attempts to legislate campaign-finance reforms. Most of the suggested reforms, however, are considered violations of First Amendment right to free speech.

Vote Videos. The newest campaign medium is the vote video, which is distributed to supporters to show friends and other prospective voters in their homes or rented halls. The videos offer razzle-dazzle productions of the candidates shaking hands, flashing smiles, throwing footballs and spitting forth popular slogans for campaign issues. The use of videos in political campaigns has brought a new dimension of political image making into the electoral process. According to some political observers, issues are no longer important in elections and have been replaced with video images.*

Direct Mail. Ranking at the top of most political consultants' lists of effective media for a number of years has been direct mail. Computerized equipment can now generate what appear to be personalized letters with the recipient's name throughout and computerized mailing lists can separate groups to receive different messages. A candidate can stress strong support for Social Security in a mailing to older citizens while emphasizing the need for government-funded day care in a mailing to younger voters.

The most effective type of direct mail, according to research by Hal Evry's Western Opinion Research Center in Los Angeles, is a letter from a personal friend or a well-respected community leader.[21] This particular technique applies the opinion-leader phenomenon (discussed earlier) to our modern high-tech mass culture.

Television Advertising. The third effective medium is, of course, television advertising. Like the vote videos, TV commercials sell images rather than discuss issues. These ads are cleverly designed and carefully produced to achieve maximum results. They are often pretested before airing (see Box 14.3).

Author George McKenna, discussing whether we are manipulated by the media, asked, "Who has not seen those 30-second spots showing shirt-sleeved candidates walking through blighted streets looking concerned? Or candidates pledging to get tough on criminals without saying how they would do it? Or a candidate listening sympathetically to *ordinary* Americans telling him their woes, while a voiceover assures us that he cares?"[22]

According to Austin Ranney, former president of the American Political Science Association, television does not necessarily depict reality, but TV's reality has become "the reality in politics." In his book *Channels of Power*, he said that television has reshaped American political culture, weakened political parties, strengthened candidates who have media charisma, weakened the presidency because the president is in the constant glare of TV's cameras and strengthened the government because it can hide from the publicity spotlight.[23]

An Opposing View. Not everyone agrees about TV's power to sell political candidates. Some feel that selective exposure, perception and retention (see Chapter 1) help voters shield themselves from these mediated images.

---

* In 1987 a large developer facing a referendum on a city council approval of a billion-dollar hotel-convention center that would transform a small upscale California bedroom community into a convention center on the scale of Las Vegas or Miami spent $50,000 to produce and mail a slick video promoting the virtues of his project to all 1,200 voters in the community. His efforts paid off, the community transformation was approved by a 56–44 percent vote.

BOX 14.3

▪ PRETESTING POLITICAL CAMPAIGN ADS ▪

Sophisticated marketing techniques used by the packaged-goods industry are being applied to political advertising campaigns as well. The cynical charge that candidates are being packaged and sold to the public like bars of soap is true to the extent that both use similar test-marketing strategies.

The latest strategy that gained popularity in the 1980s has been pretesting political television ads. According to *Advertising Age* (February 13, 1986), the number of campaigns and candidates pretesting the ads had grown three- to four-fold during the past five years.

Washington-based Democratic pollster Peter Hart says that political ad makers have followed the commercial field because dollars are scarce and the "message must be on target." Political groups are spending some $10,000 to $30,000 to pretest ads before spending hundreds of thousands or millions of dollars on statewide and national campaigns.

Some ads are pretested in studios where the commercial is shown along with other political commercials and television programs. Others are tested over the air in sample markets with follow-up polling. Other times people are shown commercial story boards and asked to select the one that appeals to them the most.

Although pretesting is more expensive, it seems to be producing results at election time.

Two political scientists, Thomas Patterson and Robert McClure, studying the 1972 Nixon-McGovern campaign, found that spot TV commercials do more to educate voters about the issues than manipulate them about the candidates.[24]

They concluded that strong evidence for advertising's ineffectiveness comes from a look at the changes in voters' images of the candidates after presidential ads were aired on television. They conducted a study using a series of George McGovern commercials, showing him in small groups designed to portray him as a man who cared about people. What they found was very little change in public attitudes.[25]

However, the study did determine that people tended to project their own political biases into the candidates' commercials and to see what they wanted to see, rather than what the advertisement intended for them to see.

Here are some of the reactions they received to the McGovern commercials:

He really cares what's happened to disabled vets. They told him how badly they've been treated and he listened. He will help them.

    —37-year-old pro-McGovern viewer

McGovern was talking with these disabled vets. He doesn't really care about them. He's just using them to get sympathy.

    —33-year-old pro-Nixon viewer

It was honest, down-to-earth. People were talking and he was listening.

    —57-year-old pro-McGovern viewer

Those commercials are so phoney. He doesn't care.

    —45-year-old pro-Nixon viewer

McGovern had his coat off and his tie was hanging down. It was so relaxed, and he seemed to really be concerned with those workers.

—31-year-old pro-McGovern viewer

He is trying hard to look like one of the boys. You know, roll up the shirt sleeves and loosen the tie. It's just too much for me to take.

—39-year-old pro-Nixon viewer[26]

Should the System Be Changed? Some political observers advocate major changes in the use of television in American elections. Claiming that politics has degenerated into an effort to sell the prettiest package, they argue that political advertising should consist only of candidates' "talking heads." Under this plan, no skillfully produced commercials designed to sell images rather than issues would be allowed.

In France, for example, political advertising is not allowed on television. Instead, French TV broadcasts five-minute statements by the various candidates following the evening news (a different candidate each evening). Many feel that such a system is preferable, because issues cannot be discussed in 30-second spots, and longer statements are needed for the voter to get a true picture of where candidates stand.

This argument has one flaw: it presumes that people will watch the longer political broadcasts. TV ratings for full-length political programs indicate otherwise. While people usually don't bother to change the channel during a 30-second commercial, they are likely to switch the channel to *Golden Girls* or *Cheers* if faced with a long broadcast by a political talking head.

Such a change would most likely take politics out of the popular culture and limit the dialogue between candidates and voters to an interested elite. Whatever its faults, at least the 30-second spot seems to reach the masses. Perhaps the new efforts by major newspapers to analyze the TV ads and point out where they stray from reality will help correct the deficiency that exists.

NEWS COVERAGE OF ELECTIONS

While most of the criticism of the American political process has been focused on how image makers use the media to sell candidates, news reporters have also been criticized for adding to campaign confusion.

Character Analysis. Following the Watergate affair, when the American people learned that the president of the United States had lied about his knowledge of illegal activities by members of his administration, the press began to pay closer attention to analyzing the character of presidential candidates. In 1987 this heightened scrutiny succeeded in derailing two presidential campaigns. The leading Democratic presidential candidate—Gary Hart—withdrew from the 1988 presidential race after the press published stories about his involvement with actress-model Donna Rice. At a press conference called to announce his decision to quit the race, an angry Hart said:

■ Actress-model Donna Rice and presidential candidate Gary Hart on the cover of the *National Enquirer* during what the tabloid called a "fun-filled weekend in the Bahamas." This kind of media coverage forced the front-runner of the 1988 Democratic nomination out of the race.

We're all going to have to seriously question the system for selecting our national leaders that reduces the press of this nation to hunters and presidential candidates to being hunted, that has reporters in bushes, false and inaccurate stories printed, photographers peeking in our windows, swarms of helicopters hovering over our roof, and my very strong wife close to tears because she can't even get in her own house at night without being harassed. And then, after all that, ponderous pundits wonder in mock seriousness why some of the best people in this country choose not to run for high office.[27]

Several months later Democratic presidential candidate Joseph Biden pulled out of the race because the media had focused on statements he had made that were either false (he had said that he had graduated near the top of his class in law school when records showed he was nearer to the bottom) or had plagiarized from speeches of others. Not long afterward, Republican candidate Pat Robertson was apologizing for hiding the fact that his marriage took place shortly before the birth of his son, rather than on the day of conception as he had said earlier. "I sowed some wild oats in my youth," he explained.

Some criticized the news media for focusing on personal characteristics rather than issues. Others, however, defended the press by saying that presidential candidates' moral character and judgment was important for voters to know about before an election.

Horse-Race Effect.   Another complaint about the press during election campaigns is that reporters tend to focus too much on who is winning the race. This criticism was probably most intense during the 1984 election between incumbent

■ No matter how hard Democratic challenger Walter Mondale and his vice-presidential running mate Geraldine Ferraro (pictured here with her husband) tried to focus on the issues in the 1984 presidential campaign, the mass media agenda focused on how much farther ahead President Ronald Reagan was in the polls.

Republican Reagan and Democratic challenger Mondale. Regardless of how hard Mondale and his running mate Geraldine Ferraro tried to talk about the issues, the front-page stories and evening news broadcasts dwelt on who was ahead in the race. This phenomenon has been characterized by some as the *horse-race* mentality of the media.

Projecting Winners.   Another election complaint is directed at television news. Ever since TV began projecting the winners of national contests in the 1960s, critics have claimed that the practice was skewing election results. TV networks usually project winners based on computer sampling of polls and surveys conducted as people leave the precincts (known as exit polling). The problem is that in the past the networks have projected winners long before the polls closed in the Western time zones.

In 1980, for example, President Jimmy Carter was televised giving his concession speech before the polls were closed in the West. Some Democratic congressional candidates said they lost their particular elections because many Democrats in these Western states didn't bother to vote after seeing Carter concede.

For two decades Congress and the public tried to persuade the networks to delay projecting winners until all the polls were closed. Network executives responded by saying that they weren't about to withhold information from the American people temporarily. Yet these same network executives regularly delayed broadcasting the 7 o'clock news in the West for three hours each night (the newscast originating in the East at 7 P.M. is actually airing at 4 p.m. Western time). In November 1986 the networks finally agreed not to predict winners in any state until the polls had closed in that state.

Positive Election Coverage.   These trends should not be interpreted as a blanket condemnation of the media in political elections, however. Some newspapers do attempt to cover issues, and the major television networks have made air time available for presidential debates on the issues. Although the ratings for the televised presidential debates seem to be slipping (it was estimated that between 70 and 80 million people watched the Reagan-Mondale debates, down from 120 million in 1980), they do draw large audiences and expose viewers to candidates discussing the issues. Some criticize the debates, however, because they are highly artificial events (ground rules must be approved by both sides before they will agree to debate) and have little resemblance to actual debates.

Television news shows like *Meet the Press* also do an effective job of getting candidates to discuss the issues. The only problem, however, is that these shows' ratings are much lower than those of the evening news, sports and sitcoms.

Political observers see positive changes in the print media's "truth boxes" that analyze TV political ads. There is hope that the more widely viewed TV news media will also begin the practice. If this happens, we may see more responsible and truthful campaign advertisements emerge.

SUMMARY

The development of a mass culture dominated by the media has made major changes in the American political system, changes some observers feel threaten the very core of American democracy.

In the 1940s the first studies were conducted to determine whether the mass media were changing American voting patterns. The studies showed that opinion leaders, not the media, were directly affecting voter behavior, although the mass media played an indirect role by influencing the opinion leaders. This discovery led to the formulation of the two-step flow theory of political communication: the mass media influence opinion leaders, who in turn influence others.

Follow-up studies in the 1960s and 1970s, however, indicated that the American political system was changing. The long-standing dominance of political parties was waning and political consultants were replacing party bosses. These consultants had advertising, public relations and opinion-polling backgrounds and had moved into the political arena to sell candidates directly to the American people through the mass media, much like others in their professions were selling soap and detergents.

During the twentieth century, the mass media and political advertising began playing significant roles in selling political images. Television, which has become one of the most dominant forms of mass communication in our culture, has emerged as a powerful influence in determining the political destiny of this country. It helped create a winning image for little-known Senator John Kennedy, who narrowly defeated Vice-President Richard Nixon in the 1960 presidential election; led to a decline in popularity of Lyndon B. Johnson; allowed Nixon to win the presidency eight years later by building a more positive television image; and gave national exposure to a little-known peanut farmer and former Georgia governor, Jimmy Carter. By the 1980s the presidency had been turned over to Ronald Reagan, who had made his living communicating in front of the camera. Through his effective use of television, he was soon regarded as one of the most effective communicators ever to hold the office of president.

American political candidates, managed by political consultants, are now using vote videos and direct mail as well as television advertising to get their messages across. Not everyone, however, gives TV so much credit for creating political images. Some studies have indicated that selective exposure, perception and retention play a bigger role in the election process. These studies contend, for example, that people project their own biases into television political commercials and see only what they want to see.

News reporters have been criticized for running stories about candidates' personal lives, downplaying issues and focusing too much on who is winning. Television news has also been criticized for projecting winners on election night before the polls have closed in the West. This has kept many Western voters away from the polls, critics contend.

Not all campaign coverage by the media has been inadequate, however. Television has been instrumental in presenting presidential debates to the American public. Newspapers are now beginning to give better coverage of campaigns by analyzing political ads and reporting on their accuracy. It is hoped that television will begin the practice and that such a trend will make advertisements more truthful and responsible.

THOUGHT QUESTIONS

1 What effect will "truth boxes" have on future political campaigns? Do you think the electronic media will follow the print media's lead in analyzing TV ads?
2 What kinds of political campaign finance reforms can be legislated without violating a candidate's free speech rights?
3 Examine some current political advertisements. Do they insult your intelligence, or are they straightforward, honest accounts of the issues?
4 What are the pros and cons of the argument that TV should ban glitzy political ads and replace them with candidates talking about issues?
5 What do you think about Hal Evry's ideas for political reform?

NOTES

1. Paul Lazarsfeld, Bernard Berelson and Hazel Gaudet, *The People's Choice* (New York: Columbia University Press, 1968), p. 148.

2. Ibid., p. 151.

3. Angus Campbell, Phillip E. Converge, Warren E. Miller and Donald E. Stokes, *The American Voter* (New York: Wiley, 1960), p. 32.

4. Robert Agranoff, *The New Style in*

Election Campaigns (Boston: Holbrook, 1976), p. 6.

5. Sidney Blumenthal, *The Permanent Campaign* (Boston: Beacon Press, 1980), p. 12.

6. Paul Simon, *The Once and Future Democrats: Strategies for Change* (New York: Continuum, 1982), p. 86.

7. John Tebbel and Sarah Miles Watts, *The Press and the Presidency: From George Washington to Ronald Reagan* (New York: Oxford University Press, 1985), p. 541.

8. Donald L. Shaw and Maxwell E. McCombs, *The Emergence of American Political Issues: The Agenda-Setting Function of the Press* (St. Paul, Minn.: West, 1977), p. 3.

9. Quoted in George McKenna, *Media Voices: Debating Critical Issues in Mass Media* (Guilford, Conn.: Dushkin, 1982), p. 91.

10. Stephen Fox, *The Mirror Makers: A History of American Advertising and Its Creators* (New York: Morrow, 1984), p. 307.

11. Ibid., p. 308.

12. Quoted in Fox, p. 310.

13. Ibid.

14. McKenna, pp. 91–92.

15. Ibid., p. 95.

16. Ibid.

17. Tebbel and Watts, p. 522.

18. Quoted in Ibid., p. 526.

19. Lester Bernstein, "The Other Side of the Story, by Jody Powell," *New York Times Book Review,* April 1, 1984, p. 7.

20. Steven H. Weisman, "The President and the Press: The Art of Controlled Access," *New York Times Magazine,* October 14, 1984.

21. Hal Evry, *The Selling of a Candidate: The Winning Formula* (Los Angeles: Western Opinion Research Center, 1977), p. 67.

22. McKenna, p. 97.

23. Austin Ranney, *Channels of Power* (New York: Basic Books, 1983), p. 69.

24. Thomas Patterson and Robert D. McClure, *The Unseeing Eye: The Myth of Television Power in National Politics* (New York: Putnam, 1976).

25. Ibid.

26. Ibid., p. 114.

27. "Hart Statement Text: I'm Not a Beaten Man; I'm an Angry, Defiant Man," *Los Angeles Times,* May 9, 1987, p. 25.

ADDITIONAL READING

Bowers, Thomas A. "Candidate Advertising: The Agenda Is the Message," in Donald Shaw and Maxwell McCombs, *The Emergence of American Political Issues: The Agenda-Setting Function of the Press.* St. Paul, Minn.: West, 1977.

Chagall, David. *The New King Makers,*

New York: Harcourt Brace Jovanovich, 1981.

Chester, Edward W. *Radio, Television and American Politics.* New York: Sheed & Ward, 1969.

Edelman, Murray. *The Symbolic Uses of Politics.* Urbana: University of Illinois Press, 1980.

Jacobson, Gary. *The Politics of Congressional Elections.* Boston: Little, Brown, 1983.

Jamieson, Kathleen Hall. *Packaging the Presidency: A History and Criticism of Presidential Campaign Advertising.* New York: Oxford University Press, 1984.

Kelley, Stanley. *Interpreting Elections.* Princeton, N.J.: Princeton University Press, 1983.

Key, V. O. *The Responsible Electorate.* Cambridge, Mass.: Harvard University Press, 1966.

Kraus, Sidney, and Davis, Dennis. *The Effects of Mass Communication on Political Behavior.* University Park: Pennsylvania State University Press, 1976.

Lamm, Richard, and Grossman, Arnold. *1988.* New York: St. Martin's, 1985.

McGinniss, Joe. *The Selling of the President, 1968,* New York: Trident Press, 1969.

Milbrath, Lester, and Goel, M. L. *Political Participation.* Skokie, Ill.: Rand McNally, 1977.

Nimmo, Dan D., and Combs, James E. *Mediated Political Realities.* New York: Longman, 1983.

O'Keefe, Garrett J., and Atwood, L. Edwin. "Communication and Election Campaigns," in *Handbook of Political Communication,* ed. Dan D. Nimmo and Keith R. Sanders. Beverly Hills, Calif.: Sage, 1981.

Patterson, Thomas E. *The Mass Media Election.* New York: Praeger, 1980.

Polsby, Nelson W., and Wildavsky, Aaron. *Presidential Elections.* New York: Scribner's, 1976.

Rivers, William. *The Opinion Makers.* Boston: Beacon Press, 1965.

Scott, Andrew M., and Wallace, Earle. *Politics, U.S.A.: Cases on the American Democratic Process,* 3rd ed. Toronto: Macmillan, 1969.

This video Walkman, introduced by Japan's Sony, is just one of a number of new electronic technologies that are rapidly moving us into the information age. The portable combination video recorder and television set weighs 2.4 pounds.

CHANGING TRENDS IN MEDIA TECHNOLOGY

The decade of the nineties is going to be one in which the traditional newspaper may face a decline, extinction or at least complete internal self-reappraisal.
—Anthony Smith,
Goodbye
Gutenberg

During the 1990s we will witness many technological changes in the way we communicate. Even books, like the one you are reading, will probably change from their 500-year-old format to exciting "user-friendly" forms enhanced by the computer age. According to futurist Alvin Toffler, books in the future will be read on book-sized video screens. These electronic devices will be able to immediately translate foreign language editions, enlarge or reduce the size of the type, change the type styles, adjust the degree of reading difficulty, and allow the readers of novels to increase or decrease the levels of violence and sexual explicitness to fit individual tastes.

All of these new "user-friendly" options along with the content itself will be delivered on tiny microchips or CD-ROMs (now used in libraries to deliver large amounts of information to computer screens).

Toffler has been forecasting technological changes since his first successful book, *Future Shock,* was published in 1970. His vision of changing trends has been remarkably accurate. In 1980, his book *The Third Wave* explained how civilization was in transition between the second and third great cycles of human history. The first cycle was the agrarian society, which existed until the second cycle, the industrial age, was ushered in during the late eighteenth and nineteenth centuries. The third cycle, which is now replacing the industrial society, is the information age.

In his latest book, *Powershift,* published in 1990, Toffler tells how the information explosion is causing turmoil among established institutions—such as governments, banks, trade unions and the media—as the industrial age gives way to the information age. According to Toffler, power is directly linked with knowledge and knowledge has become central to economic development. He sees a shifting of power in our culture, transforming such institutions as finance, politics and media. These powershifts, he contends, will create a radically different society.

In addition to economic turmoil, the information age is bringing us a wide range of new communication technologies. This technological explosion began escalating during the 1980s and seems to be gaining snowball-like momentum. Becoming commonplace in our culture are such things as coaxial cables, fiber optics, satellite communication, computers, VCRs, fax machines and cellular telephones, to name just a few. Sociologist Daniel Bell pointed out that by the 1980s the United States had more people working in the production of information than in manufacturing and agriculture combined.

COMMUNICATION REVOLUTION

What is occurring in the field of communication has been described as follows: "All modes of communication we humans have devised since the beginning of humanity are coming together into a single electronic system, driven by computers."[1]

Advances in electronic technology, particularly in the fields of telecommunication and computerization, have already affected the ways we receive radio, TV and print communication. And the combination of home computers, satellites, television, telephones and cable systems is converting some homes into communication centers. Toffler predicted the day when many homes would serve as electronic communication centers—his term is *electronic cottages*—where people work and study.[2] This trend has already started.

Finding a Niche.   How fast the new technologies will become commonplace depends on numerous factors. Just as the mass-media technologies introduced in the nineteenth century had to find a niche in our culture, so too must today's electronic inventions struggle to find their place.

■ "Telecommuting" is becoming an alternative to fighting busy freeways each day. Workers are able to use computers at home to link up to their offices so they can work at home.

Consumer acceptance of new technologies, however, is just the last step in taking a new technological development from invention to widespread use. First engineers and scientists must invent the item, then venture capitalists and shareholders must be willing to gamble on the product's success and then marketing people must sell the concept to the consumer.

Of all the new communication technologies that have been developed in recent years, cable television, satellite communication, computers and home video equipment have had the most significant impact on our culture. In this decade we may also see major changes in our culture as a result of teletext, videotext, fiber optics, digital sound, multipoint distribution service, direct broadcast satellites, and high-definition and low-power television. These innovations may bring about the day when we read our newspapers and magazines on TV screens, watch our favorite TV shows and video movies on larger-than-life screens on our living-room walls, do most of our routine banking and shopping from our computerized home information centers, and carry our telephones around in our pockets, purses or, perhaps, wear them on our wrists like watches.

CABLE TELEVISION

Cable television began in the late 1940s as a way to relay television signals to remote communities that could not receive them through the airwaves. However, following the 1975 launching of RCA's communication satellite SATCOM I, the cable industry found a new niche—serving metropolitan areas as well as rural communities with expanded TV programming.

As a technology, cable somewhat resembles the telephone, as it involves the wiring of individual homes. Some have said that the cable industry represents the "third wiring of America" (the first and second being the telegraph and the telephone).[3]

Expanded Programming.   Home Box Office (HBO), was the pioneer in expanding programming to the masses via satellite-fed cable service. In 1975 it rented a transponder on SATCOM I and made first-run movies available to cable system operators for a fee.

Cable now provides a wide variety of programming, from standard network broadcasts to a myriad of specialized channels available to cable companies via satellite. Although capable of carrying more than 100 channels on some systems, most cable companies still offer only 36 or fewer. However, even this number has greatly altered American TV viewing habits. By 1990 more than 52 million homes (57 percent) had cable and the industry was grossing nearly $16 billion a year from subscribers and an additional $2.3 billion from advertising revenue (see Box 15.1).[4]

Viewers hooked up to cable can receive a wide variety of programming, including 24-hour-a-day news, arts and entertainment, all sports, all weather, continuous congressional coverage, religious programming, movies, old TV reruns, children's programming, ethnic programs and even soft-core pornography.

Public Access.   Many cable companies also provide public-access channels that local citizens can use for public service programming. Schools sometimes use these channels for home education; some communities televise local city council meetings or other programming on local issues.

Two-Way Cable.   Although most cable TV operations involve one-way communication, cable is capable of two-way interaction, much like the telephone. One of the first of these installations was the *Qube* system, introduced in 1977 by Warner-Amex in Columbus, Ohio. The system gave viewers an unlimited range of feedback opportunities. They could, for instance, choose the endings to certain dramatic programs, participate in game shows, and instantly express opinions in polls. The *Qube* system, however, was not economically successful and went out of business in 1984 after losing $30 million.

Experimentation with two-way cable continues. A Canadian company, Videotron, has some 50,000 subscribers to an interactive TV system. In this country, GTE and J.C. Penney are experimenting with two-way cable as a home shopping service. (However, one-way cable, coupled with the use of the telephone to call in orders, has not hindered the success of home shopping channels. In 1990, there were 60 million people watching home shopping channels and placing an average of 200,000 orders a day. One such company, Home Shopping Club, has more than $1 billion in orders each year.) In addition to viewer participation and home shopping, two-way cable technology is used for home-security systems.

BOX 15.1

▪ CABLE TV ALTERS VIEWING HABITS ▪

The growth of cable TV has been phenomenal. In 1980 22 percent of American households subscribed to cable. By 1990 that figure had grown to 57 percent and was projected to increase to 65 percent by 1992.

This rapid expansion of cable into the popular culture has reduced the influence of the major over-the-air networks and curtailed the growth of their advertising revenue. For example, in 1980 advertisers spent $58 million on cable networks. Ten years later that figure had climbed 40 times for an annual expenditure of $2.3 billion. This figure is projected to double to $4.7 billion by 1995.

Because of their dual revenue stream—advertising and subscription fees—cable networks can offer more specialization in programming than the major over-the-air networks can. As a result, Americans by 1990 were spending more on cable programming than on movie attendance and videocassette rentals combined.

Advertising agencies now see the United States divided into two television universes: cable at 57 percent penetration and over-the-air broadcasts at 43 percent.

Some of the major cable networks that are competing with the over-the-air networks for advertising revenue include:

Arts & Entertainment
Black Entertainment Television
Consumer News and Business Channel
ESPN
Financial News Network
Galavision/ECO
Group W Satellite Communications
Lifetime
MTV Networks (MTV, Nickelodeon, Nick at Nite, VH-1, HA!)
Madison Square Garden Network
Movietime Channel
Prime Ticket Network
Mizlou Sports News Network
SportsChannel America
The Comedy Channel
The Discovery Channel
The Family Channel
The Learning Channel
The Nostalgia Channel
The Weather Channel
Turner Broadcasting Sales (CNN, Headline News, TBS and TNT)
USA Network

Some media critics claim that two-way cable is potentially dangerous because it is very similar to the monitoring devices used by Big Brother in Orwell's *1984*. An Orwellian-style monitoring system has already been used—on volunteers—to observe purchasing trends and advertising effectiveness (see Box 15.2).

Pay-TV.   In addition to basic cable service, most cable companies also offer to subscribers for an additional fee pay-TV channels. These include HBO, Showtime, Cinemax, The Movie Channel, the Disney Channel and the Playboy Channel.

The two largest cable companies in the United States—Tele-Communications, Inc. (TCI) and Time Warner's American Television & Communications Corporation—own controlling interests in many of these pay-TV services. Time Warner owns HBO and Cinemax and TCI owns 50 percent of Showtime.

Pay-Per-View.   Besides the above pay-TV channels there are cable TV services available for a pay-per-view cost. These services have featured primarily first-run

BOX 15.2

■ "PEOPLE METERS": HIGH-TECH MEDIA MONITORS ■

Did you know that 27 percent more spaghetti sauce is sold to soap opera fans of *Search for Tomorrow* than to fans of *All My Children*? This bit of trivia was very useful to Campbell Soup executives, makers of Prego spaghetti sauce, when they were deciding how best to spend their advertising dollars.

This and much more specific information like it is now available to advertisers through new high-tech research technology. Data about television viewing habits and consumer buying patterns are being monitored in certain parts of the country by new computerized gadgets, called *people meters*. These devices consist of a remote-control keyboard that provides data on who is watching TV. When a person turns on the television set, he or she punches a code into the hand-held keyboard. The computer automatically sends each viewer's age, sex and program choice over telephone lines to a computerized data bank.

Some marketing research firms contract with households to provide additional information. People are paid $400 a year to run a hand-held scanner over their grocery shopping receipt so that their regular purchases can also be fed into a computer. Their buying patterns are then compared to the TV advertisements that have been seen, and the ads' effectiveness is measured.

In 1987, much to the displeasure of the television networks, the A.C. Nielsen Co.—the major television rating service—began using 4,000 people meters to determine television audience sizes. (Prior to people meters, Nielsen used two systems to gather data: first, electronic meters wired to television sets in 1,700 homes recorded the channels that the set was tuned to when it was on, second, people in 2,600 other homes filled out diaries of their television-viewing habits.) The networks and advertisers have long relied on data gathered by Nielsen to calculate audience sizes for each program, which largely determine the advertising rates charged by the networks.

According to the new people-meter ratings, audiences were some 10 percent smaller than had been determined by the traditional method. The networks immediately challenged the new technology, claiming that it was biased in favor of people who were comfortable with new technology and against older, more traditional viewers who hadn't yet warmed to computer technology. Network executives also claimed that the technology exaggerated the impact of cable households, which watch less network programming.

Network dissatisfaction with the new Nielsen system in 1990 led to overtures by AGB, a British-based people-meter rating system owned by Robert Maxwell (see Chapter 3) to provide the American networks with an alternative to Nielsen. Another rating system, Arbitron, has been measuring local TV and radio audiences in the U.S. for years, but has yet to expand to national ratings. It is currently

movies and boxing matches. However, many expect that by the end of this decade a lot of the TV sports programs we currently watch on commercial and cable TV will be offered only on a pay-per-view basis. One such event may be the Super Bowl, which currently generates between $35 and $40 million in advertising revenue. That figure could climb to between $600 million and a billion dollars if the program were sold on a pay-per-view basis.

Some contend that sports fans will accept the conversion of sporting events from traditional cable TV to a pay-per-view basis because they will only be paying for the programs they watch.

Cable Deregulation.   The biggest threat to the cable industry in the early 1990s came from Congress. In 1984, Congress deregulated the cable industry. Prior to that time local governments (such as counties and city councils) controlled the

BOX 15.2 *Cont.*

using people meters in Denver and some look for it to go national as an alternative to Nielsen.

People meters seem to be just the tip of the iceberg when it comes to high-tech's invasion into the area of research on American mass-media consumption patterns. A Seattle, Washington, company has developed a device that senses, through ultrasound waves, how many viewers are in front of the television set and whether any of them leave the room while the TV set is on.

Research is also being done on devices that can identify viewers by their voice and transmit psycho-logical data by analyzing voice stress and other indicators.

Technology is even being developed to monitor print-media consumer patterns. Two New Jersey companies—Pretesting Co. in Englewood and Perception Research Service Inc. of Englewood Cliffs—are attempting to interest publishers in glasses that track reader eye movements (to show what they actually look at on a page) and digital watches that record on a microchip what magazines a person reads.

amount of money cable companies could charge for their services. Governments also set quality standards.

After deregulation the industry grew at a rapid rate. By 1990 there were some 821 cable systems in the United States. However, public criticism of the cable industry also grew. Because there was usually only one cable system serving a community, people complained that the cable business was an unregulated monopoly. The most common complaints concerned rising rates, shoddy service and long afternoons of waiting for the cable repairman to arrive.

Public criticism became so great by 1990 that numerous bills were introduced in Congress calling for a reregulation of the industry. Some of the bills even called for allowing the telephone companies to get into the business of carrying TV signals to provide people with alternatives to the local cable company. The threat of reregulation caused the bottom to drop out of cable company stocks.

SATELLITE COMMUNICATION

The new telecommunication technology ushered in by the space age has affected the mass media of radio, television and newspapers as well as cable television. The *satellite* is an electronic relay system that operates from outer space. U.S. communication satellites are placed in orbit some 22,300 miles above the equator so that they will rotate at the same speed as the earth (appearing to be stationary) and look down on the continental United States.

How It Works.   Satellites are either launched into space by rockets or placed in orbit by space shuttles. They carry transponders that pick up and retransmit signals sent from the ground. Each transponder can carry one television signal or 1,000 telephone messages at a time. Most satellites have 24 transponders, but in the future satellites are expected to carry up to 40. The more transponders, the more complicated and valuable the satellite becomes.

Prior to satellites, TV signals were sent across the nation by microwave relay stations. In many respects, satellite transmission is much like the microwave transmission. Each satellite receives messages on its transponders, amplifies them and transmits them back to earth. However, instead of manipulating microwave signals over and around mountains and into valleys, the satellite avoids ground interference by providing a direct signal into space and back to earth. Satellites are also capable of sending signals many thousands of miles, thus providing a low-cost and long-distance means of telecommunication.

Television Signals.   Most of us have seen satellite dishes people have installed to pick up TV signals. The advent of satellite television transmission has made it possible for people living in the most remote regions of the nation or world to join the telecommunications age.

Both local network television affiliates and cable operators can now get their programming signals from space. The first television network to change from microwave to satellite transmission was the Public Broadcasting Service (PBS) in 1978. NBC converted in 1985, and ABC and CBS began making the switch in 1986.

By the 1990s local television stations had numerous sources of worldwide news available to them by satellite, thus freeing them from dependence on network affiliation. However, this new technology has created new challenges and problems for the industry. The most pressing is who owns these satellite signals and how revenue is collected from them. If networks sell programs to local stations or cable companies and send them via satellite, what is to prevent others from picking up the signals directly and avoiding the locally inserted advertisements and/or monthly cable fees? By 1988 most pay TV satellite signals were being scrambled to restrict their reception to "authorized" receivers.

Radio Signals.   Satellite communication is also used extensively in radio broadcasting. Network and syndicated programming are now available to radio stations throughout the country via satellite receiving dishes. Since computerized signals make it possible for local stations to insert commercials and station identifications, the average listener has no idea that the programming is being beamed simultaneously to radio stations across the country. For example, syndicated programs like "Country Coast-to-Coast," "Stardust" and "Contemporary Top-40," all produced by Satellite Music Network, and Larry King's radio talk show are sent to stations throughout the United States by satellite.

While the new technology has improved the quality of radio programming in rural areas, it has assimilated these rural listeners into the sounds and message of a national mass audience. In many areas, regional cultures are no longer broadcast.

Newspaper Signals.   The newspaper industry is also taking advantage of satellite technology to distribute information in printed form. Satellites are used to transmit wire stories for both the Associated Press and United Press International, and Gannett's national newspaper, *USA Today*, is made possible by satellite technology (see Chapter 7). By late 1986 Gannett began publishing an international edition of *USA Today* by beaming its satellite signal to a printing plant in Switzerland.

This speed and efficiency in transmitting news and information, coupled with large chain ownerships of formerly locally owned newspapers, is contributing to the demise of the transmission of local culture in favor of national mass cultural messages.

Other Uses.   Satellite technology is also finding wide acceptance in business and personal communication. Worldwide business transactions are being conducted cheaply and efficiently via satellite-fed telephone services, teleconferencing and videoconferencing.

Home telephone users can choose from an array of long-distance carriers, such as AT&T, U.S. Sprint and MCI, that carry telephone messages on satellites as well as on telephone lines. Author James Traub has summed up the impact of satellite technology on our culture in this way:

> *The capacity of inexpensive, instantaneous nationwide transmission offered by the satellite has transformed cable television from a relay station into an immense industry; freed broadcast stations from much of their dependence on networks; increased the volume and efficiency of long-distance phone service; blurred the distinction between print and electronic media and created such wholly new technologies as videoconferencing.*[5]

Future Impact.   Because satellite dishes are expensive (usually each costs between $2,500 and $4,000), personal use of satellite TV remained primarily in the elite culture through the 1980s. By 1990 there were some 3 million satellite dishes installed in America's backyards. It is predicted that the cost and size of these dishes will soon drop and they will find their way into the popular culture. Miniature dishes—about the size of an umbrella—that can fit on a rooftop or in a window and cost between $100 and $300 are expected to be in use during the 1990s when direct broadcast satellites (DBS) find a niche in the culture.

When this happens it may place television squarely in the age of specialization, as each of us will have hundreds of TV channels available for our individual interests.

COMPUTERS

Computer technology has rapidly altered American culture. Not only have personal computers revolutionized many homes, schools and businesses, but they have had a profound impact on mass communication.

Newspaper Uses.   Computers started making inroads in the newspaper industry in the 1960s, as a tool to speed up and reduce the costs of typesetting (see Box 15.3). While this made newspaper publishing much more profitable, it also led to the demise of one of the oldest unions in the United States—the International Typographical Union.

By the 1980s newspaper reporters and editors were using computers to retrieve information, write and edit stories and design pages. Computers were also being used to program the sorting equipment that sent specialized sections of newspapers to particular geographical areas. (Large metropolitan newspapers sell space at reduced rates to advertisers who want to run their ads in copies sold in a specific region.) Newspapers' accounting and recordkeeping procedures were also computerized.

By the mid-1980s laser printers hooked up to inexpensive personal computers were producing graphics for most major newspapers. This inexpensive equipment could also be used for typesetting. Small businesses and printing operations used these computerized *desktop publishing* systems in place of typesetting equipment that cost ten times as much.

Desktop publishing systems may make it possible for newspapers to enter the stage of specialization by allowing individuals with little capital—rather than large companies or chains—to start up small newspapers aimed at a selective market or interest. Computers and laser printers that will not only typeset but perform full pagination (display the layout and design of the entire newspaper page on screen) can be purchased for less than $10,000. This may bring back the era of small individual voices transmitting specialized or regional culture.

Book Publishing.   Computer technology has also made inroads in the book publishing industry. Some authors compose books on computers and send the floppy disks to their publisher, who uses them first to edit the material and then to typeset it without additional keystroking. By the mid-1980s it was estimated that two-fifths of all published authors were using computers or word processors instead of typewriters, including former president Jimmy Carter, who wrote *Keeping the Faith* on one. The book you are now reading was written on an IBM-PC.

In 1990, McGraw-Hill used computer technology to offer college professors customized textbooks. Instructors could select from a variety of text materials and have a customized text printed for their students. (Three chapters from this

BOX 15.3

▪ COMPUTERS CAN POSE PROBLEMS ▪

Although computers have been a godsend in modernizing the typesetting function of the print media, they occasionally present a problem or two.

For example, when McClatchy's newspaper, the *Fresno Bee*, decided to refer to blacks as African-Americans, they simply programmed their computers to search their news columns for the term *black* and automatically change it to *African-American*.

Such an automated system caused them to run the following correction:

> *An item in Thursday's* National Digest *about the Massachusetts budget crisis made reference to new taxes that will help put Massachusetts "back in the African-American." The item should have said "back in the black."*

book were selected for an Introduction to Human Communication course at the University of Connecticut.)

Some envision the day when college bookstores will no longer sell printed texts but instead will manage computer data bases. Students will be able to access their textbook materials on personal computers and pay into a bookstore account for just the materials used, not for entire texts. An additional advantage will be that the materials can be kept up-to-date, something not always possible with traditional book publishing.

Libraries. Libraries are now using computers for cataloging collections, retrieving data from around the world and reducing the need for storage space. Compact

▪ Typewriters, which once dominated newsrooms, have been replaced by computer terminals, as this photo of the *Flint Journal* newsroom in Flint, Michigan, shows.

■ In libraries, computers now play a major role in conducting book searches.

disks, called CD-ROMs, are providing library users computer access to vast amounts of information from encyclopedias, periodicals and dictionaries.

The Library of Congress is putting texts and periodicals on indestructible 12-inch disks, which many people can use at one time. It is predicted that soon all printed materials will be stored in computerized memory banks at the time of publication.

Broadcasting.   In the 1980s some radio stations started using computers to operate their broadcast studios. The station's entire daily operation could now be programmed into a computer. At the appropriate second the computer could call up a tape cartridge of an announcer's voice giving the time, introducing a record or reading a commercial. The next computer cue would turn on a tape machine to play a preselected song.

As a result, some disc jockeys and radio announcers found themselves replaced by computers. However, some audiences were not ready for this new technology, and a number of stations found that the rather impersonal computers were no substitute for the disc jockey who could respond to telephone requests and had the gift of gab. By the end of the decade some radio stations had returned to the old way of doing things.

Television stations, cable companies and satellite relay systems are also using the new computer technology in their day-to-day operations.

HOME VIDEO EQUIPMENT

When Ampex introduced the first videotape recorder in 1956, its impact was slight. Although futurists predicted that the new technology would radically alter the way people watched television, only the elite could afford to pay $1,500 for one of the recorders.

Videocassette Recorders. Home video recorders did not enter the popular culture until after 1975, when Sony introduced the Betamax. At first, popular acceptance of the Betamax and a VHS model that followed was slow because of the high cost. However, within 10 years videocassette recorders (VCRs) were selling for less than $300 in some markets, and the impact of this technology could be seen everywhere.

Home video recorders freed the general public from the clutches of the TV networks. People no longer had to schedule their calendars around their favorite shows. Instead, they could tape-record programs and watch them at their convenience. They could also fast forward through commercials.

Home video equipment, which exists in more than 60 percent of U.S. households, provides an alternative to network and cable programming. If someone finds nothing of interest on TV, he or she can rent a popular movie or play home movies made with his or her own camcorder.

Video Rentals. By the 1980s, video-rental stores—which rent video movies for as little as 49 cents—could be found in every American community. People could even rent videos at their local supermarket or corner convenience store. The videocassette revolution had entered the American popular culture with a vengeance. Annual revenue from the sale and rental of videocassettes exceeded $12 billion by the end of the 1980s.

The advent of the video-rental business has affected not only the way we watch television but what we watch as well. Although the movie-rental business has hurt motion-picture theaters, it has provided an expanded market for movie producers. By the late 1980s some theaters were getting into the movie-rental business themselves.

Theaters that showed X-rated pornography were the hardest hit by the video-rental business. The ability to watch hard-core films in the privacy of one's home was much more appealing than going to a theater.

By the end of the decade many porno videos were being aimed at women. This was done by taking some of the sleaze out of the films and cleaning up the environment (more romance and foreplay before sex and clean sheets on the beds). Many of the porno producers began making hard-core imitations of soap operas and putting some of the steamy romances found in mass-market paperbacks on videotape. It was estimated that women now accounted for about 40 percent of the 100 million rentals of X-rated tapes each year.

The widespread availability of hard-core videos in stores has brought criticism from groups that fear the nation's moral fiber is being threatened. Efforts to ban such videos have failed, although some video store owners have been persuaded to locate the adult section discreetly in their stores. However, some groups are still working for a total ban.

The proliferation of hard-core video films has not been limited to the American culture. The British press, for example, has devoted numerous column inches to

■ By the late 1980s video stores had sprung up in communities all across America. Some rent tapes for as little as 49 cents.

discussing the problem of "video nasties" in the United Kingdom. Some video store owners in Britain have been jailed on obscenity charges as the authorities try to put an end to the video-porn invasion.

Religious Videos. The VCR has also generated a new line of religious materials—videotapes ranging from dramatizations of the Old and New Testaments to workout tapes featuring contemporary gospel music.

According to *Video* magazine, religious videos reach more than 8 million Christian homes, primarily through mail order and religious bookstores. They are also carried in secular video stores and in some supermarkets.

In addition to religious fitness and entertainment videos, there are instructional tapes to help people cope with rocky marriages, dating problems and the troubles of raising difficult children. Other tapes deliver sermons by such well-known speakers as Norman Vincent Peale and Billy Graham.

Flight Videos. With the introduction of Sony's "personal video" into the marketplace in 1988, airlines have begun to make these tiny TV/VCR units available to passengers on longer flights. The hand-held unit, weighing 2½ pounds and containing a 3-inch screen, is no larger than a VHS videocassete. Passengers can rent the units for under $10 and select a wide range of cassettes, from Nintendo games to movies, to occupy their time.

Video Discs. Not all home video equipment has met with success in the marketplace. In 1981 RCA announced that it would start selling videodisc players (VDPs). The discs produced better quality and made it easier to select the starting point on prerecorded material. RCA's idea was to provide inexpensive videodisc machines (the initial price was about $250) and then sell prerecorded discs, thus developing a market for disc sales similar to the one for recorded music.

RCA had a promotional budget of nearly $20 million to launch its new industry. With a new plant to produce VDPs in Bloomington, Indiana, RCA was ready to make a killing. However, at about the same time, videotape recorders were finding their own comfortable niche in the marketplace as the video rental business began to take off. To meet the demand for rentals, the price of VCRs dropped substantially.

RCA's anticipated sales of the inexpensive disc players did not materialize. Even dropping the price to $150, with discs selling for $20, didn't help. In 1984 RCA announced that it would stop making VDPs. The company closed its Bloomington plant, which had employed 750 people, and wrote off the venture as a $575 million loss.

Other companies involved in the videodisc industry—North American Phillips, MCA and IBM—abandoned their efforts after investing a quarter of a billion dollars. True to its name, Pioneer remained the lone explorer in the videodisc industry. In 1985 it developed a combination audio and video laser disc player, which promoted the perfection of the LaserVision videodisc system. This technology has started to receive acceptance in educational circles (and is expected to make another try at market acceptance during the 1990s) because of some distinct advantages over videotape players—namely the low cost of reproduction, longer life and easier program selection.

MERGING PRINT AND ELECTRONICS

The computer revolution also ushered in new technology that began to merge print and electronic mass communication. These systems, which provide print text on television screens, are called *videotext* and *teletext*. Both systems were invented in Britain in the early 1970s and to date have been far more successful in Europe than in the United States.

Videotext. The videotext system (sometimes spelled videotex) is a two-way interactive communication system between a home television set and a computer. Users can call up information from the computer's data base—as well as do their shopping and banking without leaving home.

The British Post Office, which runs Britain's telephone system, developed the first successful videotext system, Prestel. Prestel, which utilizes telephone lines to connect computerized video terminals to the system, contains thousands of pages of information that are available to subscribers for a monthly charge and a user fee (much like a long-distance telephone service).

The biggest and most successful videotext operation in the world is the French telephone system's Minitel. Some 5 million terminals are used by French citizens—who log 60 million hours a year—to receive more than 8,000 services. Users can access department stores to place orders, purchase groceries or buy opera tickets on the Minitel. However, not all the services are viewed positively. A growing and profitable use of the system in recent years has been to sell erotic messages, explicit sexual graphics, and direct sexual dialogue between individuals. This trend—called "pink Minitel"—has created concern in government circles because they fear their government-operated technology is being used for illegal purposes.

Despite the development of videotext in Europe and Japan, the technology is slower to catch on in the United States. The first experiment with videotext in this country was Viewtron, a joint venture in Florida by Knight-Ridder newspapers and AT&T. The experiment, which ran from 1983 to 1986, failed to attract enough subscribers to make it profitable. Times-Mirror also launched a videotext system in Orange County, California, in 1984, but it, too, failed. U.S. videotext systems in operation in the early 1990s included Prodigy (a joint venture of IBM and Sears, Roebuck), H & R Block's CompuServe, Trintex, Videotel and Data-Tel. Although these systems provide a wide range of services, from news, agribusiness information, weather and travel information to home banking, shopping and security systems, their ability to break out of the elite culture and find general acceptance in the popular culture has been limited.

Teletext. A system that offers one-way interactive viewing of printed text on a television screen is known as teletext. (This system should not be confused with Cabletext, where character generators are used to transmit printed text over available cable channels; Cabletext is not interactive.) In teletext, the viewer uses a hand-held program selector to call up a content listing (menu) and specific pages of information ranging from news to the latest in travel and weather information.

Teletext was invented in the 1960s by British engineers who were working on a way to provide subtitles for the hard of hearing. What emerged in the 1970s was an entirely new mass-communication medium. The British Broadcasting Corporation (BBC) has a version of teletext called Ceefax; the Independent Broadcasting Authority (IBA) version is called Oracle. The only difference between these two systems is that the IBA version carries advertising while the BBC version does not. The Oracle commercials appear at the bottom of the printed information screen.

Although first introduced in 1974, the teletext system did not receive wide acceptance in Britain until the early 1980s, when TV manufacturers started building teletext converters into their sets. By the mid-1980s more than 2 million British homes could receive teletext information. Teletext technology spread throughout Europe until every Western European and one Eastern European country—Hungary—had a system. The number of teletext users in countries other than Britain remained small, however.

Teletext information is broadcast along with the regular TV signal. In Europe the television signal consists of 625 lines of video information. Twenty-four lines that do not carry picture information are used to transmit the teletext information. (In the United States the signal consists of 525 lines, with 21 lines available for teletext information.) The space for teletext information is called the vertical blanking interval (VBI)—the blank band on a TV set that appears when the picture is out of adjustment and starts to roll.

Several hundred pages of information can be transmitted in the VBI. (Thousands of pages of information can be transmitted on blank TV channels that carry no picture information.) The teletext information is encoded at the TV station and transmitted over the VBI to the home, where a decoder converts the digitized signal back into readable form.

After a person uses a hand-held keypad to call up the information directory, he or she can then designate the page number desired and the decoder will grab the designated page as it cycles and display it on the screen.

Conflicting Systems.   In the United States, teletext, like videotext, is still trying to find a niche. Although a number of companies have experimented with teletext, the FCC has refused to designate a single standard for teletext; as a result there are two separate and incompatible systems in use in this country. One, called World System Teletext (WST), is based on the British teletext system. The other, called the North American Broadcast Teletext Standard (NABTS), is based on the French and Canadian system and is backed by RCA, NBC, Time and AT&T. Although the NABTS system delivers better graphic reproduction, it requires more expensive home decoders, which gives WST an advantage in the marketplace.

NBC began inserting NABTS teletext signals into the VBI sent to affiliates in 1983 but canceled the service in 1985. CBS also began transmitting NABTS signals in 1983, the same year Taft Broadcasting in Cincinnati began broadcasting a WST signal. Ted Turner's cable superstation WTBS carries a national WST signal. The WST teletext system was available free to those who purchased a $250 decoder. Unfortunately, the decoders worked only with a late-model Zenith television receiver. NABTS decoders cost between $800 and $1,000. They too worked only with expensive late-model television sets.

Although some local and national TV outlets are still experimenting with teletext, the technology has not lived up to a 1983 research firm's prediction that by 1990, 20 percent of all U.S. households would be teletext subscribers.

The future of videotext and teletext in the United States remains doubtful at this time. Only if and when it reaches the popular culture is this new technology going to be successful.

OTHER TECHNOLOGICAL ADVANCES

There are a number of other technologies on the horizon that may continue the transformation of American culture.

Fiber Optics.   Developed by Western Electric, fiber optics is an engineering breakthrough that makes it possible to carry 100,000 phone calls or more than 100 broadcast signals on a flexible glass strand the size of a human hair. The strand consists of tiny glass fibers that are spliced together by an intricate honeycomb crystal device, which holds them in perfect alignment so that no two are more than one eight-thousandth of an inch out of line.

Unlike wire transmission lines, fiber optics transmits signals on light beams rather than radio waves. These light beams can even go around corners. This new technology is already in use by telephone and cable companies, providing them with far more capacity to carry signals.

The possibilities for use of fiber optics are limitless. Some predict that there will be a fourth wiring of the nation, this time with fiber optics. In the future a single fiber optic cable may bring telephone, two-way television, videotext information and electronic newspapers into home communication centers.

Digital Sound.   In May 1983 a jazz-oriented recording company in New York, GRP Records, contracted with a Japanese company to produce the first album manufactured on compact disc (CD). The palm-size, wafer-thin disc of polycarbonate stored music in a numerical system in millions of microscopic pits that could be read by a low-powered laser beam. It was a remarkable new technology that produced extraordinary sounds. Later that year Sony introduced the first compact disc player in the United States. GRP Records had its CD *In the Digital Mood* waiting for the Sony units.

At first it was thought that CDs would remain a novelty for the elite for some time. However, their superior sound reproduction quickly moved them into the popular culture. Because CDs were originally targeted for the elite, most of the early recordings were classical and jazz selections and CD players sold for around $1,000. By 1986, though, CD players were priced at $200 to $300 and such popular recording artists as Bruce Springsteen and Dire Straits were releasing CDs.

By 1986 the sales of GRP Records had risen to more than $10 million, up from less than $1 million in 1984. In 1986 50 million CDs were sold in the United States, up from 800,000 in 1983. The recording industry had not seen such a technological explosion in the marketplace since the development of the long-playing album (LP) some 30 years earlier. By 1990, CDs had replaced LPs in all major music stores.

In 1990 a digital audio tape player (DAT) was introduced into the U.S. marketplace by Japanese manufacturers. Digital audio tapes, which are about the size of miniature cassette tapes but can record up to 120 minutes, reproduce the same high-quality sound as CDs. In 1991, Sony introduced a DAT Walkman that would both play and record. It is predicted that DATs will replace the standard cassette tapes in the near future.

DAT technology was originally announced by Sony in 1987, but was delayed from entering the marketplace because of a fear that people would use the tape players to reproduce and illegally distribute CD-quality recordings. To settle the dispute, and a possible ban on the product by Congress, the Japanese agreed to equip the DAT decks with copy-limiting circuitry. The circuitry allows owners to make unlimited numbers of copies of CDs, but they cannot make copies of the copies.

Multichannel, Multipoint Distribution Service (MMDS).   Another new technology allows television signals to be delivered by a multipoint distribution service that transmits multiple channels via an omnidirectional high-frequency television signal over the airwaves.

From a centrally located master transmitter in a community, the MMDS station can relay TV programming using a super-high-frequency microwave signal that can be picked up by customers by means of a special antenna. Sometimes called

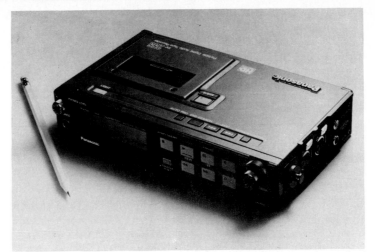

■ Digital audio tape recorders (DATs) may render the standard audio cassette recorders obsolete before the end of this decade.

wireless cable, the system is capable of providing programming similar to cable systems—but over the airwaves, thus avoiding the expensive installation of cable lines to each home. After a slow start, MMDS was available by 1990 in such cities as Cleveland, Washington, D.C., Milwaukee, New York, San Francisco, Sacramento and Sioux Falls, South Dakota.

When the cable deregulation controversy began to reach its peak in the late 1980s, the FCC suggested that MMDS should provide competition to avoid reregulation. However, cable companies worked hard to prevent wireless cable operators from obtaining popular programming owned by large cable companies.

High-Definition Television (HDTV). Most of us have seen giant-screen television sets that are in use in some homes and taverns. Magnified many times its normal size, the TV picture appears to be fuzzy and some of the colors, especially red, lose their detail.

However, the technology is available to make large-screen televisions with quality as clear as a 35-mm motion-picture film. This new high-definition TV may someday do to television what color did to black and white by bringing clear, crisp, larger-than-life images into the home.

HDTV relies on an improvement in the process of sending television signals. At the present time, TV broadcasts consist of a series of dots, called picture elements, arranged in horizontal lines. As noted earlier the United States uses a system consisting of 525 lines. The TV screen exhibits 30 of these 525-line still pictures every second, giving the illusion of motion. (In many foreign countries and most Western European nations, a 625-line standard is used, which gives a higher-quality picture.) In 1981 a coalition of Japanese companies unveiled an HDTV system that broadcasts a 1,125-line television picture. The system uses a wider screen, has better color reproduction, features stereo sound and provides a dramatic improvement in picture resolution and clarity. Projected onto a large screen, the HDTV system produces a picture with clarity and sharpness similar to that found in a motion-picture theater.

Because of the high cost of converting to the new system, both for TV signal producers and home consumers, the transition from regular TV to HDTV is expected to be gradual. (It took nearly 20 years for color TV sets to replace black-and-white sets in most American households.) Although the Japanese have been working on HDTV since 1970 and some European companies are not far behind in their research, the United States is just beginning to move forward with research and development in this area. Zenith, the only U.S. maker of television sets, is working on a joint venture with AT&T to perfect a system. Other U.S. companies exploring this field include IBM, Apple Computer and Texas Instruments.

Holding up the development of this technology in the United States has been the FCC, which did not decide until 1990 on what type of system it would allow. It finally agreed that the only system that would be approved would be one that simultaneously broadcast regular TV and HDTV so that people with the old sets would not find them obsolete. The FCC will test competing systems that follow this guideline and select what it considers to be the best system by the fall of 1992.

When HDTV does enter the American marketplace later in this decade, the cost will be high (estimated at between $3,000 and $4,000) and it will be limited to the elite culture for some period of time.

The use of this new technology is not limited to broadcasting to television screens in the home and tavern, however. Cable companies, direct broadcast satellites, videotape-rental outlets and the motion-picture industry are all expected to get involved with HDTV. The movie industry is expected to cut motion-picture distribution costs by transmitting HDTV signals via satellite to theaters around the country, thus eliminating the need for numerous prints of each picture. Theaters and video-rental outlets may be the first to utilize this new technology.

Direct Broadcast Satellites (DBS).   Another new technology on the horizon which, like MMDS, offers competition for cable companies is direct broadcast satellites. Unlike current satellite systems, which relay programming primarily to cable systems, broadcast stations and those who can afford large expensive satellite dishes, DBS is designed to relay TV programming directly to inexpensive home-satellite dishes. The system uses a new generation of high-powered satellites to send the television signals directly to rectangular-shaped receiving dishes that can be placed in a window.

Four large media and communication companies are working together on a $1 billion project to provide DBS services in the United States by 1993. They are the National Broadcasting Company, Hughes Communications, Rupert Murdoch's News Corp. and Cablevision Systems. Murdoch launched a similar system in the United Kingdom in 1989.

This U.S. DBS system will be called Sky Cable and will cost subscribers about $25 a month. The 12-by-18-inch antenna will sell for about $300. The 108-channel system is being designed to carry HDTV signals and digital sound.

Low-Power Television (LPTV).   In 1982 the FCC began issuing licenses for low-power television stations; by 1990 there were about 800 stations on the air with an average viewership of 14,500. Although these inexpensive stations can be established for under $80,000, the jury is still out as to whether they will find their intended niche of providing specialized TV programming for small audiences in limited geographic areas. The broadcast radius for these stations is between 20 and 30 miles.

There are still some 4,500 licenses available for LPTV, yet the growth of this industry remains sluggish. Stations in existence have a wide range of programming formats. They range from Native-American language lessons and political debates in Indian communities in the Southwest to tourist information in Florida. In the Bronx some 300,000 Haitians tune into an LPTV station broadcasting in their native Creole language. A video jukebox network in Florida allows viewers to make 976-telephone calls to request specific video music.

If and when LPTV finds its niche it will offer the ultimate in specialization for the medium of television. The major drawback at the moment seems to be the fact that LPTV audiences are so small and specialized that it is difficult to sell enough advertising to make the operations profitable.

IMPLICATIONS FOR THE FUTURE

Only time will tell how fast these new technologies will move into the American popular culture. The potential for our culture to be radically transformed in the near future is limitless.

Two-Way Transacting. If, for example, two-way interactive videotext finds a niche, it may become common practice for us to pay bills, order groceries and concert tickets, do our banking, read the latest news, book airline flights, check weather conditions and so on from our home computers or television sets.

Electronic Print Media. Newspapers and magazines may someday be delivered into the home electronically. The technology is already available and waiting for the cost of manual delivery to become too prohibitive to be continued. When that happens, electronic transmission will take over. This technology will allow a person to produce a hard copy (printout) of any particular story he or she might want to save.

Communication-Work Centers. Complete home communication centers where fiber-optic cables bring in a wide variety of print, radio, television, videotext and other communication services may soon become commonplace. A report commissioned by the National Science Foundation in 1983 speculated that home information systems will have as profound an impact on our culture as the automobile and commercial televison had earlier in this century. This will be accomplished by converting our homes into workplaces where people will earn a living working at home computer terminals (see Box 15.4).

Cultural Transformation. If the home communication-work centers develop as predicted, they may have a profound impact on our freeway and mass-transit

BOX 15.4

▪ WORKING AT HOME ON THE RISE ▪

In 1990, 34.3 million Americans worked at home, an increase of 29 percent over the previous year, according to a National Work at Home Survey conducted by LINK Resources Corporation, a New York–based resource and consulting firm.

This figure represented 28 percent of the total work force. Although some of this total represented home businesses, a growing percentage of home workers are employees of major businesses and corporations that are experimenting with telecommuting.

Twenty AT&T Bell Laboratories employees in Naperville, Illinois, use the latest digital telephone technology (not yet available to residences) which holds both voice and computer data on a single phone line. Many telecommuters are in immediate touch with the office via telephones, computers hooked to modems, electronic mail, teleconferencing and fax machines.

In Southern California employers are being encouraged to have a portion of their work force engaged in telecommuting to cut down on freeway congestion and air pollution. Responding to the incentive regulation adopted by the South Coast Air Quality Management District, major employers have adopted telecommuting implementation plans. In 1989, the County of Los Angeles announced plans to have 200 volunteers working at home on computer terminals before the year's end and indicated that they planned to have 2,000 of their 17,000 downtown employees telecommuting by 1994.

---

systems, our leisure activities (who will want to watch television at home after a day of staring at a home video display terminal?), our schools, libraries, shopping malls, office buildings, churches and so on.

Alvin Toffler predicts that our current practice of coming home and collapsing in front of the TV set for the evening will be reversed when the home becomes the workplace. He envisions a new trend in which couples who spend the day working together at home will want to go out in the evening. He sees a proliferation of neighborhood restaurants, theaters, pubs and clubs and a revitalization of church and voluntary group activity—all of it involving face-to-face communication.[6]

Megatrends author John Naisbitt describes this as the "high-tech, high-touch" syndrome. As people deal more and more with machines and technology in the workplace, they will want a more personal touch off the job, he says. The rise in computers has already caused the rise in human interaction groups and participatory activities like jogging, tennis, racquetball and Little League, he feels.[7]

One thing seems certain. Our rapidly changing mass-communication technology will have a profound impact on our culture. Although our civilization has changed more during the past one hundred years than it did in several thousand years before the Industrial Revolution, futurists predict that it will change even more dramatically in this decade.

SUMMARY

American culture is undergoing a technological revolution that is taking us from the industrial age to an information-based society. The rapid advance of electronic technology since the invention of the transistor in 1947 and the development of the microchip is transforming our society right before our eyes.

The acceptance of technological advances in the field of mass communication has been slower than their development. As was the case in the nineteenth century, the new technology must find a proper niche before it can enter the popular culture.

Among the major developments in mass-media technology in the 1980s were cable television, satellite communication, computers, home video equipment, fiber optics and digital sound recordings, as well as experimentation with videotext, teletext, multichannel multipoint distribution services, high-definition television, direct broadcast satellites and low-power TV. During the 1990s we will most likely see these experimental technologies find a niche in the marketplace.

Cable television, which originally brought standard TV programming to remote areas, changed in the 1970s to provide expanded and specialized programming for urban consumers.

Communication satellites made worldwide telecommunications possible by providing relay stations in outer space. Satellite transmission has affected the mass media of television, radio and newspapers, and has enabled corporations to conduct their business via teleconferencing and videoconferencing.

Computers have affected every mass-communications medium as well as the way we conduct our business and personal affairs. In the newspaper industry, computers were first used for typesetting. Today they are used to write, edit and typeset stories and to design pages. They are also used to keep books and records and to program machines so that inserts can be added to papers destined for certain geographical areas.

Radio stations use computers to replace disc jockeys, engineers and announcers. Completely computerized stations are broadcasting in today's society.

Computers have also led to the development of videotext and teletext technology, which merge print information with television. Although these technologies have not yet become established in the American culture, they have been in use in Europe since the 1970s.

Videotape recorders have transformed the way people watch television and movies and the types of programming they view. Video-rental outlets have sprung up everywhere in the United States. The rapid acceptance of VCRs has slowed the efforts to market video disc players in our culture, but that seems to be only temporary.

The development of home communication centers that will be used as workplaces as well as recreation and information centers seems imminent. This may dramatically transform our popular culture and lifestyles.

THOUGHT QUESTIONS

1   What will be some of the limitations of having books available on hand-held computer screens?
2   Do you think the cable television industry will remain financially healthy, or will new technologies replace it? What can the industry do to protect its corner on the market?

3 What major changes do you see resulting from direct broadcast satellites?
4 Can you describe how learning resource centers (college libraries, book-stores, computer centers) will operate in the year 2000?
5 Will DATs replace CDs? If not, what niche will they find in our culture?

NOTES

1. John Wicklein, *Electronic Nightmare: The New Communications and Freedom* (New York: Viking, 1981), p. 30.

2. Alvin Toffler, *The Third Wave* (New York: Bantam, 1980), pp. 194–207.

3. Les Brown, "Cable TV: Wiring for Abundance," *Channels* (November/December 1982): 8.

4. "Freedom of Choice Drives Cable's Growth," *Advertising Age,* February 19, 1990, p. 16.

5. James Traub, "Satellites: The Birds That Make It All Fly," *Channels* (November/December 1983): 8.

6. Toffler, p. 372.

7. John Naisbitt, *Megatrends: Ten New Directions Transforming Our Lives* (New York: Warner Books, 1982), pp. 211–229.

ADDITIONAL READING

Baldwin, Thomas F. and McVoy, D. Stevens. *Cable Communication.* Englewood Cliffs, N.J.: Prentice-Hall, 1988.

Bell, Daniel. *The Coming of Post-Industrial Society.* New York: Basic Books, 1976.

Brown, Ronald. *Telecommunications: The Booming Technology.* Garden City, N.Y.: Doubleday, 1970.

Martin, James. *Future Developments in Telecommunications,* 2nd ed. Englewood Cliffs, N.J.: Prentice-Hall, 1977.

Nilles, Jack M. *Exploring the World of the Personal Computer.* Englewood Cliffs, N.J.: Prentice-Hall, 1982.

Singleton, Loy A. *Telecommunications in the Information Age,* 2nd ed. Cambridge, Mass.: Ballinger, 1986.

Smith, Anthony. *Goodbye Gutenberg: The Newspaper Revolution of the 1980s.* Oxford: Oxford University Press, 1980.

Toffler, Alvin. *Future Shock.* New York: Random House, 1970.

Toffler, Alvin. *Power Shift.* New York: Bantam Books, 1990.

Weaver, David H. *Videotex Journalism: Teletext, Viewdata and the News.* Hillsdale, N.J.: Lawrence Erlbaum, 1983.

Williams, Frederick. *The Communications Revolution.* New York: New American Library, 1983.

Violence in the media, as in this scene showing Steven Seagal in the Warner Bros. action/adventure thriller Above the Law, *has raised ethical questions and has been the subject of extensive media effects research over the years.*

MEDIA ETHICS AND EFFECTS

Journalists must be free of obligation to any interest other than the public's right to know the truth.
—The Society of
Professional
Journalists

On January 22, 1987, 30 reporters and camera technicians gathered in the Pennsylvania state capital of Harrisburg for a news conference that state Treasurer R. Budd Dwyer had called to announce his resignation. He had been convicted the previous month on bribery charges.

The 47-year-old politician appeared nervous and sweaty as he delivered a rambling speech in which he referred to his 22-year political career in the past tense. He told the reporters he was innocent and criticized the prosecutor, judge,

▪ Pennsylvania State Treasurer R. Budd Dwyer holds a pistol in his hand before shooting himself in front of news cameras.

governor, justice system and the press—which he said *feasted* on him during his legal troubles. Then Dwyer pulled a .357 magnum from a manila envelope, stuck the gun barrel in his mouth and killed himself in front of the horrified onlookers.

What resulted was not just a sensational news story but some serious ethical questions as well. How vividly should the journalists who witnessed the event describe the scene? How much detail should be shown in photographs and television tapes? Some television stations showed the entire scene in living color while others merely talked about it. Some print journalists reported that Dwyer had shot himself while others described in detail what they had seen. Those who did not spare the grisly details were criticized by many of their fellow journalists and members of the public for going too far. Those criticized defended their actions by stating that as reporters they had a duty to tell and show what happened.

This is just one example of ethical considerations people working in the mass media face in their daily course of actions. Although we have looked at ethical issues and the effects that the mass media have had on our culture and on us as individuals throughout this book, it seems appropriate to conclude with a chapter that focuses on these important issues.

NEWS-MEDIA ETHICS

In 1981 Hollywood released *Absence of Malice,* a movie that dealt with news-media ethics. In the film a young Catholic woman commits suicide after a news-paperwoman, eager to get an exclusive story about a murder investigation, reports that she has had an abortion. The movie's message is clear: the newspaperwoman, played by Sally Field, should not have jeopardized the reputation (and life) of the innocent young woman for the sake of her story.

Absence of Malice was fictitious, but the issues it raised were true to life. In 1976, for example, the editors of a Dallas daily newspaper disregarded the threats of a man who said he would commit suicide if the paper printed a story accusing him of being a Soviet spy. The man killed himself the day the story appeared (see Box 16.1).[1]

In 1983 a television crew in Anniston, Alabama, became the focus of media ethics discussions when they went to a park and filmed a man setting himself on fire to protest unemployment. The man had telephoned the TV station to tell of his intentions. Although the station did call the police, the news crew made no effort to stop the man from igniting himself and went to his aid only after he was totally engulfed in flames. Chances are that if the crew had not shown up, the man would not have carried out his threat.

Honesty and Integrity.   Not all ethical considerations involving the media deal with life-threatening situations. In 1981 Janet Cooke, a *Washington Post* reporter, won the coveted Pulitzer Prize for feature writing. She had written a story entitled "Jimmy's World" about an eight-year-old heroin addict. After the prize was awarded, Cooke revealed that she had fabricated parts of her story and that Jimmy had never existed. An embarrassed *Washington Post* returned the prize and fired Cooke.

In 1978 the *Chicago Sun-Times* ran a story that exposed a series of payoffs and bribes to city and state inspectors. The newspaper had purchased a bar, called "Mirage," trained several reporters as bartenders, hid photographers behind a ventilation duct and gone into business. Throughout the summer and fall the reporters recorded the activities of inspectors who were willing to accept bribes in exchange for overlooking various fire, building and health-code violations. The story was recommended for a Pulitzer Prize by a screening committee, but it was turned down by the foundation's board.

In refusing to consider the story for the prize, Ben Bradlee, board member and executive editor of the *Washington Post,* posed the following question: "How can newspapers fight for honesty and integrity when they themselves are less than honest in getting a story?"[2]

Ethical standards for the media have changed a great deal in recent years. For example, prior to the *Chicago Sun-Times* case, Pulitzer Prizes had been awarded to reporters who had misrepresented their true occupations. The question is whether the good that comes from exposing wrongdoing outweighs questionable or deceptive behavior by the news media. Journalists line up on both sides of this issue.

Photographic Accuracy.   Journalists have long held that photographs should accurately reflect the event being portrayed. However, occasionally photographers are tempted to make pictures more eye appealing by changing the angle on the shot or cropping out certain details. The Society of Professional Journalists' Code of Ethics (see Chapter 3) states that "photographs and telecasts should give an accurate picture of an event and not highlight an event out of context."

BOX 16.1

ETHICS IN JOURNALISM: DO YOU KILL A STORY THAT MIGHT MAKE SOMEONE KILL HIMSELF?

The following article was written for FineLine, the Newsletter on Journalism Ethics, by Mike Jacobs, news anchor and head of the investigative unit at WTMJ-TV in Milwaukee. Published with permission of the author.

One story, two ethical decisions and a threat of suicide: a combination that would create a lively discussion in any newsroom.

It started as an intriguing tip: Two years ago, a suburban cop was fired because he was stopping teenage boys, threatening to give them speeding tickets, and then letting them go in exchange for sex. But the police chief did not refer the case to the district attorney for possible charges, avoiding embarrassing publicity for the department. Now, two years later, and in the wake of other allegations about a troubled police department, our sources wanted us to know about this episode.

We located two of the victims, and they confirmed what had happened. One victim, now 24 years old, even agreed to talk about it on camera, without having his identity concealed. He described, in detail, the sexual contact in the officer's apartment when he was 19 years old.

But a few days later, the young man called us back. He'd changed his mind. He did not want to be on TV.

Ethical decision number 1: Should we air the interview? He did the interview voluntarily. We had it "in the can." He was not retracting his statement,

simply asking that we not use his name or picture. We decided to use the interview, masking the man's identity electronically. We did so because he was, essentially, a sexual assault victim, and we routinely withhold the names of such victims. Furthermore, it was his information that was important, not his identity.

Ethical decision number 2 proved to be a lot more difficult. A week later, we tracked down the former officer, living in a small town 150 miles away. We surreptitiously took pictures of him working in his yard and then approached him for an interview.

When we told him why we were there, he broke down and asked to speak to me alone. He tearfully confessed to what he'd done, told me he'd tried to put that ugly period behind him, and assured me he'd had no contact with teenagers since then. He said he'd been receiving counseling from a minister. And then he asked if we were going to put his story on TV.

When I told him we were, he said, and I'll never forget his words: "Well, you've just made up my mind. I'm going to get my shotgun and go out into a farm field and kill myself. I hate myself for what I've

New computerized photo-enhancing technology, however, has made this ethical issue a concern once again. Such a device, known as "Scitex," is currently in use at many major daily newspapers. It can move, add or subtract images in any photograph. Concerns with abuses of this new device surfaced in 1989 when the *St. Louis Post-Dispatch*'s director of imaging and technology decided to remove a can of Diet Coke from a front page photograph. His decision was based on not wanting to give the product free advertising. However, the altered photograph became an issue in the *St. Louis Journalism Review* (a press watchdog publication) when it pointed out that the ethical practice of accuracy in photographs had been violated.

A bigger controversy surfaced in 1989 when *TV Guide*, which had recently been purchased by the tabloid king Rupert Murdoch, ran a cover photograph of a

BOX 16.1 *Cont.*

done. My parents don't know why I left town. And I can't stand the thought of them finding out."

I spent the next hour trying to talk the man out of committing suicide. I told him he shouldn't do anything foolish since there was a chance the story might not air, that nothing he'd done was worth dying for. I coaxed. I cajoled. I pleaded. It was, perhaps, the most difficult hour of my life.

He finally assured me he wouldn't do anything until he'd heard from me. We left and went straight to his church. We told his minister about the suicide threat. The minister agreed to visit the man immediately.

We drove back to the newsroom for discussions with news management and the station attorney. Legally, the story was clean. We had all the facts nailed down, including a confession.

Journalistically, we had a good story. But ethically, we had a problem. Could we tell this story, knowing it might cause a man to take his life?

We wrestled with other questions as well: Was it still a story since the incidents had happened a few years ago? If so, what was the most important part of the story? And was this man still using his authority to take advantage of teenagers?

We came up with these answers:

Because the officer had resigned, he was no longer in a position to use his badge to take advantage of teenagers. He had assured me he was not involved in activities that put him in contact with young people. And we knew, if we did a story, the D.A. would investigate to find out if he was telling the truth (and letting him know he was being watched).

We decided it was still a story. But we believed an equally important part of the story was the fact that the police chief had allowed the officer to resign, without referring the case to the D.A.

Yet, we did not want to do a story that might result in a man's suicide.

We decided to air the story, withholding the former officer's identity. We electronically altered our videotape of the man working in his yard so he could not be recognized. We notified him in advance, through his minister. In our story, we told the viewers about the sexual incidents. And we explained how the police chief had handled the case.

The D.A. immediately launched an investigation. Months later, after interviewing everyone involved, the D.A. decided he was not going to prosecute the former officer so long as he had no further contact with teenagers. The D.A. criticized the police chief for the way he had handled the case. But the D.A. ruled the chief had not acted criminally.

The police chief, declaring himself cleared of criminal wrongdoing and citing his age, 55, immediately resigned.

The former officer did not kill himself.

We believe we handled this case responsibly. But there is a larger issue: Can the threat of suicide be enough to kill a story? If so, some important stories probably would go unreported. Each case, we decided, must be based on its own set of facts.

slim-looking Oprah Winfrey in a bathing suit. It was later revealed that the head of Oprah had been superimposed on the body of Ann-Margret. Readers felt deceived. *TV Guide* said it would not happen again.

TV Reenactments. On a segment of *World News Tonight* in July of 1989, ABC News displayed two grainy photos that it said depicted an American diplomat handing a briefcase to a "known Soviet agent on the streets of a European capital." The man ABC identified as the diplomat had been under an official espionage investigation. However, it was later revealed that the photo did not show the diplomat or a Soviet agent but was a staged reenactment using actors. ABC acknowledged that it was a "terrible mistake" not to inform the viewers about the simulation.

By the end of the decade of the 1980s, TV simulations or reenactments by actors had become commonplace. Their popularity climbed with the development of tabloid TV, particularly shows like *America's Most Wanted* and *Unsolved Mysteries*. Soon documentaries like *Fatal Passions* were using reenactments to show murders being committed.

Public opposition to reenactments was mild in all but news shows and by the 1990s networks had shied away from using them in newscasts.

Accepting Gifts.   Another aspect of media ethics that has undergone rethinking in recent years is the acceptance of gifts or *freebies*. For many years one of the rewards of being a journalist was the many perquisites (*perks*) that came in the line of duty. Reporters often received free travel, theater passes and athletic event passes in return for stories. Reporters were often treated to lavish parties with free drinks and expensive hors d'oeuvres at the beginning of many annual news and promotional events. Of course, the reporters were expected to write about the activities to which they were invited. Journalists also routinely received free books, record albums and tapes to review.

Around holidays, like Christmas, many newsrooms resembled wedding receptions, piled high with gifts from news sources. A bottle of expensive liquor or a turkey from the mayor to the city desk was commonplace at Christmas.

As discussed in Chapter 9, in 1959 the payola scandal rocked the radio and recording industries when it was revealed that many disc jockeys had been receiving cash and/or gifts in exchange for promoting records on the air. Journalists who covered the scandal started wondering about their own attitudes toward gifts. How were they supposed to retain their credibility if they were accepting free travel, tickets and gifts from their news sources? Could a reader be expected to believe a rave review about a play, knowing that the critic had been treated to free tickets and a lavish opening-night party by the play's producers?

The Society of Professional Journalists revised its code of ethics to prohibit journalists from accepting gifts. A 1983 survey by the society found that 75 percent of the newspapers and broadcast stations responding to a questionnaire had policies regarding gifts. The policies varied greatly: some news institutions prohibited the acceptance of any gifts, while others set a monetary limit on them. The *Beaver Falls News-Tribune* in Pennsylvania, for example, allowed employees to keep a bottle of liquor but required that a case would have to be returned.

Today some newspapers pay for everything their reporters attend and even the White House now bills journalists for the price of a tourist-class airline ticket and for meals when reporters travel with the president on Air Force One.

Conflicts of Interest.   For years journalists have been reporting on the conflicts of interest of other people, particularly politicians. However, journalists are subject to similar conflicts themselves. Can a reporter who is active in the Democratic party, for example, cover political campaigns objectively? Can religious editors fairly report on developments in their own churches? Can a financial reporter write about a company in which he or she owns stock? Or can a news agency—such as a newspaper chain or television network—that has corporate holdings in other business endeavors objectively report about one of its subsidiaries?

Pro-choice demonstrations in Washington, D.C., in 1990 created problems for the *Washington Post* when it was learned by management that some of its reporters had participated in the event as private citizens. Management told its reporters to refrain from such activity for fear that it would give the impression of a conflict of interest.

In 1987 a Kansas congressman called for a congressional order to require General Electric, the nation's second largest defense contractor, to sell off its NBC network. He asked how NBC could objectively report on such matters as the Strategic Defense Initiative without appearing to have a conflict of interest.[3] In 1989, serious concerns were raised in Detroit when it was learned that the president of the business operations of two of the nation's largest newspapers— the *Detroit News* and the *Detroit Free Press*—was the brother of Charles M. Keating, the central figure in the Lincoln Savings & Loan scandal. Despite the editorial efforts to report this story accurately and thoroughly in Detroit, some people wondered if brotherly influence would creep into the news columns.

Withholding Information.   Another aspect of ethics that plagues journalists is when to withhold information. Not everything that happens in our culture is reported—nor should it be. Deciding what facts should be included in or omitted from a story is often not easy. Should a reporter write about a discovery that a prominent civic leader is having an affair? If a high-ranking government official is killed in an automobile accident and a number of pornographic magazines are found in the car, should that be reported? Should the fact that a person committed suicide or died of AIDS be included in the obituary?

The AIDS issue became an important one during the 1980s as the epidemic grew. Many newspapers developed policies on the subject. Usually a newspaper will mention AIDS if it is a cause of death of a prominent person, such as the widely reported deaths of entertainers Rock Hudson and Liberace. If the person is not well known, some newspapers will respect the wishes of the family. A common practice among many newspapers when running obituaries of gay AIDS victims is not to mention the cause of death, but to include the victim's long-term ''companion'' among the survivors. The *Washington Post,* however, refuses to run an obituary if the cause of death is not given by the family and it presses hard for the true cause when AIDS is suspected.

But what happens if AIDS is not the cause of death yet a coroner's report turns up the fact that the well-known victim had AIDS or human immunodeficiency virus (HIV)? This ethical dilemma hit the newspaper industry close to home in 1989 when C. K. McClatchy, chairman of the Sacramento (California)-based McClatchy newspaper chain, died from a heart attack while jogging. When contacted by the coroner, McClatchy's doctor reported that the publisher had tested positive for HIV. When this fact was revealed to the Sacramento press, the McClatchy paper decided against running it, citing the fact that it was not a cause of death. The rival *Sacramento Union* and one TV station ran the story as did the prestigious *Los Angeles Times*. Most other news outlets ignored the story.

When the editor of the *San Antonio* (Texas) *Light* died in February, 1989, of cryptococcal meningitis, which often is AIDS-related, the newspaper mentioned the AIDS connection in the second paragraph along with profiles of the editor, his funeral and a column discussing why they mentioned the cause of death. In the column, the editor's wife—also a journalist—said that as a journalist she understood the decision but as a wife she could not accept it.

Another common practice among journalists is not to reveal the names of rape victims. Sometimes this practice runs into trouble—say, when the rape victim is prominent or the assault occurred during a highly newsworthy crime spree. But is withholding the victim's name and details about the crime the right ethical decision? An Iowa rape victim didn't think so and for five days in 1990 her name, photograph and graphic details of her rape and subsequent experience as a witness at her assailant's trial appeared in the Des Moines *Register*. The victim and the woman editor felt that newspapers don't do enough to publicize how brutal the crime of rape is.

Invasion of Privacy.   Still another ethical problem for media personnel is the question of invasion of privacy (see legal discussion of this issue in Chapter 4). Often the press intrudes into people's private lives while pursuing a story. Television news crews have received the heaviest criticism in this area. Many viewers become irate when they see a TV reporter shove a microphone into the face of a grief-stricken person and ask how he or she feels about the loss of a loved one (see Box 16.2).

After the space shuttle *Challenger* exploded in 1986, newspapers and television networks showed pictures of the parents of Christa McAuliffe, the first teacher/astronaut, watching the explosion. When 241 U.S. servicemen were killed in Lebanon in 1983, journalists flocked to interview the victims' families. Some TV crews even filmed grieving families through the windows of their homes. However, not all journalistic behavior during that incident was inappropriate. Most families interviewed had agreed to talk to the press, and some indicated that being interviewed helped them deal with their grief. But the question still remains: when is intrusion into a person's privacy appropriate and when isn't it? Although the law has specific guidelines as to what constitutes an invasion of privacy and provides victims of such invasion with legal recourse, journalists often must weigh ethical considerations as well.

Double Standards?   Although journalists today are more concerned about their ethical behavior than at any time in American history, they are still often criticized for adhering to a double standard. Former Mobil Oil vice-president Herb Schmertz, in his critique of the media, *Good-bye to the Low Profile,* charged that the press is the only institution in the United States that avoids public scrutiny.

Whenever those in the news media have been challenged, they have grown righteously indignant. Basking in the glow of Watergate, members of the press have refused to acknowledge that they are ever on the wrong track. Never mind that reputations have been tarnished by untrue stories. Never mind that bad laws have been passed because of zealous crusading that hasn't always portrayed the whole picture. The rush into print or onto the air with evermore sensational scandals and conspiracies was, for a time, all-consuming. In the short run, it sold newspapers and it sold advertising. But in the long run, the public will ultimately be tired of it.[4]

BOX 16.2

▪ SOMETIMES INVASIONS INTO PRIVACY ARE JUST PLAIN STUPID ▪

Reporters who invade the privacy of grief-stricken relatives during times of disaster have long been criticized by American citizens. In most instances, their questions are ill-timed, inappropriate and, on some occasions, just plain stupid.

Not all invasions deal with relatives or involve the loss of loved ones—but they often display stupidity or, at best, poor judgment.

In 1990, after an airline flight crew was found guilty of flying following an evening of heavy drinking, a network TV reporter stuck a microphone into the face of the convicted pilot and asked: "If you had it all to do over again, what would you do?"

The stunned pilot responded: "You can't be serious."

In 1984, while editorializing on media ethics, *USA Today* asked the following question:

> *Journalism is a high calling. The First Amendment to the Constitution makes the news media free to serve democracy, inform the public, promote debate and scrutinize and criticize the conduct of public officials. Some have described these rights and responsibilities of the news media as a "watchdog" role. But who watches the watchdog?[5]*

Social Responsibility.   As discussed in Chapter 3, to function under the social responsibility theory, the press must report on all segments of society and it must do so honestly, openly and objectively. It also must allow divergent viewpoints to appear on its editorial pages. In other words, it must serve the entire community.

The press must be socially responsible for selfish reasons. If it is to remain an important information source in our American culture, the press must be a credible source of information. To be credible, it must be socially responsible, and social responsibility includes adherence to strict ethical standards and dedication to disclosing the truth about all institutions, including one's own.

▪ A New Jersey woman is surrounded by reporters at the Dulles International Airport just after she and 50 other passengers and crew members were released from a hijacked airliner.

MEDIA ETHICS AND ECONOMICS

Other ethical considerations arise from the fact that the American mass media are businesses designed to make a profit.

Advertiser Influence.   One fairly frequent problem occurs when advertisers—who pay the bills and produce the profits for the media—want to control their content. In the South during the civil rights movement of the 1960s, for example, some newspapers sympathetic to the civil rights cause were forced to change their positions or go out of business as the result of economic boycotts instigated by anti-civil rights readers and advertisers.

Another case occurred in Texas in the 1960s, when a newspaper publisher ran several stories about the illegal activities of one of the community's leading citizens. The stories revealed how this individual—a friend and confidant of President Lyndon Johnson—had attempted to defraud the government out of millions of dollars in grain subsidies. Community leaders reacted to these stories by starting another newspaper in the town and persuading all the local businesses to boycott the paper that ran the exposé. Even though the stories led to a jail term for the community leader, the crusading publisher was forced out of business.

PR for Advertisers.   Not all advertiser influence on media content is as malign as these examples. In small towns, for example, many newspapers run stories that are not really newsworthy but instead are publicity pieces for major advertisers. This type of story is called an *advertorial.* Tom Goldstein, in his book *The News at Any Cost: How Journalists Compromise Their Ethics to Shape the News,* cited several examples of advertorials:

> In a 1983 issue of the Reporter, *a weekly in Walton, New York, in a news column adjacent to an advertisement for the Imperial Restaurant, there was an article on the renovations that had been completed at that building. There was a picture of the new entry way with this caption: "From a newly-paved parking lot one now may enter Walton's Imperial Restaurant under a new canopy to a new entrance. Foyer includes a large hanging area for coats." A weekly in a neighboring town, the* Hancock Herald, *ran a picture of the Delaware Land Office in the spring of 1984 with the caption explaining that the real estate firm had a new "outlook" on Hancock as a result of "thermo-pane windows installed on the first floor in the front to replace the old windows that had become leaky." The office is run by a frequent advertiser.*[6]

Such advertiser-controlled hype is not limited to small-town journalism, however. Take a look at the real estate section of your nearest metropolitan newspaper. Most likely you will find the ads surrounded with "news" stories that report in glowing terms how *wonderful* some of the real estate developments in the area are and how *wonderfully* they are selling. These stories appear even when the real estate market is depressed. Such articles often are written not by journalists but by publicists for the developers or by advertising personnel at the newspaper.

Even the *Los Angeles Times,* which is regarded as one of the nation's best newspapers, runs regional real-estate hype sections for such areas as San Diego

BOX 16.3

▪ PROFILE: PEGGY CHARREN ▪

For years, Peggy Charren, founder and president of Action for Children's Television (ACT), has been battling Congress and the Federal Communication Commission over the content of television directed toward children (see Chapter 10).

Among her concerns have been the absence of educational value in children's TV programming and the belief that advertisers are allowed to sell youngsters their products with little regard for ethics or responsibility. Her frustrations mounted during the 1980s when toy manufacturers were able to produce 30-minute TV shows that promoted their products.

But Peggy Charren was a fighter who wouldn't give up. She continued to bring her concerns to the attention of the public and Congress and finally, in 1990, her dreams came true. Congress passed— and a new president signed—legislation that placed a limit on commercials during children's shows to 10.5 minutes per hour on weekends and 12 minutes on weekdays. New legislation also required the FCC to evaluate broadcasters' efforts to offer educational and informative TV for children when considering license renewals. It also established a National Endowment for Children's Educational Television programming with a funding of $2 million in 1991 and $4 million in 1992.

What made the 1990 legislation so special was that it had the endorsement of the National Association of Broadcasters, which had been fighting similar legislation in years past. An NAB spokesman said "We're pleased with the outcome. It's been a contentious issue, and we're glad to see it resolved." A similar bill had been pocket-vetoed by President Ronald Reagan in 1988.

Charren's persistence has been a key element in bringing about legislation to protect children from TV advertising abuses.

and the Coachella Valley's communities (both more than 100 miles away). Although labeled as *special advertising supplements,* these sections look like any other section of the newspaper, and many readers believe the "news" stories in these supplements (which are actually verbatim news releases) are as legitimate as any others.

Although profitable, such practices raise some ethical questions and tend to cloud a newspaper's credibility. Is the reader getting a true picture of real estate developments in the area? Has media hype influenced people to make bad real estate investments in second-home markets? Can a reader trust his or her newspaper if certain sections peddle a developer's rosy view of reality as fact?

Television Content. The influence of advertisers on TV content, particularly children's programs, raises serious ethical concerns as well. Is it ethical for toy manufacturers to produce shows that are essentially 30-minute-long commercials for their toy or doll lines? Children, who have a difficult enough time distinguishing between commercials and programs, are now being sold throughout the program by these product-oriented theme shows (see Chapter 10). Some wonder if this is ethical television programming or industry exploitation of its most impressionable audience (see Box 16.3).

Direct-Response Sales. Another concern emerged when cable systems and satellites started carrying home shopping channels, which consist entirely of direct-response advertising ("Call now for this amazing offer, 1-800-xxx-xxxx"). The hard sell of these programs encourages impulse buying—on credit—and consumers can incur unreasonable and unimaginable debts if they are not careful. This situation has the potential of becoming very serious when new technology on the horizons makes it possible for viewers to place an order by merely pushing a button on a hand-held response terminal hooked up to a two-way television set.

Chain Ownership.   The growing number of mass media owned by large chains also poses some ethical questions. Do chain-owned media owe their allegiance to the communities they serve, or are they solely responsible to their parent corporation headquartered in another area? In 1977 Panax Corporation told its eight daily and 40 weekly newspapers to run two stories critical of President Jimmy Carter on their front pages. When two of the editors refused, offering instead to run them as opinions on the editorial page, they were fired for insubordination. Despite community protests, the editors were not reinstated. Panax even refused to run letters to the editor protesting the firings.

When media baron Rupert Murdoch purchased a number of newspapers in the United States, including the *New York Post,* he turned some of them into sensationalizing publications to boost circulation. This demonstrates that he was more interested in making a profit than providing quality journalism.

MEDIA ETHICS AND ENTERTAINMENT

Entertainment in the mass media also generates some serious ethical questions. Some of the more passionately discussed issues of the early 1990s have revolved around explicit language and programming in recorded music, radio and television. Generating most of the discussion were the lyrics of rap music, sitcom programming and tabloid or trash TV, such as *Married . . . With Children.* Although this show pioneered the use of sexual innuendo and foul language on Murdoch's Fox network, it wasn't long before the major three TV networks were copying its success. The 1990–91 season saw new shows like *Married People* (ABC) and *Law and Order* (NBC) using Fox's style of foul and titillating language.

In addition to the relatively recent concern about what is good taste and how far the networks and popular music will go to challenge those standards, there is an age-old controversy over the way TV entertainment distorts cultural reality.

Cone Effect.   One way to understand better how the media influence our perceptions and often distort our view of reality is to examine how we as individuals interact with the media. One of the best diagrams of this process is Edward Jay Whetmore's *cone effect* (see Figure 16.1).[7]

According to Whetmore, all entertainment programming exaggerates and magnifies real life to make it more entertaining and interesting. What results from this process he calls *constructed mediated reality (CMR)*. To be worthy of our attention, CMR is made sexier, funnier, more intense, more violent and more colorful than real life. After all, who would want to read a novel or watch a TV show that was only as interesting as everyday life?

Next the constructed mediated reality is transmitted through a mass medium,

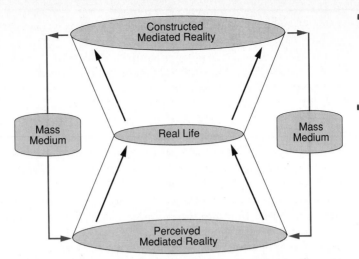

Figure 16.1 The cone effect. SOURCE: From *Mediamerica,* 3rd ed., by Edward Jay Whetmore. © 1985, 1982, by Wadsworth, Inc. Used by permission of the publisher.

such as a book or television set, to the audience. CMR consumers then interpret the messages at a perceptual level. Whetmore calls this *perceived mediated reality (PMR)*. We each interpret the mediated reality differently. An African-American ghetto child, for example, would interpret an episode of the *Cosby Show* or *Family Matters* differently from the way in which a middle-class white child would.

After people perceive this mediated reality in their own way, based on their own frames of reference (see Chapter 1), they eventually incorporate it into their own lives. This can lead to distortions if a person perceives media reality—for example, permissive sexuality on soap operas—to be the norm in modern society and changes his or her own behavior accordingly.

With the cone effect in mind, let's look at the issue of media distortion of cultural reality.

Distortions of Cultural Reality. There is a concern that the media are giving us distorted perceptions of the morals and activities of our own culture. Such charges have been leveled since the novel entered the popular culture in the early days of mass communication. Concern has progressively intensified, however, as the media's influence has become more pervasive.

Comic books came under criticism as early as the 1930s. As the youth culture enthusiastically embraced this new medium, parent groups started calling for a reduction of violence in comic books. Some people predicted that, if action weren't taken, the nation's youth would grow up with a distorted view of reality and a permissive attitude toward violence. The criticism was not totally unfounded. Many youngsters were injured by blows to the head from cap guns and other childhood accidents caused when they reenacted comic-book adventures. The comic-book industry was finally forced to adopt a code of ethics in 1954.

Concern about comic books all but vanished in the 1950s when parents and other advocacy groups turned their attention to the new, more pervasive, medium of television. Children's television entertainment started out with such innocent shows as *Kukla, Fran and Ollie, Howdy Doody, The Mickey Mouse Club* and *Time for Beany.* But then television started running old movie cartoons on Saturday mornings exclusively for children. Shows that featured the Roadrunner and the Coyote, Popeye, Bugs Bunny and numerous others were now seen for the first time as violence ridden. People started questioning whether a five-year-old's perception of reality would be distorted when he or she saw the Coyote walk away unharmed after being squashed by boulders and falling off cliffs.

During the 1980s violence-oriented Saturday children's shows continued with such programs as *He-Man and the Masters of the Universe, G. I. Joe: A Real American Hero, Transformers, She-Ra: Princess of Power, M.A.S.K. (Medical Armored Strike Command), Thunder Cats, Voltron* and *Rambo.*

Concern over violence spread to other forms of TV entertainment as well. Westerns, police and detective shows all became targets for critics. The networks, anxious over this new wave of accusations, started toning down violent programs and canceling violence-oriented shows. The motion picture industry was quick to pick up the violence themes and intensify them.

Another source of alarm was the distorted picture of American culture painted by both television entertainment and TV news. When sociologists investigated the causes of riots in American ghettos in the mid-1960s, they started getting answers that pointed a finger at television. Some ghetto residents indicated that they were rebelling against the Establishment because they felt cheated by the system. Their frustrations were traced to hours of watching such television shows as *Father Knows Best, Leave It to Beaver* and *The Adventures of Ozzie and Harriet,* which all showed happy white middle-class families living in comfortable homes with modern furniture, refrigerators and spacious fenced yards.

The latest concern over perceived efforts by television to distort cultural reality came in 1990 when Fox's cartoon comedy, *The Simpsons,* climbed to the top of the rating charts. Some critics felt that the cartoon family was not portraying American family life in a suitable fashion. After the consumer culture began selling popular Bart Simpson T-shirts with the slogan "Underachiever and Proud of It," school districts went into action, banning the wearing of such apparel.

Soap Operas.   A mainstay of daytime television from the beginning, the soap opera has also been the target of criticism. Do soap operas provide an innocent escape into the troubled lives of others, or do they, as some have charged, distort our view of reality? Do they reflect changes in our culture, or do they cause them? Is the level of permissive sex and adultery in modern soap operas in line with the level that exists in society, or is it an exaggeration? If there are distortions, how do they affect average people when they filter the PMR into real life? Is there a relationship between the tremendous increase in herpes, AIDS and teenage pregnancies and the escalation of casual sex on television?

Some media critics also worry that the exportation of shows like *Dallas* and *Dynasty* give people in foreign lands a distorted view of Americans. How many foreigners, for example, believe that all Americans are rich, beautiful and successful?

Docudramas.   The docudrama, which dramatizes an actual event, has sparked considerable controversy since the 1980s. It didn't take long before critics were asking where the facts left off and fiction began.

Among the first critics were historians, who complained about many of the historical docudramas, such as *Liberty* (discussed in Chapter 10). They worried that this distortion of history would deprive the younger generation—which gets most of its information from television—from learning from the mistakes of history.

In addition, the accuracy of several docudramas of the early 1980s was seriously challenged by those who had participated in the real events, such as the investigators and government officials involved in the arrest and conviction of Wayne Williams for a series of murders of African-American children in Atlanta, Georgia.

In 1987 two television networks aired different docudramas of the same sensational case—making people wonder which was closer to the truth. In January CBS broadcast *At Mother's Request,* a mini-series about a woman who talked her son into killing her wealthy father because he wouldn't give her money. Then in the spring, NBC televised its version, *Nutcracker: Money, Madness, Murder,* also as a well-promoted mini-series.

Criticism of docudramas continued into the 1990s. When network television broadcast *Family of Five,* about the Walker family and U.S. spy operations, the program carried the following disclaimer: "Certain events and characters have been fictionalized."

Eight months after a Boston man killed himself to avoid arrest on suspicion of murdering his pregnant wife, and before a grand jury could deliver the results of its investigation, CBS broadcast a docudrama based on the case; *Good Night, Sweet Wife: A Murder in Boston* (see Box 16.4).

The family of the victim, Carol Stuart, issued a statement that it was "very disturbing that the movie was made without their consent or participation and that such a movie is being broadcast while there is still a sitting grand jury, before anyone, even our family, knows the outcome of the criminal investigation."

When HBO broadcast the docudrama *The Tragedy of Flight 103: The Inside Story,* Pan American World Airways issued a strong statement claiming that the program contained a "reckless disregard for the facts," was an "outright fabrication" and was a "work of fiction and a cheap shot."

The ethical problem with docudramas stems from television's dual role as both an information and an entertainment medium. To get high ratings and audience shares (the percentage of TV sets in use that are tuned to a particular program), television has too often been willing to sacrifice information to provide a more entertaining program.

Media Sex and Explicit Language.   The increase of themes about casual sex and suggestive and titillating language in TV sitcoms has generated much media criticism. Fox's *Married . . . With Children* has been attacked for its sexual content and mockery of traditional family values. In 1989 a Detroit woman, Terry Rakolta, launched a campaign against the program urging advertisers to stop their sponsorship. Senator Jesse Helms called the program "trash." Even the U.S.

BOX 16.4

WERE THERE RACIAL IMPLICATIONS TO PRESS COVERAGE IN THE STUART MURDER?

It was a classic, tear-jerking murder and the press and public responded with outrage. An affluent, white, Boston-suburban couple was reportedly assaulted by a raspy-voiced African-American dressed in a jogging suit. The seven-months pregnant wife lay dying in the front seat of their car, while the seriously wounded husband called for help on his car phone. Adding drama to the event was the fact that a television crew for the popular prime-time show *911* was on duty in Boston that night and was able to film the dramatic rescue.

Headlines of newspapers across the country and network newscasts told of the gruesome details. Boston police and political leaders were quick to react, launching an all-out manhunt for the killer. African-American neighborhoods were searched and black suspects were stopped and questioned on the street. Eventually a 39-year-old African-American ex-convict was arrested for the murder.

Civic leaders, including Massachusetts Governor Michael Dukakis and the mayor of Boston, attended the funeral of the victim, Carol Stuart, while her husband remained in a hospital bed. Tears flowed at the funeral when a letter written by the 30-year-old husband, Charles, was read at the funeral by his best friend. It said: "You have brought joy and kindness to every life you've touched. Now you sleep away from me. I will never again know the feeling of your hand in mine."

The pathos of this case was so strong that police overlooked the fact that the husband had taken out large amounts of life insurance on his wife prior to the killing. After his release from the hospital, Charles Stuart identified the ex-convict in a lineup as someone who resembled the killer of his wife and child, purchased a new car and resumed his life.

Then, several months after the crime, Charles's 23-year-old brother, apparently feeling guilty that an innocent man was being held for the murder, admitted that he had been an accomplice in his brother's plot to murder his wife for the insurance money. He explained that Charles had shot Carol, then had turned the gun on himself to avoid suspicion. He told of taking Carol's purse and the gun from Charles and throwing them into the river. Charles, learning that he was now a suspect in the crime, jumped to his death from a bridge into the icy Mystic River near Boston.

The African-American community was outraged over the way the police and press handled the case. Stuart was presumed innocent until the very end because everyone believed that the killer had been black and the victims were affluent whites. African-American leaders asked whether the case would have been handled the same way if the victim had been black and the suspect white.

Journalists stand to learn an important ethical lesson from this incident. News stories should be covered objectively, based on the evidence at hand. Emotions and sensationalism can distort objective coverage and often—as in the case of the Stuarts—lead to misinformation and faulty conclusions.

Congress got into the act by passing a resolution in 1989 giving the TV industry three years to set standards.

The advent of MTV in the 1980s caused alarm and dismay among critics who claimed that many of the music videos were advocating sexual violence. Sexually violent themes in music lyrics as well have been a concern of media critics. Some critics contend that this sexual exploitation by the music industry may erode the progress women have made in their quest to avoid being stereotyped as sex objects.

Others contend that sex in the media seldom shows pleasant, enjoyable love-making in a romantic context. Instead, they note, most of the sex in the media involves some sort of violence or unpleasantness, and media programming often

■ The Bundy family in *Married . . . With Children* has been criticized for its sexual jokes and mockery of traditional family values.

suggests that participants should be punished in some way for their sexual activity. Will this type of depiction eventually change cultural attitudes toward the relationship between sex and love?

Coping with the problem of sex and sexual violence in the media is complex. Allowing pressure groups to force governmental censorship might open the door to widespread censorship of any unpopular idea. The answer seems to lie in responses to the following questions: is there any real harm in the content of media entertainment? And if there is, should the producers of constructed mediated reality exercise more social responsibility in creating this entertainment? Social scientists have been wrestling with the first question for decades and have generated a great deal of media-effects research suggesting a variety of answers.

Social responsibility seems to be the key ingredient for all mass-media operations. If our culture is to have high standards, those who shape that culture through the mass media must be extremely careful to adhere to the highest ethical practices.

MEDIA EFFECTS

As it has been noted throughout this book, the effects of the mass media are a major concern in our society—a concern incidentally that has been around since the beginning of mass communication.

Although early concerns were addressed by reactionary efforts to correct the situation—as we have seen with the burning of printers by King Henry II of France (see Chapter 2) and the book burning and banning efforts of Anthony Comstock and others (Chapter 5)—the first scientific research to explore the relationship between media content and human behavior did not begin until the 1920s when criticism of "sinful" and violent motion pictures intensified.

Mass-media studies have addressed various topics and concerns from that time forward. However, it wasn't until television became so pervasive in our culture that media-effects research increased dramatically. For example, prior to the 1970s, there were approximately 300 research studies published on media effects. During the '70s, some 2,500 new studies appeared in the literature, most of them dealing with the effects of television violence on children (see Chapter 10).

Early media-effects research was based on the *magic bullet theory* that assumed that a given message reached every eye and ear immediately and directly in the same way and that all responses were similar. It wasn't until the 1930s that research began showing that individual differences played a role in how people responded to media.

Payne Fund Studies.   The first major research efforts on media effects began in 1929 with a series of 12 studies on the effects of motion pictures. Sponsored by the well-respected Payne Fund, the studies examined such topics as how motion picture morals compared with American moral standards, whether there was a link between the making of films depicting crime and actual crime and delinquency reported in the community, and how motion pictures affected the behavior of children.

Although these studies did not come up with conclusive proof that motion pictures were damaging to our culture, the results, particularly the conclusion that teenagers had been greatly influenced by the movies, did bring pressure to bear on the government and the industry. The industry responded, in an effort to head off government censorship, by strengthening the production code of the Motion Picture Producers and Distributors of America (see Chapter 8).

Cantril Study.   Radio became the next mass communication medium to undergo media-effects research. When Orson Welles's 1938 radio drama *War of the Worlds* caused more than a million Americans to panic and believe that Martians were invading Earth, researchers went into action to find out why a radio drama, clearly identified as such, could have been believed by so many people. A study conducted by Hadley Cantril at Princeton University found that critical thinking skills were a key factor. Individuals with better educations were less likely to believe that the broadcast was real. It also listed the excellent quality of the broadcast and political tensions in Europe as contributors to the panic.

Lazarsfeld Study.   The next major study, conducted in 1940 by Paul Lazarsfeld, sought to determine if the mass media, particularly radio, were influencing the way people made political choices at election time (see Chapter 14). The study concluded that other people, known as opinion leaders, and not the mass media, influenced most people's political decisions. The study did find, however, that the opinion leaders spent more time with the mass media than the average person, thus creating the two-step flow theory of media influence that was discussed in Chapter 14.

Delinquency and Violence.   Since the very first Payne studies, society and researchers have been concerned about the effects the mass media might have on children. Of particular concern is the question of whether or not violence in the mass media causes delinquency and violent behavior in child and teenage viewers.

When comic books entered the popular culture in the late 1930s as a youth-oriented entertainment medium (see Chapter 5), action/adventure characters such as Superman became popular with young people. As previously discussed, more than one youngster was injured depicting actions of comic-book heroes. In 1952, Congress got into the business of studying media effects when Senator Estes Kefauver held hearings into the causes of juvenile delinquency. When the same committee held hearings during the 1954–55 session of Congress, it concluded that violent programming in large amounts could be potentially harmful to children.

In addition to the Kefauver hearings, two other U.S. senators held subcommittee hearings on juvenile delinquency and the media during the 1960s. They issued a warning that young people could develop antisocial behavior from watching too much violent television content. The National Commission on the Causes and Prevention of Violence, appointed by President Lyndon Johnson in 1968, concluded that a constant diet of violent behavior on television had an adverse effect on human character and attitudes. The commission stressed the need for more significant research in this area.

The Surgeon General, at the urging of Senator John Pastore, also became involved in studying TV violence as a possible public health hazard. An advisory committee issued "Television and Social Behavior: The Surgeon General's Report" and a summary report entitled "Television and Growing Up: The Impact of Televised Violence." Both reports became involved in political controversy over the committee's membership selection and research decisions, much like the Meese Commission findings on obscenity in 1986 (see Chapter 4).

Less controversial research—by Wilbur Schramm, Jack Lyle and Edwin Parker—found that violence did affect children but that it was not a simplistic action/reaction activity, but rather a complex phenomenon that created different reactions among a variety of children under similar and different situations. The study said:

> For some children, under some conditions, some television is harmful. For other children, under the same conditions, or for the same children under other conditions, it may be beneficial. For most children, under most conditions, most television is probably neither harmful nor particularly beneficial.[8]

Four Violence Theories.   As research on the relationship between violence and the media continued, different schools of thought developed. The "catharsis theory" suggests that we relieve frustrations and potential violent behavior vicariously by watching violence in the media.[9] The "aggressive cues theory" contends that TV violence increases excitement levels in viewers and triggers

■ The effect of media violence on children has long been a concern in the American culture. Today this concern is increasing as our society sees a growing number of latchkey children who spend their after-school hours alone in front of the TV set.

already learned behavior resulting in violent acts being repeated in real-life situations. A similar theory, the "reinforcement theory," suggests that TV violence reinforces behavior already existing in individuals. According to this theory, a violent individual perceives violence on television as real-life occurrences while the nonviolent person sees it as entertainment.[10] The fourth theory, the "observational theory," contends that we can learn violent behavior from watching violent programs.

Albert Bandura and his colleagues advanced the observational theory through their studies of children interacting with "Bobo" dolls. The experiments, using different groups of children, found that those who were shown pictures depicting abusive conduct with the doll imitated that behavior.[11]

The aggressive cues theory was supported by the research of Leonard Berkowitz, who conducted aggression-machine experiments where subjects were asked to administer an electric shock to another person whenever he or she gave a wrong answer to a question. Those administering the shocks had a choice of how strong to make the electrical charge. The studies showed that both children and college students participating in the research administered stronger shocks after they were exposed to TV violence.[12] Since both the Bandura and Berkowitz studies demonstrated a relationship between TV violence and aggressive behavior in the laboratory setting, they were widely quoted by groups advocating the reduction of violence on television.

Many of the studies on violence in the media used researcher George Gerbner's violence index, a technique which counted the number of violent acts in a TV program.[13] This content analysis continues to show high levels of violence in TV programming. A study released in 1990 showed that violence in children's television programming climbed dramatically during the previous three years. The study, conducted under the auspices of the University of Pennsylvania's Annenberg School of Communications, also found that prime-time levels of violence remained high but unchanged from earlier in the decade.[14]

Obscenity and Pornography.   In addition to the effects of TV program violence on children, the effect of pornography in the culture has also generated interest. As previously discussed (see Chapter 4) government commissions on obscenity and pornography came up with opposite conclusions in 1970 and 1986. However, there have been a number of other studies that have dealt with this issue.

A five-year longitudinal study of *Playboy* and *Penthouse* found in 1980 that there had been a significant increase in depictions of rape, bondage and sadism.[15]

Studies by Donnerstein and Hallam in 1978[16] and K. A. Baron in 1979[17] indicated that pornography can stimulate violent behavioral tendencies. Other studies have shown that the highest levels of sexual arousal occur in response to sexually violent pornography[18] and that a substantial number of male students observed in studies on pornography found the idea of rape attractive.[19] However, since all of these studies were conducted on male college student volunteers, care must be taken not to apply the results to sex offenders or any other group without further research.

Still, some researchers are suggesting that sexual violence shown in the media helps to cause its occurrence in real life. Research led J. H. Court to conclude that the increase in media sexual violence had caused an increase in sexual attacks on women in the Western world.[20]

Positive Effects Research.   By the 1980s, concerns over television's impact on children had been expanded to include the effects of TV advertising on children (see Chapter 10) and studies on some of the more positive aspects of media effects on young people. These latter studies focused on prosocial programs developed for children, such as *Sesame Street, The Electric Company, Mister Rogers' Neighborhood, Fat Albert and the Cosby Kids, The Harlem Globetrotters' Popcorn Machine* and *Shazam.* These programs were all developed to impart positive social values. Of all these programs, the most extensively researched has been *Sesame Street,* a show that attempts to teach rudimentary reading and counting skills as well as social skills. Much of the research suggests that children do learn from the program, but that disadvantaged children—the target audience—are the least likely to watch the show.

Unfortunately, still relatively little data has been collected on the cumulative effects of media; more longitudinal studies (studies conducted over a long period of time) would give us insight into the total effects on individuals over long periods of time from a variety of media stimuli.

■ Some media-effects research has shown that educational TV programs like *Sesame Street* have a positive effect on children.

CULTURAL CONSEQUENCES

Throughout this book we have attempted to show how our culture is shaped and changed by the mass media. Western civilization changed slowly until the invention of the printing press in the fifteenth century. Then change, assisted by mass communication, became more rapid. After the forces of industrialization, democratization and public education emerged in the nineteenth century, the expansion of the old and development of new mass media accelerated rapidly. As a result, our popular culture was radically transformed.

During the past 20 years the development of new communication technologies has been analogous to a giant snowball gathering speed as it rolls down a steep mountain, and it is safe to assume that this phenomenon is only beginning to gain momentum. As these new technologies find their niche in our culture, we are going to see dramatic changes in our lifestyles. Whether these changes will have a positive or negative impact on our culture remains to be seen.

Form vs. Content.   All technological change affects the form—the "hardware"—of the mass media. From our discussions of media ethics, we might conclude that the *content* of the mass media—the all-important "software"—has not kept pace.

What will happen if the same media content—more interest in who is winning the political race than in the issues of the campaign, distortions of reality through exaggerated entertainment programs, tasteless sitcoms and more casual sex and sexual violence—is disseminated through larger and better television sets and home information centers? Will the transfer of newspaper and magazine material from print to electronic screens mean anything if the information is not any more socially responsible than it is today? Will the availability of hundreds of TV channels transmitted into our homes by satellites or fiber optics advance our culture if the focus remains on entertainment rather than education and we continue to see the same old reruns?

If the content of our culture is to keep pace with its form, major changes need to be made in the mass media. We have learned that the media shape our culture. Perhaps it's time that we in the culture take a more active role in shaping the media. Before we do this, however, we must keep in mind the importance of the media in our free society and make sure that we maintain the delicate system of checks and balances among the judicial, legislative and executive branches of government that our nation's founders set up. Helping to protect this system is the check and balance that was added by the Bill of Rights—a free press.

Despite the various regulations that are placed on the American mass media, the press in this country still remains one of the freest in the world. This must continue to be the case if American democracy is to survive.

Importance of a Free Press.   The concept that a free press is an inherent part of a free society was based on the philosophies of John Milton, Andrew Hamilton, James Madison, Thomas Jefferson and others. As Hamilton said in his closing arguments of the John Peter Zenger trial in 1735, " . . . a free press is a cause of liberty—the liberty both of exposing and opposing arbitrary power . . . by speaking and writing the truth."

Our democracy depends on a free press to keep us informed. The temptation of government leaders, the courts and consumers to regulate our mass media is great. Thus it is important for all of us in American culture to recognize the importance of keeping our mass media free from unreasonable restraints.

Just keeping the media free is not good enough, however. Free yet irresponsible mass media that are insensitive to the needs and desires of their culture are almost as useless as a system of mass media under strict government control.

As a society, we should not tolerate shoddy, arrogant, irresponsible or inadequate performances from any of our mass media. Likewise, society should not let business interests in the media forsake responsibility for financial gains.

Consumer Awareness Needed.   It is the obligation of each of us to become aware, concerned, skeptical and demanding. We should be aware of just how well our mass media are or are not performing when it comes to social responsibility and high ethical standards. We should be concerned about inadequate performances. We should be skeptical of any movements to strengthen external regulations of the mass media (whether from government, the courts or organized consumer groups). And, most important, we should constantly demand that our mass media perform with the utmost responsibility and concern for the quality of our culture.

The fact that the mass media in the United States are businesses, dependent on making a profit, is important to remember. In any business enterprise the consumer is the most important element in the sales transaction. Without the consumer there is no sale. Television shows must be watched, news articles must be read, magazines and books must be purchased and advertised products must sell if the mass media are to stay in business.

If we were more discriminating in our consumption of the mass media, we might influence the media's content. The numbers of people listening to radio and watching television are closely monitored. When a show's ratings slip, it is canceled. TV ratings, like newspaper and magazine circulations, determine the advertising revenues a medium generates. The mass media pay close attention to what the majority of people in the culture think. We are the ones who determine whether a place in our culture exists for them. If they fail to give us what we want and demand, we have the power to phase them out of existence.

Thus if the content of the mass media remains less than of the highest quality, the fault is partially ours. Television, for example, will continue to give us *Married . . . With Children*–type programming if that is what the people are willing to watch. Sex and violence will continue to dominate movies, videos and magazines if that is what continues to sell. Whether or not the quality of mass-media content keeps pace with the new technological advances depends on each of us.

SUMMARY

The news media have come under fire in recent years for endangering people's lives, using fraud and deception to gather news stories, fabricating news, accepting gifts from news sources, having conflicts of interest and using poor judgment in determining what should and should not be covered.

Although journalists today are more concerned about ethical standards than ever before, they are still severely criticized for operating under a double standard—one that holds other institutions accountable for anything less than high ethical practices while refusing to criticize or examine their own practices.

The media also have been criticized for questionable ethical standards related to their business activities. Advertisers' attempts to control media content is a problem that has plagued the media for years. Those who pay the bills and produce the profits often feel that they should have a say in the media's editorial and entertainment content. Sometimes advertisers threaten to boycott the media if they don't get their way.

Not all advertiser influence is so blatant, however. Some media often run advertorials: news items that are publicity pieces for advertisers. Real estate sections of most newspapers are filled with advertiser hype disguised as news stories. Although these practices are profitable, they raise ethical concerns about the credibility of the news medium.

Some concerns also have been raised about television's new home shopping channels and direct-response advertising. It is feared that excessive impulse buying by consumers could result if two-way interaction with the television set were to become commonplace.

The trend toward large chain ownership of most community newspapers also threatens community journalism. Corporate dictates expressed without concern for local community sensitivities could change American journalism.

Many ethical questions are raised by the level of entertainment that the mass media provide. Concern has been focused on the distortions of cultural reality. Docudramas, sitcoms and soap operas are just some of the programs criticized. Sex and sexual violence in media content are also concerns.

All of these ethical concerns about the mass media highlight the point that a successful medium in American popular culture should be a socially responsible one.

These concerns over media content have led to numerous research studies on the effects of mass media. Most of these studies have focused on the effects of media violence on children. Since television has become the most dominant mass medium, it has been the focus of most of the media-effects research in recent years. Another topic generating media research has been obscenity and pornography.

Whether socially responsible mass-media content will keep pace with the media's rapidly expanding technology remains to be seen. If our culture is to advance with its technology, Americans must play an active role in demanding responsible content, while at the same time not forgetting the importance of a free and independent system of mass media in the American democracy.

THOUGHT QUESTIONS

1 What do you think of the various approaches used by the news media in reporting AIDS-related deaths? How would you handle such stories if you were a newspaper editor?

2 Should news media continue the practice of omitting names of rape victims? How is such a practice justified when the names of other violent-crime victims are included in stories?

3 Is there anything wrong with running favorable stories about major advertisers in the news columns? Why or why not?

4 Should the use of sexual themes and explicit language be curtailed in television entertainment? Why or why not?

5 Do you believe pornography causes an increase in crimes against women? If no, why? If yes, what should be done about it?

NOTES

1. Clifford G. Christians, Kim B. Rotzoll and Mark Fackler, *Media Ethics* (New York: Longman, 1983), pp. 114–117.

2. Steve Robinson, "Pulitzer: Was the Mirage Deception?" *Columbia Journalism Review* (July–August 1979): 14.

3. Dennis McDougal, "Congress Takes Off the Gloves at TV Hearings," *Los Angeles Times,* April 30, 1987, Calendar Section, p. 1.

4. Herb Schmertz with William Novak, *Goodbye to the Low Profile: The Art of Creative Confrontation* (Boston: Little, Brown, 1986), p. 94.

5. *USA Today* (April 5, 1984): 10a.

6. Tom Goldstein, *The News at Any Cost: How Journalists Compromise Their Ethics to Shape the News* (New York: Simon & Schuster, 1985), pp. 91–92.

7. Edward Jay Whetmore, *Mediamerica: Form, Content and Consequences of Mass Communication,* 3rd ed. (Belmont, Calif.: Wadsworth, 1985), pp. 10–12, 170–171.

8. Wilbur Schramm, Jack Lyle and Edwin Parker, *Television in the Lives of Our Children* (Stanford, Calif.: Stanford University Press, 1961), p. 13.

9. Seymour Feshbach, "The Stimulating vs. Cathartic Effects of a Vicarious Aggressive Experience," *Journal of Abnormal and Social Psychology* 63 (1961): 381–385.

10. Joseph Klapper, *The Effects of Mass Communication* (New York: The Free Press, 1960).

11. Albert Bandura and Richard Walters, *Social Learning and Personality Development* (New York: Holt, Rinehart & Winston, 1963).

12. Leonard Berkowitz, *Aggression: A Social Psychological Analysis* (New York: McGraw-Hill Book Company, 1962).

13. George Gerbner, Larry Gross, Michael Morgan and Nancy Signorielli, "The Mainstreaming of America: Violence Profile Number 11," *Journal of Communication* 30, no. 3 (Summer 1980).

14. Shawn Pogatchnik, "Kids' TV Gets More Violent, Study Finds," *Los Angeles Times,* January 26, 1990, F1.

15. N. M. Malamuth and B. Spinner, "A Longitudinal Content Analysis of Sexual Violence in the Best-Selling Erotica Magazines," *Journal of Sex Research* 16 (1980): 226–237.

16. E. Donnerstein and J. Hallam, "Facilitating Effects of Erotica on Aggression Against Women," *Journal of Personality and Social Psychology* 36 (1978): 1270–1277.

17. K. A. Baron, "Heightened Sexual Arousal and Physical Aggression: An Extension to Females," *Journal of Research in Personality* 13 (1979): 91–102.

18. N. M. Malamuth, M. Heim and S. Feshbach, "Sexual Responsiveness of College Students to Rape Depictions: Inhibitory and Disinhibitory Effects," *Journal of Personality and Social Psychology* 38 (1980): 399–408.

19. N. M. Malamuth, S. Haber and S. Feshbach, "Testing Hypotheses Regarding Rape: Exposure to Sexual Violence, Sex Differences, and the 'Normality' of Rapists," *Journal of Research in Personality* 14 (1980): 121–137.

20. J. H. Court, "Pornography and Sex Crimes: A Reevaluation in the Light of Recent Trends Around the World," *International Journal of Criminality and Penology* 5 (1977): 129–157.

ADDITIONAL READING

Anderson, Kent. *Television Fraud: The History and Implications of the Quiz Show Scandals.* Westport, Conn.: Greenwood Press, 1978.

Barron, Jerome A. *Freedom of the Press for Whom? The Right of Access to Mass Media.* Bloomington: Indiana University Press, 1973.

————, **and Dienes, C. Thomas.** *Handbook of Free Speech and Free Press.* Boston: Little, Brown, 1979.

Cline, V. H. ed. *Where Do You Draw the Line? An Exploration into Media Violence, Pornography, and Censorship,* Provo, Utah: Brigham Young University Press, 1974.

Goethals, Gregor T. *The TV Ritual—Worship at the Video Altar,* Boston: Beacon Press, 1981.

Goodwin, H. Eugene. *Groping for Ethics in Journalism.* Ames: Iowa State University Press, 1983.

Halloran, J. D. *The Effects of Mass Communication,* Leicester, U.K.: Leicester University Press, 1964.

Large, Martin. *Who's Bringing Them Up?* Gloucester, U.K.: Alan Sutton Limited, 1980.

Merrill, John C., and Odell, S. Jack. *Philosophy and Journalism.* New York: Longman, 1983.

Moody, Kate. *Growing Up on Television.* New York: Times Books, 1980.

Schramm, Wilbur. "What Is TV Doing to Our Children?" *Sight, Sound and Society: Motion Pictures and Television in America,* Boston: Beacon Press, 1968.

Sinclair, Upton. *The Brass Check: A Study of American Journalism.* Pasadena, Calif.: Published by the author, 1920.

GLOSSARY

ABC American Broadcasting Company; founded after NBC was forced to sell one of its two radio networks in 1943.

Acta diurna "Daily acts"; news sheets posted in public places by the government during the Roman Empire.

Advertorial Advertising copy written in the form of a news story. Sometimes placed in "news columns" of special sections of newspapers labeled "advertising supplement."

AFP Agence France-Presse; a Paris-based French news wire service that was organized in 1945.

Agenda setting A process whereby the mass media shape our awareness of people and events.

Alien and Sedition acts Laws passed in 1798 to silence critics of the government. These laws, which lasted only two years, represented the first U.S. government effort to restrict freedom of the press.

AM radio Amplitude modulation; a form of radio transmission in which sound waves modulate the length (or amplitude) of the carrier wave.

AP The Associated Press; the oldest American news wire service, founded in 1848.

A-T-R A model of how advertising works; stands for awareness, trial, and reinforcement.

Authoritarian theory A theory of the press that asserts that the rulers of society should control what is disseminated to the public in the mass media. Authoritarian theory has an offshoot, Soviet Communist theory. See **Libertarian theory.**

British invasion A term used to describe British rock groups bringing their version of rock-'n'-roll to U.S. audiences. The invasion began with the Beatles' U.S. tour in 1964.

Cable TV A system of sending and receiving TV signals by wire. Cable systems usually receive signals by satellite at a central facility and relay them by cable to homes for a monthly fee.

CBS Columbia Broadcasting System; founded in 1927 under the name United Independent Broadcasters /Columbia.

Chain ownership Two or more newspapers published in different communities by the same company.

Channel A term for the way we send a message. In mass communication, any one of the mass media.

Channel noise Anything that externally interferes with a message in the communication process.

Chapbooks Forerunners to the novel. These were small, pocket-sized books that were made available to the semi-literate after the fifteenth-century invention of movable type.

CNN The Cable News Network, a

24-hour television news network launched by Ted Turner in 1980.

Communication A process involving the sorting, selecting, and sharing of symbols in such a way as to help a receiver elicit from his or her own mind a meaning similar to that contained in the mind of the communicator.

Corantos Predecessors to the newspaper that consisted of a single sheet of paper containing current news. They first appeared in Germany in 1609 and in England in 1621.

Crisis management A public relations activity that reacts to corporate crises and disasters by attempting to place a positive angle on the publicity that results from the disaster. It often involves showing the company taking strong, positive actions to correct the problem.

Cult A subcultural group or movement that usually rejects and refuses to conform to mass-cultural activities or attitudes.

Cultural industries Commercial enterprises that sell not only items for use in our mass culture but items for the many subcultures as well.

Cultural niches A reference to the fact that as all new communication technologies develop, they must first find an acceptance or use in the culture before they become a part of the mass culture.

Culture Everything that occurs in a society—all the customs and practices handed down from generation to generation.

Customized textbooks Textbooks that are specifically produced for a particular class by combining a variety of chapters from one or more textbooks. The instructor of the course selects the chapters and the publisher assembles the product.

Demographic breakout A magazine production technique that enables advertisers to insert ads in only a portion of a given issue. Advertisers can target their ads to specific demographic groups, such as doctors, students, executives, or people earning above a specified income.

Desktop publishing The use of a personal computer to write, edit, typeset, design graphics, and lay out pages for a publication.

Digital sound A method of converting sound electronically into a numerical system to achieve better sound reproduction.

Direct Broadcasting Satellites (DBS) A powerful satellite system that sends signals directly to homes with small, relatively inexpensive receiving dishes.

Direct mail One of the most effective methods of disseminating information on political candidates and issues. Computerized mailings can send different messages to different audiences.

Docudrama A form of TV dramatic presentations based on current or historical events.

Drive time A term referring to the time most people commute to and from work. During this period, usually from 6 to 10 A.M. and 3 to 7 P.M., radio stations in urban areas have their largest audiences.

DuMont A TV network operating in the early days of television. Named after a pioneer in the development of TV receivers, Allen B. DuMont.

Electronic books A book reproduced, often in abridged form, on audio cassette. By the 1980s, major publishing houses like Simon & Schuster, Random House, and Bantam all had audio book divisions.

Electronic cottages A term for the homes of telecommuters, people who work at home connected to an office by a computer terminal.

EPS cycle The three stages most mass media evolve through: the elitist stage, when a medium is restricted to the educated, aristocratic, and wealthy; the popular stage, when a medium is consumed by the masses; and the specialized stage, when a medium caters to a variety of specific groups.

Equal-time provision A Federal Communications Commission requirement that all bona fide political candidates have equal opportunity to use the airwaves. (Also known as Section 315.)

Fairness Doctrine A 1949 Federal Communications Commission ruling that required broadcasters to air both sides of controversial issues. In 1987 the FCC abolished the rule, calling it unconstitutional.

FCC freeze A freeze on new television stations placed by the Federal Communication Commission in 1948 to allow time to allocate frequencies throughout the country. The freeze was lifted in 1952.

Federal Communications Commission (FCC) A government agency established in 1934 to regulate wire and radio broadcasting; its authority was later expanded to include television. It took over the duties of the Federal Radio Commission.

Federal Radio Commission (FRC) A government agency established in 1927 to regulate the airwaves and allocate frequencies for broadcasting.

Feedback Any observable response to a message in the communication process.

Fiber optics Tiny flexible glass strands capable of carrying 100,000 telephone or 100 broadcast signals on a wire the size of a human hair.

Flack A derogatory term occasionally used by journalists to refer to public relations practitioners.

FM radio Frequency modulation; a form of radio transmission in which sound waves modulate the frequency of the carrier wave.

Fotonovel A book that is part text, part picture book, and part comic book. Usually a spinoff of a popular movie or television show.

Frame of reference The set of individual experiences that each person has and uses to form an understanding in the communication process. (Sometimes called a "field of experience.")

Freebie A gratuity; usually tickets, passes, records, or books given to journalists by people seeking favorable treatment from the press.

Freedom of Information The Freedom of Information Act (FOI), passed in 1966 to give the news media and public access to the files of federal government agencies.

Gag order Court-imposed restriction on what attorneys and/or court officials may say to the media during a legal proceeding.

Gatekeeping The process whereby numerous people become involved in determining what news, information, or entertainment will reach a mass audience.

Gazetta An Italian coin that was charged for printed sheets of current news in Venice prior to the development of newspapers. When newspapers began developing in the seventeenth century, many were named "Gazette."

Glasnost The policy of "openness"

established in the 1980s by Communist Party Secretary Mikhail Gorbachev that has made news and information more readily available in the mass media of the Soviet Union.

Graphic novel A spinoff of the comic book that became popular in the 1980s. This book form consists of original, self-contained stories told in comic book format.

Green marketing A new trend where advertisers appeal to the growing interest in and concern about the environment by designing their products and advertising campaigns to be more environmentally sensitive.

Hard news The factual account of significant news events. See **Soft news.**

High-Definition Television (HDTV) An extremely clear television signal transmitted at 1,125 lines per picture (as opposed to the current 525 lines per picture of U.S. broadcasts), allowing excellent reception on larger-than-life TV screens. May one day be used to transmit motion pictures to theaters via satellite.

How-to book A specialized book giving advice on how to do something; how-to books cater to a wide range of interests.

Hybrid TV A 1980s TV genre introduced by Steve Bochco. It borrows techniques from a variety of television genres including soap operas, TV dramas, action/adventure shows, urban Westerns and sitcoms.

Industrial Revolution The social and economic upheavals of the eighteenth and nineteenth centuries that transformed America from an agrarian society to a mechanized, production-oriented culture.

Infomercials Television commercials that are designed as informational programs, usually 30-minutes in length. Topics range from money-making ideas to weight-loss programs.

Information overload A term used to describe a situation where a person is overwhelmed by too much information.

Information processing The way information is managed or used by communicators and consumers of the information.

Internal specialization A term used to describe a general-interest magazine that carries a variety of articles and allows readers to specialize by selecting articles of interest; an example is *Reader's Digest.* See **Unit specialization.**

Interpretative reporting A reporting style that developed in the 1930s to provide background for complex stories.

Instant book A book produced in only a few weeks, so it can be sold while the news event it describes is still topical.

Invasion of privacy Information published or broadcast that violates a person's right to be left alone.

Inverted pyramid A style of organizing news stories in which the essential material is placed at the beginning and subsequent paragraphs provide information in declining order of importance.

Investigative reporting News reporting that digs below the surface to uncover important information, usually political corruption or other wrongdoing.

Issues management A public relations activity that attempts to identify and correctly interpret problems before they become crises. See **crisis management.**

Kinetoscope A four-foot-high box used to show motion pictures in the nineteenth century. The device, developed in Thomas Edison's laboratory, allowed one person at a time to view the pictures. It became a penny arcade attraction.

Libel Published or broadcast information that damages an individual's reputation. There are three defenses against a libel suit: truth, privileged information, and fair comment and criticism.

Libertarian theory The theory of the press that holds that the press should serve the governed (people), not the governors. Libertarian theory has an offshoot, Social Responsibility theory. See **Authoritarian theory.**

Low-power television (LPTV) A system that can transmit television signals at lower cost to a small geographic area (usually a 15–20 mile radius). Can be used to provide special-interest programming in metropolitan areas.

Mass communication A process whereby professional communicators use technological devices to share messages over some distance to influence large audiences.

Mass culture The things in our culture that are mass-produced and/or shared through the mass media. See **Popular culture.**

Mass-market paperback Usually a romance, Western, or mystery novel that is mass-produced (a million copies or more) and mass-distributed. It is usually smaller in size than other paperbacks and printed on cheaper paper.

Message In the communication process, whatever the source or communicator attempts to share with someone else.

Metropolitan newspaper Originally called the penny press, a newspaper with a style of reporting designed for ordinary people in the popular culture.

Mini-series A multipart TV drama that runs for several consecutive nights. A popular TV genre, it is used to disrupt regular viewing habits and allow networks to promote their other programming during commercial breaks.

Motivational research (MR) Advertising research based on Freudian psychology; used to develop advertising strategies.

MTV Music Television; a cable network launched by Warner-Amex in 1981 to bring 24-hour-a-day music videos to 12- to 23-year-olds.

Muckrakers A term coined by President Theodore Roosevelt to describe reporters who specialized in exposing scandal and corruption.

Multipoint Distribution Service (MDS) A pay-TV system that broadcasts via microwave signals to small antennas. It offers an over-the-airwaves alternative to cable TV.

NBC National Broadcasting Company; founded in 1926 as a subsidiary of the Radio Corporation of America (RCA).

News ploys News events staged by public relations practitioners or political consultants to get free publicity for their clients. Sometimes called media events.

Noise See **Channel noise, psychological noise.**

Nonfiction novel Book based on a true story, but written in the style of a novel, often with invented dialogue and made-up scenes.

Novelization A book based on a successful movie; the opposite of a book made into a movie.

Op-ed page The page opposite the editorial page, where guest columns and other opinion materials usually appear.

Opinion leader A person who influences the thinking of others; usually someone who is better informed by the mass media than the average person.

Pay-per-view Cable TV channels that require a special fee to access specific programs, usually sporting events. It is predicted that many additional sporting activities in the future, including the Super Bowl, will be available only on pay-per-view channels.

Pay TV Special entertainment channels, such as HBO, Showtime and Disney, that are provided by cable operators for an additional charge.

PBS Public Broadcasting System; a noncommercial television system established by the Public Broadcasting Act of 1967.

Penny press Term first used in the 1830s to describe new American newspapers aimed at the popular culture and selling for 1 cent. Also known as **metropolitan newspapers.**

People meter A hand-held remote control device used by TV rating services to measure the size and demographics of a television audience.

Personalized book A book, usually for children, whose text is stored in a computer. When a purchaser supplies specified personal data, the computer prints out a book with these facts included in the plot.

Pictorial prints The first form of mass-produced images for popular markets. Renaissance artists, led by Albrecht Dürer, began mass producing their art using woodcuts, metal engravings and the printing press.

Political consultants People trained in opinion polling, advertising or public relations who package political candidates and/or issues and sell them to the public.

Popular culture The culture of everyone in a society. This culture is so pervasive that we seldom notice it. (Often used interchangeably with **Mass culture.**)

Popular press The popular national tabloid newspapers in the United Kingdom.

Press agents People who design and execute plans to stage events and plant stories to get publicity in the news media for their clients.

Prime time The three viewing hours on television with the biggest audiences; 7–10 P.M. in the Central and Mountain time zones, 8–11 P.M. in Eastern and Pacific areas.

Prior restraint The ability of the government to prevent something from being published or broadcast. Such activity is usually prohibited by the First Amendment.

Product brokers People who arrange for the use of their clients' products in movies and TV shows.

Protestant Reformation The religious revolt against the Catholic church in the sixteenth century that led to the establishment of Protestant churches. This was the first major social movement to use the new invention of mass communication.

Psychographics A kind of advertising research that gathers information on people's interests, needs, values and lifestyles.

Psychological noise Internal factors that can lead to misunderstanding a message: selective exposure, selective perception and selective retention.

Public access　A provision provided by some cable TV operators that allows the public to use cable channels for public service programming. Uses often include public instruction by school districts, community forums and broadcasting of local city council meetings.

Public relations　The business of creating favorable images for clients; it includes press agentry, promotion, public affairs, publicity, opinion research and advertising.

Quality press　The full-sized, elite-oriented national newspapers in the United Kingdom.

Ratings　Percentage of all households having television sets that watch a particular program. See **Share**.

Receiver　In the communication process, the person who receives the messages being shared.

Red Channels　A 1950 report on the alleged Communist infiltration of the broadcast industry. Published by a group called Counterattack, it accused 151 radio and television personalities of having Communist leanings. Most of them lost their jobs.

Regional breakouts　Copies of a magazine that are circulated only in a designated geographic region. Magazine advertisers can lower their advertising costs by designating that their ads run in certain regional breakouts.

Reuters　British news wire service; organized in the 1850s.

Satellite.　An electronic relay system that orbits 22,300 miles above the equator; it receives signals from earth, recharges them on a transponder and sends them back to earth to be received by anyone with a receiving dish.

Selective exposure　A form of psychological noise that causes people to expose themselves to information that reinforces rather than opposes their general beliefs or opinions.

Selective perception　A form of psychological noise that causes people to see, hear and believe only what they want to see, hear and believe.

Selective retention　A form of psychological noise that causes people to remember things that reinforce their beliefs and opinions better than things that oppose them.

Semantic noise　A form of message interference that occurs when the message gets through exactly as sent but is not understood because terms used are unclear in meaning.

Share　The number of TV sets turned on at a given time that are tuned to a specific program.

Sitcom　Situation comedy, a popular and long-enduring genre of broadcast entertainment. Although it is a major ingredient of today's TV programming, the sitcom originated on radio.

Social Responsibility theory　An offshoot of the libertarian theory of the press that contends that the press must be socially responsible to keep a democratic nation well-informed.

Soft news　Feature stories or background information about entertaining items of interest. It includes everything from lifestyle articles to personality profiles and Dear Abby-type columns. Sometimes called ''fluff journalism,'' soft news accounts for most of the content in today's newspapers.

Soap opera A broadcasting genre that originated on radio and now provides popular entertainment for both daytime and prime-time television. Named after the original radio sponsors, soap companies.

Source The person in the communication process who shares information, ideas or attitudes with other people.

Soviet Communist theory An offshoot of the authoritarian theory of the press that believes that the mass media should be state-owned and -operated in order to best serve the government.

Spin doctor A person who specializes in getting the news media to put a special angle or "spin" on news stories so that clients are shown in a favorable light.

Subliminal advertising A technique of hiding images in advertisements; these imbeds are supposed to appeal to the emotional instincts of sex, fear and death, triggering a subconscious response that causes the ad to be remembered.

Sunshine laws Laws that give the news media and public access to government agencies. They usually require the public agencies to hold open meetings and make their printed documents available. These laws are based on the premise that the public's business should be conducted in public.

Symbols Words, pictures or objects used in the communication process to elicit meaning in the minds of the receiver of the message.

Tabloid Any half-size newspaper; the term is often used to refer to sensational publications like the *National Enquirer*.

Tabloid TV Sensational or titillating TV programs that began in the 1980s with such Fox network productions as "America's Most Wanted," and "A Current Affair." Soon other networks were copying the format with their own versions like "Hard Copy" and "Inside Edition." Sometimes called "trash TV."

TASS The official Soviet news wire service, Telegrafnoie Agentsvo Sovetskovo Soyuza.

Teenzines Youth-oriented magazines that feature pictures, stories and profiles of rock stars. Although most of these publications are targeted at 11- to 13-year-old girls, some are aimed at boys in the same age group.

Telecommuting A new trend in urban lifestyles that encourages employers to reduce traffic congestion and air pollution by making it possible for some employees to work at home using computer terminals, modems and telephone lines.

Teleshopping channels Cable-TV channels that sell merchandise to viewers, who telephone their orders and credit card numbers to 800 numbers. Teleshopping channels feature a wide variety of products at volume discounts.

Teletext A system that provides one-way interactive viewing of printed text carried on the unused space of TV signals. A special converter on the TV set is required to receive these signals.

Televangelism Programs on broadcast and cable TV featuring preachers who use the airwaves as an electronic version of old-fashioned tent revivals.

Two-step flow theory A theory developed by Paul Lazarsfeld to describe the opinion leader concept: (1) the mass media influence certain individuals, and (2) these individuals pesonally influence others.

Two-way cable   A cable-TV system that allows the consumer to respond to programming by sending messages back to the cable station.

Underground press   Alternative or counterculture newspapers published in the 1960s and early 1970s to promote the ideas and cultural reflections that were being ignord by the Establishment press. An outgrowth of the youth subculture.

Unit specialization   A term used to describe a magazine that targets a specialized audience; *Surfer* and *Personal Computing* are examples. See **internal specialization.**

UPI   United Press International; a private news service that was formed in 1958 by the merger of United Press (1907) and International News Service (1909).

Urban Western   A term applied to the police, doctor, and detective action/ adventure shows that supplanted the Westerns on television in the 1960s.

VALS   Values and Lifestyles; psychographic research by SRI International that categorizes Americans into eight different lifestyles. Advertisers use VALS to determine the target audiences for their products.

Vaudeville   A nineteenth-century entertainment form that developed to meet the new leisure time needs created by the Industrial Revolution. It was live theater, consisting of comedy skits and musical acts. Although no longer around, its influence can still be seen in modern-day television.

Videocassette recorder (VCR)   Video tape recorders that can record TV programs and play prerecorded movies.

Video disc players   A playback unit that uses prerecorded video discs shaped much like phonograph records or CDs.

Videotext   A two-way interactive television system; viewers respond to material shown on the screen, and conduct business and other transactions via a computer keyboard. (Sometimes spelled videotex.)

Vote video   A prerecorded videocassette used to promote political candidates and issues.

Yellow journalism   A derogatory term used to describe American journalism during the turn-of-the-century circulation war between William Randolph Hearst and Joseph Pulitzer, when sensational headlines and stunt reporting were common. The name derives from a feud between Hearst and Pulitzer over the use of the "Yellow Kid" comic strip.

Zapping   Using fast-forwarding to eliminate commercials from TV programs recorded on a VCR.

Zipping   Using a remote-control device to flip from one TV channel to another during commercials.

INDEX

Absence of Malice, 400–401

Academy Awards, 197

Acquired immune deficiency syndrome (AIDS), 38, 246, 249, 405, 412

Acta diurna, 150

Action for Children's Television (ACT), 264, 318

Adams, John, 74, 154–155

Adams, Samuel, 154

Addison, Joseph, 124, 153

Addison-Wesley, 117

Adventures of Huckleberry Finn, 112

Adventures of Ozzie and Harriet, 244, 412

Advertising:

    A-T-R model, 309–310

    children's ads, 318

    Coca-Cola, 315

    consumer information environment, 310–311

    cutting edge theory, 308–309

    early examples, 304–305

    electronic advertising, 306–307

    first ad agency, 305

    government regulations, 305–306

    infomercials, 319

    minimal effects theory, 307–308

    motivational research, 320–324

    propaganda devices, 311–315

    subliminal, 315–317

    television, 317–319

    VALS, 321–323

    zipping and zapping, 319

Advertising Age, 316

Advertorial, 408

Advocacy journalism, 166–167

Advocate, 138

African-American magazines, 130, 138, 140

African-American music, 279–280

African-American newspapers, 167

Agee, Warren, 159, 315

Agenda setting, 16, 21

Agence France-Presse (AFP), 66, 172

Agnew, Spiro, 254

Agranoff, Robert, 351

Ailes, Roger, 351

Aldrich, Henry, 194

Alger, Horatio, Jr., 105–106

Alien and Sedition Acts, 74, 90, 155

Aliens, 201

Allen, Fred, 222

Allen, Gracie, 222, 224, 226, 242

Allen, Woody, 195

Allied Artists, 197

All in the Family, 13, 245

All My Children, 247–378

All the President's Men, 109

All Things Considered, 212, 231

Almodovar, Pedro, 183

Ameche, Don, 222

Amekaji, 65

American Bandstand, 282

American Bar Association, 82

American Broadcasting Co. (ABC), 17, 26, 218, 245–246, 248, 250–251, 256, 262, 267, 291, 403, 410

American Civil Liberties Union, 84

American Druggist, 141

American Football League (AFL), 33–34

American Graphophone Co., 278

American Library Association, 112, 115

American Marconi Company, 216–217

American Magazine, 125

American Minerva, 155

American Newspaper Publishers Assn., 167, 219

American Psycho, 114

American Revolution, 103, 106, 154

American Society of Newspaper Editors, 60

American Telephone & Telegraph (AT&T), 217–218, 388–389, 392

American Weekly Mercury, 151

America's Most Wanted, 250, 404

Ameringer, Oscar, 349
Amos 'n' Andy, 32, 221, 224, 226, 242
Amsterdam, Jane, 163
Anabelle, 185
Anka, Paul, 282
Annenberg, Walter, 129
Annenberg School of Communication, 419
Antitrust, 196
Apollo XI, 254
Apple Computer, 392
Appleton, Dan, 104
Arbuckle, Fatty, 190
Arena, The, 127
Arledge, Roone, 251
Armat, Thomas, 185
Arness, James, 243
Arthur, 41
Articles of Confederation, 154
As Nasty As They Wanna Be, 275, 294
Assets, 136
Associated Film Productions (AFP), 40
Associated Press (AP), 60, 66, 68,
    158–159, 162, 172, 219
Associated Press Managing Editors
    (APME), 344
Astaire, Fred, 192
A-Team, 263–264
Atlantic, 66, 126
At Mother's Request, 413
Audience, *See* Communication, receiver.
Audio books, 112
Audion, 215
Ault, Phillip H., 159, 315
Aurora, 155
Australia, 63, 249
Austria, 56
Authoritarian press theory, 51–52
Autry, Gene, 110
Avatar (Boston), 168
Avalon, Frankie, 282
Ayer, N. W., 305

B-52, 290
Baby M. 248
Bacall, Lauren, 196
Bache, Benjamin Franklin, 155
Backmasking, 294
Backpacker, 136
Baker, James, 295
Baker, Ray Stannard, 127–128
Baker, Susan, 295

Bakker, Jim and Tammy, 266–267
Ball, Lucille, 242
Ballpark, 30–35, 46, 184, 268
Bandura, Albert, 418
Barbarella, 200
Barber, Red, 212
Barbie Dolls, 108
Barnouw, Erik, 226
Barnum, P. T., 335–336
Barr, Roseanne, 238
Barrymore, John, 193
Batman, 201
Batten, Barton, Durstine & Osborn, 321
Baxter, Leona, 351
Bay Psalm Book, 102
Beach Blanket Bingo, 200
Beacon Hill, 245
Beadle, Erastus, 104
Beadle, Irwin, 104
Beatles, 200, 283–285, 288, 295
Beatty, Warren, 201
Beaver Falls (Penn.) *News-Tribune,* 404
Bee Gees, 289
Behind the Green Door, 200
Beijing, China, 48–49, 52
Being There, 41
Bell, Alexander Graham, 215, 278
Bell, Daniel, 274
Benetton, 309
Ben Hur, 197
Bennett, James Gordon, 157
Benny, Jack, 32, 211, 222, 226, 242
Bergen, Edgar, 222, 226, 242
Berkeley Barb, 168
Berkeley, Busby, 193
Berkeley, Sir William, 52
Berkowitz, Leonard, 418
Berle, Milton, 226–227, 241–242, 306
Berliner, Emile, 278
Berlin Wall, 50–51, 256
Bernays, Edward L., 336, 345
Bernstein, Carl, 109, 166, 248
Bernstein, Leonard, 252
Bernstein, Lester, 358–359
Berry, Chuck, 283
Better Homes and Gardens, 137
Bewitched, 244
Bible, 27–28, 100–102
Biden, Joseph, 365
Billboard, 290–291
Bill of Rights, 54, 421

Billy Boy, 108
Birth of a Nation, 186, 221
Blackboard Jungle, 199, 282
Black Entertainment Television (BET), 377
Blackett-Sample-Hummert, 306
Blacklisting, 197, 252–253
Black Panther, 167
Black World, 138
Blair, Linda, 263
Block, H & R, 388
Blondie, 290
Bloods, 43
Bluebird, record label, 280
Blue Velvet, 201
Blumenthal, Sidney, 351
Boating, 136
Bob and Carol and Ted and Alice, 200
Bochco, Steven, 247
Bogart, Humphrey, 192, 196
Bombeck, Erma, 170
Bonanza, 243–244
Boni & Liveright, 107
Bonnie and Clyde, 200
Bono, Sonny and Cher, 244
Books:
    censorship, 112–116
    current business trends, 116–117
    early forms, 27–29, 98–99
    early public libraries, 99–100
    middle ages, 100
    Reformation, 101–102
    Renaissance, 100
    stages of development in U.S., 102–109
    types of, 108–112
Boorstin, Daniel, 193
Born Innocent, 263
Boston Gazette, 151, 154
Boston Globe, 75
Boston News-Letter, 151
Bow, Clara, 192
Bowling Green State University, 5
Boyer, Paul, 106
Boy George, 290
Boy's Life, 137
Brackenridge, Hugh Henry, 103
Bradford, Andrew, 125
Bradford, Tom, 151, 153
Bradford, William, 151
Bradlee, Ben, 401
Brady, John, 133

Brando, Marlon, 45
Brazil, 201
Breakouts, demographic and regional, 134
Breed, Warren, 316
Breslin, Jimmy, 167
Bridal Guide, 137
Bride, 137
Bringing Up Baby, 193
Brinkley, David, 251
Bristol-Myers, 332
British Broadcasting Corporation (BBC), 63–64, 267, 388
British Marconi Company, 213
British Parliament, 51, 64
British Post Office, 215, 387
British Satellite Broadcasting, 64
Broadcast News, 255
Brokaw, Tom, 256
Brooker, William, 151
Brothers Grimm, 36, 197
Brown, Charles Brockden, 103
Brown, James, 104
Brown, Peter, 285
Brown, Sam, 358
Browne, Ray B., 7
Browning, Robert, 105
Bulgaria, 56
Bunker, Archie, 13, 245
Bunnell, David, 137
Burnett, Carol, 72, 86, 244
Burns, George, 222, 224, 226, 242
Burson-Marsteller, 342
Burton, Richard, 197
Bush, George, 166, 353, 361
Butch Cassidy and the Sundance Kid, 200
Bwana Devil, 197
Byoir, Carl, 337
Byte, 136

Cable News Network (CNN), 19, 56, 73, 76, 256–258
Cable television:
    cable deregulation, 378–379
    expanded programming, 15, 376
    pay-per-view, 377–378
    pay-TV, 377
    public access, 376
    two-way, 376–377
Cablevision Systems, 392
Caesar, Sid, 242
Cagney, James, 192

Cagney & Lacey, 38, 261
Caldwell, Erskine, 107
California Basketball, 136
California Public Utilities Commission, 318
California State University, Fresno, 249
California State University, Fullerton, 113, 296
California State University, Los Angeles, 292
California State University, Northridge, 259
Calvin, John, 102
Camcorder, 56
Camel News Caravan, 251, 306
Campbell, Angus, 351
Campbell, John, 52, 151–152, 154
Campbell, Luther, 37, 294, 297
Canadian Broadcasting Corporation (CBC), 66
Canadian Press (CP), 66
Canadian Radio-Television Commission, 67
Canons of Journalism, 60
Cantor, Eddie, 222
Cantril Study, 416
Capone, Al, 193
Capote, Truman, 109, 167
Capra, Frank, 194
Carlin, George, 80
Carnal Knowledge, 200
Carnation Co., 322
Carney, Art, 242
Carnival, 6
Carroll, Diahann, 260
Cars, 290
Car Talk, 231
Carter, Billy, 359
Carter, Boake, 219
Carter, James Earl (Jimmy), 17, 18, 76, 357–359, 366, 410
Caruso, Enrico, 278, 298
Casey, William J., 116
Cash, Johnny, 283
Catcher in the Rye, The, 112
Catholic Church, 28, 51, 101–102, 191, 341
Cave, Edward, 124
Caxton, William, 100
Ceausescu, Nicolae, 56
Censorship, 112–116, 202
Central Intelligence Agency (CIA), 116

Cerf, Bennett, 107
Challenger, 20, 255, 265, 406
Chancellor, John, 254
Chan, Charlie, 194
Channel, 8–10, 21
Channel noise, 11, 21
Chapbooks, 29
Chaplin, Charlie, 188–189, 193
Charlie's Angels, 261
Charleston, 279–280
Charren, Peggy, 264, 409
Chayevsky, Paddy, 261
Checkers, Chubby, 283
Cheers, 364
Chernobyl, 62
Chesterfield, 308
Chevron, 340
Chicago Tribune, 164
Chicago Sun-Times, 168
Child, 121, 136
Children, 136
Children's Television Workshop, 267
Christian Broadcasting Network (CBN), 266
Christian History, The, 125
Christian Science Monitor, 163
Christian rock, 289
Chusmir, Janet, 163
Cigar Institute of America, 320–321
Cincinnati Red Stockings, 30
CinemaScope, 197
Cinemax, 377
Cinerama, 197
Citibank, 322
Citizen Kane, 194
City Streets, 193
Civilisation, 267
Civil War, U.S., 106, 126, 159, 167, 186, 267, 279
Clark, Dick, 282
Clash, The, 290
Cleland, Max, 358
Clemens, Samuel. *See* Twain, Mark
Cleveland *Press,* 162
Cline, Patsy, 297
Clockwork Orange, A, 183
Close Encounters of the Third Kind, 201
Coachella Valley, 409
Coal Miner's Daughter, 297
Coasters, 283
Cobbett, William, 155

Coca-Cola, 3, 4, 41, 45, 315, 402
Coca, Imogene, 242
Codex, 100
Colbert, Claudette, 193
Cole, Nat "King," 260
Coleman, William, 155
Coles, Robert, 265
Collier's, 126–127, 129, 133
Collingwood, Charles, 251
Colonial American Press, 151–156
Color Purple, The, 204
Colt 45, 243
Columbia, 204
Columbia Broadcasting System (CBS), 17, 34, 38, 86, 218–220, 226, 241, 244–245, 251, 256, 262, 264, 267, 291, 306, 389, 413
Columbia Phonograph Record Company, 218
Columbia University, School of Journalism, 164
Commercialization of culture, 38–41
Comic books, 109–111
Comic Magazine Association of America, 110
Commission on Freedom of the Press, 57
Common Sense, 103
Communication, process of:
    channel, 8–10, 21
    channel noise, 11, 21
    channels of mass, 15, 21
    defined, 7, 14
    feedback, 10
    frame of reference, 9
    group, 8
    interpersonal, 8, 15
    intrapersonal, 8
    mass, 8, 10, 14, 26–28
    message, 8, 10, 14
    nonverbal, 9
    psychological noise, 12
    receiver, 8, 10
    semantic noise, 11
    source, 8, 10
    symbols, 8
Communications Act of 1934, 218
Communication work centers, 393
Communist party, 60–62
Como, Perry, 281
Compact disc, 6, 390
Complete Woman, 137

CompuServe, 388
Computers:
    book publishing, 382–383
    broadcasting, 384
    libraries, 383–384
    newspaper uses, 382
Comstock, Anthony, 106
Condé Nast Traveler, 122
Cone Effect, 410–411
Conrad, Frank, 217
Conrad, Paul, 12, 13
Consideration on the Nature and Extent of the Legislative Authority of the British Parliament, 103
Consumer Reports, 341
CONUS Communication, 258
Converge, Phillip E., 351
Cooke, Janet, 401
Coogan, Jackie, 188
Cool Hand Luke, 200
Coolidge, Calvin, 77, 355
Cooper, Gary, 192, 195
Cooper, James Fenimore, 104
Copley, Helen K., 163
Copley Newspapers, 163
Cop Rock, 247
Corantos, 150
Cornish, Samuel, 167
Corporation for Public Broadcasting. 267
Correll, Charles, 221, 224
Cosby, Bill, 238–239, 261
Cosby Show, The, 317, 411
Cosby, William, 153
Cosmopolitan, 126, 137, 141, 162, 305
Costello, Elvis, 290
Courier, 156
Covering, 280
Cowles, Gardner, 129
Cradle of American Journalism, 151–152
Craft, Christine, 256
Crawford, Joan, 192
Creature from the Black Lagoon, 197
Creel, George, 336
Creel Committee, 336, 345
Crips, 43
Criticism of mass society, 36–38
Cronkite, Walter, 251
Crosby, Bing, 222, 226, 242
Crouch, Paul, F., 267
Crystals, 283
Cults, in popular culture, 42–46

Cultural consequences:
    form vs. content, 420–421
    importance of a free press, 421
    need for consumer awareness, 421–422
Cultural niches, 32
Culture:
    changes, 27
    commercialization of, 38–42
    criticism of, 36–38
    cults, 42–46
    current complaints, 37–38
    definition of, 4
    elite, 6
    exporting pop culture, 41–42
    folk, 6
    high, 6
    industries, 45–46
    mass, 6, 7
    popular, 4, 5, 6, 7
    specialized, 7
Culture Club, 288
Current Affair, A, 43, 248
Czechoslovakia, 56, 63, 244

Daily Courant, 151
Daily Mirror, 62
Daily Racing Form, 63, 132
Dallas, 40, 193, 223, 247, 412
Dalton, B., 109
Daly, John Charles, 251
Data-Tel, 388
Darin, Bobby, 282
Dave Clark Five, 285
Davis, Elmer, 336
Davis, Lloyd, 318
Day, Benjamin, 156–158
Day, Doris, 281
Days of Our Lives, 38
Days of Wine and Roses, 242
Dean, James, 199
Debs, Eugene V., 75
Decent Interval, 116
Decision/Making/Information, 351
Decoder. *See* Communication, receiver
Deep Throat, 166, 200
Deer Hunter, The, 263
Defamation, 73, 85
Defenders, The, 244
Defoe, Daniel, 124
DeFoe, James, R., 316
De Forest, Lee, 190, 215, 217

Dell, 116
Demassification, 7
Demographic breakouts, 134
Denver Post, 3
Deregulation of broadcasting, 80–81
Desktop publishing, 382
Des Moines Register, 406
Destination. *See* Communication, receiver
Details, 122, 136
Detective Comics, 110
Detroit Free Press, 405
Detroit News, 405
Devil in Miss Jones, The, 200
Devo, 290
Diamond Sutra, 100
Diary of Anne Frank, The, 112, 114–115
Diary of Love, A. 112
Dichter, Ernest, 320
Dickens, Charles, 29, 104
Dickinson, John, 154
Dickson, William Kennedy, 185, 189
Diddley, Bo, 283
Digital audio tape, 390–391
Digital sound, 390
Dilenschneider, Robert L., 344
Direct Broadcast Satellites (DBS), 203,
    392
Direct mail, 362
Dire Straits, 390
Dirty Dozen, The, 200
Dirty Harry, 201
Disco, 289–290
Disney Channel, 377
Disney, Walt, 17, 201
Dixieland jazz, 279
Docudramas, 413
Dogood, Silence, 153
Domino, Fats, 283
Donahue, Phil, 246
Doors, The, 288
Dorsey, Tommy, 281
Dos Passos, John, 107
Double Dare, 264
Doubleday & Co., 116
Douglas, Norman, 303
Douglass, Frederick, 167
Dow Chemical Co., 340
Downey, Morton, Jr., 250
Doyle Dane Bernbach, 356
Dragnet, 244
Dreiser, Theodore, 107
Drive time, 214

Duck Soup, 193
Duff, Howard, 252
Dukakis, Michael, 166, 354, 361
DuMont Network, 241
Duran Duran, 290
Dürer, Albrecht, 27
Dutton, E. P., 106, 117
Dwyer, R. Budd, 399–400
Dylan, Bob, 283, 285
Dynasty, 193, 223, 247, 412

Earth Day, 24–26
Earthquake, 201
Eastern Europe, 56, 388
East Village Other, 168
Eastwood, Clint, 201
Easy Rider, 200
Easyrider magazine, 138
Ebony, 129, 138, 140
Eddy, Nelson, 222
Edison, Thomas A., 185, 189, 204,
    278–279
Editor and Publisher, 87
Edwards, Bob, 211–213
Edwards, Douglas, 251
Edwards, Jonathan, 266
Effects (media research):
    Cantril Study, 416
    delinquency and violence, 417
    four violence theories, 417–419
    Lazarsfeld Study, 416–417
    obscenity and pornography, 419
    Payne Fund Studies, 416
    positive effects research, 419
Egg, 122
Eisenhower, Dwight D., 355
Electric Company, The, 265, 267, 419
Electronic cottages, 374–375
Electronic print media, 391
Elite culture. *See* Culture
Elle, 121, 137
Ellis, Bret Easton, 114
Ellsberg, Daniel, 75
Emerson, Ralph Waldo, 104
Emery, Edwin, 159
Empire Strikes Back, The, 43, 201
Enquirer, 156
Entertainment Weekly, 135, 142
EPS cycle, 5, 6, 7, 21, 42, 101, 107, 167,
    171, 184, 187, 198, 227, 270, 322
Espionage Act of 1917, 74
ESPN cable network, 33, 268

Essanay Co., 188
Essence, 138
Establishment, 12
E.T., 201
Esquire, 131, 136
Ethics, media:
    advertiser influences, 408–409
    chain ownership conflicts, 410
    conflicts of interest, 404–405
    direct response sales, 409–410
    distortions of cultural reality, 411–412
    docudramas, 413
    double standards, 406–407
    ethics and economics, 408–410
    gifts, 404
    honesty and integrity, 401
    invasion of privacy, 406
    news media ethics, 400–407
    photographic accuracy, 401–403
    sex and explicit language, 413
    social responsibility, 407
    TV reenactments, 403–404
    withholding information, 405–406
European Travel & Life, 121–122
Everybody's, 127
Evry, Hal, 351–352, 362
Exxon Valdez, 331–332

Fabian, 282
Face the Nation, 79
Fairbanks, Douglas, 192
Fairness Doctrine, 79
Fairness in Media, 37
Falcon Crest, 223, 247
Falwell, Jerry, 37, 85, 114, 266
Fame, 122
Family Circle, 122, 137
Family magazines, 136
Family Matters, 411
Family of Five, 413
Fanning, Katharine, 163
Fanny Hill, 106
Farm Aid, 277
Farnsworth, Philo, 240
Farrow, Mia, 247
Fashion Guide, 137
Fat Albert and the Cosby Kids, 419
Fatal Passions, 404
Father Knows Best, 244, 412
Fathers, 136
Federal Aviation Administration, 81

Federal Bureau of Alcohol, Tobacco and Firearms, 81, 316
Federal Communications Commission (FCC), 58, 77–81, 218, 306, 226–227, 229, 237, 241–242, 264, 392
Federalist Papers, 155
Federalists, 74, 155
Federal Radio Commission (FRC), 77, 218
Federal Trade Commission (FTC), 81, 306
Federation of Women's Clubs, 280
Feedback, 10–11
Fenno, John, 155
Ferraro, Geraldine, 366
Fessenden, Reginald A., 215
Fiber optics, 389–390
Field of experience. See Communication, frame of reference
Field & Stream, 136
Field, Sally, 401
Fields, W. C., 193
Fifth Estate, 54
Final Days, The 248
First Amendment, 49–50, 54, 74, 79, 81, 90
Fish Called Wanda, A, 316
Flacks, 343
Flash Gordon, 194
Fleming, J. Ambrose, 215
Fly, The, 201
Flying, 136
Flynn, Errol, 116
FM Tokyo, 65
FM Yokohama, 65
Food and Drug Administration (FDA), 81, 306
Footlight Parade, 193
Ford, Gerald, 357–358
Ford Motor Company, 308
Formula, The, 41
Forsyte Saga, The, 245
For the People, 227
Fortune, 142
42nd Street, 193
Foster, Lawrence G., 342
Fotonovels, 109
Foundation for Public Relations Research and Education, 333
Fourth Estate, 54
Fox Broadcasting Co., 249, 262, 268, 410, 413, 415
Fox, Michael J., 293

Fox, Stephen, 308
Frank, Anne, 112, 115
Franklin, Ann Smith, 163
Franklin, Benjamin, 53, 102–103, 125, 151–155
Franklin, James, 151–152
Freed, Alan, 227, 281
Freedom of Information Act (FOI), 90
Freedom's Journal, 167
Freeman, Charles, 275
French Line, The, 197
Freneau, Philip, 155
Fresno Bee, 163
Friday the 13th, 201
Front, The, 195
Fun House, 264
Fuzz, 263

Gable, Clark, 40, 192–193
Gaines, William, 131
Gale Directory of Publications and Broadcasting Media, 117, 135, 228
Galella v. *Onassis,* 88
Gamble, James, 305
Gannett, 148, 170
Garbage, 138
Garland, Judy, 192
Gatekeeping, 18, 19, 21
Gazetta, 150
Gazette of the United States, 155
General Electric, 217, 405
General Hospital, 247
General Magazine, 124–125, 153
Genius of Universal Emancipation, The, 126
Gentlemen's Magazine, 124
Gentlemen's Quarterly, (GQ), 136
Gerbner, George, 264, 419
Germany, East, 56
Germany, West, 56, 117
Glamour, 137
Glasnost, 55, 60–62
Gleason, Jackie, 241–242
Go Ask Alice, 112
Godey's Lady's Book, 126
Godfrey, Arthur, 242
God's Little Acre, 107
Goebbels, Joseph, 312
Gold Diggers of 1933, 193
Golden Girls, The, 38, 364
Golden, L. L L., 331

Goldstein, Tom, 171, 408
Goldthwait, Bobcat, 26
Goldwater, Barry, 356
Gone With the Wind, 192, 194, 198
Goodbye, Columbus, 200
Good Housekeeping, 137, 141, 162
Goodman, Benny, 281
Good Morning America, 26
Good Night, Sweet Wife: A Murder in Boston, 413
Gorbachev, Mikhail, 55, 62
Gore, Albert, 295
Gore, Lesley, 283
Gore, Tipper, 295
Gosden, Freeman, 221, 224
Gould, Chester, 201
Government regulation of media, 77–81
Graber, Doris, 20
Grace, W. R., 340
Graduate, The, 200
Graham, Billy, 266
Graham, Katherine, 116, 163
Grandparents, 136
Grant, Cary, 193
Graphic novels, 110–111
Great Awakening, 266
Great Depression, 192, 219, 225, 281, 297, 336–337
Great Library in Alexandria, 99
Great Train Robbery, The, 186, 193
Greeley, Horace, 59, 157–158
Greenaway, Peter, 183
Greenfield, Patricia, 265, 318
Green Hornet, 222
Green marketing, 309
Grenada, 359
Griffith, D. W., 186–187, 221
Group W, 258
Grove Press, 117
Guardian, 152
Guess, 304
Gumbel, Bryant, 256
Guiding Light, The, 223
Gun & Ammo, 136
Guns 'n' Roses, 294
Gunsmoke, 243
Gutenberg, Johannes, 26–28, 51, 100–101, 118

Haberstroth, Jack, 316
Hadden, Britton, 128, 130

Haley, Bill, 282
Haley, Alex, 245
Halloween, 201
Hamilton, Alexander, 155
Hamilton, Andrew, 153, 421
Hammer, Armand, 340
Handlin, Oscar, 103
Happy Days, 246, 265
Hard Copy, 250
Harder, Chuck, 227
Harding, Warren G., 355
Hardy, Andy, 194
Hardy, Oliver, 189
Harlem Globetrotters' Popcorn Machine, The, 419
Harley-Davidson, 45
Harlow, Jean, 192–193
Harper, James and John, 104
Harper & Row, 117
Harper's, 66, 126–127, 305
Harper's Bazaar, 137, 141, 162
Harris, Benjamin, 151, 154
Harrison, George, 284–285
Hart, Dennis, 259
Hart, Gary, 89, 364–365
Hart, Peter, 363
Harvard Lampoon, 161
Harvard University, 102
Have Gun Will Travel, 243
Hauptmann, Bruno, 82
Hawthorne, Nathaniel, 104
Hays Offiice 191–192
Hays, Will H., 190
Hayworth, Rita, 192
Hear It Now, 252
Hearst, George, 161
Hearst, Patty, 109
Hearst, William Randolph, 33, 59, 160–162, 172, 280
Hearst Corporation, 141, 173
Hearst newspapers, 195
Heatter, Gabriel, 219
Hefner, Hugh, 131, 133
Helms, Jesse, 414
Hemingway, Ernest, 107, 116
Henderson, Fletcher, 281
Henry, Barbara, 163
Henry: Portrait of a Serial Killer, 183
Henry II (king of France), 28, 96, 102
Henry VIII (king of England), 102
Hepburn, Katharine, 192–193

Herodotus, 98
Herman's Hermits, 285
Hersh, Seymour, 166
Hershey Foods Co., 308
Hertz, Heinrich, 215
High-Definition Television (HDTV),
  391–392
High Noon, 195
High Times, 138, 141
Highway Patrol, 244
Hill, Edwin C., 219
Hill & Knowlton, 344
Hill Street Blues, 38, 247
Hindenberg, 225
Hispanic newspapers, 167
History of the Persian Wars, The, 98
Hitler, Adolf, 219, 226, 312
Hoffman, Dustin, 25
Hollywood Ten, 195
Holmes, Oliver Wendell, 74
Holt, Henry, 116
Home Box Office (HBO), 267, 291, 413
Homer, 98–99
Home Shopping Network, 268–269
Home video equipment:
  flight videos, 386
  religious videos, 386
  videocassette recorders, 385
  video discs, 386–387
  video rentals, 385
Honeymooners, The, 241–242
Hooper, John, 305
Hoover, Herbert, 25, 77
Hope, Bob, 222, 244
Hopscotch, 41
Horne, Lena, 252
Horton, Willie, 361
Hot Rod, 124
House of Wax, 197
Howdy Doody, 242, 412
Howell, Deborah, 163
Howser, Doogie, 25
How the West Was Won, 197
How-to books, 108–109
How to Stuff a Wild Bikini, 200
Houghton, Henry Oscar, 103
House Beautiful, 143
House Committee on Un-American
  Activities, 195
Hudson, Rock, 405
Hughes Communications, 392

Human immunodeficiency virus (HIV),
  405
Humphrey, Hubert, 356–357
Hungary, 56, 388
Huntley, Chet, 251
Hussein, Saddam, 40
Hustler, 85, 136
Hutchins, Maude, 112
Hutchins, Robert Maynard, 57
Hybrid TV, 247

Iconoscope, 240
Identity, 138
I Dream of Jeannie, 244
I Led Three Lives, 195
Iliad, 98
I Love Lucy, 244
I Married a Communist, 195
Impressions, 112–113
In Cold Blood, 109
Independent Broadcasting Authority
  (IBA), 64, 388
Independent Television (ITV), 64
Indiana Jones and the Temple of Doom,
  183, 201
Industrial Revolution, 6, 29, 38, 42, 44,
  104, 158, 394
Infiniti, 303
Infomercials, 319
Information Age, 7
Information-Imitation Theory, 263
Information overload, 19
Information processing:
  by consumer, 19–21
  by media, 16–19, 21
In God's Name, 109
Instant books, 109
Internal specialization, 124
International Business Machines (IBM),
  387–388, 392
International News Service (INS), 162
International Typographical Union, 382
Interpretative reporting, 164–166
Intolerance, 186–187
Invasion of privacy, 84, 87–90
Inverted pyramid, 159
Investigative reporting, 166
Iran-Contra hearings, 14, 18, 55, 255
Iraq, 256–257
Irving, Washington, 103
I Spy, 261

It Happened One Night, 193–194
It's a Wonderful Life, 194
Ives, Burl, 252
I Was a Communist for the FBI, 195
I Was a Teenage Frankenstein, 199
I Was a Teenage Werewolf, 199
Izvestia, 56, 60

Jackson, Janet, 291
Jackson, Michael, 285
Jacobs, Mike, 402–403
James, Harry, 281
Japanese Times, 64
Jaws, 201
Jazz Age, 279, 308
Jazz journalism, 164
Jazz Singer, The, 190
Jefferson Airplane, 288
Jefferson, Thomas 53–54, 74, 103,
    154–156, 421
Jenkins, Francis, 185
Jennings, Peter, 251
Jet, 138
Johnson, Don, 293
Johnson & Johnson, 332, 342–343
Johnson, Lyndon B., 356, 417
Johnson, Samuel, 124
Jolson, Al, 190
Jones, Jim, 42
Journal of Commerce, 156
Joyce, James, 107
Joy Ride, 199
Jukebox, 281–282
Julia, 260
Jungle, The, 105

Kaltenborn, H. V., 219
KDKA (radio), 217–218
Keating, Charles M., 405
Keaton, Buster, 189
Kees, Beverly, 163
Kefauver Crime Committee, 417
Keillor, Garrison, 231–233
Kelley, Kitty, 94
Kennedy, John F., 88, 116, 253, 255,
    355–356
Kennedy, Robert F., 254
Kentucky Fried Chicken, 41
Kenya, 68
Key, Wilson Bryan, 316
Keystone Film Co., 187–188

Khamenei, Ayatollah Ali, 96
Khomeini, Ayatollah, 95–96
Kid 'N Play, 276
Kid, The, 188
Kiss Me Kate, 197
Kitsch, 37
Kinescope, 241
Kinetoscope, 185
King, Larry, 227
King, Martin Luther Jr., 254
King, Stephen, 5
King, Zalman, 183
King Features Syndicate, 162
Kipling, Rudyard, 105
Klein, Calvin, 304, 314
Klopfer, Donald S., 107
KMBC-TV, 256
Knight, Arthur, 191
Knight-Ridder, 170, 388
Knots Landing, 223, 247
Knoxville Journal, 9
Koppel, Ted, 251, 256
KPIX-TV, 259
Kress, Harold, 197
Krug, Judith, 112
Ku Klux Klan, 12, 73, 75, 186

Ladies' Home Journal, 126, 305
L.A. Law, 38, 247, 261
Laine, Frankie, 281
LaserVision, 387
Last Emperor, The, 201
Last Tango in Paris, 183
Laugh-In, 244
Laurel, Stan, 189
Laurie, Piper, 242
Law and Order, 410
Lawson, Jennifer, 267
Lazarsfeld, Paul F., 350, 416
Lazarsfeld studies, 350–351, 416–417
League of Nations, 128
League of Women Voters, 79
Lear, Norman, 245
Lear's 137
Leave It to Beaver, 244, 412
Led Zeppelin, 294
Lee, Ivy Ledbetter, 335–336, 342, 345
Lee, Peggy, 281
Lee, Richard Henry, 154
Legion of Decency, 191

Lenin, V.I., 55
Lennon, John, 109, 284–285
Lennon, Julian, 285
Lesly, Philip, 333
Letterman, David, 244
Levi jeans, 5, 41
Lewin, Kurt, 18
Lewis, Sinclair, 107
Libel, 84–87, 89, 171
Liberace, 405
Libertarian press theory, 53–55
Liberty, 247, 413
Liberty Foundation, 37
Life, 43, 129–191, 134–35, 142
Lincoln, Abraham, 105
Lindbergh, Charles, 82
Lineup, The, 244
Linkletter, Art, 242
Little, Charles, 104
Little Caesar, 193
Little Richard, 283
Live Aid, 15, 277
Lloyd, Harold, 189
Locke, John, 53
Lombard, Carole, 193
London Gazette, 151–152
London Plan, 156
Lone Ranger, 222
Look, 129
Los Angeles Coliseum, 4
Los Angeles Free Press, 168
Los Angeles Herald Examiner, 168
Los Angeles Times, 12, 13, 38, 89, 139, 168, 350, 405, 408
Lorax, The, 112
Lorimar, 264
Lowenstein, Ralph, 5, 124
Low-Power Television (LPTV), 392–393
Lucas, George, 201
Luce, Henry R., 128–130
Lumiere, Auguste and Louis, 185
Luther, Martin, 28, 51, 101–102
Lux Radio Theater, 222
Lyle, Jack, 417
Lynn, Loretta, 297

McAuliffe, Christa, 265, 406
McCall's, 126, 137
McCarthy, Charlie, 222, 226, 242
McCarthy, Joseph, 252–253, 255

McCarthyism, 195, 253, 261
McCartney, Paul, 284–285
McClatchy, C. K., 405
McClure, Robert, 363
McClure, Samuel S., 126, 159
McClure's, 126–127, 159
McCombs, Maxwell, 16, 353
MacDonald, Dwight, 37
McDonald's, 4, 5, 17, 41–42, 45
McDowell, Jack, 351
McGee, Fibber and Molly, 222
McGinniss, Joe, 353, 356
McGovern, George, 357, 363–364
McGraw-Hill, 116
McKenna, George, 362
McKnaughton, John 183
Maclean's, 66
McLuhan, Marshall, 12, 28
MacWorld, 136–137
Mad, 131
Madonna, 201–202, 290–291, 297
Madison, James, 53–54, 155, 421
Madison Press Connection, 76
Magazines:
    breakouts, demographic and regional, 134
    early British publications, 124–125
    early American, 125–128
    entering popular culture, 124
    muckrakers, 126–128
    specialization of, 134–135
    types of, 135–139
Magic bullet theory, 416
Magliozzi, Tom and Ray, 231
Mailer, Norman, 167
Maisel, Richard, 140
Make Room for Daddy, 244
Man from U.N.C.L.E., 244
Mangas, 65
Manhattan Inc., 122
Mapplethorpe, Robert, 80
Marconi, Guglielmo, 215–217
Margaret, Ann, 403
Married People, 408
Married . . . With Children, 26, 237, 410, 413, 415, 422
Martin, Dick, 244
Marvelettes, 283
Marx Brothers, 192–193
Masquerade, 38

Massachusetts Spy, 154
Mass communication:
  beginnings, 26–32
  channels of, 15
  defined, 14
Mass-market paperbacks, 112
Mass media:
  chapbooks, 29, 51
  early forms, 27–29
  in mass society, 32
  pictorial prints, 27
  types, 15
  See also individual media.
Mass mediation of leisure, 33–36
Mass movement, first, 28
Masterpiece Theater, 267
Matsushita, 204–205
Maxwell, James Clerk, 215
Maxwell, Robert, 61–63
MCA/UA, 204–205, 387
Meat Inspection Act, 128
Meese Commission, 136, 417
Meese, Edwin, 84, 136
Meet the Press, 79, 367
Mein Kampf, 312
Melies, George, 185
Melville, Herman, 104
Men, 136
Men's Life, 136
Mercury Theater on the Air, 222, 225
Mergenthaler, Ottmar, 104
Merrill, John, 5, 124
Merrill Publishing Co., 116
Metalious, Grace, 247
Metro-Goldwyn-Mayer (MGM), 192, 197
Metropolitan newspapers, 30, 156–159
Meucci, Antonio, 215
M. Inc., 122, 136
Miami Herald, 89, 163
Miami Vice, 247, 292
Michael, George, 291
Middle Ages, 27, 100
Middle East, 16, 18
Midler, Bette, 24, 25
Midnight Cowboy, 183, 200
Mifflin, George Harrison, 104
Mill, John Stuart, 53
Miller v. *California,* 83
Miller, Warren E., 351
Millionaire, 138

Milton, John, 53, 421
Mini-series, 245
Minitel, 387–388
Minnesota Public Radio, 232
Minow, Newton, 237
Mirabella, 137
Miss America, 4
Missing, 41
Mission Impossible, 244
Mister Rogers, 419
Mitchell, Arnold, 322
Mitchell, Gwen Davis, 116
Mobil Oil Co., 338–341, 406
Moby Dick, 104
Model, 122
Modern Bride, 137
Modern Chivalry, 103
Modern Maturity, 132
Mondale, Walter, 359–360 366–367
Monday Night Football, 34, 246
Monogram, 197
Monroe, Marilyn, 131
Monroe, Vaughn, 281
Moonlighting, 261, 291
Moral Majority, 37
Morgan, Edward P., 97
Morning Edition, 211–212, 231
Morse, Samuel F. B., 158, 214
Motels, 290
Mother Jones, 138
Mothers Against Drunk Drivers (MADD),
  318
Motion Picture Association of America,
  181, 184
Motion Picture Producers and Distributors
  of America (MPPDA), 190, 416
Motion pictures:
  antitrust, 196
  big studio era, 192
  business of, 203–204
  censorship, 190–192, 202
  comedy, rise of, 187–189
  cultural changes, 190
  disaster films, 200–201
  early history, 184–187
  EPS cycle, 187
  film genres, 193–194
  red scare, 195–196
  sex and violence, 198–201
  sound, 189–192

Motion pictures: *continued*
  special effects, 201
  television's impact, 196–197
  video movies, 203–204
  youth films, 199–200
Motivational research (MR), 320–321
Motor, 141
Motor Boating, 141
Mouseketeers, 189
Movable type, 26–28
Movie Channel, 377
Mr. Deeds Goes to Town, 194
Mr. Smith Goes to Washington, 194
Ms., 137
Muckrakers, 126–128
Muhammad Speaks, 167
Multichannel, Multipoint Distribution
  Service (MMDS), 390–391
Munsey, Frank, 126
Munsey's Magazine, 126
Munsters, The, 244
Murder in the Rue Morgue, 197
Murdoch, Rupert, 62–63, 66, 107, 117,
  122, 130, 142, 205, 249, 292, 402, 410
Murrow, Edward R., 220, 222–223, 251,
  253
Music Television (MTV), 228, 290, 293,
  414
Mutual Broadcasting System, 218, 241
My Lai, 166
My Three Sons, 244

Naisbitt, John, 394
Napolitan, Joe, 351
Nation, The, 127
National, The, 147–148
National Association for the Advancement
  of Colored People, 186
National Association of Broadcasting, 319
National Basketball Association (NBA),
  35
National Broadcasting Co. (NBC), 17, 26,
  34, 38, 86, 216–218, 226, 239, 241, 243,
  247, 251, 256, 258, 262–263, 267, 291,
  306, 317, 389, 392, 405, 410, 413
National Commission on the Causes and
  Prevention of Violence, 417
National Council of Churches, 266
National Council on Alcoholism, 264
National Education Association, 280
National Enquirer, 62, 72, 86, 164–165

National Football League (NFL), 33–34
National Gazette, 155
National Geographic, 324
National Hockey League (NHL), 35
National Institute of Alcohol Abuse and
  Alcoholism (NIAAA), 318
National Intelligencer, 155
National Organization of Women (NOW),
  114
National Public Radio, 230–231
National Religious Broadcasters, 266
National Science Foundation, 393
NBC Nightly News, 256
Near, J. M., 76
Nelson, Ricky, 282
Nelson, Willie, 277, 283
Neuharth, Al, 148
New American Library, 117
New England Courant, 151, 153
New morality, age of, 190
Newhouse, Samuel I., 107
News Corporation, 392
Newspaper Enterprise Association (NEA),
  163
Newspapers:
  advocacy, 166
  Alien and Sedition Acts, 74, 90, 155
  basic functions, 173
  biases, 173–174
  business of, 168–171
  chain ownership, 170–171
  colonial American press, 151–156
  early origins, 150–151
  interpretative reporting, 164–166
  investigative reporting, 166
  jazz journalism, 164
  libel suits, threat of, 171
  limited specialization, 167–168
  objectivity, 163
  penny press era, 156–159
  press and the Revolution, 154
  press in the new republic, 154–155
  social responsibility, 164
  soft news, 170
  struggle against authority, 153–154
  syndicates, 159
  twentieth century press, 163–168
  watchdog function, 174
  wire services, 171–173
  yellow journalism era, 159–163
Newsweek, 122, 128

Newton, Isaac, 53
Newton, Wayne, 86
New York *American,* 280
New York *Daily News,* 164
New Yorker, The, 128
New York Gazette, 153
New York Herald, 157
New York Journal, 33, 59, 161–162
New York Post, 155, 163
New York Sun, 30, 156–158
New York Times, 59, 158, 163, 359
New York Times v. *Sullivan,* 85
New York Tribune, 59, 157–158
New York Weekly Journal, 153, 163
New York Woman, 121
New York World, 33, 59, 161–162
Nicaragua, 18, 360
Nickelodeon, 185–187, 189
Nielsen, A. C., Co., 258, 268
Nightline, 79
1984, 112
Nixon, Richard M., 76, 166, 248, 335–357,
     363–364
Nonfiction novels, 109
North American Broadcast Teletext
     Standard (NABTS), 389
North American Phillips, 387
North American Review, 126
North, Oliver, 14, 255
North Star, 167
Novanglus Papers, 103
Novel, 29
Novelization, 111
Nutcracker: Money, Madness, Murder,
     413
Nuthead, Dinah, 163
N.W.A., 294

Ochs, Adolph, 163
O'Connor, Carroll, 245
Odyssey, 98
Office of War Information, 336
Of Mice and Men, 112
Okeh, record label, 280
Oliver!, 201
Olympic games, 340
Onassis, Jacqueline, 88
O'Neal, Ryan, 247
Ono, Yoko, 285
Opinion leader, 350–351
Orwell, George, 377

Osbourne, Ozzy, 275, 294–295
Oswald, Lee Harvey, 254
Oui, 136
Outcault, Richard, 162
Out of Africa, 201
Oxford Gazette, 151

Pacific Diver, 136
Packard, Vance, 315, 320
Paine, Thomas, 103, 154
Paley, William S., 218
Palmer, Voleny, 305
Pamela, 103
Pan American World Airways, 413
Panax Corp., 410
Paramount Pictures, Inc., 196, 204
Parenting, 136
Parents' Music Resource Center, (PMRC),
     295–296
Parker, Edwin, 417
Parton, Dolly, 283
Pastore, John, 417
Pathé, 204
Patterson, Joseph Medill, 164
Patterson, Thomas, 363
Pavarotti, Luciano, 298
Payne Fund Studies, 416–417
Payola scandal, 227
PC Magazine, 136–137
PC World, 136–137
Pearl, Les, 321
Pearl Harbor, 220
Pennsylvania Gazette, 153, 304
*Pennsylvania Packet and General
     Advertiser,* 304
Pennsylvania Railroad, 342
Penny Power, 137
Penny press, 152–159
Pentagon Papers, 75–76
Penthouse, 37, 136, 290, 419
People meters, 377–379
People's Republic of China, 52
People Weekly, 122, 142
Pepsi-Cola, 315
Perceptual filters, 311
Perrier, 331–332
Perry, Richard, 290
Perry Mason, 240
Persian Gulf war, 40
Persona, 139
Personal Computing, 124

Personalized books, 109
Peter and Gordon, 285
Peterson, Theodore B., 57
Peyton Place, 247
Philadelphia Inquirer, 87
Philip Morris Co., 340
Phillip, David Graham, 127
Phillips, Sam, 281
Phoenix (Boston), 168
Photography, 32, 46
Piaget, Jean, 12
Pickford, Mary, 192
Pictorial prints, 27
Pilgrim's Progress, 127
Pioneer, 387
Platinum Blonde, 193
Plato, 99
Platters, The, 283
Playboy, 37, 131, 136, 288, 419
Playboy Channel, 377
Playgirl, 136
Playhouse 90, 261
Poe, Edgar Allan, 103–104
Poland, 56
Police, 290
Police Woman, 261
Political advertising:
    direct mail, 362
    television, 362
    vote videos, 362
Political consultants, 351–354
Political coverage, media:
    character analysis, 364–365
    horse-race effect, 365–366
    positive election coverage, 367
    projecting winners, 366
Poltergeist, 201
Poltergeist II, 201
Pompeii, 304
Poor Richard's Almanack, 102–103, 153
Pope v. *Illinois,* 83
Popular culture. *See* Culture
Porcupine's Gazette, 155
Porter, Cole, 280
Porter Edwin S., 185–186
Poseidon Adventure, The, 201
Powell, Jody, 358–359
Prairie Home Companion, 231–233
Pravda, 60–61
Premiere, 122
Presley, Elvis, 43, 200, 282, 284

Press, theories of the:
    authoritarian, 51–52
    libertarian, 53–54
    social responsibility, 57–60
    Soviet Communist, 55–57, 60–62
Press-Enterprise v. *Superior Court of California in Riverside County,* 81
Press in foreign lands, examples of:
    Canada, 66–67
    Japan, 64–65
    Mexico, 67
    Soviet Union, 60–62, 69
    Third World, 67–68
    United Kingdom, 62–64
Prestel, 387
Preston, Keith, 121
Price, Raymond K., 355
Priest, Judas, 294
Prime time, 223
Prince, 297
Prinsky, Lorraine, 296
Prior restraint, 52, 76
Prizzi's Honor, 201
Procter & Gamble, 305–307
Procter, William, 305
Product brokers, 39–41
Production Code Administration, 192
Progressive, The, 76
Propaganda, 311–315
Protestant Reformation, 28, 51, 53, 101–102
Psychological noise, 12–14
Psychology Today, 122
PTL, 266
Ptolemy, 99, 185
Public Broadcasting Service, 245, 267
Public Broadcasting Act of 1967, 231
Public Enemy, The, 193, 292
Publick Occurrences, 151
Public relations:
    activities, 339–343
    behavior modification, 339
    combined marketing and PR, 340
    controversies, 343–344
    corporate, 335–336
    defined, 333–335
    examples, 334–335
    flacks, 343–344
    government PR, 336
    history, 335–338
    issues and crisis management, 340–343

Public Relations Society of America (PRSA), 333, 342, 344
Publish, 136
Pulitzer, Joseph, 33, 59, 160–162
Pulitzer Prize, 401
Punk rock, 43–44, 290
Pure Food and Drug Act, 128, 306
Purple Rose of Cairo, The, 201
Putnam, George Palmer, 104

Qube, 376
Quinlan, Karen Ann, 12, 13

Racing Form, 63
Racing Times, 63
Racket Squad, 244
Radecki, Thomas, 264
Radio:
    AM, 229–230
    beginning of networks, 218
    CBS raid, 226
    development of, 32, 46, 214–218
    early commercial, 217–218
    electronic vaudeville, 221
    entertainment, 221–226
    FM, 229–230
    government regulations, 218
    harnessing sound waves, 214–216
    meeting cultural needs, 219
    news, 218–221
    newspaper opposition, 219
    payola scandal, 227
    public radio, 230–231
    sitcoms, 221–222
    soap operas, 222
    specialization, 227–228
    World War II, 220–221
Radio Act of 1927, 77
Radio Advertising Bureau, 214
Radio Corporation of America (RCA), 107, 216–218, 386–387, 389
Rafshoon, Gerald, 351
Raging Bull, 201
Raiders of the Lost Ark, 201
Rakolta, Terry, 413
Rambler, 125
Rand Corporation, 75
Random House, Inc., 107, 116
Ranney, Austin, 362
Rather, Dan, 256
Raymond, Henry J., 59

Reader's Digest, 66, 124, 128–130, 324
Reagan, Ronald, 18, 80, 255, 351, 358–361, 366–367
Rebel Without a Cause, 199
Receiver, 10
Recording industry:
    African-American music, 279–280
    backmasking, 294
    Beatles, 283–285
    British invasion, second wave, 285–288
    classical music, 297
    controversies, 293–297
    country-and-western, 297
    covering, 280–281
    cultural changes, 283
    disco, 289–290
    editorial statements, 293
    explicit lyrics, 294
    heavy metal, 294
    jazz, 279–280
    jukeboxes, 281
    music videos, 291–293
    new wave, 290
    Parents' Music Resource Center, 295
    punk rock, 290
    radio and sales, 281
    rap, 294
    rhythm-and-blues, 281
    rock-'n'-roll, 281–291
    sheet music, 278
    subliminal messages, 293
    talking machine, 278
    white swing, 281
Redbook, 137
Red Channels, 252
Red Lion Broadcasting Co., 79
Red Menace, The, 195
Red Scare, 195–196
Reebok, 304
Reeves, Rosser, 354
Reformation, 101–102
Regional breakouts, 134
Regulations, media:
    access to information, 90
    broadcast, 77–81
    courts, 81–82
    invasion of privacy laws, 87–89
    libel laws, 84–87
    obscenity, 82–84
    print, 74–76
    prior restraint, 76

Reid, Wallace, 190
Renaissance, 100–101
Republic, 197
Republic, The, 278
Republican, 12
Republican National Committee, 190
Requiem for a Heavyweight, 242
Return of the Jedi, 43, 201
Reuters, 66, 172–173
Review, 124
Reynolds, Burt, 263
Reynolds, Frank, 251
Rice, Donna, 89, 364–365
Rich Man, Poor Man, 245
Rifleman, The, 243
Riot in Juvenile Prison, 199
Risky Business, 38
Rivera, Geraldo, 246, 250
Riverside Press-Enterprise, 81
RKO, 192, 196
Roaring '20s, 279
Robe, The, 197
Roberts, Bill, 351
Roberts, Oral, 266
Robertson, Cliff, 242
Robertson, Pat, 266, 365
Robinson, Edward G., 192, 252
Rochester (N.Y.) *Democrat & Chronicle,*
   163
Rock Around the Clock, 199, 282
Rock concerts, 15
Rockefeller, John D., 127–128
Rock-'n'-roll, 227
Rockwell, Norman, 37
Rocky III, 40
Rogers, Ginger, 192
Rogers, Kenny, 283
Rogers, Roy, 110
Rolling Stone, 166, 168
Rolling Stones, 4, 283, 285, 290, 292
Romance of Helen Trent, The, 223
Roman Empire, 100
Romanticism, 36
Ronettes, 283
Roosevelt, Franklin D., 193, 219–220, 313,
   355
Roosevelt, Theodore, 127–128
Roots, 245
Rosenbaum, Jill, 296
Ross, Diana, 288, 290
Roth, Samuel, 82

Rowan, Dan, 244
Rowe, Sandra Mims, 163
Rubin, Ellis, 263
Runner's World, 136
Rushdie, Salman, 95
Russwurm, John B., 167
Rydell, Bobby, 282

Sacramento Union, 405
Sagal, Katey, 26
San Antonio Light, 405
San Francisco Examiner, 161
Sarnoff, David, 216–217, 252
Sassy, 121, 137
Satanic Verses, The, 95
SATCOM I, 375–376
Satellite communication:
   future, 381–382
   how it works, 380
   newspaper uses, 381
   other uses, 56, 381
   radio uses, 380–381
Saturday Evening Post, 126, 129
Saturday Night Fever, 289
Saturday Night Live, 244
Saudi Arabia, 256
Scarface, 193
Scarlet Letter, The, 104
Schenck, Charles T., 74
Schieffer, Bob, 358
Schmalensee, Richard, 308
Schmetz, Herb, 338, 341, 345, 406
Schramm, Wilbur, 57, 417
Schudson, Michael, 30, 308
Schweppes, 316
Screw, 136
Scribner, Charles, 104
Scripps, Edward W., 162–163, 172–173
Seagram's, 316
Sears-Roebuck, 388
Section 315 (FCC), 78
Sedgwick, Catherine, 104
Sedition Act of 1918, 74
Seed (Chicago), 168
See It Now, 252–253
Selective exposure, 12
Selective perception, 12, 311
Selective retention, 12, 14
Self, 137
Selling of the President, 357

Semantic noise, 11–12
Sennett, Mack, 187–188
Serling, Rod, 242
Servan-Schreiber, Jean-Louis, 140
Sesame Street, 265, 267, 419–420
Sevareid, Eric, 251
7 Days, 122
Seventeen, 63, 130, 137
Seventeenth Amendment, 161
Sex Pistols, 290
Shadow, The, 222
Shangri-Las, 283
Shape, 137
Sharon, Ariel, 86
Shaw, Donald, 16, 353
Shaw, Irwin, 245
Shazam, 419
Sheppard, Sam, 81
Shield laws, 82
Shirelles, 283,
Shirer, William L., 251–252
Shock radio, 80–81
Shore, Dinah, 281
Showtime, 377
Siebert, Fred, 57
Sigourney, Lydia, 104
Silverman, Fred, 246
Simmons Market Research Bureau, 324
Simon and Garfunkel, 288
Simon, Paul, 351
Simpsons, The, 2, 40, 43, 238–240, 412
Sinatra, Frank, 116, 281
Sinclair, Upton, 105, 107, 127–128, 335
Situation comedy (sitcom), 221, 244–245
$64,000 Question, 242
Skelton, Red, 242
Skiing, 136
Skin Deep, 38
Sky Channel, 63
Slaughterhouse Five, 112
Smart, 122
Smith, Adam, 53
Smith, Al, 313
Smith, Anthony, 373
Smith, Howard K., 251–252
Smith, Samuel Harrison, 155
Smolla, Rodney, 116
Smothers Brothers, 244
Snepp, Frank, 116
Soap operas, 222–223, 306–307, 412
Sob sisters, 162

Social Responsibility Press Theory, 57–60, 164
Society of Professional Journalists, 58–59, 399, 401, 404
Soft news, 170
Sony, 204–205, 225, 390
Sophocles, 173
Sound of Music, The, 201
Source, 8
South Africa, 52
Southern Bride, 136
Southern Pacific Railroad, 161
Soviet Communist theory of press, 55–57, 60–62
Soviet Union, 60–62, 69
Spanish-American War, 162
Specialization stages, 107–112, 134–135
Spectator, 153
Spencer, Stu, 351
Spielberg, Steven, 201
Spin, 121
Sport, 136
Sports Afield, 141
Sports Illustrated, 136
Sprague v. *Walter,* 87
Springsteen, Bruce, 390
Spy, 121
Squier, Bob, 351
SRI-International, 321–322
Srivastava v. *Harte-Hanks Communications, Inc.,* 87
Stamp Act, 154
Standard Periodical Directory, 139
Stanford, Leland, 161
Starr, Ringo, 284–285
Starsky and Hutch, 263
Star Trek, 43–44, 109
Star Wars, 201
Steele, Richard, 124
St. Elsewhere, 38, 247
Steffans, Lincoln, 127, 335
St. Louis Journalism Review, 402
St. Louis Post-Dispatch, 402
St. Paul Pioneer Press Dispatch, 163
Stephens, Ann S., 104
Stern, Howard, 80
Stevenson, Adlai, 355
Stewart, Jimmy, 192, 194
Stewart, Potter, 114
Stokes, Donald E., 351
Stowe, Harriet Beecher, 104–105

Stuart, Charles and Carol, 413–414
Students Against Drunk Drivers (SADD), 318
Style, 121
Subliminal messages, 293, 315–317
Suing the Press, 116
Sullivan, Ed, 241–242, 284
Sumerian clay tablets, 98–99
Summary View of the Rights of British America, A, 103
Summers, Donna, 289
Sun (London), 62
Sun Records, 281
Super Bowl, 4, 33–36, 40
Superman, 201
Supremes, 288
Surfer, 124
Suzuki, 341
Swayze, John Cameron, 251
Sweet Dreams, 297
Switzerland, Geneva, 28

Tabloid TV, 249–251
Taft, William Howard, 216
Talese, Gay, 167
Talking Heads, 290
Tan, 138
Tanzania, 67
Tarbell, Ida, 127–128
TASS, 60, 68, 172–173
Tatler, 124
Taxi, 122
Taylor, William Desmond, 190
Tebbel, John, 114
Technologies, mass media, 373–395
Teenzines, 137–139
Telegraph, development of, 158–159, 214–215
Telephone, 15, 32, 46, 215
Teleprompter, 359
Teleshopping, 268–269
Teletext, 387–389
Televangelism, 266–267
Television:
    business trends, 269–270
    cable, 267–268
    children's TV, 264–266
    Couch Potatoes, 262
    communist scare, 252–253
    cultural impacts, 258–267

development of, 32, 46
daytime TV, 246
docudramas, 247–249
early history, 240–242
entering popular culture, 242–250
FCC freeze, 241
hybrid TV, 247
Iran-Contra hearings, 14, 18, 255
Kennedy assassination, 253–254
live drama, 242
mini-series, 245
news, 251–259
prime time, 247
public broadcasting, 267
quiz show scandal, 242–243
religious broadcasting, 266–267
sexism, in news, 256
sitcoms, 244–245
soap operas, 247–249
space flight coverage, 254–255
sports, 245–246
tabloid TV, 249–251
technical limitations, 251–252
teleshopping, 268–269
urban Westerns, 244
variety shows, 244
Vietnam war, 244, 254
violence, 263–264
Watergate, 255
Westerns, 243–244
women in television, 262
Tellis, Gerard, 307
Temple, Shirley, 192
Temptations, 288
Ten Commandments, The, 197
Texaco Star Theater, 306
Texas Chain Saw Massacre, The, 203
Texas Instruments, 392
Thatcher, Margaret, 62
That Girl, 260
The Cook, The Thief, His Wife & Her Lover, 183–184
Theodosius I, 99
Thin Man, The, 194
Third World, 67–69
30 Seconds over Tokyo, 194
Thirtysomething, 247
Thomas, Isaiah, 106, 154
Thomas, Lowell, 219, 251
Thomas, Marlo, 260
Thompson, Dorothy, 355

Thompson, Hunter S., 166
Thompson, J. Walter, 305
Thomson, Roy, 66
Thoreau, Henry David, 104
Three Dimension (3-D) movies, 197–198
Three Men and a Baby, 40
Three's Company, 246
Tiananmen Square, 48–50, 52
Tie Me Up, Tie Me Down, 183
Time, 66, 86, 122, 128, 142, 290
Times (London), 62, 158
Times-Mirror, 170, 388
Time Warner, 117, 122, 142, 389
Titanic, 216
Today, 26, 256
Toffler, Alvin, 7, 373–374, 394
To Kill a Mockingbird, 112
Too Much Joy, 276
Top Gun, 292
Torme, Mel, 281
Touching, 116
Tower Commission, 109
Towering Inferno, The, 201
Town and Country, 141
Townshend Acts, 154
Tracy, Dick, 112, 201–202
Tracy, Spencer, 192
Tragedy of Flight 103: The Inside Story, 413
Tramp, The, 188
Traub, James, 381
Travolta, John, 40, 297
Trekkies, 43–44, 109
Triangle Publications, 129
Trinity Broadcasting Network (TBN), 266–267
Trintex, 388
Trip to the Moon, A, 185
True Stories, 292–293
Turner Broadcasting System, 33
Turner, Ted, 256–257
Truth boxes, 350
TV-Cable Week, 135
TV Guide, 63, 122, 129–130, 135, 142, 402–403
TWA hijacking, 174
Twain, Mark, 105, 114–115
20th Century, 193, 196
Twentieth Century-Fox, 63, 192
Twin Peaks, 247, 250
2 Live Crew, 37, 82–83, 275–276, 294

Two of a Kind: The Hillside Stranglers, 116
Two-step flow theory, 350–351

U-2, 291
Ulysses, 107
Uncle Buck, 239
Uncle Tom's Cabin, 105, 126
Underground press, 167
United Fruit Company, 215
United Kingdom, 62–64, 392
United Press International (UPI), 60, 66, 68, 163, 171–173, 219
UNESCO, 68
United States, 7, 18, 58, 74, 89, 104, 115, 124, 126, 135, 159, 214, 249, 285, 305, 337, 374, 410, 421
Unit specialization, 124
United States Football League (USFL), 33
University of Chicago, 57
University of Iowa, 307
University of Pennsylvania, 419
Urban Cowboy, 40, 297
USA Today, 10, 115, 148–150, 256, 407
Unsolved Mysteries, 250, 404
Upstairs Downstairs, 245, 267
U.S. Criminal Code, 77
U.S. Department of Labor, 338
U.S. Industrial Outlook, 135, 142
U.S. Information Agency, 336
U.S. News & World Report, 128
U.S. Postal Service, 81, 306
U.S. Supreme Court, 75–76, 80–83, 85, 89–90, 106, 114, 116, 196, 256
U.S. v. Paramount Pictures, 196

Valenti, Jack, 181
Values and Lifestyles (VALS), 321–323
Vanity Fair, 121
Van Gogh, Vincent, 37
Variety, 190
Vasquez Rana, Mario, 173
Vaudeville, 30–32, 46, 184–185, 221
Vertical blanking interval (VBI), 388–389
Vicary, James, 315–316
Victoria, 122
Victor Talking Machine Co., 278
Videocassette recorder (VCR), 56, 204, 319, 374, 384–386
Video magazines, 138–139
Video movies, 203–204

Videotel, 388
Videotext, 387–388
Vietnam, 12, 55, 75, 116, 166, 200, 244, 254, 283
Village Voice, 168
Violence theories, 415–417
Virginian-Pilot/Ledger-Star, 163
Virginian, The, 243
Vitaphone, 189
Vitascope, 185
Vogue, 137
Von Bülow, Claus, 116
Vote videos, 361–362

W, 137
Wallace, DeWitt and Lila, 128
Wall Street Journal, 148, 164, 168, 341, 343
Warner-Amex, 291
Warner Brothers, 142, 190, 192, 196, 204
War of the Worlds, 225–226
Washington, George, 354
Washington Post, 75, 109, 163, 166, 401, 405
Watchdog function of press, 54
Watergate, 55, 166, 248, 255
Wayne, John, 192
WDY, 217
WEAF, 217–218, 306
Webster, Noah, 103, 155
Weiner, Sandy, 351
Weisman, Steven R., 359
Welch, Raquel, 263
Welles, Orson, 194, 225–226, 252
Wells, H. G., 107, 225
West, Mae, 193
Western culture, 29
Western Electric, 217, 389
Western Europe, 67, 101, 388
Western Opinion Research Center, 262
Westheimer, Ruth, 227—228
Westinghouse, 217, 231, 240
Westmoreland, William, 86–87
WGBH-TV, 80
WGY, 217
Wheatley, William, 256
Whetmore, Edward Jay, 410–411
Whitaker, Clem, 351
White, Margaret Bourke, 131
White, Paul, 219

White swing, 281
Who (musical group), 290
Who Framed Roger Rabbit, 202
Whole Booke of Psalmes, 102
Wide World of Sports, 245, 251
Wigwam, 121
Wild Bunch, The, 201
Wild One, The, 45
Wild Orchid, 183
Wiley, John, 104
Williams, Wayne, 413
Willis, Bruce, 293
Willkie, Wendell, 350, 355
Wilson, James, 103
Wilson, James R., 248–249
Wilson, Woodrow, 186, 217, 336
Winchell, Walter, 181
Winfrey, Oprah, 244, 403
Wings of Desire, 201
Wirth, Louis, 30
Wisner, George W., 157
Wizard of Oz, The, 198
Wolfe, Tom, 167
Wonder, Stevie, 288
Wonder Years, The, 247
Woman's Day, 122, 137
Woman's Home Companion, 126
Woman's World, 137
Woodward, Bob, 109, 166, 248
Woodward, Dick, 351
Wordsworth, William, 104
Working Mother, 137
Working Woman, 137
World Cup, 35
World News Tonight, 403
World War I, 74, 90, 128, 189, 217, 311
World War II, 107, 194–195, 221, 226, 337
World Series, 35
World System Teletext (WST), 389
Writer's Digest, 133
Wyatt Earp, 243
Wylie, Frank, 338

Yallop, David A., 109
Yellow journalism, 159–163
Yellow Kid, 162
Yes Minister, 267
You Can't Take It With You, 194
Young and the Restless, 247

Young Doctor Kildare, 194
Young & Rubicam, 306
Yucaipa School Board, 112–113

Zamora, Ronnie, 263
Zenger, John Peter, 153, 163, 421

Zeta, 67
Zipping and zapping, 319
Zwingli, Huldreich, 102
Zworykin, Vladimir, 240

PHOTO CREDITS

CHAPTER 1

p. 2, Felicia Martinez/Photo Edit; p. 6, Dion Ogust/The Image Works; p. 9, Skip O'Rourke/The Image Works; p. 13, Paul Conrad; p. 16, Dan Chidester/The Image Works; p. 19, Michael S. Yamashita/Woodfin Camp & Associates.

CHAPTER 2

p. 24, Photofest; p. 31, The Bettmann Archive; p. 35, Corky Trewin/NFL Photos; p. 39, Frank Carroll/NBC/Globe Photos; p. 41, AP/Wide World; p. 42, Bernard Pierre Wolff/Photo Researchers.

CHAPTER 3

p. 48, Baldev/Sygma; p. 50, Jacques Langevin/Sygma; p. 51, Reuters/Bettmann Newsphotos; p. 54, The White House; p. 56, Bergman/Blue C/Gamma Liaison; p. 61, Sovoto; p. 65, Meredith Davenport.

CHAPTER 4

p. 72, AP/Wide World; p. 75, AP/Wide World; p. 83, Mike Schwarz/Gamma-Liaison; p. 86, Meredith Davenport; p. 88, AP/Wide World.

CHAPTER 5

p. 94, John Barrett/Globe Photos; p. 98, David Strickler/The Image Works; p. 101, Brown Brothers; p. 105, Culver; p. 113, J. Ross Baughman/Visions; p. 108, Courtesy Crown Publishers, Inc. NY, 1987.

CHAPTER 6

p. 120, Liane Enkelis/Stock, Boston; p. 124, Meredith Davenport; p. 125, Brown Brothers; p. 127, Culver; p. 130, Brown Brothers; p. 131, Margaret Bourke-

White/Life Magazine; p. 140, Cynthia Johnson/Gamma-Liaison; p. 138, Barbara Rios/Photo Researchers.

CHAPTER 7

p. 146, Alan Carey/The Image Works; p. 150, Alan Carey/Image Works; p. 152, Brown Brothers; p. 158, Lewis Hine/Culver; p. 162, The Bettmann Archive; p. 167, Brown Brothers; p. 172, Art Stein/Photo Researchers.

CHAPTER 8

p. 180, Roland Neveu/Foto Fantasies; p. 184, Camhi/Stills/Miramax Films; p. 188, The Bettmann Archive; p. 192, The Everett Collection; p. 194, Photofest; p. 196, Historical Pictures Collection; p. 198, UPI/Bettmann Newsphotos; p. 199, The Museum of Modern Art Film Stills Archive.

CHAPTER 9

p. 210, M. Grecco/Stock, Boston; p. 216, Historical Pictures Service; p. 220, UPI/Bettmann Newsphotos; p. 224, top and bottom, Culver; p. 225, Culver; p. 228, Robert McElroy/Woodfin Camp & Associates.

CHAPTER 10

p. 236, © 1991 CNN. All rights reserved; p. 240, Photofest; p. 243, Everett Collection; p. 249, Courtesy of NBC; p. 250, Sygma; p. 252, UPI/Bettmann Newsphotos; p. 253, Brown Brothers.

CHAPTER 11

p. 274, UPI/Bettmann Newsphotos; p. 279, Culver; p. 284, Culver; p. 289, AP/Wide World; p. 291, Ross Marino/Sygma; p. 292, above, The Bettmann Archive, below, UPI/Bettmann Newsphotos; p. 295, Scott Weiner/Retna.

CHAPTER 12

p. 302, Courtesy Pontiac; p. 305, The Bettmann Archive; p. 314, Sheldon Moskowitz/Contact Press Images/Woodfin Camp & Associates; p. 321, Rolex.

CHAPTER 13

p. 330, Mark Antman/The Image Works; p. 332, Courtesy of Exxon Corporation and O'Keefe, Duffy & Associates; p. 336, UPI/Bettmann Newsphotos; p. 337, Barbara Singer Collection/Culver; p. 342, Brown Brothers.

CHAPTER 14

p. 348, John Barrett/Globe Photos; p. 353, Cynthia Johnson/Gamma-Liaison; p. 354, UPI/Bettmann Newsphotos; p. 356, UPI/Bettmann Newsphotos; p. 365, AP/Wide World; p. 366, UPI/Bettmann Newsphotos.

CHAPTER 15

p. 372, Reuters/Bettmann Newsphotos; p. 375, John Coletti/Stock, Boston; p. 379, Nielsen Media Research; p. 383, Michael Heyman/Stock, Boston; p. 384, Spencer Grant/Stock, Boston; p. 386, Eli Reed/Magnum; p. 391, MIX, The Recording Industry Magazine.

CHAPTER 16

p. 398, Photofest; p. 400, AP/Wide World; p. 407, UPI/Bettmann Newsphotos; p. 415, Columbia Pictures Television; p. 418, Mark Antman/The Image Works; p. 420, Children's Television Workshop.